Encyclopaedia of
STEEPLECHASING

Other Sports Encyclopaedias published by Robert Hale Limited

Association Football
BY MAURICE GOLESWORTHY

Athletics
BY MELVYN WATMAN

Bowls
BY KEN HAWKS AND GERARD LINDLEY

Boxing
BY MAURICE GOLESWORTHY

Chess
BY ANNE SUNNUCKS

Cricket
BY MAURICE GOLESWORTHY

Flat Racing
BY ROGER MORTIMER

Golf
BY WEBSTER EVANS

Motor Cycle Sport
BY PETER CARRICK

Motor Racing
BY ANTHONY PRITCHARD AND KEITH DAVEY

Mountaineering
BY WALT UNSWORTH

Rugby League Football
BY A. N. GAULTON

Rugby Union Football
BY J. R. JONES
  (Second edition edited by Maurice Golesworthy)

Show Jumping
BY CHARLES STRATTON

Swimming
BY PAT BESFORD

Encyclopaedia of
STEEPLECHASING

Compiled by

PATRICIA SMYLY

ROBERT HALE · LONDON

ISBN 0 7091 7011 4

Robert Hale & Company
Clerkenwell House
45/47 Clerkenwell Green
London EC1R 0HT

PHOTOSET AND BOUND BY
WEATHERBY WOOLNOUGH, WELLINGBOROUGH, NORTHANTS
PRINTED IN GREAT BRITAIN BY
LOWE & BRYDONE, THETFORD, NORFOLK

Preface

Although fundamentally disapproving of prefaces in principle, I feel that some explanation of the criteria for entry must be given. Basically all winners of the jumping classics, the Cheltenham Gold Cup, the Grand National and the Champion Hurdle, are included, as are their trainers and jockeys. With regard to nineteenth-century National winners there is no official source of trainer and these are not guaranteed. Also automatically included are all champion jockeys, champion amateurs and leading trainers as far back as these can be reliably ascertained. Otherwise horses have to have won a certain number of 'pattern' races while trainers and jockeys must have trained or ridden a certain number of pattern race winners in order to qualify. These 'pattern' races have been selected by the author and do not correspond with the official pattern races recently incorporated into the Steeplechase Calendar.

In order to compress this book into a single volume, certain sections of the steeplechasing world have inevitably been cursorily dealt with. Only very influential sires and broodmares have been included. Owners may feel they have had a raw deal while racing officials and newspaper and television correspondents have been omitted altogether. Stable lads and girls, by their nature anonymous, have suffered a similar fate.

I should like to take this opportunity for thanking the Jockey Club both for permission to quote from the Rules of Racing and for prolonged use of their library and also the Thoroughbred Breeders Association not only for the run of their marvellous library during the research period but also for their support and active assistance in pursuing elusive pedigrees.

Gloucestershire, July 1978   Patricia Smyly

Illustrations

Between pages 64 and 65

1 Dual National winner ABD-EL-KADER
2 The first and only Royal National winner AMBUSH II
3 Two masters of their profession – JACK ANTHONY and Gerry Wilson
4 A famous partnership – Pat Taaffe and ARKLE
5 One of jumping's staunchest patrons, the first LORD BICESTER
6 HARRY BROWN, crack amateur and trainer
7 BULA and Paul Kelleway on their way to victory in the Champion Hurdle
8 A General view of CHELTENHAM racecourse
9 CHELTENHAM: a field of hurdlers against the backdrop of Cleeve Hill
10 CHELTENHAM – Monksfield returns to a jubilant reception
11 COMEDY OF ERRORS in full flight
12 Happy Home leads COTTAGE RAKE over the last in the 1948 Cheltenham Gold Cup
13 TOM COULTHWAITE, who saddled three National winners
14 Dick Francis and CRUDWELL
15 DEVON LOCH spreadeagles himself 50 yards from the winning post in the 1956 Grand National
16 TOM DREAPER, a master of his profession
17 EASTER HERO with Tim Cullinan

Between pages 128 and 129

18 JOSH GIFFORD, four times Champion Jockey and now a successful trainer
19 TONY GRANTHAM after his victory on Manicou in the Wimbledon H'cap Chase, Kempton, 1950
20 A happy moment for GOLDEN MILLER, Gerry Wilson and Dorothy Paget after their victory in the 1934 Grand National
21 The HON. AUBREY HASTINGS and Ascetic's Silver
22 Two great Champion Hurdlers together in the air, National Spirit and HATTON'S GRACE
23 The HON. GEORGE LAMBTON
24 The dual Gold Cup winner L'ESCARGOT with his regular pilot Tommy Carberry
25 An aerial view of LIVERPOOL
26 LIVERPOOL old style. Kellsboro' Jack and Danny Williams in the 1933 Grand National
27 A real LIVERPOOL mêlée – the 1966 Grand National

28 LIVERPOOL the tragedy – Colonel Whitbread's brave Beau Bob breaks his neck
29 LIVERPOOL the glamour – a worm's-eye view of the field streaming over Becher's
30 JAMES MACHELL who masterminded a Derby winner and four National winners
31 MANIFESTO, a dual National winner
32 LORD JOHN MANNERS
33 Liverpool-born 'TICH' MASON who was Champion Jockey six times
34 Anthony Bingham, second LORD MILDMAY, cantering to the post on Cromwell
35 ARTHUR NIGHTINGALL, a foremost professional rider of the late nineteenth century
36 A typical shot of NIGHT NURSE ridden here by Paddy Broderick

Between pages 192 and 193

37 JOHN OAKSEY
38 The legendary VINCENT O'BRIEN
39 JONJO O'NEILL
40 RODDY OWEN, one of the most distinguished amateurs of his day
41 PERSIAN WAR, a triple Champion Hurdler
42 POETHLYN pictured with his regular jockey Ernie Piggott
43 RYAN PRICE – four times Champion Trainer
44 A great supporter of steeplechasing, Mr J. V. RANK
45 RED RUM, ears pricked and on the bridle, wins his third Grand National
46 One of Steeplechasing's all-time great jockeys, F. B. REES
47 FRED RIMELL, trainer of four Grand National winners
48 Triumph for the Furlong family in the 1935 Grand National, Major Furlong and his wife lead their horse REYNOLDSTOWN
49 The first sponsored steeplechase. The 1957 running of the Whitbread Gold Cup at SANDOWN
50 SIR KEN and Tim Molony
51 GEORGE STEVENS, who rode a record five Grand National winners
52 BILLY STOTT – Champion Jockey five seasons running
53 THE COLONEL an almost black entire won the Grand National in 1869 and 1870
54 FULKE WALWYN
55 FRED WINTER, C.B.E., a man for whom superlatives pale in the face of his achievements

Picture Credits

Radio Times Picture Library, 1, 2, 30, 31, 35, 48, 52, 53; Fox Photos Ltd., 3, 6, 13, 4; Syndication International, 4, 28, 29, 42, 43, 55; Popperfoto, 5, 19, 32, 47; Central Press Photos Ltd., 7, 12, 36, 41, 50; Bernard Parkin, 8, 9; Cheltenham Newspaper Company Ltd., 10; Sport and General Press Agency Ltd., 11, 14, 16, 20, 22, 24, 45; The Associated Press Ltd., 15, 17, 54; Topix, 18; W. W. Rouch & Co. Ltd., 21, 23; Liverpool Daily Post and Echo Ltd., 25; Keystone Press Agency Ltd., 26, 34, 37; Camera Press Ltd., 27; The Illustrated London News, 33, 46; Sporting Pictures (UK) Ltd., 38, 39; The Press Association Ltd., 49; Stud and Stable, 51.

ABBOTT, T.

Abbott was an Irish amateur who won the 1851 Grand National on Abd-el-Kader for Mr J. Osborne and the Kilrue Cup three times.

ABD-EL-KADER

Bay gelding, 1842, not in the General Stud Book, Ismael—English Lass (Hit or Miss). Bred by Mr David Osborne in Co. Meath, Ireland.

A small, quality horse with splendid shoulders and a pattern-book hind leg, 'Little Ab', as he was affectionately known, won the Grand National two years running. 1850: 9-12 (C. Green) unquoted, by 11 and a dist. from The Knight of Gwynne, 11-8 (Wynne), and Sir John, 11-8 (J. Ryan). 1851: 10-4 (T. Abbott), 7/1, by ½ nk, 2l, from Maria Day, 10-5 (J. Frisby) and Sir John, 11-12 (J. Ryan). Well fancied to complete a hat-trick in 1852, an extra stone of weight, fast ground and his customary headstrong tactics proved too much and he weakened in the closing stages to finish fifth.

His dam was bought out of the Shrewsbury mailcoach and taken to Ireland where she was hunted and won steeplechases before being put to stud. Abd-el-Kader was owned and trained by his breeder's son, Mr Joseph Osborne, a considerable figure in chasing circles, being the owner of Bell's *Life* and author of the current steeplechasing *Calendar* and several books on breeding, notably *The Horsebreeders Handbook*.

ADAM, Emil (1843-1924)

A member of the famous Bavarian painting family, Emil Adam was born in Munich and brought up in the studio of his father, Benno and uncles Franz and Enger. He studied at the Hohenheim Veterinary Academy and was apprenticed to Portaels in Brussels.

He was considered to be the finest horse painter in Europe and his patrons included most of the nobility of the Austro-Hungarian Empire, the Kinskys, the Esterhazys and the Batthyanys. He also painted for M. Edmond Blanc and Baron Leopold de Rothschild while in England his biggest patron was the first Duke of Westminster, who said of him: "Emil Adam is the only artist ... who can really conceive and put on canvas the thoroughbred as he really is".

ADAMS, James

Jimmy Adams served his apprenticeship on the Flat and switched to steeplechasing when his weight necessitated it. This experience stood him in good stead for the valuable hurdle races then just nudging their way into the chasing calendar.

Among his principal successes were:

The Grand Sefton (1877) Bogue Homa
The Great Sandown Hurdle Race (1880) Blue Ruin
The Great Sandown Hurdle Race (1882) Prudhomme

After the successive National wins of Lord Manners and Count (later Prince) Kinsky, Adams was heard to remark, "What the 'ell are we a-coming to? Last year it was a blooming lord, this year it's a furrin' count and next year it'll be an ole woman most likely," and was not a little disconcerted by Count Kinksy's retort, "Yes, Jimmy, and I hope that ole woman will be yourself."

A short-legged man with the back and shoulders of a prize-fighter and a good bit more below the belt than was convenient for a jockey, Adams ended his career in a fall at Auteuil. He afterwards trained at Epsom with some success.

AFRICAN SISTER

Chestnut mare, 1932, Prestor John—Meloa (Melleray). Bred by Mr A. Baker.

A winner on the Flat at three years, African Sister won nine hurdle races and is the only mare to have won Champion Hurdle which she did in 1939, ridden by Keith Piggott and starting at 10/1, by 3l and ¼l from Vitement (E. Vinall) and Apple Peel (S. Ingham). She was runner-up to Solford in 1940. She was owned by Mr H. J. Brueton and trained at Cheltenham by Ernie Piggott's brother, Charles.

AINTREE
See LIVERPOOL.

AIRGEAD SIOS
Chestnut gelding, 1930, Werwolf—Orna (Orthos). Bred by Mr H. Boothman.

A hard-pulling front-runner and a spectacular jumper, Airgead Sios was one of the most popular chasers of the late 'thirties and was very little short of top-class. His victories included the Champion Chase, Liverpool, the Becher Chase (twice), the King George VI Chase at Kempton and the Cheltenham Grand Annual. He was owned by Sir Francis Towle and trained by C. Tabor.

ALBERGO
Brown gelding, 1954, Dante—Bill of Fare (William of Valence). Bred by Lord Astor.

After a promising beginning to his three-year-old career, Albergo developed tendon trouble and was sold to Mrs Magnier for 400 guineas at the December Sales. Trained thereafter by her husband Clem, he proved a high-class hurdler of admirable consistency and toughness. After winning a division of the Gloucester Hurdle and the Coronation Hurdle in his first season, he ran second to Another Flash in the 1960 Champion Hurdle and won the County Hurdle with 12-5 later at the meeting. Less than a fortnight later he carried 12-6 into second place in the Imperial Cup, went on to win the Liverpool Hurdle with 12-7, a valuable race in France and finally to be second in the Grande Course des Haies at Auteuil.

ALCAZAR
Bay horse, 1916, Yerres—Good Gracious (Comptive II). Bred by Mr C. Mynors.

A consistent high-class chaser and a winner of 14 races including National Hunt Handicap Chase, the Becher Chase and the Champion Chase, Liverpool, Alcazar was strongly fancied for the inaugural Cheltenham Gold Cup but had to be withdrawn on the morning of the race. In 1925 he started 8/13 favourite but was beaten convincingly by the mare Ballinode. Owned by Mr W. H. McAlpine, he was trained by George Poole and invariably ridden by F. B. Rees.

ALCIBIADE
Chestnut horse, 1860, The Cossack-—Aunt Phillis (Epirus). Bred in France.

Several National winners have but modest careers on the Flat but few can count being claimed out of a seller at Epsom as a prelude to Aintree triumph, as did the 1865 winner Alcibiade. Sold to Mr 'Cherry' Angell, he was sent to Mr Burton's Lubenham establishment to be prepared for the National. Although not given a preparatory run, he was well tried with Bridegroom, winner of the first National Hunt Chase, and placed fifth, fourth and second in successive Nationals. And Bridegroom, "who never told a lie", declared that even with 11-4 the five-year-old was worth backing. The stable plunged accordingly and with happy results, although it was only by a head that Alcibiade, ridden by Capt. Coventry, prevailed over Hall Court, 11-0 (Capt. Tempest) with the 1864 winner Emblematic, 11-10 (G. Stevens), a distance away third. Alcibiade thus became the first of five five-year-olds to win. He did not win subsequently but finished a close third in the 1868 National and fourth in 1869 to The Colonel.

ALLOWANCES
109(ii) (a) Those riders under the age of 25 years who hold a Conditional jockey's licence or a Category 'B' amateur rider's permit or who are riding under the provisions of Rule 61 and who have not won thirty races collectively under the Rules of any recognized Turf Authority shall be entitled to the following allowances in steeple chases and hurdle races which are open to professional jockeys:

7lbs until they have won 15 races. Thereafter
4lbs until they have won 30 races. Apprentices and Opportunity races under these Rules not to be included in the above totals.

The above allowances can be claimed in the steeple chases and hurdle races that are open to professional jockeys set out below with the exception of Opportunity races:
1) All handicaps except the Liverpool Grand National Steeple Chase.
2) All selling races.
3) All other races with guaranteed prize money of not more than £2,500.

ALLY SLOPER

Bay or Brown gelding, 1909, Travelling Lad—Sally in our Alley (Discord). Bred in Lincolnshire by Mr C. J. Hill.

A real 'Liverpool' horse and a winner of seven chases, including the Stanley Chase and the Valentine Chase at five years, Ally Sloper was the second of Jack Anthony's three Grand National winners, winning in 1915 carrying 10-5 and starting at 100/8, by 2l, 8l from Jacobus, 11-0 (A. Newey) and Father Confessor, 9-10 (A. Aylin).

AMATEUR

An amateur rider is one who does not receive a fee for riding in a race. The regulations governing the definition of an amateur are set out under Rules of Racing (*q.v.*). Briefly, no one who has ever been paid to ride in a race or within the past 12 months has been paid to work as a groom or a hunt-servant may ride as an amateur. All hunter chases and a few steeplechases and hurdle races are restricted to amateur riders. An 'A' Category permit is required to ride in these. A 'B' Category permit is required to ride in amateur Flat races, all steeplechases and hurdle races.

When an amateur has made more than 75 rides in races open to professional riders, a fee of £21.15 is payable to the Jockey Club when he rides a horse other than those the sole property of himself, his spouse, his mother or his father.

62. (i) The following persons are not eligible to hold Amateur Rider's permits:

(a) A person who has ever held a professional rider's licence from any recognized Turf Authority other than an Apprentice Jockey's Licence held for a period of not more than twelve months from the date of issue of his first licence. (Subject to part (c) of this sub-rule.)

(b) A person who has otherwise ever been paid directly or indirectly for riding in a race with the exception of expenses approved by the Stewards of the Jockey Club as set out in Appendix F to these Rules and any trophy advertised in the conditions of the race to be given to a rider.

(c) A person whose principal paid occupation is or at any time within the last twelve months has been to ride or groom for a licensed or permitted trainer.

(d) A person who is or who within the last 12 months has been paid as a groom in private, livery or horse dealer's stables or as a hunt-servant.

Licences

60. (iv) A Category 'A' Amateur Rider's Permit to be applied for from July 1977 and thereafter annually each July. Holders of these permits may ride in any Flat race, Steeple Chase or Hurdle race confined to Amateur Riders.

(v) A Category 'B' Amateur Rider's Permit, to be applied for from July 1977 and thereafter annually each July. Holders of these permits may ride in any Flat Race confined to Amateur Riders and in all Steeple Chases and Hurdle races except those confined to licensed jockeys.

Licence Fees

63. (iv) Category 'A' Amateur Riders' Permit – £13.50 (plus V.A.T. and including £6 to the Amateur Riders' Insurance Scheme.)

(v) Category 'B' Amateur Riders' Permit – £21.00 (plus V.A.T. and including £6 to the Amateur Riders' Insurance Scheme.)

Riders' Fees

72. In Steeple Chases and Hurdle races other than those confined to Amateur Riders: – £21.15 to the Jockey Club when an Amateur rider who has had more than 75 rides in this country in races open to professional riders rides a horse other than those the sole property of himself, his spouse, his mother or his father.

AMATEURS, CHAMPION

1945-46	Mr A. B. Mildmay	11
1946-47	Lord Mildmay	32
1947-48	Lord Mildmay	22
1948-49	Lord Mildmay	30
1949-50	Lord Mildmay	38
1950-51	Mr Peter Chisman	13
1951-52	Mr C. Straker	19
1952-53	Mr A. Moralee	22
1953-54	Mr A. Moralee	22
1954-55	Mr A. Moralee	16
1955-56	Mr A. Moralee / Mr R. McCreery	13
1956-57	Mr R. McCreery	23
1957-58	Hon. J. Lawrence	18
1958-59	Mr J. Sutcliffe	18
1959-60	Mr G. Kindersley	22
1960-61	Sir W. Pigott-Brown	28
1961-62	Mr A. Biddlecombe	30
1962-63	Sir W. Pigott-Brown	20

1963-64	Mr S. Davenport	32
1964-65	Mr M. Gifford	13
1965-66	Mr C. Collins	24
1966-67	Mr C. Collins	33
1967-68	Mr R. Tate	30
1968-69	Mr R. Tate	17
1969-70	Mr M. Dickinson	23
1970-71	Hon. J. Lawrence	17
1971-72	Mr W. Foulkes	25
1972-73	Mr R. Smith	56
1973-74	Mr A. Webber	21
1974-75	Mr R. Lamb	22
1975-76	{ Mr G. Jones / Mr P. Greenall	25
1976-77	Mr P. Greenall	27
1977-78	Mr G. Sloan	23

AMBUSH II
Bay gelding, 1894, Ben Battle—Miss Plant (Umpire). Bred by Mr Ashe.

Descended on both sides of his pedigree from the mighty Pocahontas, Ambush II, "a nice, level, old-fashioned horse with good limbs and feet", was the first and only royal National winner. Bought by Lord Marcus Beresford on behalf of the Prince of Wales (later Edward VII) and trained at the Curragh by 'Algy' Anthony, Ambush II won eight chases including the 1900 Grand National, 11-3 (A. Anthony), 4/1, by 4l, neck, from Barsac 9-12 (Halsey) and Manifesto 12-13 (G. Williamson). He looked likely to stage a repeat performance in 1903 but fell at the last.

ANATIS
Bay mare, 1850, not in the General Stud Book, King Dan—Johnstown Lass (Carlow). Bred by Mr Langan.

Originally named Bellewstown Lass, Anatis provided a thoroughly Cheltenham victory for the 1860 National. Owned by Mr Capel of Prestbury, who had owned Little Charlie, trained by William Holman and ridden by Tommy Pickernell she started 7/2 favourite on the strength of having been fifth the year before and duly won by ½l and 6l from The Huntsman, 11-8 (Capt. Townley) and Xanthus, 10-0 (F. Balchin). What her public were unaware of was that her forelegs had been so dicky that William Holman had not dared let her jump a fence since the 1859 National or give her a thorough preparation. Approaching the last she was palpably tired and with Huntsman in close attendance, her supporters held their breath but Tommy Pickernell was quite unruffled: "I had

only to be very patient with her, I knew and she would stay home. Had I ridden her *really* hard for fifty yards, she would have collapsed." Anatis started favourite for the 1861 National but was brought down when going well on the second circuit.

ANGELL, Mr Benjamin John
'Cherry' Angell was an old Etonian, a founder member of the National Hunt Committee and a leading supporter of steeplechasing. He owned Bridegroom, winner of the 1860 Grand National Hunt Steeplechase, and Alcibiade, winner of the 1865 Grand National. He was much liked and respected and very popular on the Continent as well as in this country.

ANGLO
(Formerly Flag of Convenience.) Chestnut gelding, 1958, registered in Miss Prior's Half-Bred Stud Book, Greek Star—Miss Alligator (Hyacinthus). Bred by Mr William Kennedy of Downpatrick, Northern Ireland.

After running unsuccessfully on the Flat at two years in the colours of Maj.-Gen. Sir Randle Feilden, Anglo was sold for 110 guineas and went on to win five hurdle races and nine chases including the 1966 Grand National, 10-0 (T. Norman), 50/1, by 20l, 5l, from Freddie, 11-7 (P. McCarron), and Forest Prince, 10-8 (G. Scott), thus registering a notable triumph for Fred Winter who was saddling his second National winner in his second season as a trainer. Anglo, who was owned jointly by Mr Stuart Levy and Mr Nat Cohen, was a half-brother to the 1968 National winner, Red Alligator. They are the only pair of half-brothers to have won the National, although the full-sisters Emblem and Emblematic emulated them in 1863-64. *See also* MISS ALLIGATOR.

ANOTHER FLASH
Bay gelding, 1954, Roi d'Egypte—Cissie Gay (Bagman). Bred by Mr A. Duncan.

A half-brother to several smart N.H. performers including Flash Bulb, Super Flash and the mare Flashaway, Another Flash was a fine hurdler, owned by Mr J. Byrne, who won two 'bumpers' and 11 hurdle races. Owing to the enforced absence of Fare Time he started 11/4 favourite for the 1960 Champion Hurdle and won by 2l and 3l from Albergo (D. Page) and Saffron Tartan (T. Burns). He was trained by Paddy Sleator and invariably ridden by Bobby Beasley.

ANTHONY, Algernon

'Algy' Anthony, Irish jockey and trainer, assisted H. E. Linde at Eyrefield Lodge, the Curragh, and later took over the stable for him. He trained and rode Ambush to win the 1900 Grand National for the Prince of Wales and also sent out the brilliant Troytown to win the Grand Steeplechase de Paris (1919) and the Grand National (1920).

ANTHONY, Ivor (1883-1959)

One of three Carmarthenshire brothers to distinguish themselves in the world of steeplechasing, Ivor Anthony first rode as an amateur. He won the National Hunt Chase on Timothy Titus in 1904 and was leading amateur that year. He later turned professional and was Champion Jockey in 1912. He once rode all six winners in an afternoon at Pembroke. He continued to ride after World War I, being easily conspicuous by his upright seat and long leathers, but was forced to retire after a bad fall at Ludlow. He became assistant to Aubrey Hastings at Wroughton and took over the licence on the latter's sudden death in 1929.

He trained for several Americans, notably Mr and Mrs Ambrose Clark, for whom he won the 1933 Grand National with Kellsboro' Jack, and the Bostwick brothers.

His other principal successes were:

The Cheltenham Gold Cup (1938) Morse Code
The Grand National (1937) Royal Mail
The Champion Hurdle (1934) Chenango
The Scottish Grand National (1935) Kellsboro' Jack
The Welsh Grand National (1930) Boomlet; (1933) Pebble Ridge; (1936) Sorley Boy
Champion Chase (1936, 1938) Kellsboro' Jack
The Imperial Cup (1933) Flaming
The Grand Military (1950, 1951, 1952) Klaxton

Neat, precise, punctual and a confirmed bachelor, he was the complete antithesis of his flamboyant brother, Owen. He continued to train until 1953 when Peter Hastings-Bass (son of his former 'guv'nor') took over. He then retired to Wroughton House, Kingsclere.

ANTHONY, John Randolph (1890-1954)

The youngest of the three Anthony brothers, 'Jack' Anthony came into racing via show-jumping and point-to-points. He rode his first winner in 1906 and came to public notice when replacing the injured 'Tich' Mason on the 1911 Grand National winner, Glenside. Immensely strong, tough and totally fearless, he was without peer at Aintree, won the National twice more as an amateur, in 1915 on Ally Sloper, and in 1920 on the herculean Troytown. He was Champion Jockey as an amateur in 1914 (60 winners) and turned professional in 1921. In 1922 he was again Champion Jockey (78 winners). He retired in 1927 and took out a licence to train at Letcombe Regis on the Berkshire Downs.

Among his principal patrons was the American millionaire, Mr 'Jock' Hay Whitney for whom he trained Easter Hero to win the 1929 and 1930 Cheltenham Gold Cups. Easter Hero who was so unlucky not to win the 1929 National, Thomond II (q.v.) and Brown Tony who won the 1930 Champion Hurdle were the best horses to come under his care.

It was ironic that so fearless a rider who had survived so many circuits of Aintree unscathed, should permanently lame himself stepping off a hack while on holiday in America.

ANTHONY, Owen (188?-1941)

The least known of the Anthony brothers as a jockey, Owen nevertheless rode 110 winners and was second in the 1913 Grand National on Irish Mail. He took out a trainer's licence in 1921 and the following year saddled Music Hall to win the Grand National. In 1935 he took over the delicate charge of handling Miss Paget and her horses after the fiasco of the 1935 National terminated Basil Briscoe's career in that capacity. A tough, forthright and flamboyant character, he was well able to cope with his formidable patron and roundly told her that he would not tolerate being bothered. He won her the 1936 Cheltenham Gold Cup with Golden Miller and in 1940 brought off the Cheltenham Double with Roman Hackle (Gold Cup) and Solford (Champion Hurdle). In 1941 he died suddenly from pneumonia following a cold.

ANZIO

Roan or grey gelding, 1957, Vic Day—

Lido Lady (Legend of France). Bred by the Harwood Stud.

A really brilliant performer on firm ground, Sir Thomas Ainsworth's Anzio won 10 hurdle races including 1962 Champion Hurdle (G. W. Robinson), 11/2, by 3l and 1½l from Quelle Chance (D. Dick) and Another Flash (H. Beasley), and went on to win 3 chases. He was trained by Fulke Walwyn (q.v.).

APRIL SEVENTH

Bay gelding, 1966, Menelek—Loughlahan (Artist's Son). Bred by Mr P. P. Sweeney.

A handsome, strongly made individual and a half-brother to three winners. April Seventh has won a hurdle race and 11 steeplechases including the Whitbread Trial Chase, Ascot (1976), the Whitbread Gold Cup, Sandown (1975) and the Hennessy Gold Cup, Newbury (1975). He thus joins Taxidermist, Arkle, Mill House and Charlie Potheen, the select group who have won both the two most-important long-distance handicaps in the Calendar.

He is owned by Mrs B. Meehan and trained by Bob Turnell. His Hennessy victory in the dry autumn of 1975 was a remarkably skilful piece of training for he had not run since his Whitbread victory the previous April.

ARCHER, Frederick Charles (d.1928)

A grandson of the William Archer who won the 1858 Grand National on Little Charley and a nephew of the famous Flat jockey, Frederick Archer was born into racing. As a young man he trained privately for Sir John Thursby at Highfield, the Malton Yard that used to belong to the l'Ansons. During World War I he served with the Bucks Yeomanry and afterwards went back to Highfield, this time as a public trainer. On the death of his father he moved to Newmarket from where he sent Double Chance out to win the 1925 Grand National. From 1925-27 he was private trainer to Lord Glanely and in 1928 he was killed in a car crash. He left a sum of money for the welfare of Double Chance who had been given to him by fellow Bucks Yeomanry officer, Capt. A. de Rothschild.

ARCHER, William (1826-89)

As a boy William Archer ran away from home and worked for George Taylor (uncle of famous Manton trainer, Alec).

He rode on the Flat and later spent two years, from 1843-45, working for the Tsar of Russia at Tsarkoe Zeloe. On his return he based himself at Cheltenham and rode over fences, winning the 1858 Grand National on Little Charley. On his retirement he became landlord of the Kings Arms, Prestbury, then the centre of the Cheltenham racing set which included Tom Olliver, the Holmans and Adam Lindsay-Gordon. His later life was saddened by the death of his son, William, in a steeplechase at Cheltenham and the suicide of his younger son, Fred, in 1886. His grandson, Frederick (q.v.), trained Double Chance to win the 1925 Grand National.

ARCHIVE

Bay horse, 1941. Bred by Lord Astor.

Archive			
Nearco	Pharos	Phalaris	
		Scapa Flow	
	Nogara	Havresac II	
		Catnip	
Book Law	Buchan	Sunstar	
		Hamoaze	
	Popingaol	Dark Ronald	
		Popinjay	

Despite one of the royallest pedigrees in the Stud Book, Archive proved moderate in the extreme on a racecourse. After an undistinguished two-year-old career he was sold for 470 guineas to Billy Hamnett and Timeform hazarded the hope that he might be "equal to winning long-distance handicaps in the North sooner or later". It was an optimistic estimate. Retired to Mr John Oxx's Wilmount Stud, County Meath, he immortalized himself by siring the mighty Arkle, thanks to whom, he was Leading Sire in 1964-65 with the winners of 28 races worth £38,384.

ARCTIC SLAVE

Bay Horse, 1950. Bred by Mr E. V. Kelly

Arctic Slave			
Arctic Star	Nearco	Pharos	
		Nogara	
	Serena	Winalot	
		Charmione	
Roman Galley	Man O'War	Fair Play	
		Mahubah	
	Messaline	Caligula	
		Monisima	

Arctic Slave won five races on the Flat over distances of 1-1¼m but was by no means top class. He needed give in the ground and although quite genuine, wore a hood and needed to have things his own way. He was a popular and successful stallion who held his place in the sires lists from sheer number of winners, for apart from Titus Oates, few of his stock were outstanding. For 10 consecutive seasons he finished in the first 10 of the sires list. He stood at Garryrichard House, Co. Wexford, until his death in May 1972.

ARKLE

Bay gelding, 1957. Bred by Mrs H. Baker in Co. Dublin, Ireland.

Arkle		
Archive	Nearco	Pharos
		Nogara
	Book Law	Buchan
		Popingaol
Bright Cherry	Knight of the Garter	Son-in-Law
		Castelline
	Greenogue Princess	My Prince
		Cherry Branch II

4th	1968-69	winners of 41	races worth		£19,193
3rd	1969-70	„ „ 52	„ „		£32,145
2nd	1970-71	„ „ 57	„ „		£35,000
2nd	1972-73	„ „ 71	„ „		£37,777
4th	1973-74	„ „ 74	„ „		£32,780
4th	1974-75	„ „ 66	„ „		£42,391
5th	1975-76	„ „ 69	„ „		£40,552

ARDOON

Brown horse, 1906. Bred by Mr J. H. Holdsworth.

Ardoon		
St Frusquin	St Simon	Galopin
		St Angela
	Isabel	Plebeian
		Parma
Multrue	Springfield	St Albans
		Viridis
	Helioscene	Hampton
		Sunshine

Ardoon, a fine big horse, never ran. He stood at Mr James Daly's Hartstown Stud, Clonsilla, and was one of the most influential jumping sires of the 1920s.

In the Leading Sires lists he was 3rd in 1921-22, 3rd in 1924-25, 3rd in 1926-27 and 2nd in 1928-29, while as regards numbers of winners (chases only), he was Leading Sire from 1924-28 inclusive.

ARGO

Chestnut horse, 1919, Argosy—Lady Gladys (Sundridge). Bred by Mr E. G. de Mestre.

A tough, consistent performer belonging to Lord Lonsdale, Argo won four hurdle races including County Hurdle, Cheltenham, and the Liverpool Hurdle, and went on to win four good chases. He was invariably ridden by Harry Brown.

A medium-sized bay with a classic hind leg, tremendous engine-room and a characteristically high, stag-like head carriage, Arkle was the nearest thing to a racing machine this country has ever known. He was descended on his dam's side from the great jumping family of Greenogue Princess. His dam, Bright Cherry, had been very useful at distances between 2-2½m, while his sire, Archive (q.v.) had been classically bred but useless and therefore stood at 48 guineas, a fee within the limited compass of farmer's widow, Mrs Henry Baker. Arkle was foaled at Dorothy Paget's Ballymacoll Stud, reared and broken by Mrs Baker's daughter, Alison, and sent to the August Sales at Ballsbridge as a three-year-old with the realistic reserve of £500 on him.

To the intense surprise and delight of the Bakers he became the subject of a spirited duel between Capt. Charles Radclyffe and Anne, Duchess of Westminster, to whom he was finally knocked down for 1,150 guineas, then a very good price for a store gelding.

Arkle, named after a mountain on his new owner's estate in Sutherland, spent a year in Cheshire being nagged before being offered to Tom Dreaper to be trained. Dreaper could have chosen the Duchess's other four-year-old, a handsome chestnut named Brae Flame. On looks he was undoubtedly the pick of the two but the shrewd trainer had had several of Arkle's relations and decided that blood was thicker than water.

There was no competition among the lads to 'do' the newcomer and he was assigned to 16-year-old Johnny Lumley who came from a Dublin jewellers and was a newcomer himself. As expected, Arkle was slow to mature and his first season's efforts of two hurdle victories from six outings were a great deal more promising than had been anticipated.

Early in 1962-63, however, he served notice of what was to come. In an ambitious venture, he accompanied his stable companion, Fortria, to Cheltenham for the Mackeson meeting and made his debut in England in the Honeybourne Chase, which he won by 20 effortless lengths. He went through the rest of that season unbeaten and indeed unextended and drew attention to himself as a future Gold Cup winner by winning the Broadway Novices at the National Hunt Meeting in authoritative fashion.

Standing between Arkle and any Gold Cup prospects, however, stood the massive young English champion, Mill House, also six years old, who had already graduated from novice company and won that year's Gold Cup. In November 1963, the two met at Newbury in the Hennessy Gold Cup. Arkle was set to receive 5lb and his entourage were confident of the outcome.

Mill House, as usual set off in front, jumping superbly with Arkle handily placed in about fourth place. Half-a-mile from home he began to move up and had almost joined Mill House when he sprawled landing over the open ditch three from home. His chance had gone and Mill House went on to an easy victory, with Arkle third.

The arguments were not resolved and both sides continued to regard their horse as superior. The 1964 Cheltenham Gold Cup was to be the day of reckoning and on it Arkle came out best. He allowed Mill House to lead him until the elbow and then cruised alongside. Mill House made a despairing effort to get back on terms at the last but he could do no more and Arkle strode away to win by five easy lengths.

Having cracked the English giant, there was no bar to Arkle's supremacy. During the next three years only four horses ever finished in front of him and his victories included the Irish Grand National, Fairyhouse (1964), the Hennessy Gold Cup, Newbury (1964) (in which he beat poor Mill House by 26 lengths) and 1965, the Whitbread Gold Cup, Sandown (1965), the King George VI Chase, Kempton (1965) and the 1965-66 Cheltenham Gold Cups.

His supremacy became so colossal that the Irish stewards amended their rules and instructed their handicappers to draw up two lots of weights for important handicaps: one if Arkle ran and a second to be used if he did not.

It seemed too good to be true – and it was. In December 1966, he turned out for the King George VI Chase at Kempton. The race appeared to be a formality and a huge Bank Holiday crowd were amazed to see the champion first falter and then on the run-in surrender the lead to Dormant. Their astonishment turned to dismay as Arkle returned very lame. He was found to have cracked the pedal bone inside his hoof.

A delicate operation was performed by Professor Maxie Cosgrove and he recovered sufficiently to lead a comfortable retirement, though not to race again. However by May 1970 rheumatism had set into the damaged area and, rather then allow him to suffer continuous pain, he was put down.

Arkle won a total of 27 races. He was trained throughout his career by Tom Dreaper and, after his first season, always ridden by Pat Taaffe.

His Gold Cup victories are as follows:

1964   7/4 (P. Taaffe) won by 5l and 25l from Mill House (G. W. Robinson) and Pas Seul (D. Dick).

1965   30/100 favourite (P. Taaffe) won by 20l and 30l from Mill House (G. W. Robinson) and Stoney Crossing (Mr W. Roycroft).

1966   1/10 favourite (P. Taaffe) won by 30l and 10l from Dormant (M. Scudamore) and Snaigow (D. Nicholson).

Arkle raised the sport of steeplechasing to heights of popularity it had not previously known. It seems very unlikely that any horse will ever again exercise such supremacy over his contemporaries.

ARMYTAGE, Roderick Charles (b.1934)
Roddy Armytage assisted Neville Crump and Frank Cundell before taking out a

licence in 1962. His headquarters are at East Ilsley, Berkshire. His owners number several long-standing patrons of steeplechasing, including Col. W. Whitbread and Sir John Thomson and his principal successes have come in long-distance steeplechases. They include:

The Scottish Grand National (1975) Barona; (1976) Barona
The Whitbread Northern Trophy Handicap Chase (1974) Barona
The Benson and Hedges Handicap Chase (1971) Happy Medium
The Liverpool Foxhunters (1964) Aerial III
The Tom Coulthwaite Handicap Chase (1972) Twigairy

ASCETIC
Bay horse, 1871. Bred by Mr Launde.

		Touchstone
	Newminster	
		Beeswing
Hermit		Tadmoor
	Seclusion	
		Miss Selton
Ascetic		Humphrey Clinker
	Melbourne	
		Cervantes mare
Lady Alicia		Venision II
	Testy	
		Tempa

Ascetic, a very moderate racehorse, dominated National Hunt breeding for nearly twenty years and from 1888-1904 was leading sire as regards number of chases won.

Among his stock were the National winners Cloister, Drumcree and Ascetic's Silver, Diane and Rose Graft, the dams of Troytown and Sergeant Murphy, the Liverpool specialist Leinster and the Grand Steeple winner and fine sire Royal Meath.

He stamped his stock clearly and they were described by the notable Irish breeder, J. J. Maher, thus: "the Ascetics have good fronts, splendid bone and grand straight hind legs, often a washy bay and light of back ribs and with good action".

ASCETIC'S SILVER
Chestnut horse, 1897, Ascetic—Silver Lady (Ben Battle). Bred in Ireland by Mr P. J. Dunne.

Ascetic's Silver won five races including both the Irish and English Grand Nationals. A very good-looking horse of considerable ability, his career was severely handicapped by a tendency to break blood-vessels. His first four seasons were spent in Ireland, during which time he won three races including 1904 Irish Grand National (11-7, Dowdall). In the spring of 1905 he was sent over to Liverpool for the English equivalent and although his venture ended prematurely at the third fence, he continued to jump round with zest and fluency and in fact passed the post first, greatly impressing Prince Hatzfeldt and Aubrey Hastings, who subsequently bought him. In 1906 he duly won the Grand National carrying 10-9 (A. Hastings), 20/1, by 10l, 2l, from Red Lad, 10-2 (C. Kelly) and Aunt May, 11-2 (Mr H. Persse). He did not win subsequently and was retired in 1908.

ASCOT (Group 1)
Steeplechasing has taken place at Ascot only since 1965. Many sponsors have been attracted to the best-appointed track in Britain, which, together with imaginatively framed cards, has yielded racing of a consistently high order. The hurdle and chase tracks are inside the Flat course, which places the action rather far away from the spectator, but

Best Times

Distance	Time	Horse-age-weight	Date
2m H	3m 45.3	Ronson Avenue 5-10-4	4-4-74
2m 117y H	3m 48	Burlington 11 4-11-4	9-10-65
2¼m H	4m 46.6	Mayfair Bill 7-11-7	1-4-66
3m H	5m 42.6	Exorbitant 7-10-13	28-10-65
3¼m H	6m 12.1	St Patrick's Blue 6-11-12	18-12-71
2m C	3m 48.4	I'm a Driver 7-10-11	18-11-78
2¼m C	4m 47.4	Winter Rain 6-10-4	6-4-74
3m C	6m 7.90	Balinese 7-10-13	17-11-72
3m 183y C	6m 11.8	Loyal Fort 10-10-6	2-4-66
3m 5f C	7m 54.5	Kilburn 8-10-10	17-2-66

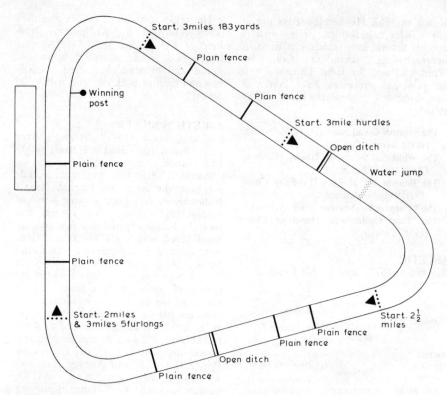

the special paddock in front of the stands has helped to minimize distances.

The track is right-handed and slightly undulating. There is a long downhill run to Swinley Bottom which many novices find taxing. Unfortunately the drainage problems have not been altogether solved and Ascot remains susceptible to waterlogging.

The most valuable race is the Black and White Whisky Gold Cup for Novices (2m, £8,106) in November. Other valuable prizes include the Berni Inns Long Distance Hurdle (April, 3m, £5,933), the Heinz Novice H'cap Chase (2m 4f), the S.G.B. H'cap Chase (December, 3m, £4,708) and the Blue Circle Cement H'cap Chase (January, 2m, £3,963).

The Buchanan Whisky Gold Cup Chase (2m)

	HORSE	OWNER	RIDER	TRAINER
1965	Flyingbolt	Mrs T. G. Wilkinson	P. Taaffe	T. Dreaper
1966	Dicky May	Mr C. Nicholson	P. Taaffe	T. Dreaper
1967	Makaldar	H.M. Queen Elizabeth	D. Mould	P. Cazalet
1968	Spanish Steps	Mr E. Courage	J. Cook	Owner
1969	Cool Alibi	Mr H. Moore	B. R. Davies	J. Bower
1970	Into View	Mrs P. Brown	P. Kelleway	F. Winter
1971	Jabeg	Lt.-Col. Whetherly	J. King	R. Turnell
1972	Pendil	Mrs C. Swallow	R. Pitman	F. Winter
1973	Bula	Capt. E. Edwards-Heathcote	R. Pitman	F. Winter
1974	*No Race*			
1975	Flashy Boy	Mr A. Watson	B. Brogan	A. Watson
1976	Tree Tangle	Mrs C. Williams	A. Turnell	R. Turnell
1977	Kybo	Mr I. Kerman	R. Champion	J. Gifford
1978	I'm a Driver	Mr E. Murphy, jnr	T. Carmody	A. Dickinson

1965-77 Run as the Black and White Whisky Gold Cup Chase

ASSAROE
Bay gelding, 1916, Battle-axe—Kroon Lady (Kroonstad). Bred by Mr D. Gleeson.

Assaroe, a useful hurdler owned by Mr Stanley Howard, won six races including the 1923 Welsh Champion Hurdle and the County Hurdle at the National Hunt Festival.

AUSTERLITZ
Chestnut horse, 1872, Rataplan—Lufra (Windhound). Bred by Lord Scarborough.

After running on the Flat at two and three years with conspicuous lack of success, Austerlitz was bought by Fred Hobson and proceeded to win two hurdle races, a 2½m chase at Sandown and the 1877 Grand National, 10-8 (Mr F. Hobson), 15/1, by 4l, neck, from Congress, 12-7 (J. Cannon) and The Liberator, 10-12 (Mr Thomas), when only a five-year-old. His trainer tried hard to dissuade Mr Hobson from riding his horse, for, although a successful amateur he had a habit of catching hold of the cantle of his saddle in mid-air which did not inspire confidence. His close friend Arthur Yates persuaded him not to yield and with the happiest results for the pair won readily after making most of the running. Austerlitz, one of many National-winning descendants of Pocahontas, was one of only five five-year-olds to win the race. Since 1931 they have been debarred from running. He ran only once subsequently and was unplaced.

AUTEUIL
Auteuil is the principal steeplechase course in France. It was founded in 1873 and in 1874 the first running of the Grand National de France was held. In 1875 it was re-christened the Grand Steeplechase de Paris which it has remained to this day. It is run in June over 6,500 metres. A list of winners appears below.

In its early days it was often raided by British stables. 'Rolly' Melgund (later Earl of Minto) won the first running on Miss Hungerford, George Lambton won on Parasang and H. E. Linde annexed it three times, with Whisper Low, Too Good and Royal Meath. Jerry M., Troytown, Silvo and Maguelonne carried the flag in the early part of this century but in nearly 50 years since Maguelonne's victory only Mandarin has been successful.

The course is very twisting and complicated being roughly a figure of eight. The fences are not uniform and although large, are made of soft privet and are designed to be jumped through rather than over, which is disconcerting for British horses. The hazards include two natural brooks, the Rivière Huit and the Rivière de la Tribune, which is right in front of the stands and comprises 4 metres of water, preceded by a hedge 1 metre high and 1 metre wide. There is also a bullfinch, 1.70 metres high and 1.60 wide, built on a stone wall, a rail, ditch and fence and a wall, previously the terror of the course, which has now been faced with turf and preceded by a small brush. Other important races at Auteuil are the Grande Courses des Haies, the Grande Course des 4 Ans (won by Beaver II in 19629 and the Prix des Drags. Jerry M., Maguelonne and Mandarin are among those honoured with a race named after them.

See also SOCIÉTÉ DE STEEPLECHASES DE FRANCE.

The Grand Steeplechase de Paris (6,500 metres)
M. stands for Monsieur and denotes amateur rider.

HORSE	RIDER
1874 Miss Hungerford	'Mr Rolly' (Vis. Melgund)
1875 La Veine	J. Page
1876 Ventriloque	Goddard
1877 Congress	J. Jewitt
1878 Wild Monarch	J. Page
1879 Wild Monarch	R. l'Anson
1880 Recruit II	Oxford
1881 Maubourguer	H. Andrews
1882 Whisper Low	M. T. Beasley
1883 Too Good	M. H. Beasley
1884 Varaville	Hatchett
1885 Redpath	T. Lowe
1886 Boissy	Benson
1887 La Vigne	Baker
1888 Parasang	M. Lambton
1889 Le Torpilleur	Mousset
1890 Royal Meath	M. H. Beasley
1891 Saida	Boon
1892 Fleurissant	Taylor
1893 Skedaddle	M. G. B. Milne
1894 Loutch	Newby
1895 Styrax	Weech

1896	Valois	Alb Johnson
1897	Solitaire	A. Roberts
1898	Marise	A. Roberts
1899	Tancarville	C. Reeves
1900	Mélibée	Campbell
1901	Calabrais	Gildon
1902	Gratin	J. Turner
1903	Veinard	H. Holt
1904	Dandolo	P. Woodland
1905	Canard	P. Woodland
1906	Burgrave II	R. Sauval
1907	Grosse Mère	R. Sauval
1908	Dandolo	A. Carter
1909	Saint-Caradec	G. Parfrement
1910	Jerry M.	E. Driscoll
1911	Blagueur II	G. Parfrement
1912	Hopper	Lancaster
1913	Ultimatum	G. Parfrement
1914	Lord Loris	A. Carter
1915-18	*No Race*	
1919	Troytown	W. Escott
1920	Coq Gaulois	W. Head
1921	Roi Belge	G. Mitchell
1922	Héros XII	G. Mitchell
1923	L'Yser	L. Barré
1924	Master Bob	J. Bedeloup
1925	Silvo	F. Rees
1926	Portmore	Piarrott
1927	The Coyote	L. Nigiaudbot
1928	Maguelonne	Bedeloup
1929	Le Touquet	L. Duffourc
1930	Le Fils de la Lune	J. Belmondo
1931	La Fregate	Roilfo
1932	Duc d'Anjou	Tremeau
1933	Millionnaire II	Chaoffour
1934	Agitato	Lock
1935	Fleuret	Bonaventure
1936	Potentate	Pelat
1937	Ingre	Bonaventure
1938	Heve	Bunker
1939	Ingre	Bonaventure
1940	*No Race*	
1941	Kerfany	Pelat
1942	Symbole	Guino
1943	Kargal	Bonaventure
1944	Hahnhof	Plaine
1945	Boum	Guino
1946	Lindor	Geffroy
1947	Lindor	Guino
1948	Redeo	Bates
1949	Bouzoulou	Beche
1950	Meli Melo	Emery
1951	Nagar	Hieronimus
1952	Tournay	Delfarguiel
1953	Pharamond III	Mashcio
1954	Orleans	Peraldi
1955	Farfatch	Maire
1956	Necor	T'Kint
1957	Bonosnap	Chancelier
1958	Sidere	Prod'homme

1959	Xanthor	Daumas
1960	Kingcraft	Philippeau
1961	Cousin Pons	Daumas
1962	Mandarin	F. Winter
1963	Loreto	Kirchhofer
1964	Hyères III	Daumas
1965	Hyères III	Daumas
1966	Hyères III	J. Daumas
1967	Cacao	G. Migeon
1968	Haroue	B. Vanheege
1969	Huron	C. Drieu
1970	Huron	C. Drieu
1971	Pot d'or	J. J. Declercq
1972	Morgex	J. P. C. Ciravegna
1973	Giquin	J. P. Creveiul
1974	Chic Type	J. P. Renard
1975	Air Landais	P. Beyer
1976	Piomares	D. Perea
1977	Corps a Corps	A. Fabre
1978	Mon Filleul	J. L. Llorens

AYALA

Chestnut gelding, 1954, Supertello— Admiral's Bliss (Admiral's Walk). Bred by Mr J. P. Phillips.

The winner of five chases including the 1963 Grand National, 10-0 (P. Buckley), 66/1, by ¾l, 5l, from Carrickbeg, 10-3 (Mr J. Lawrence) and Hawa's Song, 10-0 (P. Broderick), Ayala has had his reputation diminished by his failure to gain a place in 10 subsequent outings. In fact he was later found to have broken a small bone in his foot and this injury is thought to have occurred in his race after the National. After an unsuccessful Flat career, Ayala won three chases from 2-2½miles during season 1960-61 and the important Worcester Royal Porcelain Chase prior to his Aintree victory. He was owned by hairdresser Mr P. B. ('Teasy-Weasy') Raymond and trained at Lambourn by Keith Piggott.

AYR (Group 1)

Ayr is the principal N.H. course in Scotland. Since 1966 it has staged the Scottish Grand National (4m, 120y, £14,903). In 1967 a Scottish Champion Hurdle (2m, £5,605) was instituted. Both these races are staged at the mid-April meeting and have, in recent years, attracted a very high standard of entry.

Steeplechasing has taken place at Ayr since 1871. It is a left-handed course, about 12½f round and quite flat. The excellent drainage and proximity of the Gulf Stream make abandonments rare.

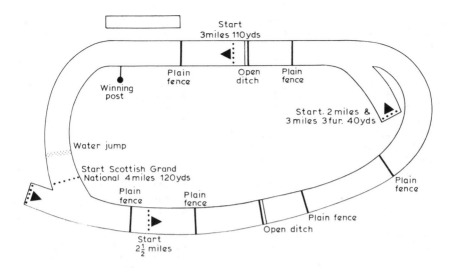

Best Times

Distance	Time	Horse-age-weight	Date
2m H	3m 30.40	Sea Pigeon 6-12-7	9-10-76
2½m H	4m 35	Moss Royal 8-9-10	19-4-74
2m 6f H	5m 13	Midao 5-11-9	14-5-77
3m H	5m 16.40	Tealing 6-9-7	10-10-70
2m C	3m 43.80	Arctic Explorer 7-11-5	18-10-72
2½m C	4m 47.20	Broncho II 5-10-12	12-10-74
3m 110y C	5m 58.90	Duffle Coat 7-11-10	11-10-75
3m 3f 40y C	6m 51.40	Straight Vulgan 8-10-8	18-11-74
4m 120y C	8m 0.40	Young Ash Leaf 7-10-2	17-4-71

William Hill Scottish Grand National (4m 120y)

	HORSE	OWNER	RIDER	TRAINER
Bogside				
1867	The Elk	Duke of Hamilton	Page	——
1868	Greenland	Mr Welfitt	G. Waddington	——
1869	Huntsman	Mr W. Forbes	Hyland	——
1870	Snowstorm	Mr A. Dunhill	Mr R. Walker	——
1871	Keystone	Capt. Machell	Mr J. M. Richardson	——
1872	Cinna	Baron Finot	Mr A. Yates	——
1873	Hybla	Lord Anglesey	J. Adams	——
1874	Duragon II	Mr J. Fearon	Mr G. Mulcaster	——
1875	Solicitor	Mr H. Houldsworth	Mr Daglish	——
1876	Earl Marshal	Lord Downe	Mr T. Spence	——
1877	Solicitor	Mr H. Houldsworth	Mr Thomas	——
1878	*No Race*			
1879	Militant	Mr J. Brodie	Levitt	——
1880	Peacock	Mr J. Lee	Mr Brockton	——
1881	Bellman	Mr C. Rouse	Mr C. J. Cunningham	——
1882	Gunboat	Mr Gardiner Muir	Capt. T. Middleton	——
1883	Kerelaw	Mr H. F. Boyd	Mr E. P. Wilson	——
1884	The Peer	Mr J. G. Muir	Capt. Lee-Barber	——
1885	Wild Meadow	Mr D. J. Jardine	Mr C. J. Cunningham	——
1886	Crossbow	Mr T. Arthur	Mr J. Mckie	——
1887	Orcadian	Mr C. Archer	Mr C. J. Cunningham	——

1888 Ireland	Mr J. Wallace	Capt. Lee-Barber	——
1889 Deloraine	Mr C. J. Cunningham	Mr C. J. Cunningham	——
1890 *No Race*			
1891 *Neither of the two runners could achieve second fence; after 25 mins race declared void*			
1892 Lizzie	Mr C. Duff	Mr C. J. Dormer	——
1893 Lady Ellen II	Mr J. McKinlay	Thornton	——
1894 Leybourne	Capt. J. M. Gordon	A. Nightingall	——
1895 Nepcote	Mr J. A. Miller	Halsey	——
1896 Cadlaw Cairn	Mr R. Stark	Tervit	——
1897 Modest Friar	Mr Turnbull	J. Walsh	——
1898 Trade Mark	Mr A. Alexander	J. Knox	——
1899 Tyrolean	Mr Meldrum	Ochiltree	——
1900 Dorothy Vane	Mr D. H. Gibbs	R. Clarke	——
1901 Big Busbie	Mr C. W. Henderson	J. Archer	——
1902 Canter Home	Mr C. E. Hunter	G. Wilson	——
1903 Chit Chat	Mr G. Paterson	Lawlor	——
1904 Innismacsaint	Mr A. Hastings	Leader	——
1905 Theodocian	Mr Bower Ismay	Capt. Rasbotham	——
1906 Creolin	Capt. M. Lindsay	A. Newey	——
1907 Barney III	Mr A. Scott	Mr A. Scott	——
1908 Atrato	Mr Wynford Phillips	I. Anthony	——
1909 Mount Prospect's Fortune	Mr P. Nelke	E. Driscoll	——
1910 The Duffrey	Mr S. Hill-Wood	J. Walsh, jun.	——
1911 Couvrefeu II	Mr A. Fitzgerald	H. Tratthen	——
1912 Couvrefeu II	Mr B. Fitzgerald	Mr A. Fitzgerald	——
1913 Couvrefeu II	Mr A. Gordon	F. Dainty	——
1914 Scarabec	Mr J. B. Charters	H. Bletsoe	——
1915 Templedowney	Maj. D. Dixon	G. Parfremont	——
1919 The Turk	Mr C. L. Willcox	T. Threlfell	——
1920 Music Hall	Mrs E. Stokes	Mr C. R. Pawson	——
1921 *Abandoned – Industrial Crisis*			
1922 Sergeant Murphy	Mr S. Sanford	Capt. G. H. Bennet	——
1923 Harrismith	Col. R. L. Birkin	F. Brookes	——
1924 Royal Chancellor	Lord Westmorland	E. Foster	——
1925 Gerald L	Mr H. Kershaw	J. Anthony	——
1926 Estuna	Mr R. Parker	A. Harraway	——
1927 Estuna	Mr R. Parker	F. Brookes	——
1928 Ardeen	Sir K. Fraser	F. Rees	——
1929 Donzelon	Col. Foljambe	R. Lyall	——
1930 Drintyre	Mr C. N. Brownhill	Mr C. N. Brownhill	——
1931 Annandale	Lady Glenapp	D. Morgan	——
1932 Clydesdale	Mr H. Collins	G. Hardy	——
1933 Libourg	Mr M. Dollar	T. Isaac	——
1934 Southern Hero	Mr J. V. Rank	J. Fawcus	——
1935 Kellsboro' Jack	Mrs A. Clarke	D. Morgan	——
1936 Southern Hero	Mr J. V. Rank	J. Fawcus	——
1937 Right'un	Mrs A. E. Phillips	J. Bissill	——
1938 Young Mischief	Mr J. V. Rank	D. Morgan	G. Evans
1939 Southern Hero	Mr J. V. Rank	J. Fawcus	H. Brown
1940-6 *No Race*			
1947 Rowland Roy	Mr A. G. Boley	Mr R. Black	F. Walwyn
1948 Magnetic Fin	Mr N. Willis	L. Vick	W. Hall
1949 Wot No Sun	Capt. T. D. Wilson	A. P. Thompson	N. Crump
1950 Sanvina	Mr J. K. M. Oliver	Owner	J. Wight
1951 Court Painter	Maj. E. D. Harris-St John	F. Carroll	C. Bewicke
1952 Flagrant Mac	Lord Grimthorpe	J. Power	R. Renton
1953 Queen's Taste	Mr W. Bailey	Mr T. Robson	H. Clarkson
1954 Queen's Taste	Mr W. Bailey	G. Slack	H. Clarkson
1955 Bar Point	Sir Stanley Bell	D. Ancil	R. Renton

1956	Queen's Taste	Mr W. Bailey	R. Curran	H. Clarkson
1957	Bremontier	Mr B. Nichols	A. Rossio	P. Taylor
1958	Game Field	Lady Barber	J. Boddy	J. Fawcus
1959	Merryman II	Miss W. Wallace	G. Scott	N. Crump
1960	Fincham	Mrs M. Milne Green	M. Batchelor	J. Wight
1961	Kinmont Wullie	Mr W. A. Stephenson	C. Stobbs	W. A. Stephenson
1962	Sham Fight	Mr R. M. C. Jeffrey	T. Robson	T. Robson
1963	Pappageno's Cottage	Mr W. G. King	T. Brookshaw	J. K. M. Oliver
1964	Popham Down	Mr W. G. Turriff	J. Haine	F. Walwyn
1965	Brasher	Mr E. D. Grosschalk	J. Fitzgerald	T. Robson

Ayr

1966	African Patrol	Miss A. H. Robertson	J. Leech	R. Fairbairn
1967	The Fossa	Mr R. Greatbatch	A. Turnell	T. F. Rimell
1968	Arcturus	Lady Hay	P. Buckley	N. Crump
1969	Playlord	Mr Attwood	R. Barry	G. W. Richards
1970	The Spaniard	Mr Rimmer	B. Brogan	J. K. M. Oliver
1971	Young Ash Leaf	Mr R. McDonald	P. Ennis	J. K. M. Oliver
1972	Quick Reply	Mr W. Thyne	M. Barnes	C. Bell
1973	Esban	Miss D. Squires	J. Bourke	R. Clay
1974	Red Rum	Mr N. le Mare	B. Fletcher	D. McCain
1975	Barona	Mr W. Whitbread	P. Kelleway	R. Armytage
1976	Barona	Mr W. Whitbread	P. Kelleway	R. Armytage
1977	Sebastian V	Mr R. Jeffreys	R. Lamb	C. Bell
1978	King Con	Mr G. Renilson	Mr P. Craggs	Owner

1867-1977 run as **Scottish Grand National**

The Scottish Champion Hurdle (2m), handicap 1967-70

	HORSE	OWNER	RIDER	TRAINER
1966	Blue Venom	Mr P. Adams	Mr P. Adams	P. Adams
1967	Originator	Mr J. McGhie	E. Wilson	J. Barclay
1968	Al Alawi	Mr M. P. Davis	P. McCarron	T. Robson
1969	Mugatpura	Dr Desai	T. Jennings	F. Walwyn
1970	Easter Pirate	Miss A. Robertson	S. Hayhurst	R. Fairbairn
1971	Dondieu	Mrs C. Attwood	B. Fletcher	D. Smith
1972	Coral Diver	Mr B. Jenks	K. White	T. F. Rimell
1973	Captain Christy	Mrs J. Samuel	H. Beasley	P. Taaffe
1974	Santon Brig	Mrs B. Stein	M. Dickinson	A. Dickinson
1975	Comedy of Errors	Mr E. Wheatley	K. White	T. F. Rimell
1976	Night Nurse	Mr R. Spencer	P. Broderick	M. H. Easterby
1977	Sea Pigeon	Mr P. Muldoon	J. J. O'Neill	M. H. Easterby
1978	Sea Pigeon	Mr P. Muldoon	J. J. O'Neill	M. H. Easterby

BACCHUS

Chestnut horse, 1874, not in the General Stud Book, Uncas—Brunette (Gamekeeper).

A game and consistent handicap chaser owned by Mr D. Dunlop and invariably ridden by Robert I'Anson, Bacchus won nearly all the big handicaps of his day including the Prince of Wales Chase, Sandown (1880), 12-7, the Great Surrey Open Chase, Croydon (1879 and 1880), 12-7, the Great Metropolitan Chase, Croydon (1879 and 1880) and the inaugural Champion Chase, Liverpool (1880).

BACHELOR'S HALL

Bay geldings, 1970, Dusky Boy—Fair Nell (Fairwell). Bred by Mr Andrew Murphy.

From modest beginnings – he won a Flat race and three hurdle races in his first three seasons – Bachelor's Hall improved rapidly in the spring of 1977 winning good chases at Liverpool and Cheltenham and sprang into chasing's upper echelons the following autumn with successive victories in the Mackeson Gold Cup, the Hennessy Gold Cup and the King George VI Chase. To date he has won nine chases for Mr P. Harris. It was thought that his best distance might be 2½ miles but his relaxed style of racing, his formidable turn of foot and the excellent understanding established with his regular partner, Martin O'Halloran, has enabled him to stay 3 miles.

His success has been a tremendous fillip to the young career of trainer Peter Cundell, son of former trainer Ken Cundell and nephew of Frank (q.v.).

BAILEY, Peter Grenfell (b.1937)

Peter Bailey served with the 4th Queen's Own Hussars, and then spent 12 months

with Peter Walwyn before taking out a licence in 1965. His small string, based at Sparsholt, near Wantage, has been regularly successful apart from two lean seasons when he was badly smitten by the virus. His best horses to date have been the smart hurdler/chaser, Canasta Lad (q.v.) and the good staying chaser Zeta's Son, who unfortunately had to be destroyed after breaking a leg in the 1977 Grand National.

His important successes include:

The Whitbread Gold Cup (1978) Strombolus
The Grand Annual Chase, National Hunt Meeting (1968) Hal's Farewell
The Welsh Champion Hurdle (1972, 1974) Canasta Lad
The Arkle Challenge Trophy (1974) Canasta Lad
The Cheltenham Trial Hurdle (1971) Canasta Lad
The Marlow Ropes John Skeaping Hurdle (1972) Canasta Lad
The Hennessy Cognac Gold Cup (1976) Zeta's Son
The Anthony Mildmay Peter Cazalet Memorial Chase (1977) Zeta's Son
The Bass H'cap Chase (1978) Prince Rock

BALDING, Gerald Barnard (b.1936)

The elder son of trainer and international polo-player, Gerald, 'Toby' Balding rode in point-to-points and took out a licence in 1957 on the sudden death of his father.

At Weyhill, Hampshire, where Willie Moore used to train, he runs a large, mixed stable concentrating more on the National Hunt element. His principal successes have been:

The Grand National (1969) Highland Wedding
The Eider Chase (1966, 1967 and 1969) Highland Wedding
The Topham Trophy (1969) Dozo
The Sweeps H'cap Hurdle (1977) Decent Fellow
The Weetabix Hurdle (1977) Decent Fellow

He is an energetic and articulate chairman of the National Trainers' Association.

BALLINODE

Chestnut mare, 1916, Machakos—Celia (Veles). Bred by Messrs Slocock.

Ballinode, 'the Sligo mare', won 12 races including the 1924 Grand Sefton, Liverpool, and the 1925 Cheltenham Gold Cup (T. Leader), 3/1, by 5l, a bad third, from Alcazar (F. Rees) and Patsey V (Mr B. Lemon). Trained at the Curragh by Frank Morgan, she was a fast, flippant fencer and not terribly easy to keep right. Morgan, who often rode her himself, came to know her very well and could be relied upon to produce her at her best for big English chases. Owned by Mr J. C. Bentley, she was the first of three mares to win the Cheltenham Gold Cup.

BALLOT BOX
Brown gelding, 1879, Candidat—Susan (Commotion). Bred by Mr W. Coleman.

A tough, game handicapper who graduated from hunter-chases, Ballot Box was a great favourite with the Nightingall family. Willie won the 1888 Grand International Chase, Sandown, on him, despite breaking a stirrup leather at the start and was third in the 1888 Grand National. Arthur rode him to most of his other victories which included the Great Metropolitan Chase, Croydon (1887) and the Great Sandown Chase (1887).

BALLYBRACK
Bay gelding, 1924, registered in Miss Prior's Half-Bred Stud Book, March-mond—May Lily (Hermit II).

Ballybrack was a very useful hunter-chaser, owned by Lt.-Col. R. W. Tweedie and ridden by his son 'Reg' (q.v.), whose 18 victories included the 1932 Liverpool Foxhunters and the 1934 Cheltenham Foxhunters.

BALLYMACAD
Bay gelding, 1907, Laveno—Ballymacar-ney (Royal Meath). Bred in Ireland by Mr J. J. Maher.

Ballymacad was sold by his breeder to Sir George Bullough for whom he was trained by Aubrey Hastings at Wrough-ton. His two victories included the 1917 War National Steeplechase at Gatwick, 9-12 (E. Driscoll), 100/9, by 8l, 4l, from Chang, 9-9 (W. Smith) and Ally Sloper, 11-10 (I. Anthony). He must be considered an extremely moderate National winner and a very fortunate one, for he would assuredly not have won had not Limerick collapsed on the run-in.

BANDALORE
Bay gelding, 1951, Tambourin—Smart Woman (Noble Star). Bred by Mrs Warman at Droitwich, Worcestershire.

Sold to Mrs Wright after winning a hurdle race as a four-year-old, Bandalore was thereafter trained by her husband Stanley and won nine hurdle races, including the 1958 Champion Hurdle, and a chase. His Champion Hurdle victory was a remarkable affair for, ridden by George Slack and starting at 20/1, he made most of the running, was given a breather going down the hill and ran on strongly to win by 2l, 3l, from Tokoroa (D. Dick) and Retour de Flamme (J. Lindley).

BANGOR-ON-DEE (Group 5)
Bangor-on-Dee together with Chepstow, are the only racecourses in Wales. National Hunt racing has been staged there since 1867 and the course retains its old country atmosphere. There are no stands but a long grass bank, on which cars can be parked, runs along the south and part of the east side of the course and provides an excellent view. The track is left-handed, about 12 furlongs round and flat. The old turf, the watering system and excellent drainage make for consistently good going. The most important race is the Sir Alfred McAlpine Welsh Champion Novice Chase (2m, 160y, £2,138) which is run in April.

Best Times

Distance	Time	Horse-age-weight	Date
2m 92y H	3m 52.70	Dee Lane 5-10-13	20-9-75
3m 68y H	6m 1.50	On the Map 6-10-2	12-4-69
2m 180y C	4m 9.80	Mighty Marine 6-11-2	6-9-75
2m 1f 94y C	4m 22	Guinea Hunter 11-12-3	21-9-68
2m 4f 81y C	4m 57.80	Royal Mark 9-10-2	20-9-75
3m 214y C	6m 21.20	Esoteric 10-12-2	18-5-77
3m 1f 42y C	6m 3.80	Vichysoise 6-12-5	19-10-68

BARBOUR, Frank

A wealthy and eccentric linen-thread manufacturer, Frank Barbour had a splendid training establishment at Trimblestown in Co. Meath where he had replicas of several famous fences, including most of the Aintree hazards, laid out on his extensive gallops. From here he sent out Koko to win the 1926 Cheltenham Gold Cup and also 'made' an explosive young horse of similar characteristics who became much more famous in Easter Hero, whom he sold to Capt. Lowenstein for £7,000 plus a £3,000 contingency should he win the National. Barbour was an M.F.H. and rode in point-to-points. Once after a fall in his Members Race, he hitched a lift to Dublin and sailed for America still in his riding clothes. In 1928 he moved to Bishop's Canning in Wiltshire. His licence was held by head-lad J. Bickley.

BARONA

Bay gelding, 1966, Neron—Barita (Berwick). Bred by Mr J. Fitzgerald.

A fine, old-fashioned type of long-distance stayer owned by one of National Hunt racing's most generous supporters, Col. W. Whitbread, and trained by Roddy Armytage, Barona has won a hurdle race and nine steeplechases including the Whitbread Northern Trophy, Newcastle (1974) and the Scottish Grand National, Ayr (1975 and 1976).

Barona is one of a long list of distinguished patients of Syd Mercer who diagnosed a blood disorder in the spring of 1975. This had been a legacy of a bad attack of the virus the previous spring from which he had never properly recovered. Barona was treated with one of the 'magic' powders and promptly sallied forth to win his first Scottish Grand National.

In all his major triumphs, Barona has been partnered by Paul Kelleway.

BARROTT, Douglas Colin (1947-73)

'Doug' Barrott was apprenticed to Willie Stephenson from 1962-67 and rode winners on the Flat before becoming too heavy. He then embarked on a highly successful but tragically brief N.H. career as first jockey to Josh Gifford, which he held until his death from multiple head injuries after a fall from French Colonist in the 1973 Whitbread Gold Cup.

His principal successes were:

The Imperial Cup (1971) Churchwood
The Benson and Hedges Hurdle (1971) Churchwood
The Stone's Ginger Wine Chase (1973) Avondhu
The Victor Ludorum Hurdle (1973) Mythical King

BARRY, R. E. (b.1943)

Ron Barry served his apprenticeship with T. Shaw in Ireland and rode his first winner in 1964. When he first came to England he was attached to Gordon Richard's Penrith stable where he remained until the beginning of 1975-76. An immensely strong, polished horseman, he was quick to make his mark and in season 1970-71 finished fourth in the Jockeys Table with 65 winners. He has twice headed the Jockey's list, in 1972-73 with 125 winners, and in 1973-74 with 94.

His total for 1972-73 was a record achievement from only 430 rides, 100 fewer than when Josh Gifford set the old record in 1966-67.

His principal successes have been:

The Cheltenham Gold Cup (1973) The Dikler
The Scottish Grand National (1969) Playlord
The Whitbread Gold Cup (1971) Titus Oates; (1973) Charlie Potheen; (1974) The Dikler
The Massey-Ferguson Gold Cup (1969) Titus Oates; (1975) Easby Abbey
The John Player Hurdle Final (1973) Dark Sultan
The Sun Alliance Novice Hurdle (1974) Brown Lad
The Wills Premier Chase Final (1977) Border Incident
The Schweppes Gold Trophy (1976) Irish Fashion
The Greenall-Whitley Chase (1975) The Benign Bishop
The Whitbread Northern Trophy (1976) Forest King
The Colonial Cup, Camden, U.S.A. (1976) Grand Canyon; (1978) Grand Canyon

BATTLESHIP

Chestnut horse, 1927, Man O'War—Quarantine (Sea Sick). Bred in America by Walker J. Salmon at Mereworth Stud, Lexington, Kentucky.

There hangs about the remarkably successful career of Battleship an aura of a fairytale. Bought as a two-year-old by millionairess Mrs Marion du Pont Scott, wife of the film star Randolph Scott, he climaxed a successful jumping career in his native land by winning the 1934 American Grand National. Sent to England to attempt the 1938 Liverpool version, he did just that. Standing barely 15.2 h.h., he was the smallest horse – trainer Reg Hobbs (who reluctantly risked £1 on his 40/1 charge "in case he had to buy the champagne") declared he would not be able to see over The Chair – and was ridden by a 17-year-old jockey. Starting at 40/1, 11-6 (B. Hobbs) he won by a head and a bad third from Royal Danieli, 11-3 (D. Moore) and Workman, 10-2 (J. Brogan).

Battleship, who won six other chases in England returned to America to become the foundation stallion for Mrs Scott's chasing stud, in which sphere he was equally successful, being leading sire on five occasions and responsible for the 1956 American Grand National winner, Shipboard. Battleship is the last 'entire' to have won the National and the only horse to have won the American and English Grand Nationals. He was put down in 1958.

BAULKING GREEN
Chestnut gelding, 1953, registered in Miss Prior's Half-Bred Stud Book, Coup de Myth—Nicotine Nelly (Irish Trout). Bred by Mr Jim Reade.

Baulking Green was the most popular hunter-chaser of recent years. A powerfully made chestnut, he won two point-to-points and 22 hunter-chases, including The Horse and Hound Cup (Stratford, 1962, 63 and 65), the Usher-Vaux Scottish Champion Hunter-Chase (Ayr) three times and the United Hunts (National Hunt Meeting) four times. On a fifth occasion, at the age of 15 he was second, beaten a short head. Owned by Old Berkshire Hunt farmer Jim Reade and named after the village where he was born, he spent his early career hunting and did not see the racecourse until he was 8, when he won a point-to-point. In 1963 he was sent to be trained by Capt. Tim Forster at Letcombe Bassett where he remained for the rest of his career. His exploits were followed by a large and devoted fan club, one of whom, Ron Liddiard, wrote an excellent book about him, published by J. H. Allen. Baulking Green was put down in 1978 at the age of 25.

BEACON LIGHT
Bay gelding, 1972, Relko—Illuminous (Rockefella). Bred by Mr H. J. Joel.

In a very competitive age for hurdlers, Mr Jim Joel's elegant, home-bred Beacon Light is, on his day, able to hold his own with the best of them. He comes from the same stable as Bird's Nest and there would not appear to be much between the pair.

He has won a flat race and six hurdle races including the William Hill Christmas Hurdle, Kempton (1977), the Lloyds Bank Champion Novice Hurdle, N.H. Meeting (1976) and the New Year's Day Hurdle, Windsor (1978). Beacon Light, who is a particularly fluent jumper of hurdles and a delight to watch, is trained by Bob Turnell.

BEASLEY, H. H. (b.1850)
The second of the five talented sons of Joseph Beasley of Atley, Co. Kildare, Harry Beasley was an effective horseman over any type of country. Less polished than his elder brother, Tommy, he was stronger and more effective on rougher mounts. He won the Grand National in 1891 on Come Away whom he also trained, having neatly contained the rash challenge of Roddy Owen on Cloister, who had tried to come between his horse and the rails. Capt. Owen afterwards objected but in vain.

Harry Beasley's other notable successes included:

The Grand Steeplechase de Paris (1883) Too Good; (1890) Royal Meath
The Grande Course des Haies (1881) Seaman

and no less than four Grand Seftons, three running, on Jupiter Jonas, Lord Chancellor, Zitella and St George.

He rode his last chase winner in the 4m Kildare Hunt Cup at Punchestown in 1918 and continued to ride on the Flat until 1935, when he finally hung up his boots after winning the Corinthian Plate (Baldoyle) at the age of 85. His two sons, H. H. and Patrick (Rufus) became distinguished jockeys on the Flat and afterwards trainers, while his grandson, 'Bobby' (q.v.), upheld the family tradition over fences.

BEASLEY, Henry Robert (b.1936)
A grandson of Harry Beasley (q.v.), Bobby Beasley was one of the strongest

and most stylish jockeys to ride over fences since World War II. His early successes included:

The Cheltenham Gold Cup (1959) Roddy Owen
The Champion Hurdle (1960) Another Flash
The Grand National (1961) Nicolaus Silver
The Mackeson Gold Cup (1963) Richard of Bordeaux

He rode for the notably successful Paddy Sleator–Arthur Thomas team, which won innumerable races including the 1966 Daily Express Triumph Hurdle with Black Ice.

At one stage a combination of a series of dreadful falls, increasing weight and an addiction to alcohol, forced him to give up riding, but in 1972 he made a triumphant comeback for Pat Taaffe's newly formed stable. Riding with all his old finesse, he won the Irish Sweeps Hurdle (1972) and the Scottish Champion Hurdle (1973) on Captain Christy and, even more incredibly, taught that insouciant character to jump fences in a reasonably respectful fashion so that the pair won six chases, including the 1974 Cheltenham Gold Cup.

At the end of 1973-74, Bobby Beasley announced his retirement. He is married to Arthur Thompson's daughter Shirley.

BEASLEY, Thomas (d.1905)

The eldest of the Beasley brothers, Tommy was a high-class Flat jockey who won three Irish Derbies. From 1872 he was associated with H. E. Linde of Eyrefield Lodge for whom he won three Grand Nationals in nine years: 1880, on Empress; 1881, on Woodbrook; and 1889, on Frigate.

In 1882 he nearly completed a hat-trick for the stable when beaten a head on Cyrus. He was also second in 1878 on Martha and third in 1879 on the same mare when no less than three of his brothers rode in the race. Victor II was ridden by Mr J. Beasley, Turco by Harry and Lord Marcus by Willie, who was killed from a fall in 1892. Tommy Beasley also won the 1882 Grand Steeplechase on Whisper Low. He was an all-round sportsman, being a fine man to hounds, a crack shot and a skilful fisherman.

BEAVER

Bay gelding, 1958, Fast Fox—Anne (Niccolo dell'Arca). Bred in France by Mme Strassburger.

Beaver, who raced in England as Beaver II, was classically bred, his dam being a half-sister to the ill-fated 1960 Derby favourite Angers, but it was as a hurdler that he made his mark. As a four-year-old he won six races including the Triumph Hurdle, Hurst Park, by 6l, the Grande Course des Haies de Quatre Ans, Auteuil, and the Mackeson Hurdle at Cheltenham. At this period he was trained at Findon by Ryan Price, in whose colours he ran, and customarily ridden by Fred Winter. He was sold to Mr Bernard Sunley before the Mackeson Hurdle. He ran only twice in the next three years during which time he was gelded and moved to Ken Cundell's establishment. On Mr Sunley's death he became the property of Mrs Cundell, in whose colours he won two more hurdle races and three novice chases.

BECHER, Capt. Martin Henry (1797-1864)

The son of a Norfolk farmer and dealer, Martin Becher was sent to Belgium in the Store-Keeper General's Department, He was stationed in Ostend and then in Brussels over the Waterloo campaign. Afterwards he joined the Duke of Buckingham Yeomanry and was given the courtesy title of Captain. He became very friendly with Thomas Coleman (*q.v.*), proprietor of the Turf Hotel, St Albans, living at his house on and off for 20 years and riding his horses.

He was one of the foremost riders in the early days of organized chasing and is chiefly remembered for his partnership with Vivian, on whom he won the Vale of Aylesbury Steeplechase (1834) and the Cheltenham Steeplechase (1837) and his fall at the first of Aintree's mighty brooks which henceforth bore his name.

Thick-set and sturdy with a rugged face and small but bright, piercing eyes, Capt. Becher was a very athletic man, whose party trick was to get round a room without touching the floor. He retired in 1847 after a very bad fall in which he broke his thigh in two places.

BEEBY, George (1904-77)

The son of famous Shires' horse-dealer, George Beeby rode a little as an amateur and took out a trainer's licence in 1924.

At first he trained only under N.H. Rules and was, for a time after World

War II, private trainer to Lord Bicester during the latter's flowering period as an owner. He then made his stable a 'mixed' one and latterly trained only under Jockey Club Rules.

Among his major N.H. successes were:

The Cheltenham Gold Cup (1939) Brendan's Cottage; (1951) Silver Fame
The King George VI Chase (1949) Finnure
The Champion Chase (1950) Finnure
The Mildmay Memorial (1951) Roimond
The Grand Sefton (1936) Delaneige; (1938) Rockquilla

His son, Harry, is a partner in Doncaster Bloodstock Sales and one of the best auctioneers in the country.

BELL, James McKie (1868-1934)
An extremely shrewd Epsom trainer who gambled successfully on a large scale, Jimmy Bell won the Imperial Cup seven times, four times for Mr Percy Heybourne who owned Trespasser (*q.v.*), 1920, 1921 and 1922 and Vermouth, 1914. His other winners were Perseus II, 1908, Peeping Tom, 1926 and Hercules, 1929.

He also won the War National (1916) with Vermouth. He trained his horses very lightly, using ponies to work them. A keen angler, he spent his summer holidays fishing in Iceland.

BELLONA
Brown mare, 1882, Lord Gough—Metz (Restitution). Bred by Mr Bernel Osborne.

The winner of six races including the Grand National Hurdle, Croydon (1886), and the Grand International Hurdle, Sandown (1887), and second in the Lancashire Chase. Bellona, "a great, raking brown mare with the grandest head you ever did see", was extremely popular and a prime favourite with her owner Hon. George Lambton. Her victory in the prestige Grand National Hurdle - her first outing - landed a tremendous gamble for her stable.

BENGOUGH, Lt.-Col. P. H. G. (b.1929)
Piers Bengough, who served in the 10th Hussars, rode as an amateur with great success. He won the Grand Military Gold Cup four times, in 1960 on Joan's Rival, and in 1970, 1971 and 1972 on Charles Dickens. Both horses were trained by Alex Kilpatrick. He was elected to the National Hunt Committee in 1965. Colours: black, silver sleeves, green cap.

BENNET, Capt. Geoffrey Harbord (1895-1924)
'Tuppy' Bennet, son of N.H. trainer Geoffrey Bennet, was a qualified veterinary surgeon and a top-flight amateur rider who won the 1923 Grand National on Sergeant Murphy. He was also leading amateur that year riding 62 winners as opposed to the leading professional F. B. Rees's 64.

On 27th December at Wolverhampton he fell from a horse called Ardeen, was kicked on the head and smashed his skull. He died 17 days later without regaining consciousness. His untimely death led to the introduction of compulsory crash helmets.

BERESFORD, Lord Marcus Talbot de la Poer (1848-1922)
A member of a distinguished Irish sporting family, Marcus Beresford was the fourth of five brothers who rode over fences. Educated at Harrow, he was commissioned into the 12th Lancers and later transferred to the 7th Hussars.

He served racing in many capacities, as an owner and amateur rider under N.H. Rules and as an owner, starter and steward under J.C. Rules. He was also Manager of the Royal Stud and Master of the Horse to Edward VII from 1902 although he had unofficially acted in that capacity since being appointed an extra equerry in 1890.

His best horses were the popular halfbred, Chimney Sweep, on whom he won races himself and who won the Sandown International Chase and ran second to Reugny in the 1874 Grand National, and Jackal who was second in the 1879 National and won the Sandown Grand International Chase. He was responsible for buying Ambush for the Prince of Wales and also Moiffa, although this was a less-successful purchase.

A contemporary said of him: "A man more delightful, more staunch and loyal and more devoted to Their Majesties, whom he loved to serve, never came into my life. He brought sunshine into the lives of all he cared to be interested in, for God had given him a rare and ready wit such as is vouchsafed to so few men. ... There was no finer judge of a horse or racing."

BERRY, Francis (b.1952)

Francis Berry was apprenticed to Mick Hurley at the Curragh and for him won the 1968 Irish St Leger on Giolla Mear when still an apprentice. He 'did' the horse, who was headstrong and difficult to ride, himself. Becoming too heavy for the Flat, he transferred to Francis Flood (*q.v.*), and in 1972 won the Cheltenham Gold Cup on the stable's Glencaraig Lady. He rode a cool race on the able but far from sure-footed mare, getting her round safely and then launching her up the hill to hold off the persistent challenges of Royal Toss and The Dikler.

Other important successes include:

The Alpen Trophy Chase (1977) Siberian Sun

The Lloyds Bank Champion Novice Hurdle (1975) Bannow Rambler

In 1975 he shared the Irish N.H. Jockeys' Championship with Tommy Carberry.

BETTING SHOPS

Betting shops became legal under the new Betting and Gaming Act of 1961, with the object of enabling working people who could not go racing and did not have a credit account with a book-maker, to have a bet. They are not allowed to have television relayed to them but they do have a 'blower' commentary relayed from most courses which provides up-to-date betting fluctuations, a commentary on the race and the official return.

Most betting shops are owned by one of the big chains – Hills, Ladbrokes, Joe Coral, Mecca or the Tote.

BEWICKE, Maj. Calverly (b.1914)

A great nephew of well-known amateur rider and trainer, Percy Bewicke, Verly Bewicke rode as an amateur rider, with some success, before World War II.

He served in the Northumberland Hussars and became a major. In 1947 he began training at his Northumberland home of Wylam-on-Tyne. Finding it too remote, he later moved down to Didcot, on the Berkshire Downs.

Among his best wins are:

The Cheltenham Gold Cup (1958) Kerstin

The Hennessy Gold Cup (1959) Kerstin

The Grand Sefton Chase (1955) Gentle Moya

The Lancashire Chase (1962) Skish

The Emblem Chase (1957) Green Drill

The National Hunt Handicap Chase (1956) Kerstin

The Scottish Grand National (1951) Court Painter

BEWICKE, Capt. Percy Wentworth (1861-1950)

A very prominent amateur rider of the late nineteenth century, Capt. Bewicke served in the 15th Hussars and won the Grand Military Gold Cup in 1892 on Ormerod. He also won the Lancashire Chase twice, in 1892 on Roman Oak and in 1896 on his own Lady Helen and the Grande Course des Haies twice, in 1897 on Soliman and in 1900 on General Peace. He was leading amateur in 1891 and 1892.

In 1909 he took out a licence to train. Mr Fred Straker was principal patron and the stable betted with considerable success. When he retired in 1927, he withdrew from the Turf completely and was quoted as saying, "I shall not mind if I never see a racecourse again."

BICESTER, Hugh Vivian Smith, 1st Baron (1867-1956)

A charming, dignified personality with a natural gift for friendship, Lord Bicester enjoyed a popularity and respect accorded to few owners.

A notable figure in the City, he was Chairman of J. S. Morgan & Co. (merchant bankers), and from 1914 Governor of the Royal Exchange Assurance. Lord Bicester became interested in chasing about 1930 and Jack Jarvis bought him his first horses who included Physician (Stanley Chase 1931). His horses were trained by Fred Withington until 1936 and thereafter by George Beeby in England and Tom Dreaper in Ireland. He was second in the Leading Owners list in 1949-50 and in 1950-51 when he won 19 races (worth £13,890) and 14 races (worth £7,955) respectively.

His horses were of a recognizable type – big, strong, short-legged animals with a bold outlook. Among the best were Silver Fame (26 races, including 1951 Cheltenham Gold Cup), Finnure (King George VI Chase, 1949), Roimond (14 chases including the Mildmay Memorial, second in the 1949 Grand National) and Royal Approach (six races including the Irish Grand National and the Cathcart Challenge Cup before breaking a leg).

His lifelong dreams to win the National died with him, though ironically he was underbidder for the 1953 winner, Early Mist, at Mr J. V. Rank's dispersal sale.

BICKLEY, J.
Held the licence for the Bishop's Canning Stable conducted by Frank Barbour (*q.v.*), which sent out the 1926 Cheltenham Gold Cup winner, Koko.

BIDDLECOMBE, Anthony
Elder brother of Terry Biddlecombe (*q.v.*), Tony Biddlecombe came from a Gloucestershire farming family. Brought up in a world of hunting, dealing, show-jumping and point-to-pointing he became a fine all-round horseman and rode briefly, but with great success, as an amateur. In 1960-1 he finished the season Champion Amateur with 30 winners.

BIDDLECOMBE, Terence Walter (b.1941)
A member of a sporting, farming Gloucestershire family, Terry Biddlecombe show-jumped, point-to-pointed and rode as an amateur before turning professional in 1960.

He joined Fred Rimell's stable in 1962-3 and remained associated with it until 1972 when he went freelance. He was Champion Jockey three times, viz.

1964-65	114 winners
1965-66	102 winners
1968-69	77 winners (equal with B. R. Davies)

and undoubtedly would have been so more often if he had been built on a slightly smaller scale. His constant battle against the scales had no visible effect on his colossal enjoyment of life and right up to his retirement in March 1974, he remained one of the strongest finishers in the game.

His principal victories were:

The Cheltenham Gold Cup (1967) Woodland Venture
The Mackeson Gold Cup (1969) Gay Trip; (1971) Gay Trip
The Daily Express Triumph Hurdle (1969) Coral Diver
The Grand Sefton (1964) Red Thorn
The Great Yorkshire Chase (1973) Charlie Potheen

He never won the Grand National, missing a winning ride on Gay Trip in 1970 through injury, and finishing second, giving 26lbs to the two-length winner, Well To Do, in 1972.

Terry Biddlecombe now runs a livery yard in Gloucestershire, breaking and schooling young horses and training point-to-pointers.

BILLY BARTON
Brown gelding, 1918, Huon—Mary le Bus (St Savin). Bred in U.S.A. by Mr A. L. Fergusson, Georgetown, Kentucky.

After a successful three-year-old career on the Flat in Cuba, Billy Barton turned cunning and was taken out of training. Sold to Mr Howard Bruce, he was hunted and raced over timber, at which he became virtually unbeatable. During 1926-7 he won the Maryland Hunt Cup, the Meadow Brook Cup, The Grand National Point-to-Point twice, The Virginia Gold Cup and the Pennsylvania and New Jersey Hunt Cups. In the autumn of 1927 he was sent to Aubrey Hastings' Wroughton yard to be trained for the Grand National. His bold schooling efforts and a facile first victory in a three-mile chase at Newbury inspired huge confidence across the Atlantic. Schools in Baltimore were given a holiday and crowds gathered in Sun Square to listen to a radio broadcast based on a telephone report of the big race. Their hopes rose high, for having avoided the schemozzle at the Canal Turn, Billy Barton jumped superbly and came to the last looking like a winner, only to capsize alongside the only other survivor Tipperary Tim. Tim Cullinan remounted to finish second. Billy Barton became difficult to train and ran only three times subsequently. He finally went home to Belmont and died in 1951 at the age of 33. A statue of him stands in the entrance of Laurel Park Racecourse.

BIRCH, A.
Won the 1904 Grand National on the giant, New Zealand-bred Moiffa.

BIRD'S NEST
Chestnut gelding, 1970, Entanglement —Fair Sabrina (Mustang). Bred by Mr G. W. Morris.

Mr Ian Scott's Bird's Nest, a handsome, well-proportioned individual, was most unlucky to have been born in the hottest generation of hurdlers for years.

On his day he is capable of beating the best of them yet he has never won a Champion Hurdle. It may be that he does not like Cheltenham for he has never run up to his best there.

His ten victories include the Fighting Fifth Hurdle, Newcastle (1976 and 1977), the Bula Hurdle (1977), and the Wolverhampton Champion Hurdle Trial (1976 and 1977). His tremendous duels with Night Nurse were one of the most exciting features of the hurdling scene during 1977 and 1978.

Bird's Nest who has lost races by veering under pressure and is undoubtedly a little wayward, is quite superbly handled by Andy Turnell and trained by his father, Bob.

BLACK, Richard
One of only two amateurs to do so, Mr Richard Black won the Cheltenham Gold Cup (1946) on the entire Fortina. He also won the Lancashire Chase (1939) on the Furlongs' Litigant and the Scottish Grand National on Rowland Roy. He later turned professional but was less successful.

BLACKLOCK
Bay horse, 1814.

			King Fergus
		Hambletonian	
	Whitelock		Grey Highflyer
			Phenomenon
		Rosalind	
Blacklock			Atlanta
			Pot 8 Os
		Coriander	
	mare by		Lavender
			High Flyer
		Wild Goose	
			Coheiress

Roundly condemned by the 'Druid' as "a plain, coarse horse with bad forelegs", Blacklock nevertheless exercised an extremely important influence on early N.H. breeding. Adam Lindsay Gordon wrote of "the lean, game head of the Blacklock breed and the resolute eye that loves the lead".

Among early Grand National winners tracing to Blacklock were Gaylad (1842) by Brutandorf by Blacklock, Vanguard (1843) probably by Belzoni by Blacklock, Freetrader (1856) out of Miss Cobden ex Blacklock mare, Little Charley (1858) by Charles XII by Voltaire by Blacklock, Half-Caste (1859) by Morgan Rattler by Velocipelo by Blacklock and Jealousy by

The Cure by Physician by Brutandorf by Blacklock.

BLACKWELL, George (1861-1942)
George Blackwell trained a few jumpers at his big (chiefly Flat) Newmarket stables and saddled Sergeant Murphy to win the 1923 Grand National. He had previously trained Rock Sand to win the Triple Crown in 1903 and thus became the third of five trainers to win both the Derby and the National. The others were James Jewitt, Richard Dawson, Willie Stephenson and Vincent O'Brien. Blackwell who was reputed to be exceedingly acute, was attached to A. Gilbert and later to Matt Dawson. He also farmed and at one time owned the Manderstown Stud Farm and Lagrange stables.

BLAIR, Morgan de Witt (d.1951)
Morgan de Witt Blair was an American amateur rider and trainer, known as 'Bam', from his habitual exclamation as he injected himself in the weighing room before riding a race. Immensely tough, he completed the 1921 Grand National on Bonnie Charlie, after no less than four falls, and again in 1925 on Jack Horner, thus landing a substantial gamble. This last effort was a remarkable affair for he rode with a scar still raw from an appendix operation a fortnight previously and had sweated off 18lbs in the previous 48 hours to do the weight. He afterwards trained, first at Rugby and later at Ewhurst, Surrey. His methods were thought to be very unorthodox but he trained winners and won the 1936 Champion Hurdle with Victor Norman.

BLARIS
Bay gelding, 1921, Achtoi—Oppliger (General Symons). Bred by Mr B. W. Parr.

Blaris, a versatile and consistent performer, won a N.H. Flat race and six hurdle races including the Liverpool November Handicap with 12-7 and the inaugural Champion Hurdle (1927), G. Duller, 11/10f, by 8l, 11 from Boddam (W. Speck) and Harpist (F. Rees). He was also a proficient chaser, most effective at two miles but able to stay three and won eleven chases including the Coventry Cup at the National Hunt Festival. He was trained by W. Payne and owned by the redoubtable Mrs Hollins, who once chased Capt. 'Tuppy' Bennet round the paddock with her umbrella after he had remounted her horse, Turkey Buzzard, no less than four times in the Grand National.

BLETSOE, Bernard

A native of Denton, Northamptonshire, Bernard Bletsoe bred, owned and trained the 1901 Grand National winner, Grudon, although the licence was held by J. Holland. The victory was largely due to Bletsoe's resourcefulness, for realizing that the race was going to be run in a snowstorm, he procured 2lb of butter from the local creamery, with which he packed Grudon's feet.

The family were noted for their fine horsemanship and 'way' with difficult horses. Bernard Bletsoe was reputed to be the only man capable of dealing with Grudon's sire, Old Buck, generally regarded as a man-eater, while his daughter Betty was thought by Arthur Nightingall to manage the far-from-easy Grudon better than anyone else. His son, Morgan (q.v.) rode Rubio to win the 1908 National.

BLETSOE, H. M.

Son of the trainer, Bernard Bletsoe (q.v.), Morgan Bletsoe was given the ride on the American-bred 1908 Grand National winner, Rubio, after stable-jockey, L. W. Bissill had rejected the ride in favour of the stable's other runner, Mattie Macgregor. He also won the Champion Chase (1897) on Grudon and the Scottish Grand National (1914) on Scarabec.

BLOOMER

Chestnut gelding, not in the General Stud Book, Blue Grass—Lady Skeffington.

Bloomer, a tough, honest gelding owned by Mr R. Bourke won 22 races including the Grand Sefton, the Champion Chase, Liverpool (1900), and the Welsh Grand National (1900).

BOGSKAR

Brown gelding, 1933, Werwolf—Irish Spring (Irishman). Bred by Mr C. Roche.

Bogskar who was owned and trained by Lord Stalbridge had a most extraordinary career. After failing to win in his first three seasons, he came good with a vengeance in 1939-40, winning four chases including the important National Trial Chase, Gatwick and the Grand National, 10-4 (M. Jones) 25/1, 4l, 6l from MacMoffat, 10-10 (I. Avder) and

Gold Arrow, 10-3 (P. Lay). He failed to win again, although continuing to race until after the war.

'BONA FIDE' MEETINGS

There were two types of 'Bona fide' meetings, Hunt which started in 1912, and Military in 1927.

"A bona fide Hunt Meeting is a Meeting held under N.H. Rules on one day only in a year by a particular Hunt or two or more adjoining Hunts over a natural or partly natural course, situated within the limits of the Hunt or of one of the Hunts joining in the promotion of the fixture and duly approved by the Stewards of the N.H. Committee after inspection by one of the Official Inspectors of Steeple Chase Courses."

"A 'bona-fide' Military Meeting is a Meeting held under N.H. Rules by a unit of the Regular Army, Navy or Air Force, approved by and over a course sanctioned by the Stewards of the National Hunt Committee."

Their rules were similar to those of point-to-points. No professional might ride. Riders were confined to members of the Hunt or Hunts staging the fixture, officers, and in the case of Hunt meetings to members of specified regiments including Yeomanry. All races were to be steeplechases and of a distance of at least three miles. No prize could exceed 20 sovereigns and any surplus was to be used, in the case of Hunt Meetings, for the Hunt or Hunts staging the fixture, and that deriving from a Military meeting, for the furtherance of N.H. Sport within the unit or units staging the fixture.

Official returns of the meetings were made and published in Steeplechases Past but a winner of a bona fide race was still considered a maiden under N.H. Rules except for the purposes of Steeplechasing at similar meetings. Bona fide meetings were abolished in 1949.

BONNIE LASSIE

Bay mare, 1882, Berserker—Hannah Ball (Rivet). Bred by Mr F. Houghton.

Bonnie Lass was a brilliant and extremely popular hurdler who won seven of her 10 races, and was only once unplaced, during 1887-88, despite invariably carrying weights in excess of 12-7. Her most notable victory was the 1888 Liverpool Hurdle with 12-10.

BORDER INCIDENT
Brown gelding, 1970, Border Chief—Cuddle Up (Coalition). Bred by Mr David Somerset.

When Border Incident, a robust, handsome individual whose appearance and pedigree strongly suggested a future chaser, won his first three hurdle races, including the Panama Cigar Final, Chepstow (1975), with incalculable ease, he was hailed as the most exciting National Hunt prospect seen in years.

Since then Richard Head's charge has been dogged by misfortune. During the next three seasons he suffered broken blood-vessels, sore shins and finally leg trouble with the result that he ran only eight times. Of these he won five chases including the Embassy Premier Chase Final in impressive fashion.

BOURTON
Bay gelding, not in the General Stud Book, by Drayton. Owned by Mr Moseley.

Bourton won the 1854 Grand National, 11-12 (Taster), 4/1f, in a common canter by 15l and 10l from Spring, 9-10 (W. Archer) and Crabbs, 9-2 (D. Wynne).

BOYCE, Charles (d.1867)
Charles Boyce won the 1857 Grand National on Emigrant with one arm strapped to his body as result of a hunting accident. In the opinion of the winning owners, Hodgeman and Green, Boyce was "so far the best . . . that I should not care to select a second". Their choice was limited by the current weight range of 8-10 to 11-2 but their confidence was fully justified by the resource of Boyce, who, observing on the first circuit that the run down to the Canal Turn was very poached, pulled his mount out on the second circuit and galloped down the towpath beside the canal. The following year flags were erected to prevent such opportunism being repeated.

BRABAZON, Aubrey (b.1920)
Aubrey Brabazon is best remembered for his association with Vincent O'Brien's treble Cheltenham Gold Cup winner Cottage Rake (1948, 1949 and 1950) and dual Champion Hurdler Hatton's Grace (1949 and 1950). He also won the King George VI Chase (1948) on Cottage Rake. A superb stylist, he was said to handle reins as though they were thin silk, and was as good on the Flat as he was over fences. He was Champion Jockey in Ireland in 1945 and also won the Irish 2000 Guineas and Oaks.

Vincent O'Brien, a man not over-given to superlatives, described him as a "really brilliant jockey . . . especially on the big occasion". He now trains a few horses at Rangers Lodge, the Curragh, where his father, Cecil, used to train.

BRAINS TRUST
Chestnut gelding, 1940, Rhodes Scholar—Easter Bonnet (Grand Parade). Bred by the Hon. Dorothy Paget.

After running unsuccessfully on the Flat at three years, Brains Trust was sold to Mr F. Blakeway, who gelded him and sent him to former Champion Jockey, Gerry Wilson, to be trained for hurdling. He won five races, four in succession in 1945, including the Champion Hurdle (T. F. Rimell), 9/2, by ¾l, the same, from Vidi (D. Butchers) and Red April (D. Jones).

BRAMBLE TUDOR
Bay mare, 1948, King Hal—Hedge Law (Within-the-Law). Bred by Capt. John Barry.

Bramble Tudor, owned by Col. 'Lord Joicey and trained by Stuart Wight, was a marvellously game and consistent mare who raced for six seasons winning 19 races. Her victories included the Cotswold Chase, N.H. Meeting (1953), the valuable Wetherby Handicap Chase, 1954 and 1956, and the Great Yorkshire Chase, 1955. She was much fancied for the 1955 Cheltenham Gold Cup but coughing interrupted her preparation and she ran below expectations. At stud she bred six living foals of whom Tudor Deal by Straight Deal, nine races, and Tudor Fort by Fortina, six races, were the best.

BREEDER
According to the Rules of Racing, the breeder "is the person or entity who owns the dam when the foal is dropped".

BRENDAN'S COTTAGE
Bay gelding, 1930, Cottage—Brendan's Glory (St Brendan). Bred by Mr M. Cunningham.

Brendan's Cottage, who was owned by Mrs Arthur Smith-Bingham and trained by George Beeby, was a very useful chaser whose seven victories included the Valentine Chase, Liverpool, and the 1939

Cheltenham Gold Cup (G. Owen), 8/1, by 5l, bad third, from Morse Code (D. Morgan) and Embarrassed (Capt. P. Herbert). His Gold Cup victory was the first leg of a Gold Cup-National double (completed by Workman) for his sire Cottage, an unprecedented achievement which he repeated in 1948 with Cottage Rake and Sheila's Cottage. Brendan's Cottage unfortunately dropped dead in 1940.

BRETHERTON, B.
Rode in most of the early Grand Nationals and won the 1840 running on Mr Elmore's second runner, Jerry.

BREWIS, Robert (b.1925)
Robert Brewis, a farmer from Belford, Northumberland, has bred, owned, trained and ridden horses with great success for a number of years. He rode as an amateur and scored his first win in 1949. His riding successes included the Liverpool Foxhunters in 1951 with Candy II, the Cheltenham Foxhunters in 1958 and 1960 with Whinstone Hill, the Emblem Chase, Manchester, in 1961 with Carmen IV, and the Kim Muir Chase in 1957 with Mighty Apollo. He trained all these except for the last-named horse, and besides saddled Carmen IV to win The Eider Chase, Newcastle, 1961. From Carmen he has bred the good mare, Scarlet Letch (1965 by New Brig) whom he trained to win nine races including the Eider Chase 1974. Colours: yellow, black hoop, check cap.

BRISCOE, A. B. (1900-51)
Basil Briscoe was a dedicated, talented, rich and self-assured old Etonian who conducted a large, mixed stable first from his family home at Longstowe and later at Newmarket. His name is indelibly linked with that of Golden Miller whom he found as a young horse, broke in, nursed through an unprepossessing fledgling stage and eventually sold to the young millionairess, Dorothy Paget, in a package deal with the hurdler, Insurance, boldly labelled, "the best chaser in the world and the best hurdler in England".

In retrospect, the highly-strung, introspective young man with a penchant for gambling was scarcely the ideal trainer for the hottest property steeplechasing had yet known and his highly individual owner, yet for three and a half years they enjoyed a run of

unbroken success. During that time Briscoe won her the Cheltenham Gold Cup four times (1932, 1933, 1934 and 1935) and the 1934 Grand National.

After the fiasco of the 1935 Grand National the idyll splintered abruptly and with it, Briscoe's career. He did continue to train until 1940 and to turn out winners and he did not, as has been suggested, die in circumstances of poverty and neglect, but he was never the same again.

BRISTOL
Steeplechasing was recorded at Bristol in the Calendar of 1832 but not repeated regularly. In March 1867, Bristol and East Somerset staged a meeting featuring two 100-sov. chases. In 1868 the winner of the principal chase, Mr Youngman on Woodbury Hill, was objected to by the second on the grounds that he was not qualified to ride as a gentleman. The matter was referred to the Stewards of the Grand National Hunt Committee. Lords Poulett, Hamilton and Westmorland and Messrs C. H. Carew, A. J. Summer and B. J. Angell, heard the case at Warwick and upheld the objection.

During the 1870s John Frail attempted a revival of Bristol's fortunes. In 1874 he laid on a Bristol and Western Counties Grand National Hunt meeting featuring a Grand Annual Handicap Hurdle worth £670 and the Bristol Royal Chase with £1000 added. This prize totalled to £1805 and was worth only £80 less than the Grand National.

Frail persuaded the Prince of Wales to attend (he stayed with Lord Fitzhardinge), a special train was chartered, the meeting was attended by thousands and the Berkeley Hunt servants kept order. A field of 20 started for the big race which was won by leading Irish amateur, Garry Moore (q.v.) on Scots Grey.

The venture did not prosper and by 1877 the value of the race had sunk to £180. Racing at Bristol continued until 1888.

BROADCASTING
The first successful broadcast of a race was the Grand National won by Sprig in 1927. *See also* TELEVISION.

BRODERICK, Patrick (b.1939)
Paddy Broderick was born in Ireland where he served an apprenticeship with Cyril Bryce Smith. He rode his first

winner at Navan in 1953 and came to England in 1961.

A long-legged, forceful horseman, his style seemed curiously old-fashioned beside the current generation of neatly-crouching jockeys. He was nonetheless extremely effective and came to prominence comparatively late in his career by virtue of his great partnership with Night Nursc (*q.v.*). He was very popular with his fellow jockeys who carried him shoulder-high into the weighing-room after his second Champion Hurdle victory. Ironically he was riding Night Nurse in the 1977 William Hill Christmas Hurdle when he sustained a heavy fall at the last flight which terminated his career. His best season was 1966-67 when he rode 50 winners.

His principal successes included:

The Champion Hurdle (1976) Night Nurse; (1977) Night Nurse
The Irish Sweeps Hurdle (1975) Night Nurse
The Welsh Champion Hurdle (1976) Night Nurse; (1977) Night Nurse
The Fighting Fifth Hurdle (1975) Night Nurse
The Scottish Champion Hurdle (1976) Night Nurse
The Mackeson Gold Cup (1966) Pawnbroker
The Welsh Grand National (1964) Rainbow Battle
The Princess Royal H'Cap Hurdle (1972) Easby Abbey

BROGAN, J. B. (b.1947)

A son of Jimmy Brogan, former professional jockey and trainer, Barry Brogan began his career as an amateur in Ireland. He was leading amateur 1964-65 and spent a year as assistant to Tom Dreaper. He briefly held a trainers' licence on the death of his father in 1966. In the autumn of 1966 he turned professional and came to England where he was attached to Ken Oliver's stable and rode second jockey to George Milburn. In 1967-68 he became first jockey to Ken Oliver for whom he rode a great many winners, notably on the very headstrong Even Keel. At the beginning of 1971-72 he came South to ride first jockey to Fulke Walwyn and was associated with The Dikler and Charlie Potheen, two very difficult horses whose improvement Walwyn attributes in great part to Brogan's strong, sensitive horsemanship. Always beset by problems of weight and very highly-strung nerves,

he handed in his licence at the end of 1972-73. He took it out again midway through the following season but the old problems recurred and terminated his career.

From 1967-72 he was consistently high up in the Leading Jockeys' table:

1967-68	57 winners	6th
1968-69	46 winners	4th
1970-71	67 winners	3rd
1971-72	70 winners	4th

His major successes are as follows:

The King George VI Chase (1971) The Dikler
The Hennessy Gold Cup (1972) Charlie Potheen
The Scottish Grand National (1970) The Spaniard
The Benson and Hedges Gold Cup (1970) Even Keel
The Black and White Gold Cup (1975) Flashy Boy

BROOKSHAW, S. J. (b.1929)

A member of a sporting, farming Shropshire family, 'Tim' Brookshaw won point-to-points, became attached to George Owen's stable and first rode as an amateur. A strong, balanced rider with an intuitive understanding of horses and a limitless bank of courage, he went straight to the top.

He was Champion Jockey in 1958-59, riding 83 winners and second in 1960-61 with 90 winners. Among his important victories were the 1963 Scottish Grand National on Pappageno's Cottage and the Grand Sefton (1962) on Eternal. He was the first man to pilot Mill House successfully round a steeplechase course. He was desperately unlucky not to win the 1959 Grand National, being beaten 21 by Oxo after riding from Bechers (second circuit) with no stirrup leathers. Next morning he was found milking his cows at 6 a.m. and offered laconically that he felt "a bit stiff".

In 1964 he became paralysed from the waist down as result of a fall. The accidents to him and Paddy Farrell highlighted the dangers constantly courted by steeplechase riders and caused the Injured Jockeys Fund (*q.v.*) to be opened. Tim Brookshaw has overcome his disabilities to an astonishing degree, he holds a trainers' licence, runs his farm and has even taken part in jockeys' show-jumping competitions.

BROTHERTON, Mrs Lurline

A Yorkshire owner who has enjoyed great success with steeplechasers trained by R. Renton, Mrs Brotherton was Leading Owner in 1949-50 when her horses won eight races worth £14,715. She was also third in 1951-52 with 32 wins worth £9,987. Her best horse was undoubtedly the 1950 Grand National winner Freebooter who also won the Grand Sefton twice, the Champion Chase and the Becher Chase. Other good horses she has owned are Q.E.D. (Lancashire Chase), Dagmar Gittell (Topham Chase), Ernest (Grand Sefton) and Scottish Sea (Wetherby Handicap Chase). She also owned Red Rum (q.v.) but sold him to Mr Noel le Mare for 6000 guineas at Doncaster Sales in August 1972. Colours: royal blue and silver halved, royal blue sleeves and red cap.

BROWN, Frank Atherton (1887-1963)

The elder of two brothers whose skill, wit, charm and personality made them leading figures of N.H. racing between the wars, Frank Brown rode fewer winners than his brother Harry but was generally considered to be the better hurdles jockey. Among his good victories was the County Hurdle (1923) on Assaroe. He was educated at Eton and served in the Royal Dragoons during the 1914-18 war. His riding career ended with a fall in a Hunters Chase at Stratford which fractured his spine. He recovered sufficiently to ride and hunt but not to race. He afterwards trained at the Bourton-on-the-Hill Stables where Weever had schooled Emblem. He regarded racing as a battle of wits and loved a good tilt at the Ring from which he did not always arise a winner.

Among his best wins were:

The Champion Hurdle (1935) Lion Courage
The Lancashire Chase (1926) White Park Bay
The National Hunt Handicap Chase (1933) Society

He did not renew his licence after World War II.

BROWN, H. A. (1889-1961)

Harry Brown, younger brother of Frank, was one of chasing's great characters. A leading jockey, later a trainer, one of the best shots in the country, first-class fisherman, raconteur and wit. He acted as racing mentor to the Prince of Wales, trained privately for Mr Rank and features as 'Charlie Peppercorn' in *Memoirs of a Foxhunter Man.* Stories about him are legion and some of his exploits were outrageous but his charm and wit were such that he could get away with a great deal.

He rode his first winner in 1907 and was Leading Amateur four times, 1918, 1919, 1920 and 1921. In 1919 he was also Champion Jockey with 48 winners and is the last amateur to lead the list.

He won 14 consecutive chases on Lord Londesborough's Dudley (q.v.) whom he also trained. These included the Grand Annual (National Hunt Meeting) 1924 and 1925 and the Victory Chase (Manchester). He also won the National Hunt Chase (1923) on Templescoby and the Cheltenham Foxhunters (1926) on his own Far Flight. He never won the Grand National but was second to Shaun Spadah in 1921 on The Bore. He had been upsides with the winner when falling at the second last and despite a broken collar bone, remounted to finish, thus landing a substantial gamble. He was also beaten a head on Conjuror II in the 1924 Cheltenham Gold Cup.

He did not renew his licence in 1930, but concentrated solely on training. For a period he was private trainer to Mr Rank for whom he won the Scottish Grand National in 1939 with Southern Hero and the Lancashire Chase (1939) with Timber Wolf.

BROWN JACK

Brown gelding, 1924, Jackdaw—Querquidella (Kroonstad). Bred in Ireland by Mr G. S. Webb.

It was for his exploits on the Flat that Sir Harold Wernher's Brown Jack, the greatest stayer of his age, became a legend in his lifetime but before he turned his attention to the more lucrative sphere of racing under Rules he proved an outstanding juvenile hurdler, winning six races including the 1928 Champion Hurdle (L. Rees), 4/1, by 1½l, 6l, from Peace River (T. Leader) and Blaris (G. Duller).

After failing to attract a bid at Goff's Sales as a yearling, Brown Jack was sold privately to Marcus Thompson who in turn passed him on to Charlie Rogers. Rogers ran him a couple of times on the

Flat for experience and, impressed by his promise, invited Aubrey Hastings to look at him on behalf of Sir Harold Wernher. A deal was done and Brown Jack was sent to Wroughton where he remained throughout his career. A well-made horse of pronounced character and exceptional intelligence, Brown Jack possessed a fine shoulder and tremendous length of rein. He stood lazily over at the knee and his forelegs were curiously bowed. Overcoming two serious bouts of illness, he swiftly made his mark on the N.H. scene with a fine first season culminating in his Champion Hurdle Victory. Among the spectators at Cheltenham that day was Champion Jockey Steve Donoghue. Asked by Aubrey Hastings to assess Brown Jack's chances of winning races on the Flat, his answer was emphatic: "Yes," he said. "he'll win on the Flat and I'll ride him." The 'old firm' were in business for seven seasons. Their victories included the Queen Alexandra Stakes six times in succession, the Ascot Stakes, the Goodwood Cup, the Chester Cup and the Ebor Handicap. It was partnership without equal on the English Turf.

BROWN LAD

Bay gelding, 1966, Sayajirao—Caicos (Cagire II). Bred by Mr J. W. Osborne in Ireland.

A game, marvellously consistent and versatile performer now owned by Mrs Peter Burrell and trained by Jim Dreaper, Brown Lad has won two Flat races, five hurdle races including the Sun Alliance Novices Hurdle, Cheltenham (1974) and the Lloyds Bank Hurdle, Cheltenham (1975) and ten chases, including the Irish Distillers Grand National, Fairyhouse (1975, 1976 and 1978). He is the first horse ever to win the race three times.

His good wins in the Thyestes Chase and the Punchestown National Trial, coupled with the absence of Captain Christy, promoted Brown Lad second favourite at 13/8 for the 1976 Cheltenham Gold Cup. However the fast conditions did not suit him and he found himself chopped for speed at half-way. He ran on well in the closing stages and in the end took clear second place from his stable companion Colebridge. He gave a similarly game performance in 1978 when chasing home Midnight Court. Brown Lad is nearly always ridden by Tommy Carberry.

BROWN TONY

Brown gelding, 1925, Jackdaw—Lady Peary (Commander Peary). Bred by Mr S. Slocock.

Although he won only two races, Mrs J. de Selincourt's Brown Tony was a distinctly useful hurdler and a very game one. After winning a maiden hurdle at Kempton on his second appearance, he went on to win the 1930 Champion Hurdle in one of the closest-fought finishes ever recorded for the race. Ridden by Tim Cullinan and starting at 7/2, he won by a head, short head from Clean Cash (G. Pellerin) and Peertoi (S. Ingham). Subsequently he was beaten a neck in the Lancashire Hurdle. In 1930-31, after being consistently placed under welter weights in big handicap hurdles, he fell in the Sandown Open Handicap Hurdle and had to be destroyed. He was trained by Jack Anthony.

BUCKINGHAM, John Anthony (b.1940)

John Buckingham grew up on Mr Edward Courage's Oxfordshire estate and drifted into the yard. Eventually he was apprenticed to Mr Courage and rode his first winner in 1959. He won the 1967 Grand National in remarkable circumstances, for his moderate mount, Foinavon, was well behind approaching the 23rd fence and was thus able to be steered clear of the carnage caused by the refusal of the riderless Popham Down. Grabbing this chance of a lifetime, John Buckingham threaded through the field which by this time resembled a battlefield, slipped his blinkered mount over the extreme right of the fence and kept him going over the remaining nine fences to cross the line 15l ahead of Honey End.

A promising career was halted by a broken leg and in 1971, depressed by his shrinking opportunities, he joined the small and select band of those most valuable servants to racing, the racecourse valets.

BUCKLEY, P. (b.1943)

A Northern jockey, Pat Buckley was apprenticed to Capt. Neville Crump (1957-62) and rode his first winner in 1961 in his first ride over fences.

At the age of 19 he won the 1963 Grand National on Ayala. Opportunities came early to him owing to the repeated injuries to stable jockey Gerry Scott, and Buckley did not waste them.

Among his other important victories have been:

The Scottish Grand National (1968) Arcturus
The Mildmay Memorial (1964) Dormant
The Whitbread Gold Cup (1963) Hoodwinked
The Whitbread Gold Cup (1964) Dormant

Both these last victories were for his trainer, Capt. Crump, and in the second of them, in which he beat Mill House three lengths, he had had to waste so stringently to do the 9st 7lb required that he was barely able to stand while the Queen Mother made the presentations. Injury forced his retirement in 1976.

BULA
Bay gelding, 1965, Raincheck—Pongo's Fancy (Golden Chain). Bred by Mr C. Purcell.

Bought privately as an unbroken three-year-old by Capt. Bill Edwards-Heathcote after the Dublin November Sales, Bula possessed the appearance and pedigree of a potential chaser. When, after the best part of a year on his owner's Somerset farm, he was sent to Fred Winter's Lambourn establishment, he did nothing to cause their view to be altered. His trainer's instructions to Stan Mellor on sending him out for his first race at Lingfield were to find out if the horse was worth persevering with. Bula answered the query with a facile victory and, partnered henceforth by Paul Kelleway, went on unbeaten through two seasons and 13 races, including a division of the Gloucester Hurdle (N.H. Meeting), the Benson and Hedges Hurdle (Sandown), the Welsh Champion Hurdle (Chepstow) 1971 and the Champion Hurdle 1971 (P. Kelleway), 15/8f, by 4l, 1l, from Persian War (J. Uttley) and Major Rose (T. Biddlecombe). His eight subsequent hurdle victories included the Ackermann Skeaping Hurdle (Sandown) and a second Champion Hurdle in 1972 (P. Kelleway) 8/11f, by 8l, 3l from Boxer (J. Uttley) and Lyford Cay (D. Cartwright), but his invincibility was dented and by the end of the season 1972-73 it was well and truly cracked. Despite five victories and having appeared, at the start of the season, to be better than ever, Bula suffered two major defeats in the Irish Sweeps Hurdle and the 1973 Champion Hurdle. His idle style

of racing combined with Paul Kelleway's pronounced waiting tactics had often induced near heart-failure among his supporters but Kelleway always maintained that only by getting the big horse to relax in the early stages of a race, could he produce the electrifying burst of finishing speed which had won so many races. However neither at Leopardstown nor at Cheltenham was it forthcoming. At Leopardstown, on rain-soaked ground, he was never in the race at any stage and finished a well-beaten fourth to runaway winner Captain Christy, while at Cheltenham he could achieve no better than fifth behind Comedy of Errors despite forceful driving from Kelleway from fully a mile out.

In 1973-74 Bula turned his attention to steeplechasing which entirely restored his enthusiasm. Few top-class hurdlers have made the transition to fences more impressively, while his turn of foot proved a lethal weapon which few three-mile chasers in England could counter.

He won a total of 13 chases including the Benson and Hedges Novices, Sandown (1973), the Black & White Whisky Gold Cup, Ascot (1973), the Blue Circle Cement Chase, Ascot (1974), the Gainsborough Chase, Sandown (1975) and the Sundew Chase, Haydock (1975 and 1976).

Sadly he was never able to emulate his hurdling triumphs over the bigger obstacles at Cheltenham. He ran a brave race to finish third to Ten Up (*q.v.*) in the 1975 Gold Cup, finding the last mile just too far in the exceptionally testing conditions. In 1976, encouraged by the absence of Captain Christy (*q.v.*) who had ruthlessly exposed his limitations when beating him 30l in that season's King George VI Chase, and the favourable ground conditions, the public made Bula favourite for the big race but he ran deplorably finishing a remote sixth to Royal Frolic (*q.v.*). In 1977 he ran instead in the two mile Champion Chase for which he was made favourite but possibly as result of a spasm, he fell heavily at the fifth fence, damaging his shoulder muscles so severely that he had eventually to be put down.

A strong, handsome gelding, Bula raced for eight consecutive seasons winning 34 of his 51 starts, an eloquent tribute to the skill of his trainer as well as to his own constitution and consistency.

BULLOCK, J.
An ex-paratrooper and prisoner of war, Johnny Bullock won the 1951 Grand National on Nickel Coin. He rode for Fred Rimell in the early fifties and won the Lancashire Chase (1950) and the Queen Elizabeth Chase (1950) on Coloured School Boy and the Emblem Chase (1962) on Stenquill.

BULLOCK'S HORN
Bay or brown gelding, 1963, Rockavon—Let It Be Me (Arctic Star). Bred by Mr G. J. Philipps.

Bullock's Horn, a doughty, staying hunter-chaser from the V.W.H., won a total of six chases. In 1973 he became the third horse since the war to win both Cheltenham and Liverpool Foxhunters in the same year. His Cheltenham win was achieved in the Stewards Room, after he had been beaten a head by Bear's Slipper in a driving finish and his Liverpool win was an equally close affair in which five horses were in with a chance at the last and less than 5 lengths separated them at the post. Bullock's Horn prevailed by a head from Dubaythorn. He was owned by Mrs E. Barker, was trained by Bob Turnell and was invariably ridden by Lord Oaksey.

BULTEEL, Sir John Crocker, K.C.V.O., D.S.O., M.C. (1890-1956)
The son of J. G. Bulteel was educated at Eton and served with distinction in the Royal Bucks Hussars, 1914-18. He became a racing official in 1926, serving as a handicapper until 1937. In 1936 he became Clerk of the Course at Aintree. He was at various times in charge of Chester, Newbury, Haydock, Hurst Park and, from 1946 until his death, Ascot. He was regarded as an outstanding racecourse official and brought imagination and flair to a profession sadly lacking in these attributes. He introduced the Queen Elizabeth Chase and the Triumph Hurdle, both of which were added to Spring Flat programmes and which proved very popular. He was also responsible for the King George VI and Queen Elizabeth Stakes at Ascot, and for the New Straight Mile and the alterations to the Stands and Paddock at that course.

BUMPER
A type of Flat race common in Ireland, confined to amateur riders and run under N.H. Rules. They are designed to introduce potential steeplechasers to racing. 'Bumper' is also a slang term for an amateur rider which derives from the supposed inability of amateurs to maintain a proper racing seat.

BUONA NOTTE
Brown gelding, 1957, Lake Placid—Jenny Lind (Norseman). Bred by Mr H. J. Joel.

Buona Notte, an almost black horse who was one of only six horses to beat Arkle after his first season, was the result of chance mating. His sire Lake Placid was the teaser at Mr Joel's Childwickbury Stud and Jenny Lind was his only mare in 1956.

After a successful season's hurdling in which he won a division of the Gloucester Hurdle, Buona Notte turned to chasing with spectacular results. His six successive victories included the Henry VIII Chase (Kempton) in which he beat Dunkirk, the T.W.W. Champion Novices Chase and the inaugural (1964) Totalizator Champion Novices Chase (N.H. meeting). After a bright start to the 1964-65 season, when he was beaten a short head by Flying Wild (rec. 6lb) with Arkle (gave 26lb) 11 away third, tragedy struck when he broke his neck and died in the 1965 Great Yorkshire Chase. He was owned by Mr H. J. Joel and trained by Bob Turnell.

BURFORD, R.
Roger Burford was a member of a Wroughton family who served the Hastings/Anthony stable for years. His father won the Welsh National (1921) on Mythical and rode Brown Jack in his early races over hurdles. He rode second jockey to Ivor Anthony and unexpectedly got the ride on the 1941 Cheltenham Gold Cup winner, Poet Prince, owing to the last-minute injury to owner, David Sherbrooke.

BURKE, John Martin (b.1953)
John Burke rode successfully in point-to-points and as an amateur for Fred Rimell before turning professional at the beginning of season 1974-75. He remained at Kinnersley and took over as

first jockey on the enforced retirement of Ken White (*q.v.*).

In 1976 he became the fifth man to achieve the Cheltenham Gold Cup (Royal Frolic) – Grand National (Rag Trade) double, the others being Tim Cullinan (1930), Gerry Wilson (1934), Fred Winter (1962) and Tommy Carberry (1975).

Other good winners include:

The Welsh Grand National (1976) Rag Trade

The Victor Ludorum Hurdle (1975) Zip Fastener

The Whitbread Gold Cup (1977) Andy Pandy

The Great Yorkshire Chase (1975) Rough House

The Daily Express Triumph Hurdle (1978) Connaught Ranger

BUTCHERS, Donald Charles Victor (1911-67)

Don Butchers rode as a professional under N.H. Rules from 1929-46, winning the Liverpool Hurdle twice, in 1936 on Armour Bright and in 1938 on Flag. In 1946 he took out a licence to train at Priam Lodge, Epsom. He took over the training of Saffron Tartan after the latter's hobday operation (Vincent O'Brien trained henceforth only on the Flat) and saddled him to win the King George VI Chase (1960) and the Cheltenham Gold Cup (1961). He also handled Gay Kindersley's Carrickbeg (six chases and second, beaten ½l, in the 1963 Grand National).

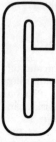

CACKLER
Bay horse, 1903, Hackler—Circe (Play Actor). Bred by Mr J. J. Maher.

A member of the celebrated Mount Royal (*q.v.*) family, Cackler's career was brief but extremely successful. Preeminently a Liverpool horse, his seven victories in the colours of Mr (later Sir) Charles Assheton-Smith included the Champion Chase and the Valentine Chase in 1908 when only a five-year-old, the Grand Sefton at six, carrying 12-3 and again in 1910 with 12-7. He died in 1911.

CAMPBELL, Lt.-Gen. Sir David, K.G.B. (1869-1936)
A member of a Liverpool family with extensive property and business interests in the area, David Campbell was educated at Clifton and joined the 9th Lancers. He had a distinguished military career, serving in South Africa (1899-1902) and being G.O.C. Baluchistan District, 1920-24. He was also Colonel-in-Chief of the 9th Lancers.

He won the Grand Military Chase twice, in 1896 on Nellie Gray and in 1897 on Parapluie. He also won the 1896 Grand National on The Soarer, whom he had bought as a young horse but sold just before the big race to Mr Hall-Walker (later Lord Wavertree).

CANASTA LAD
Brown gelding, 1966, Straight Lad—Wise Nelly (Black Rock). Bred by the executors of the late Mr J. J. O'Donnell.

A strongly made, brave and consistent horse, Canasta Lad won 10 hurdle races including the Welsh Champion Hurdle, Chepstow, twice, (1972 and 1974) beating the then Champion hurdler, Bula, in 1972. Mrs D. Hague's gelding's other victories included the Marlow Ropes-John Skeaping Hurdle (1972), the Cheltenham Trial Hurdle (1971) and the William Hill Christmas Hurdle (1972). He was much fancied for the 1973

Champion Hurdle but rapped a joint 48 hours before the race and had to be withdrawn.

Canasta Lad, who was trained by Peter Bailey throughout his career, subsequently developed into a high-class chaser winning nine chases including the Blue Circle Cement Chase (Ascot) and the Arkle Challenge Trophy (National Hunt Meeting, 1974).

CANNON, Joe (1849-1933)
Joe Cannon was apprenticed to Tom Preece. In 1876 he was appointed private trainer to Capt. Machell at Bedford Cottage, for whom he rode and trained that year's Grand National winner, Regal. Capt. Machell described him as the bravest horseman he ever saw although he was always very nervous before a race. He had great success on the Flat and won the 1877 Ascot Gold Cup with Petrarch and in 1878 the 1000 and 2000 Guineas with Pilgrimage. He later trained at Primrose Cottage (for Lord Rosebery) and from 1892 until his retirement in 1919, at Lordship Farm.

George Lambton paid him this tribute: "When I started training myself he took as much pains and trouble with me as if I had been his own son and without his help and advice I should never have got on." His son, Noel, was also a distinguished trainer who ran the astute Druid's Lodge establishment.

CANNON, Tom (1846-1945)
Elder brother of Joe (*q.v.*), Tom Cannon was a distinguished jockey and won the 1882 Derby on Shotover. He later trained at Danebury, principally on the Flat, but he saddled Playfair to win the 1888 Grand National. A "slight, delicate-looking man, good-looking and a bit of a dandy", his sons, Kempton and Mornington, became top-class jockeys and his daughter married Ernie Piggott.

CAPTAIN CHRISTY
Bay gelding, 1967, Mon Capitaine —Christy's Bow (Bowsprit). Bred by Mr George Williams.

Mrs Jane Samuel's Captain Christy burst his way into the ranks of the leading hurdlers with a runaway victory in the 1972 Irish Sweeps Hurdle from a field that included Bula. He endorsed this victory with a creditable third to Comedy of Errors in the 1973 Champion Hurdle and went on to win the Scottish equivalent at Ayr.

In 1973-74 he turned his attention to chasing with distinctly mixed results. He fell in the Irish Grand National, he blundered and unseated his jockey two out when nearly a fence clear in the Wills Premier Final and again at the same juncture when upsides with Bula in the Black and White Chase, Ascot. But he also won six chases including the Power Gold Cup and the Cheltenham Gold Cup, 7/1 (H. Beasley) by 5l and 20l from The Dikler (R. Barry) and Game Spirit (T. Biddlecombe). Brilliantly ridden by Bobby Beasley, he was held up, took the lead just before the last and despite blundering through it, produced a burst of speed to which The Dikler had no answer.

In February 1976 he sustained a tendon injury from which he has never properly recovered. Up until then he had won six hurdle races and 12 steeplechases besides finishing second in the Grand Steeplechase de Paris, Auteuil (1975) and fourth in the Colonial Cup, Carolina, U.S.A. (1975). Apart from his Gold Cup triumph his most notable successes were his consecutive victories in Kempton's Boxing Day feature, the King George VI Chase, in 1974 and 1975. In 1974 he beat Pendil by 8 lengths thus resolving arguments raised by Pendil's dramatic departure at the second last (brought down by High Ken) in that year's Gold Cup, while in 1975 he put up a staggering performance to beat England's leading staying chaser, Bula, by no less than 30 lengths. Those fortunate enough to be there reckoned it one of the most exciting exhibitions of galloping and jumping ever seen on a racecourse. In the absence of his regular jockey, through injury, Captain Christy was ridden by the young stable 'claimer', Gerry Newman.

CARBERRY, Thomas (b.1941)

Tommy Carberry is a very talented Irish jockey who has been associated with Dan Moore for years. He was apprenticed to him in 1955 but after two years transferred to J. J. Lenehan as he was too light

for a National Hunt stable. He rode many winners on the Flat and was Champion Apprentice one year but his heart was in jumping and as soon as he was heavy enough, he returned to Dan Moore, whose daughter Pamela he later married. His first big victory in this country was the Massey-Ferguson Gold Cup in 1964 on Flying Wild, in which he beat Arkle. He also won the Stone's Ginger Wine Chase on the game and popular grey mare.

Since then he has won nearly every big race in the steeplechasing calendar including:

The Cheltenham Gold Cup (1970) L'Escargot; (1971) L'Escargot; (1975) Ten Up
The Grand National (1975) L'Escargot
The Embassy Premier Chase Final (1970) L'Escargot
The Sun Alliance Chase (1976) Tied Cottage
The Daily Express Triumph Hurdle (1977) Meladon
The National Hunt Two-Mile Champion Chase (1973) Inkslinger
The Daily Express Triumph Hurdle (1977) Meladon
The Colonial Cup, Camden, U.S.A. (1971) Inkslinger

He is still light enough to ride on the Flat and is in much demand. He also rides regularly for Jim Dreaper who freely attributes much of his success to his jockey's brilliance.

CARLISLE (Group 4)

Carlisle is a right-handed, undulating, pear-shaped course about 1m, 5f round, set in attractive Lakeland countryside. Racing is not of a particularly high order and there are no really valuable prizes but the sport provided is much enjoyed by the local population. Sponsored races include the Carlisle Crown and Mitre Hotel Christmas H'cap Chase (3m, £886) in December.

N.H. racing has been recorded at Carlisle from 1849, though not continuously. The course is susceptible to waterlogging.

Best Times

Distance	Time	Horse-age-weight	Date
2m 330y H	4m 9.70	The Last Light 5-11-3	13-4-74
3m 100y H	6m 2.95	Whispering Grace 8-11-0	4-10-71
2m C	3m 58.90	Never There 7-10-0	19-9-77
2½m C	5m 11.50	Ballyroan 8-10-3	2-10-72
3m C	6m 11.10	Cumbria 7-9-11	17-9-77

CARMEN IV

Chestnut mare, 1952. Registered in Miss Prior's Half-Bred Stud Book. Bellman—Caramel II (St Tudwal). Bred by Mr G. M. Lees.

A versatile, courageous mare owned, trained and ridden by Mr R. Brewis, Carmen IV won five hurdle races and four chases including the Eider Chase, Newcastle (1961) and the Emblem Chase, Manchester (1961). She is the dam of the useful mare Scarlet Letch (nine races including the Bacal Eider Chase, 1974).

CARTMEL (Group 5)

Cartmel, a charming Lake District course, has a sharp left-handed, virtually flat track, 1m round with an 800 yard run-in. Racing has taken place at Cartmel since 1880. There are two 2-day meetings a year at the Whitsun and August Bank Holidays. Bass-Charrington sponsor the Bass-Charrington Vintners North Lonsdale Maiden Hunter Chase (3m, 470y, £485) and the Bass-Charrington Lancashire Cup H'cap Chase (3m, 470y, £443), both at the Whitsun meeting.

CASSE TÊTE

Chestnut mare, 1865, Trumpeter—Constance (Epirus). Bred by the Duke of Newcastle.

After an exceedingly modest career under Rules, Casse Tête was sold for chasing to a shrewd and successful supporter of National Hunt Racing, Mr E. Brayley. In this sphere she proved more successful, winning three chases including the 1872 Grand National, 10-0 (J. Page), 20/1 by 6l and the same, from Scarrington, 11-2 (R. I'Anson) and Despatch 10-4 (G. Waddington). A "weedy, washy chestnut", Casse Tête, who was described by *The Times* correspondent as looking "as though in training for an anatomical museum instead of a Grand National", won the National when its reputation was at its lowest ebb and must be considered a moderate winner. She did not win subsequently.

CATTERICK (Group 3)

N.H. racing has been recorded at Catterick since 1867. It is a sharp course, oval and left-handed with an uphill run on the back straight. The course has a watering system and the enterprising executive have attracted a number of sponsors, including Hills and Ladbrokes and several local firms, making the general level of prize money fairly high.

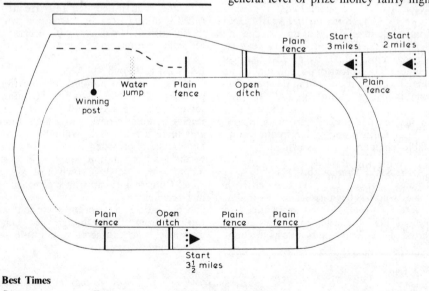

Best Times

Distance	Time	Horse-age-weight	Date
2m H	3m 36.60	Avon Bay 6-11-3	18-12-71
2m C	3m 44.60	Preston Deal 6-10-0	18-12-71
3m 300y C	6m 6.20	Bar Rock 9-10-0	29-10-77
3½m C	7m 16.40	Jolly Jester 10-10-13	17-2-62

CAUGHOO

Brown gelding, 1939, Within-the-Law —Silverdale (Vencedor). Bred by Mr P. Power.

Caughoo was bought as an unbroken two-year-old for £50 by Mr John McDowell, a Dublin jeweller and trained for him by his brother, Hector, on the outskirts of Dublin. Although he amply repaid his modest purchase price and provided the sporting McDowell family with a great deal of fun by winning two small hurdle races and the Ulster National in successive years (1945 and 1946), he did nothing in his first four seasons to suggest that a Grand National lay within his compass. However, all through the dreadful winter of 1947, Caughoo was kept fit and well on the foreshore of Sutton Strand and was consequently one of the very few of the 57 horses who lined up at rain-soaked, fog-shrouded Aintree, to have enjoyed an uninterrupted preparation. Carrying 10-0, ridden by Eddie Dempsey and starting at 100/1 he scampered home by 20l, 4l, from Lough Conn, 10-1 (D. McCann) and Kami, 10-13 (Mr J. Hislop). His jockey was afterwards involved in litigation over reports that he had taken a short cut in the fog!

CAZALET, Peter Victor Ferdinand (1907-73)

Descended from a Basque-Huguenot family who came to England as refugees, Peter Cazalet rode as an amateur before the war. He began training at Fairlawne in 1930, chiefly for himself, Edward Paget and Anthony Mildmay (q.v.). During the war he served with an anti-aircraft battery and later in the Welsh Guards with Anthony Mildmay. Together they laid plans for a big public stable which came into fruition after the war. With Jim Fairgrieve as head-lad, they formed a team whose success had few equals in chasing history.

Between 1958-70, Peter Cazalet was only once out of the list of Leading Trainers. He headed it twice; in 1959-60 with 58 races worth £22,270 and in 1964-65 with 82 races (then a record) worth £36,153.

He won the King George VI Chase four times:

Manicou (1950)
Statecraft (1951)
Rose Park (1956)
Lochroe (1958)

Other major successes include:

The Mackeson Gold Cup (1965) Dunkirk
The Imperial Cup (1963) Antiar
The Triumph Hurdle (1960) Turpial
The National Hunt 2-mile Champion Chase (1965) Dunkirk
The Hennessy Gold Cup (1970) Border Mask
The Grand Sefton (1948) Lecale Prince

Perhaps his most poignant victory of all was that of Cromwell in the 1952 Mildmay Memorial. Cheltenham was never a lucky course for him and the nearest he came to winning the Gold Cup was Lochroe's one length defeat by Pas Seul in 1960.

The Grand National exercised an even worse hoodoo on him and his runners were overcome by unbelievable misfortunes. In 1936, Davy Jones landed in the lead over the second last when going strongly and the buckle parted in Anthony Mildmay's hands, leaving him without steering and unable to prevent his mount running out at the last. In 1948, Cromwell held a winning chance when Lord Mildmay was attacked by crippling cramp and rode the last half mile to finish third, unable to lift his head from his chest. In 1957 the worst and most inexplicable blow of all fell when H.M. the Queen Mother's Devon Loch, spread-eagled 50 yards from the winning post for reasons never satisfactorily explained.

Peter Cazalet died in May 1973, after a mercifully brief illness, to the great sorrow of the racing world. He genuinely loved racing and derived as much pleasure from winning a novice chase at a West Country 'gaff' as from all his great victories on smart, park tracks. In all he trained over 1,100 winners, including 250 for the Queen Mother, whose interest in steeplechasing had been pioneered by himself and Lord Mildmay, whose horses he trained until his death. The Mildmay Memorial Chase has now been re-named the Anthony Mildmay, Peter Cazalet Memorial Chase, as a tribute to their unique partnership.

CELTIC GOLD

Brown gelding, 1962, Cash and Courage—Welsh Ballad (Mossborough). Bred by Mr H. H. Petch.

Major Cliff-McCullough's Celtic Gold was a top-class handicap hurdler who won ten races, including the Cheltenham Trial Hurdle (1969), the Ladbroke H'cap Hurdle (1970) and the Wills Hurdle (1969), He also ran second to Hill House in the 1967 Schweppes Gold Trophy. He needed to be held up for a late run and occasionally thwarted such tactics by a terrible jumping error. After rather a hesitant start he became a useful two-mile chaser and won a total of 14 chases. He was trained by W. A. Stephenson.

CHADWICK, Robert (1880-1942)

A Yorkshire-born jockey, Robert Chadwick rode a good deal for Tom Coulthwaite and achieved his greatest success for the stable when winning the 1910 Grand National on Jenkinstown. He also remounted to finish second on Rathnally in 1911 and was third on All White in 1921.

His other important victories were:

The Liverpool Hurdle (1910) Indian Runner
The Champion Chase (1909) Bloodstone; (1912) Balscadden; (1920) Iron Hard
The Lancashire Chase (1908) Albuera; (1909) Moonstruck; (1912) Wilkinstown

The Lancashire Chase was then the second most important race in the Calendar and it was no mean feat to win it three times in five years.

CHAMPION HURDLE

A level-weights classic, instituted in 1927 and run over two miles at the National Hunt Meeting at Cheltenham in March. From 1972-77 it was sponsored by Lloyds Bank. In 1978 Waterford Crystal assumed sponsorship of the race which is currently worth over £20,000 to the winner. A list of winners is included under CHELTENHAM.

From 1841-44 a Champion Hurdle was run at Liverpool at the Grand National meeting. The conditions were as follows: "Champion Hurdle race. 15 sovs each, 10 forfeit with £50 added. Billesdon-Coplow weights, winners extra."

Results:

1841 Mr Bond's **Jupiter** 11-9 T. Olliver
1842 Mr Pearce's **Defence** 12-9 Thompson
1843 Mr Raworth's **Cattonian** 11-7 Bradley
1844 Mr Raworth's **Cattonian** 12-7 Bradley

CHANDLER

Brown gelding, not in the General Stud Book, by Doctor Faustus.

Chandler, so called because he had once been the property of a purveyor of candles in Sutton Coldfield, came to steeplechasing via the hunting field. So well did he carry his owner, Captain Peel, that in 1847 that gentleman sold a half-share to another officer, Captain 'Josey' Little and Chandler was sent to Hednesford to be trained. The venture was immediately successful and, in 1847, Chandler won the Worcester Great Handicap and the Leamington Hunt Chase, then one of the principal events in the Calendar. In 1848 he won the Grand National, 11-12 (Capt. Little) 12/1 by ¼l, 1½l, from The Curate, 11-12 (T. Olliver) and British Yeoman, 11-4 (Mr Bevill).

CHARITY

Said to be a bay mare by Woodman.

Of all the early National winners, none is more difficult to establish concrete facts about than the 1841 winner, Charity. Variously described as a mare, the property of Lord Craven (Finch Mason) and a gelding, the property of Mr Vevers (Mr H. Wright's Steeplechase Calendar), all that can positively be ascertained is that she (or he) came from Gloucestershire, that she was quite fancied for the 1839 Grand National but confounded her supporters by refusing the wall, and that she won the 1841 National, 12-0 (Mr Powell), 14/1, by 2l and a neck, from Cigar, 12-0 (Mr A. McDonough) and Peter Simple, 12-0 (Walker).

CHARLES I

Bay horse, 1876, Prince Charlie—Merevale (Atherstone). Bred by H.M. Queen Victoria.

A top-class hurdler -belonging to Mr T. V. Morgan, Charles I, who was invariably ridden by Robert I'Anson, was a Croydon specialist. He won the Grand Handicap Hurdle in 1880, and the very important Grand National Handicap Hurdle in 1880 and 1881, on the same course.

CHARLIE POTHEEN

Bay gelding, 1965, Spiritus—Irish Biddy (Devonian). Bred by Mr J. T. D. Musson.

After a brief but extremely successful point-to pointing career, Charlie Potheen was sent up to Ascot Sales as a six-year-old but failed to reach his reserve. He was afterwards bought privately by Fulke

Walwyn on behalf of Mrs B. Heath, for whom he won six chases and was third in the 1973 Cheltenham Gold Cup. His victories included the Hennessy Gold Cup (1972), the John Smith Great Yorkshire Chase (1973) and the Whitbread Gold Cup (1973) by 5l with 12-0, in each case after making every yard of the running.

Formerly very headstrong and difficult to ride – he had a marked tendency to hang to the left and twice ran clean off the course in his early days – he settled remarkably well at Saxon House. His front-running tactics and bold jumping made him very popular with the racing public.

CHELTENHAM (Group 1)

Steeplechasing has been recorded at Cheltenham since 1834 when the Grand Annual Steeplechase was founded. It was then an important feature in the Steeplechase Calendar, and the centre of a festive week at the town which included meets of the local hounds, assemblies and balls. The race was won by Lottery (q.v.), in 1839 and 1840 and Adam Lindsay Gordon's well-loved lay of 'How we beat the favourite' records the 1847 running of the race, won by Mr Holman on Stanmore. The races were run round about Prestbury at various venues which included Southam, Noverton, Prestbury Park, Andoversford, Kayte Farm and the back of the cemetery.

The present course at Prestbury Park dates from 1902. In 1907 the management was taken over by Messrs Pratt who have run it ever since. The National Hunt Chase first came to Cheltenham in 1904 and became a permanent fixture in 1911. It was the third richest race in the Calendar and the March meeting at which it was run assumed importance.

Cheltenham's rise to pre-eminence among National Hunt courses dates from the founding in 1924 of the Cheltenham Gold Cup, a weight-for-age steeplechase of 3m, 2f, for five year-olds and upwards, worth £685. The race was the brainchild of Mr F. H. Cathcart whose name is commemorated by a race at the National Hunt Meeting.

The new race swiftly became popular and although it did not become very valuable until after the Second World War, from the first it attracted the best staying chasers and it has rarely been won by a bad horse.

Golden Miller heads the list authoritatively with five victories. Cottage Rake and Arkle gained three apiece, while Easter Hero and L'Escargot each won two. Golden Miller and L'Escargot are the only horses to have won both the Gold Cup and the Grand National. Tom Dreaper heads the trainers having won it five times, followed by Basil Briscoe, Vincent O'Brien and Fulke Walwyn who have each won four. Among the jockeys, Pat Taaffe has ridden four winners, F. B. Rees, Aubrey Brabazon and Tommy Carberry three and Gerry Wilson, Evan Williams and Fred Winter two each. The Hon. Dorothy Paget, owner of Golden Miller won a total of seven Gold Cups.

The success of the Gold Cup induced the executive to add a similar, level-weights classic for hurdlers in 1927. This became the Champion Hurdle over 2m, 200y. There have been three triple Champion Hurdlers: Hatton's Grace, Sir Ken and Persian War; and five dual winners: Insurance, National Spirit, Bula, Comedy of Errors and Night Nurse. No horse has won the Gold Cup and the Champion Hurdle. The nearest was Bula, third in the 1975 Gold Cup. Among the trainers, Vic Smyth trained four Champion Hurdlers, while Vincent O'Brien, Ryan Price, Willie Stephenson, Colin Davies, M. H. Easterby and Fred Winter have each trained three. Fred Winter also rode three Champion Hurdlers as did Ron Smyth and Jimmy Uttley while Tim Molony heads the list with four.

Sponsorship came to Cheltenham during the 'sixties, leading to an increase in the number of meetings and the building in 1966 of a new course. In 1976 improved drainage, a reservoir and a watering system were installed.

The course is left-handed and undulating, oval in shape and about 1½m round with a substantial down-hill gradient after the last open ditch and a testing uphill finish. It is not an easy course to jump and provides a considerable test of horse and rider.

The principal races are:

The Piper Champagne Cheltenham Gold Cup (March, 3m, 2f), £23,827

The Waterford Crystal Champion Hurdle (March, 2m, 200y), £21,332

The Daily Express Triumph Hurdle (4-y-o) (March, 2m, 200y), £7,731

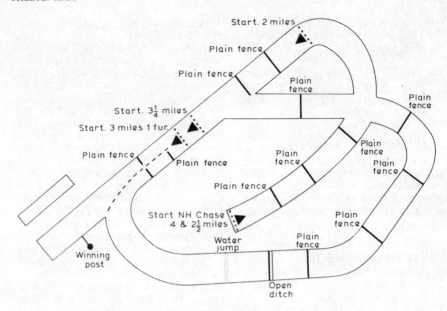

NEW COURSE

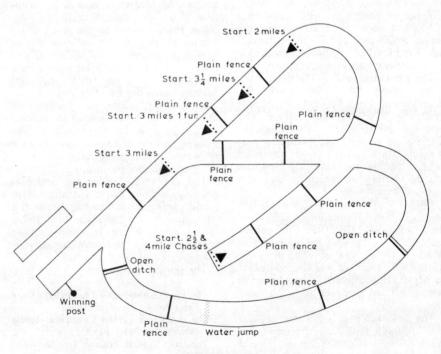

OLD COURSE

The **Sun Alliance Chase** (March, 3m), £10,053

The **Sun Alliance Novices Hurdle** (March, 2m 4f) £10,317

The **National Hunt Two-mile Champion Chase** (March, 2m), £10,619

The **Waterford Crystal Stayers Hurdle** (March, 3m), £9,949

The **Waterford Crystal Supreme Novice Hurdle** (March, 2m, 200y), £9,472

The **Arkle Challenge Trophy** (March, 2m), £9,845

The **Joe Coral Golden Handicap Hurdle Final** (March, 3m), £6,466

The **Mackeson Gold Cup Handicap Chase** (November, 2½m), £5,943

The **Massey-Ferguson Gold Cup** (December, 2½m), £7,028

The **Bass Handicap Chase** (January, 4m), £6,196

Best Times

NEW COURSE

Distance	Time	Horse-age-weight	Date
2m 200y H	3m 66.60	Spy Net 6-10-6	12-4-73
2½m H	4m 53.60	Fashion House 4-10-9	19-9-68
3m H	5m 49.10	Tirconail 8-10-0	17-4-74
2m C	3m 53.40	Spring Spirit 8-11-5	22-9-71
2½m C	5m 8-50	Inch Arran 10-10-11	17-4-74
3m 1f C	6m 26.70	Fearless Fred 9-11-12	23-9-71
3m 2f 76y C	6m 37.20	The Dikler 10-12-0	15-3-73
3m 3f C	7m 23	Snowdra Queen 8-11-11	16-3-66
4m C	8m 39	The Spaniard 11-11-1	3-1-73

OLD COURSE

Distance	Time	Horse-age-weight	Date
2m 200y H	3m 59.40	Usario 6-10-12	14-10-65
2½m H	5m 11.2	King Tan 5-10-8	26-9-73
3m H	5m 49	Apple of My Eye 6-10-12	9-10-75
2m C	3m 54.40	Hal's Farewell 7-10-10	20-3-68
2½m C	5m 0.20	Clear Cut 11-10-9	8-11-75
3m 1f C	6m 20.60	The Pooka 11-10-9	26-9-73
3m 2f 76y C (*See* NEW COURSE)			
3m 2f 170y C	6m 53	Herring Gull 6-11-12	19-3-70
4m C	8m 33.20	Foreman 7-12-1	13-3-73

The Piper Champagne Cheltenham Gold Cup (3m, 2f)

HORSE		OWNER	RIDER	TRAINER	SP
1924	Red Splash	Maj. E. H. Wyndham	F. Rees	F. E. Withington	5/1
1925	Ballinode	J. Bentley	T. Leader	F. Morgan	3/1
1926	Koko	F. Barbour	J. Hamey	J. Bickley	10/1
1927	Thrown In	Lord Stalbridge	Mr H. Grosvenor	Owner	10/1
1928	Patron Saint	F. Keen	F. Rees	H. Harrison	7/2
1929	Easter Hero	J. Whitney	F. Rees	J. Anthony	7/4
1930	Easter Hero	J. Whitney	T. Cullinan	J. Anthony	8/11
1931	*Abandoned–Frost*				
1932	Golden Miller	Miss D. Paget	T. Leader	A. B. Briscoe	13/2
1933	Golden Miller	Miss D. Paget	W. Stott	A. B. Briscoe	4/7
1934	Golden Miller	Miss D. Paget	G. Wilson	A. B. Briscoe	6/5
1935	Golden Miller	Miss D. Paget	G. Wilson	A. B. Briscoe	1/2
1936	Golden Miller	Miss D. Paget	E. Williams	O. Anthony	21/20
1938	Morse Code	Lt.-Col. D. Part	D. Morgan	I. Anthony	13/2
1939	Brendan's Cottage	Mrs A. Smith-Bingham	G. Owen	G. Beeby	8/1
1940	Roman Hackle	Miss D. Paget	E. Williams	O. Anthony	Evens
1941	Poet Prince	D. Sherbrooke	R. Burford	I. Anthony	7/2
1942	Medoc II	Lord Sefton	H. Nicholson	R. Hobbs	9/2

Year	Horse	Owner	Rider	Trainer	SP
1943	*No Race*				
1944	*No Race*				
1945	Red Rower	Lord Stalbridge	D. Jones	Lord Stalbridge	11/4
1946	Prince Regent	J. Rank	T. Hyde	T. Dreaper	4/7
1947	Fortina	Lord Grimthorpe	Mr R. Black	H. Christie	8/1
1948	Cottage Rake	F. Vickerman	A. Brabazon	V. O'Brien	10/1
1949	Cottage Rake	F. Vickerman	A. Brabazon	V. O'Brien	4/6
1950	Cottage Rake	F. Vickerman	A. Brabazon	V. O'Brien	5-6
1951	Silver Fame	Lord Bicester	M. Molony	G. Beeby	6/4
1952	Mont Tremblant	Miss D. Paget	D. Dick	F. Walwyn	8/1
1953	Knock Hard	Mrs M. Keogh	T. Molony	V. O'Brien	11/2
1954	Four Ten	A. Strange	T. Cusack	J. Roberts	100/6
1955	Gay Donald	P. Burt	A. Grantham	J. Ford	33/1
1956	Limber Hill	J. Davey	J. Power	W. Dutton	11/8
1957	Linwell	D. Brown	M. Scudamore	C. Mallon	100/9
1958	Kerstin	G. Moore	S. Hayhurst	C. Bewicke	7/1
1959	Roddy Owen	Lord Fingall	H. Beasley	D. Morgan	5/1
1960	Pas Seul	J. Rogerson	W. Rees	R. Turnell	6/1
1961	Saffron Tartan	Col. G. Westmacott	F. Winter	D. Butchers	2/1
1962	Mandarin	Mme K. Hennessy	F. Winter	F. Walwyn	7/2
1963	Mill House	W. Gollings	G. W. Robinson	F. Walwyn	7/2
1964	Arkle	Anne, Duchess of Westminster	P. Taaffe	T. Dreaper	7/4
1965	Arkle	Anne, Duchess of Westminster	P. Taaffe	T. Dreaper	30/100
1966	Arkle	Anne, Duchess of Westminster	P. Taaffe	T. Dreaper	9/100
1967	Woodland Venture	H. H. Collins	T. Biddlecombe	T. F. Rimell	100/8
1968	Fort Leney	Col. J. Thompson	P. Taaffe	T. Dreaper	11/2
1969	What a Myth	Lady Weir	P. Kelleway	H. R. Price	8/1
1970	L'Escargot	Raymond Guest	T. Carberry	D. Moore	33/1
1971	L'Escargot	Raymond Guest	T. Carberry	D. Moore	7/2 jt-f
1972	Glencaraig Lady	B. Doyle	F. Berry	F. Flood	4/1
1973	The Dikler	Mrs D. August	R. Barry	F. Walwyn	9/1
1974	Captain Christy	Mrs J. Samuel	H. Beasley	P. Taaffe	7/1
1975	Ten Up	Anne, Duchess of Westminster	T. Carberry	T. Dreaper	2/1
1976	Royal Frolic	Sir E. Hamner	J. Burke	T. F. Rimell	14/1
1977	Davy Lad	Mrs J. McGowan	D. Hughes	M. O'Toole	14/1
1978	Midnight Court	Mrs O. Jackson	J. Francome	F. Winter	5/2

The Waterford Crystal Champion Hurdle Challenge Cup (2m, 200y)

Year	HORSE	OWNER	RIDER	TRAINER	SP
1927	Blaris	Mrs H. Hollins	G. Duller	W. Payne	11/10
1928	Brown Jack	Maj. H. Wernher	L. Rees	I. Anthony	4/1
1929	Royal Falcon	Mrs W. Bulkeley	F. Rees	R. Gore	11/2
1930	Brown Tony	Mrs J. de Selincourt	T. Cullinan	J. Anthony	7/2
1931	*Abandoned–Frost*				
1932	Insurance	Miss D. Paget	T. Leader	A. B. Briscoe	4/5
1933	Insurance	Miss D. Paget	W. Stott	A. B. Briscoe	10/11
1934	Chenango	G. Bostwick	D. Morgan	I. Anthony	4/9
1935	Lion Courage	R. Fox-Carlyon	G. Wilson	F. Brown	100/8
1936	Victor Norman	Mrs M. Stephens	H. Nicholson	M. Blair	4/1
1937	Free Fare	B. Warner	G. Pellerin	E. Gwilt	2/1
1938	Our Hope	R. Gubbins	Capt. R. Harding	R. Gubbins	5/1
1939	African Sister	H. Brueton	K. Piggott	C. Piggott	10/1
1940	Solford	Miss D. Paget	S. Magee	O. Anthony	5/2

1941 Seneca	Sir M. McAlpine	R. Smyth	V. Smyth	7/1
1942 Forestation	V. Smyth	R. Smyth	V. Smyth	10/1
1943 *No Race*				
1944 *No Race*				
1945 Brains Trust	F. Blakeway	T. F. Rimell	G. Wilson	9/2
1946 Distel	Miss D. Paget	R. O'Ryan	C. Rogers	4/5
1947 National Spirit	L. Abelson	D. Morgan	V. Smyth	7/1
1948 National Spirit	L. Abelson	R. Smyth	V. Smyth	6/4
1949 Hatton's Grace	Mrs M. Keogh	A. Brabazon	V. O'Brien	100/7
1950 Hatton's Grace	Mrs M. Keogh	A. Brabazon	V. O'Brien	5/2
1951 Hatton's Grace	Mrs M. Keogh	T. Molony	V. O'Brien	4/1
1952 Sir Ken	M. Kingsley	T. Molony	W. Stephenson	3/1
1953 Sir Ken	M. Kingsley	T. Molony	W. Stephenson	2/5
1954 Sir Ken	M. Kingsley	T. Molony	W. Stephenson	4/9
1955 Clair Soleil	G. Judd	F. Winter	H. R. Price	5/2
1956 Doorknocker	C. Nicholson	H. Sprague	W. Hall	100/9
1957 Merry Deal	A. Jones	G. Underwood	A. Jones	28/1
1958 Bandalore	Mrs D. Wright	G. Slack	J. S. Wright	20/1
1959 Fare Time	G. Judd	F. Winter	H. R. Price	13/2
1960 Another Flash	J. Byrne	H. Beasley	P. Sleator	11/4
1961 Eborneezer	Dr B. Pajgar	F. Winter	H. R. Price	13/2
1962 Anzio	Sir T. Ainsworth	G. W. Robinson	F. Walwyn	11/2
1963 Winning Fair	G. Spencer	Mr A. Lillingstone	G. Spencer	100/9
1964 Magic Court	J. McGhie	P. McCarron	T. Robson	100/6
1965 Kirriemuir	Mrs D. Beddington	G. W. Robinson	F. Walwyn	50/1
1966 Salmon Spray	Mrs J. Rogerson	J. Haine	R. Turnell	4/1
1967 Saucy Kit	K. F. Alder	R. Edwards	M. H. Easterby	100/6
1968 Persian War	H. Alper	J. Uttley	C. Davies	4/1
1969 Persian War	H. Alper	J. Uttley	C. Davies	6/4f
1970 Persian War	H. Alper	J. Uttley	C. Davies	5/4f
1971 Bula	Capt. E. Edwards-Heathcote	P. Kelleway	F. Winter	15/8f
1972 Bula	Capt. E. Edwards-Heathcote	P. Kelleway	F. Winter	8/11f
1973 Comedy of Errors	E. Wheatley	W. Smith	T. F. Rimell	8/1
1974 Lanzarote	Lord Howard de Walden	R. Pitman	F. Winter	7/4
1975 Comedy of Errors	E. Wheatley	K. White	T. F. Rimell	11/8
1976 Night Nurse	R. Spencer	P. Broderick	M. H. Easterby	2/1
1977 Night Nurse	R. Spencer	P. Broderick	M. H. Easterby	5/2
1978 Monksfield	Dr M. Mangan	T. Kinane	D. McDonogh	11/2

From 1972-7 run as Lloyds Bank Champion Hurdle.

Mackeson Gold Cup (2½m)

HORSE	OWNER	RIDER	TRAINER
1960 Fortria	Mr G. Ansley	P. Taaffe	T. Dreaper
1961 Scottish Memories	Mr G. B. Sanderson	C. Finnegan	A. Thomas
1962 Fortria	Mr G. Ansley	P. Taaffe	T. Dreaper
1963 Richard of Bordeaux	Mr J. S. Schilizzi	H. Beasley	F. Walwyn
1964 Super Flash	Mr A. Wood	S. Mellor	F. Cundell
1965 Dunkirk	Mr W. H. Whitbread	W. Rees	P. Cazalet
1966 Pawnbroker	Maj. E. Cliff-McCulloch	P. Broderick	W. A. Stephenson
1967 Charlie Worcester	Mrs H. R. Price	J. Gifford	H. R. Price
1968 Jupiter Boy	Mr J. Liley	E. Harty	T. F. Rimell
1969 Gay Trip	Mr A. J. Chambers	T. Biddlecombe	T. F. Rimell
1970 Chatham	Mr C. Knott	K. B. White	T. F. Rimell
1971 Gay Trip	Mr A. Chambers	T. Biddlecombe	T. F. Rimell

1972	Red Candle	Mrs C. O'Shea	J. Fox	G. Vallance
1973	Skymas	Mr M. Magee	J. Murphy	B. Lusk
1974	Bruslee	Mrs D. Rees-Davies	A. Turnell	M. Scudamore
1975	Clear Cut	Mr J. Hemingway	D. Greaves	M. Camacho
1976	Cancello	Maj. W. Burdon	D. Atkins	N. Crump
1977	Bachelor's Hall	Mr P. Harris	M. O'Halloran	P. Cundell
1978	Bawnogues	Mrs H. Lawlor	C. Smith	M. Tate

Massey-Ferguson Gold Cup (2m, 5f)

	HORSE	OWNER	RIDER	TRAINER
1963	Limeking	Mr A. Chester-Beatty	T. Taaffe	D. Morgan
1964	Flying Wild	Mr R. R. Guest	T. Carberry	D. Moore
1965	Flyingbolt	Mrs T. G. Wilkinson	P. Taaffe	T. Dreaper
1966	The Laird	Mr H. J. Joel	J. King	R. Turnell
1967	*No Race*			
1968	Tassilo	Mr J. Joseph	A. Branford	F. Walwyn
1969	Titus Oates	Mr P. Cussins	R. Barry	G. W. Richards
1970	Simian	Mr M. F. Sanderson	D. Moore	Miss Sinclair
1971	Leap Frog	Mrs P. Burrell	V. O'Brien	T. Dreaper
1972	Arctic Bow	Mr H. J. Joel	A. Turnell	R. Turnell
1973	Pendil	Mrs C. Swallow	R. Pitman	F. Winter
1974	Garnishee	Mr J. Goldsmith	D. Mould	H. Thomson-Jones
1975	Easby Abbey	Mrs W. Blow	R. Barry	M. H. Easterby
1976	*No Race*			
1977	Even Melody	Lady Hay	C. Hawkins	Capt. N. F. Crump
1978	The Snipe	Mr G. Richmond-Watson	A. Webber	J. Webber

The Sun Alliance Chase (3m)

	HORSE	OWNER	RIDER	TRAINER
1964	Buona Notte	Mr H. J. Joel	J. Haine	R. Turnell
1965	Arkloin	Mr G. Ansley	L. McLoughlin	T. Dreaper
1966	Different Class	Mr G. Peck	D. Mould	P. Cazalet
1967	Border Jet	Lady Weir	J. Gifford	H. R. Price
1968	Herring Gull	Mrs G. A. Wilson	J. Crowley	P. Mullins
1969	Spanish Steps	Mr E. Courage	J. Cook	Owner
1970	Proud Tarquin	Col. J. Thomson	P. Taaffe	T. Dreaper
1971	Tantalum	Col. S. Green	D. Nicholson	M. B. Pope
1972	Clever Scot	Mr M. Ritzenberg	D. Mould	H. Thomson-Jones
1973	Killiney	Mrs E. Boucher	R. Pitman	F. Winter
1974	Ten Up	Anne, Duchess of Westminster	T. Carberry	J. Dreaper
1975	Pengrail	Mrs G. Morton	J. Francome	F. Winter
1976	Tied Cottage	Mr A. Robinson	T. Carberry	D. Moore
1977	Gay Spartan	Mr M. Armstrong	M. Dickinson	A. Dickinson
1978	Sweet Joe	Mr M. Ritzenberg	S. Smith-Eccles	H. Thomson-Jones

Run as Tote Champion Novices 1964-1973

Daily Express Triumph Hurdle (2m, 200y)

	HORSE	OWNER	RIDER	TRAINER
1965	Blarney Beacon	Mr F. Laker	G. Ramshaw	R. Smyth
1966	Black Ice	Mr A. Crowther	H. Beasley	A. Thomas
1967	Persian War	Mr H. Alper	J. Uttley	B. Swift
1968	England's Glory	Mrs M. Sherman	J. Uttley	S. Ingham
1969	Coral Diver	Mr B. Jenks	T. Biddlecombe	T. F. Rimell
1970	Varma	Mr C. Clore	B. Barker	M. Masson

1971	Boxer	Lord Blakenham	J. Uttley	R. Smyth
1972	Zarib	Mrs A. Hornby	W. Smith	T. F. Rimell
1973	Moonlight Bay	Mr and Mrs J. Mullion	J. Haine	J. Gifford
1974	Attivo	Mr P. O'Sullivan	R. Hughes	C. Mitchell
1975	Royal Epic	Mr R. Head	F. McKenna	V. Cross
1976	Peterhof	Mr H. Gould	J. J. O'Neill	M. W. Easterby
1977	Meladon	Mrs N. Flynn	T. Carberry	A. J. Maxwell
1978	Connaught Ranger	Mr J. McCaughey	J. Burke	T. F. Rimell

National Hunt Two Mile Champion Chase

	HORSE	OWNER	RIDER	TRAINER
1959	Quita Que	Mr D. R. Brand	Mr J. Cox	D. Moore
1960	Fortria	Mr G. Ansley	P. Taaffe	T. Dreaper
1961	Fortria	Mr G. Ansley	P. Taaffe	T. Dreaper
1962	Piperton	Mr A. H. Thomlinson	D. V. Dick	Owner
1963	Sandy Abbot	Mrs J. D. McKechnie	S. Mellor	G. R. Owen
1964	Ben Stack	Anne, Duchess of Westminster	P. Taaffe	T. Dreaper
1965	Dunkirk	Mr W. H. Whitbread	D. V. Dick	P. Cazalet
1966	Flyingbolt	Mrs T. G. Wilkinson	P. Taaffe	T. Dreaper
1967	Drinny's Double	Mr P. Mellon	O. Nash	R. Turnell
1968	Drinny's Double	Mr P. Mellon	O. Nash	R. Turnell
1969	Muir	Mr W. Willis	B. Hannon	T. Dreaper
1970	Straight Fort	Miss J. Ansley	P. Taaffe	T. Dreaper
1971	Crisp	Sir C. Manifold	P. Kelleway	F. Winter
1972	Royal Relief	Mr E. Courage	W. Smith	E. Courage
1973	Inkslinger	Mrs M. Jenney	T. Carberry	D. Moore
1974	Royal Relief	Mr E. Courage	W. Smith	Owner
1975	Lough Inagh	Mr A. Martin	S. Barker	J. Dreaper
1976	Skymas	Mr M. Magee	M. Morris	B. Lusk
1977	Skymas	Mr M. Magee	M. Morris	B. Lusk
1978	Hilly Way	Mr J. W. Sweeney	T. Carmody	P. D. McCreery

Foxhunters Champion Hunters Chase Challenge Cup (3m, 2f)

	HORSE	OWNER	RIDER	TRAINER
1920	Be Careful	Col. F. Blacker	Mr R. Roberts	— —
1921	Barca	Lord Kennmare	Mr J. Murphy	— —
1922	Connemara Black	Mr D. Tyson	Mr H. C. Alexander	— —
1923	Fairy Hill II	Maj. H. Wernher	Maj. E. C. Doyle	— —
1924	Fairy Hill II	Maj. H. Wernher	Maj. E. C. Doyle	— —
1925	Foxfoot	Mr T. Laidlaw	Mr P. Nugent	— —
1926	Far Flight	Mr H. Brown	Owner	— —
1927	Pippin II	Capt. M. E. Dennis	Owner	— —
1928	Rathpatrick	Mr J. Johnstone	Mr S. H. Dennis	— —
1929	Blennerhasset	Mr T. Parkes	Mr W. P. Dutton	— —
1930	Melleray's Belle	Mr W. Wilson	Mr G. Owen	— —
1931	*Abandoned – Frost*			
1932	Chad's Ford	Mr F. Ambrose-Clark	Mr R. C. Hobbs	— —
1933	Minstrel Boy	Maj. H. Rushton	Mr G. Bostick	— —
1934	Ballybrack	Lt.-Col. R. Tweedie	Mr R. R. Tweedie	— —
1935	Empire Night	Mr C. Nicholson	Mr A. Marsh	— —
1936	Herode Bridge	Maj. I. Straker	Mr A. Marsh	— —
1937	*No Race*			
1938	Winter Knight	Mrs E. Bailey	Mr E. Bailey	Owner
1939	Kilshannig	Mr J. Paterson	Mr L. Lillingstone	Owner
1940–45	*No Race*			

1946	Hoilo	Mrs H. Freeman-Jackson	Mr H. Freeman-Jackson	Privately
1947	Lucky Purchase	Mr S. Banks	Mr J. Nichols	Owner
1948	State Control	Mr H. Llewellyn	Owner	Owner
1949	*No Race*			
1950	Greenwood	Mr J. Tudor-Evans	Mr J. S. Evans	Owner
1951	Hallowe'en	Capt. R. Smalley	Owner	Owner
1952	Parasol II	Mr A. Walton	Mr I. Kenwood	Owner
1953	{Merry	Mr J. Ballie	Mr G. Kindersley	A. Kerr
	{Dunboy	Miss Pat Bruce	Mr C. Scott	P. Bruce
1954	Happymint	Mr A. Moralee	Owner	J. Wight
1955	*No Race*			
1956	The Callant	Mr C. Scott	Mr J. Scott-Aiton	J. Wight
1957	The Callant	Mr C. Scott	Mr J. Scott-Aiton	J. Wight
1958	Whinstone Hill	Mr R. Brewis	Owner	Owner
1959	Some Baby	Mr T. Rootes	Mr M. Thorne	Owner
1960	Whinstone Hill	Mr R. Brewis	Owner	Owner
1961	Colledge Master	Mr L. Morgan	Owner	Owner
1962	Colledge Master	Mr L. Morgan	Owner	Owner
1963	Grand Morn II	Mr G. Shepheard	Mr R. Bloomfield	Owner
1964	Freddie	Mr R. Tweedie	Mr A. MacTaggart	Owner
1965	Woodside Terrace	Mr R. Woodhouse	Owner	Owner
1966	Straight Lady	Mr W. Shepherd	Mr R. Shepherd	Owner
1967	Mulbarton	Mr I. Patullo	Mr N. Gaselee	Owner
1968	Bright Beach	Mr G. Dun	Mr C. Macmillan	Owner
1969	Queen's Guide	Mr W. Wade	Mr W. Wade	Owner
1970	Highworth	Mr R. Woodhouse	Owner	Owner
1971	Hope Again	Mr D. Windell	Mr R. Smith	Owner
1972	Credit Call	Mr C. Collins	Owner	W. A. Stephenson
1973	Bullock's Horn	Mrs E. Barker	Lord Oaksey	R. Turnell
1974	Corrie Burn	Mrs G. Fairbairn	Mr I. Williams	G. Fairbairn
1975	Real Rascal	Mrs B. Surman	Mr G. Hyatt	Owner
1976	False Note	Mr J. Horton	Mr B. Smart	Owner
1977	Long Lane	Mr R. Shepherd	Owner	Owner
1978	Mount Olive	Mr R. Shepherd	Owner	Owner

Run as Foxhunter Challenge Cup (4m) 1920-1977

The National Hunt Chase (4m)

	COURSE	HORSE	OWNER	RIDER	TRAINER
1860	Market Harborough	Bridegroom	Mr B. J. Angell	Mr Burton	——
1861	Market Harborough	Queensferry	Mr B. J. Angell	Mr Burton	——
1862	Rugby	Fidget	——	Mr Skipworth	——
1863	Market Harborough	Socks	——	Mr Goodman	——
1864	Melton	Game Chicken	Mr T. Behrens	Capt. Smith	——
1865	Wetherby	Emperor	Mr H. Chaplin	Mr Goodman	——
1866	Crewkerne	Shangarry	Mr E. Studd	Mr Goodman	——
1867	Bedford	Emperor III	Mr H. Chaplin	Mr H. Coventry	——
1868	Bedford	Tathwell	Mr Welfitt	Mr Brockton	——
1869	*No Race*				
1870	Cottenham	Schiedam	Mr Chaplin	Mr J. M. Richardson	——
1871	Burton	Daybreak	Mr J. H. Houldsworth	Capt. Smith	——
1872	Abergavenny	Red Nob	Mr Sankey	Capt. Holyoake	——
1873	Bristol	Pickles	Mr Robertson	Capt. Tempest	——
1874	Aylesbury	Lucellum	Mr Vyner	Capt. Smith	——
1875	Sandown Park	Gazelle	Mr Smyth	Mr Flutter	——
1876	Irvine	Burford	Mr Ballard	Lord M. Beresford	——
1877	Cottenham	Bear	Duke of Hamilton	Mr E. P. Wilson	——

1878	Hereford	Filbert	Mr Friend	Mr Friend	—
1879	Derby	Bellringer	Mr Vyner	Mr A. Coventry	—
1880	Liverpool	New Glasgow	Mr Peel	Capt. Smith	—
1881	Birmingham	Pride of Prussia	Mr Talbot	Mr E. P. Wilson	—
1882	Derby	Llantarnam	Mr Jenkins	Mr E. P. Wilson	—
1883	Melton	Satellite	Mr Tritton	Mr E. P. Wilson	—
1884	Leicester	Equity	Mr Howett	Mr E. P. Wilson	—
1885	Lincoln	Lady Tempest	Mr Saurin	Mr W. Beasley	—
1886	Malton	Why Not	Mr D. J. Jardine	Mr C. J. Cunningham	—
1887	Derby	Monkshood	Maj. Meysey-Thompson	Capt. E. R. Owen	—
1888	Sandown Park	Glen Thorpe	Mr E. Jay	Mr Geo. Lambton	—
1889	Cardiff	Nap	Mr B. Robson	Mr C. Thompson	—
1890	Irvine	Innisfail	Mr T. G. Arthur	Mr T. G. Arthur	—
1891	Hurst Park	Impeyan	Mr W. Low	Mr Crawley	—
1892	Derby	Royal Buck	Mr T. Cannon	Mr Yorke	—
1893	Sandown Park	Van der Berg	Capt. Crawley	Sir C. Slade	—
1894	Derby	Philactery	Sir S. Scott	Mr Ricardo	—
1895	Sandown Park	Finma-Coul II	Mr J. Arnold	Mr F. B. Atkinson	—
1896	Hurst Park	Ludgershall	Mr C. P. Shrubb	Mr H. M. Ripley	—
1897	Newmarket	Nord Ouest	Vicomte de Buisseret	M. Morand	—
1898	Gatwick	Real Shamrock	Mr F. P. Lysaght	Mr E. P. Gundry	—
1899	Hurst Park	Glen Royal	Mr W. H. Walker	Mr J. J. Fergusson	—
1900	Kempton Park	Eoos	Mr T. Bayden	Mr A. Gordon	—
1901	Melton Hunt	Friar John	Mr Barclay Walker	Mr H. Sidney	—
1902	Warwick	Marpessa	Mr J. J. Maher	Mr Persse	—
1903	Warwick	Comfit	Mr F. Bibby	Capt. R. H. Collis	—
1904	Cheltenham	Timothy Titus	Mr W. B. Partridge	Mr Ivor Anthony	—
1905	Cheltenham	Miss Clifden II	Mr D. Faber	Mr H. M. Ripley	—
1906	Warwick	Count Rufus	Mr W. Charters	Mr A. Gordon	—
1907	Warwick	Red Hall	Mr H. G. Farrant	Mr H. G. Farrant	—
1908	Warwick	Rory O'Moore	Capt. J. F. Laycock	Mr P. Whitaker	—
1909	Warwick	Wychwood	Mr R. Cartwright	Mr P. Roberts	—
1910	Warwick	Nimble Kate	Mr B. P. Steinman	Mr P. Roberts	—

(Since 1911 the race has been run at Cheltenham)

1911	—	Sir Halbert	Capt. F. D. Grissell	Mr A. Smith	—
1912	—	The Rejected IV	Mr E. Platt	Mr G. E. Cotton	—
1913	—	Kransfugl	Capt. S. P. Yates	Mr R. H. Hall	—
1914	—	War Duke	Mr H. F. Malcolmson	Mr H. Ussher	—
1915	—	Martial IV	Maj. J. H. Purvis	Maj. J. H. Purvis	—
1916-19	*No Race*				
1920	—	Prudhomme	Mr J. Daly	Mr C. Brabazon	—
1921	—	Bugler	Mr H. A. Brown	Capt. G. H. Bennet	—
1922	—	Conjuror II	Maj. C. Dewhurst	Mr C. P. Dewhurst	—
1923	—	Templescoby	Maj. H. C. Robinson	Mr H. A. Brown	—
1924	—	Patsey V	Mr B. B. Lemon	Mr B. B. Lemon	—
1925	—	Ardvasar	Maj. S. Green	Mr P. Dennis	—
1926	—	Cloringo	Mr J. C. Paterson	Mr W. P. Dutton	—
1927	—	Fine Yarn	Mrs C. Stevens	Mr J. Stevens	—
1928	—	Cryptical	Mr F. H. Bowcher	Maj. T. F. Cavenagh	—
1929	—	Big Wonder	G. S. L. Whitelaw	Capt. H. N. Weber	—
1930	—	Sir Lindsay	Mr J. H. Whitney	Lord Fingall	—
1931	—	Merriment IV	Lord Haddington	Lord Haddington	—
1932	—	Robin-a-Tiptoe	Maj. Noel Furlong	Mr F. Furlong	—
1933	—	Ego	Lt.-Col. M. Lindsay	Mr R. Harding	—
1934	—	Crown Prince	Lord Rosebery	Mr R. Strutt	—
1935	—	Rod and Gun	Mr J. H. Whitney	Mr H. Jones	—
1936	—	Pucka Belle	Mr E. W. W. Bailey	Mr E. W. W. Bailey	Owner
1937	—	Hopeful Hero	Mr H. A. J. Silley	Mr W. Dawes	Owner
1938	—	St George II	Mr A. J. G. Levenson-Gower	Mr R. Petre	Owner

1939 ——	Litigant	Maj N. Furlong	Mr R. Black	F. Furlong
1940-45 *No Race*				
1946 ——	Prattler	Mr E. Manner	Maj. D. Daly	J. Hall
1947 ——	Maltese Wanderer	Mr G. J. Wells	Maj. D. Daly	T. Yates
1948 ——	Bruno II	Maj. W. J. Anstruther-Gray	Maj. G. Cunard	W. J. Anstruther-Gray
1949 ——	Castledermot	Mrs M. H. Keogh	Lord Mildmay	M. V. O'Brien
1950 ——	Ellesmere	Lord Bicester	Mr A. Corbett	K. Cundell
1951 ——	Cushendun	Mrs L. Brotherton	Mr P. Chisman	R. Renton
1952 ——	Frosty Knight	Maj. Ian Straker	Mr C. Straker	I. Straker
1953 ——	Pontage	Lady Honor Svejdar	Mr J. Cox	D. L. Moore
1954 ——	Quare Times	Mrs Robert Smyth	Mr J. Cox	M. V. O'Brien
1955 ——	Reverend Prince	Mr P. Dufosee	Mr C. Pocock	P. Dufosee
1956 ——	Rosana III	Mr J. J. Everitt	Mr J. J. Everitt	G. G. H. Everitt
1957 ——	Kari Sou	Mr A. H. Thomlinson	Mr A. Lillingstone	A. H. Thomlinson
1958 ——	Spud Tamson	Mrs T. D. C. Dun	Mr G. Dun	T. Dun
1959 ——	Sabaria	Mr A. R. Turnell	Mr J. Lawrence	Owner
1960 ——	Proud Socks	Mr V. R. Bishop	Mr H. Thompson	Owner
1961 ——	Superfine	Mr I. Kerwood	Sir W. Pigott-Brown	F. Cundell
1962 ——	Go Slow	Mrs I. R. Millar	Mr G. Small	A. Piper
1963 ——	Time	Mr John Cheatle	Mr I. Balding	W. Stephenson
1964 ——	Dorimont	Mr M. A. Walshe	Mr C. Vaughan	T. Taaffe
1965 ——	Red Vale	Mrs C. Smith	Mr G. Small	A. Piper
1966 ——	Polaris Missile	Mr M. J. Thorne	Mr M. J. Thorne	M. J. Thorne
1967 ——	Master Tammy	Mr G. G. Guilding	Capt B. Fanshawe	G. Guilding
1968 ——	Fascinating Forties	Lord Leverhulme	Mr M. Dickinson	G. Owen
1969 ——	Lizzie the Lizard	Mr A. J. Hartnoll	Mr G. Cann	A. J. Hartnoll
1970 ——	Domason	Mr H. Dufosee	Mr R. Alner	H. Dufosee
1971 ——	Deblins Green	Mr G. H. Yardley	Mr J. Edmunds	G. H. Yardley
1972 ——	Charlie Winking	Mr L. Scott	Mr D. Scott	L. Scott
1973 ——	Foreman	Mr R. Dean	Mr W. Shand-Kydd	H. Thomson-Jones
1974 ——	Mr Midland	Mr B. Naughton	Mr M. Morris	E. O'Grady
1975 *No Race*				
1976 ——	Sage Merlin	Mr J. Bingham	Mr P. Greenall	J. Hardy
1977 ——	Alpenstock	Mr H. Thomson	Mr C. Saunders	S. Mellor
1978 ——	Gay Tie	Dr P. Morrissey	Mr J. Fowler	M. O'Toole

Arkle Challenge Trophy (2m and a few yards)

	HORSE	OWNER	RIDER	TRAINER
1969	Chatham	Mr C. Knott	T. Biddlecombe	T. F. Rimell
1970	Soloning	Mrs C. Thornton	P. Kelleway	F. Winter
1971	Alpheus	Lord Donoughmore	E. Wright	T. Dreaper
1972	Pendil	Mrs C. Kinney	R. Pitman	F. Winter
1973	Denys Adventure	Mrs R. Henriques	G. Thorner	T. Forster
1974	Canasta Lad	Mrs D. Hague	J. King	P. Bailey
1975	Broncho II	Mr F. Tyldesley	C. Tinkler	A. Dickinson
1976	Roaring Wind	Mr S. Jones	R. Crank	B. Cambidge
1977	Tip the Wink	Mr M. Simmonds	D. T. Hughes	P. Taylor
1978	Alverton	Snailwell Stud Co Ltd	G. Thorner	M. H. Easterby

Sun Alliance Novices Hurdle (2m 4f)

	HORSE	OWNER	RIDER	TRAINER
1974	Brown Lad	Mr J. Osborne	R. Barry	P. Osborne
1975	Davy Lad	Mrs J. McGowan	D. Hughes	M. O'Toole
1976	Parkhill	Mrs J. McGowan	D. Hughes	M. O'Toole
1977	Counsel Cottage	Lady Elizabeth Byng	S. Treacy	P. Mullins
1978	Mr Kildare	Mr O. Carty	T. Carmody	L. Browne

Waterford Crystal Supreme Novice Hurdle (2m 200y)

	HORSE	OWNER	RIDER	TRAINER
1974	Avec Moi	Lord Blackford	R. Rowell	Miss Sinclair
1975	Bannow Rambler	Mrs K. White	F. Berry	P. Berry
1976	Beacon Light	Mr H. J. Joel	A. Turnell	R. Turnell
1977	Mac's Chariot	Mrs A. Jordan	D. Hughes	M. O'Toole
1978	Golden Cygnet	Mr R. Rooney	Mr N. Madden	E. O'Grady

1974-1977 run as the Lloyds Bank Champion Novices Hurdle

CHENANGO

Bay gelding, 1925, Hapsburg—Will Return (William The Third). Bred by Lt.-Col. Lort Phillips.

A genuine and versatile horse owned by American amateur G. H. Bostwick and trained for him by Ivor Anthony, Chenango won seven races including the 1934 Emblem Chase (Kempton), ridden by his owner, and the 1934 Champion Hurdle (D. Morgan), 4/9f, by 5l, 6l, from Pompelmoose (P. Fitzgerald) and Black Duncan (T. Cullinan).

CHEPSTOW (Group 2)

Since the demise of Cardiff, Chepstow has housed the Corals' Welsh Grand National (February, 3m, 6f, approx. £15,000 added) and the Welsh Champion Hurdle (Easter, 2m, £8,000 added). Set in an attractive wooded park, it is a left-handed track about two miles round and undulating with a steep uphill finish which puts stamina at a premium. Other important races include the Welsh Champion Chase (April, 2m, 4f, £9,334) and the Panama Cigar Hurdle Final (March, 2m, 5-y-o, £5,885).

The opening of the M4 and the Severn Bridge, together with an enterprising executive, has made Chepstow, which dates from 1880, one of the foremost N.H. courses in the country.

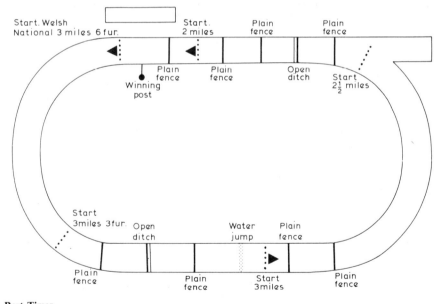

Best Times

Distance	Time	Horse-age-weight	Date
2m H	3m 46.40	Harlech Lad 4-10-13	3-10-70
2m 4f H	4m 36.20	Aileen's Cacador 9-11-3	23-4-57
2m C	4m	Vikrom 7-11-3	16-4-74
2½m C	4m 51.40	Indian Yeldah 5-10-4	11-10-69
3m C	6m 2.20	James Jacques 6-11-4	30-9-72
3m 3f C	6m 39-40	Jaunty Jane 7-12-0	26-5-75
3¾m C	7m 24	Creeola II 9-10-5	27-4-57

Welsh Grand National (3m, 6f)

HORSE	OWNER	RIDER	TRAINER
Cardiff			
1895 Deerstalker	Mr T. Cannon	Mawson	——
1896 Cloister	Mr C. Duff	Mr G. S. Davies	——
1897 Legal Tender	Mr E. Deacon	H. Brown	——
1898 Hedgehog	Mr F. W. Holden	D. Davies	——
1899 Nat Gould	Mr G. Jukes	Mr A. W. Wood	——
1900 Bloomer	Mr R. Bourke	Banner	
1901 Gangbridge	Mr H. S. Sidney	Owner	——
1902 *Appears To Have Been No Race*			
1903 *Appears To Have Been No Race*			
1904 *Appears To Have Been No Race*			
1905 Glenrocky	Mr David Faber	Barten	——
1906 Shoeblack	Mr F. P. Gilbert	Mr A. W. Wood	——
1907 *Appears To Have Been No Race*			
1908 Razorbill	Capt. R. H. Fowler	B. Flannery	——
1909 Roman Candle	Mr W. F. Stratton	E. Ward	——
1910 Caubeen	Mr F. Bibby	F. Mason	——
1911 *Appears To Have Been No Race*			
1912 Jacobus	Mr C. Bower Ismay	F. Lyall	——
1913 *Appears To Have Been No Race*			
1914 Succubus	Mr F. Lort Phillips	C. Kelly	——
1915-1919 *No Race*			
1920 Mark Back	Mr E. S. Wills	H. Smyth	——
1921 Mythical	Mr W. A. Bankier	R. Burford	——
1922 Simonides	Mr M. G. Dobbyn	T. Willmot	——
1923 Clonree	Mrs A. Blain	J. Hogan, jun.	——
1924 Dwarf of the Forest	Mr H. Kennard	G. Calder	——
1925 Vaulx	Mr C. Piggott	K. Piggott	——
1926 Miss Balscadden	Mr D. Thomas	Mr D. Thomas	——
1927 Snipe's Bridge	Capt. R. M. Thompson	W. Gurney	R. Thompson
1928 Miss Balscadden	Sir D. Llewellyn	G. Bowden	M. Lindsay
1929 Monduco	Mr A. Bendon	J. Moloney	P. Woodland
1930 Boomlet	Mr E. Large	D. Williams	I. Anthony
1931 Wise Don	Miss M. Lark	Capt. Moseley	R. Payne
1932 Miss Gaynus	Mrs A. S. Bellville	G. Wilson	J. Hall
1933 Pebble Ridge	Lord Glanely	D. Williams	I. Anthony
1934 Dream Ship	Mr J. V. Rank	J. Fawcus	G. Evans
1935 Lacatoi	Mr J. V. Rank	J. Fawcus	I. Anthony
1936 Sorley Boy	Mr F. Ambrose Clark	D. Morgan	I. Anthony
1937 Lacatoi	Mr J. V. Rank	J. Fawcus	G. Evans
1938 Timber Wolf	Mr J. V. Rank	B. Hobbs	G. Evans
1939 Lacatoi	Mr J. V. Rank	J. Fawcus	H. Brown
1940-46 *No Race*			
1947 *Abandoned – Snow*			
Newport			
1948 Bora's Cottage	Mr F. L. Vickerman	E. Reavey	H. R. Price
Chepstow			
1949 Fighting Line	Mrs C. A. Hall-Hall	R. Francis	K. Cundell
1950 Gallery	Sir A. Pilkington	A. Mullins	W. Bissil
1951 Skyreholme	Mr C. F. Booth	A. P. Thompson	N. Crump
1952 Dinton Lass	Mr E. R. Excell	A. Mullins	J. Roberts
1953 Stalbridge Rock	Mr H. W. Dufosee	Mr R. McCreery	H. Dufosee
1954 Blow Horn	Mrs S. M. Morgan	J. Hunter	T. Jarvis
1955 Monaleen	Mr H. T. Smith	P. Fitzgerald	H. T. Smith
1956 Crudwell	Mrs D. M. Cooper	R. Francis	F. Cundell
1957 Creeola II	Mr C. Nixon	M. Scudamore	T. F. Rimell

1958 Oscar Wilde	Mr T. T. Jasper	B. Lawrence	W. Wightman
1959 Limonali	Mrs G. R. Lewis	D. Nicholson	E. C. Morel
1960 Clover Bud	Mr G. G. Llewellin	D. Nicholson	Owner
1961 Limonali	Mrs G. R. Lewis	D. Nicholson	I. Lewis
1962 Forty Secrets	Mr A. G. Clark	J. Gifford	E. Jones
1963 Motel	Mr W. Lowe	P. Cowley	W. Lowe
1964 Rainbow Battle	Mr W. A. Stephenson	P. Broderick	W. A. Stephenson
1965 Norther	Mr J. G. Jones	T. Biddlecombe	D. Jenkins
1966 Kilburn	Mme Borel de Biche	T. Norman	C. Nesfield
1967 Happy Spring	Mr D. Wright	K. White	J. S. Wright
1968 Glenn	Mrs M. Joseph	E. Harty	T. F. Rimell
1969 *No Race*			
1970 French Excuse	Mr J. W. Jennings	T. Biddlecombe	T. F. Rimell
1971 Royal Toss	Mr H. Handel	P. Cowley	H. Handel
1972 Charlie H.	Mr J. Clay	J. Haine	R. Turnell
1973 Deblin's Green	Mr G. Yardley	N. Wakley	G. Yardley
1974 Pattered	Mr T. Winterton	K. White	E. Jones
1975 *No Race*			
1976 Rag Trade	Mr P. Raymond	J. Burke	T. F. Rimell
1977 *No Race*			
1978 *Abandoned – Frost*			

1895-98 Run over $2\frac{1}{2}$m
1899-1912 Run over 3m
1914 Run over 3m 100yds
1920-39 Run over $3\frac{1}{2}$m
1948 Run over 3m 4f 150yds

Welsh Champion Hurdle (2m)

HORSE	OWNER	RIDER	TRAINER
1969 Persian War	Mr H. Alper	J. Uttley	C. Davies
1970 Frozen Alive	Mrs Donald Steward	S. Mellor	H. Thomson-Jones
1971 Bula	Capt. E. Edwards-Heathcote	P. Kelleway	F. Winter
1972 Canasta Lad	Mrs D. Hague	J. King	P. Bailey
1973 Comedy of Errors	Mr E. Wheatley	W. Smith	T. F. Rimell
1974 Canasta Lad	Mrs D. Hague	J. King	P. Bailey
1975 Lanzarote	Lord Howard de Walden	R. Pitman	F. Winter
1976 Night Nurse	Mr R. Spencer	P. Broderick	M. H. Easterby
1977 Night Nurse	Mr R. Spencer	P. Broderick	M. H. Easterby
1978 *No Race*			

CHIMNEY SWEEP

Brown gelding, 1862, Ethelbert—Smut (Womersley). Bred by Lord Coventry.

Owned by Lord Coventry and not to be confused with Lord Marcus Beresford's popular half-bred (*q.v.*), Chimney Sweep was a brilliant young horse who won the Great Midland Chase (Derby), the Leamington Grand Annual and the Great Metropolitan Chase (Croydon) before his sixth birthday. Made favourite for the 1868 Grand National, he smashed a fetlock on a stone crossing the Melling Road and had to be destroyed.

CHIMNEY SWEEP

Half-bred brown gelding by Planet.

Formerly a charger in the 7th Hussars,

Chimney Sweep was assigned to Lord Marcus Beresford who decided that his mount had talents over and above the requirements of Her Majesty's Forces and turned his attention to steeplechasing. During a long and honourable career Chimney Sweep won seven races including the Grand International Chase, Sandown (1876), the Prince of Wales' Chase, Sandown (1876), the Cheltenham Grand Annual (1877), the Great Sandown Chase (1877) and the Grand Sefton, Liverpool (1878). He was also second to Reugny in the 1874 Grand National.

CHISMAN, Peter (b.1924)

Born at Epsom, Peter Chisman spent two years as a pupil trainer with Fred Rimell.

He also rode very successfully as an amateur under N.H. Rules, being Champion Amateur in 1950-51, riding 13 winners. He won the National Hunt Chase in 1951 on Cushendun and the Kim Muir twice, in 1951 on Mighty Fine and in 1952 on Menzies. He turned professional in 1952 and was based at Middleham where he rode for Neville Crump, for whom he won the Becher Chase (1952) on the ex-hunter chaser, Larry Finn.

In 1963 he took out a licence to train, at first at Stratford and latterly at Middleham. He was particularly successful with young hurdlers and won the 1973 John Player Final with Dark Sultan. He handed in his licence at the end of season 1974-75.

CHRISTIE, Hector (1905-67)

Hector Christie was educated at Eton. He fought in the 1939-45 War and was imprisoned which undermined his health. He rode as an amateur and trained privately for Countess Lindsay in Fifeshire. Later he moved to Lambourn from where he sent out Fortina to win the 1947 Cheltenham Gold Cup and Lancashire Chase for Lord Grimthorpe.

CLAIR SOLEIL (FR)

Brown horse, 1949, Maravédis—La Divine (Fair Copy). Bred by M Dupré.

Bred in France by M François Dupré and a winner of his only two races in that country, when trained by F. Mathet. Clair Soleil came to England for the 1953 Triumph Hurdle and was bought on the eve of the race by Mr Judd for £5000. Having duly won his race Clair Soleil remained in this country where, trained by Ryan Price and invariably ridden by Fred Winter, he went on to win 10 more hurdle races and a chase. His hurdle victories included the Rose of Lancaster Hurdle, Manchester (twice), the Victory Hurdle, Manchester, the Spa Hurdle, Cheltenham, and the 1955 Champion Hurdle, 5/2f (F. T. Winter) by a head, 4l, from Stroller (T. P. Burns) and Cruachan (G. Slack).

CLARK, F. Ambrose (1881-1964)

Together with his brothers, Stephen and Robert Sterling (owner of 1954 Derby winner, Never Say Die), 'Brose' Clark shared a $30 million fortune derived from the Clark Thread Company and Singer Manufacturing. He went to Columbia University, hunted and point-to-pointed and for a time kept a hunting 'box' at Melton Mowbray run by Reg Hobbs. He and his wife had steeplechasers with Ivor and Jack Anthony and later with Reg Hobbs. Mrs Clark won the 1933 Grand National with Kellsboro' Jack. He served two terms as President of the United Hunts Racing Association and won the American Grand National twice, in 1903 with Plohn and in 1961 with Hibler. He sold his entire stable in 1963. Colours: light blue, canary cap and sash.

CLERK OF THE COURSE

The Rules of Racing state as follows:

22.The Clerk of the Course (i) or his authorized substitute, is responsible for the conduct of the racing at Meetings authorized by the Stewards of the Jockey Club and is responsible, in particular, for the condition of the course and fences and for ensuring that the course is properly measured and marked. He shall also comply with the provisions of Racecourse Guidelines (Fixed Equipment) unless and to the extent that they may have been waived in writing by the Stewards of the Jockey Club.

(ii) Shall send a copy of each day's card to the Racing Calendar Office. A horse may appear on the card in the name of the nominator and the Stewards may, in special circumstances, grant permission for a horse to run in the name of the trainer or of some other person. The Clerk of the Course shall, in such latter case, make a report to the Racing Calendar Office, stating the grounds upon which the permission was granted.

(iii) See that a parade ring is provided in the paddock. All horses running at the meeting shall be saddled in the paddock and brought into the parade ring a reasonable time before the signal to mount is given. The attendants shall be provided with badges bearing numbers corresponding with those on the card. In the case of any horse not being brought into the parade ring, or a badge not being exhibited, the trainer shall be reported to the Stewards. No horse shall be admitted to the paddock unless he has been declared in to run under Rule 124, or is advertised on the race card for sale. The parade ring shall be reserved strictly for those horses which are about to run. No person shall, without special leave from the Stewards, be allowed access to the parade ring except officials of the meeting and owners, trainers and riders of horses about to run in the next race. Any person refusing to leave shall be reported to the Stewards. For the purpose of this Rule, the Stewards shall determine whether or not the Racecourse Stabling forms part of the paddock.

(iv) Shall see that a clean number-cloth, of a pattern approved by the Stewards of the Jockey Club, is provided for every horse for which a rider presents himself to be weighed out.

(v) Shall have in his possession, for the information of the Stewards, a list of persons disqualified and of persons warned off, and of trainers and riders reported, also a copy of the latest Monthly Forfeit List, and he shall not allow any horse which, or the owner or nominator of which, is in the Forfeit List to start for any race.

(vi) Shall make a return to the Racing Calendar Office of any Deputy Steward or official appointed, of all complaints to and decisions of the Stewards, of any accident during the course of a flat race and the result of the enquiry into the accident, which must be held by the Stewards, of all fines inflicted, and of all horses sold or claimed.

CLERK OF THE SCALES

The Clerk of the Scales shall:

23. (i) Weigh the riders in accordance with the Rules (*see* Parts 14 and 16).

(ii) Exhibit the number (as shown on the official card) of each horse for which a rider has been declared, together with the names of the riders and, in the case of a flat race, the draw for places, and the numbers shall not be taken down until the horses are started. He shall also furnish the Starter with a list of runners.

When the numbers have been exhibited no alteration or addition except as allowed for in Rules 27 and 28 can be made without leave of the Stewards whose reasons for such permission shall be reported to the Racing Calendar Office.

Should permission have been given for a horse's number to be added after the numbers have been exhibited, the original draw for places shall stand, and the horse added shall be given the highest number.

(iii) If extra weight or any variation from the weight appearing on the card be declared at scale, for any horse, exhibit such weight with the number, also any alteration of colours, and if a horse be wearing hood or blinkers.

The following colours on the number board shall denote allowances claimed under Rule 109:

7lb allowance - red number on a white board.

5lb allowance - black number on an orange board.

3lb allowance - white number on a blue board.

(iv) At once order such alterations on the number board as the Stewards shall sanction under sub-Rule (ii) of this Rule.

(v) Should a horse be withdrawn under Rule 28 (x) or 28 (xiii), at once withdraw the number, order a black and white flag to be hoisted, exhibit a notice on the number board stating whether such horse has come under Starter's orders or not, and immediately report to the Stewards that the number is withdrawn by order of the Starter.

(vi) In all cases, except as provided in Rule 160 (iv), weigh in the riders of the first four horses placed by the Judge, together with other riders as required by the Stewards, and report to the Stewards any rider not presenting himself to be weighed in.

(vii) Should an objection be lodged or an enquiry be called for under Rule 171 (iii), at once order the appropriate signal to be hoisted on the number board, together with the grounds for objection.

The appropriate signal shall be:

All right, Blue flag.

Objection and/or enquiry under Rule 171 (iii): Red flag with White E. This signal must also be hoisted in the event of an enquiry into matters contained in Rule 154.

Enquiry completed, placings unaltered, enquiry flag replaced by White flag. Enquiry completed, placings altered, enquiry flag replaced by Green flag.

(viii) At the close of each day's racing send a return to the Racing Calendar Office of the weights carried in every race and the names of the riders, specifying overweight, if any, and of the horses which failed to complete the course, stating the reasons.

CLINKER

Brown horse, not in the General Stud Book, by Clinker—Sancho mare. Bred in Lincolnshire by Mr Wagstaffe.

The winner of the first steeplechase recorded in Mr Wright's Racing Calendar, a £2000 match over four miles across Leicestershire, in which he beat Lord Kennedy's bay horse, Radical, Clinker was owned by Captain Ross and usually ridden by Dick Christian. In another famous match he was beaten by Mr Osbaldeston's Clasher – the Squire having dashingly stolen the lead by jumping an enormous brook which Clinker and Dick Christian had skirted in favour of a ford.

The Druid described Clinker as "a lengthy, thoroughbred, bay horse of great power, between 16-16.1 hands high, up to 14 stone with a long, lean head, long in his pasterns and very fast but rather high-tempered – as all the Clinkers are – and a very nervous water jumper".

CLOISTER

Bay gelding, 1884, not in the General Stud Book.

Cloister	Ascetic	Hermit	Newminster
			Seclusion
		Lady Alicia	Melbourne
			Tasty
	Grace II	Newminster	Touchstone
			Beeswax
		mare by Slane	Slane

Cloister was bred in Ireland by Lord Fingall from a mare so moderate that the local postman was permitted to do his morning rounds on her. But the blood of Pocahontas ran, if sluggishly, in the veins of Grace II and combined with the fine jumping and staying qualities of Ascetic, it produced one of the steeplechasing heroes in the late nineteenth century. A giant of a horse built to carry 15 stone across Leicestershire, Cloister was the beau-ideal of an old-fashioned chaser and remained a pattern until long into the twentieth century.

He began his career as a four-year-old in Ireland and during 1888-89 won seven military or hunter chases, including the Irish Grand Military at Punchestown, in the colours of Capt. J. Orr-Ewing. In 1890 he was sold to Lord Dudley and went to Richard Marsh to be trained for the 1891 Grand National. In a stirring finish he was beaten ½l by Come Away and would almost certainly have won had not his amateur rider, Captain Roddy Owen, tried to bring him between the rails and the winner, a move promptly scotched by Harry Beasley on Come Away, despite blasphemous protests from his thwarted opponent.

The following year, after a string of five victories, including the Grand Sefton with 12-7, he was second again, this time to Father O'Flynn who, receiving 26lb, beat him 20l. Shortly afterwards Cloister was sold to Mr Charles Duff (later Sir Charles Assheton-Smith) and moved to the Bishop's Sutton establishment of Arthur Yates from whence he returned a third time to Aintree, partnered by stable jockey, W. Dollery and starting 9/2f he notched one of the most scintillating performances in the history of the great race, winning in record time, with record weight, 12-7, by a record distance, 40 lengths.

It proved the watershed of his career, the rest of which was shrouded in mystery and suspicion. His preparation for the 1894 National progressed to the accompaniment of rumour and speculation which culminated in his withdrawal after injuring himself in his final gallop, which piece of information communicated itself to the bookmakers before even owner and trainer learnt of it.

Cloister was then moved to the Escotts, where after winning two races, including the Grand Sefton for the second time with 13-3, misfortune struck again in curiously similar circumstances. No further attempts were made to run him and he was retired to his owner's country seat at Vaynol Park, Caernarvonshire.

No satisfactory explanation has ever been advanced for Cloister's latter-day training troubles. Arthur Yates's theory of kidney weakness aggravated by jumping does not take into account his splendid Sefton victory of 1894. What is certain is that the Ring were reliably informed of both his breakdowns before owner or trainer.

CLONAVE

Bay or brown horse, 1868, not in the General Stud Book, Mainstay—Crystal.

Clonave, an amazingly versatile horse owned by Sir William Nugent, won both the big hurdle and the Great Metropolitan Chase at the Croydon December meeting in 1874. His other great victory was the 1877 Liverpool Hurdle with 12-2 after twice finishing second in this competitive handicap, then the most prestigious hurdle race in the Calendar.

COLEMAN, Thomas

Thomas Coleman was the first entrepreneur of steeplechasing as we know it. As a boy he was employed in the racing stables of one Wetheral who used to train a number of horses for the Plates at nearby Ascot. Round about 1815 he set up on his own in Hertfordshire, near Brocket Hall, and trained for a number of fashionable owners including Lord Melbourne and Lord Palmerston. Evidently his business prospered for he was eventually able to buy the Chequers Tavern in St Albans which he pulled down and replaced with the Turf Hotel, which contained the then unheard-of luxury of several bathrooms with hot and cold water.

The first steeplechase took place in 1830, apparently suggested by some officers of the Household Cavalry who were dining at the fashionable Turf, and the details were left to Coleman. Although cross-country races had taken place for years it was Coleman who realized that if they were to have any appeal to an audience beyond those immediately involved, it was essential that the participants should be seen at more than one point of the race. He accordingly arranged his chase from Harlington Hill to the obelisk in West Park and back to Harlington Hill. The soldiers' race was won by Captain MacDowell on Lord Ranelagh's grey, from Lord Clanricarde on Nailer. The venture was such a success that Coleman immediately put plans in train for a renewal the following year.

By 1839 the heyday of St Albans was over. The fields had dwindled in both quality and quantity and public interest waned. However Coleman's idea had not been without fruit and up at Liverpool, in the very month that the last St Albans Chase was run, William Lynn was putting the finishing touches to his new enterprise, a four-mile steeplechase twice round a more or less definable track. Public interest was colossal and one local reporter was so carried away that he labelled it "The Grand National Steeplechase".

COLLEDGE MASTER

Bay gelding, 1950, Grandmaster—Collence (Columcille). Bred by Mr A. Stafford-Smith.

A former 3-Day Eventer owned and ridden by the Australian Olympic rider, Laurie Morgan, Colledge Master won 12 Hunter Chases, including the Cheltenham and Liverpool Foxhunters twice each. His first Liverpool victory in 1957 realized the second part of his owner's ambition, namely to win the A.J.C. Derby, which he did in 1945 with Valiant Crown, and to win a chase at Aintree.

COLLINS, Christopher Douglas (b.1941)

A tall, old-Etonian amateur rider, Chris Collins maintained the fast-dying Corinthian traditions in a thoroughly up-to-date fashion. He combined his extremely successful steeplechasing career with being managing director of Goya Ltd and an International 3-Day Event rider.

He rode his first winner in 1963 and in 1965 rode his horse, Mr Jones, into third place, behind Jay Trump and Freddie in the Grand National. He was Leading Amateur twice, in 1965-6 with 24 winners and in 1966-67 with 33. He maintained a large string of high-class, mainly Irish, chasers with Arthur Stephenson. Great attention was paid to their grounding and many of them were professionally schooled by Lars Sederholm.

His best horses were Titus Oates, whom he found as a young horse and rode to win a hurdle and seven chases before selling for then a record of 14,750 guineas at Ascot Sales, Credit Call (37 chases including both Cheltenham and Liverpool Foxhunters, 1972) and Stephen's Society, on whom he became the first Englishman for more than fifty years to win the unique Gran Pardubice Steeplechase in Czechoslovakia. Chris Collins was elected to the Jockey Club in December 1972. He acts as a steward at Sandown. Colours: white, navy blue collar and cuffs, quartered cap.

COLLINS, R. John

John Collins was head-man and held the licence for the Weyhill Stable of Willie Moore (q.v.). During his time the large and successful stable sent out three Grand National winners in five years, Why Not (1894), The Soarer (1896) and Manifesto (1899).

COLLIS, Lt.-Col. Robert Henry, D.S.O.

Captain (later Lt.-Col.) Collis rode as an amateur, winning the National Hunt Chase (1903) on Comfit and afterwards trained at Kinlet, Worcestershire. He won the Stanley Chase (1906) with Lara, whom he also rode, the Grand Sefton (1908) with Caubeen and the 1911 Grand National with Glenside, the least fancied of his two runners. He was elected to the National Hunt Committe in 1905.

COLONIAL CUP, The

The Colonial Cup is an International, invitation, weight-for-age Steeplechase of 2m, 6½f run in November at Camden, South Carolina, U.S.A. It is entirely sponsored by Mrs Marion du Pont Scott, the owner of Battleship (q.v.), and in 1978 was worth £31,250 to the winner. It was instituted in 1970.

	HORSE	OWNER	RIDER	TRAINER
1970	Top Bird	Mrs Ogden Phipps	J. Aitcheson, jun.	M. Smithwick
1971	Inkslinger	Mrs M. Jenney	T. Carberry	M. Smithwick
1972	Soothsayer	Montpelier	J. Aitcheson	Montpelier
1973	Lucky Boy III	Mrs M. Valentine	C. Brittle	W. Cocks
1974	Augustus Boy	Miss J. Clark	T. Skiffington	E. Watters
1975	Café Prince	Augustin Stables	D. Washer	J. Sheppard
1976	Grand Canyon	{ Mr P. Samuel / Mr M. Buckley }	R. Barry	D. Kent
1977	Café Prince	Augustin Stables	J. Fishback	J. Sheppard
1978	Grand Canyon	Mr D. W. Samuel	R. Barry	D. Kent

Apart from the New Zealand-bred but British-trained and ridden Grand Canyon, other good British horses to have taken part include Young Ash Leaf (eighth in 1970), L'Escargot (q.v.) (fourth in 1970), Captain Christy (q.v.) (fourth in 1975), High Ken (seventh in 1975) and Lanzarote (q.v.) (fourth in 1976). Inkslinger (q.v.), the winner in 1971 and runner-up in 1972 later came to Ireland to be trained by Dan Moore and won the National Hunt Two Mile Champion Chase, while Soothsayer, the 1972 winner from the Montpelier stable of Mrs du Pont Scott, came to England to be trained by Fred Winter. He won two races and was second to Ten Up in the 1975 Cheltenham Gold Cup.

COLOURED SCHOOL BOY

Bay gelding, 1940, Grand Colours —Alpha Virginis (Empire Builder). Bred by Mrs N. Duke.

A genuine, consistent horse fractionally short of top class, Coloured School Boy raced for seven seasons and won 18 chases including the Lancashire Chase (1949), the Queen Elizabeth Chase, Hurst Park (1950) with 12-7 and the then prestigious Sandown Open Chase (1948). He was also placed twice

in the Cheltenham Gold Cup and third in the 1947 Scottish Grand National. He was owned by Mr W. F. Highnam and trained at Kinnersley by Fred Rimell.

COME AWAY

Bay gelding, 1884, not in the General Stud Book, Umpire or Cambuslang —Larkaway.

Generally agreed to have been "a really magnificent horse", Come Away ran only ten races in his life and won eight of them, including the 1891 Grand National, when carrying 11-12 (Mr H. Beasley), 4/1f, by 1l, a bad third, from Cloister, 11-7 (Capt. E. R. Owen) and Ilex, 12-3 (A. Nightingall).

A brilliant four-year-old career in which he won the Conyngham Cup ended in suspensory trouble and he did not run again for eighteen months. He came back successfully at six to win four of his five races including the Valentine Chase, Liverpool. His National victory was a closely contested affair which ended in a verbal slanging match between the two principals and an objection by the second to the winner. The objection was overruled but Come Away had more trouble to contend with. He pulled up lame and despite being fired, was never able to race again. He was owned by Mr W. G. Jameson and trained on the Curragh by Harry Beasley.

COMEDY OF ERRORS

Brown horse, 1967, Goldhill—Comedy Actress (Kingsway). Bred by Miss E. Sykes.

After winning four races on the Flat at four years when trained by Tom Corrie, Comedy of Errors was bought by Fred Rimell on behalf of Mr E. Wheatley and quickly made his mark as a juvenile

The second dual National winner, ABD-EL-KADER (1850 and 1851). This attractive, quality horse was much loved by the racing public and known as 'Little Ab'

(*Below left*) the first and only Royal National winner, AMBUSH II, 'Algy' Anthony up. H.R.H. the Prince of Wales's fine Irish chaser won in 1900.

(*Below right*) two masters of their profession, JACK ANTHONY and Gerry Wilson. Between them they were Champion Jockey nine times and rode or trained the winners of four Grand Nationals, four Cheltenham Gold Cups and two Champion Hurdles. Jack Anthony lamed himself permanently, dismounting from a hack while on holiday in the U.S.A.

A famous partnership-Pat Taaffe and ARKLE. Arkle could always be identified by his characteristically high, stag-like head carriage

One of jumping's staunchest patrons, the first LORD BICESTER, receives a trophy

HARRY BROWN, crack amateur, trainer and one of chasing's great characters, on the gallops

BULA and Paul Kelleway on their way to victory in the Champion Hurdle. This rarely defeated combination frequently gave their supporters heart-failure with the lateness of their challenge

A general view of CHELTENHAM racecourse taken from Tattersalls where the bulk of the on-course betting takes place

CHELTENHAM: a field of hurdlers streaming over what will be the last flight next time round, against the magnificent backdrop of Cleeve Hill

CHELTENHAM—an Irish victory. A scene that became painfully familiar to English racegoers at the 1978 National Hunt Festival. Champion Hurdler, Monksfield (T. Kinane) returns to a jubilant reception from the packed saddling enclosure

A fine Champion Hurdler. The big, bold and handsome COMEDY OF ERRORS (John Burke up) in full flight

Happy Home (Martin Molony) leads triple Gold Cup Winner Cottage Rake (Aubrey Brabazon) over the last in the 1948 running. Cottage Rake's finishing speed and Aubrey's flat-race expertise could always pull the race out of the fire after the last

Tom Coulthwaite started his career training athletes and applied the same techniques to horses. He saddled three National winners

Dick Francis and Crudwell. Crudwell was one of the most popular chasers of the 1950s and won a total of 50 races which is thought to be a record

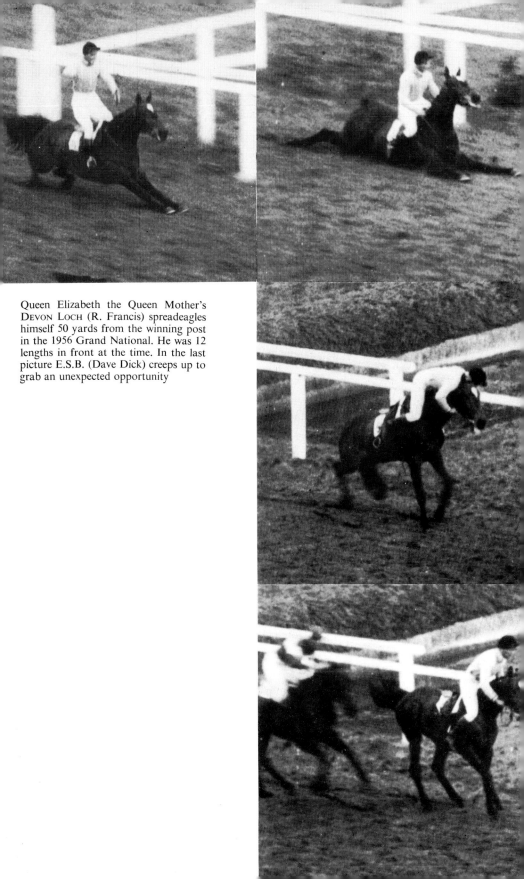

Queen Elizabeth the Queen Mother's
DEVON LOCH (R. Francis) spreadeagles
himself 50 yards from the winning post
in the 1956 Grand National. He was 12
lengths in front at the time. In the last
picture E.S.B. (Dave Dick) creeps up to
grab an unexpected opportunity

TOM DREAPER, dry of wit and unpretentious as to behaviour was a master of under-statement – and of his profession. Born and raised to be an Irish farmer, he became a trainer literally by accident and handled two of the biggest stars chasing has known in Prince Regent and Arkle

EASTER HERO, a bright and beautiful chestnut won the Cheltenham Gold Cup in 1929 and 1930. He was thought to be the handsomest chaser of his day and the best horse never to have won the National. He is pictured here with Tim Cullinan, his partner in the 1930 Gold Cup

hurdler of exceptional talent. His four victories in his first season included the Coronation Hurdle at Liverpool and he was only beaten a neck in his division of the Gloucester Hurdle. His second season opened encouragingly with facile victories in the Fighting Fifth Hurdle (Newcastle), and the Berkshire Hurdle (Newbury), but he was well beaten by Captain Christy in the Irish Sweeps Hurdle and suffered an even worse defeat in the Cheltenham Trial Hurdle. He was however found to have had tooth trouble and was allowed to take his chance in the 1973 Champion Hurdle which he won convincingly (W. Smith) 8/1, by 1½l, 2l, from Easby Abbey (R. Barry) and Captain Christy (H. Beasley) with 5/6 favourite Bula fifth. He went on to win the Welsh Champion Hurdle.

During the seasons 1973-75, Comedy of Errors was only defeated three times. His ten victories included the Ladbroke Fighting Fifth Hurdle, Newcastle (1973 and 1974), The Irish Sweeps Hurdle, Leopardstown (1973 and 1974), the Scottish Champion Hurdle, Ayr (1975), and the 1975 Champion Hurdle, National Hunt Meeting (K. B. White), 11/8, by 8l, hd, from Flash Imp (T. Stack) and Tree Tangle (A. Turnell). He thus became the first Champion Hurdler to regain his crown. He had been odds-on favourite in 1974 but Lanzarote, most enterprisingly ridden by Richard Pitman, got first run on him down the hill and held on to win by 3 lengths.

A big, strong handsome horse with a rather lazy style of racing, Comedy of Errors who won a total of 23 races, was particularly well suited to the driving talents of jockey Ken White.

CONGRESS
Brown gelding, 1866, Compromise —Countess (Slane). Bred by Mr H. G. Allen.

After running once unplaced on the Flat at four years, Congress became a chaser of the highest class whose 15 victories included the Grand Steeplechase de Paris (1877), the Grand Sefton twice (1873 and 1876), the Leamington Grand Annual (1875), the Warwick Grand Annual (1875) and the Grand International, Sandown (1877) carrying 12-7 and conceding 32lb to the second. He was second two years running in the Grand National; in 1876 beaten a neck by Regal at level weights, after being

nearly brought down, and beaten 4 lengths by Austerlitz (rec. 27lb) in 1877. His one-time owner and invariable pilot, Mr E. P. Wilson, described him as "one of the best I ever rode". He was latterly owned by Lord Lonsdale.

COOK, John Dennis (b.1937)
John Cook's parents looked after the apprentices at Kingsclere and there he served his own apprenticeship, first with Evan Williams and later with Peter Hastings-Bass. However he quickly grew too heavy for the Flat and did not get a ride. After doing his National Service with the Royal Navy he went to Fairlawne but failed to get a break there. He worked for a private trainer in the West Country and rode a few N.H. winners before returning to Kingsclere.

In the beginning of 1962 he advertised for a job with rides, which took him to the Aston Tirrold establishment of Frank Cundell and from there his career flourished.

Among his best winners were:

The Grand National (1971) Specify
The Hennessy Gold Cup (1969) Spanish Steps
The Tote Champion Novices (1969) Spanish Steps
The Schweppes Gold Trophy (1971) Cala Mesquida

He broke his leg very badly in 1972 and unhappily it did not heal sufficiently for him to race-ride again.

COOL CUSTOMER
Bay or brown gelding, 1939, Mr Toots—Never Worry (False Alarm). Bred by Mr John Burke.

A consistent and popular chaser of the highest class, owned by Major 'Cuddie' Stirling-Stuart, Cool Customer raced for six seasons and won three hurdle races and 16 chases including the Christmas Chase, Leopardstown (1946), the Leopardstown Chase (1946), the inaugural Great Yorkshire, Doncaster with 12-7 (1948) and the Victory Chase, Manchester (1949). He fell at the first fence when favourite for the 1948 Cheltenham Gold Cup and in 1949 was second, beaten 2 lengths by Cottage Rake, after leading at the last, in one of the most memorable struggles in the history of the race.

CORBETT, Hon. Thomas Anthony, M.C. (1921-76)

A son of Lord Rowallan, 'Atty' Corbett was educated at Eton and served with the Grenadier Guards. He was attached to Fred Rimell's stable and rode as an amateur, winning the National Hunt Chase (1950) on Lord Bicester's Ellesmere, the United Hunts (1950) on Monk's Crest and the Kim Muir Chase (1953) on Crudwell (q.v.). He then turned professional and rode successfully for a few years before taking out a licence to train. His biggest success was to win the Mildmay Memorial Chase (1954) on Domata. He started training with a few jumpers and had great success with the handsome, very able, but alas unsound, Blessington Esquire (nine races, including the Mackeson Novices in 1961 and 1962).

Later he concentrated solely on the Flat and turned out such good winners as Talahasse (Champagne and Gimcrack Stakes) and Queen's Hussar (Lockinge and Sussex Stakes). He died in 1976 from head injuries sustained in an accident with a motor car whilst riding out. Colours: black, white striped sleeves, black and white check cap.

CORTOLVIN

Brown gelding, not in the General Stud Book, by Chicken or Cheerful Horn.

Cortolvin was bred in Ireland by Lord Poulett and in his colours ran second to Salamander in the 1866 Grand National. He was afterwards bought by the Duke of Hamilton, at the suggestion of Harry Lamplugh, the French-based Yorkshire jockey, and went on to win the 1867 running, carrying 11-13 (J. Page) 16/1, by 5l, 4l, from Fan, 10-3 (Thorpe) and Shangarry, 10-13 (Mr Thomas), to the great surprise of his many detractors who had previously rated him a non-stayer and soft. He never ran in England after that season.

COSTELLO, W.

W. Costello held the licence for the Danebury establishment of Fred Withington that sent out Rubio and Mattie Macgregor, first and second in the 1908 Grand National. Rubio who was distinctly unsound, was by far the least fancied of the two.

COTTAGE

Brown horse, 1918. Bred by Baron de Rothschild.

		Sainfoin
	Rock Sand	
Tracery		Roquebrunne
	Topiary	Orme
		Plaisanterie
Cottage		
	Marco	Barcaldine
		Novitiate
Casetta		
	Crème Simon	St Simon
		Settlement

One of the most influential jumping sires of the twentieth century, Cottage was bred by Baron Edouard de Rothschild and raced only on the Flat at four years, winning the Fitzwilliam Plate, Doncaster. He was stood by Mr Michael Magnier in Fermoy, County Cork. He was leading sire on four occasions, second three times and third once. His stock included the Grand National winners Workman (1939), Lovely Cottage (1946) and Sheila's Cottage (1948) and the Gold Cup winners Brendan's Cottage (1939) and Cottage Rake (1948, 1949, 1950). In 1939 and again in 1948 he sired the winners of both the Gold Cup and the Grand National.

Leading Sire Figures:

1938-39	winners of	30	races worth	£10,502½
1945-46	„ „	29	„	„	£12,823
1947-48	„ „	51	„	„	£23,465½
1948-49	„ „	30	„	„	£12,395

COTTAGE RAKE

Brown gelding, 1939. Bred by Dr Vaughan.

		Rock Sand
	Tracery	
Cottage		Topiary
	Casetta	Marco
		Crème Simon
Cottage Rake		
	Hartford	Swynford
		My Dear
Hartingo		
	Stellingo	By Jingo
		Zamora

Although Cottage Rake was a son of one of the great Irish jumping sires, he was not cast in the traditional mould, being a light-framed, quality individual with a high stag-like head carriage. This stag-like impression was accentuated by the fact that he used to run up very light. Moreover it was his speed and class rather than stamina and jumping ability that served as his principal weapon in a career that encompassed four Flat races, including the Irish Cesarewitch, and twelve chases, including the 1948 King George VI Chase and three Cheltenham Gold Cups.

Cottage Rake was bred in Mallow on the Blackwater and when, as a five-year-old, he was returned unsold from Ballsbridge Sales, Dr Vaughan sent him to a young trainer up the road who was just embarking on his career. Cottage Rake promptly won bumpers at Limerick and Leopardstown and became a very marketable proposition. Prospective buyers were not lacking but two deals had foundered, because of an alleged wind infirmity, before he was offered to the stable's first patron, Bradford wool merchant, Mr Frank Vickerman. Mr Vickerman's vet also failed the horse but through some type of Irish misunderstanding the deal went through and Cottage Rake was sold for £3,500.

A young trainer who could persuade his first patron to pay £3,500 (in 1945) for a horse who had failed three different vets, deserves to prosper. The young man was Vincent O'Brien poised to take the first bound up the ladder of his amazing career.

Cottage Rake was ridden in nearly all his chase victories by Aubrey Brabazon, whose cool, quiet horsemanship and tactical brain perfectly complemented his mount's qualities. The Brab, who was said to hold the reins as though they were thin silk, was as good on the Flat as over fences and the combination of his flair and Cottage Rake's formidable turn of foot was deadly.

> Aubrey's up, the money's down
> The frightened bookies quake
> Come on my lads and give a cheer
> Begod, 'tis Cottage Rake.

ran the war-song that preceded the pair to Cheltenham.

Cottage Rake's Gold Cup victories were as follows:

1948 (A. Brabazon) 10/1 won by 1½l and 10l from Happy Home (M. Molony) and Coloured School Boy (E. Vinall).

1949 (A. Brabazon) 4/6 favourite won by 2l and 6l from Cool Customer (P. J. Murphy) and Coloured School Boy (E. Vinall)

1950 (A. Brabazon) 5/6 favourite won by 10l and 8l from Finnure (M. Molony) and Garde Toi (Marquis de Portago).

Of these, the 1949 running, postponed until April, when Cottage Rake and Cool Customer engaged in a sustained duel from the last open ditch which was not resolved until less than 100 yards from the post, is always rated one of the highlights of the Gold Cup's history. After his 1950 victory he declined with frightening rapidity and failed to win a race in his last four seasons. In the spring of 1953 he joined Gerald Balding, with whom he had always stayed on his visits to England, and there he passed the twilight years of his great career.

COTTON, Gilbert Egerton (1880-1971)

A distinguished N.H. official, Gilbert Cotton was Clerk of the Course at Bangor-on-Dee and Inspector of Courses for 50 years (1920-70). He was responsible for filling-in the ditch in front of the fence at the Canal Turn at Aintree after the debacle caused by Easter Hero in 1928 and wished to eliminate fence 23 because, he maintained, the horses had insufficient time to balance themselves after the drop. Had this suggestion been carried out, the shambles of 1967 would have been avoided. Another innovation for which he was responsible, together with Brigadier Tony Teacher, was the sloping of the fences, carried out in 1960-61, which, more than anything else, has brought high-class horses back to Aintree. He rode as an amateur before World War I and won the National Hunt Chase (1912) on The Rejected IV.

COULTHWAITE, Tom (1862-1948)

A somewhat eccentric, very blunt Lancastrian, Tom Coulthwaite never sat on a horse in his life. He trained athletes and applied the same principles to horses with markedly successful results.

He trained at Hednesford in Staffordshire and was regarded as one of the shrewdest trainers of the early twentieth century. So shrewd in fact as to arouse the suspicion of the Stewards of the N.H.C. In 1913 they enquired into the running of Bloodstone (at Hurst Park) and Jacobus (Birmingham), pronounced themselves dissatisfied and warned him off. He came back again after the war and trained with undiminished success until 1932.

Among his major successes were:

The Grand National (1907) Eremon; (1910) Jenkinstown; (1931) Grakle

The National Hunt Chase (1922) Conjuror
II; (1930) Sir Lindsay
The Champion Chase (1909) Bloodstone
The Stanley Chase (1910) Rathnally;(1927)
Gregalach
The Lancashire Chase (1907) Eremon

He bought both Grakle and Gregalach
as young horses for Mr T. K. Laidlaw.
When the latter went abroad and his
horses were sold, Coulthwaite advised
Mr Taylor to buy Grakle. He was particularly fond of the horse and delayed
his retirement to see his career through.
He once gave Ted Leader a cigarette case
inscribed "actions speak louder than
words" – when that jockey caught the
riderless Grakle and brought him back to
the unsaddling enclosure after winning
the 1932 Gold Cup on Golden Miller.

In his later years he became very much
the Grand Old Man of British chasing.
He was known as 'Old Tom' and the
Prince of Wales used to ride out with his
string. He possessed an iron hut on
Cannock Chase to which he used to retire on occasions. After Grakle's National
victory he answered letters of congra-
tulations from there, giving his address as
the Castle.

He was a meticulous stableman and
would get up at 2 a.m. to give an extra
feed to a shy feeder. The Haydock Park
executive named a steeplechase after
him.

COURAGE, Edward Raymond (b.1906)
A member of the brewing family,
Edward Courage was crippled by polio in
1938 and is confined to a wheelchair.
From his Oxfordshire home he trains,
under permit, an enormously successful
yard of horses, all of whom are descended from his mare Drumrora V (*q.v.*)
whom he purchased in 1946. In 1969-70
he achieved the unprecedented feat of
being Leading Owner (14 races worth
£20,001), Leading Breeder and seventh in
the Leading Trainers List.
Among his major successes are:

The Hennessy Gold Cup (1969) Spanish
Steps
**The National Hunt Two Mile Champion
Chase** (1972) Royal Relief; (1974) Royal
Relief
The Tote Champion Novices (1969) Spanish
Steps

The Benson and Hedges Gold Cup (1970)
Spanish Steps
The Grand Sefton Chase (1958) Tiberetta

Mr Courage is a Trustee of the Injured
Jockeys' Fund. He was elected to the
National Hunt Committee (now incorporated with the Jockey Club) in July
1967.

COUVREFEU II
Bay Gelding, 1904, Curfew—Regime
(Raeburn). Bred by Lord O. Beauclerk.
Couvrefeu II won a total of nine
chases, including the Scottish Grand
National two years running (1912-13)
and the Champion Chase, Liverpool
(1915).

COVENTRY, Arthur (1852-1925)
A younger brother of Capt. Henry ('Bee')
Coventry (*q.v.*) and a grandson of the
eighth Earl, Arthur Coventry was
unquestionably born into racing. A
highly strung, dandified individual who
took immense pains over his boots and
gaiters, he liked to call himself "the
ugliest man in England", while fully
aware of the charm he could and did
exercise.

He was regarded as the best amateur
of his day and, while equally proficient
over fences and hurdles, his finesse was
more effective over hurdles. In the
preface to the Badminton Volume on
Racing and Steeplechasing, the Duke of
Beaufort described him as "the first
Gentleman Rider of the day; he has
wonderful hands and emphatically rides
with his head . . . he successfully holds
his own against the very first flat-race
jockeys of the day".

Among his more important successes
were:

The National Hunt Chase (1879) Bellringer
The Grand Metropolitan Chase (1882) The
Scot
The Grande Course des Haies (1883) Brutus

In 1890 he became Jockey Club Starter
and he was also Secretary of Hurst Park
Race Club.

**COVENTRY, George William,
ninth Earl of (1838-1930)**
A founder member of the N.H.C., on
which he served till he died in 1930, and
the owner of the National-winning

sisters, Emblem (1863) and Emblematic (1864), Lord Coventry was indeed one of steeplechasing's grand characters.

A contemporary wrote of his "cultivated tastes, strong religious convictions with an almost boyish gaiety of temperament and inflexible uprightness of character with the most winning manners. He was as familiar and well-informed at Christie's and Sotheby's as at Ascot and Newmarket and he could discourse on the details of the more than 60 Derbies he had seen as well as on pictures and porcelain". His family seat was Croome Court, Worcestershire, near Kinnersley where his chasers were trained. Colours: brown, blue cap.

COVENTRY Capt. Henry (1842-85)

Elder brother of Arthur Coventry (q.v.) and a cousin of the ninth earl, 'Bee' Coventry served in the Grenadier Guards and was a successful amateur rider, winning the 1865 Grand National on Alcibiade and the 1867 National Hunt Chase on Emperor III.

COVERTCOAT

Bay gelding, 1906, Hackler—Cinnamon (Concha). Bred by Mr J. J. Maher.

Covertcoat was a full-brother to several good winners including Coverthack and a member of the Mount Royal family (q.v.). In a brief and curious racing career he won but two races in his life but these were the important Hurst Park Trial H'cap Chase (1913) and the Grand National (1913), 11-6 (P. Woodland), 100/9, by a distance and the same from Irish Mail, 11-4 (Mr O. Anthony) and Carsey, 12-0 (Mr H. Drake).

He was described by Major Hurst as a "weak, leggy animal hardly worth the name of a racehorse", but Major Hurst, a contributor to the *Bloodstock Breeders Review* dismissed the entire Mount Royal family, whose remarkable success under N.H. Rules had attracted some attention, as "too bad or too slow to win anything else". Covertcoat, who failed to win another race and retired at the end of 1914, was owned by Sir Charles Assheton-Smith and trained at Findon by Robert Gore.

COWLEY, P.

Paddy Cowley was Champion Jockey in 1908 riding 65 winners. He won the Champion Chase (1908) on Cackler, and the Stanley Chase twice, in 1902 on Thomondgate and in 1908 on Jerry M. whom he rode in all that horse's early races in this country. Tragically he was killed soon after winning the Championship, when falling through the wing of a hurdle at Hooten Park and smashing his skull. An Irishman, he was quiet and reserved. He rode very short and was reckoned a fine judge of pace.

CRASH HELMETS

Crash helmets became compulsory in 1924 following the death of leading amateur Captain 'Tuppy' Bennet (q.v.) from being kicked on the head by a following horse after a fall at Wolverhampton. Various modifications have taken place over the years, the most significant of which was the addition of a chin-strap adopted from Australia in the early 1960s. Since 1976 trainers are required by the Rules of Racing to ensure that their staff wear approved protective headgear at exercise.

CREDIT CALL

Brown gelding, 1964, Reverse Charge —Atout Noir (Atout Royal). Bred by Mr J. V. Leavy.

A very fine hunter-chaser, owned and ridden first by Mr Christopher Collins and latterly by Mr Joey Newton, Credit Call won 37 races, including the Horse and Hound Cup, Stratford, four times (1971, 1972, 1973 and 1975) and both the Cheltenham and Liverpool Foxhunter Cups in 1972. He won the Liverpool Foxhunters twice more in 1975 and 1976 and was second in the 1976 Cheltenham Foxhunters. Much fancied in the ante-post market for the 1973 Grand National, he was prevented from taking part by his owner-rider breaking his arm in a hunting accident.

CRICKMERE, Mr

He rode as an amateur and won the 1844 Grand National on Discount. The previous year he had been third on Dragsman. He was said to ride "with great skill and judgement".

CRISP (AUS)

Brown gelding, 1963, Rose Argent —Wheat Germ (Ingo). Bred by Sir Chester Manifold in Australia.

A magnificent-looking gelding, standing nearly 17 h.h., Crisp was raced by his breeder, Sir Chester Manifold, and won two Flat races, five hurdle races and six steeplechases including the Melbourne Cup Chase and the Carolina Hunt Cup, Camden, before coming to England in the winter of 1970. Here he won nine chases including the 2m Champion Chase, National Hunt Meeting (1971) by 25 lengths from a talented field including Royal Relief and Muir, the Coventry Chase, Kempton (1972) and the Gainsborough Chase Sandown (1972).

He was also fifth in the 1972 Gold Cup and second in the 1973 Grand National after putting up one of the most stunning performances in the history of the race. Carrying 12-0 and ridden by Richard Pitman, he adopted his customary, front-running tactics, treating the mighty fences like hurdles. By Becher's on the second circuit he was a fence ahead of the rest of the field, of whom only Red Rum could be seen to be making the slightest impression. At the second last he still had an apparently unassailable lead but at this point his trainer, Fred Winter, who had watched for nearly nine minutes in stoical silence, turned to his owner and said "start praying Sir Chester, for you're going to be beat". Halfway along the run-in Crisp began to wander and two strides from the post he was caught and beaten by Red Rum (rec. 23lb). The pair beat the course record by 19 sec. After winning two races in the autumn of 1973, Crisp developed leg-strain and had to be rested for the rest of the season. He made a brief come-back but was then finally retired to the hunting field.

CROMWELL
Bay gelding, 1941, Landscape Hill—Fort Defiance (Defiance). Bred by Captain J. A. Hornsby.

A slashing stamp of old-fashioned chaser, owned first by Lord Mildmay and latterly by his sister, the Hon. Mrs Helen Mildmay-White, Cromwell won 22 chases including the Prince's Chase, Sandown (1950), the Emblem Chase, Manchester (1951) and, most poignantly, the race staged in memory of his former owner, the Mildmay Memorial, Sandown (1952). He was also third to Sheila's Cottage in the 1948 Grand National after his owner-rider had been afflicted by the cramp in his neck that finally killed him, and had therefore ridden the last half mile unable to raise his eyes from his horse's neck. Cromwell was trained at Fairlawne by Peter Cazalet. *See also* Anthony Bingham, 2nd Baron Mildmay of Flete.

CROSS, Vernon Bertram
From 1932-52 Vernon Cross looked after Lord and Lady Stalbridge's horses and was thus associated with Bogskar (Grand National, 1940) and Red Rower (Cheltenham Gold Cup, 1945). For five years after Lord Stalbridge's death he trained privately for Lady Stalbridge and handled Red Rower's good half-brother Red April (23 races including the Queen Elizabeth Handicap Chase). He then became a public trainer with his headquarters at Chattis Hill, Stockbridge, where 'Atty' Persse used to train. His most notable victory in recent years has been the 1975 Daily Express Triumph Hurdle with Royal Epic.

CROYDON
According to Nimrod, Croydon could claim to have staged some of the earliest race meetings in the country but there was no permanent home for a racecourse until 1877, when the Woodside course was opened. It enjoyed a brief but very successful career and attracted good-class horses to its principal races, namely the Grand Metropolitan Chase, the United Kingdom Handicap Chase and the Grand International Hurdle. A contemporary correspondent described the Metropolitan Chase as "second in interest only to the Liverpool". When in 1890 local magistrates refused to renew Croydon's licence the principal races were transferred to Gatwick (*q.v.*).

CRUDWELL
Bay gelding, 1946, Noble Star—Alexandrina (Tangiers). Bred in Crudwell, Wiltshire, by Mr A. Large.

Crudwell's racing career, during which he won seven Flat races, four hurdle races and 39 steeplechases, spanned the whole decade of the 'fifties. It was a period when the sport of steeplechasing was burgeoning and Crudwell was one of the stars responsible for the boom. He displayed a toughness and tenacity unequalled since the days of Lord Lonsdale's Dudley (*q.v.*) and when on 15th September 1960, Michael Scudamore steered him into the winner's enclosure at Wincanton after his fiftieth and last victory, he struck a chord of rare emotion in the hearts of the watching racegoers.

Although in his latter years, Crudwell was habitually ridden by Michael Scudamore, it was with Dick Francis that he was usually associated. Among the pair's more important victories were the Welsh Grand National (1956) and the Sandown Open Chase (1957) in which they beat Pointsman by two lengths at level weights.

CRUMP, Neville Franklin (b.1910)

The son of a Master of the South Oxfordshire Foxhounds, Neville Crump was educated at Marlborough and Balliol College, Oxford. He hunted, rowed and point-to-pointed. From 1931-35 he served with the 4th Hussars and rode as an amateur under N.H. Rules. He became assistant to J. L. Hall at Russley Park and in 1937 took out a licence to train. During World War II he served with the Royal Armoured Corps and afterwards moved to Middleham, Yorkshire, where he has trained ever since.

A consistently successful trainer, noted for his high-class staying chasers, he has twice been Leading Trainer and between 1949-64 was in the leading six on ten occasions.

| 1951-52 | 41 races worth | £19,357 |
| 1956-57 | 39 „ „ | £18,495 |

His major successes include:

The Grand National (1948) Sheila's Cottage: (1952) Teal: (1960) Merryman II
The Scottish Grand National (1949) Wot No Sun: (1959) Merryman II: (1968) Arcturus
The Welsh Grand National (1951) Skyreholme
The Whitbread Gold Cup (1957) Much Obliged: (1963) Hoodwinked (1964) Dormant
The Hennessy Gold Cup (1962) Springbok
The Champion Novices Chase (1961) Rough Tweed
The Mackeson Gold Cup (1976) Cancello
The Massey-Ferguson Gold Cup (1977) Even Melody

A large, bluff, outspoken man, he puts tremendous enthusiasm into racing and inspires great loyalty among his owners, jockeys and staff.

CULLINAN, Thomas Brady

In 1930 Tommy Cullinan achieved the unique treble of winning the Cheltenham Gold Cup (Easter Hero), the Champion Hurdle (Brown Tony) and the Grand National (Shaun Goilin). The last victory must have been a most pleasant surprise for he had been engaged for the ante-post favourite, Easter Hero, who had been withdrawn, lame, four days before the race. Shaun Goilin, who won a most exciting race by a neck, was a chance ride. Cullinan was unlucky not to win the 1928 National, for on the tough, American stayer, Billy Barton, he had been upsides with the very slow Tipperary Tim going to the last but had fallen. This treble marked the high-spot of his career. During World War II he joined up as a private in an English anti-aircraft unit and shot himself in a fit of depression.

CUNARD, Sir Guy Alick, 7th Bt (b.1911)

A Yorkshireman of lean, not to say cadaverous appearance and extreme toughness, Guy Cunard served with the 4th/7th Royal Dragoon Guards (1931-49), becoming a major. During World War II he saw active service in France, Belgium and the Western Desert.

He began riding and training his own horses as a young officer and became one of the best and most successful point-to-point riders of all time, winning 251 races. Although weight problems severely limited his opportunities under Rules, he nevertheless won 61 races, including The National Hunt Chase (1948) on Bruno II and the Liverpool Foxhunters (1948) on San Michele.

He held a permit from the start of the scheme and from 1968-69 has held a trainer's licence. He has a small string of jumpers at his Malton home, the best of whom he appears to inculcate with something of his own brand of toughness. His most successful horse to date has been Bountiful Charles (14 races and a respectable second to Killiney in the 1973 Tote Champion Novices). Colours: royal blue, white belt and cap.

CUNDELL, Francis Lawrence (b.1908)

Frank Cundell is the nephew of a distinguished trainer and son of the veterinary surgeon who pioneered the use of electrical treatment in horses. He qualified as a veterinary surgeon and in 1931 joined the Royal Army Veterinary Corps. While serving, he rode as an amateur under N.H. Rules and completed both Liverpool Foxhunters (second) and the Grand National (sixth on Blue Peter III in 1934). He also won the Indian Grand National in 1934 when serving in that country. After leaving the Army he spent three years in India as Veterinary Officer and Stipendiary Steward to the Royal West India Turf Club. He returned to England and assisted his uncle before taking out a licence on his own account in 1939. Shortly afterwards war broke out and he returned to military service. After the war he set up a stable at Aston Tirrold, Berkshire, where he trained until 1975 with great success under both Rules.

His best-known chaser was perhaps Crudwell, whom he trained to win 50 races, including the Welsh Grand National (1956). Other important successes for the stable have been:

The Great Yorkshire Chase (1958) Hall Weir; (1964) King's Nephew
The Mackeson Gold Cup (1964) Super Flash
The S.G.B. Chase (1965) Vultrix
The National Hunt Chase (1961) Superfine
The Mildmay Memorial (1954) Domata

CUNNINGHAM, C. J. (1849-1906)

Charlie Cunningham was a leading amateur of the late nineteenth century. A member of an old Ayrshire family, he measured 6 feet 1 inch and had to waste a good deal. He was amusing and very outspoken and, despite an excitable temper, very popular. In his youth he had the good luck to own three horses out of the same half-bred mare by Russborough. They were Percy (by Hotspur), Merryglass (by Laughing Stock) and Douglas (by Sincerity) and between them they won him 51 races and gave him a great start.

He was Leading Amateur 1882-83 with 47 winners. He won the Scottish Grand National four times in eight years: 1881, Bellman; 1885, Wild Meadow; 1887, Orcadian; 1889, Deloraine.

He was second in the 1889 Grand National on Why Not and won the 1886 National Hunt Chase on the same horse.

Arthur Nightingall who later won the National on Why Not, admired him but remarked that he had bad hands. Colours: olive, primrose hoops, red cap.

CUNNINGHAM, T.

Cunningham won the 1849 Grand National on Peter Simple after being vainly offered £1,000, £2,000, £3,000 and finally, in desperation, £4,000 to pull his horse in the last ½m by Captain Darcy, whose Knight of Gwynne (second) was plainly beaten. The going was very heavy that year and three horses were killed.

CURE-ALL

Brown gelding, not in the General Stud Book, by Physician.

Cure-All "a stocky, short-legged, compact horse, rather coarse-looking", was bred in Yorkshire and was bought by Mr Walter Loft of Healing, Lincolnshire, for £60 at Horncastle Fair after laming himself being tried over some rails. Mr Loft's groom, Kitty Crisp, restored Cure-All to soundness and, after a lengthy spell of walking and trotting exercise, the horse was fit enough to give his new owner some decent runs with the Brocklesby and to run second in a steeplechase. Thus encouraged, Mr Loft entered Cure-All for the 1845 Grand National and thither the little horse and Kitty Crisp set forth on foot. A sharp frost caused racing to be postponed until 5 p.m. and many people considered the ground still unfit. Very little was thought of the chances of Cure-All and his owner/rider but however inexperienced Mr Loft might have been at steeplechasing, he possessed an excellent eye for a country and spotting a tow path bordering the stretch of heavy plough running up to the Canal Ditch, he was able to conserve a good deal of energy and land Cure-All (11-5) the winner by 2 lengths and the same from Peter Simple, 11-12 (Frisby) and The Exquisite, 11-12 (Byrne). Cure-All returned to a triumphant reception in Healing and presumably spent his retirement in the hunting-field since he never ran again.

CURRAN, Richard Thomas (b.1924)

A Yorkshireman, Richard Curran was apprenticed to John Beary and rode first jockey to Stewart Wight (*q.v.*) from 1945-57. Between 1951-55 he finished four times in the Leading Jockeys list, his best season being 1952-53 when he rode 72 winners and finished second to Fred Winter. He was associated with Lord Joicey's fine mare, Bramble Tudor, on whom he won the Great Yorkshire Chase (1955) and the Wetherby Handicap Chase (1956).

CUSACK, Thomas

Tommy Cusack won the 1954 Cheltenham Gold Cup on Four Ten. He also won the Queen Elizabeth Chase (1951) on Red April and the Imperial Cup (1950) on Secret Service.

DALY, James (1846-1917)

A very well-known dealer of Liffey Bank, Dublin, James Daly started his career in remounts and hunters. In 1880 he extended his interests to thoroughbreds and bought the Hartstown Stud where he stood Hackler (*q.v.*). He had few equals as a judge of a potential chaser and among the horses who passed through his hands were Why Not, Cloister, Eremon, Jenkinstown, Mattie McGregor and Royal Meath.

DANIELS, William

Bill Daniels won the 1887 Grand National on Gamecock.

DAVENPORT, Stephen George (b.1944)

Yet another product of George Owen's school of jockeys, Stephen Davenport rode his first winner in 1961 and was Champion Amateur in 1963-64 with the fine total of 32 winners. He thus became the fourth of Owen's protégés to become a Champion (the others being Dick Francis, Tim Brookshaw and Stan Mellor). He then turned professional for a few years before taking out a licence to train. His best season was 1965-66 when he rode 34 winners and his victories included the 1968 Topham Trophy on Surcharge. He ran a small string of jumpers from his Cheshire home for a few years but gave up in 1975 to concentrate on show-jumpers. He is married to show-jumping star, Jean Goodwin.

DAVIES, Bertram Robert (b.1946)

Bob Davies comes from a farming family and in fact gained a B.Sc in Agriculture. He rode from his earliest days and won a point-to-point aged 14. He began riding as an amateur and rode his first winner in 1966. He retained amateur status for two seasons, winning 20 races and turned professional at the beginning of 1967-68. He shot to the top in an astonishingly rapid fashion, owing a good deal to his retainer with the prolific winner-producing stable of David Barons. Since 1975 he has ridden first jockey for David Morley's strong stable.

He has been Champion Jockey on three occasions:

1968-69	77 winners (equal with Terry Biddlecombe)
1969-70	91 winners
1971-72	89 winners

His victories include the 1978 Grand National on Lucius, the Black and White Gold Cup (1969) on Cool Alibi and the Imperial Cup (1970) on Solomon II.

He is married to Terry Biddlecombe's sister, Susan.

DAVIES, Colin Hughes

The son of a Cardiff property developer, Colin Davies served with the Fleet Air Arm from 1947-49. A man of drive and vigour and an astute businessman, he was also an accomplished racing driver who held the lap record at Aintree and won the Grand Prix des Frontieres at Chimay (Belgium). However his grand-mother was an Anthony and the call of horse-racing would not be denied. He rode in point-to-points and as an amateur, winning the Lady Dudley Cup and the United Hunts (Cheltenham). He also completed the 1964 National on Claymore.

In 1963 he took out a licence to train and established a very modern complex at Oakgrove, near Chepstow. By far the best horse he has handled is the triple Champion Hurdler, Persian War (1968, 1969, 1970) with whom he also won the Welsh Champion Hurdle (1969) and the Schweppes Gold Trophy (1968). He also won the Imperial Cup (1968) with Persian Empire.

DAVY JONES

Chestnut horse, 1929, Pharos—Panic (Hurry On). Bred by Maj. J. S. Courtauld.

A tubed horse, standing nearly 17 h.h., Davy Jones ranks high on the list of luckless National losers. After winning five races on the Flat and two chases, he was bought by Lord Mildmay for his son, Anthony, to ride. The pair got off to a great start by winning a 2-mile chase at Gatwick, before lining up for the 1936 Grand National. They made every yard of running and landed over the second last well clear; here however the reins parted at the buckle and with his steering gone, Anthony Mildmay was powerless to prevent Davy Jones from running out at the last.

Davy Jones was thereafter plagued with unsoundness and won only one more race before retiring to stud at Fairlawne. His stud career was severely curtailed by the war but he was responsible for several N.H. winners notably the Imperial Cup winner, Peggy Jones.

DAVY LAD
Bay gelding, 1970, David Jack—Château (Amour Drake). Bred by Mrs K. Westropp-Bennett.

A strong, tough, workmanlike gelding trained in Ireland by Mick O'Toole, Mrs McGowan's Davy Lad had proved a fine money-spinner for his stable, having won six hurdle races, including the Sun Alliance Novices Hurdle, National Hunt Meeting (1975) and four chases including a Wills Premier Qualifier and the Wetherby Pattern Chase, but he was nevertheless demonstrably several pounds below top class and his prospects of winning a Cheltenham Gold Cup seemed remote.

However, in 1977, profiting from the absence of the established stars, the testing underfoot conditions and the mistakes and misfortunes of the relatively inexperienced field, Davy Lad (D. Hughes) turned in a dour display of galloping and jumping and at 14/1, won by 6l, 20l, from Tied Cottage (T. Carberry) and the broken-down Summerville (J. King).

DAWSON, Richard Cecil (1865-1955)
The son of an Irish trainer and breeder, Richard Dawson went to Dublin University and came to England in 1896, bringing with him a young chaser, Drogheda. In 1897 he took out a licence to train at Whatcombe, Berkshire, and the following year saddled Drogheda to win the Grand National. Later he concentrated chiefly on the Flat, winning the Derby three times (Fifinella, 1916; Trigo, 1929; and Blenheim, 1930) and being Leading Trainer in 1916, 1924 and 1929. He retired in 1945.

DEMPSEY, Edward
An Irish jockey, Eddie Dempsey won the 1947 Grand National on the 100/1 outsider, Caughoo. He was later accused of taking a short cut through the fog from the fence before Bechers and joining in again after Valentine's. The story seems pure Banjo Patterson but nevertheless it involved Eddie in a punch-up and later a lawsuit in which he was completely vindicated. Eddie Dempsey rode Prince Regent in his early races and won three times on him.

DEVON AND EXETER (Group 4)
An undulating but testing track, right-handed and nearly two miles round, Devon and Exeter provides excellent racing and is extremely popular with trainers. The bulk of its meetings are in the summer, at the beginning and end of the season, when holiday crowds are attracted. Racing was recorded from 1840-44 but did not become a regular feature until 1898. Important races include the December H'cap Hurdle (3m 1f, £1,002), the Foxtor Challenge Cup H'cap Chase (April, 2m 3f, £1,201), the Torbay Challenge Trophy H'cap Chase (April, 2m 40yds, £1,031), and the Westward Television H'cap Chase (May, 2m 3f, £1,124).

Best Times

Distance	Time	Horse-age-weight	Date
2m 40y H	3m 58.80	{ Zeus Girl 6-11-8	7-10-72
		{ Hemon 8-10-11	6-8-75
2m 3f H	4m 25.60	Latan Furze 5-11-1	21-9-72
3m 1f H	6m 10	Snaggle Puss 5-10-7	18-8-71
2m 40y C	4m 8.20	Shawnigan 8-12-0	21-9-72
2m 3f C	4m 37.20	Dolly Boy 13-10-0	27-5-75
3m 1f C	6m 18.60	Brokopondo 7-10-0	8-8-74

DEVON LOCH

Brown gelding, 1946, Devonian—
Coolaleen (Loch Lomond). Bred by Mr
W. A. Moloney.

A very popular chaser owned by Her
Majesty Queen Elizabeth the Queen
Mother and the winner of six chases,
Devon Loch started favourite for the
1956 Grand National and was undoubtedly the unluckiest loser ever. Having
jumped the last well clear, apparently full
of running, he spread-eagled 50 yards
from the post and although he righted
himself, his shaken jockey, Dick Francis,
dismounted and led him home. After the
race Devon Loch showed no symptoms
of distress or undue fatigue and no really
satisfactory explanation has ever been
advanced for his collapse. Theories range
from shock at hearing the deafening
volume of applause anticipating a Royal
victory (Dick Francis), a ghost jump over
the shadow of the adjoining water jump
(most of the popular Press) and cramp
causing a sudden, temporary muscular
seizure (Ivor Herbert). This last suggestion is supported by his subsequent performance in the Mildmay Memorial and
is on balance the most plausible
explanation.

Devon Loch won two good chases the
following season and was second in the
King George VI Chase, Kempton Park,
but after running fourth in the Mildmay
he developed leg trouble and was retired.
Trained, like most of the Queen Mother's
horses by Peter Cazalet at Fairlawne,
Devon Loch was given to another royal
trainer, Noel Murless, for use as a hack.

DICK, David Victor (b. 1924)

Swashbuckling Dave Dick was one of the
'characters' among post-war jump
jockeys. He was also one of the best. The
son of an Epsom trainer, he grew up with
Fred Winter and attended, irregularly,
the same school. He was apprenticed to
his father (1936-38) and won the 1941
Lincolnshire Handicap on Gloaming at
7st 4lb, a fact that his broad-shouldered,
six-foot form makes difficult to assimilate. In 1956, profiting from Devon
Loch's collapse, he won the Grand National on ESB and thus became the only
jockey to win the Spring Double. He first
came to prominence in 1951, when he
was engaged to ride Miss Dorothy
Paget's horses, then trained by Fulke
Walwyn. The following year he won the
Cheltenham Gold Cup on Miss Paget's
Mont Tremblant.

Among his other successes are:

The Whitbread Gold Cup (1961) Pas Seul
**The National Hunt Two Mile Champion
Chase** (1962) Piperton: (1965) Dunkirk
The Champion Novices Chase (1962)
Piperton

He has become something of a legend
and a book (alas unprintable) could be
devoted to his exploits and sayings. Had
he been constructed on a slightly smaller
scale, he would undoubtedly have been
Champion Jockey for his contemporaries
numbered few stronger finishers and no
braver man. He currently manages Wyld
Court Stud.

DICKINSON, Anthony Edward (b.1915)

The sudden rise to prominence of the
Dickinson family of Gisburn, Lancashire,
has been one of the most remarkable
features of National Hunt racing during
the last few seasons. Previously they had
farmed, hunted and been very successful
in point-to-points. Tony Dickinson was
leading point-to-point rider in 1954 and
his wife, formerly Miss Birtwhistle, was a
very distinguished lady rider, but they
were not involved with racing proper
until 1967-68 when Tony Dickinson took
out a permit to train a few horses for his
son Michael (*q.v.*) to ride. His success was
instantaneous and in 1968-69 he went
public. In 1973-74, with 25 horses in his
yard, he turned out the winners of 63
races, worth £31,820, and the flow has
never faltered.

His select string of horses is hallmarked as much by the fastidious scru-
tiny paid to their conformation and
pedigree as by their meticulous preparation and schooling.

His principal successes include:

The Sun Alliance Chase (1977) Gay Spartan
The Arkle Challenge Trophy (1975) Broncho
II
The Scottish Champion Hurdle (1974) San-
ton Brig
The Heinz Chase (1974) Winter Rain
The Mildmay Chase (1974) Winter Rain
The Panama Cigar Hurdle Final (1977)
French Hollow
The Tote Northern H'cap Chase (1978) Gay
Spartan
The Buchanan Whisky Gold Cup Chase
(1978) I'm a Driver

DICKINSON, Michael (b.1950)

A son of trainer Tony Dickinson (*q.v.*), Michael Dickinson started riding in point-to-points and won the Lord Grimthorpe Cup in 1968 on Shandover. Previously he had done spells with Frenchie Nicholson, and Vincent O'Brien. He rode his first winner in 1968 and in 1969-70 he was Champion Amateur, riding 23 winners. He turned professional the following season and, riding chiefly for his father, enjoyed steadily increasing success. The father-son combination were particularly successful with their young chasers who all jumped confidently and well.

His principal victories included:

The Great Yorkshire Chase (1972) Slave's Dream
The Scottish Champion Hurdle (1974) Santon Brig
The Sun Alliance Chase (1977) Gay Spartan
The National Hunt Chase (1968) Fascinating Forties
The National Hunt H'cap Chase (1973) The Chisler
The Mildmay Chase (1974) Winter Rain
The Heinz Chase (1974) Winter Rain
The Tote Northern H'cap Chase (1976) Shifting Gold
The Panama Cigar Hurdle Final (1977) French Hollow
The Benson and Hedges H'cap Chase (1974) Dorlesa
The Tote Northern H'cap Chase (1978) Gay Spartan

A horrible fall in the Spring of 1978 forced this fine horseman into premature retirement.

DISCOUNT

Chestnut horse, 1838, Sir Hercules—Minikin (Manfred). Bred by Mr Fowler.

Discount's original name of Magnum Bonum proved singularly inappropriate for he turned out to be desperately slow on the Flat and passed from dealer to dealer until he finally became the property of Mr Quartermaine of Piccadilly for a sum that steadily diminished as the deal wrangled on – hence his name. Better things were to come, however, and in 1844 he became the first horse registered in the General Stud Book to win the Grand National. Starting 5/1 favourite and ridden by Crickmere (10-12), he overcame torrential rain and dreadful conditions to win by 20l, 1l

from The Returned, Scott (12-0) and Tom Tug, Rackley (10-7), landing something of a gamble for his connections in the process.

He went on to win two more races including the important Royal Birthday Stakes, Worcester, beating Tom Olliver's Vanguard (*q.v.*), after which he was sold for 1,100 guineas at Tattersalls. No subsequent record can be found of him.

DISTEL

Bay gelding, 1941, by Rosewell—Laitron (Soldennis). Bred by Col. A. J. and Mr I. J. Blake.

In an all-too-brief career, the Hon. Dorothy Paget's Distel won three Flat races and eight hurdle races including the Scalp Hurdle, Leopardstown, and the 1946 Champion Hurdle (R. O'Ryan) 4/5f, by 4l, ½l, from Carnival Boy (T. F. Rimell) and Robin O'Chantry (J. Goodgame). Shortly after being pulled up in the 1947 Champion Hurdle, he died of a brain tumour. He was trained in Ireland by Charlie Rogers.

DISTURBANCE

Bay horse, 1867, Commotion—Polly Peachum (Collingwood). Bred by Mr Barber.

A small, clean-winded and immensely tough horse, Disturbance won seven Flat races, three hurdles and three chases including the 1873 Grand National, Mr J. M. Richardson (11-11), 20/1, by 6l, 10l, from Ryshworth, Boxall (11-8) and Columbine, Harding (10-9). This last was an extremely fine performance for Ryshworth was a class horse who had been fourth in the 1869 Derby and won the Grand Sefton, with 12-7 by 10 lengths in a hack canter, the day after the National.

Disturbance had an extremely busy Flat career, running 40 times in three seasons and besides his seven victories he once ran Flying Childers to a length at Kelso, at a difference of only 14lb. After his hurdling successes he was sold to that astute judge and trainer, Capt. Machell, together with Reugny and Defence for a total of £1,200. Two years later, after the National victories of Disturbance and Reugny, Capt. Machell passed the trio on to Mr Gerard Leigh for £12,000 but Mr Leigh had little joy out of his investment. Disturbance, in particular, quite failed to appreciate his new and unorthodox training methods and was never any use again. He was later sold as a stallion to Lord Hastings and stood at Melton Constable, but, although he lived to be 29, he achieved no particular success.

DODD, John
John Dodd ran a small yard in Shropshire and won the 1928 Grand National with Tipperary Tim.

DOLLERY, William (d.1936)
Bill Dollery was one of the stable jockeys to the large and successful Bishop's Sutton establishment of Arthur Yates. Like all the Bishop's Sutton jockeys he started as a stable lad (and before that had been a shepherd) and continued to carry out stable duties after he had made his name.

He won:

The Grand National (1893) Cloister
The Champion Chase (1888) Johnny Longtail; (1890) Gamecock
The Grand Sefton (1892) Cloister

He had the enviable knack of falling light and during his whole career did nothing worse than break a collar bone.

His worst fall occurred in his last ride in a chase at Folkestone. Fearing that he had broken several ribs, the first-aid people wished to take him back to the weighing room on a stretcher. Dollery refused point-blank, saying he had never yet returned in such a fashion and had no intention of starting now.

DONCASTER (Group 1)
Although steeplechasing was recorded at Doncaster in 1849 and in 1852, it did not become a regular feature until after World War II. Since then the 2-mile, left-handed, pear-shaped track with its easy bends and fine fences has become recognized as one of the fairest and best in the country. The principal race is the William Hill (formerly John Smith) Great Yorkshire Chase run in January (3m 2f, £4,724) which is nearly always won by a high-class horse. The Princess Royal H'cap Hurdle (February, 2m 150yds, £2,929) is always a very competitive race as is the William Hill H'cap Hurdle (January, 2m 150y, £2,233).

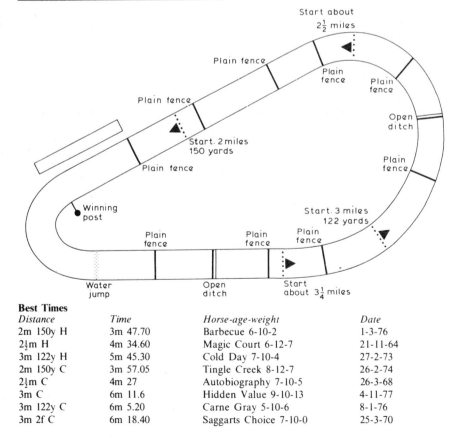

Best Times

Distance	Time	Horse-age-weight	Date
2m 150y H	3m 47.70	Barbecue 6-10-2	1-3-76
2½m H	4m 34.60	Magic Court 6-12-7	21-11-64
3m 122y H	5m 45.30	Cold Day 7-10-4	27-2-73
2m 150y C	3m 57.05	Tingle Creek 8-12-7	26-2-74
2½m C	4m 27	Autobiography 7-10-5	26-3-68
3m C	6m 11.6	Hidden Value 9-10-13	4-11-77
3m 122y C	6m 5.20	Carne Gray 5-10-6	8-1-76
3m 2f C	6m 18.40	Saggarts Choice 7-10-0	25-3-70

William Hill Great Yorkshire Chase (H'cap) (3m, 40y)

HORSE	OWNER	RIDER	TRAINER
1948 Cool Customer	Maj. R. Stirling Stuart	P. Murphy	J. Fawcus
1949 Old Mortality	Mr T. E. Ward	R. Turnell	T. F. Rimell
1950 Freebooter	Mrs L. Brotherton	J. Power	R. Penton
1951 Arctic Gold	Mr J. H. Whitney	T. Molony	G. Balding
1952 No Race (Funeral of H.M. King George VI)			
1953 Knock Hard	Mrs M. Keogh	T. Molony	M. V. O'Brien
1954 No Race			
1955 Bramble Tudor	Col. Joicey	R. Curran	J. Wight
1956 No Race			
1957 E.S.B.	Mrs L. Carver	T. Molony	T. F. Rimell
1958 Hall Weir	Mr H. Sumner	W. Rees	F. Cundell
1959 No Race			
1960 Knightsbrook	Mr W. J. Roach	G. Slack	W. A. Hall
1961 Chavara	Mrs I. Evans	S. Mellor	G. R. Owen
1962 Nicolaus Silver	Mr C. Vaughan	H. Beasley	T. F. Rimell
1963 No Race			
1964 King's Nephew	Mr Allen Wood	S. Mellor	F. Cundell
1965 King of Diamonds	Mr C. F. Gilman	J. Kenneally	G. Vergette
1966 Freddie	Mr R. R. Tweedie	P. McCarron	R. R. Tweedie
1967 Spear Fir	Mrs M. W. Darling	J. Leech	R. Fairbairn
1968 Sixty Nine	Mr J. Lisle	B. Fletcher	D. Smith
1969 Playlord	Mr P. Cussins	R. Barry	G. W. Richards
1970 Freddie Boy	Mrs E. Vestey	R. Pitman	F. Winter
1971 Two Springs	Mr D. H. Barnes	R. Edwards	G. R. Owen
1972 Slave's Dream	Mrs L. Carr	M. Dickinson	R. Hall
1973 Charlie Potheen	Mrs B. Heath	T. Biddlecombe	F. Walwyn
1974 Cuckolder	Mrs J. Rogerson	A. Turnell	R. Turnell
1975 Rough House	Mrs W. Brown	J. Burke	T. F. Rimell
1976 No Race			
1977 No Race			
1978 Autumn Rain	Mr S. Marsh	C. Tinkler	A. Dickinson

1948-69 run as Great Yorkshire Chase - 1970-75 run as John Smith Great Yorkshire Chase

DONE UP

Bay gelding, 1950, Donatello II—Fasten (Fastnet). Bred by the Maharaja of Kashmir.

A classically bred horse from the Pearl Maiden family, Done Up was owned throughout his N.H. career by Mr J. U. Baillie and trained at Findon by Ryan Price.

After winning two hurdle races in 1953-54 he broke down twice and was off the course for three seasons before coming back to win seven chases including the Hurst Park Grand National Trial (1959) and the Whitbread Gold Cup (1959), by an infinitesimally short head, from Mandarin. A very game little horse, he was also incorrigibly lazy and was invariably ridden by the mighty Fred Winter. When the latter was injured on the eve of the Whitbread, a suitable replacement was not easy to find and the choice fell upon ace hurdles rider, Harry Sprague. After his triumph, Sprague, an exceptionally strong jockey, was sick from his exertions.

DOORKNOCKER

Chestnut gelding, 1948, registered in Miss Prior's Half-Bred Stud Book, Cacador—Shady Girl II (Pickpocket).

A fine, big stamp of gelding, bred in Ireland, Doorknocker won a bumper, a chase and six hurdle races including the 1956 Champion Hurdle (H. Sprague), 100/9, by $\frac{3}{4}$l, 4l, from Quita Que (Mr J. Cox) and Baby Don (T. Molony). He was bought as a yearling by Paddy Sleator on behalf of Mr Clifford Nicholson and won first time out over hurdles at Mallow. Shortly afterwards, however, he knocked himself so badly that he was not able to run for two years, after which he came to England to be trained, like most of Mr Nicholson's horses, by W. A. Hall.

DORMANT

Chestnut gelding, 1957, Domaha—Miss Victoria (Devonian). Bred by Mr H. G. Gregson.

A game, consistent gelding and something of a giant-killer. Dormant survived a bewildering number of changes of stable with unshakeable placidity. His seven victories included the Whitbread Gold Cup, Sandown (1964), beating Mill House, the Mildmay Memorial, Sandown (1964) and the King George VI, Kempton (1966), beating Arkle. He was owned by Mrs Wells-Kendrew.

DOUBLE CHANCE

Chestnut gelding, 1916, Roi Herode or Day Comet—Kelibia (Upas). Bred by Mr L. de Rothschild.

Double Chance had but modest success on the Flat, winning two small races for Capt. A. de Rothschild who finally gave him to Fred Archer, a trooper in his squadron of the Royal Bucks Yeomanry who had just started training. Fred Archer was a grandson of William Archer (*q.v.*) and a nephew of the famous jockey whose namesake he was. Double Chance was cut and soon won a selling chase for his new owner but shortly afterwards developed leg trouble and was off the course for two seasons. After a spell of hunting he returned to the racecourse and during 1924-25 he won eight chases including the 1925 Grand National, 10-9 (Maj. J. P. Wilson), 100/9, by 4l, 6l, from Old Tay Bridge, 11-12 (J. Anthony) and Fly Mask, 11-11 (E. Doyle). Shortly before his Aintree victory, Fred Archer sold a half-share to Mr Goold, a Liverpool cotton-broker, whose colours he carried in the big race.

DOWDESWELL, John (b.1917)

Few braver men have ridden under N.H. Rules than Jack Dowdeswell. He served his apprenticeship with Ted Gwilt and for a while rode on the Flat. World War II, during which he served with the Royal Horse Artillery, interrupted his career and after it he was too heavy. Although almost too light for jumping and the wrong shape, with his big head, broad shoulders and short legs, his unlimited courage and effective finish stood him in good stead and he won a great many big races including the Queen Elizabeth Chase (1955) on Limb of the Law, the

Imperial Cup (1954) on The Pills and the Grand Sefton (1947) on Good Date. He was Champion Jockey in 1946-47 riding 58 winners. Despite his success, his opportunities were limited and he rode some really bad horses who gave him some horrifying falls. He broke his collar bones so often that he had them removed and wore a kind of cricket pad with a hole for his head over his shoulders.

Finally medical advice forced him to give up and in 1960 he took out a licence to train in his native village of Lambourn. Although he made the most of the modest horses he was sent, he was undercapitalized and could not cope with soaring overheads. In 1970 he handed in his licence and became headman to David Nugent. His brother, Tom, is head-man to Arthur Budgett.

DOYLE, Maj. Edward Cecil, D.S.O. (1886-1954)

Paddy Doyle, an officer in the R.A.V.C., was a leading amateur rider of the 'twenties. He won the Cheltenham Foxhunters (1923 and 1924) on Maj. (later Sir Harold) Wernher's Fairy Hill II. He also won the 1923 National Hunt Chase but was disqualified, Harry Brown on Templescoby getting the race. In the end of 1925, after finishing third in the Grand National on Fly Mask, the Stewards obliged him to turn professional but his career was almost immediately terminated by a bad fall. From 1926-29 he trained and then took up an appointment as Judge and Veterinary Officer in Malaya. On his return he ran a private practice in Naas. He was an extremely distinguished vet with decided ideas on equine nutrition.

DREAPER, James Thomas (b.1951)

The son of Tom Dreaper (*q.v.*), Jim Dreaper rode very successfully as an amateur and was a close second in the 1971 Grand National on Black Secret. He took over his father's Kilsallaghan establishment in 1972 and continued to run it on its slightly unorthodox but supremely successful lines. He inherited its marvellous, long-established staff and to replace retiring Pat Taaffe he enjoyed the priceless advantage of Tommy Carberry's jockeyship.

He was leading N.H. trainer in Ireland in his first season, a position he maintained for five consecutive years.

His successes include:

The Cheltenham Gold Cup (1975) Ten Up
The Irish Distillers Grand National (1974) Colebridge; (1975) Brown Lad; (1976) Brown Lad; (1978) Brown Lad
The W. D. & H. O. Wills Premier Chase Final (1972) Colebridge
The National Hunt Two Mile Champion Chase (1975) Lough Ineagh
The Schweppes Gold Trophy Handicap Hurdle (1972) Good Review

Brown Lad, whose successes in the Irish National made him the first-ever triple winner, was also second in two Cheltenham Gold Cups (1976 and 1978). In the first of those years, Jim Dreaper was involved in a controversy over the running of Ten Up, a habitual breaker of blood vessels, to whom a coagulant, Estro, was normally administered prior to a race. This procedure was, at the time, permissible in Ireland provided the stewards were notified in advance. The stewards of the N.H. Meeting, however, pointed out that according to Rule 200 of the Rules of Racing "any person administering or causing to be administered any amount of any substance (other than a normal nutrient) ... which ... could affect the racing performance of a horse is guilty of a breach of the Rules and may be declared a disqualified person or otherwise penalised", and that if the coagulant were administered, Dreaper would have to bear the consequences if the dope test the stewards would undoubtedly order, proved positive. In the event Dreaper withdrew his horse and was fined for not running him.

DREAPER, Thomas William (1898-1975)
A dedicated, unassuming and extremely shrewd Irishman, Tom Dreaper trained jumpers from his farm at Greenogue, Kilsallaghan, from the early 'thirties until 1971 when he relinquished the licence to his son, Jim (*q.v.*). His big chance in racing came quite by chance when Bobby Power, a vet who was breaking some youngsters, including Prince Regent for Mr J. V. Rank, was killed when changing a tyre on the road to the Dublin Horse Show and the horses were sent to Dreaper. After the horses had been broken and hunted they went to Gwyn Evans at Druids Lodge but when in the summer of 1938, he too was killed, Prince Regent returned to Greenogue where he remained for the rest of his career.

Tom Dreaper concentrated on producing high-class chasers, regarding hurdling just as a means to an end. He valued and would seek out the established Irish jumping strains and took great pains to give his horses a thorough jumping education. Dreaper horses were schooled twice a week throughout their careers, although the rest of their preparation was unorthodoxly light. He believed in giving them time and went to considerable trouble to keep them individually happy and fresh.

His results were spectacular and consistently so. Four really great horses passed through his hands, Prince Regent, Royal Approach, Flyingbolt, and Arkle, besides many others that a lesser man would have happily called great. He inspired tremendous loyalty and his relationships with owners, jockeys and staff were permanent ones. His two principal patrons were each rewarded with a really great horse, Mr Rank with Prince Regent and Anne, Duchess of Westminster with Arkle. His partnership with Pat Taaffe, which started in 1950, ended in their mutual retirement.

His major winners include:

The Cheltenham Gold Cup (1946) Prince Regent; (1964) Arkle; (1965) Arkle; (1966) Arkle; (1968) Fort Leney
The Irish Grand National (1942) Prince Regent; (1949) Shagreen; (1954) Royal Approach; (1960) Olympia; (1961) Fortria; (1962) Kerforo; (1963) Last Link; (1964) Arkle; (1965) Splash; (1966) Flyingbolt
The King George VI Chase (1965) Arkle
The National Hunt Two Mile Champion Chase (1960) Fortria; (1961) Fortria; (1964) Ben Stack; (1966) Flyingbolt; (1969) Muir; (1970) Straight Fort
The Hennessy Gold Cup (1964) Arkle; (1965) Arkle
The Whitbread Gold Cup (1965) Arkle
The Mackeson Gold Cup (1960) Fortria; (1962) Fortria
The Massey-Ferguson Gold Cup (1965) Flyingbolt; (1971) Leap Frog
The Black and White Gold Cup (1965) Flyingbolt; (1966) Dicky May
Wills Premier Chase (1971) Leap Frog

He twice featured in the Leading Trainers lists in England, finishing third in 1964-65 when three horses won him

£28,890, and second in 1965-66 with four horses winning £38,861.

DRISCOLL, Edmund Walter

Before World War I, Ernie Driscoll was attached to Robert Gore's Findon stable. He won six races, including the 1910 Grand Steeplechase de Paris, on Jerry M. and was second to Jenkinstown in the 1910 National. He also won the Grand Sefton (1909 and 1910) on Sir Charles Assheton-Smith's Cackler and the Scottish Grand National (1909) on Mount Prospect's Fortune. In 1917 he won the 'War' National at Gatwick on Ballymacad.

DROGHEDA

Bay gelding, 1892, not in the General Stud Book, Cherry Ripe—Eglantine (Hollywood). Bred in Ireland.

An extremely plain son of an Irish Grand National winner, Drogheda was bought out of Ireland, after winning four chases in that country, by Richard Marsh. In England he added to that tally to the tune of a hurdle race and two more chases including the 1898 Grand National, 10-12 (J. Gourley), 25/1, by 3l, 4l, from Cathal, 11-5 (Mr R. Ward) and Gauntlet, 10-13 (W. Taylor) in just about the filthiest conditions on record.

DRUMCREE

Bay gelding, 1894, registered in Miss Prior's Half-Bred Stud Book, Ascetic—Witching Hour (Midnight). Bred by Mr C. Hope.

Originally bought in Ireland by Owen Williams for the well-known amateur Charles Newtown to hunt, Drumcree showed such aptitude that he was sent to Sir Charles Nugent to be trained for steeplechasing. He won eight chases and after running second to Grudon in the 1901 Grand National, won the 1903 running, 11-3 (Percy Woodland), 13/2f, by 3l, 20l, from Detail, 9-13 (A. Nightingall) and Manifesto, 12-3 (G. Williamson). Drumcree bears the name of one of Miss Prior's most distinguished families and from his own-sister, Pride of Mabestown (six chases), descends Mr Edward Courage's famous foundation mare, Drumrora V (q.v.).

DRUMRORA V

Bay mare, 1935, registered in Miss Prior's Half-Bred Stud Book. Bred by Mrs M. B. Smyly.

Drumrora V		
Friar Gray	Friar Marcus	Cicero
		Prim Nun
	Pharsalia	Roi Herode
		Lacroma
Pride of Drumrora	Fra Diavolo	Teufel
		Loyse
	Mabestown	St. Gris
		Pride of Mabestown

Descended from a distinguished line of jumpers, Drumrora V did not race. In 1946 she became the property of Mr Edward Courage for whom she founded a remarkably successful family. Her four daughters were:

French Colleen 1946 (Lobau) won a point-to-point and was dam of the winners:
Noble Pierre (Kingstone), one hurdle
Certainement (Doubtless II), four chases
Royal Relief (Flush Royal), two hurdles and 13 chases
Tiberina 1947 (Tiberius) won four chases and was dam of the winners:
Royal Exile (Le Jacobin), one chase
Neapolitan Lou (Flush Royal), six hurdles and four chases
Lira (Souverain), one hurdle and four chases
San Angelo (Fortina), ten chases
Attribute (Doubtless II), two chases
Saccone (Flush Royal), two hurdles and two chases
Tikitas (Tangle), three hurdles
Galley Light (Sailing Light), one chase
Tiberetta (q.v.) 1948 (Tiberius) won 11 chases and was dam of the winners:
Chamoretta (Chamossaire), three chases and three point-to-points
Tamoretta (Chamossaire), one hurdle and five chases
Spanish Steps (q.v.) (Flush Royal), four hurdles and 12 chases
Trajan (Flush Royal), eight chases
Quintus (Quorum), four chases
Lictor (Right Boy), one hurdle race and two chases
Mafia King (Tycoon II), two chases
Colleen's Fancy 1952 (Your Fancy) won one chase.

DUDLEY

Bay gelding, 1914, registered in Miss Prior's Half-Bred Stud Book, Rhosmarket—mare by Succoth. Bred by Mr J. C. Carroll.

Dudley, a Limerick-bred gelding

owned by the 'Yellow' Earl Londesborough and trained and ridden by
Harry Brown, raced for nine seasons and
won 44 races, thus establishing a record
which stood for 30 years until being
bettered by Crudwell. During 1924-25
he won 18 races, 15 of them in succession including the Grand Annual at the
National Hunt Meeting, two years in
succession, and the valuable Victory
Chase, Manchester. Dudley's best distance was two miles but he was as versatile as he was tough and his tally
included National Hunt Flat races,
hurdle races and three-mile chases.

DULLER, George Edward (1892-1962)

Some say that George Duller was the
greatest hurdles jockey ever. Short and
strongly built he revolutionized the art
of N.H. race-riding by adopting a
pronounced crouch seat which enabled
him to get his horse fast away from their
hurdles without breaking their rhythm.
He rarely rode over fences but did once
in the National (1920 on Silver Ring
when he fell). His father trained trotters
'on the clock', from whence he derived
his exceptional judgement of pace.

Appreciating that this was one of his
greatest assets he liked to dictate the pace
from in front and such was his mesmeric
effect on other jockeys that he was
usually allowed to do this. If some bold
spirit ventured to take him on early in a
race, his plans were sometimes over-
turned. He was Champion Jockey in
1918, riding 17 winners. Between 1920-28
he rode 358 winners, his best season being 1922 with 97 winners from 239 rides.

Among his best victories were:

The Champion Hurdle (1927) Blaris
The Imperial Cup (1914) Vermouth;(1920)
  Trespasser; (1921) Trespasser; (1922)
  Trespasser; (1926) Peeping Tom; (1929)
  Hercules; (1930) Rubicon II
The County Hurdle (1920) Trespasser;
  (1924) Argo; (1926) Checktaker
The Liverpool Hurdle (1922) Count Ross;
  (1928) Stuff Gown

He rode Easter Hero over hurdles in
his 'prep' races for the 1929 Gold Cup.

In 1930 he took out a licence and
trained under both Rules. His patrons
included Prince Rajpipla, the Aga Khan
and Prince Aly, to whom he taught
something of the art of race-riding. He
won the Imperial Cup twice with

Rubicon II (1930) and Mange Tout
(1939).

Apart from his racing activities, he flew
his own aircraft and drove at Brooklands.
He spent his retirement at Epsom and
continued to ride work after World War
II. A hurdle race is named after him at
Cheltenham.

DUNKIRK

Brown gelding, 1957, Domaha—Toll-
down (Davy Jones). Bred by Mr F. J.
Akerman.

National Hunt enthusiasts of the 1960s
knew few more exciting sights than that
of Col. W. Whitbread's flying Dunkirk in
action. A specialist two-miler, he won a
hurdle race and eight chases including
the National Hunt Two Mile Champion
Chase, National Hunt Meeting (1965)
and the Mackeson Gold Cup, Cheltenham (1965) but is perhaps best
remembered for his sensational performance in the Frogmore Chase, Ascot
(1965), when, in winning by 15 lengths,
he recorded a time four seconds faster
than the current hurdle record and faster
than the average Flat-race over that distance.

Dunkirk died tragically in the 1965
King George VI Chase at Kempton,
from a haemorrhage of the lungs which
caused him to fall heavily through the
last open ditch and break his neck. It was
thought that he died before hitting the
ground. He was trained at Fairlawne by
Peter Cazalet.

DUTTON, William Parker (1901-58)

Son of a Cheshire country gentleman,
William Dutton went to Cambridge and
was articled to his uncle, Mr T. Moore
Dutton, passing his law finals in 1928. By
this time, however, he was riding as an
amateur with conspicuous success and
was disinclined to pursue a legal career.
He won both Foxhunters, the Liverpool
in 1925 on Upton Lad and the Cheltenham in 1929 on Blennerhasset and the
1926 National Hunt Chase on Cloringo.
In 1928 he achieved his greatest success
winning the Grand National on the unconsidered, tubed, 100/1 outsider
Tipperary Tim.

He afterwards trained at Hednesford,
Staffordshire. He was noted for his
handling of sprinters, notably Pappa
Fourway, Right Boy and Vigo and also
won the 1956 Cheltenham Gold Cup
with Limber Hill.

EARLY MIST

Chestnut gelding, 1945, Brumeux—Sudden Dawn (Hurry On). Bred by Mr D. J. Wrinch.

The career of Early Mist serves to underline the irony that is never far from the surface in racing. He slipped tantalizingly through the fingers of the first Lord Bicester and Mr J. V. Rank, two lavish supporters of steeplechasing whose lifelong ambition to win the Grand National died with them. Mr Rank did own the big, handsome chestnut that Vincent O'Brien had guided so successfully through a novice career that included a hurdle race (from his only outing) and six chases including the Carrickmines Chase and the Christmas Chase, but he died in January 1952 and his horses were put up for sale.

At the dispersal sale Lord Bicester tried hard to buy Early Mist but at £5,300 he was outbid by Mr Joe Griffin, a Dublin businessman and a newcomer to racing. Little more than a year later, Early Mist realized the dreams of both late and would-be owners and won the 1953 Grand National, 11-2 (B. Marshall) 20/1, by 20l, 4l, from Mont Tremblant, 12-5 (D. Dick) and Irish Lizard, 10-6 (R. Turnell).

Early Mist broke down the following year and although he continued to race for four seasons winning two more chases and running fourth in the 1955 Gold Cup, he never regained his early form. He was not a natural jumper, being rather hesitant and Vincent O'Brien attributes his Aintree success to the brilliant horsemanship of Bryan Marshall.

EASBY ABBEY

Bay gelding, 1967, Narrator—Memoire Cheri (Mossborough). Bred by Mr W. Steel.

Easby Abbey, a strong, well-made but not very big gelding, has a Flat-race pedigree and is half-brother to several winners on the Flat, but was himself conspicuously unsuccessful in this department and achieved only one third place from seven outings at two, three and four years.

However, under the shrewd tutelage of Peter Easterby, he developed into a fine, consistent hurdler, just short of top class, whose 13 wins included the Princess Royal Handicap Hurdle (Doncaster) twice. He was also second to Comedy of Errors in the 1973 Champion Hurdle.

In 1974-75 he turned his attention to fences and ably assisted by Ron Barry, he became a top-class 2½mile chaser and won nine chases including the London and Northern Securities Future Novices Championship, Ayr (1975), the Benson and Hedges Handicap Chase, Sandown (1975) and the Massey-Ferguson Gold Cup, Cheltenham (1975).

These performances coupled with the prevailing firm ground made him quite fancied for the Cheltenham Gold Cup but sadly leg trouble intervened and he had to be laid off.

EAST, Henry John

A Northern-based jockey attached to Neville Crump, Harry East rode a lot of winners in the late 1950s and early 'sixties. Strong and forceful, he excelled on the big staying chasers his yard specialized in.

Among his best victories were:

The Whitbread Gold Cup (1957) Much Obliged
The Mildmay Memorial (1957) Much Obliged
The Wetherby Handicap Chase (1958) Much Obliged
The Haydock Park Grand National Trial (1957) Goosander
The Victory Chase (1958) Northern Echo
The Topham Trophy (1957) Roughan
The Champion Novices Chase (1961) Rough Tweed

EASTERBY, Miles Henry (b.1929)

'Peter' Easterby comes from a racing family. He assisted his Uncle Walter and spent three years with Frank Hartigan at Weyhill. He joined the Royal Army Veterinary Corps, becoming a lance-corporal, and rode in point-to-points.

He inherited Habton Grange, near Malton, Yorkshire, with 550 acres and took out a licence in 1950. He started with four horses and saddled his first winner in 1953. In recent years the stable has prospered mightily with many successes under both Rules.

His principal N.H. victories have been:

The Champion Hurdle (1967) Saucy Kit; (1976) Night Nurse; (1977) Night Nurse

The Scottish Champion Hurdle (1976) Night Nurse; (1977) Sea Pigeon; (1978) Sea Pigeon

The Welsh Champion Hurdle (1976) Night Nurse; (1977) Night Nurse

The Massey-Ferguson Gold Cup (1975) Easby Abbey

The Fighting Fifth Hurdle (1975) Night Nurse; (1978) Sea Pigeon

The Irish Sweeps Hurdle (1975) Night Nurse

The Arkle Challenge Trophy Chase (1978) Alverton

His handling of the dual Champion Hurdler, Night Nurse, earned him universal praise. In 1975-76 he pioneered that horse, unbeaten through a campaign that included the Irish Sweeps Hurdle and a grand slam of the English, Scottish and Welsh Champion Hurdles. Night Nurse's earnings boosted his trainer into fourth place in the Trainer's List with 29 winners worth £57,521. His best season to date was 1977-78 when he turned out the winners of 60 races worth £80,080.

EASTER HERO

Chestnut gelding, 1920, registered in Miss Prior's Half-bred Stud Book, My Prince—Easter Week (Outbreak). Bred by Mr Larry King.

A small but beautifully fashioned gelding of a quality rarely found in chasers of his age, Easter Hero was a member of the famous Arab Maid family. He was foaled near Greenogue, Co. Dublin, and sold as a five-year-old for little money to Mr Bartholomew, an Englishman regarded by his Irish contemporaries as "a bit of a chancer", who owned and trained a few horses. Easter Hero showed signs of considerable ability which was however tempered by pronounced inaccuracy of jumping. From eight runs, he fell or blundered himself out of contention four times. When in the summer of 1927 Mr Bartholomew was obliged to sell, Easter Hero became the property of Frank Barbour, a rich, eccentric and extremely shrewd linen-thread manufacturer, who owned and trained the previous year's Gold Cup winner, Koko.

Mr Barbour trained Easter Hero to win eight chases during 1927-28 including the Molyneux and Becher Chases at Liverpool, but it was not until the last of these, the prestige $3\frac{1}{2}$-mile Coventry Chase at Kempton, which he won with 12-7, that the big battalions sat up and took notice. Hitherto their admiration had been qualified; one scribe thought him "full of quality but rather lacking in substance", another wondered "where he finds all his powers of jumping and endurance". By proving himself able to stay an extra mile in top-class company, Easter Hero became a star overnight and was to preserve the status for the rest of his brilliant and sensation-strewn career.

Briefly, he won 12 more chases, including two Cheltenham Gold Cups and was an infinitely gallant second in the 1929 Grand National under 12-7, despite being handicapped by a grotesquely twisted plate over the last mile. But that is only the bare bones of the story. On the strength of his Coventry Chase victory his appearance at the 1928 National Hunt Meeting was eagerly awaited, but on the eve of the Gold Cup it was announced without a heralding whisper that he had been sold to an unknown purchaser for some undisclosed, astronomical sum and would wait for the National. The racing world throbbed with speculation, finally dispelled when the buyer was announced to be Capt. Lowenstein, a Belgian financier, and the price £7,000 plus a £3,000 contingency should he win the Grand National.

Easter Hero went to Aintree amid a buzz of anticipation. Everyone was agog to see how the flamboyant and spectacular horse would acquit himself. Not until the fourth attempt were the 42-strong field despatched and, predictably, Easter Hero went straight into the lead, flicking the upright fences with apparent impunity until he reached the Canal Turn, then an open ditch. Here he took off outside the wings and landed plumb on top. Within seconds there was a gigantic pile-up. To onlookers it appeared that men and horses were being mown down with machine-guns. Only nine horses emerged to continue the race and of these only the 100/1 outsider, the tubed Tipperary Tim, reached the winning post unscathed.

Easter Hero then went to Paris for the Grand Steeple but, evidently displeased at F. B. Rees's unwillingness to cooperate in his customary front-running tactics, he refused the water jump in front of the stands and shot the hapless Rees off. A few days later he redeemed his reputation by winning the Prix des Drags in easy fashion, which turned out to be his only success in his new owner's colours. Barely a month later Capt. Lowenstein vanished out of his private plane over the North Sea and no trace was ever found of him. So for the second time that year Easter Hero was sold, this time to the American millionaire, Mr 'Jock' Hay Whitney, who sent him to the Letcombe stables of Jack Anthony.

From here he was sent out next season to win four minor hurdle races, the Cheltenham Gold Cup by 20 effortless lengths and finally to his heroic run at Aintree. In an age when the National was reckoned the main objective of all chasers with any pretensions to class, Easter Hero was widely rated the best horse never to have won it. Next year after winning 3 chases, including a second Gold Cup, Easter Hero developed tendon trouble which necessitated his being withdrawn four days before the National, but the breakdown was only minor and he was back on a racecourse by the end of 1930. He won three of his four preparatory races for the 1931 National and was only beaten a head in the fourth, giving 23lb to the winner, Desert Chief. Starting favourite at 5/1 for the National, he was knocked over at Becher's on the second circuit but was not thought to be travelling like a winner at the time. Pulled out again the very next day for the Champion Chase, he managed to force a dead-heat with Coup de Château. As Coup de Château was rated a much inferior animal and they were meeting at level weights, this was considered an irrefutable sign of decline and Easter Hero was retired forthwith. It is however difficult to visualize a current National contender, trained for 4½ miles and having completed two-thirds of that most gruelling course, being hauled out again the next day to do battle against fresh, specialist two-milers. Easter Hero was shipped across the Atlantic where he gave his owner many a fine day with hounds over the post-and-rails of Virginia and lived in much-fêted retirement to the ripe old age of 28.

EBORNEEZER
Bay horse, 1955, Ocean Swell—Priory Princess (Precipitation). Bred and owned by Dr Pajgar.

Eborneezer proved a fair stayer under Jockey Club Rules, winning three races including the Queen's Prize, after which he embarked on a brief but extremely successful hurdling career under the aegis of Ryan Price. From five runs, he won four races including the 1961 Champion Hurdle, 4/1 (F. Winter) by 3l, 1½l, from Moss Bank (J. Rafferty) and Farmer's Boy (D. Nicholson). He has achieved a certain amount of success as a sire of National Hunt winners, his stock including Ebony Prince, Persian Majesty, Eborneezersdouble and Ernie Wiltshire.

EDE, George Matthew (1834-70)
George Ede rode under the name of Mr Edwards. Despite a frail constitution and precarious health he was the finest Gentleman Rider of his day, winning a total of 306 races, including the 1867 Grand National on The Lamb for his great friend, Lord Poulett.

The twin son of a Hampshire gentleman, he was educated at Eton where he was a notable cricketer. Together with Lord Poulett, he founded the Hampshire Cricket Club and in 1863 scored 1,200 runs. He was coached in race-riding by Ben Land (*q.v.*) and his other big wins included the 1869 Old Baden-Baden Hunt Chase on Benazet. He died three days after a shocking fall from a horse called Chippenham in the 1870 Grand Sefton.

EDWARDS, David Roy (b.1933)
A member of a Shropshire farming family, Roy Edwards rode his first winner in 1957. During the 1960s he consistently finished high up in the list of leading jockeys without ever becoming Champion.

1962-63	50 winners	3rd
1963-64	55 winners	4th
1966-67	64 winners	4th
1967-68	59 winners	4th (equal)
1969-70	48 winners	4th

His best victory was the 1967 Champion Hurdle on Saucy Kit. He now trains and also owns and manages the Blakeley Stud, Shrewsbury, where Saucy Kit stands.

EDWARDS, Lionel (1878-1966)

One of the most popular depicters of modern racing, Lionel Edwards was a West Countryman who had the gift of capturing and preserving on canvas, the essence of all field sports. He is best remembered for his painting of movement and his ability to record individual characteristics of horse, hound or weather.

EMBLEM

Chestnut mare, 1856, Teddington—Miss Batty (The Hydra). Bred in Wales by Mr R. Swale.

After a Flat career not nearly as mediocre as has been supposed – she won seven races including a five length victory as a two-year-old at the Newmarket October meeting – Emblem was bought by Lord Coventry and sent to Tom Golby at Northleach, to be trained for jumping. This almost proved to be an insuperable task, for Emblem appeared to have neither aptitude nor inclination for her new rôle in life. However, during the course of a day with the North Cotswold Hounds in Northwick Park, she managed to achieve a small hurdle in the wake of a reliable cob and, thus emboldened, was able to pursue a successful chasing career. Her successes included the 1863 Grand National, 10-10 (G. Stevens), 4/1, by 20l, 2l from Arbury, 11-2 (Mr Goodman) and Yaller Girl, 10-13 (Mr Dixon), and the 1863 Cheltenham Steeplechase.

At stud she bred four foals, three colts and a filly, of whom Deerhurst (by Tim Whiffler) won over hurdles. She died in 1871. *See also* EMBLEMATIC.

EMBLEMATIC

Chestnut mare, 1858, Teddington—Miss Batty (The Hydra). Bred by Mr R. Swale.

A weedy little mare, very on-the-leg and nothing approaching the conventional stamp of chaser, Emblematic was a full-sister to Emblem (*q.v.*). They are the only pair of full-sisters ever to have won the National which they did in successive years, for the same owner and ridden by the same jockey. Owned by Lord Coventry, Emblematic won her National in 1864, 10-6 (G. Stevens), 10/1, by 3l, a bad third, from Arbury, 11-12 (Ben Land) and Chester, 10-0 (W. White). The following year she carried 11-10 into third place behind Alcibiade. At stud she

bred three fillies for Lord Coventry and was then exported to Prussia in foal to Breadalbane with a Blackdown foal at foot.

EMERY, René

René Emery rode a number of winners during the 1950s, his best season being 1953-54 when he rode 54 winners and finished second in the Jockeys' Table.

He was second in the 1956 Gold Cup on Vigor and won:

The Mildmay Memorial (1953) Whispering Steel
The Sandown Open Chase (1956) Vigor
The Lancashire Hurdle (1955) Didoric
The Imperial Cup (1951) Master Bidar; (1957) Camugliano

He afterwards trained without a great deal of success.

EMIGRANT

Bay gelding, 1846, not in the General Stud Book, Melbourne—Pandora by Cadland or Cain.

Emigrant was produced by old Ben Land but during the Shrewsbury races of 1855, old Ben had a shocking run at cards and became so much in debt to a pair of bookmakers, Hodgeman and Green, that he finally sold them Emigrant for £590 plus £100 contingency if he won at the meeting, which he duly did, landing his new owners a gamble in the process.

Emigrant was henceforth trained at Epsom under the supervision of Hodgeman. His preparation was very light and he was schooled only over hurdles, a regime rare in those days of 4 mile gallops over fence but evidently one that suited Emigrant, who won the 1857 Grand National, 9-10 (C. Boyce), 10/1, by 2l, and a distance, from Weathercock, 8-12 (C. Green), ironically owned by the Lands, and Treachery, 9-0 (Poole). Emigrant won his joint-owners a fortune in the process for not only had they backed him heavily to win but also to be first over the water. He rose at this obstacle upsides with Westminster but his jump was swifter and cleaner and he landed a length up.

EMPRESS

Chestnut mare, 1875, Blood Royal—Jeu des Mots (King Tom). Bred by Mr Thomas Lindesay (in Ireland).

Named after the Empress Elizabeth of Austria, Empress was owned by Mr P. Ducrot and trained at Eyrefield Lodge, the Curragh by H. E. Linde. The winner of five of her seven races, Empress was one of five five-year-olds to win the Grand National which she did in 1880, 10-7 (Mr T. Beasley), 8/1, by 2l and a head, from The Liberator, 12-7 (Mr G. Moore) and Downpatrick 10-7 (Gavin). Few horses could withstand a Linde preparation for long and Empress was no exception. She was never able to run again but retired to stud where she bred the exceptionally brilliant Red Prince II (*q.v.*).

EREMON

Bay gelding, 1900, Thurles—Daisy (Lord Gough). Bred by Mr James Cleary.

A half-brother to the dual Cambridgeshire winner, Christmas Daisy, Eremon was descended on both sides of his pedigree from Pocahontas. He was bought in Ireland by James Daly on behalf of Mr Stanley Howard for only £400 on account of his being thick-winded and did not see a racecourse till he was six years old.

In his first season he won two Hunter Chases and the first-ever chase at Newbury. He went on to win four of his five races in 1907 including the Grand National, 10-1 (A. Newey), 8/1, by 6l, a bad third, from Tom West, 9-12 (H. Murphy) and Patlander, 10-7 (J. Lynn) after an exhibition of fast, flippant fencing such as had not been seen at Aintree for years, which Alf Newey had to cope with stirrupless for he lost an iron at the second fence and rode the rest of the way without. Ten days later Eremon won the Lancashire Chase with a 12lb penalty and all seemed set for a brilliant career. Unhappily he got loose at exercise shortly afterwards and injured himself so badly that he had to be put down. He was trained at Hednesford by Tom Coulthwaite.

E.S.B.

Bay or brown gelding, 1946, Bidar —English Summer (Blue Ensign). Bred by Miss S. Burke.

A tough, sound, courageous horse, E.S.B. carried the colours of Mrs Carver for 11 seasons, winning one hurdle race and 22 chases including the 1956 Grand National, 11-3 (D. V. Dick) by 10l and same, from Gentle Moya, 10-2 (G. Milburn) and Royal Tan, 12-1 (T. Taaffe).

E.S.B.'s achievements have always been shrouded by the fact that he undoubtedly owed his Liverpool victory to the sensational collapse of Devon Loch 50 yards from the winning post. This is unfair as he was a fine horse in his own right whose victories included the Great Yorkshire, Doncaster (1957), the Lancashire Chase, Manchester (1959) and the Lord Stalbridge Memorial Cup, Wincanton (1955).

His owner, Mrs Leonard Carver was a first-class horsewoman and (as Miss Pierce) was the first lady to win the Daily Mail Championship at Olympia. E.S.B. was trained for brief spells by Sid Mercer and by his owner but he spent the greater part of his career with Fred Rimell at Kinnersley.

ESCART III

Chestnut horse, 1955. Bred in France by M H. Coulon.

			Ksar
		Tourbillon	
			Durban
	Turmoil II		Blue Skies
		Blue Iras	
Escart III			Iras
			Firdaussi
		Escamillo	
	Escalade		Estoril
			Dark Legend
		Cle de Mi	
			Clemi

Escart III won seven races in France from one mile to $13\frac{1}{2}$ furlongs including the Prix de Madrid. He was bought by Sir Adrian Jarvis and came to England where he shortly jarred himself. He went to George Owen and had one run in a novice hurdle, finishing fourth, before developing leg trouble. He was then bought by Mr Frank Latham for the Blackrath Stud where he stood five seasons before dying of a thrombosis in the autumn of 1966. He got the dual Gold Cup and Grand National winner L'Escargot in his first crop and his other good winners include Esban, Moonlight Escapade, Interview II and Collingwood.

By the end of season 1977-78 he had sired the winners of 234 races worth £214,067, an incredible achievement from only nine crops. He was leading sire in 1972-73 with 73 races worth £42,611 and in 1974-75 with 23 races worth £53,889.

ESCOTT, Anthony

A son of Harry Escott (*q.v.*), Anthony Escott was a leading jump jockey during the 'twenties and for a time first jockey to Frank Barbour (*q.v.*). His principal victories were the Lancashire Chase twice, in 1922 on Keep Cool, and 1931 on Solanum, and the Grand Sefton twice, 1922 on Keep Cool and 1923 on Silvo.

ESCOTT, H. (d.1948)

Harry Escott was apprenticed to William Day of Danebury where his fine horsemanship and light hands soon made an impression. However he quickly grew too heavy for the Flat and transferred to National Hunt racing with great success. He won the Lancashire Chase in 1897 on Knight of Rhodes and 1900 on Uncle Jack, and also the Stanley Chase in 1900 on the same horse. He trained at the same time at Lewes on the Sussex Downs.

He was sent Cloister after that horse's breakdown prior to the 1894 National. He trained and rode the great horse to win that year's Grand Sefton in smashing style but could not get him to the post for the 1895 National. Among his other good horses were Lutteur III, whom M. James Hennessy sent to him to complete his preparation for the 1909 National and Poethlyn whom he trained to win the Grand Nationals of 1918 and 1919 and the Lancashire Chase of those years. His son Anthony (*q.v.*) was a well-known steeplechase jockey   ,

ETERNAL

Chestnut gelding, 1951, The Phoenix —Constant Nymph (Dastur). Bred by Mr Myerscough.

Owned and trained by Lt.-Col. Fenwick-Palmer, Etnal was a doughty campaigner who raced for 12 seasons winning 14 races including the Grand Sefton, Liverpool (1962), the Lancashire Chase, Manchester (1960 and 1961) and the Emblem Chase, Manchester (1960). Lt.-Col. Fenwick-Palme is the author of a best-selling manual on training the steeplechaser entitled *Out of the Ruck*.

EVANS, Gwyn (d.1938)

Gwyn Evans rode as an amateur under N. H. Rules and assisted George Poole at Lewes. In 1933 he became private trainer to Mr J. V. Rank (*q.v.*). He won:

The Welsh Grand National (1934) Dream Ship; (1935) Lacatoi; (1937) Lacatoi; (1938) Timber Wolf
The Scottish Grand National (1934) Southern Hero; (1936) Southern Hero; (1938) Young Mischief
The Imperial Cup (1937) Le Maestro
The Liverpool Hurdle (1937) Beachway

Tragically he was killed in a car crash in 1938 at the age of 46.

EVEN MONEY

Brown horse, 1955. Bred by Capt. Maguire.

			Pharos
		Nearco	
			Nógara
	Krakatao		
			Solario
		Life Hill	
Even Money			Lady of the Snows
			Dark Legend
		Legend of France	
			Francille
	Vendome		
			King Salmon
		Corvette	
			Molly Brawn

Even Money, a robust handsome individual owned by Mr C. H. Palmer and trained by Vincent O'Brien, had a brief but successful racing career winning three races including the Ascot Gold Vase (1959) in record time. In 1960 he retired to Grange Stud, Co. Fermoy where he stood until his death in July 1970 and became an extremely successful sire of jumpers. He stamped his stock with much of his own robust good looks and they quickly became sought after. Although he sired no outstandingly good horse, he was responsible for many good chasers including Even Keel (Benson and Hedges Chase, Sandown), Even Melody (Massey-Ferguson Gold Cup and Sun Ratings Chase) and the prolific winner, Even Dawn.

For the past three seasons he has been consistently high up in the lists of Leading Sires.

3rd	1975-76	winners of 63 races worth	£50,873
2nd	1976-77	„ „ 60 „ „	£48,293
2nd	1977-78	„ „ 37 „ „	£45,435

EVERETT, Lt. Robert (R.N.), D.S.O. (d.1942)

Bob Everett was born in Australia. He served in the Royal Navy and first rode as an amateur until 1928 when he turned professional. A daring, courageous and resolute rider, he achieved a great deal of success on far from high-class horses. He won the 1929 Grand National on Gregalach and the Irish Grand National (1934) on Poolgowan. In 1939 he returned to the Navy and served with the Fleet Air Arm until listed as missing, presumed dead, in February 1942. He was awarded a posthumous D.S.O. for his "bravery, skill and tenacity in many hazardous operational flights in the protection of shipping".

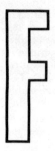

FAKENHAM (Group 5)

Fakenham, a small country meeting in Norfolk, has staged steeplechasing since 1839 and retains an old-fashioned, point-to-point style. There are no important races and many of the more valuable prizes are for Hunter Chases and Amateur Riders. The track is left-handed, square-shaped and about seven furlongs round. The sandy soil drains well and there is a watering system.

Best Times

Distance	Time	Horse-age-weight	Date
2m 120y H	3m 56.20	The Coral Horse 3-11-0	10-9-77
2m 200y H	3m 56.80	Saint Angelo 4-11-5	14-9-74
2m 6f 100y H	5m 25	Red Wolf 6-10-10	31-5-71
3m 35y H	6m 3.50	Grecian Fighter 5-9-8	12-11-77
2m 55y C	4m. 3	Jave River 8-11-8	10-9-77
2¼m C	5m 11.50	Guards Cake 8-10-8	9-10-70
2m 300y C	4m 26.40	Red Rally 6-12-5	31-5-71
3m C	6m 14.20	Nicky Brown 10-12-0	14-9-74

FAN

Bay mare, 1862, Volunteer—Miss Harkaway (Sir Tatton Sykes). Bred and owned by Mr Barber.

Principally due to the great regard which the racing public entertained for her owner's shrewdness, Fan was very much fancied for the 1867 Grand National in which she ran second, beaten 5l by Cortolvin (gave 10lb). Thereafter she immortalized herself by declining to proceed beyond the second fence in the succeeding three Nationals since when the obstacle in question has carried her name.

FARE TIME

Bay gelding, 1953, Thoroughfare—Septime (Caracalla II). Bred by the Hon. Mrs Macdonald-Buchanan.

Fare Time was bought as a yearling by Mr G. C. Judd for 490 guineas and won on the Flat at 3 years before turning his attention to hurdling. He won a total of nine hurdle races including 1959 Champion Hurdle (F. Winter), 13/2, by 4l, 1l, from Ivy Green (P. Taaffe) and Prudent King (T. P. Burns). The following year, he won the Otley Hurdle and was ante-post favourite for the Champion but struck into himself and had to be withdrawn. Fare Time was trained at Findon by Ryan Price. His owner, Mr G. C. Judd, owned another Champion Hurdler in Clair Soleil.

FARRELL, P. A. (b.1930)

An Irishman, Paddy Farrell was apprenticed to Paddy Sleator (1944-48). He came to England in 1953 to ride first jockey to W. A. Hall. Arthur Stephenson had second claim. He consistently finished high up in the Jockeys' Table, riding:

39 winners	1958-59	5th
39 winners	1959-60	6th
45 winners	1960-61	6th

His major victories included the Queen Elizabeth Chase (1956) on State Secret, the Mildmay Chase (1959) on The Liquidator, and the Emblem Chase (1953) on Stormhead. He was also third in the 1961 Grand National on O'Malley Point.

Tragically he broke his back when Border Flight fell at the Chair in the 1964 Grand National and is now paralysed from the waist down. It was as a result of this injury and a similar one to Tim Brookshaw that the Injured Jockeys Fund (*q.v.*) was founded.

FATHER O'FLYNN
Bay gelding, 1885, not in the General Stud Book, Retreat—Kathleen (Master Bagot).

A small horse, measuring barely 15.2 but, if Adrian Jones's portrait is to be relied upon, of rare quality with a fine shoulder and an excellent foreleg, Father O'Flynn won one Flat race and 17 chases including the 1892 Grand National, 10-5 (Capt. E. R. Owen), 20/1, by 20l, 2l, from Cloister, 12-3 (Mr J. C. Dormer) and Ilex, 12-7 (A. Nightingall).

Father O'Flynn, who was Owen's pick of six mounts for the big race, belonged to a succession of amateurs who invariably rode him themselves and in fact most of his victories were gained in Hunter chases. He won the National in the colours of Mr J. C. Wilson.

FAWCUS, Capt. John (1908-67)
'Jack' Fawcus came from an old Northumbrian family, long connected with horses. He started riding as an amateur and was Champion Amateur in 1931-32. He then turned professional and rode a good deal for Mr Rank with tremendous success. He won:

The Scottish Grand National (1934) Southern Hero; (1936) Southern Hero; (1939) Southern Hero
The Welsh Grand National (1934) Dream Ship; (1935) Lacatoi; (1937) Lacatoi; (1939) Lacatoi
The Imperial Cup (1937) Le Maestro
The National Hunt H'cap Chase (1937) Teme Willow
The Lancashire Chase (1935) Cooleen; (1939) Timber Wolf
The Coventry Cup (1936) Windermere Laddie
The Liverpool Hurdle (1932) Windermere Laddie; (1935) Beachway; (1937) Beachway; (1939) Aldine

During the war he was in a prison camp which crippled his health. An attempt to rebuild his career was not successful and he began training at Ashgill, Middleham. His best horse was Maj. 'Cuddie' Sterling-Stuart's Cool Customer who won 19 races, including the Princess Margaret Chase (twice) and the 1948 Great Yorkshire. He also won the Scottish Grand National (1958) with Game Field and the Wetherby H'cap Chase (1961) with Dandy Tim. He was killed in a car-crash in May 1967 on his way to Uttoxeter races.

FEES
The Rules of Racing state:
71. In Steeplechases and Hurdle races the fee to a jockey shall be £21.15 (plus V.A.T. where applicable).

In addition when a jockey is requested to leave home for the purpose of riding, the cost of travelling expenses and £1 per day for living may be charged to the owner or divided between the owner and whose request he left home. Every jockey sending in a charge for expenses at a meeting shall state at the same time what charge has been made to other owners for attending.
74. On each occasion when a jockey's fee becomes payable under Rule 70 or 71, or a fee in respect of an Amateur Rider becomes payable under Rule 72, the owner shall pay the sum of £2 to the Trustees of the Racehorse Owners Compensation Fund for Jockeys, for application under the Trusts thereof.

FIRING
Firing is a veterinary operation for the treatment of sprained or damaged tendons and involves the application of an electrically heated iron laid in bar fashion across the skin over the affected area. This contracts and strengthens the underlying tendons and if a sufficient period of rest can then be given, the horse can often be successfully trained again. Modern veterinary surgeons are continually seeking a more scientific treatment to supersede this somewhat barbarous but effective cure.

FLAME GUN
Chestnut gelding, 1951, Flamenco—Lady Mustang (Mustang). Bred in Ireland by Mr P. Quinlan.

A member of a very distinguished Irish jumping family whose dam was a granddaughter of the dam of Kellsboro' Jack, Flame Gun won six hurdle races and 11 chases including the Champion Novices Chase, Manchester (1959) and the Cotswold Chase, N.H. Meeting (1959). Owned by Mr (later Sir) Michael Sobell, he was a brilliant two miler and a

Sandown specialist whose spectacular, if not always accurate, jumping made him very popular. A somewhat delicate horse who suffered from very thin soles, he was handled with much perception by Ivor Herbert.

FLETCHER, B. (b.1948)

An extremely successful North Country jockey, Brian Fletcher was apprenticed to Denys Smith for whom he won the 1968 Grand National on Red Alligator when only 19. He later won the National twice more (1973 and 1974) on Red Rum (*q.v.*) thus becoming the second jockey this century to achieve a hat-trick.

A quiet, sensitive horseman, he rode with great coolness, well demonstrated in his first victory on Red Rum when he made up a conservative 100 yards over the last three fences, never giving up or losing his rhythm in a situation many men would have regarded as hopeless. He also won several good races on the smart hurdler, Dondieu, including the Scottish Champion Hurdle (1971), and the Fighting Fifth Hurdle (1972). His best season to date was 1967-68 when he rode 77 winners and came second to Josh Gifford in the Jockey Championship. As a result of repeated head injuries, Brian Fletcher retired in 1976 on medical advice.

FLOOD, Francis

An Irish trainer and a former leading amateur rider, Francis Flood was for some time attached to the Grange Con establishment of Paddy Sleator (*q.v.*) He now trains next door and his biggest successes to date include:

> The Cheltenham Gold Cup (1972) Glencaraig Lady
> The S.G.B. Chase (1970) Glencaraig Lady
> The Irish Grand National (1970) Garoupe
> The Alpen Trophy Chase (1977) Siberian Sun

FLYINGBOLT

Chestnut gelding, 1959, Airborne —Eastlock (Easton). Bred in Ireland by Mr R. E. Way.

A tall, angular horse of a rather washy chestnut colour, Flyingbolt made such an auspicious start to his career that he was seriously compared to Arkle from whose stable he came. After winning two

bumpers, Mrs T. G. Wilkinson's youngster won four hurdle races, including his division of the Gloucester Hurdle (N.H. Meeting) without tasting defeat. During the next two seasons he won eleven chases including the National Hunt Two-Mile Champion Chase (N.H. Meeting) by 15 lengths and the Irish Grand National (1966) with 12-7. He was also third in the Champion Hurdle. Thereafter training difficulties beset him. He came to England and though both Ken Oliver and Roddy Armytage tried hard to restore his health, he never recaptured his former brilliance and won only one more chase.

FOINAVON

Brown gelding, 1958, Vulgan—Ecilace (Interlace). Bred by Mr T. H. Ryan.

As a young horse owned by the Duchess of Westminster, trained by Tom Dreaper and the winner of two novice chases in Ireland, Foinavon's future seemed bright but he failed to live up to his promise. He was weeded out of the classy Greenogue establishment and came to England to be trained by John Kempton, where nothing much was heard of him until March 1967 when fame was thrust upon him in totally unforeseen circumstances.

As the Grand National field went down to the 23rd fence, Foinavon, who had made a bad mistake at Becher's, was practically tailed off, which enabled him to avoid the wholesale carnage caused by the riderless Popham Down swerving across the fence. Rider John Buckingham steered smartly to the right and nipped through on the rails. Not until he had completed several more fences did he appreciate that there was no-one in front of him and that he and Foinavon had in fact been the only pair to achieve the 23rd at the first attempt. Foinavon, 10-0, (J. Buckingham), 100/1, kept going and at the line had 15l, 3l, to spare over Honey End, 10-4 (J. Gifford) and Red Alligator, 10-0 (B. Fletcher). Neither owner nor trainer was present to see his triumph. John Kempton watched in stunned disbelief at Worcester Races, whither he had gone to saddle and ride a novice hurdler while his father did duty for the stable's Liverpool long-shot.

Foinavon won two more races, one in curiously similar circumstances at Uttoxeter in October 1968. He was owned by Mr Cyril Watkyns.

FOLKESTONE (Group 4)

Steeplechasing is recorded at Folkestone in 1849 and 1870 but did not become a permanent feature until 1898. A popular seaside track, right-handed and approximately one mile, three furlongs round, it calls for handiness and adaptability. The principal race is the Gay Record Challenge Trophy H'cap Chase in March (2m, 3f, £1,606).

Best Times

Distance	Time	Horse-age-weight	Date
2m 200y H	4m 2.40	Omar Straits 6-10-5	11-9-72
2½m H	4m 43	Coriolis 7-10-10	17-9-62
2m 50y C	3m 59.50	Regal Arch 8-11-3	30-4-62
2m 100y C	4m 8.40	Chief of Staff 9-10-0	19-3-73
2m 3f C	4m 48.60	Prince Gin 10-10-13	1-5-67
3m C	5m 58.70	Smilbo Smaggins 11-11-7	26-4-76
3m 600y C	6m 59-50	Brilliant Knight 10-12-0	20-3-72

FONTWELL PARK (Group 3)

Fontwell is an attractive, undulating figure-of-eight course in a pretty park setting between Chichester and Arundel. The track is only a mile round and speed and handiness are essential. It is a course for specialists, one of whom, Certain Justice, has a chase named after him. The course was built in 1924 and Queen Elizabeth the Queen Mother had her first winner there in 1948 with Monave'en (owned jointly with the then Princess Elizabeth). Although it cannot claim to be an important course, the general level of prize money is quite good and the racing is of a fair order. The principal race is the National Spirit Trophy Pattern Hurdle in February (2m 1f, £4,206).

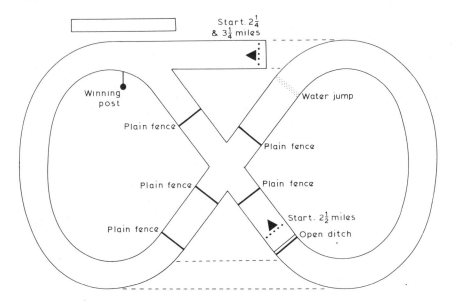

Best Times

Distance	Time	Horse-age-weight	Date
2m 1f H	3m 54.90	Darjeeling Boy 4-10-10	19-8-71
2m 6f H	5m 13.40	Hardivim 5-10-0	12-8-75
2¼m C	4m 14-6	Major Owen 9-10-5	29-5-78
2½m C	4m 41-30	Mighty Marine 7-10-13	11-8-76
3¼m C	6m 12.80	Barleycroft 7-11-10	3-10-62

FORBRA

Black or brown gelding, 1925, Foresight—Thymbra (Rochester). Bred by Mr H. Glover.

Forbra, one of the finest jumpers of his day, was known as the horse that could not fall. He won three hurdle races and four chases including the Coventry Chase, Kempton (1933) and the 1932 Grand National, 10-7 (J. Hamey), 50/1, by 3l, a bad third, from Egremont, 10-7 (Mr E. Paget) and Shaun Goilin, 12-4 (D. Williams). He was also sixth in the 1933 National and fourth in 1934. Owned by Mr E. Parsonage, ex-chorister, ex-book-maker and town-councillor of Ludlow, he was trained at Kinnersley by Tom Rimell whose son Fred helped in his preparation.

Forbra was only seven when he won the National, unusually young in the twentieth century. He had in fact been earmarked for the novice Stanley Chase but rendered himself ineligible by winning unexpectedly at Taunton, which resulted in a bolder policy being adopted.

Forbra broke a leg and had to be destroyed at Newbury in January 1935.

FORD, James John (b.1910)

Jim Ford rode in point-to-points and as an amateur before the war. He also broke in and dealt in young horses. In 1948 he took out a licence to train at Chitterne, Wiltshire. His best winner was Gay Donald, hero of the 1955 Cheltenham Gold Cup, the longest-priced winner of the race and one of the easiest, who sadly broke down irreparably not long afterwards. A race is named after him at Wincanton.

FORESTATION

Bay gelding, 1938, Felicitation—Woodciss (Gainsborough). Bred by Sir Woodman Burbidge.

A classically bred horse, Forestation won on the Flat at three and four years before going to win seven hurdle races including the 1942 Champion Hurdle (R. Smyth), 10/1, by 3l, 3l, from Anarchist (T. Isaac) and Southport (F. Rickaby). His victory was a triumph for the Smyth family for he was owned and trained by Ron's uncle, Victor.

FOREST KING

Bay gelding, 1969, not in the General Stud Book, Rubor—Workington Wanderer (All Red). Bred by Mr K. Tuer.

An immensely tough, rather plain but workmanlike gelding. Forest King is trained in a distinctly unorthodox fashion in the fells above Penrith by his owner, permit-holder Ken Hogg, who bought him from his breeder for £125 as a yearling. Forest King, who is a full-brother to two winning hurdlers, is only debarred from the Stud Book by a technicality. Both his sire and dam and full-brothers are registered but apparently no returns were made for him.

To date he has won five hurdle races and eleven chases including the Eider Chase, Newcastle (1976), the Northern Trophy Handicap, Newcastle (1976) and the Haydock National Trial (1976). He ran fifth in the 1977 Grand National.

FORSTER, Timothy Arthur (b.1934)

Tim Forster was a regular Army officer and served with the 11th Hussars from 1954-60. On demobilization he went as a pupil to crack Newmarket trainer Geoffrey Brooke and later assisted Derrick Candy. He took out a licence in 1962 and now controls a medium-sized stable of jumpers at Letcombe Regis, a little village on the edge of the Berkshire Downs.

His first good horse was the doughty hunter-chaser, Baulking Green (q.v.), who won 22 chases including the United Hunts no less than four times. Other good winners include Rueil, Grand Military Gold Cup (1965), Mr Wonderful, Fred Withington Chase (1965), Denys Adventure, Arkle Chase (1973), Royal Marshal II, King George VI Chase (1976) and Hennessy Cognac Gold Cup (1974) and that horse's half-brother Well To Do, left to him in the will of Mrs Heather Summer whose early death from cancer was a terrible blow to her many friends, winner of the 1972 Grand National.

This last victory made Forster Leading Trainer 1971-72 (and fourth in the Owners' list) with 50 races worth £49,436. He is the first owner-trainer to win the National since the war. He also produced the winning jockey, Graham Thorner, the season's champion, who had come to Letcombe Regis as a 15-year-old schoolboy.

FORTINA

Chestnut horse, 1941, Bred in France.

		Bruleur
	Ksar	
		Kizil Kourgan
Formor		
		Clarissimus
	Formose	
Fortina		Terre Neuve
		Sans Souci II
	La Farina	
		Malatesta
Bertina		
		Gouvernant
	Thea	
		Theorie

The only entire, and one of only four six-year-olds to win the Cheltenham Gold Cup, Fortina came to England in 1946, having won a hurdle race and four chases in his native France, and won his only two starts, namely the Lancashire Chase, Manchester, with top-weight and the 1947 Cheltenham Gold Cup (Mr R. Black), 8/1, by 10l, 6l, from Happy Home (D. Moore) and Prince Blackthorn (R. Turnell).

He was owned by Lord Grimthorpe and trained by Hector Christie, whose head-lad Charlie Mallon was to turn out another Gold Cup winner in Linwell. Fortina was stood by the Magniers at the Grange Stud, Fermoy in Co. Cork and after a shaky start established himself as one of the most influential sires of the century. Never leading sire, he was second on seven occasions:

1960-61	winners of 50	races worth			£22,586
1961-62	„ „ 43	„	„		£12,235
1962-63	„ „ 28	„	„		£14,013
1964-65	„ „ 46½	„	„		£25,994
1966-67	„ „ 49	„	„		£21,541
1967-68	„ „ 42	„	„		£22,984
1971-72	„ „ 31	„	„		£29,357

By the end of 1978 he had sired the winners of 666 races worth £297,102. He was responsible for the winners of two Gold Cups – Fort Leney (1968), and Glencaraig Lady (1972); also for four Irish Nationals – Olympia (1960), Fortria (1961), Last Link (1963) and Splash (1965); for two American Nationals – Bampton Castle (1966 and 1968); for one Scottish National – Brasher (1965); and for a Welsh National – Forty Secrets (1962).

Fortina was put down in May 1968 when suffering from severe arthritis of the knees.

FORT DEVON
Chestnut gelding, 1966, Fortina—Devoncourt (Devonian). Bred by Mr R. Burke.

In recent years several horses have crossed the Atlantic from the U.S.A., to make their mark in British steeplechasing but few have had a more curious history than Mr C. Bird junior's Fort Devon, who like many a slow-maturing, chasing-bred youngster, began his career over fences in point-to-points. Far from showing any marked aptitude he failed to win in five outings at six years and was described by Messrs. Sale and Mackenzie, in their splendidly forthright annual *Point-to-Pointers*, as having "plodded round" in such relatively undistinguished contests as the Oxford University Maiden Race.

He was therefore sold and went to the U.S.A. where he spent several seasons hunting over the formidable timber fences of the South. He then reverted to steeplechasing and won six races, including the Maryland Hunt Cup (1976) and the Butler Grand National.

He returned to England in 1976 to the Saxon House yard of Fulke Walwyn and since then has won four chases, including the Yellow Pages Pattern Chase (1978). He also ran Royal Marshal II to ½ length in the 1976 King George VI Chase and was second (beaten a neck) to Bachelor's Hall (rec. 14lbs) in the 1977 Hennessy Gold Cup. He started favourite for the postponed 1978 Cheltenham Gold Cup but ran disappointingly. He was afterwards said to have broken a blood vessel.

FORT LENEY
Bay gelding, 1958, Fortina—Leney Princess (Roi d'Egypte). Bred by Colonel Sir John Thomson.

The first produce of the famous maré Leney Princess (q.v.), Fort Leney was raced by his breeder, Colonel Sir John Thomson, and trained in Ireland by Tom Dreaper. In a career that spanned five seasons he won a bumper, a hurdle race and 16 chases including the Leopardstown Chase, 1967 and the Cheltenham Gold Cup, 1968 (P. Taaffe), 11/2, by a neck, 11, from The Laird (J. King) and Stalbridge Colonist (T. Biddlecombe).

Among his near misses, he was beaten by half a length by Buona Notte in the first Tote Champion Novices, N.H. Meeting (1964) and carried 12-0 into second place in the 1968 Whitbread Gold Cup.

FORTRIA

Bay gelding, 1952, Fortina—Senria (Sun Yat-sen). Bred by Mr A. Craigie.

A full-brother to the dual N.H. Handicap Chase winner Sentina, Fortria was a very fast, tough horse who raced for seven seasons, winning two hurdle races and 18 chases. Although he won an Irish National, Fairyhouse (1961) and was twice second in the Gold Cup (to Mandarin in 1962 and to Mill House in 1963) he was at his best over two miles and his successes include the Cotswold Chase, N.H. Meeting (1958), the National Hunt Two Mile Champion Chase, N.H. Meeting (1961) and the Mackeson Gold Cup, Cheltenham (1960 and 1962).

Fortria was owned by Mr George Ansley and trained at Greenogue, Co. Dublin, by Tom Dreaper. He was the first of many top class jumpers sired by the Cheltenham Gold Cup winner, Fortina (q.v.).

FOSTER, Eric

A vigorous, unstylish but effective rider, Eric Foster was Champion Jockey in 1925. His success was short-lived and his best victory was the 1924 Scottish Grand National on Royal Chancellor.

FOULKES, Charles William (b.1932)

A hunting farmer from Hilton in Derbyshire, Bill Foulkes has ridden as an amateur and in point-to-points with great success for many years and for a while trained under permit. He was Champion Amateur in 1971-72 riding 25 winners and his victories include the Liverpool Foxhunter (1962) on Dominion, the Kim Muir Chase (1973) on Hinterland and the Town of Warwick Champion Hunters Chase on Bear's Slipper (1974). This last success did not come out of turn for in 1973 he and Bear's Slipper met with two luckless reverses. They won the Cheltenham Foxhunters after a desperate struggle with John Oaksey on Bullock's Horn (q.v.) only to lose the race in the Stewards' room, and they also lost the valuable Midlands Grand National in

the last stride by a head to Rip's Lyric. Colours: red and green quartered, black cap.

FOUR TEN

Bay gelding, 1946, Blunderbuss—Undue Praise (Felicitation). Bred by Mr A. Strange.

Point-to-pointing has thrown up several National winners but until 1954 no Gold Cup winner. The precedent established by Mr A. Strange's slashing, home-bred Four Ten was however swiftly followed by Limber Hill (1956), Linwell (1957), Woodland Venture (1967) and The Dikler (1973).

Bred in Dorset where he won four point-to-points, Four Ten was sent to the Cheltenham trainer John Roberts for his N.H. career which spanned seven seasons and brought him 18 victories, all in chases. Besides the Gold Cup, 100/6 (T. Cusack), 41, the same, from Mariner's Log (P. Taaffe) and Hallowe'en (G. Slack), Four Ten won the N.H. Handicap Chase, N.H. Meeting (1953), the Charlton Park Handicap Chase, Cheltenham (1953), the Golden Miller Chase, Cheltenham (1956) and the Walter Hyde Chase, Kempton (1956).

A resolute galloper and jumper, Four Ten was particularly well suited to heavy ground.

FRANCIS, Richard Stuart (b.1920)

A member of a prominent showing-dealing family, Dick Francis was from the first a beautiful horseman and would have made a success of whatever branch of equestrianism he had chosen.

After serving in the R.A.F. as a pilot from 1940-45, he went to that leading producer of National Hunt jockeys, George Owen, and rode as an amateur with some success.

He turned professional in 1948 and opportunities quickly came his way. He was retained by Lord Bicester, as second jockey to Martin Molony, which gave him the ride on some of the best chasers in England. He won the King VI Chase on Finnure (1949) and was second in the 1949 Grand National on Roimond. He won the Welsh Grand National twice, in 1949 on Fighting Line and in 1956 on that popular character Crudwell, with whom he got on better than anybody else. In 1953-54 he was Champion Jockey riding 76 winners.

In 1953 he was retained by Peter

Cazalet which gave him the opportunity of riding for H.M. Queen Elizabeth the Queen Mother, and with it the tragedy of his career. He was leading in the 1956 Grand National on the Queen Mother's Devon Loch when 50 yards from the post the horse, well clear, undistressed and full of running, for reasons never satisfactorily explained, spread-eagled himself and slid to the floor, leaving E.S.B. to win at his leisure.

Francis retired in 1957 and since then has made a considerable name for himself as a writer. He has written a modest and articulate autobiography, a popular weekly column for the *Sunday Express* and a string of highly successful thrillers which have won numerous awards and some of which are being filmed.

FRANCOME, John (b.1952)

The son of a Swindon building contractor, John Francome came into racing via the Pony Club and show-jumping. Despite coming from a non-horsey family, he quickly displayed an inborn aptitude for horses. He was a member of the V.W.H. Pony Club team that reached the finals of the Prince Philip Cup in 1963 and of the winning British Team at the Junior European Championships, St Moritz, 1970.

By this time he had an introduction to Fred Winter who, although doubtful about the size of his hands and feet which suggested future weight problems, was impressed by his horsemanship and agreed to give him a trial. The fine tuition of Winter and his jockey, Richard Pitman, grafted on to his own innate abilities, swiftly bore fruit and John Francome was immediately successful. In 1974-75 he rode 70 winners, finishing second to Tommy Stack in the Jockeys' Championship and on the retirement of Richard Pitman in the spring of 1975, he was given the plum job of first jockey to Fred Winter. At the end of his first season in this capacity he was Champion Jockey having 96 winners.

His principal successes have been:

The Piper Champagne Cheltenham Gold Cup (1978) Midnight Court
The Sun Alliance Chase, N.H. Meeting, (April 1975) Pengrail
The Embassy Premier Chase, Haydock (1976) Floating Pound; (1978) The Dealer
The Panama Cigar Hurdle Final, Chepstow (1975) Border Incident

The Kirk and Kirk Hurdle, Ascot (1974) Lanzarote
The Victor Ludorum Hurdle, Haydock, (1977) Rathconrath

FREDDIE

Brown gelding, 1957, registered in Miss Prior's Half-Bred Book, Steel Chip —Nell (Soldado). Bred in Ireland by Miss Ringwood.

The story of Freddie is a fairy-tale that did not quite come true. The career of the handsome, dark-brown horse with the distinctive crooked blaze epitomized the unique character of British steeple-chasing. Reared in the Buccleugh country on the Scottish Borders, Freddie underwent his early education in the hunting field and first appeared on a racecourse as a five-year-old in his Hunt Race. He finished second. Next season he went through one point-to-point and four Hunter Chases unbeaten and indeed unextended. By the time he was seven he was reckoned near invincible in hunter company and after hacking up in three confined events including the Foxhunter, N.H. Meeting (1964) he was upgraded to handicaps. Thrown in the deep end he was set to carry top-weight in the 1964 Scottish Grand National and failed most gallantly by only ½l to concede 22lb to Popham Down.

Thereafter he confined his activities to steeplechasing proper although continuing to be trained at home by his owner, Mr R. R. Tweedie. In all he won seven handicap chases including the Mildmay Memorial, Sandown (1965), the Great Yorkshire, Doncaster (1966) and the Gallagher Gold Cup, Sandown (1966), but he is best remembered for his heroic failure in the 1965 Grand National when, after a titanic struggle, he was beaten ¾l by Jay Trump (rec. 5lb). He was also second in 1966, this time beaten 20l by Anglo (rec. 21lb). Freddie was ridden in point-to-points and Hunter Chases by Mr Alan Mactaggart and afterwards by Pat McCarron.

He was subject of a book by Vian Smith, *A Horse called Freddie*.

FREEBOOTER

Bay gelding, 1941, Steel-point—Proud Fury (Free from Pride). Bred in Co. Waterford by Mr W. F. Phelan.

An immensely strong, impeccably designed horse, Freebooter was originally bought by Dan Moore as an unbroken three-year-old for 620 guineas. After winning two bumpers he was sold to Mrs Lurline Brotherton for 3000 guineas and was henceforth trained in Yorkshire by Bobby Renton. Freebooter was perhaps the best jumper of Liverpool's fences since the war. In a career that spanned eight seasons, he won a hurdle race and 17 chases including the Great Yorkshire, Doncaster (1950), the Becher Chase, Liverpool (1953), the Champion Chase, Liverpool (1949), the Grand Sefton, Liverpool (1949 and 1951) and the 1950 Grand National, 11-11 (J. Power), 10/1 joint-favourite, 15l, 10l, from Wot No Sun, 11-8 (A. P. Thompson) and Acthon Major, 11-2 (R. O'Ryan).

Although almost infallible at Liverpool, Freebooter never really fathomed the stiff birch fences and shifting gradients of Cheltenham and his record there was deplorable – in fact he rarely completed the course. He must not, though, be regarded solely as a Liverpool horse for he won decent chases at Birmingham, Hurst Park, Wetherby and Doncaster.

Throughout most of his career Freebooter was associated with Jimmy Power. However, in his last outing in the autumn of 1953 when 12 years old, he went out for the Becher Chase partnered by George Slack who had not yet won over the big fences. Bobby Renton opined that Freebooter would put that right and so it proved. Bringing the old horse in to a tumultuous reception, Slack announced that he had just had a conducted tour round Aintree.

FREE FARE
Chestnut gelding, 1928, Werwolf—Bachelor's Fare (Tredennis). Bred by Mr A. Lowry.

A very consistent horse, equally at home on the Flat and over hurdles, Free Fare kept his form over a remarkably long period. Owned by Mr B. Warner, he was trained at Saxon House, Lambourn, by Ted Gwilt and usually ridden by G. Pellerin.

Free Fare won a total of 11 races on the Flat, the most important being the Manchester November Handicap (1935), and 12 hurdle races including the Liverpool Hurdle (1933) and the 1937 Champion Hurdle, N.H. meeting (G. Pellerin), 2/1f, 2l, short head, from Our Hope (Capt. R. Harding) and Menton (S.

Ingham). He also ran second to Victor Norman in 1936.

FREEMAN, Arthur Robert (b.1926)
A nephew of the famous Pytchley huntsman, Frank Freeman, Arthur Freeman was apprenticed to George Lambton. After the war, he was retained by Peter Cazalet's stable and rode a number of winners for H.M. Queen Elizabeth the Queen Mother. He was associated with the gallant, little Lochroe, on whom he won the King George VI Chase (1958), and won the 1958 Grand National on Mr What by 30l, despite putting up 6lb overweight.

He finished well up the Jockeys' Table on three occasions:

1956-57	35 winners	5th
1957-58	53 winners	3rd
1958-59	49 winners	3rd

Increasing weight and a bad skull fracture forced him to give up and for a while he trained at Newmarket with some success, but sadly his health has been poor of recent years.

FREETRADER
Bay or brown horse, 1849, The Sea—Miss Cobden (Stockport). Bred by Mr H. B. Powell.

Freetrader, one of 15 entires to win the National, was owned by Mr W. Barnett and ridden at Aintree by George Stevens for whom he provided the first of five victories. Formerly a fair horse on the Flat, he won twice and was thought good enough to run at Royal Ascot. Freetrader also won over hurdles before turning his attention to steeplechasing. In 1855 he ran second to Wanderer in the Grand National while in 1856 he went one better, 9-6 (G. Stevens), 25/1, winning ½l, the same, from Minerva, 9-10 (Sly, jun.) and Minos, 9-4 (R. James).

FRENCHMAN'S COVE
Chestnut gelding, 1955, Airborne—Frenchman's Creek (Mieuxcé). Bred by The Snailwell Stud.

A classy horse both in pedigree and appearance, Frenchman's Cove was owned by Mr Stanhope Joel and trained at Newmarket by Harry Thomson-Jones. In all he won 15 races including the Whitbread Gold Cup, Sandown (1962) and the King George VI Chase, Kempton (1964). He was also fourth in the

1961 Gold Cup after making most of the running and was thought to have been going particularly well when being brought down at the nineteenth fence in the 1962 Grand National. A bold, front-running horse and spectacular jumper, Frenchman's Cove was an exciting horse to watch and had many followers despite several disappointing displays. Frenchman's Cove did not race after 1966 and spent his retirement hunting in Warwickshire.

FRIGATE

Bay mare, 1878, Gunboat—Fair Maid of Kent (Gladiateur). Bred by Mr M. Maher.

A small mare standing barely 15.3 and all wire and whipcord, Frigate can have had few equals for gameness, consistency and long service. Trained at Eyrefield Lodge, the Curragh, by H. E. Linde, she won the Conyngham Cup as a five-year-old and went on to win two chases round Liverpool and run second to Voluptuary in the Grand National aged six. She finished second twice more in the National, to Roquefort in 1885 and, desperately unluckily, to Playfair in 1888 after being practically knocked off the racecourse by the broken-down Usna, before her turn finally came in 1889. Carrying 11-4 (Mr T. Beasley), 8/1, she won by 1l, a bad third, from Why Not, 11-5 (Mr C. Cunningham) and M.P., 10-9 (A. Nightingall).

FURLONG, Lt.-Cdr. Francis, R.N.V.R. (1910-44)

A member of a sporting Irish family settled in Leicestershire, Frank Furlong was commissioned into the 9th Lancers and, living up to the traditions of the regiment that produced David Campbell (*q.v.*) and Fulke Walwyn (*q.v.*), became a fine amateur rider. Riding horses owned and trained by his father, many of them home-bred, he won the National Hunt Chase (1932) on Robin-a-Tiptoe, was second in the 1933 Grand National on Really True and won the 1935 Grand National on Reynoldstown. He became too heavy to continue riding and the following year Reynoldstown was ridden by his friend and brother officer, Fulke Walwyn.

In World War II he joined the Fleet Air Arm. After experiencing the torpedoing of the *Bismarck* and surviving 72 hours in a rubber dinghy after an amphibian bomber had crashed into the Atlantic, south of Iceland, he crashed a damaged light aircraft on Salisbury Plain when returning from a reconnaisance flight and was killed.

FURLONG, Maj. Noel Charles Bell (d.1963)

The Furlongs came from Fermoy, Co. Cork, and had been connected with hunting and chasing for years. They came to England during the troubles and settled at Skeffington Hall, Leicestershire. Noel Furlong trained, with great success, horses owned, and some of them bred, by himself and ridden by his son Frank (*q.v.*) until the latter became too heavy.

His victories included:

The National Hunt Chase (1932) Robin-a-Tiptoe: (1939) Litigant
The Grand National (1935) Reynoldstown: (1936) Reynoldstown

A very popular man he generated tremendous enthusiasm and possessed an infectious sense of humour. He was elected to the N.H. Committee in 1952. Colours: straw, pale blue sleeves and cap.

GALLOWAY BRAES
Brown gelding, 1945, Norwest—Isola (Irish Trout). Bred in Ireland by Mr M. McGuinness.

A raking, big dark-brown horse, who knew only one way of running – in front – and whose attitude to fencing bordered on the foolhardy, Galloway Braes won a hurdle race and 18 chases and was probably the most popular chaser on Park tracks during the 'fifties.

Owned by Lady Orde, trained by Alec Kilpatrick and usually ridden by Bert Morrow, whose courage and limpet-like qualities perfectly complemented his own reckless talents, Galloway Braes won the Queen Elizabeth Chase, Hurst Park (1953 and 1954) and the King George VI Chase, Kempton (1953) in record time carrying 12-6. He was also twice second in the King George in 1954 and 1955, in the latter of which he was beaten just a neck by the Gold Cup winner Limber Hill (rec. 4lb) after jockey Fred Winter had made a most uncharacteristic error of judgement and dropped his hands halfway up the run-in. Galloway Braes was also very successful at Cheltenham where he won the Holman Cup twice, the Charlton Park Handicap Chase and was third in the 1953 Gold Cup. In the end the fences claimed him, for he had to be destroyed after falling in the 1956 King George VI Chase, thus making a black Boxing Day for his many supporters.

GAMECOCK
Bay gelding, 1879, registered Miss Prior's Half-Bred Stud Book, Revolver—Lightfoot (Gamekeeper).

A supremely tough, game, consistent horse, a great stayer and a fine jumper, particularly round Aintree, Gamecock raced for seven seasons and won 28 chases including nearly every important race in the Calendar. He won the Great Sandown Chase (1885), the Grand International, Sandown (1886), the Great Metropolitan Chase, Croydon (1889), the Hampton Court Chase with 13-5 at the inaugural Hurst Park meeting (1890), the Champion Chase, Liverpool, twice, in 1887 with 12-12 and in 1890 with 12-13, and the 1887 Grand National, 11-0 (W. Daniells), 20/1, by 3l, a bad third from Savoyard, 10-13 (T. Skelton) and Johnny Longtail, 10-6 (Childs). Gamecock who was owned by Mr E. Jay, was a great favourite in the Bishop's Sutton yard of Arthur Yates where he was trained for most of his career. He had a two-mile chase named after him at the Kempton March Meeting.

GATLAND, James (b.1846)
James Gatland was born near Alfriston, Sussex. He was assistant to William King and later trained on his own account. His biggest success was the 1895 Grand National with Wild Man from Borneo. He also won the Lancashire Chase (1892) with Roman Oak, and handled the prolific hunter/Flat-race-winning mare, Lady Villikins, grandam of My Prince. Roddy Owen rode a good deal for the stable and got many horses into the yard.

GATWICK
The Sussex racecourse, on the site of the present airport, was built on land bought in 1890 from Mr John Farlow by a group headed by George Venali, racecourse judge, Charles Edward Robinson and others of the Croydon executive. The principal races from Croydon, namely the Grand Metropolitan Chase, the National Hurdle and the International Hurdle, were transferred and the first meeting was held in December 1891.

It was an immediate success. The *Victoria County History* described Gatwick as "in many respects the best enclosed meeting in the kingdom. It possesses a noble course, a fine range of stands, a spacious club enclosure and a very large paddock. No fault can be found with the added money or with the management". The writer omitted to mention the station with a special platform for unloading horses, the free stabling for 120 horses, the excellent accommodation for lads, the racecourse hospital and garage repair pit.

The course, reckoned the severest outside Liverpool, was also popular. It was well protected with peat and moss litter and, from the start, good horses were attracted. Manifesto, Poethlyn and Golden Miller were among the great horses that ran there.

It was one of the few courses to keep going during World War I and for three years staged a substitute Grand National, run over 4½ miles with specially reconstructed fences supervised by Frank Hartigan, Robert Gore, Aubrey Hastings, Percy Whitaker and Fred Withington.

Results:

1916	Vermouth	J. Reardon
1917	Ballymacad	E. Driscoll
1918	Poethlyn	E. Piggott

From 1930 a valuable Grand National Trial was run at the March meeting, of which the best winners were Southern Hero (1934) and Bogskar (1940).

In 1941, Gatwick was requisitioned by the Air Ministry who in 1946 passed it to the Ministry of Civil Aviation. In 1955 the land was sold to the Ministry and the company was wound up, and in 1958 the International Airport opened.

GAY DONALD

Bay gelding, 1946, Gay Light—Pas de Quatre (Royal Dancer). Bred by Mr Harry Frank.

Gay Donald, a big strong gelding, best described as workmanlike, was one of the only pair of half-brothers to win the Cheltenham Gold Cup which he did in 1955 (Pas Seul completed the double in 1960). Bought cheaply as an unbroken four-year-old by the Cholderton trainer, Jim Ford, on behalf of Mr P. J. Burt, Gay Donald won a total of 13 chases including the 1955 Gold Cup (A. Grantham), 33/1, by 10l, 8l, from Hallowe'en (F. Winter) and Four Ten (T. Cusack). His victory, achieved in storming fashion on soft, slippery ground, was widely regarded as a fluke but his detractors were obliged to eat large portions of humble pie when nine days later he gave weight and a beating to Mont Tremblant over three miles round Sandown. *See also* Pas de Quatre.

GAY LAD

Bay gelding, 1834, not in the General Stud Book, by Brutandorf.

Reliable information about Gay Lad, the 1842 Grand National winner, is extremely hard to come by. He was owned by John Elmore, whose Lottery also ran in the race, and ridden by Tom Olliver,

for whom he provided the first three winners. The race was still a level-weights affair and Gay Lad, who was returned at 7/1 won by 5l, from Seventy-Four (Powell) and Peter Simple (Mr Hunter). Six days after his Aintree victory Gay Lad, who must have had a constitution of an ox, won a valuable race at Oxford carrying 13-1 beating Roderic Random (rec. 18lb) by a head. Later that season he won at Nottingham and Chelmsford. He never ran in the National again but won several minor races for Mr Davey to whom he was sold.

GAY SPARTAN

Bay gelding, 1971, Spartan General —Copper Lace (Copernicus). Bred by Mrs B. Glendinning.

Gay Spartan, a strongly-built, imposing gelding typical of his sire has proved a most useful and resolute gelding. To date he has won a bumper, two hurdle races and eight steeplechases including the Sun Alliance Chase, N.H. Meeting (1977), the Tote Northern Chase, Haydock (1978) and the Wetherby H'cap Chase (1978). Like all the products of the Dickinson stable, Gay Spartan, who is owned by Mr M. Armstrong, is a superb jumper. He is particularly suited by soft ground.

GAY TRIP

Bay gelding, 1962, Vulgan—Turkish Tourist (Turkhan). Bred by Mr F. D. Farmer.

Small but very deep, beautifully proportioned and as versatile as he was tough, Gay Trip won one Flat race, two hurdles and eight chases including the Heinz Chase, Ascot (1968), the Mackeson Gold Cup, Cheltenham (1969 and 1971) and the 1970 Grand National, 11-5 (P. Taaffe), 15/1, by 20l, ½l, from Vulture, 10-0 (S. Barker) and Miss Hunter, 10-0 (F. Shortt). In 1972 he took the honours if not the prize when running second, beaten 2l, by Well To Do (rec. 22lb).

In his early days when trained in Ireland by Dan Moore, Gay Trip was regarded as a two-mile specialist and indeed apart from his National victory, he never won over more than 2½ miles. He was by no means the first horse whose ability to jump found him an extra two miles at Aintree. Gay Trip was prepared for the National by Fred Rimell and won in the colours of Mr A. J. Chambers. An exuberant little horse, he was exciting to watch and a great favourite with the racing public.

GIBSON, Maj. W. D. (b.1925)

David Gibson was educated at Harrow and served with the Welsh Guards, from 1944-57. During that time he rode successfully in point-to-points and as an amateur. He won the Grand Military Gold Cup four times, in 1950, 1951 and 1952 on Klaxton and in 1956 on Cottage Lace. He was elected to the National Hunt Committee in 1959 and served as a Steward from 1963-66. From 1969-70 he was Deputy Senior Steward of the Turf Board. Colours: black, with red, white and blue sash and cap.

GIFFORD, Joshua Thomas (b.1941)

Josh Gifford is the son of a Fitzwilliam farmer who was himself a fine point-to-point rider. He was apprenticed to Cliff Beechener and later to Sam Armstrong and rode 51 winners on the Flat including the Chester Cup and the Irish Lincolnshire Handicap. However, he grew too heavy and before the end of his apprenticeship was riding over jumps for Ryan Price as number two to Fred Winter. He rode his first winner in 1959 and when Winter retired, took over as first jockey for the powerful Findon stable.

He was Champion Jockey four times:

1962-63	70 winners
1963-64	94 winners
1966-67	122 winners (then a record)
1967-68	82 winners

He won the Schweppes Gold Trophy four times in five years; Rosyth (1963 and 1964), Le Vermontois (1966) and Hill House (1967).

He was suspended for a month after Rosyth's second victory.

His other good victories include:

The Mackeson Gold Cup (1967) Charlie Worcester
The Tote Champion Novices (1967) Border Jet
The Triumph Hurdle (1962) Beaver II
The Whitbread Gold Cup (1969) Larbawn
The Welsh Grand National (1962) Forty Secrets

In 1970 he took out a licence to train under N.H. Rules using one of his former employer's yards at Findon. Success came quickly to his stable and among the good races it has won are:

The Daily Express Triumph Hurdle (1973) Moonlight Bay
The Victor Ludorum Hurdle (1973) Mythical King
The Stone's Ginger Wine Chase (1973) Avondhu
The Imperial Cup (1976) Nougat
The Black and White Whisky Gold Cup (1977) Kybo

His best season to date was 1977-8 when he turned out the winners of 82 races worth £79,385 and finished fifth in the Trainers' List

Josh Gifford is married to former international show-jumper, Althea Roger-Smith.

GIFFORD, Macer Charles (b.1944)

The younger brother of Josh Gifford, Macer Gifford started as an amateur. He rode his first winner in April 1964 and became Champion Amateur the following season riding 13 winners including the Horse and Hound Cup on Royal Phoebe. His biggest success was the 1968 Whitbread Gold Cup on Larbawn, on whom he also won the Golden Miller H'cap Chase. Head injuries forced him to retire in 1976.

GILBERT, John Christopher

A fine hurdles rider from the famous Wootton academy, Johnny Gilbert once rode 10 winners in succession in 1959 which remains a record. His best season was 1959-60 when he rode 38 winners and finished sixth in the Jockeys' Table.

His winners included:

The Triumph Hurdle (1959) Amazon's Choice
The Lancashire Hurdle (1948) Agramante; (1956) French Flyer; (1956) Rosati
The Imperial Cup (1948) Anglesey; (1949) Secret Service
The Liverpool Hurdle (1952) Rahsas
The Cheltenham Hurdle (1952) Avec Toi

In 1973 he was appointed Racing Instructor to the Joint Racing Board Apprentice Training Scheme at the National Equestrian Centre, Stoneleigh.

GLENCARAIG LADY

Chestnut mare, 1964, Fortina—Luckibash (Turbulent). Bred by Mr J. F. Hogan.

In 1972 Glencaraig Lady, hitherto regarded as useful but distinctly unlucky, emulated her sire and became the third mare to win the Cheltenham Gold Cup. Prior to that she had won three hurdle races and seven chases including the S.G.B. Chase, Ascot (1970) but had fallen at the last when challenging strongly for the Tote Champion Novices, N.H. Meeting (1970) and again at the third last in the 1971 Gold Cup. Even her victory was tinged with drama for after coming home first (F. Berry), 4/1, by $\frac{3}{4}$l, a head, from Royal Toss (N. Wakley) and The Dikler (B. Brogan), she had to survive an objection lodged by Nigel Wakley before being declared the winner. Glencaraig Lady was owned by Mr P. Doyle and trained by the young Irish trainer Francis Flood.

GLENSIDE

Bay gelding, 1902, St Eris—Kilwinnet (Kilwarlin). Bred by Mr W. G. Peareth.

A one-eyed horse, plagued with unsoundness, Glenside achieved immortality by being the only horse to survive the unspeakable conditions of the 1911 Grand National which he won, 10-3 (Mr J. Anthony), 20/1, by 20l, 3l from Rathnally, 11-0 (R. Chadwick) and Shady Girl, 10-5 (G. Clancy) both of whom were remounted. Glenside, who won four other chases, was owned by Mr Frank Bibby and trained at Kinlet by Capt. R. H. Collis. The engagement of Jack Anthony to ride at Aintree was a last-minute arrangement caused by stable jockey Tich Mason breaking a leg.

GOLDEN CYGNET

Bay gelding, 1972, Deep Run—Golden Cygneture (Golden Vision). Bred by Mr J. T. O'Brien.

Few youngsters have made a more impressive Cheltenham début than Mr Raymond Rooney's Golden Cygnet when winning the 1978 Waterford Crystal Supreme Novice Hurdle. Racegoers could scarcely believe their eyes when as the high-class, competitive field qickened down the hill, they realised that the handsome Golden Cygnet was literally running away. He won on a tight rein by 15 lengths in a time 0.3 of a second faster than the Champion Hurdle later that afternoon. It was the fifth successive victory for the elegant, bright bay gelding bought by trainer Eddie O'Grady for 980 guineas as an unbroken three-

year-old. He went on to win another race in Ireland before tackling his seniors in the Scottish Champion Hurdle. Apart from Monksfield, all the top-class hurdlers were in the line-up. Golden Cygnet moved smoothly up to the leaders two flights out and seemed likely to take up the running at the last when he pitched and fell heavily. He appeared to be unhurt but he had fractured two vertebrae in his neck and died two days later. It was a tragic loss, not only to his connections but to National Hunt racing as a whole. Golden Cygnet was ridden in all his races by Mr Neil Madden.

GOLDEN MILLER

Bay gelding, 1927. Bred by Mr L. Geraghty.

Golden Miller			
Goldcourt	Gold Miner	Gallinule	
		Seek and Find	
	Powerscourt	Atheling	
		Waterfall	
Miller's Pride	Wavelets' Pride	Fernandez	
		Wavelet	
	Miller's Daughter	Queen's Birthday	
		Allan Water	

Comparisons between great horses of different generations are as impossible as they are futile, but it can be stated incontrovertibly that the outstanding stars of the twentieth century have been Arkle, Golden Miller and Red Rum. If Arkle established a more formidable ascendancy over his contemporaries and Red Rum reigned supreme at Aintree, it is equally true that Golden Miller's achievement of retaining his form and his soundness over nine consecutive seasons, of never falling in 52 races, of winning 28, including five Cheltenham Gold Cups and a Grand National under top-weight and in record time, has never been approached and is exceedingly unlikely to be so.

Several people discerned seeds of greatness in the young Golden Miller, notably the shrewd Tipperary farmer dealer Paddy Quinn, who bought him as a yearling for 120 guineas at Ballsbridge Sales, and Leicestershire hunter-dealer, Capt. Farmer, who picked him out of a field as an unbroken three-year-old and bought him for 500 guineas on behalf of Basil Briscoe. The horse's admirers did not however include his new trainer who viewed the gangling newcomer with marked lack of enthusiasm which the first few months at Longstowe did nothing to dispel. A day with the Fitz-william Hounds and an extremely moderate run in a lowly hurdle at Southwell served only to emphasize the stable's opinion that he was slow, un-willing and a thoroughly bad jumper. Head-lad Sam Tidy's caustic comment, that Golden Miller was a damned good name for a damned bad horse, was representative of the general feeling.

Yet Briscoe's patrons included another admirer and, shortly after the débâcle at Southwell, Mr Philip Carr bought Gol-den Miller for £1,000 from his perplexed and dubious trainer. Within the month Mr Carr's judgement was vindicated and Golden Miller had run a good third in an all-aged handicap at Newbury, causing jockey Bob Lyall to enthuse: "one of the best three-year-olds I've ever ridden". Three victories and three places from his next six runs confirmed Lyall's judgement and on learning that Mr Carr wished to dispose of his horses, Briscoe confidently informed a prospective new owner, the Hon. Dorothy Paget, that he could offer her the best chaser in the world and, should she be interested, the best hurdler in England. The temerity of the boast evidently appealed to the young millionairess and for £10,000 she bought Golden Miller and Insurance who, within 15 months, won her two Cheltenham Gold Cups and two Cham-pion Hurdles.

Despite four prior victories that season, Golden Miller went to the post for the 1932 Gold Cup little fancied to beat 10/11 favourite Grakle. Whether or not he would have done so remained a mat-ter for conjecture for, at the fence before the water, Grakle swerved on landing to avoid the prostrate Kingsford and un-seated Mr Jack Fawcus, leaving Golden Miller to win as he pleased.

Next season Golden Miller went un-beaten through five races including a second Gold Cup before being asked to tackle Aintree for the first time. Carrying 12-2 and ridden by Ted Leader, he started favourite at 9/1 and ran very well until Becher's on the second circuit where he blundered horribly. His confidence shaken, he made an even worse mistake at the next which was sufficient to unship Ted Leader. Percipient correspondents wondered whether Golden Miller's fast, low-pitched style of jumping was suitable

for Aintree but in those days the tower-ing, un-aproned fences rendered the mathematical chances of a horse getting round at less than 8/1 and this opinion was by no means widely held. There followed two seasons of almost unbroken dominance, including his record-shatter-ing triumph at Aintree – surely one of the great moments in the history of the race – which culminated in his fourth and finest triumph in the Cheltenham Gold Cup.

Basil Briscoe had viewed the race as a suitable preliminary to the Grand National, at £6,545 worth nearly ten times as much, and therefore sent Gol-den Miller to the post just short of peak fitness. What he had not reckoned on was the presence of Mr 'Jock' Hay Whitney's Thomond II, switched at the last minute from the two-mile Coventry Cup. Thomond II was an exceptionally fast, tough, little horse, trained to the minute and ideally suited, as the Miller was not, to the prevailing hard ground.

Golden Miller was to be ridden by Gerry Wilson, Thomond II by Billy Speck. The field was made up by Kells-boro' Jack (winner of 13 chases includ-ing the Grand National, the Scottish National and the Champion Chase twice), Avenger and Southern Hero (winner of 18 chases including three Scottish Grand Nationals). Southern Hero set a cracking pace until the third last where he withdrew, leaving the two principals in command. Down the hill they flew, stride for stride, over the last locked level and not until they were halfway up the hill to the winning post, did the superior strength of Golden Miller assert himself and he drew ahead to win by ¾l.

It is still reckoned to be the finest race ever run for the Gold Cup and it was the rider of the second, Billy Speck who spoke its epitaph. After the excitement and tumultuous reception of the prin-cipals had died away, he and Gerry Wilson were having a drink with Sir John Grey. Speck raised his glass to his old friend and rival and said: "Well done mate. Well there's one thing, when we are old and grey, sitting back and en-joying a drink, we can tell them how we did ride at least one great horse-race, one day in our lives." Alas, poor Speck was never able to sit back and tell that glorious tale for he broke his back in a fall off a moderate animal in a seller at the next Cheltenham meeting and died six days later.

Golden Miller and Thomond II went on to Aintree with neither of their chances improved by this epic dual. Golden Miller, at 2/1 the shortest-priced favourite in the history of the race, was never going at any stage of the race and was well behind by the time the field reached the fence before Valentine's. Here he attempted to refuse but driven on, bucked and twisted through the fence ejecting the luckless Wilson like a cork from a bottle. Thomond II, by contrast, ran a heroic race and in fact landed first over the final obstacle but his lack of physique told in the final $\frac{1}{4}$ of a mile and he finished third to Reynoldstown.

Connections and public alike were mystified by the performance of Golden Miller, and having passed a veterinary examination, the champion turned out again the following day to contest the Champion Chase. Unequivocally stating his point of view, he repeated his antics, this time at the very first fence.

In the ensuing rumpus, the reputations of owner, trainer and jockey all suffered. The already tenuous relationship between Briscoe and Miss Paget terminated abruptly and Miss Paget's horses were transferred first to her cousin Donald Snow and thence to Owen Anthony where Golden Miller remained for the rest of his career.

Gerry Wilson survived the cataclysm but the following autumn Golden Miller ran out with him at Newbury after which he too was axed. The rumour and speculation that yapped around this top-class and entirely straight jockey persisted even after his death is fully discussed under his own entry. Suffice it to say that Wilson informed both owner and trainer a full week before the race that he had been offered a bribe to stop Golden Miller which he had turned down and that his account of Golden Miller's antics at the fateful fence were fully corroborated not only by on-the-spot spectators but, incontrovertibly by the evidence of the film camera.

Golden Miller ran in two subsequent Nationals and in neither would he proceed beyond the fence before Valentine's. Fulke Walwyn did induce him to compete the 1936 Becher Chase and finished second but he reported that "the old fellow groaned as he touched down over the drop-fences".

Away from Aintree, however, the old sparkle still dazzled. He won another Gold Cup (and would surely have won in 1937 had the weather permitted it to be run). He ran one of the bravest races of his career to win the Prince Chase, Sandown (1938) giving 34lb to the second, and finally he ran an infinitely gallant second to Morse Code in his last Gold Cup. It was his first and only defeat at Cheltenham and it was ironic that it should have happened in the race whose status he had so firmly established and which he had made so peculiarly his own.

Golden Miller lived in much fêted retirement until 1957 when he was finally put down at the age of 30.

Details of major victories:

Cheltenham Gold Cup

1932   (T. Leader), 13/2, won by 4l, a bad third from Inverse (R. Lyall) and Aruntius (D. McCann).

1933   (W. Stott), 4/7f, won by 10l, 5l, from Thomond II (W. Speck) and Delaneige (J. Moloney).

1934   (G. Wilson), 6/5f, won by 6l, 6l, from Avenger (R. Lyall) and Kellsboro' Jack (D. Morgan).

1935   (G. Wilson), 1/2f, won by $\frac{3}{4}$l, 5l, from Thomond II (W. Speck) and Kellsboro' Jack (D. Morgan).

1936   (E. Williams), 21/20, won by 12l, 2l, from Royal Mail (Mr F. Walwyn) and Kellsboro' Jack (D. Morgan).

The Grand National

1934   12-2 (G. Wilson), 8/1, won by 5l, 5l, from Delaneige, 11-6 (J. Moloney) and Thomond II, 12-4 (W. Speck).

GOODMAN, Alexander

A leading amateur rider of the mid-nineteenth century, Alex Goodman was easily distinguishable by his full beard. He was said by a contemporary trainer to be a master at presenting his horse correctly at a fence. He won the Grand National twice, in 1852 on Miss Mowbray and in 1866 on Salamander. Some histories state that he was persuaded out of retirement to ride this race but, as he won the National Hunt Chase in 1863 on Socks, in 1865 on Emperor and in 1866 on Shangarry and also the Warwick Grand Annual in 1867 on Shakespeare, the theory does not hold water.

GORDON, Adam Lindsay (1830-70)

Adam Lindsay-Gordon may not have ranked among the major poets of the nineteenth century, indeed some of his writing has been labelled, not altogether undeservedly, as doggerel, but at his best he was able more than anyone else, to convey vividly the atmosphere of the early days of steeplechasing. In particular did he capture the vigour, the reckless courage, the tough chivalry and the insouciant attitude to life that characterized the Cheltenham Chasing set of the 1840s and 'fifties. It is to him that we are indebted for the vivid portraits we have of the Archers, the Holmans and the man he hero-worshipped, Tom Olliver.

The son of a soldier and a mother who suffered from acute depression, he was educated at Cheltenham. He was interested in and adept at riding and boxing and also in Greek and Latin literature with which, in later life, he used greatly to bore less-intellectual, Australian friends.

After a prematurely terminated scholastic career and abortive attempts to embrace both military and ecclesiastical professions, he committed the crowning indiscretion of falling in love 'out of his class' and was forthwith bundled off to Australia, then considered the ideal repository for unsatisfactory sons. He worked as a mounted policeman until he threw a pair of boots, which he had been ordered to clean, at a superior officer's head.

He broke horses, rode over fences and won the Adelaide Grand Steeplechase. He then became interested in politics and stood as member for Victoria District, South Australia, which he won by three votes. He soon became disillusioned and resigned. He suffered from chronic insomnia and melancholia and finally shot himself before his fortieth birthday.

GORDON, Robert

The son of a parson, Bert Gordon was known as "the blue monkey" for his small, wiry frame, impish face and permanent blue shadow. He rode very long and was noted for his windmill finishes. He was Champion Jockey in 1909, riding 45 winners.

GORE, Robert George (1859-1941)

An Irishman descended from the Earls of Arran, Robert Gore held a commission in the militia for a while. He came to England during the 1880s and was attached to William Murland's stable as assistant trainer and amateur rider. In 1887 he set up on his own at Findon while continuing to ride. He frequently took strings of horses to Germany, Austria and Denmark to win races and sell on and in 1890 gave up his licence, spending his summers in Germany and his winters with Garry Moore at Littleton near Winchester.

In 1899 he went back to Findon where he continued to train with great success until 1941. His owners included Sir Charles Assheton-Smith, Lords Buchanan and Woolavington and Mr Paul Nelke. Among his best victories were:

> **The Grand National** (1912) Jerry M.; (1913) Covertcoat
> **The Grand Steeplechase de Paris** (1910) Jerry M.
> **The Paris Hurdle** (1900) General Peace
> **The Champion Chase** (1907) Mount Prospect's Fortune; (1908) Cackler
> **The Grand Sefton** (1909) Cackler; (1910) Cackler

GOURLEY, John

John Gourley won the 1898 Grand National on Drogheda. The race was run in a snowstorm and Gourley was given a life-pension by the grateful joint-owners, Mr G. Adams and Richard Dawson (*q.v.*).

GRAKLE

Brown gelding, 1922, Jackdaw—Lady Crank (Machakos). Bred by Messrs Slocock.

A rather plain but exceptionally well-constructed gelding, Grakle won 12 chases including the 1931 Grand National, 11-7 (R. Lyall), 100/6, by 1½l, 10l, from Gregalach, 12-0 (J. Moloney) and Annandale, 10-7 (T. Morgan). He was also placed three times in the Cheltenham Gold Cup being second in 1927 to Thrown In, third in 1929 to Easter Hero, and second to Easter Hero again in 1930. In 1932 he started 10/11 favourite in the race won by Golden Miller, and was going exceptionally well when he swerved to avoid the falling Kingsford and unshipped Mr Jack Fawcus. Ted Leader on Golden Miller caught the riderless Grakle after passing the post and brought him back to the unsaddling enclosure, for which quixotic gesture

Grakle's trainer Tom Coulthwaite gave him a silver cigarette case inscribed "actions speak louder than words".

Originally owned by Mr T. K. Laidlaw for whom he won the National Hunt Juvenile Chase, N.H. Meeting, and ran second in the 1927 Gold Cup, Grakle was then sold for £4,000 to Mr C. R. Taylor.

Although very game Grakle could not be hit and was inclined to hang under pressure, which problems Bob Lyall overcame with the utmost coolness in the close finish to the 1931 National. Tom Coulthwaite was particularly attached to Grakle whom he had found as a young horse and delayed his retirement to see his career out. Grakle gave his name to a type of crossed noseband often used for controlling headstrong horses.

GRANTHAM, Anthony

The son of a famous Sussex dealer and livery man, Tony Grantham was for a period stable jockey to Peter Cazalet and rode H.M. Queen Elizabeth the Queen Mother's first winner (owned jointly with the then Princess Elizabeth), Monave'en at Fontwell. In all he rode five winners for the stable's royal patron, including the Queen Elizabeth Chase on Monave'en. His best victory was the 1955 Cheltenham Gold on Gay Donald and he also won the King George VI Chase on Statecraft. His best season was 1949-50 when he rode 42 winners, finishing fourth in the Jockeys' Table. He now runs a high-class dealing yard in Sussex.

GREEN, Christopher

The son of a Norfolk farmer, Chris Green was a noted N.H. jockey of the mid-nineteenth century. He won the Grand National twice, in 1850 on Abd-el-Kader and in 1859 on Half-Caste. On the suicide of Ben Land (q.v.) he became private trainer to Lord Poulett and saddled The Lamb to win the 1871 Grand National.

GREENALL, Peter (b.1953)

A member of the brewing family who sponsor the valuable Greenall-Whitley Chase at Haydock. Peter Greenall has come swiftly to prominence on the National Hunt scene both as an owner and as an amateur rider. With a large string

of horses, chiefly with W. A. Stephenson, at his disposal, he shared the Amateur title with George Jones (q.v.), in 1975-76 with 25 winners and won it outright in 1976-77 with 27 victories.

His principal winners are the National Hunt Chase (1976) on Sage Merlin and the John Corbett Hunter Chase, Stratford (1977) on Timmie's Battle.

GREGALACH

Chestnut gelding, 1922, My Prince—St Germanie (St Luke). Bred in Ireland by Mr M. Finlay.

A strikingly handsome individual Gregalach was, like Grakle, bought by Tom Coulthwaite as an unbroken three-year-old on behalf of Mr T. K. Laidlaw. He did not see a racecourse until he was five years old and then made a very auspicious start, winning four chases including the Stanley Chase, Liverpool (1927), after which he was sold for £5,000 to Mrs Gemmell and transferred to Tom Leader's Newmarket establishment.

The sun did not shine upon Mrs Gemmell's new purchase, for Gregalach set up a depressingly long sequence of seconds; as result of falling in his tune-up race just eight days before the 1929 Grand National, went to Liverpool least fancied of his stable's fleet of five runners. Not even his owner was present to see Gregalach, 11-4 (R. Everett), 100/1, win by 6l, a bad third, from the hot favourite, Easter Hero, 12-7 (J. Moloney) and Richmond II, 10-6 (W. Stott) in a record field of 66.

Gregalach won five more chases including the Coventry Chase, Kempton (1930) and ran a marvellous race under 12-0 in the 1931 National, being just run out of it in the last 50 yards by his ex-stable companion, Grakle (rec. 7lb) in a time only two-fifths of a second outside the record.

GRIFEL

Chestnut horse, 1953, Grof II—Festina.

A small, handsome Russian-bred entire and winner of the 1960 Pardubice Steeplechase, Grifel was sent to England to contest the 1961 Grand National. Automatically handicapped with top-weight (12-0) Grifel and his partner, Vladimir Prakhov, a Red Army Officer, fell at Becher's on the first circuit: Prakhov remounted but the pair pulled up after completing a circuit.

GRIFFIN, J. H.

A Dublin-born businessman who made a fortune in the canning-trade, thus earning the sobriquet of "Mincemeat Joe", Mr Griffin's appearance in the ranks of owners was as brief as it was dramatic. Within three years he won two Grand Nationals, headed the Owners List twice and was bankrupted for £80,000. At the dispersal sale following the death of Mr J. V. Rank in 1952, he outstayed Lord Bicester to secure Early Mist at 5,300 guineas. The following year Early Mist won the National, thereby hoisting his owner to the top of the list with two races worth £10,015. Following this he bought, on trainer Vincent O'Brien's advice, the luckless Royal Tan and the hurdler, Galatian, for a total of £5,000.

Rumours as to his solvency were rife in Ireland that winter but not until the eve of the National did matters come to a head. Bryan Marshall, who had ridden Mr Griffin a winner that afternoon, was still owed £500 from his previous year's victory and a hideous scene was just averted by the diplomacy of Dermot O'Brien, brother of the trainer.

Next afternoon, Mr Griffin, unable to obtain credit from bookmakers on the rails, watched Royal Tan win the National and Galatian, the Liverpool Hurdle. Their victories won him £10,707 and again put him at the top of that years Owners List but it was not sufficient to avert bankruptcy proceedings later that year in which Bryan Marshall figured as a creditor for £2,781.

GROSVENOR, Hon. Hugh (1904-28)

The only son of the 2nd Baron Stalbridge, 'Puck' Grosvenor was the first of only two amateurs and the only Oxford undergraduate to win the Cheltenham Gold Cup, which he did in 1927 on his father's Thrown In. Later he joined the 7th Hussars and went to Australia as A.D.C. to the Adjutant-General, Lord Gowrie. Shortly afterwards he was killed in an air crash.

GRUDON

Brown horse, 1890, registered in Miss Prior's Half-Bred Stud Book, Old Buck—Avis (Sugarplum). Bred by Mr H. Bletsoe.

Grudon, who was owned and trained by his breeder, won a hurdle race and 13 chases including the Champion Chase, Liverpool (1897) and the 1901 Grand National, 10-0 (A. Nightingall), 9/1, by 4l, 6l, from Drumcree, 9-12 (Mr H. Nugent) and Buffalo Bill, 9-7 (H. Taylor).

The Bletsoes were a Northamptonshire family, all of whom were involved with racing. The son, Morgan, was a jockey and won the 1908 Grand National on Rubio, while the daughter Betty hunted Grudon and rode him in all his work. Arthur Nightingall reckoned that the horse, not an easy ride, went better for her than for anyone else.

Grudon owed his National triumph to the resource of Mr Bletsoe who, realizing that the race was going to be run in a snowstorm, procured 2lb of butter from the local dairy with which he packed the soles of his horse's feet. Thus equipped Grudon scampered over the slithery snow and came home a very easy winner. Shortly afterwards Grudon broke down when going very well in the Lancashire Chase and it was not found possible to restore him to racing soundness. He stood as a sire for some years but was not conspicuously successful in this sphere.

GUBBINS, Roderic Joseph Beresford

Roderic Gubbins owned and trained the 1938 Champion Hurdler, Our Hope, ridden by amateur Capt. 'Perry' Harding.

There have only been three other home-trained winners of the hurdling classic, Merry Deal (1957), Bandalore (1958) and Winning Fair (1963); and curiously enough, Winning Fair was ridden by the only other amateur to win the race, Alan Lillingstone.

GWILT, Edward Douglas (1875-1946)

The son of a Sussex rector, Ted Gwilt was brought up at Kilsby in Northamptonshire. He hunted with Pytchley and rode in point-to-points before taking out a licence to train under both Rules in 1909. He served with the King's Own Scottish Borderers in the 1914-18 War and resumed his licence in 1919.

His best N.H. horse was Free Fare who won 11 Flat races including the Manchester November Handicap and 12 hurdle races including the Liverpool Hurdle and the 1937 Champion Hurdle. He trained at Saxon House, Lambourn, where Fulke Walwyn now trains.

HACKETT, J. F.

Jem Hackett trained privately for bookmaker Ambrose Gorham, at Telscombe on the Sussex Downs. He saddled the 1902 Grand National winner, Shannon Lass.

HACKLER

Bay horse, 1887. Bred by Mr G. A. Baird

		Newminster
	Lord Clifden	
		The Slave
Petrarch		
		Orlando
	Laura	
Hackler		Torment
		Marsyas
	Albert Victor	
		Prince of Wales
Hackness		
		Le Maréchal
	Cicely Hackett	
		Meg o'Marley

Hackler, who won three races on the Flat, stood at Mr James Daly's Hartstown stud and was extremely successful as a sire of jumpers. He is said to have dominated N.H. breeding for the first decade of the twentieth century, but no statistics have come to light.

He stood 16.1 and possessed a grand front, a fine, straight hind leg and was a particularly fluent mover. He nicked particularly well with mares of the Mount Royal family and matings on this pattern produced Covertcoat (Grand National, 1913) Cackler (Champion Chase, Valentine Chase and Grand Sefton Chase twice), Hackwatch (Stanley Chase and Grand Sefton twice) and Ballyhackle (11 chases). He also sired the 1910 National winner, Jenkinstown. He was leading sire 1911-12, siring the winners of 34 races worth £5,376 and 1912-13 with 29 races worth £6,043.

HACKWATCH

Bay gelding, 1900, Hackler—On the Watch (Aughrim). Bred by Mr H. Turnstall-Moore.

Hackwatch, a brilliantly precocious youngster owned by Mr H. Turnstall-Moore, was unbeaten in seven outings as a five-year-old and his victories included the Stanley Chase, Liverpool, and the Grand Sefton. He won the Grand Sefton again by six lengths, carrying 12-7 in 1906, but unhappily never ran again.

HAINE, John (b.1942)

A member of a family of hunting farmers from the Duke of Beaufort's country, Johnnie Haine was apprenticed to Bob Turnell in 1958. He modelled himself on Scobie Breasley and rode 30 winners on the Flat before switching to jumping with immediate success. A natural 10-stoner, blessed with a fine judge of pace, he was easily conspicuous by his streamlined position and stylish finish.

Among his major victories were:

The Champion Hurdle (1966) Salmon Spray
The Tote Champion Novices Chase (1964) Buona Notte
The Welsh Grand National (1972) Charlie H
The Topham Trophy (1970) Charter Flight
The Wills Hurdle (1971) Chapman's Peak
The Stone's Ginger Wine Chase (1968) Bowgeeno
The Imperial Cup (1967) Sir Thopaz
The Daily Express Triumph Hurdle (1973) Moonlight Bay

He handed in his licence in 1977 and now trains near Gloucester.

HALF CASTE

Brown horse, 1853, not in General Stud Book, by Morgan Rattler.

Little can be established about Mr Willoughby's half-bred entire who won the 1859 Grand National, 9-7 (Chris Green), 7/1, by a short neck, 11, from two other entires, the Frenchman Jean du Quesne, 9-9 (H. Lamplugh) and Huntsman, 11-2 (Ben Land). It was Half Caste's first and only attempt at the race.

HALL, William Arthur (1903-77)

A Yorkshireman based at Tadcaster and the elder brother of successful Flat trainer, Sam Hall, 'Charlie' Hall's principal successes were for Mr Clifford Nicholson for whom he trained the 1956 Champion Hurdler, Doorknocker. That season he was Leading Trainer with 41 winners of £15,807 and in 1959-60 he was fifth with 29 winners of £11,500.

His other good victories were:

The Scottish Grand National (1948) Magnetic Fin

The Queen Elizabeth Chase (1956) State Secret

The Emblem Chase (1952) Stormhead; (1953) Stormhead; (1959) Knightsbrook

The Haydock Grand National Trial (1953) Witty

The Topham Trophy H'cap Chase (1950) Culworth; (1951) Culworth; (1953) Stormhead; (1955) Stormhead; (1974) Clear Cut

The National Hunt H'cap Chase (1969) Chancer

The Mildmay Chase (1959) Liquidator

In 1975 he retired and handed the stables over to his stepson, Maurice Camacho, who trained Clear Cut to win the Mackeson Gold Cup that year.

HALLOWE'EN

Brown gelding, 1945, Court Nez—My Blue Heaven (Tai-Yang). Bred by Mr F. E. Woodman.

A small horse graphically described by his regular professional jockey, Fred Winter, as "a bouncy little blanker, all backside and heart", Hallowe'en started life in a very modest way and progressed via the hunting field and point-to-points, to win 15 chases, including the King George VI Chase twice (1952 and 1954) and to become one of the most popular chasers of the 'fifties.

Hallowe'en was bought as an unbroken three-year-old for £90 by Capt. R. B. Smalley who trained and rode him to win two point-to-points in 1950. Next season he was sent to Bill Wightman to be trained for Hunter Chases and there he remained for the rest of his career. In 1951 he won five Hunter Chases including the Foxhunter Challenge Cup (N.H. Meeting) after which Capt. Smalley was unable to refuse an £8,000 offer from the Contessa di St Elia.

Hallowe'en's entry in handicap company was far from auspicious for in his first two races ridden by two top-class professional jockeys he negotiated no more than four fences. Captain Smalley was then recalled to the colours and rode his old partner to victory in two amateur chases. When, finally, Fred Winter was asked to try his hand with the unpredictable little brown horse, he took the sensible step of enquiring from the former owner what he did. "Nothing", proved to be the answer, Hallowe'en furiously resented restraint or 'placing' from on top and would launch himself from outside the wings if this was attempted. Left to his own devices by Fred Winter, he proved one of Britain's top chasers and would undoubtedly have increased his winning record had he not been deprived of the latter's services for the whole of season 1953-54.

Hallowe'en was placed three times running in the Cheltenham Gold Cup, but the Gloucestershire course never brought out the best in him, probably because his lack of front proved an insuperable handicap in the vital downhill run to the last fence.

HAMEY, James Henry (b.1905)

'Tim' Hamey, a Cheltenham-based jockey, won the 1926 Cheltenham Gold Cup on Koko and the 1932 Grand National on Forbra. Other important victories for him were the Coventry Cup twice, in 1932 on Brave Cry and 1934 on Thomond II, and the Stanley Chase in 1935 on Provocative. He afterwards trained. His son Rex was also a N.H. jockey and won the 1956 Mildmay Memorial on Linwell. He now manages Willie Stephenson's Tudor Stud near Buntingford, Hertfordshire.

HANDEL, Charles William Herbert

A West Country farmer, dealer, wholesale butcher and permit-holder, Herbert Handel has had great success with a handful of mostly home-bred, beautifully produced and schooled chasers. Chief among them was Royal Toss (*q.v.*) bred from a good mare, Spinning Coin II (10 point-to-points and two Hunter Chases), with whom he won 12 races including:

The Whitbread Gold Cup (1970)
The Mildmay Memorial (1972)
The Welsh Grand National (1971)
The Gainsborough Chase (1973)
The Mandarin H'cap Chase (1972)

In 1972 he very nearly pulled off the ultimate triumph of any trainer when Royal Toss failed by just $\frac{3}{4}$l to catch Glencaraig Lady in the Cheltenham Gold Cup. Colours: pale blue, red and white check cap.

HANDICAP

A handicap is a race in which the weights to be carried by the horses are adjusted for the purpose of equalizing their chances of winning. Official handicappers are appointed by the Jockey Club for this function and since 1974 they have been assisted by a computer at Weatherbys, into which all relevant information is fed and which produces a central list from which the handicapper bases his calculations.

The first recorded handicap in N.H. racing was at Eglinton Park on 1st May 1841. It was won by Mr Wentworth Hope-Johnstone on The Returned. At Newport Pagnell on 19th November that year, another handicap was run in which Mr Elkins' Luck-All, 11-5 (Goddard) beat Mr Elmore's Lottery, 13-6 (Mason) by a length. The Grand National became a handicap race in 1843.

HANDICAPPERS

(i) Handicappers, in making a handicap, shall allot the weights to be carried in accordance with the definitions of a handicap and a handicap rating and the provisions of Rules 94 and 95. The weights for all handicaps shall be published in the Racing Calendar, and no alteration shall be made to a weight allotted by the handicappers after publication, except that by express permission of Stewards of the Jockey Club a weight may be affixed for a horse duly entered but whose name or weight has been omitted for the handicap, or a correction may be made when, through an error in transmission or transcription, an incorrect weight has been published. Such alterations or additions may only be made up to noon on the Friday before the first declaration of forfeit, or, in races for which there is only one declaration of forfeit, not later than 48 hours before the time for declaration of forfeit under Rule 120 and shall whenever possible be published in the next succeeding edition of the Racing Calendar.

(ii) Handicappers shall attend Meetings as required by the Stewards of the Jockey Club.

HANLON, J.

J. Hanlon won the 1855 Grand National on Wanderer.

HAPPYMINT

Bay gelding, 1945, registered in Miss Prior's Half-Bred Stud Book, Happy Thoughts—Countermint (Bargany). Bred by Mr H. Laing.

A tough staying hunter-chaser, owned and ridden by Mr Danny Moralee (q.v.) and trained by Stuart Wight, Happymint won 10 chases including the Heart of All England, Hexham (1952), the Cheltenham Foxhunters (1954) and the Liverpool Foxhunters (1955).

HAPPY SPRING

Bay gelding, 1956, Tambourin—Smart Woman (Noble Star). Bred by Mr J. S. Wright.

A good staying chaser owned by Mrs J. S. Wright and trained by her husband Stan (q.v.), Happy Spring won ten chases including the Rhymney Breweries H'cap Chase (1962), the Golden Miller H'cap Chase (1963) and the Welsh Grand National (1967). He was also second to Mill House in the 1963 Hennessy Gold Cup with Arkle third. He was a very game horse and an excellent jumper.

HARDING, Maj.-Gen. Sir Reginald Peregrine, D.S.O. (b.1905)

A brave and distinguished soldier who joined the 5th Royal Inniskilling Dragoon Guards in 1925 and served until 1958, 'Perry' Harding won the 1938 Champion Hurdle on Our Hope. He is one of only two amateurs to have won the hurdlers' classic. He also won the National Hunt Chase in 1933 on Ego.

HARRISON, Herbert Stanley (1880-1956)

Stanley Harrison was born near Liverpool and educated at Bradfield College. He rode successfully as an amateur in England and Ireland and also Germany and Austria-Hungary, where he trained for some years. Between the wars he trained at Bangor and won the 1928 Cheltenham Gold Cup with the five-year-old Patron Saint. A shrewd, clever trainer, he excelled at selling races and won a tremendous number with Golden Fleece. He trained up until the outbreak of World War II and then retired near Camberley, Surrey.

HARTIGAN, Frank (1880-1952)

A member of a very prominent Irish racing family, Frank Hartigan was the son of an Irish veterinary officer and the nephew of Willie Moore (q.v.), whom he succeeded at Weyhill. After a successful riding career both as an amateur and a professional, he took out a licence to train in 1905. A great horsemaster in the Irish tradition, his horses always looked bright and bonny and he won over 2,000 races under both Rules. He won the 1000 Guineas twice, with Lord Rosebery's Vauclause (1915) and Roseway (1919). He also trained Wrack (*q.v.*), for Lord Rosebery (5th Earl) with whom he won six hurdle races as well as 10 Flat races.

His principal N.H. success was the 1930 Grand National with Shaun Goilin and he was second twice (1925 and 1926) with the luckless Old Tay Bridge.

Several future distinguished trainers learnt their craft at Weyhill, among them Noel Murless and Hartigan's son Joe who assisted him from 1936-40 and from 1945-52 before setting up on his own at Middleham.

HART ROYAL

Chestnut gelding, 1948, Atout Royal —Roe Deer (Craig an Eran). Bred by Maj. E. I. Scott.

A stout-hearted, staying chaser, Hart Royal won 12 chases including the Lancashire Chase twice (1957 and 1958), The Herne the Hunter Chase at Windsor (1958), and the Worcester Royal Porcelain Chase (1959). He was trained by Mrs Rosemary Lomax (although the licence was held by her husband), owned first by his trainer and then by Mr L. C. Denton and usually ridden by P. Pickford.

HARTY, Edward Patrick (b.1937)

The son of Capt. Cyril Harty, a leading trainer who won the 1944 Irish Grand National with Knight's Crest and was an international show-jumper of some repute, Eddie Harty is the only man to have represented his country in an Olympic 3-Day Event (he was ninth in Rome, 1960) and to have won the Grand National (Highland Wedding, 1969).

A charming, voluble Irishman, Eddie Harty was more or less born in the saddle, he rode in his first hurdle race at 14, won more than 50 point-to-points and won his first chase, as an amateur in 1953, when only 16. He then spent two years in America working as a cowboy. He turned professional in 1960-61, starting with ex-champion Tim Molony and graduating to Fred Rimell, Fred Winter and finally Toby Balding.

Apart from his National victory, which was a chance ride as he was deputizing for injured Owen McNally, Eddie Harty won:

The Welsh Grand National (1968) Glenn
The Mackeson Gold Cup (1968) Jupiter Boy
The Topham Trophy (1965) Hopkiss; (1969) Dozo

In 1972 he took out a licence to train. His headquarters are at Strawhall House, the Curragh, Co. Kildare.

HASTINGS, the Hon. Aubrey (1878-1929)

The third son of the 13th Earl of Huntingdon, Aubrey Hastings trained and rode the 1906 Grand National winner Ascetic's Silver. He had to waste severely to ride at 10-9 and was thought by onlookers to have won the race with a beautiful jump at the fence just before the racecourse. This fence has an awkward dip in front of it and every other runner still in the race with a chance, hit it hard.

Hastings sent out three more National winners from his Wroughton stables, Ally Sloper (1915), Ballymacad (1917) and Master Robert (1924). This feat remained unequalled until 1976 when Fred Rimell (*q.v.*) gained his fourth National success with Rag Trade.

Hastings also found Brown Jack and Kellsboro' Jack as young horses and trained Brown Jack to win the 1928 Champion Hurdle.

In May 1929 he collapsed and died very suddenly after a game of polo. His stable was taken over by his widow and his former assistant, Ivor Anthony (*q.v.*). His son, Peter Hastings-Bass, was also a distinguished trainer who died tragically young, leaving his Kingsclere stables to his young assistant, Ian Balding.

HATTON'S GRACE

Bay gelding, 1940, His Grace—Hatton (Mr Jinks). Bred by Mr J. W. A. Harris.

One of three triple Champion Hurdlers (the others being Sir Ken and Persian War), Hatton's Grace was a good-class performer on the Flat whose victories included the Irish Lincolnshire Handicap (1949) and the Irish Cesarewitch (1949 and 1950).

Hatton's Grace was owned by Mrs Keogh and trained from 1948 onwards by Vincent O'Brien in Cashel, Co. Tipperary. In all he won 10 hurdles and a chase. His Champion Hurdle victories, achieved in successive years, were as follows: 1949 (A. Brabazon), 100/7, by 6l, 1l, from Vatelys (R. Bates) and Captain Fox (K. Mullins); 1950 (A. Brabazon), 5/2f, by 1½l, 2l, from Harlech (M. Molony) and Speciality (K. Mullins); 1951 (T. Molony), 4/1, by 5l, ½l, from Pyrrhus III (A. Gill) and Prince Hindou (A. Larraun).

Hatton's Grace was a small, insignificant horse of somewhat under-nourished appearance who did not achieve anything outstanding on a racecourse until he was nine years old. Together with Cottage Rake he lit the torch of the trail-blazing career of Vincent O'Brien.

HAYDOCK PARK (Group 1)
Despite its proximity to Lancashire's industrial centres, Haydock Park has an agreeably attractive, parkland setting. The track is oval, left-handed and un-dulating, about one mile, five furlongs in length. Some of the fences have a slight drop on the landing side which makes it a valuable pre-Aintree testing ground.

N.H. racing has been staged there since 1883. Previously the two most important races were the Tom Coulthwaite Chase and the Hurst Park Grand National Trial. In recent years, under the dynamic direction of first John Hughes and latterly Peter Firth, a spate of sponsors have been attracted, so that some of the most competitive racing in the North is held there. The principal races include:

The Tote Northern H'cap Chase (January, 3m, £6,186)
The Embassy Premier Chase Final (January, 2m 4f, £10,182)
The Greenall Whitley H'cap Chase (March, 3m, £7,780)
The Victor Ludorum Hurdle (March, 4-y-o, 2m, £6,685)
The Royal Doulton H'cap Hurdle (May, 2m, £20,085)

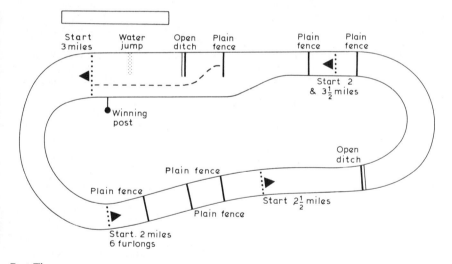

Best Times

Distance	Time	Horse-age-weight	Date
2m H (Old)	3m 49	Tamorn 5-10-7	12-3-65
2m H (New)	3m 41.10	Royal Gaye 5-10-0	1-5-78
2m 1f 192y H	4m 25.50	Booney 10-10-7	6-2-64
2m 4f H	4m 50.20	Gintop 6-11-1	30-5-78
2m 6f H	5m 21	Pattern Maker 6-11-4	28-1-78
2m 7f H	5m 32	Colonel Imp 9-11-9	4-2-71
3m H	5m 46.20	Garliestown 8-11-8	16-10-75
2m C	3m 55.40	Teddy Bear II 9-10-0	5-3-76
2½m C	5m 1.9	The Alikadoo 8-11-4	1-5-78
3m C	6m 8.25	Royal Frolic 6-10-6	15-10-75
3½m C	7m 17.90	Rubstic 8-10-0	1-12-77

Embassy Premier Chase Final (2½m)

HORSE	OWNER	RIDER	TRAINER
1970 L'Escargot	Mr R. Guest	T. Carberry	D. Moore
1971 Leap Frog	Mrs P. Burrell	V. O'Brien	T. Dreaper
1972 Colebridge	Mrs P. Burrell	V. O'Brien	J. Dreaper
1973 Balinese	Mr H. J. Joel	A. Turnell	R. Turnell
1974 Credibility	Mrs I. Dewhurst	R. Pitman	F. Winter
1975 Ben More	Mr P. Harper	S. Holland	J. Hardy
1976 Floating Pound	Mrs E. Boucher	J. Francome	F. Winter
1977 Border Incident	Mr A. Warrender	R. Barry	R. Head
1978 The Dealer	Mrs D. Hague	J. Francome	F. Winter
1979 Silver Buck		T Carmody	A. Dickinson.

Greenall Whitley H'cap Chase (3m)

HORSE	OWNER	RIDER	TRAINER
1971 Rainbow Valley	Mrs A. Dickinson	M. Dickinson	A. Dickinson
1972 Young Ash Leaf	Mr R. McDonald	T. Stack	J. K. M. Oliver
1973 Tregarron	Mr H. Blyth	C. Tinkler	J. K. M. Oliver
1974 Glanford Brig	Mr P. Harper	S. Holland	J. Hardy
1975 The Benign Bishop	Mr D. Oliver	R. Barry	J. K. M. Oliver
1976 Royal Frolic	Sir E. Hamner	J. Burke	T. F. Rimell
1977 General Moselle	Mrs F. Metcalf	I. Watkinson	H. Wharton
1978 Rambling Artist	Mr E. Robbins	J. J. O'Neill	T. Gillam

Victor Ludorum Hurdle (2m)

HORSE	OWNER	RIDER	TRAINER
1971 Nerak	Mr P. Hinchcliff	S. Taylor	S. Norton
1972 North Pole	Mr C. Cleary	K. White	T. F. Rimell
1973 Mythical King	Mr E. Adkins	D. Barrott	J. Gifford
1974 Relevant	Mrs E. Dedman	G. Griffin	R. Edwards
1975 Zip Fastener	Mr R. McAlpine	J. King	T. F. Rimell
1976 Sweet Joe	Mr M. Ritzenberg	I. Watkinson	H. Thomson-Jones
1977 Rathconrath	Mrs M. Valentine	J. Francome	F. Winter
1978 Mixed Melody	Mr J. Latham	D. Goulding	G. W. Richards

Tote Northern Trophy H'cap Chase (3m)

HORSE	OWNER	RIDER	TRAINER
1974 Tartan Ace	Mr D. Adams	T. Stack	W. A. Stephenson
1975 The Benign Bishop	Mr D. Oliver	R. Barry	J. F. K. Oliver
1976 What A Buck	Lord Vestey	J. King	D. Nicholson
1977 Shifting Gold	Mr R. Russell	M. Dickinson	K. Bailey
1978 Gay Spartan	Mr M. Armstrong	M. Dickinson	A. Dickinson

Royal Doulton H'cap Hurdle (2m)

1978 Royal Gaye	Sir J. Hamner	C. Tinkler	T. F. Rimell

HAYHURST, S. G. (b.1933)

One of the most competent Northern-based jockeys of recent years, Stan Hayhurst came from the Border country and was apprenticed to Major Bewicke. He was attached to the stable for some years and won the 1958 Cheltenham Gold Cup and the Hennessy Gold Cup (1959) on Kerstin. The Gold Cup was only his third ride at Cheltenham. More recently he rode for Bobby Fairbairn for whom he won the 1970 Scottish Champion Hurdle on Easter Pirate. He retired at the end of season 1972-73 and has become a racing official.

HERBERT, Edward Ivor Montgomery (b.1925)

An old-Etonian, Cambridge graduate and former Guards officer, Ivor Herbert is scarcely a typical product of these venerable establishments. Possessed of both wit and charm he can also be disconcertingly perceptive and paralysingly blunt and delights in pricking the pretensions of the pompous.

An author, journalist and playwright, he has written a number of books about National Hunt racing. The best known are *Arkle, The Story of a Champion; A Winter's Tale*, a study of life behind-

Best Times

Distance	Time	Horse-age-weight	Date
2m H	3m 50.60	Seething Lane 5-10-1	12-5-71
2½m H	4m 49.50	Tangles Brother 6-10-7	29-5-78
3m H	5m 47	Coraliety 7-11-9	29-5-78
2m C	4m 3.10	Golden Express 9-10-0	29-5-78
2½m C	5m 1.90	Pan-Man 7-10-7	26-3-73
3m C	6m 10.30	The Fencer 6-11-7	29-5-78

the-scenes in Fred Winter's yard; and *Red Rum*.

Apart from a brief period in the early 'sixties, he trained from 1952-69. During the years 1952-54 he was a private trainer to Mr (later Sir) David Brown, after which the stable became public. As the Stewards of the National Hunt Committee considered that his activities as a racing journalist precluded him from doing so, the licence was held by headlad, Charlie Mallon (*q.v.*).

In 1957 he became one of the youngest trainers ever to saddle a Cheltenham Gold Cup winner in Linwell. Linwell won 18 other races, including the Mildmay Memorial (1956). He also trained the very fast Flame Gun who won the Champion Novices Chase (1959) and the Cotswold Chase.

HEREFORD (Group 5)

A pleasantly situated, right-handed and almost square course, Hereford provides modest but entertaining sport on the Welsh borders in spring and autumn. The track, which is almost level, is about 1½ miles round and the bends are easy. The clay soil can get very hard and does not drain well naturally but considerable improvements have been made.

National Hunt racing has flourished since 1842 and while there is no race of real importance, there are several sponsored handicap hurdles including the Bulmer Strongbow Novices H'cap Hurdle (March, 2m 4f, £1,058). The principal chases include the Sun Valley Novices Chase (March, 3m, £1,589).

HEXHAM (Group 5)

Steeplechasing has been recorded at Hexham since 1869. A left-handed course, conical in shape and about 1½ miles in length, it has an uphill run to the last fence so stamina and good jumping are essential here. A sporting, informal atmosphere prevails and there is a splendid natural grandstand.

The principal race is the Heart of All England Maiden Hunters Chase (April, 3m, £1,054), a long-established race which has been won by such as The Callant, Happymint and Macmoffat. Teal fell but was remounted to finish third. Another important race is the Hugh Joicey Memorial H'cap Chase (March, 3m, £1,061).

HICKEY, O.

O. Hickey trained the New Zealand-bred Moiffa to win the 1904 Grand National for Mr Spencer Gollon.

HIGHLAND WEDDING

Brown gelding, 1957, registered in Miss Prior's Half-Bred Stud Book, Question—Princess (Corbridge). Bred by Mr John Caldwell, Prestwick, Ayrshire.

A fine, if somewhat plain stamp of old-fashioned chaser, Highland Wedding was produced by permit-holder and veterinary surgeon Peter Calver to win six point-to-points and run second in the Royal Artillery Gold Cup, Sandown. He was then sold to Mr D. J. Jackson and trained thereafter by Toby Balding, went on to win 12 chases including the Whitbread Trial, Ascot (1966), the four-

Best Times

Distance	Time	Horse-age-weight	Date
2m H	3m 42.20	Tasty Son 10-10-1	11-3-73
2½m H	4m 52.40	Nereo 4-10-12	29-8-70
3m H	5.48.8	Mezzofanti 6-10-2	3-5-78
2m C	3m 52	Napoleon 7-11-5	24-8-74
2½m C	4m 57.60	Coolure 7-10-13	11-5-66
3m C	6m 2.50	Stanhope Street 10-12-0	6-5-76
3m 3f 116y C	7m 2.20	Stanhope Street 8-11-11	18-5-74

mile Eider Chase, Newcastle, three times (1966, 1967 and 1969), and the 1969 Grand National, 10-4 (E. Harty), 100/9, by 12l, 1l, from Steel Bridge, 10-0 (R. Pitman) and Rondetto, 10-6 (J. King).

A most resolute horse who stayed extreme distances and loved the mud, Highland Wedding won the National in the colours of Mr Thomas Hall McKoy, jun., who took him home to Canada in March 1970.

HILL, William (1903-71)

William Hill's activities as an owner and breeder were confined to Flat-racing but the firm of bookmakers he founded and which bears his name, serves racing as a whole. The William Hill Organization is now firmly established as the leading firm of bookmakers in the country and sponsor a number of races under N.H. Rules, including the valuable conditions William Hill Christmas Hurdle on Boxing Day and the Imperial Cup.

William Hill was born in Birmingham. He was one of a family of 11 and left school at the age of 12 to work as a farm boy. He began 'making a book' during World War I when serving an apprenticeship with B.S.A. He moved to London in 1929 and made his mark as a bookmaker by laying against Big Game for the 1942 Derby. He contended, accurately, that the horse would not stay.

He founded studs at Sezincote and Whitsbury and among the good horses he bred are the fine sire Grey Sovereign, the St Leger winner Cantelo, and the Gimcrack winner Be Careful.

HILL HOUSE

Bay gelding, 1960, By Thunder! or Indian Blue—Pretty Baby (Kingsway). Bred and owned by Mr L. Colville.

Hill House won a total of three hurdle races, the last of which, a 12-length victory in the 1967 Schweppes Gold Trophy, Newbury, only eleven days after running fourth under 10-12 in a modest handicap at Sandown, sparked off one of the biggest controversies of the 'sixties. After his victory, which was greeted with sustained booing, Hill House was dope tested and the result showing a high concentration of cortisone, there followed an inquiry which lasted 171 days.

In order to assist the stewards in their deliberations, Hill House was sent on 13th May to the Equine Research Station at Newmarket where he remained until 9th June, after which the following report was issued:

"In the first 48 hours after admission of Hill House the urine contained abnormally high concentrations of cortisol. These were of the same magnitude as that found in sample A.B.810 obtained from this horse at Newbury Racecourse on February 18th, 1967.

"After the first 48 hours at the Equine Research Station the concentration of cortisol in the urine of Hill House fell to approximately one-third the initial concentration but remained consistently higher (four to five times) than that found in the urine of apparently normal racehorses."

It was therefore concluded that Hill House manufactured some of his own cortisone and the enquiry was closed.

Hill House, who had been trained by Ryan Price, was then sold for £12,700 to bookmaker John Banks. During the next three seasons he ran 23 times without success and indeed often refused to start. A spell of point-to-pointing proved no more successful and he was finally retired.

HOBBS, Bruce, M.C. (b.1920)

The son of N.H. trainer, Reg Hobbs (q.v.), Bruce Hobbs was born in America. A beautiful, natural horseman with long legs and quiet hands, he started riding in point-to-points when only 14 and turned professional in 1937. The following year he became the youngest rider ever (17) to win the Grand National on Mrs du Pont Scott's Battleship. He also won the Welsh Grand National in 1938 on Timber Wolf and the Cedarhurst Grand National, U.S.A., before breaking his back.

During World War II, he served with the Queen's Own Yorkshire Dragoons, became a captain and won the Military Cross. He also won the Palestine Grand National. When hostilities ceased he weighed 14½ stone. He shed three stone in three weeks but the effort was too severe and he abandoned his riding career.

From 1945 to 1951 he trained a small string of jumpers, chiefly for Mr and Mrs John Rogerson, for whom he won the 1946 Grand Sefton with War Risk. When this arrangement was terminated he did a spell as assistant to several trainers before starting to train under Jockey Club Rules, at first privately for Mr David Robinson and later a large and extremely successful public stable at Palace House, Newmarket.

HOBBS, Reginald

Father of former N.H. professional jockey and current leading Flat-trainer Bruce (q.v.), Reg Hobbs was for a time Master of Horse to Mr Ambrose Clark (q.v.) in the U.S.A. In 1922 he returned to England and looked after Mr and Mrs Clark's hunters at Melton Mowbray until they gave up hunting in 1931. That year he set up a stable of jumpers in Lambourn to which Mr Clark sent a few horses.

He was Leading Trainer in seasons 1940-41 and 1941-42. His best winners were Medoc II, with whom he won the 1942 Cheltenham Gold Cup for Lord Sefton, and Battleship who, ridden by his son, won the 1938 Grand National. Hobbs was so pessimistic about the chances of his diminutive horse (Battleship measured 15.2), who he averred would not be able to see over the Chair, that he refused to have a bet until he was persuaded to accept £1,000-£15 "in case he had to buy the champagne".

He continued to train after the war and had charge of the smart hurdler, Vidi, with whom he won the 1946 County Hurdle.

HOBSON, F. G. (b.1842)

Fred Hobson, known affectionately as "the Squire" won the 1877 Grand National on his own Austerlitz. He had to overcome considerable opposition from his stable who were not impressed by his habit of catching hold of the back of the saddle when landing over a fence and wished to put up a 'pro'. In fact "the Squire", who was a great friend of Arthur Yates, was a very competent amateur and headed the list in 1867 with 36 winners, beating such as George Ede and Arthur Yates.

A kindly man with a neat wit, he once replied to a large tough who had evidently lost money on him at Croydon races and enquired belligerently whether he could fight, "No, at least not with a great big fellow like you . . . but I can run like the devil."

His wife divorced him and subsequently married Arthur Yates.

HOLLAND, J.

J. Holland held the licence for the Denton-based stable of Bernard Bletsoe

that trained the 1901 Grand National winner, Grudon.

HOLMAN, George (d.1896)

A member of the famous Cheltenham racing family, George Holman was the second son of William (q.v.).

A leading N.H. jockey he, like his father, won the Cheltenham Grand Annual on five occasions, in 1862 on Penarth, in 1869 on Brick and 1873, 1875 and 1876 on Master Mowbray. He also won the Grand Metropolitan Chase in 1866 on Globule and the 1873 Liverpool Hurdle on Fidele.

The nearest he came to winning the Grand National was 1870 when he rode The Doctor and was beaten a neck by The Colonel. Spectators could not recall a finer finish to the great race but their view was not shared by a visiting R.S.P.C.A. Inspector who instigated a summons against George Stevens for excessive whipping and spurring of his mount.

HOLMAN, William (b.1810)

William Holman was a leading member of the Cheltenham racing set and the founder of a famous N.H. family. He trained three Grand National winners, Freetrader (1856), Little Charley (1858) and Anatis (1860), and rode the winner of the Cheltenham Grand Annual on no less than five occasions. He won on Xeno (1841), Stanmore, twice (1842 and 1847), The Page (1843), and Sir Peter Laurie (1852).

His six sons included George (q.v.), John, a prominent N.H. jockey, Alfred, a trainer and manager of Cheltenham Racecourse, William, a vet, and Walter and Frederick, both keen amateurs. Frederick's granddaughter married 'Frenchy' Nicholson and thus he is the great-grandfather of David Nicholson (q.v.).

HOPE-JOHNSTONE, Capt. Wentworth William (d.1910)

A member of a well-known Dumfriesshire family, Wenty Hope-Johnstone served in the 7th Hussars and was one of the leading amateurs of his day. He rode 352 winners and was Champion Amateur in 1876 riding 45 winners. He won the Grand Military three times, in 1873 on Revirescat, 1875 on Lady Sneerwell and

1876 on Earl Marshal. He was elected to the N.H.C. in October 1893. On his retirement from the saddle he farmed in Kent and stewarded at Gatwick, Plumpton and Lingfield.

HORSERACE BETTING LEVY BOARD

The Levy Board was established by the Betting Levy Act of 1961. The first chairman was Field-Marshal Lord Harding. Under the Betting, Gaming and Lotteries Act of 1963, which consolidated all previous legislation, the Levy Board is responsible for assessing and collecting monetary contributions from bookmakers and the totalisator and for applying the money thus raised to the following purposes:

(a) the improvement of breeds of horses;

(b) the advancement and encouragement of veterinary science and education;

(c) the improvement of horseracing.

The Board is composed of a Chairman and two members appointed by the Home Secretary, who must be persons with no interest connected with horseracing which might prevent them from discharging their duties in an impartial manner. These are joined by the Chairman of the Bookmakers' Committee, the Chairman of the Horserace Totalisator Board and members of the Jockey Club. The present Chairman is Sir Desmond Plummer.

HORSERACE TOTALISATOR BOARD

The Horserace Totalisator Board evolved from the Racecourse Betting Control Board set up in 1929 (*see* THE TOTE). The Board's Constitution and powers are embodied in the Horserace Totalisator and Betting Levy Board Act of 1972. The Board comprises a chairman and four members, all appointed by the Home Secretary.

The Chairman of the Board is *ex-officio* a member of the Horserace Betting Levy Board.

The 1978 composition of the Board is – Chairman: Mr Woodrow Wyatt; Director-General: Dr Geoffrey Ardron, M.B.E.; Secretary: J. M. Burns, Esq.; Members: Sir Leonard Barford, Sir Alexander Glen, Dame Elizabeth Ackroyd, Dr Geoffrey Ardron, M.B.E.

HOWARD, Stanley McKnight (d.1956)

The son of Col. Henry Howard of Stone House, Kidderminster, Stanley Howard was one of the luckiest owners in steeplechasing. James Daly found most of his horses and it was said that he never owned a bad one.

He trained with Tom Coulthwaite (*q.v.*), until the latter lost his licence in 1913, and won the Grand National twice, with Eremon in 1907 and Jenkinstown, 1910. He sold his horses when Coulthwaite lost his licence but resumed owning after the war. Alf Newey (*q.v.*) who had ridden Eremon, trained for him and won the County Hurdle and the Welsh Champion Hurdle with Assaroe. Colours: Eton blue, olive-green sash.

HUDSON, Frank (1896-1971)

A former jockey, Frank Hudson took out a licence in 1927. His yard, a mixed one, was in Henley-in-Arden, Warwickshire, and when he saddled Sundew to win the 1957 Grand National, the magnificent chestnut was the only chaser in the yard. He also trained the fine stayer Bitter Sweet, who won the Queen Alexandra Stakes twice.

HUGHES, Desmond T.

The story of 'Dessie' Hughes is something of a fairytale. After serving an apprenticeship with Dan Kirwan on the Curragh, he grew too heavy for Flat-racing and came to England to try his luck as a National Hunt jockey. He was attached to Reg Akehurst but found it hard to make his mark and was not prospering when a very bad fall put him in hospital for months. He returned to Ireland and was out of racing until he joined up with Mick O'Toole (*q.v.*). He now acts as first jockey and right-hand man to the big and powerful stable and achieved the highlight of his career at the 1977 National Hunt Meeting when he rode a treble including the Gold Cup on the outsider, Davy Lad (*q.v.*).

His principal victories are:

The Cheltenham Gold Cup (1977) Davy Lad

The Arkle Challenge Trophy (1977) Tip the Wink

The Lloyds Bank Champion Novice Hurdle (1977) Mac's Chariot

The Sun Alliance Novices Hurdle (1975) Davy Lad; (1976) Parkhill

The Lloyds Bank Hurdle (1976) Bit of a Jig

The Templegate Hurdle (1978) Monksfield

HUGHES-ONSLOW, Maj. Arthur (1862-1914)

An old Etonian and an officer in the 10th Hussars, Maj. Hughes-Onslow was the leading military rider of his day.

He won the Grand Military three times, in 1888 on Bertha, 1898 on County Council and in 1903 on Marpessa. He also won the Irish Grand Military at Punchestown three times and the Conyngham Cup in 1899, 1901 and 1903 on Covert Hack. He was killed in action in 1914.

HUNTERS' STEEPLECHASE

A hunters' steeplechase is a weight-for-age steeplechase confined to horses certified by a Master of Hounds to have been hunted during the current year, and ridden by amateur riders.

HUNTINGDON (Group 4)

Huntingdon, a right-handed, flat, oval-shaped course about $1\frac{1}{2}$ miles in length, with easy bends, has staged N.H. racing since 1886. The turf is old and the gravel subsoil ensures good drainage. The sport provided is of a modest quality but several sponsors have been attracted and recently the level of prize money has been raised.

Good prizes include the Lord Protector H'cap Hurdle (April, 2m 4f, £1,207), the Fitzwilliam H'cap Chase (March, 3m 100yds, £1,318) and a group of races sponsored by Ward Hill Bookmakers at the February meeting.

Best Times

Distance	Time	Horse-age-weight	Date
2m 200y H	4m 2	Blue Bidder 5-10-6	25-10-75
2½m H	4m 49.70	Linden Dolly 4-10-12	3-5-77
3m H	5m 54	Silkstone 5-10-5	14-4-73
2m 100y C	4m 7.20	Clare Dawn 7-10-9	25-10-75
2½m C	5m 3.20	Vultown 8-10-6	14-4-73
3m 100y C	6m 16.20	Mickey Mouse 8-10-0	22-10-77

HUNTSMAN

Bay horse, 1853, not in the General Stud Book, by Tupsley.

A Liverpool 'hardy annual' of the mid nineteenth century, Huntsman was produced by Ben Land for whom he ran third in the 1859 Grand National. The following year he went one better, being beaten just ½l by Anatis (rec. 26lb) after which he was bought by French-based Yorkshireman, Harry Lamplugh on behalf of his patron the Vicomte de Namur, who had been trying to win the National for years. In 1862 Huntsman enabled him to realize this ambition, carrying 11-0 (H. Lamplugh), 3/1f, he won by 4l, a distance, from Bridegroom, 10-13 (B. Land) and Romeo, 8-12 (Mr C. Bennett).

HURST PARK (1890-1962)

The Hurst Park Club Syndicate was formed in 1889 under the chairmanship of Mr Joseph Davis. The venture was a great success and became a public company and gained a quote on the Stock Exchange, soon afterwards. The first jumping fixture was held in 1890 and apart from stoppages from 1916-18 and 1940-49 when it became a military camp, jumping continued until its closure. From the start racing was of a high standard. The gravelly sub-soil ensured good going, the prize money was uniformly high and the calibre of management exceptional.

The best-known races were the Grand National Trial, instituted in 1950 and run at the March meeting, the Queen Elizabeth Chase (1949) and the Triumph Hurdle (first run in 1939 but not resumed until 1950). These last two races were the brain-children of Sir John Crocker Bulteel, one of the most distinguished of all racing officials. The Queen Elizabeth Chase was attached to the otherwise Flat Whitsun meeting and was enormously popular with the public, although trainers of high-class horses found it too late in the year. Nevertheless the success of Sandown's Whitbread Gold Cup (in April) shows the validity of Sir John's idea. The first Queen Elizabeth Chase was won, appropriately enough, by the Queen Elizabeth and the then Princess Elizabeth's Monave'en. Monave'en broke his leg and was destroyed during the 1951 running of the race and is buried near the stables. In October 1962 the racecourse was closed to make way for a housing estate.

The Queen Elizabeth Chase (Hurst Park, 3m, 180y)

	HORSE	OWNER	RIDER	TRAINER
1949	Monave'en	H.R.H. Princess Elizabeth	A. Grantham	P. Cazalet
1950	Coloured School Boy	Mr W. F. Highnam	J. Bullock	T. F. Rimell
1951	Red April	Lord Stalbridge	T. Cusack	V. Cross
1952	*No Race*			
1953	Galloway Braes	Lady Orde	R. Morrow	A. Kilpatrick
1954	Galloway Braes	Lady Orde	R. Morrow	A. Kilpatrick
1955	Limb of Law	Mr E. Bee	J. Dowdeswell	T. Yates
1956	State Secret	Mr Clifford Nicholson	P. A. Farrell	W. Hall

Triumph Hurdle (4-y-o, 2m, 100y)

	HORSE	OWNER	RIDER	TRAINER
1939	Grey Talk	Mr James Hennessy	S. Rochet	In France
1950	Abrupto	M. E. Marchant	R. Mantelin	E. Diggle
1951	Blue Song II	M. D. Saint	F. Thirion	G. Pelat
1952	Hoggar	M. M. Fabiani	R. Triboit	J. Cunnington
1953	Clair Soleil	Mr G. C. Judd	F. T. Winter	F. Mathet
1954	Prince Charlemagne	Mr L. Lipton	L. Piggott	T. H. Carey
1955	Kwannin	Mme L. Chataignoux	P. Delfarguiel	A. Head
1956	Square Dance	Mrs V. G. Cardy	M. Scudamore	F. Walwyn
1957	Meritorious	Mr J. W. Hart	D. Dillon	P. Thrale
1958	Pundit	Mrs M. Aitken	H. Sprague	S. Ingham
1959	Amazon's Choice	Mr H. J. Verrall	J. Gilbert	P. Thrale
1960	Turpial	Mrs A. T. Hodgson	A. Freeman	P. Cazalet
1961	Cantab	Miss E. Chanelle	F. T. Winter	H. R. Price
1962	Beaver II	Capt. H. R. Price	J. Gifford	H. R. Price

See also CHELTENHAM (*Daily Express* Triumph Hurdle).

HYDE, Timothy Joseph (d.1961)

A former show-rider, Tim Hyde is said to have become a professional jockey at the insistence of trainer J. Ruttle, who insisted that "only Hyde was right for Workman". It was an inspired choice because together Hyde and Workman won the 1939 Grand National.

His other big wins included the Irish Grand National twice, in 1938 on Clare County and in 1942 on Prince Regent. It is for his association with Prince Regent that Hyde is best remembered. The pair won the 1946 Cheltenham Gold Cup and were third and fourth in the Nationals of 1946 and 1947.

In 1951 he was partially paralysed by a fall and spent the rest of his life in a wheelchair. He trained a few horses at his home in Cashel, Co. Tipperary, assisted by his son Tim.

I'ANSON, Robert

The son of William I'Anson who bred, owned and trained the Derby winners, Blink Bonny and Blair Athol, Robert I'Anson was considered to be the best jockey of his day. Despite being over six feet tall, he was incredibly neat and stylish. He was also tremendously popular, both with the public and in the weighing-room and was invariably kind to young jockeys. His major victories included:

The Grand Steeplechase de Paris (1879)
Wild Monarch
The Leamington Grand Annual (1869)
Scipio
The Liverpool Hurdle (1871) Stradbroke
The Great Sandown Chase (1876) Palm
The Surrey Grand Open Chase (1876)
Shifnal
The Sandown Grand International (1878)
Shifnal
The Great Metropolitan Chase (1878)
Citizen; (1880) Bacchus; (1881) Bacchus
The Champion Chase (1881) Bacchus
The Prince of Wales' Chase (1880) Bacchus;
(1881) Bacchus
The Grand National Hurdle (1880) Charles
I; (1881) Charles I

He afterwards trained in the Burgh Heath stables, Epsom, later occupied by Arthur Nightingall and saddled Austerlitz to win the 1877 Grand National.

ILEX

Chestnut gelding, 1884, not in the General Stud Book, Rostrevor—Vatonia (Master Bagot).

Ilex, who won the 1890 Grand National, 10-5 (A. Nightingall), 4/1 f, by 12l, a bad third, from Pau, 10-5 (Hasley) and M.P., 11-5 (Mr W. H. Moore), was always associated with the Nightingall family with whom he was a special favourite. Arthur first saw the horse as a four-year-old at Leicester where he had been engaged to ride it in a seller. He was distinctly unimpressed with the rather shaggy chestnut with no front, a large belly and four ominous bandages. These last were however removed by the owner who materialized mysteriously on the way to the start, remarked that they were more ornamental than useful and that Ilex would win by the length of the street without them, which he duly did, impressing Arthur so much that he persuaded George Masterman to buy the horse who was henceforth trained at Epsom by Arthur's father, John.

Ilex also won the prestigious Lancashire Chase, Manchester (1890) and was twice third in subsequent Grand Nationals. In 1891 under 12-3, he was beaten ½l, a bad third, by Come Away (11-12) and Cloister (11-7) and in 1892 with 12-7, was beaten 20l and 2l, by Father O'Flynn (10-5) and Cloister (12-3). He broke down so badly in this race that his leg was in plaster for weeks and he was never able to run again.

Arthur Nightingall, the outstanding professional of his age, winner of three Grand Nationals and just about every important steeplechase in Britain, France, Austria and Germany, rated Ilex "absolutely the best I ever rode".

INGHAM, S. W. H. (1908-77)

'Staff' Ingham was apprenticed to Stanley Wootten and rode on the Flat with brilliant success before becoming too heavy. Among his most important successes was the Royal Hunt Cup on H.M. King George V's Weathervane. He subsequently rode with flair and polish over hurdles, winning the Imperial Cup (1936) on Negro and the Coventry Hurdle (1935) on Polly Steven. He was frequently placed in the Champion Hurdle.

He served with the R.A.F. during World War II, becoming a Squadron Leader. Afterwards he trained at Epsom, at first under both Rules, but latterly only on the Flat. He won the Imperial Cup (1948) with Anglesey and the Triumph Hurdle twice, in 1958 with Pundit and 1968 with England's Glory. He also produced some fine jockeys in the Wootten tradition, including ace hurdles-rider, Jimmy Uttley (q.v.).

INJURED JOCKEYS FUND

The Injured Jockeys Fund was set up in 1964 after the terrible accidents to Tim Brookshaw and Paddy Farrell which left them both paralysed below the waist. Mr Edward Courage and Mr Clifford Nicholson launched an appeal on their behalf to which the response was so great that it was decided to set up a fund so that, in future, assistance could be made to any jockey or his family that might be killed or injured in the course of his profession.

The fund pays for legal advice on questions affecting the interests of injured jockeys and also the accommodation expenses of jockeys attending the Medical Rehabilitation Centre. In addition it will pay all medical expenses on application; in a number of cases, of jockeys injured many years ago, the Trustees have recommended and paid for treatment which have improved the beneficiary's health and enjoyment of life. It gives weekly assistance to jockeys whose earning capacity has been damaged and makes loans to enable injured jockeys to buy a home and set up a small business. Widows living in rural areas have been provided with a car and, in some cases, assistance with school fees for children in areas where there is no satisfactory state school.

The fund raises its money from voluntary contributions, Christmas-card sales and various fund-raising activities. As it does not have enough capital to support the weekly grants made, which are currently running at £40,000 a year, the Trustees are dependent on continuing public support. Mrs Susan Mills, Mrs Rosemary Preston and Mrs Hilary Kew act as voluntary almoners, seeing that cases are referred to the Trustees and keeping in constant touch with beneficiaries.

The headquarters have recently moved from London to Market Place, Ely, Cambridgeshire and Mr J. W. P. Richardson acts as Secretary. The Trustees are Mr Edward Courage, C.B.E., Lord Oaksey, Mrs Lester Piggott, Mr Brough Scott, Mr F. T. Winter, C.B.E., Mr R. J. McCreery and Col. J. A. T. Barstow, D.S.O., T.D.

INKSLINGER

Bay gelding, 1967, Bronze Babu—Laurel Wreath (Arden). Bred in the U.S.A. by the Glade Valley Farms Inc.

Inkslinger, bought as a yearling for $5,500, became a leading fencer in the U.S.A. winning 10 races including the Colonial Cup, Camden (1971) as a four-year-old. On this occasion he was ridden by his trainer Mike Smithwick's cousin, Tommy Carberry. When his owner, Mrs Martha Jenney, decided to send her champion to be trained in Ireland, it was to Tommy Carberry's trainer and father-in-law, Dan Moore (q.v.), that he was despatched.

At the National Hunt Meeting of 1973, Inkslinger achieved a memorable double winning the National Hunt 2-mile Champion Chase and the Cathcart Chase.

A remarkably tough and versatile horse, Inkslinger won only one more race in Europe but he ran some fine races notably when second to Pendil (q.v.), in the 1973 King George VI Chase, third to The Dikler (q.v.) in the 1974 Whitbread Gold Cup, and fourth to Tartan Ace in the 1973 Irish Grand National.

INSURANCE

Bay gelding, 1927, Achtoi—Prudent Girl (Juggernaut). Bred by Mr E. J. Hope.

A fair horse on the Flat who won four races including the Welsh St Leger, Insurance went on to prove a fine hurdler whose nine victories included two Champion Hurdles. In 1932 ridden by Ted Leader, 4/5 favourite, he won with contemptuous ease by 12l, a bad third, from Song of Essex (W. Parvin) and Jack Drummer (T. Cullinan), and the following year ridden this time by Willie Stott and again odds-on favourite at 10/11 he won by ¾l, 8l, from Windermere Laddie (S. Ingham) and Indian Salmon (G. Pellerin).

Insurance, who also won a two-mile chase at Newbury, was owned, like Golden Miller, by Mr Philip Carr. When in the autumn of 1931, the latter learnt of his incurable illness, both horses were sold to the Hon. Dorothy Paget (q.v.). Insurance was trained by Basil Briscoe.

IRISH LIZARD

Bay gelding, 1943, Irish Trout—Kiki (Tredennis). Bred by Mr T. D. McKeever.

An indomitable little horse and a rare stayer owned by the 7th Earl of Sefton, Irish Lizard raced for eight seasons and won 13 chases. His two favourite courses were Cheltenham where he won the then important 4m Fred Withington Chase (1953 and 1954), and Liverpool where he won the Grand Sefton (1952), the Topham (1953) the Christmas Cracker (1953 and 1955). He was also third in two Grand Nationals, in 1953 to Early Mist and in 1954 to Royal Tan. Irish Lizard was trained at Cheltenham by 'Frenchie' Nicholson.

IRISH RACING

National Hunt racing in Ireland is in some respects a nursery for the sport in Great Britain. The warm, wet climate and marvellous limestone grass is ideal for producing steeplechasers and a high proportion of Britain's top-class jumpers come from Ireland as do a number of our top jump-jockeys.

Steeplechasing in Ireland is run by the Irish National Hunt Steeplechase Committee whose headquarters is at 25 Merrion Square, Dublin. The Stewards of the Committee are *ex-officio* members of the British Jockey Club. The Committee use Weatherbys as their Registry Office and Receiver of Entries.

There is no close season in the Irish jumping calendar and their rules permit Flat races for maiden steeplechasers (known as 'bumpers', as they are confined to amateur riders), races that many British trainers are glad to have seen adopted in their own country as they provide immature young chasers with a far less traumatic introduction to racing than the present overcrowded novice hurdles, usually dominated by speedy recruits from the Flat.

The principal courses are Leopardstown and Fairyhouse and the most important races the Irish Grand National at Fairyhouse and the Irish Sweeps Hurdle at Leopardstown.

The Irish Grand National (3m 4f)

	HORSE	OWNER	RIDER	TRAINER
1870	Sir Robert Peel	Mr L. Dunne	Boylan	——
1871	The Doe	Mr Kirkwood	Boylan	——
1872	Scots Grey	Maj. Browne	Mr G. Moore	——
1873	Torrent	Mr P. J. Reynolds	Toole	——
1874	Sailor	Capt. S. Gubbins	W. Ryan	——
1875	Scots Grey	Maj. Browne	Mr S. Moore	——
1876	Grand National	Mr M. Taylor	Mr T. Beasley	——
1877	Thiggin-thue	Mr J. Gubbins	Mr T. Beasley	——
1878	Juggler	Mr Moore	Mr J. Beasley	——
1879	Jupiter Tonans	Mr Lee Barber	Owner	——
1880	Controller	Mr W. Brophy	Mr H. Beasley	——
1881	Antoinette	Mr J. R. Andrews	S. Fleming	——
1882	Chantilly	Mr Fanning	D. Canavan	——
1883	The Gift	Mr P. J. Reynolds	T. Kelly	——
1884	The Gift	Mr P. J. Reynolds	T. Kelly	——
1885	Billet Doux	Count Zborowski	Mr W. Murland	——
1886	Castle Lucas	Mr J. G. Blake	Mr Atkinson	——
1887	Elegantine	Mr Gradwell	Mr R. Brabazon	——
1888	The Maroon	Mr Richards	Mr W. McAuliffe	——
1889	The Citadel	Mr H. Beasley	Owner	——
1890	Greek Girl	Mr H. Gore	Owner	——
1891	Old Tom	Mr S. Kelly	Capt. Burn-Murdoch	——
1892	Springfield Maid	Mr S. A. Leonard	Mr L. Hope	——
1893	Thurles	Maj. Bunbury	L. Ryan	——
1894	The Admiral	Mr F. W. Mitchell	Owner	——
1895	Yellow Girl II	Mr E. Rooney	Mr J. Ennis	——
1896	Royston Crow	Mr G. V. Briscoe	Mr Parsons	——
1897	Breemount's Pride	Mr J. O'C. Murphy	Hopper	——
1898	Porridge	Mr E. Delany	T. Collier	——
1899	Princess Hilda	Mr L. Hope	Mr J. Clarke	——
1900	Mavis of Meath	Mr F. J. Kelly	J. Kelly	——
1901	Tipperary Boy	Mr T. B. Holmes	T. Moran	——
1902	Patlander	Mr M. J. Cleary	J. Cheshire	——
1903	Kirko	Mr T. A. Hartigan	J. Scully	——

	HORSE	OWNER	RIDER	TRAINER
1904	Ascetic's Silver	Mr P. J. Dunne	Dowdall	———
1905	Red Lad	Mr E. M. Lucas	C. Kelly	———
1906	Brown Bess	Mr V. Wall	J. Bresname	———
1907	Sweet Cecil	Mr M. Dawson	Mr T. Price	———
1908	Lord Rivers	Mr P. McLoughlin	Mr R. H. Walker	———
1909	Little Hack II	Mr N. Markey	Mr R. H. Walker	———
1910	Oniche	Mrs F. McDonnell	Mr F. Malone	———
1911	Repeater II	Mr W. L. Goulding	Mr J. A. Trench	———
1912	Small Polly	Mr R. H. Walker	Owner	———
1913	Little Hack II	Mr N. Markey	S. Mathews	———
1914	Civil War	Mr L. King	Capt. P. O'B. Butler	———
1915	Punch	Mr F. Barbour	Mr R. H. Walker	———
1916	Allsorts	Mr J. Kiernan	J. Lynn	Peary
1917	Pay Only	Mr W. P. Hanly	W. S. Sankey	W. P. Hanly
1918	Ballyboggan	Mr E. W. Hope-Johnstone	C. Hawkins	Featherstonehaugh
1919	*No Race*			
1920	Halston	Major Dixon	D. Colbert	J. Ruttle
1921	Bohernore	Mr A. Wills	D. Colbert	C. Brabazon
1922	Halston	Major Dixon	J. Moloney	J. Ruttle
1923	Be Careful	Mrs F. Blacker	J. Moloney	Mrs F. Blacker
1924	Kilbarry	———	W. Horan	Dawson
1925	Dog Fox	———	Jos. Doyle	Featherstonehaugh
1926	Amber Wave	Mr E. A. Kirwan	Mr J. E. O'Brien	W. P. Hanley
1927	Jerpoint	Mr J. M. Barbour	P. Powell	Pardy
1928	Don Sancho	Mr V. H. Smith	T. B. Cullinan	Withington
1929	Alike	Mr F. W. Wise	Owner	Owner
1930	Fanmond	Mr G. Griphin	K. Lenehan	Harry Usher
1931	Impudent Barney	Mrs B. Webster	Mr T. E. McKeever	C. Rogers
1932	Copper Court	Mrs B. Webster	T. Cullen	C. Rogers
1933	Red Park	Lady McCalmont	D. Kirwan	Barry
1934	Poolgowran	Sir J. Nelson	R. Everett	Maj. R. H. Scott
1935	Rathfriland	Mr J. Marskey	J. Regan	F. McKeever
1936	Alice Maythorn	Mr J. Osborne	Mr C. Prendergast	J. Osborne
1937	Pontent	Mr G. Malcomson	F. McKeever	C. Brabazon
1938	Clare County	Mr T. O'Gorman	T. Hyde	Cunningham
1939	Shaun Peel	Mr N. Dixon	J. Wade	C. Creed
1940	Jock Chaucer	Mr H. Egen	J. Lenehan	C. Brabazon
1941	*No Race*			
1942	Prince Regent	Mr J. Rank	T. Hyde	T. Dreaper
1943	Golden Jack	Hon. D. Paget	D. Moore	C. Rogers
1944	Knight's Crest	Mrs W. Moloney	M. Molony	C. Harty
1945	Heirdom	Mr H. Quinn	J. Maguire	J. Kirwan
1946	Golden View II	Mrs L. Lillingston	M. Molony	R. O'Connell
1947	Revelry	Mr J. Doyle	D. Moore	J. Brogan
1948	Hamstar	Mr B. Hamilton	P. Doyle	W. O'Grady
1949	Shagreen	Mr J. Rank	E. Newman	T. Dreaper
1950	Dominic's Bar	Mrs P. Kiely	M. Molony	T. Hyde
1951	Icy Calm	Mr P. Gray	P. Doyle	W. O'Grady
1952	Alberoni	Mr H. Stanley	L. Stephens	M. V. O'Brien
1953	Overshadow	Mrs J. Wood	A. Power	C. Magnier
1954	Royal Approach	Lord Bicester	P. Taaffe	T. Dreaper
1955	Umm	Mr D. Rooney	P. Taaffe	G. Wells
1956	Air Prince	Mrs J. McClintock	T. O'Brien	J. McClintock
1957	Kilballyowen	Mrs M. Lynch	G. W. Robinson	P. Norris
1958	Gold Legend	Mrs J. Murphy	J. Lehane	J. Brogan
1959	Zonda	Mrs St. J. Nolan	P. Taaffe	M. Geraghty
1960	Olympia	Lord Donoughmore	T. Taaffe	T. Dreaper
1961	Fortria	Mr G. Ansley	P. Taaffe	T. Dreaper
1962	Kerforo	Mr F. Stafford	L. McCloughlin	T. Dreaper
1963	Last Link	Mr A. Craigie	P. Woods	T. Dreaper

HORSE	OWNER	RIDER	TRAINER
1964 Arkle	Anne, Duchess of Westminster	P. Taaffe	T. Dreaper
1965 Splash	Mr A. Craigie	P. Woods	T. Dreaper
1966 Flyingbolt	Mr T. Wilkinson	P. Taaffe	T. Dreaper
1967 Vulpine	Mr T. Nicholson	M. Curran	P. Mullins
1968 Herring Gull	Mrs G. A. J. Wilson	J. Crowley	P. Mullins
1969 Sweet Dreams	Mrs P. Meeham	R. Coonan	K. Bell
1970 Garoupe	Mrs F. Williams	C. Finnegan	F. Flood
1971 King's Sprite	Mr R. McIlhagga	A. Moore	G. Wells
1972 Dim Wit	Mr J. J. O'Neill	M. Curran	P. Mullins
1973 Tartan Slave	Mrs S. Graham	J. Cullan	T. Costello
1974 Colebridge	Mrs P. Burrell	E. Wright	J. Dreaper
1975 Brown Lad	Mrs P. Burrell	T. Carberry	J. Dreaper
1976 Brown Lad	Mrs P. Burrell	T. Carberry	J. Dreaper
1977 Billycan	Mr V. Kilkenny	M. Morris	A. Maxwell
1978 Brown Lad	Mrs P. Burrell	G. Dowd	J. Dreaper
1979 *TIED COTTAGE*		*A. ROBINSON*	

Irish Sweeps Hurdle (2m)

HORSE	OWNER	RIDER	TRAINER
1969 Normandy	Mr B. Jenks	T. Biddlecombe	T. F. Rimell
1970 Persian War	Mr H. Alper	J. Uttley	A. Pitt
1971 Kelanne	Mr J. M. Kelly	W. Smith	W. Marshall
1972 Captain Christy	Mrs J. Samuel	H. Beasley	P. Taaffe
1973 Comedy of Errors	Mr E. Wheatley	W. Smith	T. F. Rimell
1974 Comedy of Errors	Mr E. Wheatley	K. B. White	T. F. Rimell
1975 Night Nurse	Mr R. Spencer	P. Broderick	M. H. Easterby
1976 Master Monday	Mr P. Quirke	J. P. Harty	L. Quirke
1977 Decent Fellow	Brig.-Gen. Kilbride	R. Linley	G. Balding
1978 Chiniullah	Mr R. Eastwood	G. Newman	M. O'Toole

1979 IRIAN   *ANN FERRIS*

JACK HORNER

Chestnut gelding, 1917, Cyllius—Melton's Guide (Melton). Bred by Mr John Musker at the Melton Stud.

Jack Horner was sold as a yearling to Lord Barnby and for several seasons carried the Blankney Hunt Servants and on one occasion the Master, Colonel Willey, in a historic 14-mile point. After changing hands several times, Jack Horner was sent chasing and ran seventh to Double Chance in the 1925 Grand National thus landing a substantial gamble for his American amateur rider Morgan de Witt Blair, who had had his appendix out just 16 days previously and sweated off 16lb at the last 48 hours in order to do the weight. A month later Jack Horner came up at the Sandown Spring Sales and was sold for £1,250 to the Hon. Kenneth Mackay for whom he proved a veritable goldmine. After winning two chases, Mr Mackay passed him on through the agency of Hon. George Lambton to American, Charlie Schwartz, for £4,000 plus a £2,000 contingency should he win the National. George Lambton thought it a grossly inflated sum but Charlie Schwartz wanted to win the National and was not concerned with the price necessary to achieve it. The deal took place only weeks before the National and Jack Horner remained in Jack Leader's yard to his great advantage for Jack Leader had been conspicuously successful in developing the horse's lamentably deficient speed by working him with the two-year-olds. In the event Jack Horner, 10-5 (W. Watkinson), 25/1, won by 3l, 1l, from Old Tay Bridge, 12-2 (J. Anthony) and Bright's Boy, 11-8 (E. Doyle).

Poor Watkinson was killed within a month as a result of a fall at Bogside and Jack Horner broke down in preparation for the 1927 National. He was shipped across the Atlantic and spent his retirement in the U.S.A.

JAY TRUMP

Bay gelding (U.S.A.), 1957, Tonga Prince—Be Trump (Bernborough). Bred at Jay Sessenich, Lancaster, Pennsylvania.

After an unsuccessful career on the Flat, Jay Trump turned to steeplechasing with vastly improved results, winning nine chases including the 4½-mile Maryland Hunt Cup over timber twice. In 1964 his owners, Mrs M. Stephenson and Mr Tommy Smith (who regularly rode him) sent him to England to be trained by Fred Winter for the 1965 Grand National. After winning three of his preliminary races, Jay Trump, 11-5 (Mr T. Smith), 100/6, got the better of a titanic struggle with the indomitable Freddie, 11-10 (P. McCarron) winning by just ¾l, with Mr Jones, 10-13 (Mr C. Collins) 20l away third.

Jay Trump thus became the third American horse to win the National, the others being Rubio and Battleship. After his Aintree triumph Jay Trump went to France and attempted to bring off an unprecedented international treble by winning the Grand Steeple. Although he failed, he ran a great race to finish third, beaten a total of 2½l, to Hyeres III.

He then returned to his native land and spent his retirement carrying Mrs Stephenson with the Camango Hounds, Ohio. Jay Trump was the subject of a book *The Will to Win*.

JEALOUSY

Brown mare, not in General Stud Book, by The Cure—dam's pedigree untraced.

One of the many National winning descendants of Brutandorf (The Cure, like Cure-All (*q.v.*), was bred from The Physician, a son of Brutandorf), Jealousy belonged to Mr J. Bennett and was evidently a mare of some account for when the weights for the 1861 National were published, George Stevens, the leading professional, immediately picked her out and turned down 13 rides in order to ride her. Alas for his prescience, he was claimed by one of his retainers whose horse could not run and Jealousy, 9-12, was ridden by Kendall and starting at 5/1 second favourite won by 2l, the same, from The Dane, 10-0 (W. White) and Old Ben Roe, 10-7 (G. Waddington). Kendall rode a waiting race, made ground steadily from Becher's on the second circuit and came away from the last to win readily.

In 1863 Jealousy was made favourite at 3/1, but, under 11-10, more forcing tactics were adopted and after making the running until Becher's on the second circuit, she faded to finish sixth.

JENKINS, W. H. P.

Born in Monmouthshire, 'Jenks' Jenkins was educated at Rugby and Merton College, Oxford, from which he derived the pseudonym of Mr Merton, under which he rode as an amateur under N.H. Rules with considerable success. He was also a very good man to hounds and was well known with the Beaufort.

He married Lady Caroline Villiers, a daughter of the sixth Earl of Jersey and after his retirement from the saddle, trained for himself and a few friends.

He kept open house for young men fond of riding and kept them as fit and well as their horses. A rigorous schooler, his horses rarely fell and his most notable feat was the training of Zoedone and her owner-rider, Prince Charles Kinsky, to win the 1883 Grand National.

JENKINSTOWN

Bay gelding, 1901, by Hackler—Playmate (Play Actor). Bred in Ireland by Mr P. Leonard.

After winning two chases in Ireland as a six-year-old when owned by Mr James Daly, Jenkinstown was sold for £600 to Mr Stanley Howard and was sent to Tom Coulthwaite's Hednesford establishment. Either he took time to acclimatize or else his talents were admirably concealed, for apart from winning a small race in 1909, he revealed no special merit until the 1910 Grand National in which, carrying 10-5 (R. Chadwick), he was by no means unfancied at 100/8 and won readily by 3l, the same, from the mighty Jerry M., 12-7 (E. Driscoll) and Odor, 9-8 (Mr R. H. Hall). Jenkinstown never won another race, fell in two subsequent Nationals and died in 1912.

JERRY

Not in General Stud Book, Catterick— Sister to Jerry (Bellerophon).

Like many early National winners, Jerry's particulars are incomplete and obscure. Thanks to Mr Henry Wright, it is possible to establish his racing career with some clarity but the problem of his ownership is quite another matter.

Jerry first sprang to prominence in 1837 when he won the big chase at Leamington beating Vivian. He appears to have drawn a blank in 1838 but the following year he won at Northampton and Daventry and after being disqualified at Waltham Abbey for not going between the flags, he won the 1840 Grand National, 12-0 (Mr Bretherton), 12/1, by 4l, the same, from Arthur, 12-0 (Mr A. McDonough) and Valentine, 12-0 (Mr Power). Jerry was indubitably fortunate to win, for not only did his stable companion Lottery make a rare error of judgement at the wall and bring down The Nun, Columbine and Seventy-Four in his wake, but Arthur (later the sire of The Lamb) somewhat unluckily pitched over at Valentine's and made up a tremendous amount of ground to finish second.

A contemporary described Jerry as idle, by no means brilliant but one who, if allowed to start quietly, could go on for ever.

Jerry was variously ascribed as belonging to John Elmore, Lord Sheffield and Mr Villebois. Henry Wright, the most reliable statistician of the time, plumps for John Elmore, a theory supported by the fact that Jerry was habitually ridden by Elmore's stable jockey, Jem Mason and that he features in C. B. Spalding's charming study of Elmore's horses (Lottery, Jerry and Sailor). It seems probable that Jerry was leased on occasions to Lord Sheffield and/or Mr Villebois both of whom are known to have had dealings with John Elmore.

Jerry ran only once subsequent when he was fourth to Lottery in the big chase at Leamington.

JERRY M.

Bay gelding, 1903. Bred in Co. Limerick, Ireland, by Miss Kate Hartigan.

		Lord Clifden
	Hampton	
		Lady Langden
Walmsgate		
		Doncaster
	Flying Footstep	
Jerry M.		Atalanta
		Beauclerk
	Luminary	
		Stella
Luminary Mare		
		Sam Chifney
	Quinine	
		Talipes

A slashing, bright bay Aintree type, once described as "powerful enough to pull a brewer's dray", Jerry M. defied wind, back and leg troubles for four brief seasons and was unquestionably the outstanding horse of his age. He won 14 of his 20 races including the 1912 Grand National, 12-7 (E. Piggott), 4/1, joint favourite, by 6l, 4l, from Bloodstone, 11-6 (F. Lyall) and Axle Pin, 10-4 (I. Anthony), the Grand Steeple, Auteuil (1910) and four chases over Liverpool. He was also second in the 1909 Grand Steeple and the 1910 Grand National.

Unlike most big, strong staying chasers, Jerry M. wasted no time in revealing his exceptional ability and before his sixth birthday had won four of his first five races in Ireland, in a style that had English owners and trainers thrusting eagerly for their cheque-books. They included Tommy Lushington, Hubert Hartigan, Sir Edward Hulton and Robert Gore, on behalf of Sir Charles Assheton-Smith (who, as Mr Duff, had won the National with Cloister). Sir Edward Hulton actually concluded a deal which fell through when the horse was pronounced thick-winded and failed to pass his veterinary examination. Sir Charles Assheton-Smith's vet also spun the horse and it was somewhat against his better judgement, that Sir Charles became the owner of Jerry M. for £1,200.

Nor had he any reason to doubt his trainer's judgement in the course of the following two triumphant seasons, culminating in the momentous Grand Steeple victory. For the next 18 months, however, it was not found possible to run Jerry M. and although his connections were not disposed to divulge the reasons, it seems reasonable to suppose that he was afflicted by back and leg troubles and that the enforced inactivity aggravated his wind infirmity. It was noticed that on his reappearance in 1912, he was heavily bandaged.

For the 1912 National, however, Jerry M. shrugged aside his disabilities in magnificent fashion. He jumped immaculately the whole way, Ernie Piggott recalls him jumping clean over a horse lying across the fence at the Canal Ditch – "cleared the lot without touching a thing", and making light of 12-7, stormed away after the last to win by six easy lengths. It was a performance seldom equalled and never surpassed. For the record only four horses have ever won the National with 12-7 – Cloister, Manifesto, Jerry M. and Poethlyn.

Jerry M. never ran again and had to be put down in the autumn of 1914.

JOCKEYS

Since 1879 jockeys have been required to be licensed.

60. Subject to the provisions of Rule 61 no person shall ride under these Rules in any race until he has attained the age of sixteen years and he has obtained from the Stewards of the Jockey Club subject to such restrictions as the Stewards consider necessary, a licence or permit as follows:

(ii) For Steeple Chases and Hurdle races, a Steeple Chase and Hurdle race jockey's licence, to be applied for each season.

62. (ii) During the term of his licence no jockey may

(a) be the owner or part-owner of any horse being entered or run under these Rules or the Rules of any recognised Turf Authority with the exception of horses taking part in Hunters' Steeple Chases only.

(b) bet on horse racing. This rule applies to a bet wherever placed and to a horserace wherever run.

(c) receive presents in connection with a race from persons other than the owner of the horse he rides in that race.

And any jockey who may be proved, to the satisfaction of the Stewards of the Jockey Club to have contravened any of the above conditions appropriate to his licence or permit will have his licence or permit withdrawn.

Fees

63. The following fees are payable in respect of each licence or permit to ride:

(ii) Steeple Chase and Hurdle race jockey's licence – £12 (plus V.A.T.) of which £2 is to be applied as the jockey's subscription to the Rendlesham Benevolent Fund.

(iv) Conditional jockey's licence (to be paid by the trainer) – £7 (plus VAT) of which £1 is to be applied as the jockey's subscription to the Rendlesham Benevolent Fund.

64. No jockey or Category B amateur rider other than those riding under the provisions of Rule 61 may ride in a steeplechase or hurdle race open to professional riders unless he has obtained a Medical Record Book from the Stewards of the Jockey Club. The holder of a Medical Record Book must produce it on every occasion when he rides in a steeplechase or hurdle and if he fails to do so will be fined not less than £4 or more than £16.50 unless he satisfies the

(*Above left*) Josh Gifford, four times Champion Jockey is now a most successful trainer. His stables are at Findon, Sussex next door to his former guv'nor, Ryan Price. (*Above right*) jumping's best-loved patron, H.M. Queen Elizabeth (now the Queen Mother) with H.R.H. Princess Elizabeth greeting Tony Grantham, the first jockey to win in the familiar blue and buff stripe, black velvet cap and gold tassel, after his victory on Manicou in the Wimbledon H'cap Chase, Kempton 1950

A happy moment for Golden Miller, Gerry Wilson and Dorothy Paget after their victory in the 1934 Grand National which completed a unique Gold Cup/National double in the same year. But the straight-shouldered Golden Miller did not like the towering Liverpool fences with their juddering drops and was extremely unwilling to essay them again. His obstinacy caused terrible ructions between Miss Paget and her trainers and jockeys

The Hon. AUBREY HASTINGS and Ascetic's Silver which he rode and trained to win the 1906 Grand National. Hastings trained three more National winners, a feat that remained supreme until 1976 when Fred Rimell equalled it

Two great Champion Hurdlers together in the air at the last flight of the 1951 Champion Hurdle. The blinkered and bandaged dual winner National Spirit (D. Dillon), still fractionally in the lead, falls leaving HATTON'S GRACE and Tim Molony to record their third and last victory at leisure

The Hon. George Lambton, later known for his enormous success as a trainer on the Flat and for his evocative and beautifully-written memoirs, began his career in racing as a distinguished amateur rider under N.H. rules. His irresistible charm, dandified appearance and propensity for gambling made him one of the principal personalities in a flamboyant age

The dual Gold Cup winner L'escargot with his regular pilot Tommy Carberry return to the saddling enclosure after the second of their Cheltenham victories. Proud owner Mr Raymond Guest (a former U.S. ambassador to Ireland) leads him in. L'Escargot later won a Grand National thus becoming only the second horse to win both races

An aerial view of Liverpool. The oval Flat course is seen in the foreground while the National course juts out across the Melling Road (*bottom right*) down to Becher's Brook and the Canal Turn

LIVERPOOL old style. Kellsboro' Jack and Danny Williams lead over the water on their way to victory in the 1933 Grand National. Danny Williams swings his body backwards so that he almost touches the horse's quarters in the accepted fashion of the day

A real LIVERPOOL mêlée. The sloping of the fences in 1960 was intended to minimize the falls that litter the National's unique history, but did not always achieve it as this shot of the 1966 running shows. Freddie the foxhunter (2nd) and Pat McCarron nimbly avoid the tangle of feet in their path. Anglo (winner) and Tim Norman are recovering from a stumble. Beyond them another pair are about to fall victim to Captain Becher's notorious Brook

LIVERPOOL the tragedy –
Colonel Whitbread's brave
Beau Bob (Jeremy Glover)
breaks his neck in this sicken-
ing fall. Becher's Brook 1975

LIVERPOOL the glamour – a
spectacular worm's-eye view
of the field streaming over
Becher's in 1971. Note the
frighteningly short leathers
and bold forward crouch of
the modern jockeys

JAMES MACHELL, the impoverished son of a distinguished family, began his career in an unfashionable regiment before turning to the Turf with conspicuous success. He masterminded a Derby winner and four National winners and gambled on a spectacular scale. He was able to buy back his family estates, but gout and suspicion clouded his triumphs and he was not a happy man

Emil Adam's charming study of MANIFESTO, a dual National winner (and thrice placed) and, before Red Rum, the acknowledged maestro of Aintree

LORD JOHN ('Hoppy') MANNERS, an archetypal
Victorian buck. A fine hunting man who decided
to give steeplechasing a try, to which end he
bought two good Irish chasers. Within a single
season he fulfilled the dreams of every soldier-
rider in winning the Grand Military Gold Cup and
the Grand National.

A great pro. Liverpool born 'Tich' MASON
dominated steeplechasing in the Edwardian decade
and was Champion Jockey six times

Perhaps the best-loved amateur of them all. Anthony Bingham, second LORD MILDMAY cantering to the post on Cromwell, on whom he was so unlucky not to win the 1948 Grand National. After Lord Mildmay's tragic death Cromwell raced for his sister Helen and won the first running of the Mildmay Memorial at Sandown

(*Below left*) ARTHUR NIGHTINGALL, member of a most prominent Epsom racing family, was a foremost professional rider of the later nineteenth century and afterwards trained successfully. (*Below right*) a typical shot of the front-running, bold-jumping NIGHT NURSE ridden here by his regular partner, Paddy Broderick. A dual Champion Hurdler, Night Nurse has already made an auspicious start to his career over fences

Stewards on the day of racing that this is due to circumstance outside his reasonable control. Medical Record Books are returnable to the Stewards of the Jockey Club on demand and are issued subject to the instructions contained therein.

A fee of £3 (plus V.A.T.) is payable in respect of each Record Book issued to an amateur rider.

65. Any horse ridden in a race in contravention of Rules 60, 61 or 66 of these Rules, shall, on objection, be liable to be disqualified by the Stewards of the Jockey Club.

66. (i) An amateur rider or a jockey whose permit or licence has been suspended by the Stewards of the Jockey Club or by any other recognised Turf Authority shall not ride in any race during the period of his suspension.

(ii) If an amateur rider or a jockey becomes a disqualified person his permit or licence is thereby revoked.

67. A list of the amateur riders and licensed jockeys shall be published in the Racing Calendar.

JOCKEYS, CHAMPION
Prior to season 1925-26 statistics are for the Calendar year.

(* Record)

1900	Mr H. S. Sidney	53
1901	F. Mason	58
1902	F. Mason	67
1903	P. Woodland	54
1904	F. Mason	59
1905	F. Mason	73
1906	F. Mason	58
1907	F. Mason	59
1908	P. Cowley	65
1909	R. Gordon	45
1910	E. Piggott	67
1911	W. Payne	76
1912	I. Anthony	78
1913	E. Piggott	60
1914	Mr J. R. Anthony	60
1915	E. Piggott	44
1916	C. Hawkins	17
1917	W. Smith	15
1918	G. Duller	17
1919	Mr H. Brown	48
1920	F. B. Rees	64
1921	F. B. Rees	65
1922	J. Anthony	78
1923	F. B. Rees	64
1924	F. B. Rees	108*
1925	F. B. Rees	76
1925-26	T. Leader	61

1926-27	F. B. Rees	59
1927-28	W. Stott	88
1928-29	W. Stott	76
1929-30	W. Stott	77
1930-31	W. Stott	81
1931-32	W. Stott	77
1932-33	G. Wilson	61
1933-34	G. Wilson	56
1934-35	G. Wilson	73
1935-36	G. Wilson	57
1936-37	G. Wilson	45
1937-38	G. Wilson	59
1938-39	T. F. Rimell	61
1939-40	T. F. Rimell	24
1940-41	G. Wilson	22
1941-42	R. Smyth	12
1942-43	*No Racing*	
1943-44	*No Racing*	
1944-45	H. Nicholson / T. F. Rimell	15
1945-46	T. F. Rimell	54
1946-47	J. Dowdeswell	58
1947-48	B. Marshall	66
1948-49	T. Molony	60
1949-50	T. Molony	95
1950-51	T. Molony	83
1951-52	T. Molony	99
1952-53	F. T. Winter	121*
1953-54	R. Francis	76
1954-55	T. Molony	67
1955-56	F. T. Winter	74
1956-57	F. T. Winter	80
1957-58	F. T. Winter	82
1958-59	T. Brookshaw	83
1959-60	S. Mellor	68
1960-61	S. Mellor	118
1961-62	S. Mellor	80
1962-63	J. Gifford	70
1963-64	J. Gifford	94
1964-65	T. W. Biddlecombe	114
1965-66	T. W. Biddlecombe	102
1966-67	J. Gifford	122*
1967-68	J. Gifford	82
1968-69	B. R. Davies / T. Biddlecombe	77
1969-70	B. R. Davies	91
1970-71	G. Thorner	74
1971-72	B. R. Davies	89
1972-73	Ron Barry	125*
1973-74	Ron Barry	94
1974-75	T. Stack	82
1975-76	J. Francome	96
1976-77	T. Stack	97
1977-78	J. J. O'Neill	149*

JOCKEYS ASSOCIATION
The Jockeys Association was formed in 1969 by an amalgamation of the Associations of Flat and National Hunt jockeys. This followed the amalgamation

of the Jockey Club and the National Hunt Committee. The National Hunt Jockeys Association was formed in 1966. The original president was Lord Trevethin and Oaksey (father of the present Lord Oaksey) and Stan Mellor was Vice-President. The present Association is constituted as follows:

President		Robert Sangster
Vice Presidents	North	D. Atkins
		J. Lowe
	South	L. Piggott
		R. Atkins
Secretary		Peter Smith

In addition there are eight Council Members, two Flat and two Jumping for both northern and southern areas.

The association is a non-profit-making limited liability company whose function is to provide a service for all jockeys and to represent their interests.

JOCKEY CLUB, The
(incorporating the National Hunt Committee by Royal Charter, 1970)

Patrons:
Her Majesty The Queen
Her Majesty Queen Elizabeth the Queen Mother

Stewards:
Lord Howard de Walden (Senior Steward)
Major M. G. Wyatt (Deputy Senior Steward)
R. N. Richmond-Watson, Esq. (Chairman, Disciplinary Committee)
J. Hambro, Esq. (Chairman, Administration and Finance)
The Lord Manton (Chairman, Race Planning Committee)
J. B. Sumner, Esq. (Chairman, Licensing Committee)

Members:
*H.R.H. the Prince Philip, Duke of Edinburgh
Marquess of Abergavenny
Viscount Allendale
The Hon. J. J. Astor
J. U. Baillie
Lt.-Col. P. H. G. Bengough
Sir Henry Benson
Col. the Hon. Julian Berry
R. A. Bethell
Gen. Sir Cecil Blacker
T. F. Blackwell
M. Marcel Boussac
A. M. Budgett
Maj.-Gen. Sir George Burns

Earl Cadogan
Maj. E. M. Cameron
Lt.-Col. J. E. S. Chamberlayne
Viscount Chelsea
Sir Rex Cohen
Lt.-Gen. Sir George Collingwood
E. S. M. Collingwood-Cameron
C. D. Collins
E. R. Courage
Lord Crathorne
J. B. Daly
Maj.-Gen. J. A. d'Avigdor-Goldsmid
Earl of Derby
Duke of Devonshire
Sir William S. Dugdale, Bt
T. E. S. Egerton
Lord Fairhaven
Maj.-Gen. Sir Randle Feilden
Lt.-Col. D. Forster
Louis Freedman
Maj. W. D. Gibson
Lt.-Col. Sir Martin Gilliat
Capt. H. M. Gosling
Brig. H. Green
*Raymond Guest
Earl of Halifax
Jocelyn Hambro
Brig. C. B. Harvey
Mrs P. Hastings
J. R. Henderson
J. L. Hislop
Maj. R. Hoare
Edward Holland-Martin
T. D. Holland-Martin
L. Brook Holliday
R. D. Hollingsworth
Lt.-Col. J. D. Hornung
Lord Howard de Walden
B. P. Jenks
H. J. Joel
Mrs G. T. Johnson-Houghton
Lord Kilmany
Lord Leigh
Viscount Leverhulme
Lt.-Col. H. M. Llewellyn
C. L. Lloyd
Sir Edwin McAlpine
R. J. McAlpine
Sir Robin McAlpine
Maj. V. McCalmont
A. J. McDonald-Buchanan
Capt. J. Macdonald-Buchanan
Maj. Sir Reginald Macdonald-Buchanan
Lord Manton
Lord Margadale
J. A. Marshall
Brig. M. S. K. Maunsell
*Paul Mellon
A. Milday-White
Maj. J. C. Vernon Miller

The Hon. James Morrison
Sir Noel Murless
Lt.-Col. R. B. Moseley
Brig. F. B. B. Noble
Sir Philip Oppenheimer
Maj. H. M. Peacock
Sir Thomas Pilkington
The Hon. J. P. Philipps
Col. Sir John Carew Pole, Bt
Lord Porchester
Earl of Ranfurly
*Sir Gordon Richards
R. N. Richmond-Watson
J. Rogerson
R. E. Sangster
The Earl of Scarborough
J. S. Schilizzi
D. D. Sieff
Lord Soames
Sir Michael Sobell
The Hon. Richard Stanley
J. B. Sumner
Duke of Sutherland
Sir Richard Tatton-Sykes, Bt
Sir John Thomson
R. R. Tweedie
Wg.-Cdr. P. D. O. Vaux
J. J. Watt
A. T. A. Wates
*P. M. Weatherby
The Hon. G. A. Weir
Lord Westbury
W. H. Whitbread
*J. H. Whitney
Maj. Derek Wigan
R. S. Wilkins
Lord Willoughby de Broke
Maj. M. G. Wyatt
Marquis of Zetland
*Honorary Member

Ex-Officio Members:
The Queen's Representative at Ascot:
Marquess of Abergavenny
The Queen's Racing Manager: Lord
Porchester
The Manager of The Queen's Stud:
W. R. M. Oswald
The Stewards of the Turf Club, Ireland:
Maj. V. McCalmont, Denis McArthy,
R. W. McKeever, J. J. Byrne
The Stewards of the Irish National Hunt
Steeple Chase Committee: The
Marquis of Waterford, Brigadier
A. D. R. Wingfield, The Lord
Hemphill
The President of the Société d'En-
couragement pour l'amelioration des
Races de Chevaux in France: M.
Hubert de Chaudenay

The four Stewards of the Société: M.
Claude Guerlain, Marquis de
Talhouet-Roy, Comte Bertrand de
Tarragon, Duc de Noailles
The Chairman of the Jockey Club, New
York: Nicholas F. Brady
The Chairman of Committee of the
Australian Jockey Club, New South
Wales: J. H. B. Carr
The Chairman of Committee of the
Victoria Racing Club: P. J. R. Steele,
Esq.
The Chairman of the Jockey Club
Limited (Canada): E. P. Taylor
The President of the New Zealand Rac-
ing Conference: A. M. Hughes
The Chairman of the Executive Stewards
of the Jockey Club of South Africa:
A. M. Snijman

Jockey Club Representatives on the
Horserace Betting Levy Board: T. F.
Blackwell, The Hon. J. J. Astor, Lt.-
Col. P. H. G. Bengough
Jockey Club Representatives on Tatter-
salls Committee: T. E. S. Egerton, The
Hon. James Morrison

JOHNNY LONGTAIL
Chestnut gelding, 1878, not in General
Stud Book, Polardine—Debonnaire
(Newminster).
   A popular half-bred whose consistent
career encompassed 18 victories, Johnny
Longtail was owned by and usually rid-
den by leading amateur Willie Moore.
After winning a string of hunter-chases
and the Royal Artillery Gold Cup with
13-7, he went on to win the Champion
Chase, Liverpool (1888), the Grand In-
ternational, Sandown (1887) and the
Great Metropolitan, Croydon (1888).

**JOICEY, Lt.-Col. Hugh Edward, 3rd
Baron Joicey, D.S.O. (1881-1969)**
Lord Joicey was educated at Harrow and
served with distinction with the 14th
Hussars and the Suffolk Regiment in
South Africa and World War I. He was
Master of the North Northumberland
Hounds for five spells totalling 14 years
and owned a number of high-class
chasers trained for him by Stuart Wight
and after his retirement, Neville Crump.
The best of these were Bramble Tudor
(21 chases including the Great Yorkshire
and the Wetherby H'cap Chase twice)
and Springbok (Hennessy Gold Cup).
   Lord and Lady Joicey figured three
times in the Leading Owners tables:

1954-55		4th	16 races	£4,575
1962-63	Lady Joicey	2nd	6 races	£9,594
1962-63	Lord Joicey	5th	4 races	£5,978

Colours: pink, olive green sleeves, pink cap.

JONES, Arthur Whitfield (b.1923)
A Shropshire farmer, Arthur Jones took out a licence in 1952 and in 1957 saddled his own Merry Deal to win the Champion Hurdle. Our Hope, Bandalore and Winning Fair are the only other Champion Hurdlers to have been owner-trained. Merry Deal also won him the Victory Hurdle (1957) and the Princess Royal Hurdle (1957). Jones trained another smart hurdler in Man of the East.

JONES, D. L. (b.1907)
A Cheltenham-based jockey, Davy Jones was apprenticed to Ben Roberts and won the 1945 Cheltenham Gold Cup on Red Rower, carrying no less than three stone of dead weight. He once rode a winner on the Flat, over hurdles and over fences in the same afternoon at Liverpool and continued to ride and win races in Kenya, where he later settled, until well into his sixties. His son, T. M. ('Buck') Jones was a useful jockey to Ryan Price and won the 1964 Imperial Cup on Invader. He now has a small yard near Guildford.

JONES, George
George Jones shared the Champion Amateur title in 1975-76 with Peter Greenall (q.v.). They each rode 25 winners. In the autumn of 1976 he turned professional. His biggest success has been the County Hurdle, National Hunt Meeting (1976) on Java Fox.

JONES, Harry Thomson (b.1925)
Tom Jones was educated at Eton and served with the 1st Royal Dragoon Guards. He assisted R. Featherstonehaugh for two years and afterwards F. Armstrong and took out a licence in 1951.

He runs a highly successful 'mixed' stable in Newmarket and is now one of jumping's chief bulwarks at the Headquarters of the Turf. He does particularly well with his young hurdlers who always look well and are thoroughly schooled. In 1973-74 he saddled the winners of 43 races worth £35,973, which took him into fifth place in the Trainers List.

On the Flat he has won the 1971 St Leger with Athens Wood and the William Hill Cheveley Park Stakes (1978) with Devon Ditty, while over fences his major victories have been:

The King George VI Chase (1964) Frenchman's Cove
The Whitbread Gold Cup (1962) Frenchman's Cove
The Tote Champion Novices Chase (1972) Clever Scot
The National Hunt Chase (1973) Foreman
The Grand Military Gold Cup (1957) Easter Breeze
The Massey-Ferguson Gold Cup (1974) Garnishee
The Victor Ludorum Hurdle (1976) Sweet Joe
The Sun Alliance Chase (1978) Sweet Joe

Tom Jones is one of the more amusing members of the racing fraternity and is also something of an amateur poet.

JONES, J. G.
John Jones, the Epsom jockey and trainer, was a major character in late nineteenth-century chasing. He used to ride first jockey to 'Fogo' Rowlands at Pitt Place but in 1876 he went to Priam Lodge where he trained and rode for Lord Marcus Beresford and some of his friends, who included H.R.H. the Prince of Wales.

Among his good victories were:

The Grand National (1878) Shifnal
The Grand Sefton (1878) Chimney Sweep (h.-b.)
The Croydon Grand National Hurdle (1876) Woodcock; (1883) Theocrastus
The Croydon International Hurdle (1881) Lord Clive; (1885) Serge II

He became a well-known Epsom figure and one of the foremost followers of the local Draghounds. His son, Herbert, a top-class Flat jockey, won the Derby twice for H.M. Edward VII, on Diamond Jubilee (1900) and Minoru (1909).

JONES, Mervyn Anthony (1920-42)
A nephew of the Anthony brothers, Mervyn Jones's promising career as a jump jockey was halted by World War II. He joined the R.A.F. and became a pilot-sergeant.

In 1940, owing to the injury to Eric Foley, he was offered the ride on Lord Stalbridge's Bogskar in the Grand National. His air-commodore in giving his permission, enquired whether Jones had passed his navigation exam. On being answered in the affirmative, he ordered: "Well, go and navigate Bogskar round Aintree and if you don't, we'll put you through another navigation examination." Mervyn Jones successfully accomplished his mission, but in April 1942 he was reported missing, presumed dead.

JUDGE, The

27. (i) The Judge, or his authorized substitute, must occupy the judge's box at the time the horses pass the winning-post, or the race shall be void. He must announce his decision immediately, or after consulting the photograph, and shall determine the winner according to the part of the horse's head, excluding the ears, which is first pass the winning post, the remaining placings being determined in a similar manner. Such decision shall be final, unless an objection to the winner, or any placed horses, is made and sustained provided that this Rule shall not prevent a judge from correcting any mistake, such correction being subject to confirmation by the Stewards.

(ii) The Judge shall, at the close of each day's racing, sign and send a report of the results of each race to the Racing Calendar Office.

Judges are appointed by and are responsible to the Jockey Club. The senior judge, known as the Jockey Club Judge, officiates at the Classics and other principal meetings. There are normally four junior judges and a number of part-trained judges, styled 'casuals', who officiate at minor N.H. meetings on Bank Holidays and similar occasions when there are too many meetings for the full-time judges.

KAVANAGH, T.

An Irish jump jockey, Terry Kavanagh rode chiefly for Mr H. M. Dyas and Henry Linde.

He won the 1897 Grand National on Manifesto and the Lancashire Chase (1895) on Gentle Ida. Other victories included:

The Grand Sefton (1890) Choufleur
The Jubilee Handicap (1892) Niblick
The Sandown Grand Prize (1893) Gillstown

KELLSBORO' JACK

Bay gelding, 1926, Jackdaw—Kellsboro' Lass (Oppressor). Bred in Co. Meath, Ireland, by Mr J. Hutchinson.

A stout-hearted and consistent horse who was, in the opinion of his trainer Ivor Anthony, the finest jumper of Liverpool in his memory, Kellsboro' Jack won 13 chases including both English and Scottish Grand Nationals, the Stanley Chase, Liverpool (1932) and the Champion Chase, Liverpool, twice (1936 and 1938).

Bred in Co. Meath, he was bought as a yearling by Mr F. Ambrose Clark, the American sewing-machine millionaire whose brother Robert won the Derby with Never Say Die. At four years Kellsboro' Jack joined the Wroughton establishment of Ivor Anthony and swiftly proved himself a youngster of rare promise winning chases at Cheltenham, Liverpool and Newbury in his first season, but his trainer felt he was not lucky and suggested a change of ownership. For the sum of £1 Kellsboro' Jack became the property of Mr Clark's wife Florence, in whose colours he won the 1933 Grand National, 11-9 (D. Williams), 25/1, by 3l, a neck, from Really True, 10-12 (Mr F. Furlong) and Slater, 10-7 (Mr M. Barry).

Mrs Clark refused to allow her young champion to risk the hazards of the National again but he continued to race for five more seasons, winning his share every year and running third to Golden Miller three times running in the Cheltenham Gold Cup, before being retired to the U.S.A. He was buried along with Clarks' Welsh National winner, Sorley Boy, on the summit of one of the foothills of the Adirondacks.

KELLEWAY, P. A. (b.1940)

Paul Kelleway was apprenticed to Harry Wragg and rode his first winner in 1955. However he quickly grew too heavy for the Flat and had a considerable struggle to establish himself over fences. He was retained by both Ryan Price and Fred Winter but from the end of 1971-72 rode freelance until his retirement at the end of 1976-77. He now trains at Newmarket and in only his second season turned out the Group I Champion Stakes winner, Swiss Maid.

A strong, fearless jockey, he was particularly well suited to lazy horses.

His successes include:

The Cheltenham Gold Cup (1969) What A Myth
The Champion Hurdle (1971) Bula; (1972) Bula
The National Hunt Two Mile Champion Chase (1971) Crisp
The Whitbread Gold Cup (1966) What A Myth
The Mildmay Memorial (1966) What A Myth
The Mackeson Hurdle (1963) Cash
The Whitbread Northern Trophy (1974) Barona
The Scottish Grand National (1975) Barona; (1976) Barona

KELSO (Group 4)

A left-handed, squarish course of marvellous old turf which has staged N.H. racing since 1869, Kelso provides modest but entertaining sport in the Border country. The track is undulating and about one mile, two furlongs in length.

The principal races are the Anthony Marshall Trophy H'cap Chase (October, 3m, £1,226), the King's Own Scottish Borderers Cup H'cap Chase (March, 3m, £1,242) and the Tennant-Quaich H'cap Hurdle (March, 2m, 4f, £1,226).

Best Times

Distance	Time	Horse-age-weight	Date
2m H	3m 43.90	Golden End 7-9-12	9-5-78
2½m H	4m 45.10	Blue Chrome 5-12-0	15-10-77
3m 1f 120y H	6m 11.30	Lochar Moss 8-11-2	31-3-73
2m 196y C	4m 7.70	Arctic Explorer 7-11-7	8-11-72
2¾m C	5m 46	Bar Haze 7-11-12	28-4-76
3m C	6m 8.40	Hidden Value 10-11-8	9-5-78

KEMPTON, John Henry (b.1938)

John Kempton rode as an amateur and as a professional under N.H. Rules. He took out a licence to train in 1958, when still riding, and had a small yard in Compton, Berkshire. His major triumph was to win the 1967 Grand National with the Dreaper reject, Foinavon. He was not even at Aintree but watched the race, in growing disbelief, on the television at Worcester Races where he had just won a novice hurdle.

KEMPTON PARK (Group 2)

Kempton Park, a right-handed, triangular, more or less flat course, whose stiff fences and sharp turns have always made it a jockeys' course, was built in 1878 and has staged N.H. racing from the beginning. It was not until 1890 however that jumping became an important feature with six annual meetings, the most important of which were the Christmas meeting and the March meeting with its £1,000 handicap hurdle. The emergence of Kempton and other park tracks such as Sandown and Newbury with their

smart London crowds and comparative affluence produced a new style of chaser, classier and faster, who might not survive four miles of Aintree but who could earn his keep from the good prizes on the London tracks.

The Coventry Chase (now the Yellow Pages Pattern Chase, February, 3m, £4,968) instituted after World War I, proved an immediate success for it provided a convenient prep. race for the Gold Cup and National and was nearly always contested by a good-class field. Easter Hero first vaulted to fame by winning the Coventry Chase.

Kempton's most famous race the King George VI Chase (December, 3m, £7,373) was first run in February 1937 and was won by Mr J. V. Rank's Southern Hero. It became a permanent feature in 1947. Other important races include the William Hill Christmas Hurdle (formerly the Lonsdale Hurdle. December, 2m, £8,526) and the Yellow Pages Hurdle (4-y-o, February, 2m, £2,927).

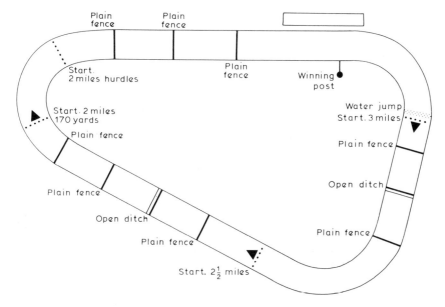

Best Times

Distance	Time	Horse-age-weight	Date
2m H	3m 40.90	Gently Does It 5-10-12	15-10-77
2½m 90y H	4m 51.60	Grand Canyon (NZ) 7-11-8	15-10-77
3m H	5m 45.60	Esmenella 7-10-6	17-10-64
2m C	3m 55.60	Big Bill 7-10-10	23-1-53
2m 170y C	4m 2.40	Jabeg 7-11-10	4-11-72
2½m 90y C	5m 4.40	The Dealer 7-11-0	16-11-77
3m C	5m 59.40	Jimmy Scot 13-10-4	18-10-69
3½m C	7m 2.30	Maniwaki 10-10-0	15-10-77

King George VI Chase (3m)

	HORSE	OWNER	RIDER	TRAINER
1937	Southern Hero	Mr J. V. Rank	J. Fawcus	G. Evans
1938	Airgead Sios	Sir Francis Towle	T. McNeil	C. Tabor
1939-46	*No Race*			
1947	Rowland Roy	Hon. D. Paget	B. Marshall	F. Walwyn
1948	Cottage Rake	Mr Vickerman	A. Brabazon	M. V. O'Brien
1949	Finnure	Lord Bicester	R. Francis	G. Beeby
1950	Manicou	H.M. Queen Elizabeth	B. Marshall	P. Cazalet
1951	Statecraft	H.M. Queen Elizabeth	A. Grantham	P. Cazalet
1952	Hallowe'en	Contessa di St Elia	F. Winter	W. Wightman
1953	Galloway Braes	Lady Orde	R. Morrow	A. Kilpatrick
1954	Hallowe'en	Contessa di St Elia	F. Winter	W. Wightman
1955	Limber Hill	Mr G. Lawrence	J. Power	W. Dutton
1956	Rose Park	Mr J. Davey	M. Scudamore	P. Cazalet
1957	Mandarin	Mme Hennessy	P. Madden	F. Walwyn
1958	Lochroe	Hon. Mrs Mildmay-White	A. Freeman	P. Cazalet
1959	Mandarin	Mme Hennessy	P. Madden	F. Walwyn
1960	Saffron Tartan	Col. G. R. Westmacott	F. Winter	D. Butchers
1961	*No Race*			
1962	*No Race*			
1963	Mill House	Mr W. Gollings	G. W. Robinson	F. Walwyn
1964	Frenchman's Cove	Mr S. Joel	S. Mellor	H. T. Jones
1965	Arkle	Anne, Duchess of Westminster	P. Taaffe	T. Dreaper
1966	Dormant	Mrs Wells-Kendrew	J. King	J. Wells-Kendrew
1967	*No Race*			
1968	*No Race*			
1969	Titus Oates	Mr P. Cussins	S. Mellor	G. W. Richards
1970	*No Race*			
1971	The Dikler	Mrs August	B. Brogan	F. Walwyn
1972	Pendil	Mrs C. Kinney	R. Pitman	F. Winter
1973	Pendil	Mrs C. Kinney	R. Pitman	F. Winter
1974	Captain Christy	Mrs J. Samuel	R. Coonan	P. Taaffe
1975	Captain Christy	Mrs J. Samuel	G. Newman	P. Taaffe
1976	Royal Marshal II	Mr J. Sumner	G. Thorner	T. Forster
1977	Bachelor's Hall	Mr P. Harris	M. O'Halloran	P. Cundell
1978	Gay Spartan	Mr M. Armstrong	T. Carmody	A. Dickinson

1978 Silver Buck. *T. Carmody* *A. Dickinson.*

KERSTIN

Brown mare, 1950, Honour's Choice—Miss Kilcash (Knight of Kilcash). Bred in Ireland by Mr C. Burke.

The winner of a hurdle race and 11 chases and one of only three mares to win the Cheltenham Gold Cup, Kerstin was bought privately as an unbroken four-year-old by her trainer, Maj. Verly Bewicke and passed on to Mr G. H. Moore in whose colours she raced for the whole of her career. She was first-cousin to another Gold Cup winner, Linwell, their dams both being daughters of Toy Fish, and curiously enough their careers touched on several occasions.

Kerstin wasted no time in revealing her exceptional ability and won eight races before her seventh birthday including the National Hunt Handicap Chase, National Hunt Meeting (1956) and the Christmas Cracker Chase, Liverpool (1956). As a result of which she started favourite for the 1957 Gold Cup but was beaten just a length by Linwell. The following year she redeemed herself (S. Hayhurst), 7/1, by ½l, a bad third, from Polar Flight (G. Slack) and Gay Donald (F. Winter) after a hard-fought race.

The season of 1958-59 was blank despite a great run for the Hennessy when she was beaten a short head by Taxidermist, after appearing to have the race well won, but she ended her career on a triumphant note, winning the Hennessy Gold Cup, Newbury (1960) by five lengths. She was put down in 1976, having bred three winners of whom the most notable was the game Fashion House who won 14 races before breaking a leg in 1972.

KILLINEY
Bay gelding, 1966, Tiger—Killiney Hill (Hill Gail). Bred by the Confey Stud Farm.

The fatal fall of Killiney in the Heinz Chase, Ascot (1973) resulting in a broken shoulder and inevitable destruction, terminated the career of the most promising young staying chaser to have appeared for years.

A fine, big horse, known affectionately as 'the gentle giant', Killiney's career was plotted with infinite sagacity by Fred Winter. After a 'bumper' victory in Ireland, Killiney won six hurdle races, including the Players No. 6 National Championship Final and was beaten six lengths by Persian Majesty in his division of the Gloucester Hurdle, National Hunt Meeting (1971). A fall at Newbury in November 1971 resulted in a damaged hock which laid him off for the rest of the season but the enforced absence probably allowed him to furnish his vast frame and he reappeared for the season 1972-73 better than ever. An unbeaten string of eight chases, including an effortless victory in the Tote Champion Novices, National Hunt Meeting, were the prelude to the Ascot tragedy in what was to have been his last race of the season.

Killiney, who was owned by Mrs Enid Boucher, has given his name to a novice chase at the Ascot December meeting.

KILMORE
Bay gelding, 1950, Zalophus—Brown Image (Ut Majeur). Bred in Ireland by Mr A. G. C. Webb.

When, at 12 years of age, Kilmore won the 1962 Grand National, 10-4 (F. Winter), 28/1, by 10l, the same, from two more twelve-year-olds, Wynburgh, 10-9 (T. Barnes) and Mr What, 10-9 (J. Lehane), in particularly testing conditions, it was held to be a triumph of dour staying-power over youth and speed. Yet Kilmore's earlier career in no way suggested him to be a plodding stayer: It encompassed victories in two bumpers, three hurdle races and 10 chases, all but three of which were over distances short of three miles.

He was trained in Ireland by M. Browne and sold in February 1961 for £3,000 to Ryan Price acting on behalf of Messrs Nat Cohen and B. Rosenfeld who wanted a National runner. Right well did Kilmore reward them, running a grand race to finish fifth behind the speedy Nicolaus Silver. He failed to win another race for his co-owners but finished sixth in the 1963 National. Only three 12-year-olds have won the National this century, the others being L'Escargot (1975) and Red Rum (1977).

KILPATRICK, Alec Stuart (1898-1976)
Alec Kilpatrick trained at Collingbourne Ducis from 1933 to 1973. His best-known horses were Sir Percy and Lady Orde's heart-stopping pair, Pointsman and Galloway Braes.

His good victories include:

The King George VI Chase (1953) Galloway Braes

The Queen Elizabeth Chase (1953) Galloway Braes; (1954) Galloway Braes

The National Hunt Handicap Chase (1960) Isle of Skye

The Mildmay Memorial (1953) Whispering Steel

The Haydock Park Grand National Trial (1967) Bassnet

The Grand Military Gold Cup Chase (1954) Pointsman; (1958) Stalbridge Park; (1960) Joan's Rival; (1961) Stalbridge Park; (1970) Charles Dickens; (1971) Charles Dickens; (1972) Charles Dickens

KINANE, Thomas (b.1933)
Tommy Kinane served his time with Tim Hyde (q.v.) and Tom Yates but failed to get a breakthrough and for a time left racing. He later took out a licence in

Ireland and rode his first winner in 1958. He remained freelance and while riding his share of winners, remained outside the public eye until 1978 when he won the Waterford Crystal Champion Hurdle on Monksfield. Another big success was the County Handicap Hurdle, N.H. Meeting (1977) on Kilcoleman.

KINDERSLEY, Gay (b.1930)

Gay Kindersley was educated at Eton and served with the 7th (Queen's Own) Hussars. He rode as an amateur under both Rules with great success from 1948 until 1965, when he broke his back. Strictly against doctor's orders he continued to ride on the Flat until 1969. He was Champion Amateur (N.H.) in 1959-60 with 22 winners and second in 1960-61 with 16. He dead-heated for the Cheltenham Foxhunters (1953) with Merry and won the Kim Muir (1959) on Irish Coffee. He owned a half share of Carrickbeg, so narrowly beaten in the 1963 Grand National.

He was elected to the N.H.C. in 1962, was Hon. Secretary of the Amateur Riders Association of Great Britain and acted as a Steward (N.H.) at Kempton, Ascot, Newbury and Windsor. At the beginning of 1973-74, however, he resigned from the Jockey Club in order to become a public trainer. A progressive thinker, he is also a witty and charming companion with an extensive repertoire of Irish folk songs.

KING, Jeffrey Steven (b.1941)

Jeff King was for several years reckoned to be the finest N.H. jockey riding. He has never been Champion Jockey and is unlikely to be and he has yet to win any of chasing's classics but for sheer consistency and confidence-giving horsemanship, on any type of horse and on any course, he has no equal.

He was apprenticed to Sir Gordon Richards and rode his first winner in 1960. He then joined Bob Turnell, that great trainer of horses and jockeys, and under his guidance achieved the perfection he demanded in himself.

His best season was 1971-72 when he rode 66 winners, coming sixth in the Jockey's Table. His victories include:

The Hennessy Gold Cup (1967) Rondetto
The Topham Trophy (1964) Red Tide
The Massey-Ferguson Gold Cup (1966) The Laird

The Welsh Champion Hurdle (1972) Canasta Lad; (1974) Canasta Lad
The Black and White Gold Cup (1971) Jabeg
The Imperial Cup (1965) Kildavin; (1974) Flash Imp
The Schweppes Gold Trophy (1973) Indianapolis
The Mackeson Hurdle (1964) Sky Pink
The Arkle Challenge Trophy (1974) Canasta Lad
The Whitbread Gold Cup (1976) Otter Way

KINSKY, Prince Charles (1868-1919)

Prince Charles Kinsky was a member of an ancient Bohemian family who had been counts since 1326 and princes since 1746.

His mother, a princess of Liechtenstein, was a noted horse-woman and employed an English Master of Horse, Rowland Reynolds. This officer taught young Charles to speak English, to ride and above all to balance his horse and embued him with notions of hunting and taking part in the world's most famous steeplechase. Accordingly in 1878 he accompanied the Empress Elizabeth on her hunting expedition to the British Isles. In 1881 he became attached to the Austro-Hungarian Embassy where he remained for fifteen years, a leading member of society and a devoted admirer of Lady Randolph Churchill.

He shared a hunting box in Leicestershire with "Bay" Middleton and with the proceeds of a successful bet on Corrie Roy in the Cesarewitch, bought a good young staying mare, Zoedone, which he sent to W. Jenkins (q.v.) at Upton, to be trained for the Grand National. The pair's comfortable victory in the 1883 running of the big race was holloaed home by "Bay" Middleton and other choice spirits from Leicestershire where Charles Kinsky was immensely popular. The following year the pair were made favourite to repeat their victory but the combination of top-weight and fast ground proved too great and after leading to the last, they weakened to finish fourth. In 1885 his beloved mare became the victim of a vicious gang of dopers who damaged her so badly that she was never able to race again.

Prince Kinsky remained a confirmed Anglophile. He was made an honorary member of the Jockey Club and of the French Steeplechase Society. In 1906 he was elected to the N.H.C. His later years were tragically clouded by the outbreak of the 1914-18 war which made him an enemy alien from the country of his adoption and his friends. Seeking employment as far away from Europe as possible, he volunteered for the Russian Front and spent two years with the cavalry. He died in 1919, heartbroken by the ruin of his own country and his inability to return to England.

KIRKLAND
Chestnut gelding, 1896, not in the General Stud Book, Kirkham—La Princess (Perigonious). Bred in Ireland by the Rev. E. Clifford.

A rangy chestnut with tremendous limbs, whose half-brother Kirkham had won the Irish Grand National, Kirkland was bought out of Ireland by Liverpool-born manufacturer, Mr Frank Bibby. He started his career in auspicious fashion and before his sixth birthday had won 10 chases including the 1902 Grand Sefton. Perhaps this precocious activity sapped his energies for there followed two blank seasons redeemed only by a fourth in the 1903 Grand National, beaten a head for third place by the evergreen Manifesto, and a second in 1904, beaten eight lengths by Moiffa (rec. 3lb). However he emerged triumphant in 1905, winning his only two starts, including the Grand National, 11-5 (F. Mason), 6/1, by 3l, 4l, from Napper Tandy, 10-0 (P. Woodland) and Buckaway II, 9-11 (A. Newey). Six times champion jockey, "Tich" Mason, was like owner, Frank Bibby, Liverpool-born, thus providing a thoroughly popular local victory.

Kirkland did not win subsequently and did not in fact run very frequently although he started favourite for the 1908 National in which he finished seventh after being remounted. Kirkland was yet another National-winning descendant of Pocahontas for his dam, La Princess, was out of a mare by East Lancashire by Rataplan ex Pocahontas.

KIRRIEMUIR
Brown gelding, 1960, Tangle—Jonquille II (Royalhunter). Bred by Mrs F. B. Watkins.

After a modest success on the Flat at three years when trained by Peter Payne-Gallwey, Kirriemuir turned to National Hunt racing with conspicuous success, winning a chase and 12 hurdle races and became the longest-priced winner of the Champion Hurdle on record when winning the 1965 running at 50/1 (G. W. Robinson), by 1l, 1½l, from Spartan General (T. W. Biddlecombe) and Worcran (D. Nicholson). Had he maintained his form of 1963-64 when he had won seven races in succession and finished a good third in the Champion Hurdle, he would not have started at anything like those odds but he had blotted his copybook badly prior to Cheltenham. Kirriemuir was owned by Mrs D. Beddington, an aunt of Mrs Fred Winter, and trained by Fulke Walwyn.

KLAXTON
Brown gelding, 1940, Mr Toots—Orchardstown Lass (Gallio). Bred by Mr F. Purcell.

A stout-hearted and consistent staying chaser, owned and ridden by National Hunt Steward Maj. W. D. Gibson, Klaxton won eight chases, including the Grand Military Gold Cup, Sandown, three times in succession (1950, 1951 and 1952) and the important Hurst Park Grand National Trial (1954). Klaxton was trained by Ivor Anthony until he retired and subsequently by Bob Turnell.

KNIGHT OF THE GARTER
Bay horse, 1921. Bred by Mr J. J. Parkinson.

Knight of the Garter	Son In Law	Dark Ronald	Bay Ronald
			Darkie
		Mother-in-Law	Matchmaker
			Be Cannie
	Castelline	Cyllene	Bona Vista
			Arcadia
		Cassine	Xaintrailles
			Crowflower

Bought as a foal by Lord Marcus Beresford on behalf of H.M. King George V, Knight of the Garter proved as classy as his pedigree suggested. His three victories as a two-year-old included the Coventry Stakes at Royal Ascot and he was also second in the Richmond Stakes, Goodwood and third in the Middle Park. After running unplaced in the 2000 Guineas, on his only outing at three years he developed heel bug and was unable to run again. He took up stud duties in 1927 and stood at Mr Patrick Rogers' Ratoath Stud, Co. Meath. His influence on National Hunt breeding was considerable for not only was he leading sire (Ireland only) in 1944-45, but he was second on three occasions and third twice.

1st
1944-45 10 winners of 12½ races worth £1,516

2nd
1936-37 17 winners of 29 races worth £3,555½
1938-39 14 winners of 26 races worth £3,499¼
1945-46 17 winners of 30 races worth £5,756

3rd
1937-38 13 winners of 25 races worth £3,320
1946-47 19 winners of 31½ races worth £5,227

He also became a noted sire of broodmares. He nicked well with My Prince mares, notably Greenogue Princess who bred four winners to him, including Bright Cherry, seven races and dam of three winners, including Arkle. He died in 1944.

KNOCK HARD
Chestnut gelding, 1944, Domaha—Knocksouna (Beresford). Bred by Mr T. J. Sheahan.

A good-class horse on the Flat and the winner of the Irish Lincoln, Knock Hard went on to win eight chases including the Great Yorkshire, Doncaster (1953) and the 1953 Cheltenham Gold Cup (T. Molony), 11/2, by 5l, 2l, from

Hallowe'en (F. T. Winter) and Galloway Braes (R. Morrow), after appearing to have no chance at the bottom of the hill. He had run a very similar race in the 1952 event and was rapidly catching Mont Tremblant when he fell at the second last.

Knock Hard was a fourth Gold Cup winner for Vincent O'Brien who described him as having no natural aptitude for jumping. A fine, big horse owned by Mrs Keogh, he was at his best on top of the ground.

KOKO
Brown gelding, 1918, Santoi—Persister (Persimmon). Bred and owned by Mr Frank Barbour.

A handsome, spectacular horse who went best when allowed to bowl along in front, Koko won 18 chases, including the 1926 Cheltenham Gold Cup (J. Hamey), 10/1, by 4l, 5l, from Old Tay Bridge (J. Hogan) and Ruddyglow (Mr W. Filmer-Sankey). He broke a blood vessel and faded to finish a poor third when 4/5 favourite to complete the double in 1928 and fell after repeated mistakes when restraining tactics were attempted in 1929. Among his other important victories was the 1928 Hurst Park National Trial with 12-7. He continued to run and win until 1931.

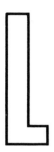

LAD

All stable employees are known as 'lads' regardless of age or sex. They are the unsung heroes of racing. Their names never go into the record books beside the horses they have looked after, yet the fate of their valuable charges is largely dependent on their skill and understanding. They feed, muck out, groom and usually ride their horses every day. They take them to the races, tend them when they are sick, injured or exhausted and exult in their triumphs.

A lad usually 'does' two or three horses. At the top of the hierarchy is the head lad who is responsible for all inmates of the yard, both equine and human, for 24 hours a day. He rarely, if ever, goes to the races. The travelling head-lad accompanies runners and their lads to the races and is responsible for them during their absence from the yard.

All lads must hold a card from Weatherbys which is applied for by their trainers. At racecourse stables, where strict security operates, this card must be produced. Head-lads have their own association and they and other lads may belong to the T.G.W.U.

LADY RIDERS

As a result of the Sex Discrimination Act of 1975 the Jockey Club were obliged to permit ladies to ride in steeplechases from January 1976. Despite the furore and prognostications of doom provoked at the time, the innovation has made very little difference. In amateur company the ladies are well able to hold their own against the men.

The first lady to ride a winner was Miss Diana Thorne in February 1976 in the Nimrod Hunter Chase, Stratford, to be followed ten days later by her twin sister Jane at Warwick.

The first lady rider to win as a professional in Great Britain was Miss

Lorna Vincent, whose first success at Cheltenham was swiftly followed by the important Buchanan Whisky H'cap Hurdle, Ascot (1978).

LAMB, Ridley

The son of Northumberland trainer, Reg Lamb, Ridley Lamb progressed from point-to-points to N.H. racing and rode as an amateur for several years, culminating in season 1974-75 when he rode 22 winners and finished Champion Amateur. The following season he turned professional, riding chiefly for his father but for several other Northern trainers as well.

His principal success to date is the 1977 Scottish Grand National on the headstrong Sebastian V on which he finished a close second in the 1978 Grand National. He also won the Kim Muir Chase, National Hunt Meeting (1975) on Quick Reply.

LAMBTON, Hon. George (1860-1945)

The fifth son of the 2nd Earl of Durham, George Lambton was a man who did all things well. He was an amateur rider of distinction and later became a trainer of even greater repute. He was recognized as being one of the leading judges of a yearling in the country, while his autobiographical *Men and Horses I Have Known* ranks as a classic among racing books. He was elegant in person, dandified in his dress and possessed of enormous personal charm. He never won the Grand National but came nearest to it in 1889 when Savoyard, who was in the lead and going well, crossed his forelegs and somersaulted a stride after the second last. His best victories were:

The Grand Steeplechase de Paris (1888) Parasang
The National Hunt Chase (1888) Glenthorpe
The Great Sandown Hurdle (1886) Ducat
The Grand National Hurdle (1886) Bellona
The Grand International Hurdle (1887) Bellona
The Champion Chase (1885) The Captain

The cumulative effect of several bad falls forced him to give up riding for training in 1892.

He was one of the first 'gentlemen' trainers to use his own name and from small beginnings quickly became one of the leading members of his profession. At first he trained under both Rules but in

1893 he was appointed private trainer to the 16th Earl of Derby. On the earl's death in 1908, the Stanley House stables passed to the 17th earl for whom Lambton continued to train. He was leading trainer on three occasions and saddled 13 classic winners, including Hyperion (Derby and St Leger).

LAMPLUGH, Harry (d. c1867)

The son of a Yorkshire jump jockey, Harry Lamplugh was taught by John Scott and is reputed to have schooled Miss Mowbray (*q.v.*). At the age of 17, he got the opportunity to go to France where he rode many winners for Mr Higgins and Major Morgan. He then moved to Chantilly to become trainer/jockey to the de la Motte family, then the leading family in French chasing. He had charge of the legendary Franc Picard and also Jean du Quesne, who failed so narrowly in the 1859 Grand National. He bought Huntsman for the Vicomte de Namur and trained and rode him to win the 1862 Grand National. Later he managed the Duke of Hamilton's chasers in France. He suffered internal injuries from a fall at Angers, from which he never properly recovered and which undoubtedly caused his early death.

LANZAROTE

Brown gelding, 1968, Milesian—Slag (Mossborough). Bred and owned by Lord Howard de Walden.

Lanzarote, a half-brother to the Cesarewitch winner Scoria, won on the Flat at three years when trained by Ernie Weymes but his form was no more than moderate and, being a well-grown, rangy sort, it was thought worth sending him to Fred Winter to be trained for jumping.

He won a novice hurdle as a four-year-old but did not appear to be a champion hurdler in the making, nor did his early efforts of season 1972-73 suggest any such possibility. However in the spring of 1973 he improved with startling rapidity and won four races off the reel culminating in the Imperial Cup, Sandown, with 12-4.

In 1973-74 he went through six races unbeaten culminating in the Champion Hurdle (R. Pitman), 7/4, won by 3l, 8l, from Comedy of Errors (W. Smith) and Yenisei (H. Beasley).

Lanzarote was normally ridden from behind, coming with a smooth burst at the finish and it was widely anticipated that the more experienced, stout-hearted Comedy of Errors would out-gallop and out-jump his younger rival and take the edge off his speed before the uphill finish. However, enterprisingly ridden by Richard Pitman, Lanzarote took on the ex-champion at his own game and when Comedy of Errors challenged at the last, it was Lanzarote who found a little in reserve and went away to win convincingly.

During the next two seasons Lanzarote won eight more hurdle races including the Welsh Champion Hurdle, Chepstow (1975) and in the autumn of 1976 he seemed as good as ever. His season opened with an eight-length victory over Sea Pigeon, a short-head defeat by Night Nurse in the Marlow Ropes Skeaping Hurdle, and a game fourth to Grand Canyon (beaten less than three lengths) in the Colonial Cup, Camden, his first attempt at fences. On his return to this country he won three good-class novice chases with complete authority and, with all the established top three-mile chasers on the sidelines, was allowed to take his chance in the Cheltenham Gold Cup for which he was strongly fancied. Alas, the bad luck that haunted his trainer for years at the National Hunt Meeting did not relent and, having made a mistake at the seventh (open ditch), he slipped landing over the ninth, fractured a hind leg above the hock and had to be destroyed.

LARBAWN

(Late Copper Delight.) Bay gelding, 1959, Vulgan—Fly Book (Flyon). Bred by Mr W. H. Cory.

A full-brother to the 1966 Champion Hurdler, Salmon Spray, Larbawn won three hurdle races and 15 chases including the Mildmay Memorial, Sandown (1970) and the Whitbread Gold Cup, Sandown, twice (1968 and 1969).

A very popular horse, owned and trained by Warwickshire permit-holder Michael Marsh and usually ridden by Macer Gifford, Larbawn was a great battler, loved firm ground and was effective at any distance from 2m to 3m, 5f.

LEADER, Harvey (1894-1972)

A brother of Tom, Frank and Colledge, all of whom were trainers, 'Jack' Leader was an all-round sportsman. He was Master of the Cambridge Harriers, a keen polo-player and a fine shot. He was also said to be a fine judge of a horse and an even better one of form.

As a boy he rode on the Flat but soon got too heavy and switched to fences. A bad fall schooling left him with a damaged kidney and he missed the 1914-18 war. He took out a licence to train in 1918, taking over his father's string. At first he conducted a mixed stable but later concentrated on the Flat with great success. He bought Jack Horner for an American patron, Charlie Schwartz, and trained him to win the 1926 Grand National. He was unable to see his charge first past the post for, in his excitement, Mr Schwartz hit him so hard across the shoulders that he fell off the stand.

LEADER, Thomas Edward (b.1903)

A member of a famous racing family, 'Ted' Leader was a son of the well-known jump trainer, T. R. (Tom) Leader (q.v.) and a nephew of several good Flat trainers. Because of a weak chest, he could not go to school and was apprenticed to his uncle, Harvey. A strong, stylish rider, he grew too heavy for the Flat but quickly established himself under National Hunt Rules, being particularly effective on large and lazy horses. He was Champion Jockey in 1925-26, riding 61 winners.

His principal winners were:

The Cheltenham Gold Cup (1925) Ballinode;
   (1932) Golden Miller
The Grand National (1927) Sprig
The Champion Hurdle (1932) Insurance
The Champion Chase (1926) Aisle; (1928)
   Mount Etna
The Grand Sefton (1924) Ballinode
The Imperial Cup (1928) Royal Falcon

In 1934 he took out a licence to train and took over his uncle Colledge's yard at Machell Place, Newmarket. Since then apart from serving with the R.A.F. during World War II, he has trained continuously.

Among the good races he has won are the Queen Alexandra Stakes. three years in succession, and the Goodwood Cup with Predominate, the Middle Park, the St James's Palace and the Queen Elizabeth II Stakes with Major Portion and the Champion Stakes twice with Wychwood Abbott.

He ranks among seven jockeys to have

won the Gold Cup, the Grand National and the Champion Hurdle, The others are H. Beasley, T. Cullinan, F. B. Rees, G. W. Robinson, G. Wilson and F. T. Winter.

LEADER, Thomas Richard (1879-1945)

Tom Leader was the eldest son of 'Old' Tom Leader who was head-lad to Tom Olliver, took over the latter's Wroughton stable when he died in 1874 and saddled George Frederick to win the Derby later that year. He began training at an early age when his father moved to Wroughton House, Newmarket, leaving him the Wroughton establishment where he made his name as a trainer of jumpers. In 1906 he moved to Newmarket. Among his greatest successes were the 1927 Grand National with Sprig, ridden by his son, Ted (q.v.). He won again in 1929 when Gregalach, the least fancied of his five runners, upset the favourite, Easter Hero.

He was a licensed preacher and an active Freemason, being Master of Ethelreda Lodge, Newmarket.

LEHANE, Johnny (1935-69)

An Irishman, Johnny Lehane knew something of the ups and downs of racing. He ran away from home at the age of 14 and got himself apprenticed to Dick Morrison. He moved on to Jimmy Brogan, for whom he won the 1958 Irish Grand National on Gold Legend.

About that time he came to England to ride chiefly for Bill Marshall, who admired him greatly and attributed his best N.H. season to Lehane's handling of his horses. He wrote: "His great love for horses and his kindness and patience with difficult ones had to be seen to be believed. The most unmanageable became like lambs under his beautiful handling."

He twice finished fourth in the Jockeys' Table, riding 47 winners in 1958-59 and 41 in 1959-60 and his best victories included the Lancashire Chase (1962) on Skish and the Eider Chase on Pontin-Go. Latterly he worked as head-lad to Derek Crossman and died in 1969 at the age of 34.

LEICESTER (Group 3)

A right-handed, rectangular, undulating course, 1¾ miles round. Leicester is a severe track which puts stamina at a premium. The hurdles course can get

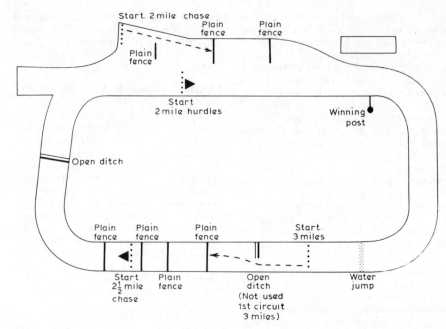

extremely heavy. It has staged racing since 1870 and is very much a trainers' course, providing mid-week fixtures with plenty of opportunities for novice and moderate horses.

The principal races are the Golden Miller Pattern Hurdle (January, 2m, £2,607) and the Leicestershire Silver Fox H'cap Chase (November, 2½m, £1,679).

Best Times

Distance	Time	Horse-age-weight	Date
2m H	3m 41.20	Greenhills Lad 5-11-1	10-11-64
3m H	5m 48	King Tarquin 5-10-6	1-4-67
2m C	4m 10.20	Noon 4-10-2	2-11-71
3m C	5m 55.40	Sorbus 10-10-7	24-4-67

LEINSTER

Brown gelding, 1898, Ascetic—Secret (Cameliard). Bred in Ireland by Mr G. L. Walker.

A full-brother to the Sefton winner, Hidden Mystery, Leinster began his career in smashing fashion, winning three races as a five-year-old, including the 1903 Grand Sefton with 12-7 and going unbeaten through his six-year-old season with four victories including the Champion Chase, Liverpool (1904).

In the spring of 1904 he went to France where he won two chases the following season. He did not race in England again until 1908 by which time his lustre seemed to have dimmed, but at 12 years old he staged a remarkable come-back, winning three chases including the Valentine Chase, Liverpool, and the Champion Chase, Liverpool (1910), for the second time.

Leinster was owned by Sir T. Gallwey and trained and ridden by Percy Woodland (q.v.) who reckoned him the best horse he ever rode.

LENEY PRINCESS

Brown mare, 1949. Bred by Mr E. Tormey.

Leney Princess			
Roi d'Egypte	Van B.		Alcantara II
			Annarella
	Menthe Poivrée	Pot Au Feu	
			Minieh
Biddy The Hawk	Sun Yat Sen	Santoi	
			Nesta
	Triple Alliance	Mighty Power	
			Allies Offensive

After winning two point-to-points, Leney Princess broke a bone in her knee and was sold privately as a broodmare to Colonel (later Sir) John Thomson who had owned her sire Roi d'Egypte, winner of the Cathcart Challenge Cup, National Hunt Meeting, and a full-brother to the Gold Cup winner Medoc II.

Her foaling record was as follows:

1958 bay gelding (Fortina) **Fort Leney** (14 races including the Cheltenham Gold Cup, Leopardstown Chase (twice), Power Gold Cup, John Jameson Gold Cup

1959 brown gelding (Fortina) **Prince Tino** (20 races)

1960 gelding (Arctic Slave) **King Frost** (three races)

1961 gelding (Buckhound) **Buck Regis** (put down)

1962 filly (Black Tarquin) (put down)

1963 brown gelding (Black Tarquin) **Proud Tarquin** (nine races, including Tote Champion Novices.)

1964 brown gelding (Black Tarquin) **Tuscan Prince** (15 races, also the Whitbread Gold Cup, disqualified.)

1966 bay gelding (Bowsprit) **Lean Forward** (16 races, including Leopardstown Chase 1974.)

1967 filly (Little Buskins) **Theatre Royal** (never ran, dam of bay filly 1973 (Sir Herbert.)

1968 colt (Little Buskins) (killed by lightning.)

1969 filly (Arctic Chevalier) **Dame Leney**

1970 filly (No Argument) **Legal Argument**

1971 colt (Raise You Ten) **Princely Bid**

1972 colt (Mugatpura)

All Leney Princess's living progeny were reared, broken and hunted by Cecil Ronaldson and with the exception of King Frost, who was sold, all have remained in Sir John's ownership and have been trained by Tom (and now Jim) Dreaper in Ireland or Roddy Armytage in England.

By the end of season 1977-78 the progeny of Leney Princess had won 77 races.

LE PAILLON

Bay horse, 1942, Fastnet—Blue Bear (Blenheim). Bred by the Comte A. de Foucher de Careil.

Le Paillon is the only Prix de l'Arc de Triomphe winner to have run in the Champion Hurdle – and not won it! He did in fact run National Spirit to a length in 1947 and might have won had his rider, Alec Head (subsequently a most distinguished trainer), been more familiar with Cheltenham's bends and gradients. La Paillon who won a total of seven Flat and 10 hurdle races went on to win the Grand Course des Haies, Auteuil (1947) and the Arc later that year. He was owned by Mme Head and trained by her husband, Willie.

L'ESCARGOT

Chestnut gelding, 1963. Bred by Mrs B. O'Neill.

L'Escargot			
Escart III	Turmoil II	Tourbillon	
		Blue Iras	
	Escalade	Escamillo	
		Cle de Mi	
What a Daisy	Grand Inquisitor	His Reverence	
		High Prestige	
	Lady Sunderlin	J'Accours	
		Duchess of Pedulas	

A strongly made, tough, courageous gelding of extreme versatility, Mr Raymond Guest's L'Escargot is one of a select band of five horses to have won more than one Cheltenham Gold Cup. He also won on the Flat, he was a top-class juvenile hurdler, he raced and won in the United States and he won and was twice placed, under big weights, in successive Grand Nationals.

In all he won a bumper, three hurdle races, including the Osbertown Hurdle and the division of the Gloucester Hurdle, National Hunt Meeting (1968), and nine chases including the Grand National (1975), the W. D. and H. O. Wills Premier Final, Haydock (1970), the Meadowbrook Chase, U.S.A. (1969) and the Cheltenham Gold Cup twice, in 1970 (T. Carberry), 33/1, by 1½l, 10l, from French Tan (P. Taaffe) and Spanish Steps (J. Cook), and again in 1971 (T. Carberry), 7/2 joint favourite, by 10l, 15l, Leap Frog (V. O'Brien) and The Dikler (B. Brogan).

After that, advancing age began to blunt his speed but his courage remained undaunted. Although he only won two races in his last four seasons he was fourth in the 1973 Gold Cup and third to Red Rum and Crisp in the Grand National a fortnight later. In 1974 he went one better and finished second to Red Rum, while in 1975 his career ended on a fairy tale note when he became the first Gold Cup winner since Golden Miller to win the Grand National, 11-3 (T. Carberry), 13/2, by 15l, 8l, from Red Rum, 12-0 (B. Fletcher) and Spanish Steps, 10-3 (W. Smith).

L'Escargot was trained throughout his career by Dan Moore, in Ireland.

LILLINGSTONE, Alan (b.1935)

The son of well-known amateur rider and M.F.H., Capt. Luke Lillingstone, and a half-brother of the Earl of Harrington, Alan Lillingstone is one of only two amateurs to have won the Champion Hurdle, which he did in 1963 on Winning Fair. The other was Capt. 'Perry' Harding on Our Hope (1938). Alan Lillingstone also won the National Hunt Chase (1957) on Kari Sou. He now owns and manages the Mount Coote Stud, Co. Limerick. His wife, Vivienne, is a daughter of the Marquis of Abergavenny.

LIMBER HILL

Chestnut gelding, 1947, Bassam—Mindoon (Gainsborough). Bred in Lincolnshire by Mr J. Davy.

The only winning son of his sire, Bassam, Limber Hill was broken by his owner-breeder, hunted with the Brocklesby and won five of his six point-to-points ridden by Mr P. Fox. Transferred to Bill Dutton's Malton Yard, he posed something of a problem for no rug or roller could be found big enough to fit the slashing, roman-nosed six-year-old. An anguished call to the local saddler produced one which would, he said, fit any horse foaled. So it proved – but only by the last hole!

Limber Hill soon proved to have speed as well as jumping and staying powers and during his first season under Rules, he won four hurdle races. Switched to the bigger obstacles he proved near invincible for two seasons, winning eight chases including the National Hunt Handicap Chase (1955), the Emblem Chase, Manchester, the King George VI, Kempton, and the 1956 Cheltenham Gold Cup (J. Power), 11/8f, by 4l, 1½l, from Vigor (R. Emery) and Hallowe'en (F. T. Winter), after a foot-perfect display of jumping which had him the race won two fences from home.

Limber Hill, who needed very little preparation and ran best when fresh, continued to race until 1959 but did not win another race.

LINDE, Henry Eyre

A farmer from Co. Kildare who, after a spell in the Royal Irish Constabulary, settled at Eyrefield Lodge, the Curragh, Henry Eyre Linde was the most brilliantly successful Irish trainer of the nineteenth century. His beginnings were modest and it was a £25 mare, Highland Mary, who won him several races and bred his first good horse, Eyrefield, who laid the foundations of his fortune. He was fortunate that nearby his Curragh establishment lived the Beasley brothers (q.v.), all of whom, and particularly Tommy, help him train, school and ride his glittering team.

Linde's methods were rigorous and severe even by the standards of his age and few horses withstood them for long. Nevertheless they were supremely successful. He won the Grand National three times in ten years with Empress (1880), Woodbrook (1881) and Frigate (1889), and was second five times (once with Cyrus who was beaten a short head by a stable reject, Seaman, who had been discarded because of unsoundness), and third once.

He won the Grand Steeplechase de Paris in 1882 with Whisper Low, 1883 with Too Good, 1890 with Royal Meath, and in 1893 with Skedaddle. He also won the Lancashire Chase in 1888 with Spahi and 1893 with Empress's son Red Prince II whom he bred.

LINGFIELD PARK (Group 2)

Lingfield is set in a pretty 350-acre park in an undulating stretch of Surrey downland somewhat susceptible to waterlogging. Constructed in 1890 by the Beckwith-Smith family who until recently owned and managed it, the first chasing meeting was held in 1891.

Although no really important race under National Hunt Rules is run there, the framing of the races and the general level of prize money have always attracted good horses. The executive have always commemorated great horses in their race programmes and among the National Hunt performers in whose honour a race is named are Cloister, Hidden Mystery, Jerry M., Manifesto, Trespasser and Troytown. The most valuable races are Ladbroke Leaders H'cap Hurdle (December, 2m, 4f, £3,984 to the winner) and the Summit Junior Hurdle (December, 2m, £2,824).

In the autumn of 1974 the Beckwith-

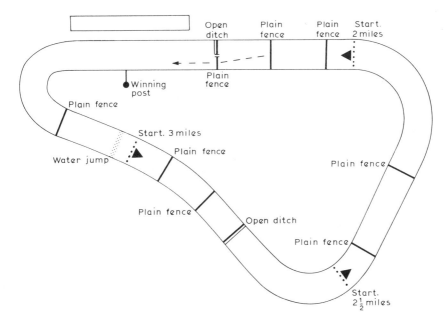

Smiths announced that they could no longer practically run it as a private, family concern and offered it for sale. It was bought by the Ladbroke Group, the first venture of its type by a bookmaking firm, and is now run by a committee.

Best Times

Distance	Time	Horse-age-weight	Date
2m H	3m 45.20	Gay Light 8-11-7	23-2-34
2½m H	5m 12.60	Dragon Hill 10-10-3	4-3-76
2¾m H	5m 32.20	Cameraman III 8-11-0	19-12-47
2m C	3m 57.20	Zambomba 7-11-5	30-10-72
2½m C	5m 7.30	Garva 6-10-6	30-10-72
3m C	5m 50.10	Jack Palmer 7-10-8	30-10-72

LINWELL
(Formerly Floral Tribute.) Brown gelding, 1948, Rosewell—Rubia Linda (Arran Chief). Bred in Ireland by Mr James Delany.

After showing some promise in bumpers in Ireland, Linwell was bought for £750 by Ivor Herbert on behalf of Mr (later Sir) David Brown as a likely point-to-pointer. He did not in fact prove wholly successful in this sphere, falling at the very first fence in his first race and finishing third on his only other outing.

Switched to racing proper, however, he made an immediate impact and became one of the most consistent, high-class, staying chasers of the late 'fifties. In 44 outings between 1954-59 he was only seven times unplaced. His 19 victories included the Mildmay Memorial, Sandown (1956) and the 1957 Cheltenham

Gold Cup (M. Scudamore), 100/9, by 1l, 5l, from Kerstin (G. Milburn) and Rose Park (G. Nicholls). His trainer reckoned him a 10lb better horse at Cheltenham than anywhere else and he was probably unlucky not to win at least one more Gold Cup. In 1958 he was distracted by Mandarin's antics at the water and fell, leaving the field clear for the previous year's runner-up Kerstin (incidently his first-cousin, their dams both being daughters of Toy Fish) and in 1959 he was severely hampered by the last-fence fall of Pas Seul, when beaten three lengths by Roddy Owen.

LION COURAGE
Bay or brown gelding, 1928, Jackdaw —Lullaby (Lord Savile). Bred by Mr M. J. Gleeson.

A high-class hurdler trained by Frank Brown, Lion Courage won nine races including the Imperial Cup, Sandown (1934) and the 1935 Champion Hurdle (G. Wilson), 100/8, by $\frac{1}{2}$l, $\frac{3}{4}$l, from Gay Light (S. Ingham) and Hill Song (G. Pellerin). Lion Courage changed hands on more than one occasion but he won the Champion Hurdle in the colours of Mr R. Fox-Carlyon. He subsequently won two races including a three-mile chase at Gatwick.

LITTLE, Capt. James Lockhart (1821-77)

A leading amateur rider and a founder member of the National Hunt Committee, 'Josey' Little was a small, dark, finely-built man, reputed to have a way with women, and beautiful 'hands'. Commissioned into the King's Dragoon Guards, he lost money in a bank failure and transferred to the less expensive 81st Foot Regiment.

He had been coached in the art of steeplechase riding by Tom Olliver and lack of funds did not prevent him from acquiring a half-share in Chandler, whom he rode to victory in the 1848 Grand National, beating The Curate (ridden by Tom Olliver!) by $\frac{1}{2}$l in a driving finish. Later he bought Peter Simple from Finch Mason and with Tom Olliver up, the gritty bay stayed home best to win the 1853 National.

Captain Little's other good successes included the Worcester Grand Annual (1847). Colours: white, black sleeves and cap.

LITTLE CHARLEY

Bay gelding, not in the General Stud Book, by Charles XII.

Little Charley won the Grand National in 1858, the year the race was postponed for three days on account of appalling weather. As it was, the race was run in gale-force winds and snow and a crowd of barely 500 watched Little Charley, 10-7 (W. Archer), 100/6, win by 4l, 50 yards, from Weathercock, 11-7 (Mr G. Ede) and Xanthus, 11-0 (F. Balchin). Only two others of the sixteen starters finished. The result proved a great triumph for Cheltenham for owner, Mr Christopher Capel of Prestbury House, trainer W. Holman and jockey William Archer were all natives of the town.

Previously Little Charley had run in three Nationals, being knocked over in

1855, finishing fifth in 1856 and unplaced in 1857.

LIVERPOOL (Group 1)

Steeplechasing at Liverpool dates from 1836 and a Grand Liverpool Steeplechase, sometimes styled the first Grand National, was run at Maghull from 1836-38. However, the Aintree course, which Mr William Lynn (q.v.) leased from the second Earl of Sefton, was first used in 1839.

The first National was a level-weights affair over four miles for gentleman riders. Lord Molyneux, later third Earl of Sefton, acted as umpire. There were 29 fences and the course was chiefly plough. The two great brooks were christened by riders who fell into them. Captain Becher was disunited from his mount Conrad at Brook Number One in 1839 while Brook Number Two was named after Mr Power's Irish horse, Valentine.

In 1843 the race became a handicap and in 1847 it was for the first time styled 'The Grand National'. During the 1850s and early 'sixties the race and the course fell into disrepute. However, wise and able men were involved in steeplechasing at the time and the decade saw the birth of the National Hunt Committee, an official Calendar, Steeplechases Past and a code of Rules. The sport revived dramatically and by the 1890s Liverpool was a very different affair. The National was worth nearly £2,000 and the course was all grass with a running rail and regulation furze fences, much as they are now, only upright. The 'aprons' were added in 1960 after a dreadful spate of accidents when four horses were killed in the first two days of the meeting. During the nineteenth and early twentieth centuries, Liverpool was by far and away the most important steeplechase course in the country. Not only was the Grand National the most valuable and prestigious race in the Calendar, but some of the supporting races and the Autumn Meeting gained in significance. The Grand Sefton Chase (Autumn Meeting 1867-1965 and briefly revived in 1972) was foremost among these. The Topham Trophy (Autumn) was also important, as were the Liverpool Hurdle, the Foxhunter Steeplechase for Amateurs and the Stanley Chase for novices, all in March. This last was a real graveyard for novices and on more than one occasion all the runners fell. Previous winners include Ally Sloper, Sprig, Gregalach, Kellsboro' Jack and Southern Hero. In 1953 at the instigation of Lord Mildmay a small circuit was built inside the main course with scaled-down replicas of the big fences. It was known as the Mildmay course and the Stanley Chase was renamed the Mildmay. The course was not a success and now has regulation birch fences.

The Grand National exercises world-wide fascination. Horses from all over the world have been sent over to try to win and many have been successful. The New Zealand Moiffa won in 1904, the Australian Crisp was an infinitely gallant second in 1973 while the French were successful in 1862 with Huntsman and 1909 with Lutteur II. The Americans,

after their narrow miss with Billy Barton who fell at the last in the lead in 1928 and was remounted to finish second, were successful in 1938 with Battleship and 1965 with Jay Trump. The Russians sent Reljef and Grifel over in 1961 but neither completed.

The race was the first to be broadcast in 1927, the year of Sprig's victory. In 1951 Mrs Topham, the racecourse manager, became involved in a dispute with the B.B.C. and staged her own broadcast. It was not successful. The race was first televised in 1960.

Only one horse has won the Grand National three times, Red Rum. He was also second twice, thus establishing a record of consistency only approached by Manifesto who won twice and was three times third, carrying weights that would not be allowed nowadays (12-7, 12-13 and 12-8). There have been six other dual winners, Peter Simple Abd-el-Kader, The Colonel, The Lamb, Poethlyn and Reynoldstown. Among the jockeys George Stevens rode five winners while Tom Olliver, Mr T. Beasley, Arthur Nightingall, Ernie Piggott, Jack Anthony and Brian Fletcher rode three apiece. Aubrey Hastings and Fred Rimell head the trainers with four wins each, while Henry Linde, Tom Coulthwaite and Neville Crump each trained three. Captain Machell was in fact responsible for four winners, but Regal (1876) is officially credited to Joe Cannon and Seaman (1882) to James Jewitt.

The Topham family have been associated with Liverpool since 1857, as Clerks of the Course and Managers. In 1949 Mrs Mirabel Topham bought the course from the 7th Earl of Sefton, subject to a covenant restricting its use to racing and agriculture. In the post-war years she found it very difficult to make the course an economically viable proposition and in 1964 arranged its sale to Capital and Counties for redevelopment. Lord Sefton sought an injunction to restrain her and was given judgement, which was upheld in the House of Lords but reversed on appeal. From 1964-73 Mrs Topham soldiered on, but she received little help and the course became increasingly shabby and run down. Admission prices rose steeply and television coverage became so professional that the public stayed away.

In November 1973 she sold the course for £3 million to William Davies' Walton Group and for two years the course's future hung in the balance. Mr Davies acquired a generous new sponsor in the *News of the World*, but he then tried to force the Jockey Club's hand into giving him a £75,000 grant towards the course and permission to stage a 1½m Aintree Derby as his condition for staging the Grand National. He finally accepted a compromise of £50,000 in return for a guaranteed six days' racing, but no Aintree Derby. In May 1975 he announced the sale of the course to Irishman, Patrick McCrea. However, the deal never materialized and in August was called off. The Levy Board offered £400,000 for the course and Ladbrokes £1¼ million. In December 1975 the Jockey Club issued an ultimatum that if agreement was not reached by 29th December the race would go to Doncaster. On 22nd December the deal was announced. Ladbrokes guaranteed to stage the race until 1978. They were to pay Davies £200,000 a year to run the course for 1976 and 1977 with an option to renew for a further five years at £225,000 for the first two years and £250,000 for the final three years.

Ladbrokes installed John Hughes (already running Lingfield for them) as Clerk of the Course and working at breakneck speed he attracted a host of generous new sponsors and staged a meeting worthy of the big race. By 1977 a real festival on a par with the National Hunt Meeting was organized, and the crowds came pouring back to enjoy some great racing and a fairytale climax as Red Rum became the first horse to win three Grand Nationals.

The course is left-handed, triangular in shape, perfectly flat and approximately 2¼ miles long (the Mildmay course being 1¼ miles). The Turf is the finest in the country with perfect drainage, and the going is rarely anything but good, whatever the weather conditions.

The principal races are:

The Sun Grand National (March, 4m, 4f, £41,140)

The Sun Ratings Chase (March, 2m, £7,302)

The Templegate Hurdle (March, 2m 5½f, £7,253)

The Gillette Trophy Chase (Mildmay Course, March, 2m, £3,492)

The Topham Trophy Handicap Chase (March, 2m 6f, £4,441)

The Sporting Chronicle Handicap Chase (Mildmay Course, March, 2m 4f, £4,818)

The Kennedy Construction Handicap Hurdle (March, 2m 100y, £4,025)

The Papermate Hurdle (4-y-o, March, 2m, £3,817)

The Whisky Haig Foxhunter Chase (Amateurs, March, 2m 6f, £2,905).

Best Times (Mildmay Course)

Distance	Times	Horse-age-weight	Date
2m H	3m 47.30	Beparoejojo 4-10-0	31-3-78
2m 100y H	3m 48.60	Spartan General 5-11-0	29-10-64
2m 1f few y H	4m 0.80	Hasty Word 6-10-11	31-3-73
2m 5f H	5m 10.80	Ulandi 8-11-5	1-12-55
2m 5f 100y H	5m 0.4	Raleighstown 7-11-8	31-3-78
2m C	3m 51.40	Menehall 3-10-2	3-4-76
2m 4f C	4m 54.90	King or Country 7-11-2	30-3-78
3m 1f C	5m 56	Mr Snowman 9-10-10	31-3-78
3m 1f 130y C	6m 25.60	Irish Lizard 12-11-6	30-11-55

(Grand National Course)

Distance	Times	Horse-age-weight	Date
2m 80y C	3m. 59	Glenn 6-11-11	7-4-67
2m 5f C	5m 20.40	Inch Arran 8-11-7	28-10-72
2m 6f C	5m 31.8	Inch Arran 9-11-2	29-3-73
2m 7½f C	5m 53.60	Red Thorn 8-11-1	31-10-64
4m 856y C	9m 1.90	Red Rum 8-10-5	31-3-73

The Grand National

	HORSE	OWNER	RIDER	TRAINER	S.P.
1839	Lottery	Mr Elmore	J. Mason	——	5/1
1840	Jerry	Mr Elmore	B. Bretherton	——	12/1
1841	Charity	Lord Craven	Powell	——	14/1
1842	Gay Lad	Mr Elmore	T. Olliver	——	7/1
1843	Vanguard	Lord Chesterfield	T. Olliver	——	12/1
1844	Discount	Mr Quartermaine	Crickmere	——	5/1
1845	Cure All	Mr Crawford	Loft	——	←
1846	Pioneer	Mr Adams	Taylor	——	—
1847	Matthew	Mr Courtney	D. Wynne	——	10/1
1848	Chandler	Capt. Little	Capt. Little	——	12/1
1849	Peter Simple	Mr J. Mason	T. Cunningham	——	20/1
1850	Abd-el-Kader	Mr Osborne	C. Green	——	—
1851	Abd-el-Kader	Mr Osborne	T. Abbott	——	7/1
1852	Miss Mowbray	Mr T. Mason	Mr A. Goodman	——	—
1853	Peter Simple	Capt. Little	T. Olliver	——	9/1
1854	Bourton	Mr Moseley	Tasker	——	4/1
1855	Wanderer	Mr Dennis	J. Handon	——	25/1
1856	Free Trader	Mr W. Barnett	G. Stevens	——	25/1
1857	Emigrant	Mr G. Hodgman	C. Boyce	——	10/1
1858	Little Charley	Mr C. Capel	W. Archer	——	100/6
1859	Half Caste	Mr Willoughby	C. Green	——	7/1
1860	Anatis	Mr C. Capel	Mr Thomas	——	7/2
1861	Jealousy	Mr J. Bennett	J. Kendall	——	5/1
1862	Huntsman	Vicomte de Namur	H. Lamplugh	——	3/1
1863	Emblem	Lord Coventry	G. Stevens	——	4/1
1864	Emblematic	Lord Coventry	G. Stevens	——	10/1
1865	Alcibiade	Mr B. Angell	Capt. Coventry	——	100/7
1866	Salamander	Mr Studd	Mr A. Goodman	——	40/1
1867	Cortolvin	Duke of Hamilton	J. Page	——	100/6
1868	The Lamb	Lord Poulett	Mr Edwards	——	10/1
1869	The Colonel	Mr Weyman	G. Stevens	——	13/1
1870	The Colonel	Mr M. Evans	G. Stevens	——	4/1
1871	The Lamb	Lord Poulett	Mr Thomas	——	5/1
1872	Casse Tête	Mr E. Brayley	J. Page	——	20/1
1873	Disturbance	Capt. Machell	Mr J. Richardson	——	20/1
1874	Reugny	Capt. Machell	Mr J. Richardson	——	5/1
1875	Pathfinder	Mr H. Bird	Mr Thomas	——	100/6
1876	Regal	Capt. Machell	J. Cannon	——	25/1
1877	Austerlitz	Mr F. Hobson	Mr E. Hobson	——	15/1
1878	Shifnal	Mr J. Nightingall	J. Jones	——	7/1
1879	Liberator	Mr G. Moore	Mr G. Moore	——	5/1
1880	Empress	Mr P. Ducrot	Mr T. Beasley	——	8/1
1881	Woodbrook	Capt. Kirkwood	Mr T. Beasley	——	6/1
1882	Seaman	Lord Manners	Lord Manners	——	10/1
1883	Zoedone	Count C. Kinsky	Count C. Kinsky	——	100/8
1884	Voluptuary	Mr H. Boyd	Mr E. Wilson	T. Wilson	10/1
1885	Roquefort	A. Cooper	Mr E. Wilson	J. Swatton	100/30
1886	Old Joe	Mr A. Douglas	T. Skelton	——	25/1
1887	Gamecock	Mr E. Jay	W. Daniells	Jordan	20/1
1888	Playfair	Mr E. Baird	G. Mawson	——	40/1

HORSE	OWNER	RIDER	TRAINER	S.P.
1889 Frigate	Mr M. Maher	Mr T. Beasley	——	8/1
1890 Ilex	Mr G. Masterman	A. Nightingall	J. Nightingall	4/1
1891 Come Away	Mr W. Jameson	Mr H. Beasley	——	4/1
1892 Father O'Flynn	Mr G. Wilson	Capt. R. Owen	——	20/1
1893 Cloister	Mr M. C. Duff	W. Dollery	J. Swatton	9/2
1894 Why Not	Capt. C. Fenwick	A. Nightingall	J. Collins	5/1
1895 Wild Man from Borneo	Mr J. Widger	Mr J. Widger	J. Gatland	10/1
1896 The Soarer	Mr W. Walker	Mr D. Campbell	J. Collins	40/1
1897 Manifesto	Mr H. Dyas	T. Kavanagh	W. McAuliffe	6/1
1898 Drogheda	Mr G. Adamson	J. Gourley	E. Woods	25/1
1899 Manifesto	J. Bulteel	G. Williamson	R. Collins	5/1
1900 Ambush	H.R.H. Prince of Wales	A. Anthony	A. Anthony	4/1
1901 Grudon	Mr B. Bletsoe	A. Nightingall	J. Holland	9/1
1902 Shannon Lass	Mr A. Gorham	D. Read	J. Hackett	20/1
1903 Drumcree	Mr H. Morrison	P. Woodland	Sir C. Nugent	13/2
1904 Moifaa	Mr S. Gollans	A. Birch	O. Hickey	25/1
1905 Kirkland	Mr F. Bibby	F. Mason	Thomas	6/1
1906 Ascetic's Silver	Prince Hatzfeldt	Hon. A. Hastings	A. Hastings	20/1
1907 Eremon	Mr S. Howard	A. Newey	T. Coulthwaite	8/1
1908 Rubio	Maj. F. D-Pennant	H. Bletsoe	W. Costello	66/1
1909 Lutteur III	Mr J. Hennessy	G. Parfrement	H. Escott	100/9
1910 Jenkinstown	Mr S. Howard	R. Chadwick	T. Coulthwaite	100/8
1911 Glenside	Mr F. Bibby	Mr J. Anthony	Capt. Collis	20/1
1912 Jerry M.	Sir C. Assheton-Smith	E. Piggott	R. Gore	4/1
1913 Covertcoat	Sir C. Assheton-Smith	P. Woodland	R. Gore	100/9
1914 Sunloch	Mr T. Tyler	W. Smith	T. Tyler	100/6
1915 Ally Sloper	Lady Nelson	Mr J. Anthony	Hon. A. Hastings	100/8
1916 Vermouth	Mr P. Heybourne	J. Reardon	J. Bell	100/8
1917 Ballymacad	Sir G. Bullough	E. Driscoll	Hon. A. Hastings	100/9
1918 Poethlyn	Mrs H. Peel	E. Piggott	A. Escott	5/1
1919 Poethlyn	Mrs H. Peel	E. Piggott	A. Escott	11/4
1920 Troytown	Maj. T. Gerrard	Mr J. Anthony	A. Anthony	6/1
1921 Shaun Spadah	Mr M. McAlpine	F. Rees	G. Poole	100/9
1922 Music Hall	Mr H. Kershaw	L. Rees	O. Anthony	100/9
1923 Sergeant Murphy	Mr S. Sandford	Capt. G. Bennett	G. Blackwell	100/6
1924 Master Robert	Lord Airlie	R. Trudgill	Hon. A. Hastings	25/1
1925 Double Chance	Mr D. Gould	Maj. J. Wilson	F. Archer	100/9
1926 Jack Horner	Mr A. Schwartz	W. Watkinson	H. Leader	25/1
1927 Sprig	Mrs M. Partridge	T. E. Leader	T. E. Leader	8/1
1928 Tipperary Tim	Mr H. Kenyon	Mr W. Dutton	J. Dodd	100/1
1929 Gregalach	Mrs M. Gemmall	R. Everett	T. R. Leader	100/1
1930 Shaun Goilin	Mr W. Midwood	T. Cullinan	F. Hartigan	100/8
1931 Grakle	Mr C. Taylor	R. Lyall	T. Coulthwaite	100/6
1932 Forbra	Mr W. Parsonage	J. Hamey	T. Rimell	50/1
1933 Kellsboro' Jack	Mrs F. Clark	D. Williams	I. Anthony	25/1
1934 Golden Miller	Miss D. Paget	G. Wilson	A. B. Briscoe	8/1
1935 Reynoldstown	Maj. N. Furlong	Mr F. Furlong	N. Furlong	22/1
1936 Reynoldstown	Maj. N. Furlong	Mr F. Walwyn	N. Furlong	10/1
1937 Royal Mail	Mr Lloyd Thomas	E. Williams	I. Anthony	100/6
1938 Battleship	Mrs M. Scott	B. Hobbs	R. Hobbs	40/1
1939 Workman	Sir A. Maguire	T. Hyde	J. Ruttle	100/8
1940 Bogskar	Lord Stalbridge	M. Jones	Lord Stalbridge	25/1
1946 Lovely Cottage	Mr J. Morant	Capt. R. Petre	T. Rayson	25/1
1947 Caughoo	Mr J. McDowell	E. Dempsey	H. McDowell	100/1
1948 Sheila's Cottage	Mr J. Proctor	A. Thompson	N. Crump	50/1
1949 Russian Hero	Mr W. Williamson	L. McMorrow	G. Owen	66/1
1950 Freebooter	Mrs L. Brotherton	J. Power	R. Renton	10/1
1951 Nickle Coin	Mr J. Royle	J. Bullock	J. O'Donoghue	40/1

	HORSE	OWNER	RIDER	TRAINER	S.P.
1952	Teal	Mr H. Lane	A. Thompson	N. Crump	100/7
1953	Early Mist	Mr J. Griffin	B. Marshall	V. O'Brien	20/1
1954	Royal Tan	Mr J. Griffin	B. Marshall	V. O'Brien	8/1
1955	Quare Times	Mrs W. Welman	P. Taaffe	V. O'Brien	100/9
1956	E.S.B.	Mrs L. Carver	D. Dick	T. F. Rimell	100/7
1957	Sundew	Mrs G. Kohn	F. Winter	F. Hudson	20/1
1958	Mr What	Mr D. Coughlan	A. Freeman	T. Taaffe	18/1
1959	Oxo	Mr J. Bigg	M. Scudamore	W. Stephenson	8/1
1960	Merryman II	Miss W. Wallace	G. Scott	N. Crump	13/2
1961	Nicolaus Silver	Mr C. Vaughan	H. Beasley	T. F. Rimell	28/1
1962	Kilmore	Mr N. Cohen	F. Winter	H. R. Price	28/1
1963	Ayala	Mr P. Raymond	P. Buckley	K. Piggott	66/1
1964	Team Spirit	Mr J. Goodman	W. Robinson	F. Walwyn	18/1
1965	Jay Trump	Mrs M. Stephenson	Mr C. Smith	F. Winter	100/6
1966	Anglo	Mr S. Levy	T. Norman	F. Winter	50/1
1967	Foinavon	Mr G. Watkins	J. Buckingham	J. Kempton	100pS
1968	Red Alligator	Mr J. Manners	B. Fletcher	D. Smith	100/7
1969	Highland Wedding	Mr T. McKoy, jun.	E. Harty	G. Balding	100/9
1970	Gay Trip	Mr A. Chambers	P. Taaffe	T. F. Rimell	15/1
1971	Specify	Mr F. W. Pontin	J. Cook	J. E. Sutcliffe	28/1
1972	Well To Do	Capt. T. A. Forster	G. Thorner	T. Forster	14/1
1973	Red Rum	Mr N. le Mare	B. Fletcher	D. McCain	9/1
1974	Red Rum	Mr N. le Mare	B. Fletcher	D. McCain	11/1
1975	L'Escargot	Mr R. Guest	T. Carberry	D. Moore	13/2
1976	Rag Trade	Mr P. Raymond	J. Burke	T. F. Rimell	14/1
1977	Red Rum	Mr N. le Mare	T. Stack	D. McCain	9/1
1978	Lucius	Mrs D. Whitaker	B. R. Davies	G. Richards	14/1
1979	Rubstic	J. Douglas	M. Barnes	J. Leadbetter	

The Whisky Haig Hunters Chase (2m, 6f)

	HORSE	OWNER	RIDER	TRAINER
1923	Gracious Gift	Mr R. Gresson	Capt. G. H. Bennett	——
1924	Patsey V	Mr B. Lemon	Owner	——
1925	Upton Lad	Mr J. Paterson	Mr W. P. Dutton	——
1926	L'Aiglon II	Mrs P. Cholmondeley	Mr D. D. Williams	——
1927	Seti the First	Mr E. Craig-Tanner	Owner	——
1928	Pippin II	Capt. M. Dennis	Mr G. S. Poole	——
1929	Agden	Mr O. Moseley	Mr D. P. G. Moseley	——
1930	Milltown	Mr R. Cohen	Mr L. Whitfield	——
1931	Hank	Mr H. Cherry-Downes	W. R. Bissill	——
1932	Ballyback	Lt.-Col. R. Tweedie	Mr G. Elliot	——
1933	Half Asleep	Mrs C. Leyland	Sir P. Grant-Lawson	——
1934	Moorland View	Mr A. Nicholson	Mr E. Paget	——
1935	Freetown	Sir I. Walker	Mr G. Wint	——
1936	Don Bradman	Mr S. Wilkinson	Mr A. Marsh	——
1937	O'Dell	Maj. H. Rushton	Maj. O. Prior-Palmer	Owner
1938	O'Dell	Maj. H. Rushton	Maj. O. Prior-Palmer	Owner
1939	Nushirawan	Mrs G. Lees	Capt. P. Herbert	A. Bankier
1940-46	No Race			
1947	Lucky Purchase	Mr S. Banks	Mr J. Nichols	Owner
1948	San Michele	Mr H. Metcalfe	Maj. Cunard	Owner
1949	Ballyhartfield	Mrs J. Makin	Mr J. Staker	Owner
1950	Hillmere	Mr L. H. Dalton	Mr P. Brookshaw	Owner
1951	Candy II	Mr R. Brewis	Owner	Owner
1952	Pampeene	Col. H. T. Alexander	Owner	Owner
1953	Solo Call	Mr M. Brewis	Owner	Owner
1954	Dark Stranger	Mr L. Colville	Mr J. Boseley	Owner
1955	Happymint	Mr A. Moralee	Mr A. H. Moralee	J. Wight
1956	Mister Shanks	Mr J. Keith	Mr J. Everitt	Owner

1957 Colledge Master	Mr L. Morgan	Owner	Owner
1958 Surprise Packet	Mrs S. Richards	Mr T. Johnson	Owner
1959 Merryman II	Miss Wallace	Mr C. Scott	N. Crump
1960 April Queen	Mr M. Fear	Mr J. Daniel	Owner
1961 Colledge Master	Mr L. Morgan	Owner	Owner
1962 Dominion	Mr K. Beeston	Mr C. Foulkes	Owner
1963 Sea Knight	Mr F. Nicholson	Mr P. Nicholson	Owner
1964 Aerial III	Mr M. Fear	Mr J. Daniel	R. Armytage
1965 Sea Knight	Mr F. Nicholson	Mr P. Nicholson	W. Stephenson
1966 Subaltern	Mr C. T. Alexander	Hon. J. Lawrence	Owner
1967 Minto Burn	Miss B. Johnson	Mr B. Surtees	Owner
1968 Juan	Mr P. J. Wills	Owner	Owner
1969 Bitter Lemon	Mr V. H. Rowe	Owner	Owner
1970 Lismateige	Mr P. Wates	Mr A. Wates	Owner
1971 Bright Willow	Mr A. Cure	Mr R. Chugg	Owner
1972 Credit Call	C. Collins	Owner	W. A. Stephenson
1973 Bullock's Horn	Mrs E. Barker	Lord Oaksey	R. Turnell
1974 Lord Fortune	Mrs J. Brutton	Mr D. Edmunds	Owner
1975 Credit Call	Mrs R. Newton	Mr J. Newton	W. A. Stephenson
1976 Credit Call	Mrs R. Newton	Mr J. Newton	Owner
1977 Happy Warrior	Mr N. Henderson	Owner	F. Winter
1978 Spartan Missile	Mr M. J. Thorne	Owner	Owner

1923-77 run as **Liverpool Foxhunters**

Sun Ratings Chase Limited Handicap (2m)

HORSE	OWNER	RIDER	TRAINER
1976 Menehall	Mrs R. Shand	M. Floyd	F. Walwyn
1977 Skymas	Mr M. Magee	M. F. Morris	J. Lusk
1978 Even Melody	Mr S. Green	C. Hawkins	N. Crump

LOCHROE
Bay gelding, 1948, King Hal—Loch Cash (Knight of Kilcash). Bred in Ireland by Mr B. O'Donnell.

A neatly-made, elegant, little horse whose fighting qualities were out of all proportion to his physique, Lochroe raced for nine consecutive seasons and won a Flat race, three hurdle races and 27 chases including the King George VI Chase, Kempton (1958), the Henry VIII Chase, Hurst Park (1955), the Golden Miller Chase, Cheltenham (1957) and the Kim Muir, National Hunt Meeting (1958). He was also second, beaten 1 length to Pas Seul in the 1960 Cheltenham Gold Cup. He is best remembered for his titanic struggle with the subsequent Gold Cup winner, Roddy Owen, in the 1958 King George which he won by a head in one of the most exciting and emotional finishes on record.

Lochroe, who was bought in Ireland as a four-year-old for Mrs Helen Mildmay-White and trained thereafter by Peter Cazalet, possessed real star quality and acted as a magnet to any racecourse at which he ran.

LOFT, W. J.
William Loft, the youngest son of a general with an estate in Lincolnshire, farmed the family land and was well known with the Brocklesby Hounds.

He bought Cure-All for £60 at Horncastle Fair after that horse, sent up with a hefty reserve, had crippled itself being tried over some rails. Cure-All was restored to soundness by Loft's groom, Kitty Crisp, and in 1845 his owner rode him to a surprise victory in the Grand National.

Apart from a preliminary race at Lincoln, in which he finished second, despite going the wrong side of a flag and having to return and falling at the last, there is no record of William Loft riding in any other steeplechase. His good eye for a country assisted him in his one great victory for he noticed a narrow strip of stubble bordering the heavy plough going down to the Canal Turn, which he took thereby saving precious energy.

LOTTERY
(Formerly Chance.) Bay gelding, 1830. Bred by Mr Jackson.

		Dick Andrews
	Tramp	
Lottery		Gohanna mare
		Pot 8 Os
	Mandane	
Lottery		Young Camilla
		Soothsayer
	Welbeck	
		Pledge
Parthenia		
	Mare by	Grog
	Grog	

Despite being a narrow, unfurnished youngster, Lottery won two minor races on the Flat at four years before being turned away to mature. He was then sent to Horncastle Fair, an established market for hunters and jumpers, where he was bought for 120 sovereigns by John Elmore (q.v.) to be trained for steeplechasing. During a long and honourable career which spanned eight seasons he won five hurdle races and 16 chases including the first Grand National (1839) then a level-weights affair (J. Mason), 5/1f, by 3l, a bad third, from Seventy Four (T. Olliver) and Paulina (Mr Martin). His other important successes included the Daventry Grand Steeplechase (1838) and the Cheltenham Steeplechase (1839 and 1840). This last victory was a mixed blessing for the conditions of the 1841 and 1842 Nationals contained the proviso that the winner of the Cheltenham Steeplechase 1840 should carry an 18lb penalty, raising his weight to a ludicrous 13-4. All over England, clerks of courses conspired to diminish the daunting superiority of Lottery but none more simply and effectively than the official of Horncastle, who framed a race "open to all horses except Mr Elmore's Lottery"!

A contemporary described Lottery as "a peculiarly made horse, short in his quarters, deep in his girth but light in his middle and back ribs with a perfect snaffle mouth, fine speed and a very trap to follow ... he stands 16 hands high ... and his shoulders are remarkably fine". He must also have been remarkably tough. A few classy, Flat stables had followed the lead of Lord George Bentinck and acquired horse-drawn vans to convey their charges, but humble chasers walked. In 1840 between 5th March and 8th April, Lottery ran six times at Liverpool, Fakenham, Leamington, Northampton, Cheltenham and Stratford. All the races were over four miles; in all he carried 12-0 except at Cheltenham when he shouldered a mighty 13-3 and he won the last four. Small

wonder that racegoers and sportswriters of his age were adamant that they should not look upon his like again.

Lottery was ridden in all his races by his owner's son-in-law, Jem Mason, a beautiful horseman who was reckoned the outstanding cross-country rider of his day. For most of his career he was trained at Epsom by George Dockeray who used him as a hack when his racing days were over.

LOVELY COTTAGE
Bay gelding, 1937, registered in Miss Prior's Half-Bred Stud Book. Cottage —The Nun III (Zadkiel). Bred in Co. Cork, Ireland, by Mr M. J. Hyde.

The son of a top-class point-to-point mare, Lovely Cottage made his early appearances in Hunter company and during 1943-44 won three chases including the important Conyngham Cup for Mrs L. Hyde. In December 1945 he was sold to Mr John Morant and came to England to be trained near Winchester by Tommy Rayson who saddled him to win two races including the 1946 Grand National, 10-8 (including 3lb overweight) (Capt. R. Petre), 25/1, by 4l, 3l, from Jack Finlay, 10-2 (W. Kidney) and Prince Regent, 12-5 (T. Hyde).

Lovely Cottage, a most resolute stayer won the race clearly on merit and has suffered in that the great grief felt by the racing world over the defeat of the gallant Prince Regent, has overshadowed his achievement.

LUCIUS
Bay gelding, 1969, Perhapsburg— Matches (Bakhtawar). Bred by Dr Margaret Lloyd.

Lucius, bought by his trainer Gordon Richards as an unbroken three-year-old for 1,800 guineas at Doncaster Sales and passed on to Mrs Fiona Whitaker, had proved an admirable investment and provided a great deal of fun for his connections by winning five hurdle races and twelve chases. He was rated one of the best and most consistent of the northern handicap chasers and when he turned up for the 1978 Sun Grand National had only been out of the first two once in nine previous outings that season. None of which however seemed likely to put him into the record books. This he proceeded to amend. Given a marvellous ride by Bob Davies, he jumped superbly the whole way and after a protracted duel with Sebastian V found a little extra on the run-in to see him home. Carrying 10-9 (B. R. Davies) 14-1, he won by ½l, a neck from Sebastian V, 10-10 (R. Lamb) and Drumroan, 10-10 (G. Newman).

Bob Davies was a last minute substitute for stable jockey David Goulding, who had chosen Lucius of the two stable runners but was prevented from riding him by a recurring back injury. If this was cruel misfortune for Goulding, it was poetic justice for Davies who had been prevented from riding the 1971 winner, (Specify) by an injury to himself.

If the 1978 National was deficient in class it was one of the most exciting and competitive on record. Seven horses were there with a chance approaching the last and less than 3 lengths separated the first five at the winning post.

LUCKY PURCHASE
Bay gelding, 1938, Allagash—Shahrinaz (Abbots' Trace). Bred by Sir Charles Pulley.

Lucky Purchase, who was owned and trained by Mr S. C. Banks and ridden by Mr J. Nichols, won five Hunter Chases including both Cheltenham and Liverpool Foxhunters in 1947. At Liverpool he fell but was remounted and still won by a distance.

LUDLOW (Group 4)
A very attractive, right-handed, oval course, about 1½ miles round and more or less flat, Ludlow has staged jumping since 1868 and has always been an extremely popular local track.

There are no big prizes but several attractive trophies including the Forbra Gold Challenge Handicap Chase (March, 3m, £1,295) presented by Mr W. Parsonage, a Ludlow man, in honour of his 1932 National winner, Forbra.

LUTTEUR III
Chestnut horse, 1904, St Damien— Lausanne (Fra Diavolo). Bred in France by M. Gaston-Dreyfus.

Lutteur III was bought as a yearling by M. James Hennessy and sent him to G. Batchelor to be trained. He was troubled by extremely dubious joints and proved of little account on the Flat and still less over hurdles, finishing last on his only outing. However at chasing he proved more adept and after winning at his first attempt in France he was sent in March 1909 to Harry Escott's Lewes establishment to complete his preparation for the National. Having served notice of his quality by winning the Champion Chase at Hurst Park by 6l, he started 100/9 joint favourite, 10-11 (G. Parfremont) he won by 2l, and a bad third, from Judas, 10-10 (R. Chadwick) and Caubeen, 11-7 (F. Mason). Lutteur who was the fifth and last five-year-old and the second of the two French-breds to win the race, proved difficult to train thereafter and won only two more races. He ran in two subsequent Nationals, finishing fifth under 12-3 in 1911, after being brought down and remounted, and third under 12-6 in 1914.

LYALL, Robert Vincent
Bob Lyall was the youngest of five steeplechasing sons of Lincolnshire trainer J. G. Lyall. His eldest brother, Frank, was second in the 1912 Grand National on Bloodstone.

He rode Golden Miller to win his first race and achieved his greatest triumph in 1931 when he won the Grand National on Grakle. This was a cool feat of horsemanship as Grakle disliked the whip and could not be hit. On the run-in, Gregalach (the 1929 winner) drew level but Lyall remained cool, riding him with hands and legs. He gave him one crack

---

Best Times

Distance	Time	Horse-age-weight	Date
2m 150y H	3m 58.90	Master H. 6-10-12	30-10-75
2m 1f 30y H	3m 58.8	Ronson Avenue 4-10-22	10-4-74
2m 1f 100y H	4m 5	Stolen Flight 6-11-8	26-4-67
3m H	5m 59.20	Hamoun 6-10-1	28-4-60
3m 1f 85y H	6m 12	Ibrahim Hussain 5-11-2	23-10-63
2m C	3m 51.50	Master Eye 9-11-8	4-10-72
2½m C	4m 54.60	Red Ruler 6-10-9	8-10-7.0
3m C	5m 57	Moonlight Escapade 8-12-2	11-4-74
3m 3f C	6m 48	Mickley Seabright 8-10-10	4-3-76

100 yards from the post which saw him home by 1½ lengths.

He also won the 1929 Scottish Grand National on Donzelon. In 1935 he covered the Grand National as a B.B.C. commentator.

LYNN, William

The proprietor of the Waterloo Hotel and reputed to be the best fish cook of his day, William Lynn organized Flat racing in Liverpool for some years before being tempted to turn his hand to jumping. Emboldened by the success of the St Albans venture, he laid out a steeplechase course at Maghull which was used from 1836 to 1838.

In 1839 for various reasons, not least being the link of rail and macadam roadway between Manchester and Liverpool, a course was laid out at Aintree. Public interest was unprecedented and William Lynn did not feel equal to the task of management.

Instead he turned the meeting into a company of 1,000 proprietorships of £25 each. The course was vested in five trustees, headed by Lord Stanley and a committee including Lord Derby, Lord Sefton, Lord George Bentinck and Mr Lloyd Mostyn were appointed to look after its racing affairs. William Lynn retained a stake and intended to serve in a advisory capacity but the venture grew beyond him. He was unable to retain his position and died in impoverished obscurity.

MACHELL, Capt. James (1838-1902)

Born at Beverley, Yorkshire, of a distinguished but impoverished family, James Machell served in an unfashionable line regiment. He gained a reputation for being a superb athlete and judge of a horse, particularly of a chaser, and in 1862 he resigned his commission and established himself at Newmarket where he bought, sold, trained, managed and backed horses, generally to the advancement of himself and those who employed him.

He won the Grand National three times, with Disturbance (1873) and Reugny (1874) whom he bought in a package deal with Defence for a total of £1,200 and passed on 18 months later for £12,000. These two horses were trained (and ridden) by Maunsell Richardson but Regal (1876), although officially trained by Joe Cannon, Machell managed himself as also was the case with Lord Manner's Seaman (1882) who was officially credited to James Jewitt. He was also responsible for the 1867 Derby winner, Hermit. Accounts as to his split with Maunsell Richardson vary but Finch Mason's in *Heroes and Heroines of the Grand National*, dedicated to and proofed by the man in question, seems likely to contain the germs of truth. This was that after the trial which suggested that the 1874 Grand National lay within Reugny's grasp, Machell was uncharacteristically slow to get his money on and consequently his price was taken by Richardson's friends. Capt. Machell was furious and delivered himself of some extremely unkind remarks culminating with the insult that he did not keep horses for Lincolnshire farmers to bet on. Despite Reugny's victory, the association terminated and Richardson did not in fact race-ride again.

Machell's success on the Turf enabled him to buy back his family estate in Westmorland but his declining years were clouded by gout and depression and he told George Lambton that suspicion had been the curse of his life and made him an unhappy man.

MADDEN, Peter Gerald (b.1931)

Gerry Madden was apprenticed to Willie O'Grady and rode his first winner in 1950 at Limerick Junction. He came to England and was attached to Fulke Walwyn for whom he rode Mandarin to win the Hennessy Gold Cup and the King George VI Chase twice. Unfortunately for him he shot to fame faster than was good for him and was not able to maintain his good form.

MAGEE, Sean

Sean Magee won the 1940 Champion Hurdle on Miss Dorothy Paget's Solford.

MAGIC COURT

Brown gelding, 1958, Supreme Court —Blue Prelude (Blue Peter). Bred by Mr T. Lilley.

A strong, attractive and beautifully bred horse whose half-sister, Bleu Azur, bred the dual classic winner Altesse Royale, Magic Court won on the Flat at three years when trained by Noel Murless. He was then bought by the shrewd North-country trainer and vet, Tommy Robson, for £1,300 on behalf of Mr J. McGhie in whose colours he won three more Flat races and 10 hurdle races including the Princess Royal Hurdle, Doncaster (1964), the Trial Hurdle, Cheltenham (1965) and the 1964 Champion Hurdle (P. McCarron), 100/6, by 4l, $\frac{3}{4}$l, from Another Flash (H. Beasley) and Kirriemuir (G. W. Robinson). Magic Court was also second to Grey of Falloden in the 1964 Cesarewitch. Later in life he went hunter-chasing but though he was placed on several occasions, he did not win.

MAHER, James J. (1862-1934)

James Maher was a very influential figure in Irish racing circles. Educated at Downside, he afterwards returned to Ireland to manage his father's farms and ride as an amateur until he got too heavy. He afterwards trained and bred at Williamstown near Dublin. Among the good chasers who passed through his hands were Wild Man From Borneo, Jenkinstown and Ballymacad, while he bred both Covertcoat (whose sire, Hackler, he stood), winner of the 1913

National and Manna (2000 Guineas and Derby, 1925). He was a member of the Irish Turf Club and the Irish National Hunt Committee, Chairman and Managing Director of Baldoyle and Chairman of the Conyngham Club.

MAIDEN

For the purposes of steeple chases and hurdle races a maiden is a horse that has never won a steeple chase or a hurdle race, other than a match or a private stake, a National Hunt Flat race or a steeple chase at a point-to-point meeting, at any recognized meeting in any country. Unless otherwise stated, a maiden means a maiden at the time of the start.

MANCHESTER

The first race under National Hunt Rules at Manchester was run in May 1872. The following year, two hurdle races were added to the September card, after which chasing became a regular feature.

From 1867 to 1901 racing took place on the New Barns Course on a site now occupied by the Salford Docks Ship Canal and it was there that the Lancashire Chase was instituted in 1884. The race swiftly established itself as a classic and for a brief period was worth more than the Grand National.

In 1901, under the guidance of Mr John Davis, the racecourse moved back to its old Castle Irwell home. Mr Davis remained chairman until his death in 1919 at the age of 84. The Castle Irwell course was long, narrow and wasp-waisted. There were separate tracks for Flat, hurdles and chases and the stands which included a covered paddock for wet weather, were the most luxurious in England.

Racing was interrupted by the World War II and resumed in 1946-47. In November 1947 the £1500 Emblem Chase was instituted. The course was closed in November 1963.

Great Lancashire Chase (3¾m)

	HORSE	OWNER	RIDER	TRAINER
1884	Saville	Mr T. Cannon	Mr E. M. Owen	——
1885	Redpath	Mr Zigomala	Capt. Lee-Barber	——
1886	Unice	Mr J. G. Muir	Capt. Lee-Barber	——
1887	Savoyard	Baron Schroder	T. Skelton	——
1888	Spahi	Mr J. Gubbins	T. Kavanagh	——
1889	Magic	H.R.H. the Prince of Wales	A. Hall	——
1890	Ilex	Mr Masterman	A. Nightingall	——
1891	Why Not	Mr C. Perkins	W. Nightingall	——
1892	Roman Oak	Sir H. de Trafford	Capt. Bewicke	——
1893	Red Prince II	Mr H. E. Linde	W. Hoysted	——
1894	Manifesto	Mr H. M. Dyas	T. Kavanagh	——
1895	Gentle Ida	Mr H. M. Dyas	T. Kavanagh	——
1896	Lady Helen	Capt. Bewicke	Owner	——
1897	Knight of Rhodes	Mr F. B. Atkinson	H. Escott	——
1898	Keelson	Mr C. J. Cunningham	A. Nightingall	——
1899	Breemount's Pride	Mr G. Edwards	D. Morris	——
1900	Uncle Jack	Lord Beresford	H. Escott	——
1901	Coragh Hill	Mr J. Lonsdale	Hogan	——
1902	Fairland	Mr T. Bater	J. Phillips	——
1903	Fairland	Mr T. Bater	Goswell	——
1904	Lord James	Mr G. Edwardes	R. Woodland	——
1905	Seisdon Prince	Mr T. Ashton	F. Mason	——
1906	Theodocian	Mr C. Bower-Ismay	A. Newey	——
1907	Eremon	Mr S. Howard	A. Newey	——
1908	Albuera	Sir P. Walker	R. Chadwick	——
1909	Moonstruck	Mr R. B. Henry	R. Chadwick	——
1910	The Duffrey	Mr S. Hill-Wood	S. Walkington	——
1911	The Duffrey	Mr S. Hill-Wood	A. Anthony	——
1912	Wilkinstown	Mr C. Bower-Ismay	R. Chadwick	——
1913	Irish Mail	Mr W. T. Drake	Mr H. W. T. Drake	——
1914	Eugenist	Mr E. S. Wills	H. Smyth	——
1915	Vermouth	Mr P. F. Heyburn	J. Reardon	——

HORSE	OWNER	RIDER	TRAINER
1916-17 *No Race*			
1918 Poethlyn	Mrs H. Peel	E. Piggott	––
1919 Poethlyn	Mrs H. Peel	E. Piggott	––
1920 Dumadry	Mrs A. Blair	T. Hulme	––
1921 Black Lamb	Mr W. H. Dixon	Capt. G. H. Bennett	––
1922 Keep Cool	Mr W. H. Midwood	A. Escott	––
1923 Southampton	Lord Woolavington	A. Robson	––
1924 Maureen Bawn	Mr E. L. Lloyd	P. Lynch	––
1925 Knight of the			
Wilderness	Mr G. White	S. Regan	––
1926 White Park	Maj. J. T. North	S. Dennis	F. Brown
1927 Trump Card	Mr G. Newell-Nairn	S. Dennis	W. Denwick
1928 Tusker	Mr H. R. Lawrence	W. Scott	Magee
1929 Kilbrain	Mr E. A. Longworth	Fish	A. Bickley
1930 East Galway	Mr J. S. Shepherd	T. McNeil	(in Ireland)
1931 Solanum	Hon. D. Paget	A. Escott	A. Law
1932 Huic Holloa	Mr W. Waddington	Hodgkinson	Owner
1933 South Louth	Maj. H. D. Beamish	J. Lynn	(in Ireland)
1934 Avenger	Mrs V. Mundy	W. Speck	D. Harrison
1935 Cooleen	Mr J. V. Rank	J. Fawcus	R. Gore
1936 Right'un	Mrs A. E. Phillips	T. Carey	W. Bissill
1937 Antipas	Lady Lindsey	W. Parvin	Private
1938 Royal Danieli	Mr H. C. McNally	D. Moore	(in Ireland)
1939 Timber Wolf	Mr J. V. Rank	J. Fawcus	H. Brown
1940 Bachelor's			
Folly II	Mr J. Davey	I. Alder	J. Russell
1941-46 *No Race*			
1947 Fortina	Lord Grimthorpe	Mr. R. Black	H. Christie
1948 Bronze Arrow	Mr J. Straker	Mr J. Straker	V. Smyth
1949 Coloured School			
Boy	Mr W. F. Highnam	R. Bates	T. F. Rimell
1950 Coloured School			
Boy	Mr W. F. Highnam	J. Bullock	T. F. Rimell
1951 Q.E.D.	Mrs L. Brotherton	R. O'Ryan	R. Renton
1952-54 *No Race*			
1955 Tudor Line	Mrs E. Truelove	G. Slack	R. Renton
1956 Pippikin	Mr R. D. Darragh	J. Power	S. Parker
1957 Hart Royal	Mr L. C. Denton	P. Pickford	I. Lomax
1958 Hart Royal	Mr L. C. Denton	P. Pickford	I. Lomax
1959 E.S.B.	Mrs L. Carver	T. Brookshaw	T. F. Rimell
1960 Eternal	Lt.-Col. Fenwick-Palmer	R. Langley	Owner
1961 Eternal	Lt.-Col. Fenwick-Palmer	R. Langley	Owner
1962 Skish	Mr J. Westholl	J. Lehane	C. Bewicke
1963 Rough Tweed	Mr S. L. Green	G. Scott	N. Crump

Champion Novice Chase (2m)

HORSE	OWNER	RIDER	TRAINER
1956 Glorious Twelfth	Mr H. J. Joel	B. Wilkinson	R. Renton
1957 Northern King	Mr J. E. Wood	M. Pumfrey	E. Cousins
1958 Pas Seul	Mrs J. Rogerson	W. Rees	R. Turnell
1959 Flame Gun	Mr M. Sobell	F. T. Winter	C. Mallon
1960 Sandy Abbot	Mrs J. D. McKechnie	S. Mellor	G. R. Owen
1961 Rough Tweed	Mr S. H. Green	H. East	N. Crump
1962 Piperton	Mr A. H. Tomlinson	D. V. Dick	Owner
1963 Too Slow	Mr A. Watson	J. Leech	C. Bell

Also see CHELTENHAM (Sun Alliance Chase).

MANDARIN

Bay gelding, 1951, Deux pour Cent—Manada (Canot). Bred in France by Mme Hennessy.

As the winner of two hurdle races and 17 chases, including the Cheltenham Gold Cup (1962), the Grand Steeplechase de Paris (1962), the King George VI Chase twice (1957 and 1959) and the Hennessy Gold Cup twice (1957 and 1961), it is incredible that prior to his last season Mandarin was regarded as a very good, gallant, somewhat unlucky little horse who was just short of top class. Nor did it seem probable that at nearly 11 years old, after seven incident-packed seasons peppered with falls, defeats, a broken bone and a breakdown which had necessitated firing, he would ever achieve anything likely to alter this view.

But season 1961-62 was for Mandarin and his entourage a kind of *annus mirabilis,* an unbroken string of five victories starting on 25th October with a little conditions race at Ludlow, going on to a second Hennessy (the race founded by his owner's family firm) with 11-5, the Walter Hyde H'cap Chase, Kempton with 11-11, the Cheltenham Gold Cup, (F. Winter), 7/2, by 1l, 10l, from Fortria (P. Taaffe) and Cocky Consort (C. Stobbs), and finally and most triumphantly the Grand Steeplechase de Paris. Everything conspired to defeat Mandarin: the ground, always watered and softened by scudding June rain, the condition of jockey Fred Winter, wasting himself hideously to do 9-10 required for Beaver II later in the afternoon, the rubber bit which snapped in his mouth landing over the third fence leaving 18 fences and 3½ miles of Auteuil's figure-of-eight course to be negotiated with neither brakes nor steering and finally his patched-up legs which gave out four fences from home. All these hazards Mandarin and Fred Winter overcame to beat the French horse, Lumino, by a rapidly dwindling short head. For the little crowd of English fans it was Agincourt, Trafalgar and Waterloo rolled into one.

Behind Mandarin's stony way to the top lay the genius of two men: the first was his trainer Fulke Walwyn into whose care he came as a small, badly broken three-year-old, who coaxed condition and muscle on to a frame rendered spare by poor appetite and wayward behaviour, who put back the confidence constantly sapped by falls and defeat and cherished his legs through eight seasons and 51 races. The second was Fred Winter who finally got the slovenly youngster jumping hurdles, who thought that he could be taught to jump fences, and who finally partnered him in his two greatest triumphs at Cheltenham and Auteuil – victories which raised their partnership to the ranks of the immortals.

MANICOU

Bay horse, 1945, Last Post—Mylael (Blue Ensign). Bred in France by M. P. Zizine.

Originally bought by Peter Cazalet for Lord Mildmay from France, where he had been unbeaten at three years, Manicou had a triumphant first season, winning six races culminating in a division of the Broadway Novices, National Hunt Meeting. Following the tragic death of his owner, he became the property of H.M. Queen Elizabeth the Queen Mother for whom he won three chases including the 1950 King George VI and Queen Elizabeth Chase, Kempton, beating the subsequent Gold Cup winner, Silver Fame, by three lengths at a difference of only 8lb, a remarkable performance for a five year-old.

Thereafter Manicou trained off badly and did not win again. He stood at the Godden's Gable Stud, Sussex, until his death in 1971 and had some success as a sire of jumpers. By the end of season 1977-78 he had sired the winners of 172 races worth £77,479. His best winners were The Rip, Man of the West, Man of the East and Isle of Man.

MANIFESTO

Bay gelding, 1888 Man o'War—Vae Victis (King Victor). Bred in Co. Meath, Ireland, by Mr H. M. Dyas.

A raw-boned, somewhat plain but tremendously powerful horse, Manifesto raced for 13 consecutive seasons and won a hurdle race and seven steeplechases including the Irish Champion Chase, Leopardstown (1892), the Lancashire Chase, Manchester (1894), the Grand International Chase, Sandown (1897) and the Grand National twice, in 1897, 11-3 (T. Kavanagh), 6/1f, by 20l, a head, from Filibert, 9-7 (Mr Beatty) and Ford of Fyne, 10-7 (Mr Withington), and again in 1899, 12-7 (G. Williamson), 5/1, by 5l, 2l from Ford of Fyne, 10-10 (E. Matthews) and Elliman, 10-1 (E. Piggott). Manifesto ran in six other Grand Nationals, finishing fourth in 1895, third with 12-13 in 1900, third with 12-8 in 1902, third yet again in 1903 with 12-3, and sixth in 1904.

Like most successful staying chasers of his age, Manifesto was descended from Pocahontas through his sire, Man o'War, who was by Ben Battle by Pocahontas's son Rataplan.

His early career was handled with patience and percipience by his owner-breeder Mr Harry Dyas, a man much respected by the racing fraternity who was as successful as he was shrewd and did not hesitate to put his money where his mouth was. Mr Dyas made a killing out of Manifesto's first National victory and on the strength of it sold him for £4,000 to Mr (later Sir) John Crocker Bulteel. In 1899 however he was less fortunate for believing, from past experience, Manifesto to be incapable of giving his own Gentle Ida a stone, he laid heavily against him, only to have his hopes confounded when Gentle Ida fell at Valentine's on the first circuit. Mention must be made of Manifesto's victory in the Lancashire Chase for it was at the time the most valuable race in the Calendar and it was a fine performance for a six-year-old to win with 11-3.

For his first five seasons Manifesto was trained at home in Ireland. In the autumn of 1896 he came to England to the Eversleigh stable of Willie McAuliffe who saddled him to win the 1897 National. After his sale to Mr Bulteel, he was transferred to Willie Moore at Weyhill (the licence was held by John Collins) where he remained for the rest of his career.

In his later years Manifesto became something of an institution in racing circles and when he made his final National appearance at the age of 16 in 1904, a large crowd gathered to watch him do his morning work. Among them was the famous Flat-race jockey, Mornington Cannon, who begged to be allowed to hop up on the old horse's back for a few minutes.

MANNERS of Foston, Lord John, third Baron (1852-1927)

Lord Manners, known to his friends as 'Hoppy', served in the Grenadier Guards and was reckoned a beautiful horseman and a very good man to hounds. He was Master of the Quorn for a period but had never ridden in a steeplechase before 1881 when he purchased two useful horses from the famous Eyrefield Lodge trainer, Henry Linde. These were Lord Chancellor, a Grand Sefton winner, and Seaman, winner of the Conyngham Cup and the Grand Course des Haies. The following season, from very few rides, he won the Grand Military Gold Cup on Lord Chancellor (13-7) and the Grand National on Seaman, beating Tommy Beasley, the leading professional of the day on the Linde-trained second-favourite Cyrus, a short head. The feat was all the more remarkable in that Seaman broke down so badly at the last fence that he was never able to run again.

Lord Manners then hung up his boots and returned to the Quorn leaving a record unequalled in the annals of amateur riders.

MARCO

Chestnut horse, 1892. Bred by Mr F. Luscombe.

Marco			
Barcaldine	Solon	West Australian	
		Daslings' Dam	
	Ballyroe	Belladrum	
		Bon Accord	
Novitiate	Hermit	Newminster	
		Seclusion	
	Retty	Lambton	
		Fern	

The winner of 10 races on the Flat including the 1895 Cambridgeshire, Marco exerted a tremendous influence on National Hunt breeding, being the maternal grand-sire of Cottage (ex Casetta by Marco) (q.v.) and the paternal grand-sire of My Prince (ex Marcovil by Marco) (q.v.) He sired the 1927 National winner Sprig and appears close-up in the pedigrees of the National winner Bogskar, the Gold Cup winner Silver Fame, and the Champion Hurdler Free Fare.

MARKET RASEN (Group 3)

A progressive, well-laid-out course dating from 1868, Market Rasen is pleasantly situated, looking across the Lincolnshire Wolds. The track is right-handed, oval in shape and about 1¼ miles round. The soil is light and quick draining, while a watering system ensures reasonable going in dry weather.

Thanks to some imaginative sponsoring, a better class of horse has been attracted recently. The principal races include:

The Victor Lucas Memorial Long Distance Novice Hurdle (March, 3m, £1,447)
The Lincoln H'cap Chase (January, 3m, £2,282.)
The Lincolnshire Poacher Pattern Hurdle (December, 2m, £1,745)

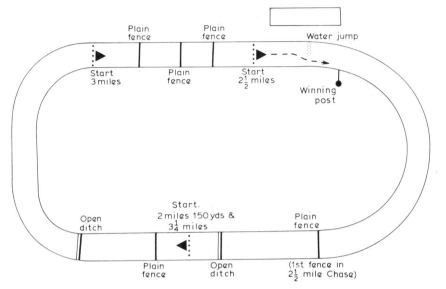

Best Times

Distance	Time	Horse-age-weight	Date
2m H	3m 54.40	Border River 4-10-9	30-7-77
2m 100y H	4m 11.20	Stoney Hill 6-11-10	12-8-65
2½m H	5m 3.80	Pandolfi 4-10-6	3-10-70
3m H	5m 52.50	Owenogue 10-9-7	26-9-75
2m C	4m 13.70	King Crocket 7-11-4	23-8-75
2m 150y C	4m 18.40	Touch Lime 9-11-4	26-8-67
2m 5f C	5m 30.50	Humber Light 8-10-3	14-10-77
3m C	6m 5.20	Dingle Poke 8-10-3	31-5-75
3¼m C	7m 33.40	Royal Phoebe 8-12-3	9-5-64

MARSH, Alec (b.1908)

A highly competent amateur rider, Alec Marsh rode a total of 163 winners (including 21 on the Flat) and was Leading Amateur in 1934-35, 1935-36 and 1936-37. He won the Cheltenham Foxhunters twice, in 1935 on Empire Night and 1936 on Herod Bridge, the Liverpool Foxhunters (1936) on Don Bradman and deadheated for the Grand Sefton that year on the same horse.

He was appointed a starter in 1947 and was Jockey Club starter from 1953-1972.

MARSH, Michael Leo (b.1915)

Michael Marsh, a farmer and company director, has held a permit since 1954

and operated a small but highly efficient stable from his Warwickshire house. His best horse to date has been Larbawn (*q.v.*) who won him the Whitbread Gold Cup (1968 and 1969), the Golden Miller Chase (1967, 1968 and 1969) and the Mildmay Memorial (1970) and whose winnings twice boosted him into the Leading Owners table. In 1967-68 he finished fourth, winning five races worth £9,909, and in 1968-69 sixth with six races worth £10,846.

MARSH, Richard John (1851-1933)

Richard Marsh was the son of a Kentish hop-farmer who followed racing closely and encouraged his sons into the game. Richard quickly grew too heavy for the Flat but he made a considerable name for himself under N.H. Rules. He was particularly effective over hurdles and won nearly all the big hurdle races at Croydon and Kempton including the first Grand International H'cap Hurdle, Croydon (1880) on Thornfield and the first Grande Course des Haies at Auteuil. He was also third in the 1881 Grand National on Thornfield. He rode his last winner at Kempton in 1881.

He began training at Newmarket in 1874 when he was still riding and made his name training jumpers for the Duke of Hamilton. He won the Grande Course des Haies three times, twice for the Duke.

In 1892 he moved to Egerton House and took over the Prince of Wales's horses. Thereafter he concentrated on the Flat with enormous success. He handled the Prince's (later King Edward VII) three Derby winners, Persimmon (1896), Diamond Jubilee (1900) and Minoru (1909), and also Jeddan (1898).

He married twice, firstly a sister of Dan Thirwell's and secondly a daughter of the famous Beckhampton trainer, Sam Darling. Their son, Marcus, became a very successful trainer.

MARSHALL, Bryan A. (b.1916)

Bryan Marshall the son of an international show-jumper was one of the best N.H. jockeys of the post-war period. He was apprenticed in the tough but effective school of 'Atty' Persse and then spent five years with Martin Hartigan and three with Noel Murless. At the outbreak of World War II he joined up and was commissioned into the 5th Royal Iniskilling Dragoon Guards. He became a captain and was demobilized in 1946 after which he embarked on a National Hunt career.

Strong, stylish with an intuitive grasp of horses' requirements and a marked penchant for the shortest route, he was immediately successful. He was Champion Jockey in 1947-48 riding 66 winners, besides being runner-up three times and third once in a comparatively brief period.

He won the Grand National twice in successive years for Vincent O'Brien, in 1953 on Early Mist and in 1954 on Royal Tan, victories which O'Brien attributed in great part to his superb horsemanship.

His other important victories included:

The King George VI Chase (1947) Rowland Roy; (1950) Manicou
The Mildmay Memorial (1952) Cromwell
The Liverpool Hurdle (1954) Galatian
The County Hurdle (1952) Ballymacan

Repeated injuries caused his premature retirement and in 1954 he took out a licence to train. He was less successful in this sphere although turning out a number of winners. He became a respected and widely sought-after teacher of jockeys.

MASON, F.

Liverpool-born 'Tich' Mason was a very successful Flat jockey and was in fact Champion Jockey in Ireland before turning his attention to N.H. racing in which sphere he dominated affairs during the first decade of the twentieth century.

He was Champion Jockey six times, in 1901 (58 winners), 1902 (67), 1904 (59), 1905 (73), 1906 (58) and 1907 (59).

His big victories included:

The Grand National (1905) Kirkland
The Champion Chase (1902) Killmallog
The Imperial Cup (1910) Black Plum
The Lancashire Chase (1905) Seisdon Prince
The Grand Sefton (1898) Shaker; (1902) Kirkland; (1908) Caubeen

He would have ridden Glenside (1911) but for breaking a leg just before, thus giving Jack Anthony a fortunate chance ride.

He rode long, was considered a little rough and ready but strong, effective and very cool.

MASON, James (d.1866)

Jem Mason was the foremost cross-country rider of his day and the first crack jockey in chasing's history. He was the son of a Leicestershire coaching stable proprietor and his family moved down to Hertfordshire whilst he was still in his teens. Here his sensitive hands and intuitive horsemanship soon created a demand for his services as a nagsman in the big dealing yards in the area. Finally he became permanently attached to John Elmore's Uxendon establishment and cemented the relationship by marrying Miss Elmore.

His principal victories included:

The Grand National (1839) Lottery
The St Albans Steeplechase (1834) The Poet
The Cheltenham Steeplechase (1839) Lottery; (1840) Lottery
The Leamington Grand Annual (1840) Lottery

He also rode abroad and won the first big chase in Paris on St Leger.

A gentle man, pale-faced and dark-haired, with an aquiline nose, he was universally liked and respected. His principal rival, the rough, half-gypsy Tom Olliver declared he would fight "up to his knees in blood" on Mason's behalf and, even more generously, that he had "never ridden beside him without envying the perfection of his style".

Something of a dandy, he enjoyed his success and took immense pains with his dress. He always rode in white gloves and patronized the most fashionable tailors and bootmakers of the day. In fact it took the combined effort of Messrs Bentley of Oxford Street, who built the legs and Messrs Wrens of Knightsbridge who constructed the feet, to achieve the perfection he demanded in his boots.

He retired while still at the top of his profession and ran a fashionable dealing business in Mount Street. He died in 1866 from cancer of the throat. His obituary claimed that "it was at putting a horse at a fence that he chiefly excelled, always bringing him to the jump at the right place and in his right stride".

MASTER MOWBRAY

Bay horse, 1865, Mowbray—mare by Footstool *ex* Bird's Nest. Bred by Mr John Goodliff.

Master Mowbray a tough, consistent campaigner raced for his breeder and won nine races including the Cheltenham Grand Annual on three occasions (1873, 1875 and 1876). He ran in three Nationals always finishing in the first six without ever achieving a place. He was nearly always ridden by George Holman.

MASTER OWEN

Bay horse, 1956. Bred by Mrs A. W. Riddell-Martin

Many good jumping sires have had but modest careers on the racecourse but it is small wonder that Master Owen took time to become established as a sire for at the end of his three-year-old career, by

which time he had not reached the frame, he was dismissed by Timeform as "of no account" and his solitary success was achieved in an amateur Flat race at four years in Ireland. However with the benefit of hindsight it is seen that his pedigree was ideal for a sire of jumpers. Not only were his sire and both grand-sires Derby winners (and the line of Owen Tudor has proved particularly effective in producing good jumpers) but his bottom line traces directly to the important jumping influence of Marcovil (the sire of Miss Matty) and Marco (*q.v.*).

			Gainsborough
		Hyperion	
			Selene
	Owen Tudor		
			Pharos
		Mary Tudor II	
Master Owen			Anna Bolena
			Blandford
		Trigo	
			Athasi
	Miss Maisie		
			Truculent
		Miss Matilda	
			Miss Matty

He was standing at the Garryrichard House Stud at the time of his death in the autumn of 1976.

Master Owen, understandably, made a slow start to his career but a steady flow of modest jumpers brought better mares to him and during the past few seasons, he came right to the fore. He was Leading Sire twice, in 1976-77 and 1977-8 when he had winners of 33 races (worth £53,602) and 40 races (worth £56,168) respectively.

He holds his place with a steady stream of winners and has not to date produced an outstanding individual. The best of his stock would be the 1976 Sweeps Hurdle winner, Master Monday, and the high-class staying chaser, Master H.

MASTER ROBERT

Chestnut gelding, 1913, Moorside II—Dodds (Dazzle). Bred by Mr McKinlay in Co. Donegal, Ireland.

In a career plagued by navicular and thick-windedness, and which included a spell in a plough, Master Robert won five chases including the 1924 Grand National, 10-5 (R. Trudgill), 25-1, by 4l, 6l, from Fly Mask, 10-12 (J. Moylan) and Silvo, 12-2 (G. Goswell).

Originally trained on the Curragh by Algy Anthony, he accompanied Troytown in some of his work but was thought to be moderate on the whole and was sent home. Later brought to England by Harry Fordham as a potential point-to-pointer, he won a race at the Hertfordshire point-to-point by the length of the proverbial street. A subsequent sale fell through on the grounds of thick-windedness and he was eventually sold to Lord Airlie and Major Green for Lord Airlie to ride in the Scottish Military Chase at Perth. This objective he accomplished carrying 13-13, including a remarkable 37lb overweight. Now trained at Wroughton by Aubrey Hastings, Master Robert won good chases at Newbury, Cheltenham and Liverpool but was being increasingly troubled by navicular. Only constant poulticing enabled him to be trained at all and despite this he was intermittently lame. Master Robert was a chance National ride for Bob Trudgill after more fashionable jockeys had turned him down. In the race he was badly outpaced early on but kept persevering and finally wore down the leaders to win going away. He was not asked to race again.

MATTHEW

Brown gelding, 1838, by Vestrius. Bred by Mr John Westropp.

Matthew, described as a "mealy, brown horse, rather stilty on his hindlegs and the said legs very straight . . . carried his head proudly and had a bold, confident look of the eye", won the 1847 Grand National, being the first Irish horse to do so. Heavily supported by his fellow countrymen, it was said that half of them would have emigrated had he not won, Matthew, 10-6 (D. Wynne), 10-1 jt-f, won by 11, the same, from St Leger, 12-3 (T. Olliver) and Jerry, 11-6 (Bradley). Strongly fancied to repeat his victory in 1848, he was knocked over in atrocious going.

MAWSON, George

George Mawson won the 1888 Grand National on Playfair, thanks to some friendly assistance from Arthur Nightingall who pulled him back from a precarious position on Playfair's head, just in time to avert calamity. Which chivalrous gesture drew the thankful response: "Thank the Lord! It ought to be a pinch for me now."

Other notable victories included:

The Manchester Jubilee H'cap (1891) Dornock
The Great Sandown Hurdle (1891) Master Charlie; (1892) Yorkshireman

McAULIFFE, W.

Willie McAuliffe ran a large jumping stable at Eversleigh, Hampshire. From November 1866 to February 1888 he had charge of Manifesto who he saddled to win the 1887 Grand National.

McCAIN, Donald (b.1930)

'Ginger' McCain has a small yard tucked surprisingly away behind the Southport garage he owns. His exercise grounds are the tree-lined suburbs of Southport and the adjacent beach his gallops.

After doing his National Service with the R.A.S.C. he took out a permit in 1952 and a full licence in 1967. His principal patron is octogenarian Mr Noel le Mare, for whom he bought Red Rum at the Doncaster August Sales 1972 for 6,000 guineas. In his charge, Red Rum won 16 races including three Grand Nationals (1973, 1974 and 1977) and the Scottish Grand National (1974). For the same patron, he also bought Glenkiln (10 races including the B.P.-sponsored Grand Sefton). In 1972-73 he was sixth in the table of Leading Trainers winning 18 races worth £37,404 and in 1973-74 he was fourth, saddling the winners of 20 races worth £50,729.

A tall, spare, unassuming man, his success has left him apparently unmoved and he has made no effort to transfer himself to a more fashionable set-up which he could undoubtedly command.

McCARRON, Patrick (b.1937)

An accomplished North-country jockey, Pat McCarron was apprenticed to Harry Blackshaw. His first big win was the 1964 Champion Hurdle on Magic Court. He was also associated with the gallant and popular Freddie on whom he won the Gallagher Gold Cup, the Great Yorkshire and the Mildmay Memorial as well as finishing second in both 1965 and 1966 Grand Nationals. Other good victories include the Scottish Champion Hurdle (1968) on Al Alawi and the Heinz Chase on Bobbie Corbett.

McCREERY, Robert James (b.1930)

The son of General Sir Richard

McCreery who won the 1928 Grand Military Gold Cup on Dash o'White, Bob McCreery was a highly successful amateur rider under both Rules, winning approximately 150 races between 1949-63. He was leading amateur (N.H.) in 1955-56 with 13 winners (jointly with Mr A. Moralee), and in 1956-57 with 23 winners. He also rode winners in France, the U.S.A., Spain and Sweden. He won the Welsh Grand National (1953) on Stalbridge Rock. His best horse was Gold Wire who won him 21 races, including the Prix St Saveur (Auteuil).

He now owns and manages the highly successful Moreton Paddox Stud in Warwickshire which has already bred the 2000 Guineas winner, High Top. Colours: green, black collar, cuffs and cap.

McDONAGH Desmond

Des McDonagh trains a small string in Co. Meath and hit public notice with a series of important successes achieved with his very game hurdler, Monksfield (*q.v.*). These include:

The Champion Hurdle, N.H. Meeting (1978)
The Templegate Hurdle, Liverpool (1977)
    (d.-h. with Night Nurse)
The Templegate Hurdle, Liverpool (1978)

He rode as an amateur until a badly broken leg enforced his retirement. He learnt his profession from the late Cyril Bryce-Smith whose daughter, Helen, is his wife.

McDONOUGH, Alan (1804-88)

A well-known Irish amateur, Alan McDonough was born in Co. Galway and rode from an early age. He won his first race, the Tipperary Hunt Cup, in his first ride over fences. He came to England in the late 1830s and rode with such success that he made himself very unpopular in some quarters. He was once deliberately charged and bowled over in a race at Dunchurch, breaking two ribs and a collar bone. Happily for native honour, Captain Lamb (the owner of Vivian) caught the offender and thrashed him with a horsewhip.

He won many races on the able but temperamental Sir William but missed the ride through injury when that horse won the Liverpool Steeplechase in 1838. He was associated with a high-class mare,

Brunette, on whom he won a £500 match at Melton, beating Jem Mason on Jerry.

His other good victories included the famous Horncastle race from which Lottery was excluded on Cigar, the Dunchurch Chase (1841), on Cigar, the Warwick Chase (1841) and the Worcester Royal Birthday H'cap (1842) on Roderic Random.

McDOWELL, Hector

A Co. Dublin veterinary surgeon and small trainer, Hector McDowell won the 1947 Grand National with his brother's Caughoo. He had previously won the Ulster National at Down Royal in 1945 and 1946 with the same horse who was nearly scheduled to attempt a hat-trick instead of going to Aintree.

McDowell was able to use the beach at Sutton Strand to work Caughoo whereas practically every other trainer had been held up by the worst winter in living memory.

McMORROW, Liam

Larry McMorrow was an Irish jockey based in Yorkshire who won the 1949 Grand National on the unconsidered Russian Hero. Notwithstanding his success, his affairs did not prosper and he eventually went to the United States where he rode for Paddy and Mick Smithwick, cousins of Dan Moore. He was later killed in a car smash.

MEDOC II

Bay gelding, 1934, Van—Menthe Poivrée (Pot au Feu). Bred in France by the Comte Dauger.

A full brother to Roi d'Egypte, winner of 1942 Cathcart Cup and sire of Leney Princess (*q.v.*), Medoc II won three Flat races in France, two hurdles and nine chases including the National Hunt Juvenile Chase and the 1942 Cheltenham Gold Cup (H. Nicholson), 9/2, by 8l, 4l, from Red Rower (D. Morgan) and Asterabad (T. Carey). Medoc II was owned by Lord Sefton and trained by Reg Hobbs. There was no further racing in England for three years and Medoc II went to Ireland but was not successful.

MELLOR, Stanley Thomas Edward (b.1937)

Stan Mellor is one of the great figures of post-war jumping and not only for his prowess as a jockey which was considerable. Intelligent, articulate and immensely competent he did an enormous amount for the safety, standards and public relations of his profession. He has also done a great deal for the Injured Jockeys Fund. In 1972 he was awarded the M.B.E. for his services to N.H. Racing, an honour which previously only Fred Winter had been accorded.

The general public loved him for his unquenchable determination to win while, for the *cognoscenti*, the sight of his curiously upright figure 'winding' a horse up for the last, was one to be treasured long after his retirement. He was attached to George Owen and first rode as an amateur in 1952.

He was Champion Jockey three times, in 1959-60 with 68 winners, 1960-61 with 118 and 1961-62 with 80. In January 1972 he rode his 1,000th winner in Britain on Ouzo, which is thought to be a record.

His important wins include:

The King George VI Chase (1964) Frenchman's Cove; (1969) Titus Oates
The National Hunt Two Mile Champion Chase (1963) Sandy Abbot
The Whitbread Gold Cup (1962) Frenchman's Cove
The Hennessy Gold Cup (1966) Stalbridge Colonist
The Mackeson Gold Cup (1964) Super Flash
The Great Yorkshire (1961) Chavara; (1964) King's Nephew
The Welsh Champion Hurdle (1970) Frozen Alive

He retired at the end of 1972 and took out a licence to train under N.H. Rules. He has a burgeoning yard at Lambourn and looks set to make a similar success of this branch of his profession.

Good winners for the stable include: The National Hunt Chase (1977) Alpenstock

MENELEK
Bay gelding, 1957 Bred by Major D. McCalmont.

His best years in the Leading Sires lists are:

1973-74	3rd	winners of 56 races worth	£33,122
1974-75	2nd	„ „ 39 „ „	£43,819
1975-76	1st	„ „ 57 „ „	£93,198

Menelek was Leading Sire in 1975-76 and seems likely to fill the gap left by the deaths, in quick succession, of Fortina, Arctic Slave and Vulgan. A robust, attractive individual, he was a tough, consistent, middle-class handicapper on the Flat, winning 11 races, including the Swaffham Handicap at the Newmarket Craven meeting and the Old Newton Cup at Haydock. He raced in the colours of Major D. McCalmont and was trained by Geoffrey Brooke at Newmarket. He stayed well but was most effective at about 1½ miles and was particularly well suited by a firm surface. He continued to race until he was six and was sold for 3,000 guineas at the Newmarket December Sales in 1963. He now stands at the Ballinscala Stud, Co. Limerick, Ireland.

			Bois Roussel
		Tehran	
	Tulyar		Stafaralla
			Nearco
		Neocracy	
Menelek			Harina
			Bahram
		Persian Gulf	
	Queen of Sheba		Double Life
			Buen Ojo
		Ojala	
			Dursilla

His stock are generally strongly made and tough and are usually slow to mature.

His best winners to date are Rag Trade (*q.v.*) (eight races, including the 1976 *News of the World* Grand National), April Seventh (*q.v.*) (twelve races, including the Whitbread and Hennessy Gold Cups, 1975) and Lough Ineagh (National Hunt Two-Mile Champion Chase, 1975). Other good winners include High Ken, Menehall, I'm Smart, Quick Reply, Ballyrichard Again and Half a Sixpence.

MERRY DEAL
Bay gelding, 1950, Straight Deal—Merryland (Mieuxcé). Bred by the Hon. Dorothy Paget.

A fine stamp of horse who took some time to mature, Merry Deal became the hurdler of the highest class whose 17 victories included the Princess Royal H'cap Hurdle, Doncaster (1957), the Victory Hurdle, Manchester (1957) and

the 1957 Champion Hurdle (G. Under-
wood), 28/1, by 5l, the same, from Quita
Que (Mr J. Cox) and Tout ou Rien (R.
Emery).

Merry Deal, who was owned and
trained by Arthur Jones, continued to
win hurdle races until he was 12 before
embarking on a chasing career. He won
two chases during season 1963-64 and
was placed in a point-to-point in the
spring of his sixteenth year after which
he was retired.

MERRYMAN II

Bay gelding, 1951, registered in Miss
Prior's Half-Bred Stud Book. Carnival
Boy—Maid Marion (Star and Garter).
Bred by the Marquess of Linlithgow.

A grand stamp of old-fashioned
chaser, Merryman II was sold by his
breeder's executors to Miss Winifred
Wallace as an unbroken five-year-old.
Miss Wallace broke him, hunted him and
trained him to win two point-to-points
and a hunter chase as a seven-year-old.

The following season he was qualified
with hounds and then sent to the
Middleham stables of Captain Neville
Crump, where he remained for the rest
of his racing career. In all, Merryman II
won five chases including the Liverpool
Foxhunters (1959), the Scottish Grand
National, Bogside (1959) and the 1960
Grand National, 10-12 (G. Scott), 13/2f,
by 15l, 12l, from Badanloch, 10-9 (S.
Mellor) and Clean Profit, 10-1 (B.
Wilkinson).

He ran a most gallant second (beaten
5l) to Nicolaus Silver (rec. 25lb) in the
1961 National after being kicked at the
start.

Merryman II was the last horse to win
the National over the old-style upright
fences. By 1961 they had been given
helpful, sloping 'aprons' which have
made the race a good deal safer but
taken away the advantage previously
enjoyed by really bold, clever jumpers of
which Merryman II was such a fine
example.

Merryman II spent his retirement in
the hunting field and died in November
1966 at a meet of the North Northumberland Hounds.

METROPOLITAN RACECOURSE BILL

The Metropolitan Racecourse Bill of
1879 prohibited racing within a 15-mile
radius of central London. Its casualties included Bromley, West Drayton, Kings-
bury, Streatham, Sutton Park and most
important, Croydon.

MIDNIGHT COURT

Bay gelding, 1971, Twilight Alley
—Strumpet (Umberto). Bred by the
Airlie Stud.

The only son of the Ascot Gold Cup
winner Twilight Alley to distinguish
himself over fences, Midnight Court, a
handsome medium-sized gelding was
transformed in the season of 1977-78
from a promising novice chaser to the
unbeaten winner of seven high-class
chases including the S.G.B. Chase (Ascot) and the Piper Champagne Cheltenham Gold Cup.

He began his career in Ireland when,
owned by Lord Petersham and trained
by T. Costello, he won two of his four-
teen races between 1974 and 1976. He
was then sold to Mrs O. Jackson and
came to Fred Winter's magic hands. The
transformation was not instantaneous.
From six runs in 1976-77 he won two
handicap hurdles and a chase and was
second in the important Heinz Chase.

His Gold Cup victory achieved at the
postponed April fixture ((J. Francome),
5/2, by 7l, 1l from Brown Lad (T. Carberry) and Master H (R. Crank)) brought
to an end the series of unbelievable
misfortunes that have dogged Fred
Winter's runners at the N.H. Festival and
aroused scenes of enthusiasm and emotion round the unsaddling enclosure
which one would not expect so
supremely professional and undemon-
strative a man to evoke.

Midnight Court is an accurate,
economical jumper, blessed with a formidable turn of foot and an apparently
perfect racing temperament. At only
seven years old he seems likely to
dominate the ranks of top staying chasers
for some years to come.

MIDNIGHT STEEPLECHASE

It is very unlikely that this stirring subject
of Alken's famous prints ever took place
at all. It is supposed to have taken place
just before Christmas in 1803 and to have
been the outcome of a challenge given by
Lieutenant Hansum in the mess-room of
Ipswich barracks that he would engage to
beat any of his brother-officers over a
country. The challenge was taken up and
as the moon was full and the spirits of
the revellers high, it is supposed to have

taken place there and then, the officers wearing night shirts and caps over their regimentals. No mention was made of the affair at the time but some years later a detailed account appeared in the *New Sporting Magazine.*

MILBURN, George

George Milburn, a competent, Northern-based jockey was attached to Verly Bewicke and later to Ken Oliver. He never won one of chasing's classics despite coming very close on several occasions. He was second in the 1957 Cheltenham Gold Cup on Kerstin, second in the 1956 Grand National on Gentle Moya and third in 1958 on Green Drill.

His victories included:

The Grand Sefton (1955) Gentle Moya
The Emblem Chase (1957) Green Drill
The National Hunt H'cap Chase (1956) Kerstin
The Mildmay Chase (1955) Wise Child
The Cheltenham H'cap Chase (1956) Lancelot

His best season was 1955-56 when he rode 38 winners and was fifth in the Jockeys' Table.

MILDMAY OF FLETE, Lord Anthony Bingham, second Baron (1909-50)

Tall and frail-looking, with a pale, sensitive face and sad eyes, Anthony Mildmay was by no means a natural athlete nor even a natural horseman yet by mental determination and physical discipline he made himself a thoroughly proficient amateur rider able to compete on terms with the leading professionals of his age while his courage, example, courtesy and the sheer magnetism of his personality made him one of the most important and best-loved figures in the history of steeplechasing.

When he died, tragically and inexplicably in May 1950, people far beyond his immediate circle felt bereaved and their emotion was best caught by *The Times,* who called him "The Last of the Corinthians" and wrote: "There never was a harder rider, a better loser or a more popular winner; and though he always valued the race more than the victory and the victory more than the prize, he would not perhaps have disdained the reward he has won – which is a kind of immortality among the

English." He went through Eton and Cambridge without any undue distinction and while at university rode, rather moderately in point-to-points. The turning-point of his career was his meeting Peter Cazalet, a fellow Etonian but older and more distinguished than himself. From their friendship, which ended only with his death, was born a rider and an administrator of the highest class, the mighty Fairlawne training establishment and the introduction to chasing of its principal patron, H.M. Queen Elizabeth. No such grandiose schemes were evident at the beginning. It was just a case of two friends with a common interest in training and riding chasers and since Cazalet's family home offered the most convenient base, Mildmay moved in. It was an arrangement which happily survived his friend's two marriages and lasted until his death.

Anthony Mildmay rode his first winner in 1933 on Good Shot. In 1936 his father bought him Davy Jones to ride in the National. The horse was tubed and thought moreover to have distinct stamina limitations but he was a safe jumper, likely to give an amateur a good ride. The pair started at 100/1 and with nothing to lose, set out to make the running. They were still in the lead approaching the second last but as they landed, the brand-new reins parted at the buckle. With his steering gone, Davy Jones ran out at the last leaving Reynoldstown to win at his leisure. Anthony Mildmay had deliberately not tied a knot in his reins because "Davy has such a tremendously long neck, I needed the full extent of rein for those drop-fences."

From 1939-45 he served with the Welsh Guards along with Peter Cazalet and it was during this time that they laid their plans for the establishment they would found at Fairlawne. It was a dream that in the immediate post-war years gave every appearance of coming true. Mildmay resumed his riding career with an authority he had previously lacked. Young horses, chosen carefully from France and Ireland, arrived at Fairlawne and under the watchful care of Cazalet and his head-lad, Jim Fairgrieve, blossomed into winning material. The cry of "Come on m' lord" echoed all over Britain's racetracks and it was often efficacious.

Mildmay was Champion Amateur five

years in succession. In 1945-46 he rode 11 winners, in 1946-47 32, in 1947-48 22, in 1948-49 30 and in 1949-50 38, the total which took him into sixth place in the professional ranks. That season Cazalet headed the Trainers List, winning 75 races worth £18,427.

Mildmay also took his integrity, wisdom and foresight into chasing's Stewards' Rooms and became an administrator of exceptional merit.

H.M. Queen Elizabeth and her daughter the Princess Elizabeth, fired by his enthusiasm, had ventured into ownership. Their first two runners had both won and Queen Elizabeth began to broaden her interest. There was just one blot on the horizon. Cromwell, the big Irish chaser who, it was hoped, would succeed where Davy Jones had so lucklessly failed, was going like a winner in the 1948 Grand National when, half a mile from home, paralysing cramp gripped Mildmay's neck. Unable to assist his horse in any way or even to raise his eyes from his neck, he rode on to be third to Sheila's Cottage. It was very tantalizing but there would be other Nationals and then, as the triumphant season of 1949-50 drew to its close, he took some friends down for a quiet weekend at his Devonshire home. As was customary he went down to the beach for a pre-breakfast swim and was never seen again.

MILDMAY

The Mildmay course at Liverpool was designed by Lord Mildmay and Sir John Crocker Bulteel to introduce novice horses to Aintree. The Mildmay Chase, run at the National meeting, was instituted in 1954 and replaced the Stanley Chase.

For the Mildmay Memorial Chase *see* SANDOWN.

MILL HOUSE

Brown gelding, 1957, King Hal—Nas na Riogh (Cariff). Bred by Mrs B. Lawlor in Co. Kildare, Ireland.

When the six-year-old Mill House won the 1963 Cheltenham Gold Cup (G. W. Robinson), 7/2, by 12l, 4l, from Fortria (P. Taaffe) and Duke of York (F. Winter), he was hailed as the new Golden Miller.

It was not unreasonable; Fulke Walwyn's young giant had strength, speed, stamina, incredibly effective jumping

which could take him past six horses in the air at a single jump and although he was prone to the occasional blunder, such was his strength and his balance that these aberrations seemed to affect him hardly at all. Moreover in Fulke Walwyn he had someone whose skill and experience in training high-class steeplechasers had few equals.

Mill House had been bred by the Lawlors, a catering family in Co. Kildare. He had been broken as a three-year-old, hunted, ironically by Pat Taaffe who was later to encompass his downfall, and had had three runs over hurdles. He won one and ran a tremendous race for the Martin Mahoney Champion Novices Hurdle until falling three from home when still pulling Dave Dick's arms out. Pat Taaffe opined that he would be the horse of the century, Dave Dick was inclined to agree and told the shrewd bloodstock agent, Jack Doyle, that the horse must be bought. Doyle touted him unsuccessfully round the smarter stables and finally placed him with Epsom trainer Syd Dale, former head-lad to Ryan Price. Mill House's new owner was Mr W. H. Collings and his price a reputed £7,500. Mill House's first season was curious and his results uneven. He ran in two novice hurdles, a conditions hurdle, a novice chase and a handicap chase at Cheltenham. He fell twice, won a novice hurdle at Wincanton and the Ledbury Handicap at Cheltenham.

Next season, for reasons not fully acceptable to Syd Dale, he was moved to the Saxon House establishment of Fulke Walwyn where he remained for the rest of his career. During the next 18 months he won seven races including the King George VI Chase, Kempton (1963), the Hennessy Gold Cup, Newbury (1963), beating Arkle, and the 1963 Cheltenham Gold Cup.

Not surprisingly he came to Cheltenham 1964 odds-on favourite to repeat his victory. Arkle's supporters were sure that but for the slip, their horse would have won. Fulke Walwyn disagreed. He maintained that Arkle made the most fantastic improvement between the Hennessy and the Gold Cup. The defeat, by five conclusive lengths was shattering, not only to owner, trainer and jockey, all convinced they had the best horse in the world, but to the horse himself. Six weeks later, trying to give 42lb to the Mildmay winner, Dormant, in the 3m 5f

Whitbread Gold Cup, he faltered 50 yards from the post and was beaten 3l.

These two defeats totally sapped him and though he won six more races including the 1967 Whitbread Gold Cup, he was never the same again. It was hoped that Arkle's retirement might allow him a brief Indian summer but back and leg trouble intervened and after falling in the Cheltenham and Whitbread Gold Cups of 1968 he was finally retired.

MISS ALLIGATOR
Chestnut mare, 1946, registered in Miss Prior's Half-Bred Stud Book. Bred by Mr W. Kennedy.

		Gainsborough
	Hyperion	
		Selene
Hyacinthus		
		Cygnus
	Sweet Wall	
		Dark Eyes
Miss Alligator		
		Spion Kop
	Landscape Hill	
		Young Stella
Girl o'the Hills		
		Sea Serpent
	Wily Girl	
		Lucky Girl

Miss Alligator shares with Miss Batty the distinction of being the only mares to breed two Grand National winners, namely Anglo (1966) and Red Alligator (1968).

After a modest career as a racehorse, she was placed at three years and finished sixth in Musidora's Oaks – she was brought for 70 guineas by Mr William Kennedy of Downpatrick, Northern Ireland.

Her breeding records is as follows:

1952 grey mare (Magic Red) **Fernet Branca** (five races).
1953 chestnut gelding (Speckled Band) **Wild Roses** (six races).
1955 chestnut gelding (Merry Boy) **Generous Token.**
1956 chestnut gelding (Magic Red) **Generous Joe** (one Flat race, three hurdle races).
1958 chestnut gelding (Greek Star) **Anglo** (five hurdle races, nine chases).
1959 chestnut gelding (Magic Red) **Red Alligator** (one hurdle race, 11 chases).

MISS BATTY
Chestnut mare, 1845. Bred by Mr Batty.

Mr R. Swale's Miss Batty, who did not race, was the first mare to breed two National winners, namely Emblem

		Whalebone
	Sir Hercules	
		Peri
The Hydra		
		Partisan
	Zebra	
Miss Batty		Venom
		Orville
	Muley	
		Eleanor
Sister to Malibran		
		Soothsayer
	Prima Donna	
		Tippitywichit

(1863) and Emblematic (1864). It was not until 1968 that Miss Alligator emulated this achievement.

Miss Batty's full breeding record was as follows:

1850 chestnut colt (Scamander).
1855 chestnut colt (half-bred horse).
1856 chestnut filly (Teddington) **Emblem.**
1858 chestnut filly (Teddington) **Emblematic.**
1861 bay or tan colt (Watlock) **Sprite.**
1863 brown filly (Knight of Kars).

She died in 1864.

MISS MOWBRAY
Bay mare, not in the General Stud Book, Lancastrian—Norma.

A fine staying mare and by all accounts an excellent hunter, Miss Mowbray won the 1852 Grand National, 10-4 (Mr A. Goodman), unquoted, by 1l, 1½l, from Maurice Daley, 9-6 (C. Boyce) and Sir Peter Laurie, 11-2 (W. Holman). Among her other successes were the Warwickshire Hunt Cup and the Leamington Open Steeplechase in 1851.

Miss Mowbray, who was owned by Mr T. F. Mason, ran in three subsequent Nationals but was dogged by misfortune. In 1853 she ran a brave race in heavy going which she disliked, to be second, beaten four lengths to Peter Simple (gave 2lb). The next year she was made ante-post favourite and Jem Mason was coming out of retirement to ride her but on the eve of the race she was 'got at' and a blister applied to her near fore which effectively prevented her from running.

Well fancied again in 1855, she was well up with the leaders on the second circuit when she caught the lip of the bank landing over Becher's Brook and broke her back and neck.

MOIFFA
Brown gelding, 1896, Natator—Denbigh (The Painter). Bred in New Zealand.

A giant of a horse measuring over 17 hands and extremely ugly, Moiffa won chases in New Zealand and was then shipped to England by his owner, Mr Spencer Gollam. Moiffa won the 1904 Grand National, 10-7 (A. Birch), 25/1, by 8l, a neck, from Kirkland, 10-10 (F. Mason) and The Gunner, 10-4 (Mr J. W. Widger).

On the strength of this victory, Moiffa was then purchased by Lord Marcus Beresford on behalf of King Edward VII. Unfortunately he was almost immediately beset by wind problems and never won for his royal owner. He ran very well in the 1905 National until his wind gave out on the second circuit. He was afterwards given to Colonel Brocklehurst and spent his retirement hunting in Leicestershire.

There is a legend that on his way to England, Moiffa was shipwrecked off the coast of Ireland and given up for lost until being found by some fishermen, parading angrily up and down a narrow strand of sand about half a mile from the shore.

MOLONEY, Jack (1898-1969)

Peter Cazalet once said that when he died the words "Grand National" would be found engraved on his heart. The same might be true of Jack Moloney, the calm, soft-spoken Irishman whose beautiful, natural horsemanship excited the admiration of all his contemporaries.

In 1929 he was second on Easter Hero, conceding 17lb and a wickedly twisted hindplate to Gregalach. Afterwards he commented: "I couldn't take a whip to the Hero. If he slowed down you knew he'd given all he had." Ironically he was second again two years later on Gregalach, beaten 1½ lengths by Grakle (rec. 7lb). He was second on Delaneige in 1934, the year of Golden Miller's record-breaking run and lastly on Black Hawk in 1939, was upsides with the winner, Workman, at the last open ditch when they bumped in mid-air and Black Hawk got the worst of it and came down.

His victories included:

The Welsh Grand National (1929) Monduco
The Coventry Trial Chase (1936) Brienz
The Grand Sefton (1930) Drin; (1936) Delaneige (dead-heat)
The Stanley Chase (1931) Physician
The National Hunt H'cap Chase (1930) Don Sancho

The Hurst Park Trial Chase (1935) Brienz
The Irish Grand National (1922) Halston; (1923) Be Careful

He spent his retirement at Newmarket where he was much in demand as a work-rider and died following a road accident in 1969.

MOLONY, Martin

It is commonly agreed that Martin Molony was the most brilliant jockey to emerge in the post-war period. He was compared, by those whose memory stretched that far, to Dick Rees and his brand of excellence was something akin to genius. He was a quiet and deeply religious man. He refused to live in England and, because his career was cut short by a bad fall, it is his elder brother, Tim (q.v.), who figures more prominently in steeplechasing's annals.

He was a polished Flat rider as well and finished third in the 1951 Derby on Signal Box. He won the Irish Grand National three times, 1944 on Knight's Crest, in 1946 on Golden View II and 1950 on Dominic's Bar.

Despite his refusal to live in England he was retained as first jockey to Lord Bicester and commuted by aeroplane to ride. At one stage his winning average in England was in the region of 33 per cent. The highlight of his career was his victory, by a short head, on Silver Fame in the 1951 Cheltenham Gold Cup. It was said that no other jockey riding would have won. After his retirement he lived in Co. Limerick where he owns and manages the Rathmore Stud.

MOLONY, Tim (b.1919)

The elder of the Molony brothers, Tim rode as an amateur from 1936-40 and as a professional from 1940-58. He rode approximately 900 winners and was Champion Jockey five consecutive seasons (1948-52). His best season was 1950-51 with 99 winners. Although considered to be slightly less brilliant than his brother, he was nevertheless absolutely top class, equally at home on park tracks and at Aintree and as effective over hurdles as he was over fences.

His principal successes were:

The Cheltenham Gold Cup (1953) Knock Hard
The Champion Hurdle (1951) Hatton's Grace; (1952) Sir Ken; (1953) Sir Ken; (1954) Sir Ken

The **Mildmay Memorial** (1951) Roimond
The **Grand Sefton** (1952) Wot No Sun;
(1956) Key Royal
The **Great Yorkshire Chase** (1951) Arctic
Gold; (1953) Knock Hard; (1957 E.S.B.
The **Emblem Chase** (1949) Wot No Sun
The **Champion Chase** (1948) Luan Casca;
(1949) Freebooter
The **Stanley Chase** (1947) Billykin; (1949)
Carmody
The **Mildmay Chase** (1956) Sir Ken

He took out a trainer's licence in 1960 and trains at Wymondham near Melton Mowbray, where his patrons include Mr Maurice Kingsley, owner of Sir Ken.

MONAVE'EN
Bay gelding, 1942, Landscape Hill—Great Double (Stefan the Great). Bred by Mr G. Flood.

The winner of nine races including the 1950 Queen Elizabeth H'cap Chase at Hurst Park, Monave'en was the first horse to be owned by H.M. Queen Elizabeth and her daughter H.R.H. Princess Elizabeth. Monave'en was chosen for his royal owners by Lord Mildmay and trained by Peter Cazalet. He ran in the colours of Princess Elizabeth and carried them into fifth place behind Freebooter in the 1950 Grand National.

Sadly he broke a leg and had to be destroyed after falling at the water during the Queen Elizabeth Handicap Chase Hurst Park in December 1950.

MONKSFIELD
Bay horse, 1972, Gala Performance—Regina (Tulyar). Bred by the Hamwood Stud.

Monksfield, a small but stout-hearted and beautifully made entire was shrewdly bought at Ballsbridge by trainer Des McDonagh, for only 740 guineas. He has won five Flat races and ten hurdle races, including the Templegate Hurdle, Liverpool (1977 (dead-heated with Night Nurse) and 1978), and the 1978 Champion Hurdle (T. Kinane), 11/2, by 2l, 6l, from Sea Pigeon (F. Berry) and Night Nurse (C. Tinkler).

He was also second to Night Nurse in the 1977 Champion Hurdle and ran a very gallant race when failing by $\frac{3}{4}$l to give 28lbs to Royal Gaye in the most valuable handicap hurdle in the British Isles, the Royal Doulton Handicap Hurdle, Haydock (1978).

His small stature and fighting heart have made him very popular with the race-going public and being the first entire to win the Champion Hurdle since Saucy Kit, and having plenty of class in his pedigree, he should be equally popular at stud.

MONT TREMBLANT
Chestnut gelding, 1946, Gris Perle—Paltoquette (Tom Pinch). Bred in France by M. James Hennessy.

Mont Tremblant won on the Flat and over hurdles in France before coming to England as a four-year-old. Owned thereafter by the Hon. Dorothy Paget and trained for her by Fulke Walwyn, he won two hurdle races and 11 chases including the Coventry Chase, Kempton (1952), the Grand International Chase, Sandown (1954), the Mildmay of Flete, National Hunt Meeting (1955) and the 1952 Cheltenham Gold Cup (D. Dick), 8/1, by 10l, 4l, from Shaef (F. Winter) and Galloway Braes (R. Morrow).

A big, handsome chestnut horse with a white blaze, Mont Tremblant began his chasing career in spectacular fashion and as he was barely out of the novice stage when he won the Gold Cup, it was not absurdly fanciful to speculate whether Miss Paget had not another Golden Miller in the making. However tendon trouble set in and although Mont Tremblant was successfully fired and ran many fine races subsequently, notably to be second with 12-5 to Early Mist in the 1953 National, he never recaptured his early brilliance. Later he was plagued by a hock injury and sinus and it is a great tribute to the skill of his trainer that he was able to retain winning form for so long.

MOONRAKER
Bay gelding, not in the General Stud Book.

A leggy horse standing 16.1 h.h., Moonraker was brought for £20 at Birmingham Fair and became one of the best-known chasers of his day, winning eight races including the St Albans Chase (1831 and 1832). After his first victory in that race, then the most important in England, he was bought by John Elmore (*q.v.*) and afterwards usually ridden by the Marquis of Clanricarde. His speed was said to be "far inferior to his great, raking style at a fence and he was fired and very tender on both his front legs".

MOORE, Daniel L. (b.1910)

Dan Moore, a member of a famous Irish chasing family, rode as an amateur (1932-37) and as a professional under both Rules (1937-48). He was Leading Jockey in Ireland in 1940 and Leading N.H. Jockey in Ireland six times. He won the Irish Grand National twice, in 1943 on Golden Jack and 1947 on Revelry, and the Lancashire Chase (1938) on Royal Danieli on whom he was beaten a head by Battleship in the 1938 Grand National.

For a while he rode for Charlie Rogers and Miss Paget. It was a much-feared team who did not hesitate to put its money down. The Irish National victory of Golden Jack landed a tremendous gamble for the stable which had repercussions. The local stewards enquired into the running of Golden Jack but accepted the explanations given. The Stewards of the National Hunt Committee however most unusually intervened and although they took no action they "severely censured and cautioned" Charlie Rogers and added that the handicapper Paddy Kirwan "was greatly to blame as he appeared not to have taken the horse's previous form into consideration".

Dan Moore retired in 1948 and immediately took out a licence to train. He currently runs a large and efficient team at Ballysax Manor, Curragh Camp, and his patrons include a number of Americans including Mr Raymond Guest, owner of his dual Gold Cup winner L'Escargot.

The big races he has won include:

The Grand National (1975) L'Escargot
The Cheltenham Gold Cup (1970) L'Escargot; (1971) L'Escargot
The National Hunt Two mile Champion Chase (1959) Quita Que; (1973) Inkslinger
The Mildmay Memorial H'cap Chase (1960) Team Spirit
The Massey-Ferguson Gold Cup (1964) Flying Wild
The W. D. & H. O. Wills Premier Chase (1970) L'Escargot
The Meadowbrook Chase, Belmont Park, U.S.A. (1969) L'Escargot

A large blunt and jovial man, he is irresistibly good company. He possesses a fine eye for a potential young chaser and found both Freebooter and Team Spirit as unbroken three-year-olds in Ireland.

His son Arthur was a very good N.H. jockey who won the 1971 Irish Grand National on King's Sprite. He is now also a trainer.

MOORE, Garrett (d.1908)

The eldest son of John Moore of Jockey Hall, the Curragh, both Garry and his brother Willie (q.v.) spent their lives with chasers. A beautiful natural horseman coached by Alan McDonough (q.v.), he was said to combine skill, strength and elegance to a rarely equalled degree. He won the 1879 Grand National on The Liberator and was second the following year to Empress. Other important victories included the first Bristol Chase (worth £1,000) on Scots Grey, and the 1875 Great Metropolitan Chase, Croydon, on Fawley.

Being well over six foot and a natural 12 stoner, he was forced to abandon riding in the early 1880s. He then took up training and established himself at Seven Barrows where Peter Walwyn now trains. His biggest success was the 1891 Eclipse Stakes with Surefoot.

Although an intuitive horsemaster, he was a poor businessman and the despair of his gambling owners. He coached a number of budding amateurs and sent one out for his first ride with following sterling injunction: "Wish you luck. Really sorry I cannot be there. You will not come unstuck. Wear a low rein, a stiff chin, keep your elbows in—and go like the merry winds of Hades."

He was also a director of Hurst Park.

MOORE, W. H.

Willie Moore was the younger brother of Garrett (q.v.) and like him, brought up at Jockey Hall on the Curragh. He too rode as an amateur and though his principal successes were abroad he also won the £1,000 Champion Hurdle (H'cap) at Kempton on Theodolite (1890). He won the Old Baden Hunt Chase four times for Herr Oscar Oehlschlager, in 1883 on Lady of the Lake, 1884 on Bell Tower and 1886 and 1887 on Adare.

He then turned his attention to training and set up a huge establishment at Weyhill in Hampshire where Toby Balding now trains. The licence was held by head-lad John Collins (q.v.) as was customary among gentleman trainers of his age and the stable sent out three National winners in five years. These were Why Not (1894), The Soarer (1896) and Manifesto (1899).

Like all his family Willie was built on a large scale and he was also cantankerous; the combination commanded wide respect. Later in his career he was assisted and finally succeeded by his nephew, Frank Hartigan (q.v.).

MORALEE, Andrew Hall (b.1916)
A member of a farming family from Alnwick, Northumberland, Danny Moralee rode very successfully as an amateur during the 1950s. He was Champion Amateur four times: 1952-53 with 22 winners, 1953-54 with 22, 1954-55 with 16 and 1955-56 (jointly with Bob McCreery), with 13. His victories included the Cheltenham Foxhunters (1954) and The Liverpool Foxhunters (1955) on his own Happymint (q.v.) the Kim Muir (1956) on Filon d'Or and he was beaten a head, by Alan Lillingstone on Kari Sou, for the 1957 National Hunt Chase.

MORGAN, D. J. (b.1912)
Danny Morgan, a nephew of Frank Morgan (q.v.) was apprenticed to Basil Jarvis and rode and won on the Flat. He had the distinction of riding for three kings of England – and winning for Edward VIII and George VI.

He grew too heavy for Flat and turned to 'the sticks', in which sphere he reached the highest class. He rode chiefly for Ivor Anthony and his principal victories included:

The **Cheltenham Gold Cup** (1938) Morse Code

The **Champion Hurdle** (1934) Chenango; (1947) National Spirit

The **Scottish Grand National** (1931) Annandale; (1935) Kellsboro' Jack; (1938) Young Mischief

The **Welsh Grand National** (1936) Sorley Boy

The **Champion Chase** (1933) Thrumster; (1936) Kellsboro' Jack; (1938) Kellsboro' Jack

The **Grand Sefton** (1935) Castle Irwell

The **Liverpool Hurdle** (1946) King of the Jungle

He surrendered his licence in 1947 and the following year took out one to train. His headquarters were at Kellsboro', Newbridge, Co. Kildare and his greatest triumph was the 1959 Cheltenham Gold Cup victory of Roddy Owen. He retired in 1973. His wife, Lilian, is a daughter of Hubert Hartigan.

MORGAN, Frank (1867-1970)
Frank Morgan was born in Co. Waterford and served his apprenticeship with Michael Dawson. He won many races on the Flat, including the 1904 Irish Derby on James Daly's Royal Arch.

He afterwards rode and trained under National Hunt Rules at the Curragh. He was an extremely skilful trainer, prone to mount successful raids on rich English races, in the fashion pioneered by Harry Dyas (q.v.) and, more recently, Paddy Sleator, with a string of perfectly prepared horses.

He produced Dudley (q.v.) which he sold to Lord Londsborough but his most famous horse was Ballinode, the Sligo mare with whom he won the 1924 Grand Sefton and the 1925 Cheltenham Gold Cup. He had been going to ride her himself but was taken ill the night before and engaged Ted Leader instead.

His four sons, Dick, Frank, Tommy and Joe, were all successful jockeys as was his nephew, Danny (q.v.).

MORROW, Robert Henry
Bert Morrow, a small, popular and immensely tough Irishman used to hold jumping crowds of the 'fifties spellbound by his reckless courage and limpet-like adherence to those hair-raising fencers Galloway Braes and Pointsman. He won the King George VI Chase and the Queen Elizabeth Chase on Galloway Braes.

MORSE CODE
Bay or chestnut gelding, 1929, The Pilot—Heliograph (Heliotrope). Bred by Col. D. P. Part.

Morse Code who traced back to the 1880 National winner Empress (her son, Red Prince II (q.v.) sired his second dam, Revolving Light) was raced by his breeder in partnership with Capt. Bridges. Unsuccessful over hurdles, he became a top-class steeplechaser over park tracks and won 14 chases including the Grand Annual, National Hunt Meeting (1936), the National Trial Chase, Gatwick (1937) and the 1938 Cheltenham Gold Cup (D. Morgan), 13/2, by 2l, 3l, from Golden Miller (H. Nicholson) and Macaulay (D. Butchers). It was Golden Miller's first and only defeat at Cheltenham and poor Morse Code was not accorded the reception he deserved. In 1939 he was odds-on to repeat his victory but ran an unaccountably lack-lustre race to finish a tired second to Brendan's Cottage. Morse Code was trained throughout his career by Ivor Anthony.

MOULD, David Stephen (b.1940)
David Mould was apprenticed to Staff Ingham and had the recognizable polish of products of the Wootten/Ingham school of jockeyship. He then transferred to Peter Cazalet for whom he rode a number of winners, including several for H.R.H. Queen Elizabeth the Queen Mother, and finally rode for Tom Jones's Newmarket Stable. He retired in 1975.

His best victories include:

The Tote Champion Novices (1966) Different Class; (1972) Clever Scot
The Hennessy Gold Cup (1970) Border Mask
The Heinz Chase (1967) Three No Trumps
The Imperial Cup (1963) Antiar
The Mackeson Hurdle (1965) Makaldar; (1966) Rackham
The Benson and Hedges H'cap Chase (1973) Tingle Creek
The Massey-Ferguson Gold Cup (1974) Garnishee

He is married to international show-jumper, Marion Coakes.

MOUNT ROYAL
Bay mare, 1877, Monarch of the Glen—Keerawn (Bandy). Bred by Lord Gormanstown.

Mount Royal did not race but, at Mr J. J. Maher's Stud, she founded a remarkable family of jumpers.

MUNNINGS, Sir Alfred J., K.C.V.O. (1878-1959).
Sir Alfred Munnings, perhaps the most distinguished painter of horses this century has yet produced, was the son of a miller and was born and bred in East Anglia. He served an apprenticeship in a lithograph studio in Norwich and then equipped himself with a caravan and some horses and settled down on the Ringwood hills to paint.

He became a fine painter of landscape in the style of Constable. Later a distin-guished critic wrote: "a show devoted exclusively to Sir Alfred's landscapes would place him undoubtedly among the masters of the English scene".

He lost an eye at the age of 21 which precluded him from serving in World War I but he was chosen as a War artist and attached to the Canadian Cavalry Brigade. Afterwards he concentrated on equestrian studies.

He began to exhibit at the Royal Academy at the beginning of the century and was President from 1944-49. He made a sensational speech denouncing the attitude of critics towards sporting art at the banquet marking the end of his term of office. He is largely responsible for the tremendous resurgence in sporting art and good examples of his work have a world-wide demand and are currently fetching five-figure sums in London salerooms.

MR WHAT
Bay gelding, 1950, Grand Inquisitor—Duchess of Pedulas (Duke of Buckingham). Bred in Co. Westmeath, Ireland, by Mrs Barbara O'Neill.

After being bought for £500 by Tos Taaffe as a just-broken five-year-old, Mr What won a maiden hurdle at Navan in March 1956 and was sold to Mr D. J. Coughlen. He remained in Tos Taaffe's yard and went on to win another hurdle race and five chases including the Troytown Chase and the 1958 Grand National, 10-0 (car. 10-6) (A. Freeman), 18/1, by 30l, 15l, from Tiberetta, 10-6 (G. Slack) and Green Drill, 10-10 (G. Milburn). He did not win again but was third to Oxo in the 1959 National and third again to Kilmore in 1962.

MUCH OBLIGED
Black or brown gelding, 1948, Cameron—May Sen (Sun Yat Sen). Bred by Mr Isdale.

Much Obliged, a strongly built horse was brought privately as an unbroken four-year-old by Captain Charles Radclyffe, who broke and hunted him and then passed him to Mr H. Draper, a patron of Neville Crump. Much Obliged raced for eight seasons and won 15 chases, including the Wetherby Handicap Chase (1958), the Mildmay Memorial, Sandown (1957) and the first Whitbread Gold Cup, Sandown (1957) beating Mandarin (q.v.), a neck in a most exciting finish.

MUSIC HALL

Bay gelding, 1913, not in the General Stud Book, Cliftonville—Molly. Bred by Mrs F. Blacker in Co. Kildare, Ireland.

After a very successful campaign in 1920 during which he won seven races including the Scottish Grand National for Mrs E. Stokes, Music Hall was sold to Mr Hugh Kershaw and transferred to Owen Anthony's stable. The following year he developed leg trouble after winning a minor race at Nottingham and was off the course for over a year.

In 1922 he came back to win two prestige chases, the Hurst Park National Trial and the Grand National, 11-8 (L. B. Rees), 100/9, by 12l, 6l, from Drifter, 10-0 (W. Watkinson) and Taffytus, 11-0 (T. Leader). The first three were the only horses to complete the race without a fall.

MY PRINCE

Bay horse, 1911. Bred by Lord St Davids.

A good-class Flat horse owned by Lord St Davids, My Prince won three races including the Union Jack Stakes, Liverpool, and the Gordon Stakes, Goodwood. Retired to Mr A. H. Maxwell's Corduff Stud, Lusk, Co. Dublin, he

			Barcaldine
		Marco	
			Novitiate
	Marcovil		
			Hagioscope
		Lady Villikins	
My Prince			Dinah
			Galopin
		St Simon	
			St Angela
	Salvaich		
			Scottish Chief
		Muirninn	
			Violet

became a most important sire of National Hunt horses.

His stock include the Grand National winners Gregalach (1929), Reynoldstown (1935 and 1936) and Royal Mail (1937) and the Gold Cup winners Easter Hero (1929 and 1930) and Prince Regent (1946).

He was leading sire on five occasions:

1928-29	winners of	12	races worth		£14,934
1934-35	„ „	26	„	„	£9,349
1935-36	„ „	12	„	„	£8,587
1936-37	„ „	16	„	„	£7,266
1941-42	„ „	11	„	„	£1,696

He was also a noted sire of broodmares, one of the most influential being Greenogue Princess.

NATIONAL ASSOCIATION OF BOOKMAKERS LTD

A main object of the National Association of Bookmakers as defined in its Articles is "to pay particular regard to the interests of bookmakers and persons interested in betting, whether on or off the racecourse". A non-profit-making organization, it is recognized by the Government and sporting authorities as representing and competent to speak for responsible bookmakers throughout Britain, both on course and off course.

Its network of affiliated associations covers every county in Britain, the constituent associations preserving their own identity and autonomy on local matters and collaborating through the National organization to define uniform policy on major issues affecting the profession as a whole. Membership is open to all eligible bookmakers.

The associations are responsible to the racing authorities for pitch-control administration and screening of new bookmakers at all racecourses. Apart from their own specialist committees, they also supply representatives for the Bookmakers' Levy Committee (a statutory Committee under the Home Office) and for the Advertising Bookmakers' Investigation Committee (a joint committee with the Press). The profession's monthly newspaper, *The British Bookmaker,* is published by the National Association.

The executive members, both national and regional, are practising bookmakers who serve without remuneration and are elected annually by the members in general meeting. The associations have been serving bookmakers, the betting public and the Turf for over half a century.

Chairman: Mr A. Bruce (Fife)
Vice-Chairman: Mr E. Barber (Manchester)
Treasurer: Mr F. J. Stock (Stratford-on-Avon)

NATIONAL HEAD LADS ASSOCIATION

The National Head Lads Association aims to secure and maintain proper conditions of employment for its members. To negotiate on behalf of its members in general or any member or members in particular, with employers or any person or organization connected with the horse-racing industry. To provide, so far as may be practicable, benefit for any member or members during unemployment, sickness or industrial dispute and to promote the well-being of the horse-racing industry in general and Head and Travelling Head Lads in particular.

Chairman: Mr R. V. King
Vice-Chairman: Mr G. Walker-Williams
Secretary/Treasurer: Mrs R. V. King

NATIONAL HUNT CHASE

The National Hunt Chase, the second oldest race in Cheltenham's calendar is held at the National Hunt Meeting in March. It was instituted in 1859 by 'Fogo' Rowlands (*q.v.*) as an attempt to provide a race for genuine steeplechasing hunters over a suitable course with local hunts subscribing to and supporting the race.

The first running met with a very disappointing response but the following year, at Market Harborough, it was a resounding success. The race, over four miles, was for maidens at starting. It cost £10 to run and £500 was added to which the following hunts subscribed:

The Duke of Beaufort's
The Monmouthshire
Lord Fitzwilliam's
The Warwickshire
Lord Stamford's (Quorn)
The North Warwickshire
Lord Dacre's
The Cambridgeshire
Lord Tredegar's
The Oakley
Mr T. T. Drake's (Bicester)
The Heythrop

There were 31 runners and it was won by the favourite, 'Cherry' Angell's Bridegroom.

In 1861 there were two races, one at Market Harborough which fielded 17 runners and was won by 'Cherry'

Angell's Queensferry, and one at Cleeve Hill, Cheltenham, over 2¼ miles, organized by 'Fogo' Rowlands and won by George Ede on The Freshman.

The race then became a moveable event and was staged at 25 different venues before coming to Cheltenham in 1904. After five intervening years at Warwick it finally settled at Cheltenham in 1911.

The National Hunt Chase used to carry a great deal of prestige. When the Gold Cup was instituted in 1924 it was worth £685 to the winner, whereas the National Hunt Chase at £1,285 was the third most valuable in the Calendar.

No really good horse has won the race but two, Why Not (1886) and Quare Times (1954) went on to win the Grand National, while Conjuror II (1922) was a fair performer who was placed in both the Gold Cup and the Grand National.

For a list of winners *see* CHELTENHAM.

NATIONAL HUNT COMMITTEE

During the early 1860s it became increasingly clear to steeplechasing men that their sport was in considerable disrepute. Such rules as there were, were ineffectively enforced because suspensions and penalties for abuse were only effective at meetings run by the same Stewards as had imposed them. Moreover the Jockey Club did not recognize steeplechasing so the most heinous steeplechasing offenders found sanctuary under Jockey Club Rules.

Envious eyes were cast at Flat-racing with the authority of Admiral Rous and its governing body to adjudicate, plan and rule. Fortunately for steeplechasing, many of its supporters were also members of the Jockey Club. In 1862, Mr 'Cherry' Angell and Mr W. G. Craven (shortly to be Senior Steward of the Jockey Club) wrote an anonymous letter to *Bell's Life,* enclosing a proposed set of Rules for steeplechases. This was followed by a letter from Admiral Rous with some suggestions and amendments. In 1863 Mr Angell and Mr Craven co-opted Lord Grey de Wilton to their National Hunt Committee and within the year they were being asked to adjudicate on disputes. By 1866 they had reached agreement with the Jockey Club that a separate entity with similar powers should be established to govern the affairs of steeplechasing.

The 1866 committee comprised: B. J.

Angell, C. H. Carew, Viscount Chaplin, Lord Coventry, Capt. Henry Coventry, W. G. Craven, Sir Frederick Johnstone, Capt. James Little, George Payne, Lord Poulett, Lord Westmorland, and Lord Grey de Wilton.

They were a well-qualified committee. Josie Little and 'Bee' Coventry had each ridden a National winner. 'Cherry' Angell had owned one in Alcibiade and Lord Coventry had owned two in the sisters Emblem and Emblematic. Lord Poulett was a very successful rider who was later to lease The Lamb.

For nearly 100 years the National Hunt Committee ran their own shop but in 1963 a new step was taken. A joint authority known as the Turf Board was set up under the chairmanship of the Senior Steward of the Jockey Club and made up of Stewards from both organizations. The idea was for the Turf Board to lay down general policy while the Jockey Club and the National Hunt Committee were to be responsible for the day-to-day running of racing. In 1969 the Jockey Club and the National Hunt Committee amalgamated.

The current Board comprises a Senior Steward, a Deputy Senior Steward, and four stewards.

The present board comprises:

Senior Steward:
Lord Howard de Walden

Deputy Senior Steward:
Maj. M. G. Wyatt

Stewards:
Lord Manton
Mr J. B. Sumner
Mr Louis Freedman
Mr L. B. Holliday

Patrons:
H.M. The Queen, H.M. Queen Elizabeth The Queen Mother

Founders:
Viscount Andover (afterwards Earl of Suffolk and Berkshire), B. J. Angell, Esq., E. C. Burton, Esq., and W. G. Craven, Esq.

Members, past and present, with date of election, revised to 1969:

His Royal Highness the Duke of York (afterwards King George VI) (14th May 1934);
His Royal Highness the Duke of Gloucester (14th May 1934);

His Royal Highness the Duke of
Windsor (1st February 1921);

Abergavenny, Henry Gilbert Ralph,
3rd Marquess of (9th October 1905);

Abergavenny, Guy Temple Montacute
Larnach-Nevill, 4th Marquess of
(9th October 1916);

Abergavenny, John Henry Guy Nevill,
5th Marquess of, O.B.E. (14th
December 1942);

Angell, Benjamin John (Original
Member)

Anglesey, Sir Henry William George,
3rd Marquess of (17th April 1871);

Anstruther-Gray, Major Sir William
John, Bt, P.C., M.C. (19th July
1948);

Astley, Sir John Dugdale, Bt (31st
December 1870);

Aylesford, Heneage, Earl of (25th
October 1872);

Baird, Brig. Gen. Edward William
David, C.B.E. (10th October 1892);

Barclay, Maj. Hedworth Trelawny
(14th December 1885);

Bass, Sir William Arthur Hamar, Bt
(16th July 1923);

Bassett, Ralph Thurstan (12th October
1869);

Beaufort, Sir Henry Charles FitzRoy,
8th Duke of, K. G. (Co-opted 3rd
April 1866);

Bengough, Maj. Piers Henry George
(1st March 1965);

Benson, Sir Henry, G.C.B. (December
1969);

Beresford, Lord Marcus Talbot de la
Poer, C.V.O. (12th April 1875);

Beresford, Col. Lord William Leslie de
la Poer, V.C., K.C.I.E. (11th
December 1880);

Bibby, Frank (10th October 1898);

Bibby, Captain Frank Brian Frederic
(9th December 1918);

Bicester, Vivian Hugh Smith, 1st Baron
(16th July 1928);

Bicester, Randal Hugh Vivian Smith,
2nd Baron (21st July 1958);

Bingham, Maj.-Gen., the Hon. Sir
Cecil Edwards, K.C.M.G., C.B.,
G.C.V.O. (10th October 1921);

Blacker, Maj.-Gen. Cecil Hugh,
O.B.E., M.C. (13th December 1954);

Brabazon, Maj.-Gen. Sir John Palmer,
K.C.B., C.V.O. (8th May 1905);

Brassey, Major Harold Ernest (8th
October 1900);

Bulkely, Col. Charles Rivers, C.B. (8th
December 1884);

Bullough, Sir George, Bt (14th
December 1914);

Bulteel, John Crocker, D.S.O., M.C.
(16th July 1923);

Bulteel, John George (12th May 1902);

Burton, Edmund Charles (14th
December 1897);

Byrne, Maj.-Gen. Thomas Edmond
(12th April 1875);

Cadogan, William Gerald Charles
Cadogan, 7th Earl, M.C. (17th July
1939);

Calthorpe, Sir Frederick Henry
William, 5th Baron (25th November
1868);

Cambaceres, Comte Delaire de (10th
May 1920);

Campbell, Gen. Sir David Graham
Muschet, K.C.B. (16th July 1928);

Carew, Charles Hallowell (Original
Member);

Carington, Rupert Clement George,
4th Baron Carrington, C.V.O.,
D.S.O. (11th July 1881);

Case-Walker, Thomas Edward (17th
June 1871);

Champion de Crespigny, Brig.-Gen.
Sir Claude Raul, Bt., C.M.G.,
D.S.O. (10th October 1921);

Chaplin, Henry, 1st Viscount (Original
Member);

Chelsea, the Viscount (July 1967);

Chetwynd, Sir George, Bt (16th
December 1872);

Cholmondeley, George Henry Hugh,
4th Marquess of (19th December
1889);

Christie-Miller, Major Edward Goff
(14th December 1914);

Clermont-Tonnerre, Comte Robert de
(12th May 1913);

Collis, Lt.-Col. Robert Henry, D.S.O.
(9th October 1905);

Combe, Maj.-Gen. John Frederick
Boyce, C.B., D.S.O. (15th July
1946);

Cooper, Capt. William Henry (3rd
January 1870);

Cotes, Lieut.-Col. Charles James (9th
October 1911);

Cottenham, John Digby Thomas
Pepys, 7th Earl of (11th October
1954);

Courage, Commander Archibald
Vesey (16th July 1934);

Courage, E. R. (July 1967);

Coventry, George William, 9th Earl of,
P.C. (Original Member);

Coventry, Capt. the Hon. Charles John, C.B. (8th October 1900);

Coventry, Capt. Henry Amelius Beauclerk (Original Member);

Cowley, Henry Arthur Mornington, 3rd Earl (9th December 1895);

Craven, William George Robert, 4th Earl of (21st June 1873);

Craven, William George (Original Member);

Curtis, Sir William Michael, Bt (9th December 1901);

Daly, Maj. D. R. (July 1967);

Denman, Sir Thomas, 3rd Baron, P.C., G.C.M.G., K.C.V.O. (19th July 1920);

Derby, Sir Edward George Villiers Stanley, 17th Earl of, K.G., G.C.B., G.C.V.O. (20th July 1936);

de Trafford, Sir Humphrey Edmund, Bt. M.C. (9th December 1929);

de Tuyll, Baron Francis Charles Owen, M.B.E. (8th December 1919);

Douglas-Pennant, Lieut.-Col. Frank (succeeded as 5th Baron Penrhyn on (26th June 1949) (10th May 1915);

Drogheda, Henry Francis Seymour, 3rd and last Marquess of, K.P. (13th July 1885);

Du Bos, Auguste (9th December 1912);

Dudley, William Humble, 2nd Earl of, P.C., G.C.B., G.C.M.G., G.C.V.O. (8th October 1900);

Dufosee, Henry William (4th March 1963);

Eden, Sir William, Bt (9th December 1889);

Egerton, Charles Augustus (9th December 1889);

Egerton, Commander Hugh Sydney, D.S.C. (13th October 1952);

Enniskillen, Sir Lowry Egerton, 4th Earl of, K.P. (13th October 1890);

Essex, George Devereux de Vere, 7th Earl of (9th October 1905);

Feilden, Maj.-Gen. Sir Randle Guy, K.C.V.O., C.B., C.B.E. (11th October 1954);

Fetherstonhaugh, Major Frederick Howard Wingfield (14th December 1914);

Filmer, Sir Robert Marcus, Bt (14th October 1907);

Fisher-Childe, Col. Ralph Bromfield Willington, C.B. (9th December 1912);

Fitzhardinge, Francis William Fitzhardinge, 2nd Baron (January 1884);

Fitzwilliam, The Hon. William John Wentworth (12th December 1887);

Forestier-Walker, Lieut.-Col. Roland Stuart, D.S.O. (14th December 1914);

Forsyth-Forrest, Capt. Philip Maurice (12th October 1953);

Foster, Capt. James (13th May 1907);

Foster, Maj. John Bentley (20th July 1931);

Furlong, Maj. Noel Charles Bell (13th October 1952);

Garratt, Lieut.-Col. John Arthur Thomas (9th July 1883);

Gheest, Maurice de (13th October 1919);

Gibson, Maj. William David (12th October 1959);

Gilliat, Lieut-Col. Sir Martin John, K.C.V.O., M.B.E., D.L. (12th October 1964);

Gillois, Col. A. M. (13th October 1919);

Gordon, Major John Maxwell (10th December 1906);

Gordon-Smith, Sir Allan Gordon, K.B.E. (10th October 1949);

Gosling, Edward Lambert (15th July 1946);

Gosling, Capt. Henry Miles (1st March 1965);

Gowrie (Brig.-Gen. the Hon. Sir Alexander Gore Arkwright Hore-Ruthven), 1st Earl, V.C., P.C., G.C.M.G., C.B., D.S.O. (12th December 1921);

Gresson, William Jardine (13th May 1929);

Grimthorpe, Sir Ralph William Ernest Beckett, 3rd Baron, T. D. (19th July 1926);

Haddington, George Baillie-Hamilton, 12th Earl of, K.T., M.C., T.D. (18th July 1932);

Halifax, Charles Ingram Courtenay Wood, 2nd Earl of (9th October 1950);

Hamilton and Brandon, William Alexander Louis Stephen, 12th Duke of, K.T. (6th March 1868);

Hanmer, Sir Griffin Wyndham Edward, Bt (11th December 1933);

Hardinege, Henry Charles, 3rd Viscount, C.B. (12th October 1903);

Harewood, Sir Henry George Charles Lascelles, 6th Earl of, K.G., G.C.V.O., D.S.O. (13th December 1938);

Harford, Lieut.-Col. Frederick Henry (17th June 1871);

Harrington, Charles Augustus, 8th Earl of (10th July 1882);

Harvey, Brig. C. B., D.S.O. (December 1969);

Hastings, Sir George Manners, 20th Baron (12th July 1886);

Hathorn, Lieut.-Col. John Fletcher (9th February 1874);

Helmsley, William Reginald Duncombe, Viscount (12th July 1880);

Henderson, Charles William Chipchase (11th December 1905);

Henderson, John Ronald, M.B.E. (19th July 1965);

Heneage, Edward, 1st Baron Heneage (31st December 1870);

Herbert, William Reginald Joseph Fitz-Herbert (29th April 1869);

Hoare, Maj. Robert, M.C. (8th October 1956);

Holland-Martin, Edward (28th August 1940);

Hope-Johnstone, Capt. Wentworth William (9th October 1893);

Howard, the Hon. Cecil Molyneux (12th July 1880);

Hughes-Onslow, Major Arthur (12th October 1908);

Hungerford, Henry Vane Forester Holdich (17th April 1882);

Huntington, Maj. Arthur William, D.S.O. (21st July 1930);

Ilchester, Edward Henry Charles James Fox-Strangways, 7th Earl of (15th July 1946);

Jarvis, George Eden (8th October 1900);

Jenkins, William Henry Phillips (9th July 1883);

Jersey, George Henry Robert Child-Villiers, 8th Earl of (11th December 1905);

Joel, Harry (10th May 1965);

Johnstone, Sir Frederick John William, Bt (Original Member);

Johnstone, Lt.-Col. George Charles Keppel (Co-opted 23rd January 1867);

Johnstone, The Hon. Gilbert, Vanden Bempde (10th December 1906);

Johnstone, John (21st July 1924);

Joicey, Lt.-Col. Sir Hugh Edward, 3rd Baron, D.S.O. (14th December 1948);

Ker, Lord Charles John Innes (5th January 1872);

Kidston, A. M. G. (December 1969);

Kindersley, Gay (16th July 1962);

King, Thomas Poole (10th May 1915);

Kinsky, Prince (14th May 1906);

Knox, Col. George Williams (25th November 1868);

La Rochefoucauld, Comte Jean de (10th May 1915);

Lascelles, Henry Ulick Lascelles, Viscount, 5th Earl of Harewood (1st December 1873);

Lawson, Col. Sir Peter Grant, Bt (18th July 1932);

Leeds, Sir George Godolphin, 10th Duke of (10th April 1887);

Legard, Sir Charles, Bt (25th November 1868);

Leigh, Rupert, William Dudley, 4th Baron (25th February 1952);

Leigh, John Gerard (15th December 1873);

Leverhulme, Sir Peter William Bryce Lever, 3rd Viscount, T.D. (9th October 1961);

Leveson-Gower, Maj. Granville Charles Gresham (19th July 1938);

Lewis, Brig. James Charles Windsor, D.S.O., M.C. (25th February 1952);

Lindsay, Lt.-Col. Henry Edzell Morgan (12th October 1903);

Little, Capt. James Lockhart (Original Member);

Llewellyn, Lt.-Col. Henry Morton, C.B.E. (15th July 1946);

Lloyd, Sir Marteine Owen Mowbray, Bt (12th May 1902);

Londesborough, Hugo William Cecil, 4th Earl of (13th December 1920);

Londonderry, Sir Charles Stewart, 6th Marquess of, K.G. (14th July 1879);

Lonsdale, Sir Hugh Cecil Lowther, 5th Earl of, K.G., G.C.V.O. (13th December 1915);

Lumsden, Lt.-Gen. Herbert, D.S.O., M.C. (19th July 1937);

McCalmont, Col. Harry Leslie Blundell, C.B. (9th October 1899);

McCreery, Gen. Sir Richard Loudon, G.C.B., K.B.E., D.S.O., M.C. (11th December 1944);

Machell, Capt. James Octavius (10th April 1876);

McAlpine, Sir Edwin (June 1969);

McKie, Lt.-Col. John, D.S.O. (9th October 1899);

Mainwaring, Charles Francis Kynaston (8th May 1905);

Manners, John Thomas, 3rd Baron (10th July 1882);

Marshall, Major Anthony Charles (10th May 1948);

Marshall, John Anthony (11th May 1959);

Meux, Admiral of the Fleet, the Hon. Sir Hedworth, G.C.B., K.C.V.O. (19th July 1920);

Middleton, Capt. William George (8th July 1878);

Mildmay of Flete, Francis Bingham, 1st Baron, P.C. (19th July 1937);

Mildmay of Flete, Anthony Bingham, 2nd Baron (14th December 1942);

Montrose, Sir Douglas Beresford Malise Ronald, 5th Duke of, K.T. (8th April 1878);

Morgan, Col. the Hon. Frederic Courtenay (10th April 1866);

Morrison, the Hon. James (June 1969);

Moseley, Lt.-Col. Roger Bright (13th December 1948);

Mountain, Sir Brian, 2nd Bt. (October 1970);

Murat, Prince, G.C.V.O. (12th May 1913);

Murland, William (13th May 1901);

Neuflize, Baron de (12th May 1913);

Newton, Charles Stancliffe (17th June 1895);

Noble, Brig. Frederick Babington Bridgeman, O.B.E. (13th December 1965);

Norfolk, Bernard Marmaduke Fitzalan-Howard, 16th Duke of, E.M., K.G., P.C., G.C.V.O. (18th July 1938);

Normanton, Edward John Sidney Christian Welbore Ellis Agar, 5th Earl of (9th May 1960);

Norrie, Lt.-Gen. Sir Charles Willoughby Moke, 1st Baron, G.C.M.G., G.C.V.O., C.B., D.S.O., M.C. (19th July 1937);

Orr-Ewing, Maj. James Alexander (9th December 1889);

Owen, Hugh Darby Annesley (23rd March 1877);

Owen, Morris Williams Lloyd (10th December 1906);

Paget, Lord Berkeley Charles Sidney (9th February 1874);

Paget, Edward Catesby (20th July 1936);

Paget, Sir George Ernest, Bt (12th July 1880);

Part, Lieut.-Col. Sir Dealtry Charles, O.B.E. (9th December 1946);

Payne, George (Original Member);

Payne-Gallwey, Lt.-Col. Peter, D.S.O. (11th December 1944);

Paynter, Brig.-Gen. Sir George Camborne Beauclerk, K.C.V.O., C.M.G., D.S.O. (9th October 1911);

Peacock, Major Hugh Myddleton (10th October 1955);

Penrhyn, George Sholto Gordon, 2nd Baron (Co-opted 14th December 1867);

Penrhyn, Edward Sholto, 3rd Baron (13th December 1926);

Penrhyn, Hugh Napier Douglas-Pennant, 4th Baron (17th July 1933);

Phillips, the Hon., James Perrott, T.D. (21st July 1958);

Phillips, Lt.-Col. John Frederick Lort (12th December 1898);

Platt, Eric James Walter (14th December 1914);

Pole, Col. Sir John Gawen Carew, Bt, D.S.O., T.D. (11th December 1950);

Poulett, William Henry, 6th Earl (Original Member);

Queenborough, Almeric Hugh Paget, 1st Baron, G.B.E. (21st July 1927);

Queensberry, Sir John Sholto, 8th Marquess of (27th April 1872);

Ranfurly, Thomas Daniel Knox, 6th Earl, K.C.M.G. (June 1969);

Rank, James Voase (16th July 1951);

Rankin, Brig.-Gen. Charles Herbert, C.B., C.M.G., D.S.O. (13th October 1919);

Rendlesham, Frederick William Brook, 5th Baron (13th October 1890);

Richardson, John Maunsell (4th May 1874);

Richmond-Watson, R. N. (June 1969);

Rogerson, John (12th December 1949);

Rose, Sir Charles Day, Bt (19th October 1892);

Rosebery, Sir Albert Edward Harry Meyer Archibald Primrose, 6th Earl of, K.T., P.C., D.S.O., M.C. (10th December 1934);

Rossmore, Henry Cairns, 4th Baron (1st December 1873);

Rossmore, Derrick Warner William, 5th Baron (14th July 1884);

Rushout, Sir Charles Fitzgerald, Bt (1st December 1873);

St Davids, Sir John Wynford, 1st Viscount (11th December 1905);

Sassoon, Capt. Reginald Ellice (18th July 1932);

Schilizzi, J. S. (July 1967);

Sefton, Sir Osbert Cecil, 6th Earl of, G.C.V.O. (12th October 1903);

Sefton, Sir Hugh William Osbert Molyneux, 7th Earl of (11th May 1936);

Shrewsbury and Waterford, John George Charles Henry Alton Alexander Chetwynd Chetwynd-Talbot, 21st Earl of (10th October 1955);

Smith, Gerald Dudley (14th December 1914);

Speed, Brigadier Elmer John Leyland, M.C. (9th December 1946);

Stalbridge, Hugh Grosvenor, 2nd Baron, M.C. (19th July 1926);

Stamford and Warrington, George Harry, 7th Earl of (25th November 1868);

Stanley, Edward Montague Cavendish, Lord (8th December 1919);

Stanley, Brig.-Gen. the Hon. Ferdinand Charles, C.M.G., D.S.O. (8th October 1900);

Stirling, Maj. Gilbert Chalmers (21st April 1875);

Staker, Maj. Ian Allgood (19th July 1920);

Straker, John Joicey, McC. (12th October 1953);

Suffield, Sir Charles, 5th Baron (1st June 1868);

Suffolk and Berkshire, Henry Charles, 18th Earl of (Co-opted 3rd April 1866);

Suffolk and Berkshire, Henry Molyneux Paget, 19th Earl of (8th October 1906);

Sumner, Arthur Holme (Original Member);

Sumner, J. B. (December 1971);

Sumner, John Richard Hugh, C.B.E. (12th December 1955);

Tempest, Capt. Arthur Cecil (3rd January 1870);

Thomas, Hugh Lloyd, C.V.O., C.M.G. (10th December 1934);

Thompson, Col. Reginald, D.S.O., T.D. (15th July 1946);

Thomson, Colonel John, T.D. (11th October 1965);

Throckmorton, Sir Nicholas William George, Bt (5th November 1868);

Tomkinson, Brig. Henry Archdale, D.S.O. (11th May 1936);

Tredegar, Sir Godfrey Charles, 1st Viscount (10th April 1866);

Tweedie, R. R. (June 1969);

Vaux, Wing-Commander Peter Douglas Ord (12th October 1953);

Vyner, Henry Frederick Clare (12th April 1875);

Walker, Sir Peter Carlaw, Bt (9th December 1901);

Ward, Capt. the Hon. Reginald, D.S.O. (8th December 1902);

Westmacott, Col. Guy Randolph, D.S.O. (15th July 1946);

Westminster, Sir Hugh Richard Arthur Grosvenor, 2nd Duke of, G.C.V.O., D.S.O. (9th December 1901);

Westmorland, Francis William Henry, 12th Earl of, C.B. (Original Member);

Westmorland, Vere Anthony Francis St Clair Fane, 14th Earl of (18th July 1932);

Weyland, Capt. Mark (18th July 1927);

Whichcote, Sir Thomas, Bt (31st December 1870);

Whitbread, William Henry (16th July 1956);

White, Col. the Hon. Charles William (16th December 1872);

White, Capt. the Hon. Luke, 3rd Baron Annaly, C.B. (11th December 1882);

Whitney, John Hay (15th July 1957);

Wickham, Major George Lamplugh (11th December 1893);

Wigan, Major Derek (14th December 1964);

Wilkins, Richard Sinclair (19th July 1965);

Williams, Charles Crofts Llywellyn, M.C. (19th July 1938);

Williams, Owen (8th October 1900);

Willoughby de Broke, Henry, 18th Baron (4th May 1874);

Willoughby de Broke, John Henry Peyto Verney, 20th Baron, M.C., A.F.C. (9th December 1940);

Wilson-Todd, Sir William Pierrepont, Bt (13th December 1915);

Wilton, Arthur Edward Holland, 3rd Earl of (Original Member);

Withington, Frederick Edward, C.B.E. (11th May 1931);

Wolverton, George Grenfell, 2nd Baron (2nd January 1884);

Wyatt, Maj. M.G. (December 1969);

Wyndham, Col. the Hon, Everard Humphrey, M.C. (9th December 1918);

Yarborough, Charles, 3rd Earl of (31st December 1870);

Yarborough Charles Alfred Worsley, 4th Earl of (8th December 1884);

Yardley, Lt.-Col. John Watkins, C.M.G., D.S.O. (9th December 1912).

See also JOCKEY CLUB.

NATIONAL HUNT TRAINERS' ASSOCIATION

The objects of the Association are to consider and promote the interests of all National Hunt trainers and to encourage a close liaison between the Association, the Jockey Club, and all organizations with National Hunt Racing.

Chairman: G. B. Balding Esq., Fyfield House, Andover, Hants. Tel: Weyhill 2278.

There is a committee of members for each training centre in Britain and in addition a northern sub-committee with its own secretariat. The Association is now amalgamated with the Flat Trainers and known as the National Trainers Federation (*q.v.*).

NATIONAL SPIRIT

(Formerly Avago). Chestnut gelding, 1941, Scottish Union—Cocktail (Coronach). Bred by Mr L. A. Abelson.

A big rangy chestnut, a superlative jumper and a fine stayer, National Spirit raced for eight seasons and won 14 Flat races and 19 hurdles including the Princess Elizabeth Handicap Hurdle, Doncaster, and the Champion Hurdle twice each. In 1947 (D. Morgan), 7/1, by 1l, 2l, from Le Paillon (A. Head) and Freddy Fox (R. Smyth), and 1948 (R. Smyth), 6/4f, by 2l, ¾l, from D.U.K.W. (J. Maguire) and Encoroli (M. Connors).

He was considered fortunate to beat Le Paillon in 1947, which view was handsomely substantiated by the latter's victory in the Prix de l'Arc de Triomphe that autumn. National Spirit ran in four more Champion Hurdles being fourth to Hatton's Grace in 1949, fourth to the same horse in 1950 after blundering badly at the last, falling at the last when still in the lead in 1951 and being fourth again in 1952.

National Spirit was virtually unbeatable in his prime and in fact was only beaten twice over hurdles between the Spring of 1946 and January 1949. He was raced by his breeder and trained throughout his career, by Vic Smyth at Epsom.

NEWBURY (Group 1)

Although racing was recorded at Newbury as early as 1839, the present course dates from 1906. The track is left-handed, pear-shaped, slightly undulating and about 1 mile, 7 furlongs round. Very well run and accessible both to race-goers, via

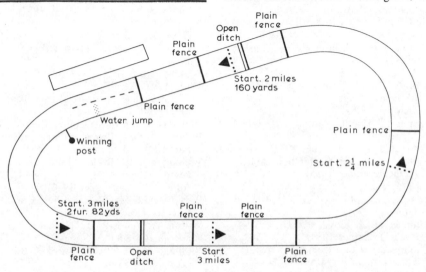

the M4 motorway and train services, and to trainers from the Lambourn area, it has proved exceptionally popular since its inception. It was the brain-child of John Porter, the famous trainer of nearby Kingsclere, who often passed the site on the train to London and thought it an ideal spot for a racecourse.

Its most famous N.H. race is the Hennessy Gold Cup Handicap Chase (November, 3m 2f 85y, £8,972) which has been run at Newbury since 1960, three years after its institution. Other important races include The Schweppes Gold Trophy H'cap Hurdle (February, 2m, £12,724) for years the most valuable and controversial hurdle race in the Calendar.

Best Times

Distance	Time	Horse-age-weight	Date
2m H	3m 36.50	Night Nurse 4-10-12	23-10-75
2½m H	3m 48.70	Beacon Light 6-11-9	21-10-77
2½m 120y H	4m 57.40	Blackheath 5-10-2	10-2-60
3m H	5m 57	Victor's Venture 9-11-8	1-1-55
3m 120y H	5m 57.90	Croftamie 7-10-8	6-11-75
2m 160y C	3m 59.40	Inch Arran 7-11-1	4-11-71
2½m C	4m 55.50	Game Spirit 9-11-6	25-10-75
3m C	5m 51.70	Grey Sombrero 7-10-10	3-11-71
3m 2f 82y C	6m 30.80	Spanish Steps 6-11-8	29-11-69

Hennessy Cognac Gold Cup (3¼m)

Cheltenham

	HORSE	OWNER	RIDER	TRAINER
1957	Mandarin	Mme Hennessy	G. Madden	F. Walwyn
1958	Taxidermist	Mrs P. Hastings	Hon. J. Lawrence	F. Walwyn
1959	Kerstin	Mr G. H. Moore	S. Hayhurst	C. Bewicke

Newbury

	HORSE	OWNER	RIDER	TRAINER
1960	Knucklecracker	Maj. L. S. Marler	D. Ancil	D. Ancil
1961	Mandarin	Mme Hennessy	G. W. Robinson	F. Walwyn
1962	Springbok	Col. Lord Joicey	G. Scott	N. Crump
1963	Mill House	Mr W. Gollings	G. W. Robinson	F. Walwyn
1964	Arkle	Anne, Duchess of Westminster	P. Taaffe	T. Dreaper
1965	Arkle	Anne, Duchess of Westminster	P. Taaffe	T. Dreaper
1966	Stalbridge Colonist	Mr R. Blindell	S. Mellor	K. Cundell
1967	Rondetto	Mr A. Mitchell	J. King	R. Turnell
1968	Man of the West	Mr D. Drewery	G. W. Robinson	F. Walwyn
1969	Spanish Steps	Mr E. Courage	J. Cook	E. Courage
1970	Border Mask	Mrs Arnold	D. Mould	P. Cazalet
1971	Bighorn	Maj. Vernon-Miller	D. Cartwright	C. Vernon-Miller
1972	Charlie Potheen	Mrs B. Heath	B. Brogan	F. Walwyn
1973	Red Candle	Mrs C. O'Shea	J. Fox	G. Vallence
1974	Royal Marshal II	Mr J. Sumner	G. Thorner	T. Forster
1975	April Seventh	Mrs B. Meehan	A. Turnell	R. Turnell
1976	Zeta's Son	Mr M. Buckley	I. Watkinson	P. Bailey
1977	Bachelor's Hall	Mr P. Harris	M. O'Halloran	P. Cundell
1978	Approaching	Maj. D. Wigan	R. Champion	J. Gifford
1979	Fighting Fit		R. Linley	K. Oliver

Schweppes Gold Trophy (2m)

(Liverpool)

	HORSE	OWNER	RIDER	TRAINER
1963	Rosyth	Mr J. W. Sankey	J. Gifford	H. R. Price

(Newbury)

	HORSE	OWNER	RIDER	TRAINER
1964	Rosyth	Mr J. W. Sankey	J. Gifford	H. R. Price
1965	Elan	Mr R. Tucker	D. Nicholson	J. Sutcliffe
1966	Le Vermontois	Mrs S. Jones	J. Gifford	H. R. Price
1967	Hill House	Mr L. A. Colville	J. Gifford	H. R. Price
1968	Persian War	Mr H. Alper	J. Uttley	C. Davies
1969	*No Race*			
1970	*No Race*			
1971	Cala Mesquida	Mr Pontin	J. Cook	J. E. Sutcliffe
1972	Good Review	Mrs P. Burrell	V. O'Brien	J. Dreaper
1973	Indianapolis	Mr D. Wickens	J. King	J. E. Sutcliffe
1974	*No Race*			
1975	Tammuz	H.M. Queen Elizabeth	W. Smith	F. Walwyn
1976	Irish Fashion	Mrs N. O'Dowd	R. Barry	M. Cunningham
1977	True Lad	Mrs W. Swainson	T. Stack	W. Swainson
1978	*No Race*			
79	WITHIN THE LAW		A BROWN	M WEASTERBY
80	BOOTLACES		P LEACH	D BARRONS

NEWCASTLE (Group 1)

Attractively laid out in Gosforth Park, Newcastle's left-handed, triangular course of 1 mile 6 furlongs with its easy turns and uphill finish, makes heavy demands of stamina and courage. It is a very well-run course dating from 1839, with every amenity for the racegoer, including a paddock in front of the stands, and a number of attractive, competitive races.

They include the Bellway Fighting Fifth Handicap Hurdle (November, 2m 120y, £10,735), the Ladbroke Trophy H'cap Chase (January, 3m 6f, £3,843) and the Bacal Eider H'cap Chase (February, 4m 1f, £3,544).

Best Times

Distance	Time	Horse-age-weight	Date
2m 60y H	3m 42.30	Dondieu 6-11-7	27-10-71
2m 120y H	3m 53.40	Doonside 4-11-12	15-5-75
2½m H	4m 48.60	Sarona 4-10-9	27-10-71
3m H	5m 45	Pandolfi 4-10-1	25-10-70
2m 120y C	4m 1.40	Crofton Hall 8-12-3	30-4-77
2½m C	4m 54	Southern Lad 6-11-1	19-5-73
3m C	5m 48.10	Even Swell 8-10-4	30-10-75
3m C	5m 53.20	Slaves Dream 7-10-4	6-11-71
4m 350y C	8m 45.40	Vice Regent 7-9-12	8-2-64

Ladbroke Trophy H'cap Chase (3m 6f)

	HORSE	OWNER	RIDER	TRAINER
1974	Barona	Col. W. Whitbread	P. Kelleway	R. Armytage
1975	Tee-Cee-Bee	Mr T. C. Bell	Mr G. McMillan	Owner
1976	Forest King	Mr K. Hogg	R. Barry	Owner
1977	*No Race*			
1978	Rambling Jack	Maj. A. Baillie	J. J. O'Neill	J. K. M. Oliver

Bellway Fighting Fifth Hurdle (2m 120y)

	HORSE	OWNER	RIDER	TRAINER
1969	Mugatpura	Dr Desai	G. W. Robinson	F. Walwyn
1970	Inishmaan	Mr J. A. Dillon	T. Biddlecombe	T. F. Rimell
1971	Dondieu	Mrs C. Attwood	B. Fletcher	D. Smith
1972	Comedy of Errors	Mr E. Wheatley	W. Smith	T. F. Rimell
1973	Comedy of Errors	Mr E. Wheatley	W. Smith	T. F. Rimell
1974	Comedy of Errors	Mr E. Wheatley	K. White	T. F. Rimell
1975	Night Nurse	Mr R. Spencer	P. Broderick	M. H. Easterby
1976	Bird's Nest	Mr I. C. G. Scott	S. Knight	A. R. Turnell
1977	Bird's Nest	Mr I. C. G. Scott	A. Turnell	A. R. Turnell
1978	Sea Pigeon	Mr P. Muldoon	I. Watkinson	M. H. Easterby

NEWEY, Alfred (1882-1940)

Alf Newey, born at Halesowen, Worcestershire, started life as a miner and never rode until he was 18. He joined Tom Coulthwaite's Hednesford establishment and took out a licence in 1902. He quickly made his mark for besides being strong and brave and a powerful finisher, he used his head and was blessed with an imperturbable nature. He was also totally dependable. Stan Howard, for whom he won the 1907 Grand National on Eremon, said "Alf Newey never lets you down." It was a marvellous feat of horsemanship to win for he broke a stirrup leather at the second fence and rode the rest of the way without.

He also won:

The Lancashire Chase (1906) Theodocian;
    (1907) Eremon
The Stanley Chase (1910) Rathnally
The Liverpool Hurdle (1905) St Hubert;
    (1907) One Away
The Scottish Grand National (1906) Creolin

His best season was 1905 when he rode 41 winners and was second in the Jockeys' Table. He renewed his licence after World War I and won The Welsh Champion Hurdle (1923) on Assaroe. He afterwards trained at Hednesford but was not so successful although he won several races, including the Liverpool Foxhunters (1923) with Gracious Gift. He retired to Cleeve Hill near Cheltenham.

NEWTON ABBOT (Group 3)

Newton Abbot in Devonshire which dates from 1880, forms part of the West Country circuit. The track is left-handed, rectangular, quite flat and about one mile in length. The proximity of the river supplies a watering system which greatly assists the early and late-season racing but frequently threatens the mid-winter fixtures with waterlogging. The general level of prize money at this sporting, popular track is higher than might be expected but there are no big races. The most valuable are the Haccombe H'cap Chase (2m 5f), the Allen Park H'cap Chase (3m 2f 100y) and the Buckland H'cap Chase (2m 150y) all at the April meeting and all worth approximately £1400, and the Brixham H'cap Hurdle (May, 2m 5½f, £1,431).

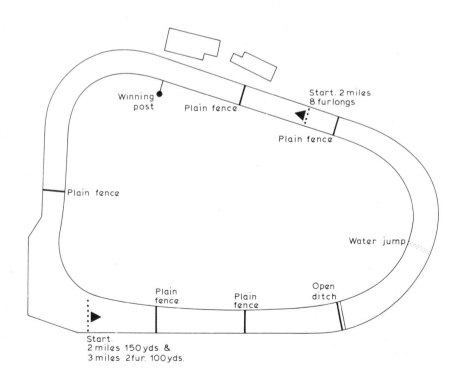

Winning post
Plain fence
Start. 2 miles 8 furlongs
Plain fence
Plain fence
Water jump
Plain fence
Plain fence
Open ditch
Start.
2 miles 150 yds. &
3 miles 2 fur. 100 yds.

Best Times

Distance	Time	Horse-age-weight	Date
2m 150y H	3m 50	El Basque 5-10-7	1-8-77
2m 5f H	5m 5.60	Seaward Bound 5-9-10	4-8-75
2m 5½f H	5m 10.20	Sarah's Choice 8-10-1	31-7-76
3m 2f H	6m 29	Hogan Hills 6-10-9	2-9-75
3m 2f 100 yds H	6m 29.80	Arctic Heir 9-11-2	24-5-78
2m 150y C	4m 1.60	Mighty Marine 7-11-13	10-9-76
2½m C	4m 43.60	Pay Pol 8-10-12	17-9-66
2m 5f C	5m 15	Captain George 7-11-1	31-7-76
3m 2f 105y C	6m 29.30	Pine Lodge 11-11-3	11-8-77

NICHOLSON, Clifford (1892-1972)

A successful farmer both in Lincolnshire and Natal, Mr Clifford Nicholson was a long-standing patron of National Hunt racing. He was a successful breeder, owner and, for a short while, trainer and he was a founder of the Injured Jockeys Fund.

His best horses were Doorknocker (*q.v.*) whom he bred (Champion Hurdle 1956), The Heron (*q.v.*), Stormhead (*q.v.*) (Emblem Chase, 1952 and 1953, and Topham Trophy, 1955), Witty (Haydock Park National Trial) and Billykin, whom he trained himself (Stanley Chase, 1947). He tried for years to win the National but the nearest he got was sixth with Limestone Edward in 1946.

He was regularly in the lists of Leading Owners (five times between 1948-49 to 1958-59) his best season being 1955-56 when he was second with 13 races worth £10,069.

He owned the Limestone Stud, Lincolnshire and the Tara Stud, Co. Meath. His trainers were himself, W. A. Hall and Paddy Sleator. Colours: grey, scarlet sleeves, collar, braid and cap.

NICHOLSON, David (b.1939)

If ever a man was born to ride steeplechasing it was long-legged David Nicholson, known as 'the Duke' who is descended on the one side from the Holmans (*q.v.*), Cheltenham's most-famous racing family, and on the other from one of the most distinguished race-riding tutors of the century. Nor did he disappoint expectations. He left school early to become apprenticed to his father and rode his first winner from his first ride at Chepstow in 1955.

Despite being exceptionally tall for a jockey, his fine hands and long legs stood him in good stead and he rose swiftly to the leading echelons of his profession. He regularly finished high up in the Jockeys' Table, his best season being 1966-67 when he rode 63 winners.

Although he rode the mighty Mill House, and won the 1967 Whitbread Gold Cup on him, it was in the twilight of that horse's sad career and he reckons the dual Mackeson Novice winner, Blessington Esquire, the best he ever rode.

He also won:

The Imperial Cup (1960) Farmers Boy
The Schweppes Gold Trophy (1965) Elan
The Welsh Grand National (1959) Limonali; (1960) Clover Bud; (1961) Limonali
The Tote Champion Novices (1971) Tantalum
The Stone's Ginger Wine Chase (1962) Rough Tweed

In 1968 he took out a licence to train while continuing to ride. His headquarters are Cotswold House, Condicote, where he has built up a strong team to run under both Rules. He gave up riding in 1972 in order to concentrate on training and after a slow start, looks like becoming equally successful in this branch of his profession. His principal successes have been with L'Escargot's half-brother, What a Buck, which he bought as a young horse for his principal patron, Lord Vestey, and has trained to win 11 races including the S.G.B. Chase (1975) and the Tote Northern Trophy (1976).

NICHOLSON, Herbert Denton Charles (b.1913)

'Frenchie' Nicholson's father was Master of the Pau Foxhounds and he was first apprenticed to C. Clouet in Chantilly from whence he derives his nickname. He then came to England and was transferred to Stanley Wootten (*q.v.*), an experience that stood him in good stead for the rest of his life.

He became a National Hunt Jockey of the highest class, his biggest successes being the 1942 Cheltenham Gold Cup on Medoc II for Lord Sefton, who remained a lifelong patron, the 1936 Champion Hurdle on Victor Norman and the 1947 Imperial Cup on Tant Pis. He also rode Golden Miller to several victories and would undoubtedly have won the 1937 Gold Cup on him, had it not fallen victim to the weather. In 1944-45 he shared the Jockeys' Championship with Fred Rimell.

He took out a licence to train in 1946 while continuing to ride, his biggest patron being Lord Sefton whose Irish Lizard won him four chases at Liverpool including the Topham Trophy and the Grand Sefton and was twice placed in the National. He also trained and rode Mr Fitz to win the 1947 Liverpool Hurdle.

He still trains at Prestbury but in recent years it is as a trainer of jockeys that he is best known. Among his legion successful protégés on the Flat are Paul Cook, Tony Murray and Pat Eddery, while for jumping he has turned out his son, David (*q.v.*), Brough Scott, Michael Dickinson and Tim Holland-Martin.

NICKEL COIN
Bay mare, 1942, Pay Up—Viscum (Walter Gay). Bred by Mr R. Corbett.

Nickel Coin was bought as a yearling for 50 guineas by Mr Jeffrey Royle but was sold on and then bought back after the war. She achieved some success as a show-jumper before being sent to Jack O'Donaghue's Reigate yard to be trained for chasing. She proved a resolute stayer and, as might be expected, a thoroughly reliable jumper and despite possessing little speed, had won six races including the Sandown Open Chase (1950) before achieving her last and most notable victory in the 1951 Grand National, 10-1 (J. Bullock), 40/1, by 6l, a bad third from Royal Tan, 10-13 (Mr A. O'Brien) and Derrinstown, 10-0 (A. Power). The first two were the only members of the 36-strong field to complete the course without incident. Nickel Coin was the thirteenth mare to win the National. At stud she bred three foals of whom King's

Nickel, a bay gelding, 1954, by Kingsmead, won four races.

NICOLAUS SILVER
Grey gelding, 1952, Nicolaus—Rays of Montrose (Montrose). Bred by Mr James Hefferman.

A strikingly handsome individual, Nicolaus Silver won two hurdle races and seven chases including the 1961 Grand National, 10-1 (H. Beasley), 28/1, by 5l, a neck, from Merryman II, 11-12 (D. Ancil) and O'Malley Point, 11-4 (P. A. Farrell). Just four weeks later he ran a splendid race to finish second to Pas Seul (gave 2lb) in the Whitbread Gold Cup.

Nicolaus Silver was originally submitted to the Newmarket October Yearling Sales but failed to make his reserve. He was therefore gelded and 'stored' until a three-year-old when he was broken, hunted and finally put into training with Dan Kirwan.

Nicolaus Silver won the National in the colours of Mr Charles Vaughan, on whose behalf Fred Rimell had bought him for £2,000 at Goffs Sales the previous November.

NIGHTINGALL, Arthur (1868-1944)
A member of the famous Epsom racing family, Arthur Nightingall was the son of trainer, John (*q.v.*).

The finest professional jockey of his day, he was noted for his coolness and judgement and his exceptional strength in a finish. After the close finish to the 1894 Grand National which he won on Why Not, correspondents claimed he could have won on any of the first three, a judgement which he hastened to refute.

He was a noted exponent of the 'lean-back' seat and his tall spare frame could be seen swinging gracefully back, almost touching the horse's quarters, as he landed over Aintree's drop-fences.

In all he won the National three times, his other victories being on Ilex (1890) and Grudon (1901).

Among his other big wins were:

The **Lancashire Chase** (1890) Ilex: (1898) Keelson
The **Scottish Grand National** (1894) Leyburn
The **Grand Sefton** (1893) Why Not
The **Liverpool Hurdle** (1890) Toscano
The **Grand International Chase** (1890) M.P.
The **Great Sandown Hurdle** (1900) Spook: (1901) Goldfinder

He also rode many winners in France, Austria and Germany, including the big chase in Baden-Baden on Pampero.

He subsequently became a fine trainer, taking over Priam Lodge from Jack Jones. His patrons included H.R.H. the Prince of Wales and Lord Marcus Beresford. He paid meticulous attention to horse management and to schooling, and his horses rarely fell. A gentle man himself with an aesthetic face and beautiful manners, he was widely loved and respected in Epsom and when he died his ashes were sprinkled over the Derby course. He wrote an excellent autobiography entitled *My Racing Adventures* published by T. Werner Laurie.

NIGHTINGALL, John

The father of the famous racing family, John Nightingall trained at South Hatch, Epsom, as did his son William and his grandson, Walter. He saddled two Grand National winners in Shifnal (1878) and Ilex (1890) who was ridden by his son Arthur (*q.v.*).

His son described him as "a very careful man with horses" and he possessed the intuitive eye of a real horsemaster. He believed in rigorous and regular schooling and the stable owned a private steeplechase and hurdle course at Walton Heath.

NIGHT NURSE

Bay gelding, 1971, Falcon—Florence Nightingale (Milesian). Bred by Cloghran Stud Farm.

Night Nurse was bought by trainer M. H. (Peter) Easterby for 1,300 guineas at the Newmarket Houghton Sales. Racing thereafter in the phenomenally successful colours of Mr Reg Spencer, he won three races on the Flat but was only moderate. He wore blinkers and achieved a Timeform rating of only 85.

However he proved a hurdler of exceptional merit and had by the end of 1976-77 won 18 of his 22 outings including an unprecedented 'grand slam' during the season 1975-6 of the Irish Sweeps Hurdle and the English, Scottish and Welsh Champion Hurdles.

In 1977 he repeated his victories in the English and Welsh Champion Hurdles. In 1976 at five years Night Nurse became the youngest Champion Hurdler since Kirriemuir in 1965.

Starting 2/1 favourite and ridden as usual by P. Broderick, he made all the running and won by 2½l, 8l, from Bird's Nest (A. Turnell) and Flash Imp (R. Mann). He thus preserved his trainer's remarkable record for the race in which his previous runners had been Saucy Kit, victorious in 1967, and Easby Abbey, second to Comedy of Errors in 1973.

In 1977, his reputation dinted by two consecutive mid-season defeats including a bewildering 15 lengths by Bird's Nest (subsequently attributed to damaged back muscles), Night Nurse went to the post for the Champion Hurdle only fourth favourite at 15/2. Bird's Nest, the Irish Sweeps winner Master Monday, and his Kempton conqueror, Dramatist, were all preferred in the betting. On heavy ground, Night Nurse (P. Broderick) ran a most resolute race, responding gamely to hard driving and held on by 2 lengths, the same, from Monksfield (T. Kinane) and Dramatist (W. Smith).

By the following season, age appeared to be dragging those flying feet. He won only one of his ten races, though placed seven times including third to Monksfield and Sea Pigeon in the Champion Hurdle. Moreover in his uncharacteristic fall at the last flight of the William Hill Christmas Hurdle, he lost the services of his old comrade-at-arms, Paddy Broderick, who was so badly concussed that he had to retire. After Night Nurse had run unplaced in a handicap at Newcastle in May, it was thought that he too might retire. However those who so thought had reckoned without the inborn horsemastership of Peter Easterby and the invigorating effects of a new challenge. Fences more than restored Night Nurse's zest for life and after unseating his rider on his debut, he won three chases in succession culminating in an Embassy Premier Chase (qualifier) by no less than a furlong from the far-from-useless Lord Greystoke.

NORMAN, Timothy (b.1944)

A West-country man, Tim Norman started riding as an amateur and rode his first winner at Fontwell in 1961. He then became attached to Fred Winter's stable for whom he won the 1966 Grand National on the 50/1 outsider Anglo.

NOTTINGHAM (Group 3)

Nottingham, a sharp, left-handed, oval

If modern steeplechasing has a man for all seasons, it is surely JOHN OAKSEY who, whether in the saddle, with his pen, with a microphone on television or as a Trustee of the Injured Jockeys Fund, has put the maximum energy and skill into the sport

The Master of Ballydoyle. The legendary VINCENT O'BRIEN who started training jumpers in a very modest way and rose with astonishing rapidity to bestride the 'fifties like a Colossus. Four Cheltenham Gold Cups and three Grand Nationals featured among his myriad victories. He then switched his attention totally to the Flat and, having a business acumen to match his training skill, has created a multi-million complex in the depths of Tipperary

JONJO O'NEILL, a young man who appears to possess the skill, courage and determination, all touched with genius, that characterized F. B. Rees, Martin Molony and Fred Winter. In 1977-8, his first season as a freelance, he rode a record 149 winners

A romantic study of a soldier-rider who was a very figure of romance, although he would have strongly deprecated the term. RODDY OWEN was one of the most distinguished amateurs of his day and after winning the Grand National applied for foreign service. He died of cholera in the desert on the Dongola campaign

Brave PERSIAN WAR a triple Champion Hurdler, dominated his branch of the sport for two-and-a-half seasons. He moved stables on several occasions but was always ridden by ace hurdles jockey, Jimmy Uttley

A very fine chaser whose opportunities were curtailed by World War I, POETHLYN nevertheless won the Grand National twice. He is pictured here with his regular jockey Ernie Piggott

The shrewd, seamed face of RYAN PRICE. Four times champion trainer in the 'fifties and 'sixties, he now concentrates almost entirely on the Flat. Nevertheless his few hurdlers are always regarded with much respect

A great supporter of steeplechasing, Mr J. V. RANK, seen here with his Flat trainer Noel Cannon

The king of Aintree. RED RUM, ears pricked and on the bridle, wins his third Grand National. Tommy Stack emits a whoop of triumph echoed by Ginger McCain's lads perched on the rails

(*Above left*) indisputably one of steeplechasing's all-time great jockeys, five times champion F. B. REES. (*Above right*) FRED RIMELL of Kinnersley has trained no less than four Grand National winners. He is one of only two men who head the N. H. lists both as a jockey (four times) and as a trainer (four times)

A family affair. Triumph for the Furlong family in the 1935 Grand National. Major Furlong (bowler hat) and his wife lead their horse REYNOLDSTOWN, trained by Major Furlong and ridden by their son Frank. Reynoldstown won again in 1936 but Frank could not do the weight so the ride was taken by his friend and brother officer, Fulke Walwyn

The first sponsored steeplechase. The 1957 running of the Whitbread Gold Cup, at SANDOWN. Mandarin (*left*, Gerry Madden) just leads Much Obliged (H. J. East) at the last. In an exciting finish Much Obliged prevailed by a neck. The famous white hunter-chaser, The Callant, had parted with Mr Scott-Aiton and his bridle much earlier in the proceedings

SIR KEN and Tim Molony who went through three seasons and 16 races including three Champion Hurdles undefeated. Note the length of leathers adopted by crack hurdle jockeys of the fifties

Frail, gentle GEORGE STEVENS from Cheltenham rode a record five Grand National winners. He was killed out hacking near his home on Cleeve Hill

Wootten trained BILLY STOTT was Champion Jockey five seasons running from 1927-32. His career was cut short by heart trouble

THE COLONEL, a fine-looking, almost black entire won the Grand National in 1869 and 1870. He was later exported to Germany as a stallion and founded a line of some influence

FULKE WALWYN, a former crack amateur rider forced to retire by injury, started training just before World War II and has been at the forefront of his profession for over 30 years. Since the death of Peter Cazalet he has handled the Queen Mother's horses

FRED WINTER, C.B.E., a man for whom superlatives pale in the face of his achievements. He was Champion Jockey four times and has topped the trainers' list seven times to date. He has ridden and trained the winner of every important race in the Calendar

course, 1½ miles round, dates from 1867 and is, like Leicester, a trainer's course providing mid-week racing, chiefly for novice and, less-than-top-class horses. Recently however, some imaginatively framed races have attracted better horses. Important races include The Nottingham Champion Chase (January, 2m, £1,746) which has twice been won by Tingle Creek, The Nottingham Novice Chase

(February, 2m, £1,746) and the Merit Hurdle, (3-y-o, November, 2m, £1,698).

It was at Nottingham that Stan Mellor rode his 1000th winner in this country on Ouzo on 18th December 1971. He is thought to be the first N.H. jockey to have achieved this feat, in commemoration of which The Ouzo Chase and The Stan Mellor Cup are staged at the December meeting.

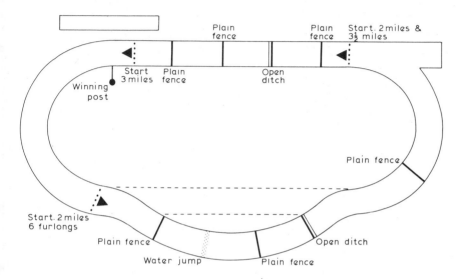

Best Times

Distance	Time	Horse-age-weight	Date
2m H	3m 39.50	Boy Marvel 4-11-7	22-5-78
2½m H	4m 44	Rupununi 8-11-12	29-10-63
2¾m H	5m 0.50	Given 5-10-0	23-5-76
2m C	3m 48	Stanway Lad 6-11-13	23-5-76
2¾m C	5m 15.60	Lothian Brig 13-11-7	22-5-78
3m C	6m 2.80	Auckland Girl 7-12-3	18-5-70
3½m C	6m 53.80	Bourdon 10-9-13	23-5-76

NOTTING HILL

The Notting Hill Hippodrome, London, was the brain-child of Mr John Whyte. Built on 200 acres of meadowland rented from a Mr Ladbroke, it ran parallel to the Portobello Road and was the first modern chase course, boasting three tracks, one for Flat, one for hurdles and chases and one for training. The chase course was approximately 2½ miles in length and intersected by natural brooks and hedges. The middle of the course featured a natural mound which provided a primitive grandstand and other amenities included 75 boxes, near the

present Underground station, an enclosure round the whole area and a "large space . . . railed in and allotted to persons on foot where they can enjoy the various amusements on offer without danger of molestation".

The course opened in 1837 and Lottery won a chase on the opening day. Unhappily the venture was not a success financially and in 1841 the land was sold for building. The Kensington and Chelsea Public Library owns a set of Henry Alken prints representing the last chase run there.

NOVICE

For the purposes of hurdle races, a novice is a horse which has not won a hurdle race at the time of starting *or* at the time of closing; and for steeplechases, a horse that has not won a steeplechase at the time of starting *or* at the time of closing.

NUGENT, Sir Charles, 5th Bart (1847-1927)

A second son, Sir Charles succeeded his brother Sir Hugh in 1863 when the latter accidentally shot himself. He rode as an amateur and lost a great deal of money betting.

In 1896 he began training at Cranborne, Dorset. He won the Grand Sefton (1899) with Hidden Mystery which was ridden by his son, Hugh, and in 1903 he saddled Drumcree to win the National. Drumcree was also to have been ridden by Hugh who had been second on him in 1901 but he was injured and replaced by Percy Woodland. Hugh Nugent was killed from a fall in a hurdle race at Ostend later that year. Sir Charles later moved to Bourton-on-the-Hill and thence to Lambourn.

OAKSEY
See TREVETHIN AND OAKSEY.

O'BRIEN, V.
Val O'Brien is a young Irish jockey attached to Jim Dreaper's stable. His major successes include the Massey-Ferguson Gold Cup (1971) with Leap Frog, the Schweppes Gold Trophy (1972) with Good Review, and the Embassy Premier Chase Final (1971) with Leap Frog and (1972) with Colebridge.

O'BRIEN, Michael Vincent (b.1917)
Vincent O'Brien, who rode as an amateur before taking out a licence in 1944, is a shrewd, dedicated, planning man, a perfectionist, who would have succeeded in whatever profession he had essayed. A man who had sufficient vision to persuade his first patron to buy for £3,500 a horse that two vets had spun for his wind and one for a foreleg. That horse was Cottage Rake who won for O'Brien three successive Cheltenham Gold Cups (1948, 1949 and 1950) and the King George VI Chase (1948).

It was the start of one of the most amazing decades in chasing history. During it O'Brien won a fourth Gold Cup with Knock Hard (1953), three Champion Hurdles (1949, 1950 and 1951) with Hatton's Grace, three successive Grand Nationals with Early Mist (1953), Royal Tan (1954) and Quare Times (1955) and no less than 10 divisions of the Gloucester Hurdle.

He was the first man to airlift horses to save them the fatigues of the long sea and rail journey, he was the first also to weigh them regularly which enabled him to gauge how much any race had taken out of them.

In 1959 he abandoned N.H. racing entirely in order to devote himself to the Flat and apart from a spell in 1960 when he briefly lost his licence after dope tests on Chamier had proved positive, his career has been one unbroken run of success. He has won 30 classics including five Derbys with Larkspur (1962), Sir Ivor (1968), Nijinsky (1970), Roberto (1972) and The Minstrel (1977) and the Triple Crown with Nijinsky, a feat which had not been achieved since before the war.

Chamier's subsequent performances in the Gallinule Stakes and the Irish Derby suggested that he was scarcely in need of stimulant to win a maiden plate.

O'DONAGHUE, J.
Jack O'Donaghue, a soft-spoken, twinkling Irishman, rode in point-to-points and was apprenticed to Jack Lombard in Ireland before taking out a licence to train in 1948. He has a small yard in Reigate, Surrey from which he sent Nickel Coin out to win the 1951 Grand National.

He used to number H.M. the Queen Mother among his owners, handling any of her horses which were not suited to the Fairlawne regime and had notable success with the fretful Gay Record with whom he secured Her Majesty's hundredth victory.

OLD JOE
Bay gelding, 1879, Barefoot—Spot (Chevalier d' Industrie). Bred by Mr E. H. Banks.

Old Joe won 13 races including the United Kingdom Chase, Croydon (1889) and the 1886 Grand National, 10-9 (T. Skelton), 25/1, by 6l, 5l, from Too Good, 11-12 (Mr H. Beasley) and Gamecock, 10-12 (W. E. Stephens).

A tissue of romance has shrouded his career, most of which is palpably untrue. He was neither Irish nor a half-bred and it is extremely unlikely that he ever pulled a cart or engaged in any show-jumping. On the contrary he was a registered thoroughbred, born in Cumberland, hunted with the Dumfriesshire hounds by Mr Joseph Graham, after whom he was named and was then sold again, this time to Mr A. J. Douglas, in whose colours he won the National. Henceforth he was trained at Burgh-by-Sands by George Mulcaster, and usually ridden by leading amateur, Capt. 'Wenty' Hope-Johnstone. It is presumed that Capt. Hope-Johnstone was not able to do the weight for the National.

The winter of 1886 was extremely severe and Old Joe was one of the few runners able to enjoy an uninterrupted preparation.

OLD TAY BRIDGE

Chestnut gelding, 1914, Bridge of Earn—Broken Reed (Tredennis). Bred by Mr A. Lowry.

A consistent, unlucky horse owned by Mrs W. H. Dixon, Old Tay Bridge won 10 races including the National Trial Chase, Gatwick (1926). He was favourite for the 1925 National when finishing second, beaten four lengths to Double Chance. He was second again in 1926 this time beaten three lengths by Jack Horner and was also second, beaten four lengths by Koko, in the 1926 Cheltenham Gold Cup.

OLIVER, James Kenneth Murray (b.1914)

A former successful amateur rider whose biggest success was to win the Scottish Grand National (1950) on Sanvina, Ken Oliver took out a permit in 1959 and a full licence in 1960 and is currently one of the most successful trainers in the north of England.

He is also a farmer, an active member of his local hunt, Chairman and Managing-Director of Andrew Oliver and Son, Auctioneers and Estate Agents, and a Partner in Doncaster Bloodstock, so inevitably much of the training is done by his wife, who as Miss Rhona Wilkinson, bred and produced Wyndburgh (q.v.).

The stable at Hawick, Roxburghshire, regularly turns out a high percentage of winners and its victories include:

The Scottish Grand National (1963) Pappageno's Cottage; (1970) The Spaniard; (1971) Young Ash Leaf

The Eider Chase (1970) China Cloed

The Fred Withington Chase (1963) Pappageno's Cottage; (1964) Pappageno's Cottage

The Benson and Hedges Gold Cup (1970) Even Keel

The Greenall Whitley Handicap Chase (1972) Young Ash Leaf; (1973) Tregarron; (1975) The Benign Bishop

The Heinz Chase (1971) Bobby Corbett

The Tote Northern Trophy H'cap Chase (1975) The Benign Bishop

The Mildmay Chase (1975) Tom Morgan

The Ladbroke Northern H'cap Chase (1978) Rambling Jack

OLLIVER, Tom (d.1874)

Swarthy-faced and black-haired, of Spanish-gypsy blood, gay, brave and generous, hopeless with money and women and brilliant at riding horses across country, Tom Olliver stands head-and-shoulders above the personalities of nineteenth-century jumping.

He was born in Sussex, one of a family of 16. There was no money, no schooling and very often no shoes in the Oliver family (Tom added the extra 'l', feeling it as well to have an extra £ at hand!) but Tom could do anything with horses and soon worked his way into the burgeoning world of hunting and steeplechasing.

His phenomenal success brought him fame but not fortune, although fortunes could be made, as litigation in which he was involved, shows. Against a background of stableboys earning £10 a year, top-flight jockeys expected £5 a ride and £10 a winner while for an important victory in which a gamble had been landed, £50 was considered reasonable.

But Olliver, who would put his hand into his pocket for every chance-met beggar when he was in funds was permanently on the verge of bankruptcy and was frequently imprisoned for debt. Usually the officers of the locally stationed regiments, many of whom he coached in the art of cross-country riding, came to his aid during these confinements. To one request from an Oxfordshire regiment who enquired how they might serve him, he replied characteristically: "Send me a d——d good wall-jumper."

He won the Grand National three times, in 1842 on Gay Lad, 1843 on Vanguard and 1853 on Peter Simple. He was also second three times and third once, and won the Liverpool Steeplechase at Maghull in 1838 on Sir Henry. Other important victories included, The Cheltenham steeplechase, 1841 on Grayling (dead-heating with William Holman on Xeno).

For a time he was landlord of 'The Star' at Leamington, but later he moved to Prestbury, near Cheltenham, where he became an important figure.

He coached a bevy of Cheltenham-based jockeys including Tommy Pickernell, George Stevens, William Holman, William Archer and 'Josie' Little, who repaid him by beating him ½l on Chandler for the 1848 National. He also coached a rebel Cheltenham schoolboy who hero-worshipped him. Adam Lindsay-Gordon later immortalized him in his racy ballads of hunting and chasing.

> He cares not for the bubbles of fortune's fickle tide
> Who like Bendigo can battle and like Olliver can ride.

Later in life he became a trainer with headquarters at Wroughton and proved himself just as skilful in that branch of his profession. He handled the 1874 Derby winner, George Frederick, although he died without seeing the fruits of the victory, leaving the honour and his priceless store of knowledge to his head-lad, Tom Leader.

His wit never deserted him. Later in life he returned to the lengthy query of a fussy owner over the staying capacity of an extremely slow horse with the glorious reply: "Honoured Sir, your horse can stay four miles but takes a h—l of long time to do it."

O'NEILL, John Joe (b.1952)

'Jonjo' O'Neill was apprenticed to M. Conolly for three years and rode his first winner at the Curragh in 1970. He came to England in 1973 and was attached to Gordon Richards' Penrith stable.

His strong, stylish brand of riding made its mark immediately and his services were much in demand. After Ron Barry had left the stable in the autumn of 1975 he took over as first jockey and had a marvellous season riding 64 winners to finish fourth in the Jockeys' Table, despite an injury in April which grounded him for the rest of the season. At the beginning of the 1977-78 season he parted amicably from Gordon Richards and went freelance. Those who wondered whether he would be able to maintain his position without the support of a big, powerful stable were answered in brilliant fashion when he rode a record 149 winners. During the afternoon in which he passed Ron Barry's previous record, he rode five winners at Perth. His prodigious strength and unquenchable will to win are reminiscent of Fred Winter and barring injuries he seems likely to dominate N.H. racing for some time to come.

His principal successes have been:

The Scottish Champion Hurdle (1977) Sea Pigeon; (1978) Sea Pigeon

The Daily Express Triumph Hurdle (1976) Peterhof

The Allied Manufacturing H'cap Hurdle (1977) Sea Pigeon

The Stone's Ginger Wine H'cap Chase (1974) Erring Burn

The Yellow Pages Pattern H'cap Chase (1976) Canadius

The Greenall Whitley H'cap Chase (1978) Rambling Artist

O'RYAN, Robert Joseph

An Irish jockey who won the 1946 Champion Hurdle on Distel.

OSBORNE, Joseph

Joseph Osborne was an influential figure in early chasing circles. He owned and trained Abd-el-Kader, the dual National winner whom his father bred.

He was also a journalist who contributed to *Bell's Life*, wrote *The Horse-breeders Handbook* and edited a Steeplechase Calendar throughout the 1850s which serves as a link between Mr Henry Wright's Calendar, 1826-40, and the official *Steeplechases Past*, which began in 1866.

O'TOOLE, Michael A. (b.1931)

The large, genial, flamboyant figure of Co. Kildare trainer Mick O'Toole is a comparatively new one to British racecourses and one whose presence is increasingly making itself felt. The former greyhound trainer first took out a licence in 1966 and from small beginnings has assembled a large and talented team. He deals and gambles on a large scale and during the past few seasons has been winning races to match.

His chief triumphs include:

The Cheltenham Gold Cup (1977) Davy Lad

The Sun Alliance Novices Hurdle (1975) Davy Lad; (1976) Parkhill

The Lloyds Bank Hurdle (1976) Bit of a Jig

The Lloyds Bank Champion Novice Hurdle (1976) Mac's Chariot

The National Hunt Chase (1978) Gay Tie

He also trains on the Flat and won the Ascot Stakes (1972) with Belios. His first jockey-cum-assistant, cum-head-lad is D. T. ('Dessie') Hughes (*q.v.*).

OUR HOPE

Grey gelding, 1929, registered Miss Prior's Half-Bred Stud Book, Son and Heir—Here's Hoping (Irawaddy). Bred by Mr W. E. Robinson.

Our Hope, who was owned and trained by Mr R. Gubbins, won three Flat races and six hurdle races including the 1938 Champion Hurdle (Capt. R. Harding), 5/1, by 1½l, 10l. from Chuchoteur (M. Plaine) and Lobau (H. Nicholson). In the previous year he had run second to Free Fare.

OWEN, Maj. E. R., D.S.O. (1856-96)

'Roddy' Owen was one of the most famous military riders of all time. He was born in Prestbury near Cheltenham and he and his brother grew up with horses and hunted with the Cotswold, along with the Archers, the Holmans, Tom Olliver and Adam Lindsay-Gordon.

He was commissioned into the 20th (East Devonshire) Regiment and later transferred to the Lancashire Fusiliers. He did ten years strenuous soldiering, serving in Canada, Cyprus, Malta and India and served as A.D.C. to both the Viceroy of India and the Lord-Lieutenant of Ireland before returning to England to embark on a race-riding career. This he tackled with characteristic energy and success and in the period 1882-92, it is estimated that he rode 254 winners from 812 mounts. Inevitably his military duties were neglected and on one occasion when nominally stationed at Aldershot, he encountered his Divisional Commander, General Sir Evelyn Woods, who greeted him frostily with: "Captain Owen, I have been here two months and have not yet had the pleasure of your acquaintance." To which the recalcitrant captain, rarely lost for words, replied: "My loss General, not yours."

His principal victories included:

The National Hunt Chase (1887) Monkswood
The Grand International Chase (1889) Kilworth
The Sandown Grand Prize (1890) Francisca; (1891) Maypole
The Grand Military Gold Cup (1889) St Cross

He also won this race in 1887 on H.R.H. the Prince of Wales's Hohenlinden but to the considerable embarrassment of the authorities, Hohenlinden was objected to, on the grounds of his owner not being a serving officer, which the stewards had perforce to uphold.

In 1891 he was second in the Grand National on Cloister, beaten ½ length by Harry Beasley on Come Away, after a piece of over-opportunist riding which Beasley neatly thwarted despite his opponent's vociferous rage.

The following year he finally attained his ambition and brought Father O'Flynn home 20 lengths clear of Cloister. He promptly caught the next train to London and applied for foreign service. He served with Colonel Francis Scott's Gold Coast Constabulary, in the Chitral campaign in India and the Dongola campaign in Egypt. On this last campaign, cholera set in as he recorded in his journal: "I am seated on a rock, surrounded with desert, the only European here with seven cases of cholera on the 5th, 6th and 7th July (1896) but I think we've tackled it. . . . We must stick to Khartoum and bar European complications, the dream of Cecil Rhodes looks likely of accomplishment."

He died the following day and was buried in the desert. The Moslems levelled his grave and marked it with stones, a rare compliment to a Christian soldier.

OWEN, George Richard (b.1907)

George Owen rode with great success as an amateur from 1925-33 and as a professional from 1933-39. His victories included the Cheltenham Foxhunters (1930) on Melleray's Belle, the Champion Chase (1939) on The Professor and the Cheltenham Gold Cup (1939) on Brendan's Cottage.

After the war he took out a licence to train, at first from his Cheshire farm and later from the Cholmondley Castle stables.

His winners included:

The National Hunt Chase (1968) Fascinating Forties
The Grand National (1949) Russian Hero
The National Hunt Two Mile Champion Chase (1963) Sandy Abbott
The Champion Novices Chase (1960) Sandy Abbott
The Great Yorkshire Chase (1961) Chavara
The Haydock Park National Trial (1960) Highland Dandy; (1964) Reproduction
The Mildmay Chase (1968) Brian's Best

He also has the distinction of having produced, from amateurs, three Champion Jockeys in Dick Francis, Tim Brookshaw and Stan Mellor. He relinquished his licence to train in 1976.

OWNERS, LEADING

Owner	Horses	Races	
1940-41 Miss D. Paget	12	15	£ 1,325
1941-42 Mr V. Smyth	2	5	£950
1942-45 *No Racing*			
1945-46 Mr J. Morant	1	2	£9,001
1946-47 Mr J. J. McDowell	1	1	£10,007
1947-48 Mr J. Proctor	3	5	£9,801
1948-49 Mr Williamson	1	4	£10,350
1949-50 Mrs L. Brotherton	4	8	£14,294
1950-51 Mr J. Royle	1	3	£10,221
1951-52 Miss D. Paget	19	50	£14,191
1952-53 Mr J. H. Griffin	2	2	£10,015
1953-54 Mr J. H. Griffin	3	4	£10,457
1954-55 Mrs W. H. E. Welman	1	1	£8,934
1955-56 Mrs L. Carver	1	5	£10,683
1956-57 Mrs G. Kohn	1	2	£9,618
1957-58 Mr D. J. Coughlan	1	1	£13,719
1958-59 Mr J. E. Bigg	1	3	£14,558
1959-60 Miss W. H. S. Wallace	1	1	£13,134
1960-61 Mr C. Vaughan	1	2	£20,700
1961-62 Mr N. Cohen	2	3	£20,852
1962-63 Mr P. B. Raymond	1	2	£22,095
1963-64 Mr J. K. Goodman	1	1	£20,280
1964-65 Mrs M. Stephenson	1	4	£23,237
1965-66 Anne, Duchess of Westminster	1	4	£24,572
1966-67 Mr C. P. T. Watkins	1	1	£17,630
1967-68 Mr H. S. Alper	3	7	£18,240
1968-69 Mr B. P. Jenks	8	25	£20,618
1969-70 Mr E. R. Courage	6	14	£20,001
1970-71 Mr F. Pontin	3	5	£24,999
1971-72 Capt. T. A. Forster	2	3	£26,302
1972-73 Mr N. H. le Mare	3	8	£34,196
1973-74 Mr N. H. le Mare	2	7	£37,386
1974-75 Mr R. Guest	1	1	£38,005
1975-76 Mr P. B. Raymond	1	2	£45,325
1976-77 Mr N. H. le Mare	1	2	£41,791
1977-78 Mrs O. Jackson	3	13	£49,791

OXO

Bay gelding, 1951, Bobsleigh—Patum (Portlaw). Bred in Dorset by Mr A. C. Wyatt.

A strongly-built, old-fashioned stamp of chaser, Oxo was brought as a yearling for 400 guineas by Mr Geoffrey Mason for whom he won two point-to-points as a six-year-old. Mr Mason then submitted him to the Newmarket October Sales where he caused something of sensation by realizing £3,200 guineas. His new owner Mr J. Bigg sent Oxo to the Royston stables of Willie Stephenson from whence he was sent out to win five chases including the 1959 Grand National, 10-13 (M. Scudamore), 8/1, by 1½l, 8l, from Wyndburgh, 10-12 (T. Brookshaw) and Mr What, 11-9 (P. Taaffe). Oxo broke down in preparation for the 1960 National. He continued to race for three more seasons but failed to win again.

National double. She bred the 1956 Champion Hurdler Merry Deal, and it was at her Ballymacoll Stud that Arkle was foaled in 1957.

Her trainers included Basil Briscoe, Owen Anthony, Fulke Walwyn, Charlie Rogers and 'Frenchie' Nicholson. Although she did some unpopular things early in her career and undoubtedly treated Basil Briscoe very badly, her later trainers speak of her with warmth and no one has filled the gap her death left.

PAGE, John

Warwickshire-born John Page was apprenticed to William Day of Danebury but became too heavy for Flat-racing and switched to steeplechasing with great success. Together with Robert I'Anson he was reckoned to be the best of his generation. He rode a good deal for the Duke of Hamilton for whom he won the 1867 Grand National on Cortolvin. He won again in 1872 on the little-considered Casse Tête and also won the Grand Steeplechase de Paris twice, in 1875 on La Veine and in 1878 on Wild Monarch.

PAGET, Hon. Dorothy Wyndham (1906-60)

Daughter of the 1st Lord Queenborough, rich beyond the dreams of avarice, eccentric, one of the heaviest betters of her generation, both imperious and morbidly shy, devastatingly capricious yet capable of endearing loyalty, Dorothy Paget numbers among chasing's most remarkable patrons. A fine all-round horsewoman in her youth, she hunted, showed and point-to-pointed until she grew too heavy. She was lured into steeplechasing by the success of her cousin, Mr 'Jock' Hay Whitney and remained a lavish supporter until her death.

She won the Cheltenham Gold Cup seven times, five times with Golden Miller (1932-36), Roman Hackle (1940) and Mont Tremblant (1952). She also won the Grand National with Golden Miller (1934) and the Champion Hurdle four times, in 1932 and 1933 with Insurance, 1940 with Solford and 1946 with Distel. She won a total of 1,532 races and was Leading Owner three times, 1933-34, 1940-41 and 1951-52.

She also won a wartime Derby with Straight Deal and remains the only woman to have achieved the Derby-

PARDUBITZ STEEPLECHASE

The Gran Pardubitz Steeplechase was founded in 1874 and is Eastern Europe's equivalent to the Grand National. It is held in Czechoslovakia, in a part that used to be Bohemia, about 25 miles east of Prague. It is run over four miles of complex, unrailed, country, including long stretches of plough and there are 29 fences including open waters, banks, post and rails and the notorious Taxis fence which consist of a hedge five feet high and six feet wide flanking 16 feet of water. It is quite common for the whole field to be felled by this obstacle and although the riders usually remount, there have been two occasions, 1909 and 1920, when the race has been declared void because no one finished within the time limit. Two Russian winners, Gyi Lovam (1927) and Grifel (1960) came to try their luck in our Grand National but neither completed.

English horses and riders used to compete regularly and the first running was won by an English jockey, Sayers, on Frantome. However after World War I such ventures died out until 1973 when Chris Collins decided to challenge for it with his slow but reliable hunter-chaser, Stephens Society. It was a brave venture, richly repaid and he became the first Englishman to win for over half a century. He returned in 1974 and finished third, despite two falls.

PARFREMONT, Georges (d.1923)

Georges Parfremont is the only French jockey to have won the Grand National, which he did in 1909 at his first attempt on M. James Hennessy's Lutteur III. A very strong jockey, he won the Grand Steeple three times, in 1909 on St Caradec (beating Jerry M.), 1911 on Blagueur II and 1913 on Ultimatum. He also won the Grand International Chase, Sandown (1915) on Lord Marcus, and

(1919) on Mask Off and the Imperial Cup (1923) on North Waltham. Barely a month later he was killed in a fall at Enghien from a horse called Field Marshal.

PAS DE QUATRE
Bay mare, 1938. Bred by Mr F. Darling.

			Swynford
		Blandford	
	Royal Dancer		Blanche
			Royal Realm
		Queen of the Ballet	
Pas De Quatre			Lady Lightfoot
			Prunus
		Weissdorn	
	Baroness II		Weiner Maedel
			Teddy
		American Beauty	
			Maillezais

Pas de Quatre, who was bred by the famous Beckhampton trainer, Fred Darling, is the only mare to have bred two individual Gold Cup winners, namely, Gay Donald (1955) and Pas Seul (1960). She was choicely bred, being a daughter of the good race mare Baroness VI, who won 14 races in France, but, because of the war, was sold cheaply to Wiltshire farmer Harry Frank as a yearling.

Some years after the birth of Gay Donald, Harry Franks gave Pas de Quatre to that horse's owner Mr Burt. Although she had been covered by Erin's Pride, she had frequently shown herself to be in use and had twice been certified as empty. During the spring of 1953 she took part in three Hunter-trials and two ladies' point-to-points, ridden by Mr Burt's girl groom. Mr Burt then died and Harry Franks gave the mare to Bob Turnell (q.v.) who sent her to the Littleton Stud where she was covered by Royal Tara. A few weeks later she gave birth to Pas Seul. The foal was given back to the Franks and was later brought from them by Bob Turnell on behalf of Mr John Rogerson. Apart from her Gold Cup winners she bred three fillies by Henry Tudor (1948), Your Fancy (1951), Erin's Pride (1952), and a filly and two geldings by Domaha of whom Travel Alone (1956), won as a four-year-old and seemed promising but who afterwards became difficult to train.

PAS SEUL
Bay or brown gelding, 1953, Erin's Pride—Pas de Quatre (Royal Dancer). Bred by Mr H. Frank.

The romantic background to Pas Seul is told under the entry of his dam Pas de Quatre. A half-brother to the 1955 Gold Cup winner, Gay Donald, he won two hurdle races and 15 chases including the Champion Novices, Manchester (1958), the Whitbread Gold Cup, Sandown (1961) and the 1960 Cheltenham Gold Cup (W. Rees), 6/1, by 1l, 5l, from Lochroe (D. Mould) and Zonda (G. W. Robinson). Pas Seul was clear when he fell at the last in the 1959 Gold Cup and ran third to Arkle and Mill House in 1964.

At his peak Pas Seul, who was owned by Mr John Rogerson and trained by Bob Turnell, was a very high-class horse indeed. Unfortunately he broke down during the 1962 Whitbread Gold Cup, missed the whole of the next season and never recovered his former brilliance.

PASSPORT
A racehorse passport is the approved diagrammatic document of identity issued on the authority of the Stewards of the Jockey Club or that of any recognized Turf authority.

PATHFINDER
Bay gelding, 1867, not in the General Stud Book, by Mogador.

Not a great deal is known about the 1875 Grand National winner Pathfinder. He was the last of Tommy Pickernell's five winning rides and carrying 10-11, won by ½l, 3l, from Dainty, 11-0 (Mr Hathaway) and La Venie, 11-12 (J. Page).

Pathfinder was very lightly raced and appears to have only won two other races. At one stage he was owned by Mr Coupland, Master of the Quorn hounds, and regularly carried the huntsman Tom Firr. However, he ran at Aintree in the colours of Mr T. H. Bird and the Marquis of Huntly.

Tommy Pickernell afterwards reported that Pathfinder was so blown by Becher's on the second circuit that had he been on his own, he would have pulled up.

PATRON SAINT
Brown gelding, 1923, St Girons—V.M.C. (Common). Bred by Mr A. B. Barrow.

A precocious youngster owned first by Colonel Foljambe and then by Mr F. W. Keen, Patron Saint had won eight chases before his sixth birthday. The most important of these were the National Hunt Juvenile Chase (1927) and the 1928 Cheltenham Gold Cup (F. Rees), 7/2, by 4l, 2l, from Vive (L. Rees) and Koko (P. Powell). Koko, who had won the race the previous year, was favourite at 4/5 and ran greatly below expectations. He was afterwards found to have broken a small blood vessel. Patron Saint thereafter became difficult to train. He ran very seldom and won only one more race. He was trained by H. Harrison.

PAYNE, W. H. (1891-1961)

Bill Payne was the son of a prosperous Essex farmer and M.F.H. He came into racing via hunting and at one stage whipped-in to Percy Whitaker with the Oakley Hounds.

He was Champion Jockey in 1911 riding 76 winners and his principal successes included the Grand Sefton (1912) on Carsey, the Champion Chase (1911) on Rory O'Moore and the Stanley Chase (1909) on Autocar. He afterwards trained, first at Burgh Lodge, Epsom, and latterly at Seven Barrows, Lambourn. He retired in 1954.

His principal patron was Mrs Hollins for whom he trained Blaris to win the first Champion Hurdle (1927) and the Coventry Cup (N.H. Meeting) and Colliery Band (Champion Chase and Molyneux Chase). After World War II he concentrated on the Flat and saddled Tangle to beat Abernant in the King's Stand Stakes at Ascot. His son Bill was also a successful steeplechase jockey and took over his stable in 1954.

PELLERIN, Georges Augustin

Georges Pellerin was a very fine hurdles rider who won the 1937 Champion Hurdle on Free Fare. He also won the Imperial Cup (1931) on Residue, the Liverpool Hurdle (1933) on Free Fare, the Coventry Cup (1930) on Blaris and the County Hurdle (1930) on Gone Dry.

PENDIL

Bay gelding, 1965, Pendragon—Diliska (Distinctive). Bred by Mr R. E. Bebb.

A neat, athletic-looking horse, Pendil won six hurdle races and 21 chases including the Arkle Challenge Trophy, N.H. Meeting (1972), the Massey-Ferguson Gold Cup, Cheltenham (1973)

and the King George VI Chase, Kempton, twice (1972 and 1973).

Between the autumn of 1971 and the end of season 1973-74 he was only beaten twice. The Dikler beat him a short head in the 1973 Gold Cup, while in the 1974 running of that race, he was brought down at the second last when in third place and having every chance.

Pendil's early efforts on a racecourse did not lead anyone to suppose that he was a budding champion. He won a novice hurdle at Catterick in October 1968 and was sent up to Ascot Sales where Fred Winter bought him for 1,800 guineas on behalf of Mrs C. Kinney. The following season he won two handicap hurdles and a further three hurdle races in 1970-71, including the Cheltenham Trial Hurdle following the disqualification of Dondieu, but he was far from invincible and had once or twice appeared not to relish a struggle.

Pendil broke down in February 1975 when finishing third in the Yellow Pages Pattern Chase at Kempton. The injury kept him off the course for 22 months but then, nursed back to soundness with the skill we have come to expect from his trainer, he reappeared at Kempton, his favourite course, to win a 2½-mile chase with much of his old élan. He won two more races but just as another chance at his bogey race, the Cheltenham Gold Cup, became a distinct possibility, he slipped up on the road, damaged his neck and had to be retired.

A fast, fluent jumper with a rare turn of foot he stood head and shoulders above his contemporaries at distances of 2½-3 miles. Whether he also possessed the stamina to last out the extra two furlongs of the Cheltenham Gold Cup remains a matter of conjecture as recurring leg trouble has now terminated his career. Pendil was always ridden by stable jockey, Richard Pitman.

PERMIT

Persons wishing to train only for themselves, their wives, sons, parents or unmarried daughters, may do so under permit. The scheme was introduced in season 1948-49. In 1963-64 a permit became necessary to run horses in Hunter Steeplechases. As ladies were not at the time permitted to hold licences or permits, considerable hardship was caused to several ladies who had prepared such horses for years, including Miss Lucy Jones and Mrs Jackie Brutton. Since 1966 ladies have been permitted to hold licences or permits. A restricted permit confines their runners to amateur races but once they have trained a winner and their premises have been approved by a Jockey Club inspector, they have the same facilities as a licensed trainer. The most notable permit-holder in recent years is Mr Edward Courage (*q.v.*). It is not necessary to have a permit in order to run horses in steeplechases confined to hunters or for the Grand Military Gold Cup.

PERMIT-HOLDERS ASSOCIATION
The Permit-Holders Association was founded in 1973 under the Chairmanship of Mr W. Shand-Kydd with Mr M. J. Thorne as Vice-Chairman. The Council consists of seven area representatives (one of whom is Mr Thorne) and two co-opted members.

The Association has a secretariat at 42 Portman Square, London W.1. Recently it has achieved something of a breakthrough for its members with regard to restricted permits. Previously it was necessary to train a winner for the granting of a full permit even to be considered, which, as the races open to horses trained by holders of such permits are extremely limited, particularly in the early part of the season, created a considerable problem. The Jockey Club have now agreed to drop this condition provided the applicant has proved himself competent and fulfils the other necessary requirements.

PERSIAN WAR
Bay gelding, 1963, Persian Gulf—Warning (Chanteur II). Bred by the Astor Studs.

One of three horses to win the Champion Hurdle three times (the others were Hatton's Grace and Sir Ken) Persian War won twice on the Flat at three years when trained by Tom Masson, who then sold him for £3,000 to Mr David Naylor-Leyland. He won three times for his new owner before being sold again to Mr Henry Alper who moved him to the Epsom stables of Brian Swift.

In all Persian War won 18 hurdle races and apart from his Champion Hurdle victories which are set out below, he won every big event in the Calendar including the *Daily Express* Triumph Hurdle, Cheltenham (1967), the Schweppes Gold Trophy, Newbury (1968), the Welsh Champion Hurdle, Chepstow (1969), and the Irish Sweeps Hurdle, Leopardstown (1970). He won the Champion Hurdle in:

1968 (J. Uttley), 4/1, by 4l, 5l, from Chorus (A. Turnell) and Black Justice (B. Scott).
1969 (J. Uttley), 6/4f, by 4l, 2½l, from Drumikill (B. Brogan) and Privy Seal (J. Cook).
1970 (J. Uttley), 5/4f, by 1½l, the same, from Major Rose (J. Gifford) and Escalus (D. Mould).

Persian War was trained by Colin Davis during the peak of his career. Later he was moved to Arthur Pitt, from thence to Dennis Rayson and lastly to Jack Gibson. Never a brilliant jumper, he won most of his races from his bottomless reserves of stamina and courage. Jimmy Uttley who rode him to nearly all his victories called him "the most genuine animal I've ever ridden". Towards the end of his career, Persian War suffered from wind infirmities and had to have a series of operations.

PERSSE, Henry Seymour (1869-1960)
'Atty' Persse's principal achievements lay in the field of Flat-racing – he handled The Tetrarch and won four classics – but in his youth he was a fine amateur rider under N.H. Rules, winning a large number of races including The National Hunt Chase (1902) on Marpessa and the Conyngham Cup (1902) on Sweet Lavender. He was also third in the 1906 Grand National on Aunt May.

PERTH (Group 5)
A right-handed, rectangular track, quite flat and about 1¼ miles long, Perth is laid out in the glorious wooded grounds of Scone Palace and is the northernmost course in Britain. Racing takes place in spring and autumn when the old turf usually provides good going.

The most important races are The Perthshire Memories H'cap Chase (April, 3m, £1,646), the Tamerosia Challenge Cup H'cap Chase (September, 2m, £1,125) and the Perthshire Challenge Cup H'cap chase (September, 3m, £1,186).

Best Times

Distance	Time	Horse-age-weight	Date
2m H	3m 40.40	Molly Fay 4-11-8	23-9-71
2½m H	4m 45.90	Twidale 5-10-12	17-5-78
3m H	5m 48.10	Sun Lion 7-11-0	19-4-77
2m C	3m 50.20	Clareman 8-12-2	27-4-67
2½m C	4m 58.80	Another Guy 9-11-6	17-4-73
3m C	5m 55.8	Chandigar 9-12-5	17-4-73

PETER SIMPLE

Grey horse, 1834, not in the General Stud Book, by Arbutus.

A hard-pulling horse affectionately known as 'Old Peter', Peter Simple won nine chases and was placed in three Grand Nationals. He was third to Charity in 1841, third to Gay Lad the following year and second to Cure-All in 1845.

A contemporary described him as "a grey, light-fleshed, varmint-looking horse, not very big but all muscle and wire and be the fence what it may he would have it some way or the other ... such light actions as his are rarely seen and this knack of moving was peculiar to all the stock of Arbutus".

Peter Simple changed hands on numerous occasions but he was usually ridden by Frisby.

PETER SIMPLE

Bay gelding, 1838, not in the General Stud Book, by Patron.

Some doubt exists as to whether Peter Simple deserves the title of the first dual Grand National winner. It is curious that Finch Mason, who owned the horse when he won in 1849, 11-0 (Cunningham), 20/1, by 3l, a distance, from Knight of Gwynne, 10-7 (Capt. D'Arcy) and Prince George, 10-10 (T. Olliver), makes very little account in his *Heroes and Heroines of the Grand National* of his former horse's second victory particularly as Peter Simple defeated the author's own pair, Miss Mowbray and Oscar.

It has also been thought odd that Peter Simple who carried 11-0 when he won in 1849 and 12-2 in 1850, should have only been allotted 10-10 in 1853 when, starting at 9/1 and ridden by Tom Olliver he won by four lengths, the same, from Miss Mowbray, 10-12 (Mr Gordon) and Oscar, 10-2 (Mr A. Goodman). The truth is that Peter Simple, although a grand jumper and stayer was extremely slow and only came into his own in really testing conditions which prevailed in 1849 and 1853. Furthermore he was 15 in 1853 so it was quite reasonable that he should have gone down somewhat in the weights.

PETRE, Capt. Robert Charles

Bobby Petre served in the Scots Guards and as a young officer was a great friend of Fulke Walwyn and Frank Furlong. On one memorable day in 1930 all three (then cadets) won races at the Garth point-to-point. He was Leading Amateur 1937-38 and won the National Hunt Chase (1938) on St George II. His greatest triumph came in 1946 when he won the Grand National on Lovely Cottage. His riding career came to an end when he broke a leg on a breakwater and had to have it amputated. He trained for a short while but lost his licence after one of his horses was found to have been doped, this being the statutory penalty at the time.

PICKERNELL, Thomas (1834-1912)

Tommy Pickernell was born at Witley in Worcestershire and attended Cheltenham College with Adam Lindsay-Gordon. He was coached in the art of cross-country riding by Tom Olliver and Will Holman and then went to Australia to further his riding experience.

Although Pickernell's claim to be a gentleman was not questioned, his amateur status was a matter of acrimonious dispute. In Tasmania he rode with such success that the local pro's got up a petition imploring him to desist. Leading jockey David Richardson painted a harrowing picture of "poor men – and some of them with large families" being deprived "of their usual and legitimate and only means of subsistence" by his questionable activities. More seriously it caused a duel in France between a French duke and a young English journalist which resulted in the death of the journalist.

Pickernell who rode in England as 'Mr Thomas' was something of a rough diamond and, towards the end of his career, a hard drinker but he was a sympathetic horseman who reckoned that "more races were lost than won by the use of the flail".

He won three Grand Nationals, 1860 on Anatis, 1871 on The Lamb (see THE LAMB for the story of Lord Poulett's curious dream) and 1875 on Pathfinder. He retired in 1877 after a more than usually horrific fall which he broke his jaw in three places and lost an eye. He became the first N.H. Inspector of Courses and held the post until 1885 when he resigned and went to live in King's Heath, Birmingham. He became very popular with the locals who got up a testimonial for him in 1895.

PIGGOTT, Charles (1875-1956)
A brother of Ernie Piggott (q.v.), Charles Piggott was born at Walls Hall, Shropshire. His father farmed and he hunted and point-to-pointed as a young man. During World War I he served with the 3rd Btn, The Worcestershire Regiment, and on his demobilization he set up a training establishment at Cleeve Lodge, Cheltenham. One of his earliest successes was with his own horse, Vaulx, who he had bought as a yearling for £10 in 1915 and named after the village of Vaulx-Vraucourt on the Somme where he had been heavily engaged. Vaulx won him the valuable National Hunt H'cap Chase (1922 and 1924) and the 1925 Welsh Grand National, ridden on the last occasion by Charles's nephew, Keith. His chief patron was Mr Horace Brueton for whom he won the 1939 Champion Hurdle with African Sister. For the most part he trained moderate animals most effectively and his technical skill, individual attention and perceptive assessment of the opposition were much valued by his patrons to most of whom profit was important.

PIGGOTT, Ernest (1879-1967)
A younger brother of Charles Piggott, Ernie Piggott rode a great deal in France and Belgium in his youth and did not settle permanently in England until after his 1912 National victory on Jerry M. He rode approximately 300 winners on the continent and a further 700 in this country. He was Champion Jockey in 1910 (67 winners), 1913 (60) and 1915 (44).

Besides Jerry M. he won the National on Poethlyn (1918 at Gatwick and 1919 at Liverpool) and also the Lancashire Chase twice on the same horse. Other important victories included the Imperial Cup (1913) on Rathlea. He retired shortly after Poethlyn's second victory and trained at the Old Manor House, Letcombe Regis. He achieved only modest success and retired in 1940 to live at Oxford. His wife was a sister of Mornington and Kempton Cannon and their son, Keith (q.v.), became an accomplished jockey and later a trainer.

PIGGOTT, Keith (b.1904)
Keith Piggott is the son of the famous National Hunt jockey, Ernie (q.v.), and father of the even more famous Flat jockey, Lester. He was apprenticed to Bert Lines and rode his first winner at Newbury on his fifteenth birthday. He soon became too heavy however and switched his attention to National Hunt racing. In all he rode 350 winners, his principal successes being the Welsh Grand National (1925) on Vaulx, the Grand Sefton (1927) on Trump Card and the 1939 Champion Hurdle on African Sister. Both horses were trained by his uncle, Charles (q.v.). He took out a licence to train in 1945 and gained his biggest success when Ayala won the 1963 Grand National. This victory made him leading trainer for the season 1962-63 with four winners of six races worth £23,091.

PIGOTT-BROWN, William Brian, 3rd Baronet (b.1941)
Sir William Pigott-Brown's career as a N.H. amateur was brief but extremely successful. Riding chiefly his own horses which were trained by Frank Cundell, he was Leading Amateur in 1960-61 with 28 winners and 1962-63 with 20. In 1961 he won the National Hunt Chase on Superfine, thus emulating his grandfather, Gilbert Cotton (q.v.), who had won it in 1912 on The Rejected IV.

Colours: dark blue and grey stripes, red cap.

PIONEER
Bay gelding, 1840, not in the General Stud Book, by Advance.

Pioneer who was owned by Mr Adams, won the 1846 (five-mile) Grand National,

11-12 (Taylor), unquoted, by 3l, the same, from Culverthorpe, 11-4 (Rackley) and Switcher, 12-4 (Wynne). The distance of the race was extended in error. Pioneer who was described in the paddock as "a rough-looking fellow, poor in condition", went on to win the important Leamington Grand Annual later the same year and was afterwards sold to Captain Peel (*q.v.*) for £1,000. Captain Peel rode him into fourth place behind Matthew in the 1847 National.

PIPPIN II

Bay gelding, not in the General Stud Book.

Pippin II who was usually ridden by his owner, Capt. M. E. Dennis, won six hunter-chases, including the Cheltenham Foxhunters, N.H. Meeting (1927), and the Liverpool Foxhunters (1928).

PITMAN, Richard Thomas (b.1943)

Although he was born within sight of Cheltenham racecourse, Richard Pitman had no interest in racing until his sister Pam married jump-jockey Paddy Cowley (now a trainer). His progress was modest at first but when Fred Winter was about to retire from the saddle he asked if there would be any place for him at the new establishment and thus the foundations of his career were laid. He rode his first winner for the Winter stable in December 1964 on Indian Spice and his first important victory was the Imperial Cup 1966 on Royal Sanction.

In 1972 he became first jockey to the all-powerful Winter stable and the opportunity to ride such marvellous horses gave him the boost and the confidence he needed to join the top league.

His successes include:

The Champion Hurdle (1974) Lanzarote
The King George VI Chase (1972) Pendil; (1973) Pendil
The Benson and Hedges Gold Cup (1972) Pendil
The Wills Premier Chase (1974) Credibility
The Black and White Gold Cup (1972) Pendil; (1973) Bula
Imperial Cup (1966) Royal Sanction; (1973) Lanzarote
The Whitbread Gold Cup (1970) Royal Toss
The Tote Champion Novices Chase (1973) Killiney
The Massey-Ferguson Gold Cup (1973) Pendil
The Arkle Trophy (1972) Pendil

The Great Yorkshire (1970) Freddie Boy
The Welsh Champion Hurdle (1975) Lanzarote

He was also second, beaten by desperately narrow margins, in both the 1973 Gold Cup (on Pendil) and Grand National (on Crisp). Since his retirement in 1975 he has worked as a B.B.C. television racing commentator.

PLASTIC FENCES

Owing to the high cost and scarcity of birch, experiments have been made with sectionalized fences of plastic simulated birch, aproned with green mock gorse. The first set were on view at the National Hunt Meeting at Cheltenham 1972 and later a set travelled round the principal training centres.

One fence was jumped at a public meeting at Stratford but, although without incident, several jockeys were doubtful as to the safety of the high metal retaining rail on the far side of the fence and made representations through their association. No further attempts have been made to introduce such fences for the time being.

The Stewards of the Irish National Hunt Committee have adopted them as a acceptable alternative.

PLAYFAIR

Black gelding, 1881, not in the General Stud Book, Rippendem—half-bred mare (Rattlebones).

Playfair, an attractive, lop-eared black gelding standing over a lot of ground, started his career on modest lines when as a six-year-old he won a Farmers Hunt Race for non-thoroughbreds for his owner, Mr Hunt. He was then sold to Mr H. T. Barclay, for whom he won a Hunter Flat race, and finally to Mr E. W. Baird for whom he won two Hunter-chases and the 1888 Grand National, 10-7 (G. Mawson), 40/1, by 10l, 4l, from Frigate, 11-2 (Mr W. Beasley) and Ballot Box, 12-4 (W. Nightingall).

Subsequently Playfair ran out in Sandown's Grand International and never ran again. He was trained by Tom Cannon.

PLUMPTON (Group 3)

A sharply undulating, left-handed, oval track just over a mile round with an uphill finish, Plumpton, in Sussex, calls for handy horses with plenty of speed and, like nearby Fontwell, is very much a course for specialists. It is susceptible to waterlogging and has had its share of drainage problems. It dates from 1890 and while it has never aspired to feature top-class racing is nevertheless a popular and sporting fixture. Among the more valuable races are the Ian Buchanan Memorial Challenge Trophy H'cap Chase (April, 3m, £1,584), the Kybo H'cap Chase (April, 2m 750 yds, £1,772), the John Courage H'cap Hurdle (October, 2m, 4f, £1,082) and a series of races sponsored by Playboy Bookmakers at the October meeting.

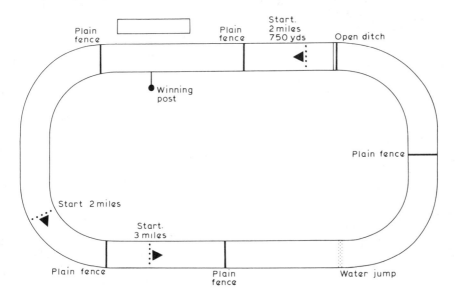

Best Times

Distance	Time	Horse-age-weight	Date
2m H	3m 34.8	Favedo 7-11-11	30-8-76
2½m H	4m 43	Nova Light 5-10-2	5-5-69
3m H	5m 49.20	Arch Point 7-11-2	2-5-65
2m C	3m 51.40	Inch Arran 6-11-3	22-9-70
2m 750y C	4m 53	Retrospect 6-10-5	11-9-73
3m C	5m 58.50	Dark Highway 6-10-12	23-9-69

POCAHONTAS

Bay mare, 1837, Glencoe—Marpessa (Muley). Bred by Mr Greatrex.

Pocahontas, a very plain mare about 14.3 h.h., was useless as a racehorse and a roarer. She was also extremely strong, lived to be over 30 and exercised a remarkable influence on the breeding of steeplechasers.

The Colonel, Empress, Ambush, Manifesto, Cloister, Poethlyn, Jerry M., My Prince and Jackdaw of Rheims are among those that trace their descent from her.

The bulk of these trace their descent through four of her sons, Stockwell, King Tom, Knight of Kars and Rataplan and of these Rataplan, graphically described by The Druid, would hardly appeal to prospective N.H. breeders today. "He stands about 16 hands, possessing a plainish head ... with white legs and cow hocks; a bad walker and a terrible slug in his slow paces." His temperament, too, left much to be desired and he once ran away with John Porter and killed three sheep.

POETHLYN

Bay gelding, 1910, registered in Miss Prior's Half-Bred Stud Book, Rydal Head—Fine Champagne (King Crow). Bred by Maj. H. Peel.

A weak, sickly yearling who was sold to a Shrewsbury hotelier for £7 and then bought back by his breeders for £50 when a two-year-old, Poethlyn took some time to reach maturity and it may not have been unfortunate that the war interrupted his early career.

In all he won 15 races and during seasons 1918-19 he went unbeaten through 10 races including the Prince of Wales Chase, Sandown, the Lancashire Chase twice, each time carrying over 12 stone, and the Grand National twice.

In 1918 he won the War National at Gatwick, 11-6 (E. Piggott), 5/1jt-f, by 4l, a bad third, from Captain Dreyfus, 12-7 (J. Reardon) and Ballymacad, 11-3 (I. Anthony). In 1919 the race returned to Aintree and this time Poethlyn, favourite at 11/4, carried top-weight of 12-7 (E. Piggott), and won by 8l, 6l, from Ballybogan, 11-10 (W. Head) and Pollen, 11-4 (A. Escott).

Poethlyn was favourite for the 1920 National but fell at the first fence and was afterwards retired to the Peels' Shropshire home. He was trained at Lewes by Harry Escott.

POET PRINCE
Chestnut gelding, 1932, Milton—Welsh Princess (Hapsburg). Bred by Capt. J. G. Sherrard.

As a young horse Poet Prince was thought to be wrong in the wind and thus was brought cheaply by amateur rider/veterinary surgeon, David Sherbrooke for whom he won nine races including the Stanley Chase, Liverpool (1940) and the 1941 Cheltenham Gold Cup, (R. Burford), 7/2, by 3l, a short head, from Savon (G. Archibald) and Red Rower (D. Morgan). Poet Prince was usually ridden by his owner but a fall on the previous day prevented Mr Sherbrooke from taking the ride in the Gold Cup.

The war interrupted Poet Prince's career just as it reached its peak but he went back into training afterwards and won four more races. He was trained at Wroughton by Ivor Anthony for most of his career but spent his last two seasons with Fulke Walwyn.

POINT-TO-POINTING
As the nineteenth century progressed and the sport of steeplechasing became more sophisticated with enclosed courses and professionally trained and ridden horses, more and more of whom were thoroughbred, the sporting amateur and his hunter, who had originated the sport, found himself out in the cold. Therefore attempts were made among hunting men to stage races over natural country from which proper racehorses and professional riders were rigidly excluded.

Dr 'Fogo' Rowlands (q.v.) of Cheltenham started The National Hunt Chase, in 1859, feeling that if there was a worthwhile prize for proper hunters, farmers would be encouraged to breed them. After a shaky start the race prospered, but by 1875 it was taking place over the new enclosed course at Sandown and although the race continued to be confined to horses who had been hunted and were maidens at starting, it was idle to suppose that the contestants for what was for a long time the third richest race in the Calendar were proper hunters.

More successful were various Hunt ventures. The Worcestershire Hunt have records of sporadic Hunt meetings at the Madresfield estate of Earl Beauchamp from 1836. Mr W. E. Oakley, Master of the Atherstone, claimed to be the first to stage an annual hunt point-to-point meeting dating from the 1870s. In 1888 the Midland Sportsman's races at Kineton were established with five Hunts, including the Warwickshire, the Pytchley, the Bicester and the Heythrop. These were shortly followed in 1892 by the Stock Exchange point-to-point and in 1895 by the Pegasus Club. University races appear to date at least from the 1880s. Thomas Hitchcock, the famous American chasing supporter, won the Christ Church Grind in 1882.

All these meetings had their own rules and it was not until 1913 that the Master of Hounds Point-to-Point Association established a set of rules. These did not include any prohibition of lady riders taking part, which they frequently did – often side-saddle. In 1929 ladies were channelled into races confined to their own sex.

During the 1920s and 1930s the sport was given a great fillip by the participation of the Prince of Wales. His Highness, who was coached by Harry Brown (q.v.), was said to be more enthusiastic than skilful but he won 13 races before his family and advisors put a brake on this undeniably hazardous branch of his equestrian activities.

By 1934 the National Hunt Committee was growing increasingly disturbed at the professional trend of point-to-pointing and for the season of 1935 they ran the sport under a specially framed set of rules, while an advisory committee was formed consisting of three members of the National Hunt Committee and three members of the Master of Foxhounds Association. In 1937 the Masters' point-to-point committee was dissolved.

The broad outline of the rules was that:

(i) No horse was eligible that had, since January 1st of the year in question, been in a licensed trainer's yard.

(ii) Professional riders were banned. This included Hunt Servants, grooms, apprentices, stable lads or anyone who had "ridden for hire" in any capacity.

(iii) Courses had to be approved by an official Inspector of Courses.

By and large these rules still hold good. The date by which horses may not have been in a licensed trainer's yard has been frequently shifted, back to November, then to July and now back to November again. The "ridden-for-hire" clause has been relaxed with regard to Lady riders and modified for men (*see* RIDDEN FOR HIRE). Lady riders have since 1967 been permitted to ride in their Hunt races and the Sex Discrimination Act of 1975 has opened all races to them. In fact it is now only possible to stage a race confined to lady riders when the programme includes a race of similar conditions confined to men. The ceiling of prize money has also been raised a little. Since 1975 any race may be worth £40 and this does not have to include the value of the memento, while Open races (including Ladies' and Restricted) may be worth £50

Point-to-points which used to be run for the sport of hunt members and as a means of entertaining the farmers are now a major public attraction and are the principal source of revenue for most hunts. They continue to be a valuable nursery for young horses and riders, many of whom graduate successfully to National Hunt Racing. Teal, Merryman II, Hallowe'en, Four Ten, Limber Hill, Linwell, Woodland Venture, The Dikler and Charlie Potheen all started their careers in the point-to-point field, while the list of jockeys, trainers and racing officials is interminable. At the Garth point-to-point in 1930, three races were won by Frank Furlong, Fulke Walwyn and Bobby Petre. All three went on to win the National.

POINT-TO-POINT STEEPLECHASES

Point-to-point steeplechases are held under the sanction of the Jockey Club and under regulations entitled *Jockey Club Regulations for Point-to-Point Steeplechases* published from time to time by the Stewards of the Jockey Club and every person taking part in these races shall comply with these regulations.

In order to run in a point-to-point steeplechase a horse must have a hunter's certificate, registered with Weatherbys, signed by the Master of the Hounds with which he has been qualified, to the effect that he has been hunted with these Hounds and that his owner is a member or subscriber to the Hunt or is a farmer farming within the boundaries of the country. The owner must further declare that his horse has been regularly and fairly hunted.

In order to ride in a point-to-point, a person must be a member, subscriber or farmer of a recognized Hunt or their respective spouse or child and must obtain from his Hunt Secretary a certificate declaring him to be such, which he must produce for the Clerk of the Scales at any meeting at which he proposes to ride. Serving members of Her Majesty's Forces may be permitted to ride if so provided by the conditions of the race.

The principal point-to-point steeplechases are the Lady Dudley Cup (Worcestershire), the Lord Ashton of Hyde Cup (Heythrop) and the Lord Grimthorpe Cup (Middleton). From 1968-74 Players Gold Leaf sponsored a series of Open races, the winner of which qualified to compete for the Players Gold Leaf Trophy, held on a racecourse in May. Since 1974 a similar series has been sponsored by B.M.W. with finals for both Ladies and Gentlemen at Chepstow.

Point-to-point results are not tabulated in *The Racing Calendar* or in *Steeplechases Past* and a winner of a point-to-point steeplechase is still a maiden under National Hunt Rules.

Every horse that runs in Hunter chases and point-to-points is covered by Geoffrey Sale and Iain McKenzie's admirable and highly individual annual *Point-to-Pointers and Hunterchasers*.

There is a Point-to-Point Secretaries Association, the officers of which are:

Chairman: Col. A. Clerke-Brown; Vice-Chairman: J. Baylis; Hon. Secretary: C. R. Glyn.

POOLE, George Calcutt (1880-1952)

George Poole was the son of a trainer

and rode his first chase winner aged 13. He made hunters, point-to-pointed, rode as an amateur and assisted Teddy Woodland and his son Percy before taking out a licence in 1912. His stables were near Lewes in Sussex and his partner and principal owner was newspaper proprietor, Tommy Edge. The Rees brothers rode for the stable which became the most formidable in Southern England. In 1921 he won the Grand National for Mr (later Sir) Malcolm McAlpine with Shaun Spadah and very nearly completed the Spring double when Senhora was second in the Lincoln.

A reserved, somewhat terse man, who showed his great kindness and considerable sense of humour only to his immediate circle, George Poole did not renew his licence after World War II.

POTTS, Henry (b.1811)

A Cheshire gentleman and a keen hunting man, Henry Potts won the 1838 Liverpool Steeplechase on Alan McDonough's Sir William, owing to McDonough's injury. He appears to have been one of the few people, other than McDonough, for whom the wayward Sir William would co-operate.

POWELL, A.

A Gloucestershire man and a bit of a rough diamond, A. Powell won the 1841 Grand National on Charity. He also won the 1838 Cheltenham Steeplechase on Cannon Ball.

POWER, James Joseph

A highly accomplished Northern jockey, Jimmy Power rode a good deal for Bobby Renton and won the 1950 Grand National on Freebooter after surviving a hair-raising moment at The Chair where Freebooter took off a length too early and had the luckless Power literally clinging to his ears. His major triumph was the 1956 Cheltenham Gold Cup on Limber Hill.

He also won:

The Lancashire Chase (1956) Pippikin
The Grand Sefton (1949) Freebooter; (1950) Shagreen; (1951) Freebooter
The Scottish Grand National (1952) Flagrant Mac

The Great Yorkshire Chase (1950) Freebooter
The Topham Trophy (1956) John Jacques

His best season was 1955-56 when rode 37 winners and finished sixth in the Jockeys' Table.

PRICE, Henry Ryan (b.1912)

A leading point-to-point rider of the 1930s, Ryan Price took out a licence to train in 1937. From very small beginnings, he created at Findon in Sussex one of the most consistently successful stables chasing has ever known and won every important race in the Calendar.

From 1958-70 he was never out of the leading six in the trainer's table. He was Leading Trainer on four occasions:

1958-59	with 52 races worth	£26,550
1961-62	„ 64 „ „	£40,950
1965-66	„ 65 „ „	£42,276
1966-67	„ 73 „ „	£41,222

His principal successes are:

The Cheltenham Gold Cup (1969) What A Myth
The Grand National (1962) Kilmore
The Champion Hurdle (1955) Clair Soleil; (1959) Fare Time; (1961) Eborneezer
The Triumph Hurdle (1961) Cantab; (1962) Beaver II
The Grand Course des Haies de quatre ans (1962) Beaver
The Schweppes Gold Trophy (1963) Rosyth; (1964) Rosyth; (1966) Le Vermontois; (1967) Hill House
The Tote Champion Novices Chase (1967) Border Jet
The Whitbread Gold Cup (1959) Done Up; (1966) What A Myth

The bulk of his winners were ridden by his two great jockeys, Fred Winter and Josh Gifford, and it was to the latter that he handed over one of his yards and his jumpers in 1970 in order to concentrate on the Flat.

Predictably the move has been totally successful and already he has won the Oaks (1972) with Ginevra, the Champion Stakes (1974) with Giacometti and the St Leger (1975) with Bruni. Jumping, however, remains his first love. All his old favourites are pensioned off near his house and during the last few seasons he has not been able to resist the temptation of having a few hurdlers during the winter months.

PRINCE REGENT

Bay gelding, 1935. Bred by Mr A. H. Maxwell.

Prince Regent			
My Prince	Marcovil	Marco	
		Lady Villikins	
	Salvaich	St Simon	
		Muirnin	
Nemaea	Argos	Sundridge	
		Mesange	
	Capdane	Captivation	
		Little Denmark	

Prince Regent was bought as a yearling at Goff's Sales by Harry Bonner on behalf of Mr J. V. Rank. At the time the stock of My Prince were carrying all before them. He was Leading Sire for the third time, his sons had won two Cheltenham Gold Cups and three Grand Nationals in eight years. Two of the Nationals had been won by Reynoldstown whom Mr Rank could have bought as a young horse but did not on account of his black colour.

Prince Regent was sent to Bobby Power to be broken and when the young vet was killed, changing a tyre on the road to Dublin Horse Show, he was transferred along with several of Mr Rank's other youngsters to Tom Dreaper, then a substantial farmer with a few horses. His education completed, he was sent to England to Gwyn Evans who controlled the National Hunt side of Mr Rank's Druid Lodge establishment. Not long afterwards, Evans too was killed in a motor accident and Prince Regent sailed back across the Irish Sea to the land of his birth. He returned to Tom Dreaper's Kilsallaghan farm where he remained until the final two seasons of his great career.

It was a curious situation. Marooned on their tiny island by the war, a whole generation of fine Irish chasers normally exported to race all over Europe, instead ran furiously against each other for chicken feed stakes. It is necessary to appreciate this in order to assimilate that Arkle had to win two Cheltenham Gold Cups before Tom Dreaper conceded that "he might be the Prince's equal".

Prince Regent won twelve races in Ireland between 1941 and 1945 when he first came to race in England. They included the 1942 Irish Grand National carrying 12-7. He became a legend in his own country and when he made his first eagerly awaited visit to England, he was surrounded with all the panoply of a star. Nor were his public disappointed. In his first major test he won the 1946 Cheltenham Gold Cup by five lengths. The press and public were eulogistic but jockey Tim Hyde's post mortem was not: "it took me a moment or two to beat that fellow today, Tom", he quietly informed his trainer, realising in the moment of triumph that peace had come too late. The brilliance had gone and Prince Regent, now eleven, was just too old to stamp his glory on the English Turf.

At Aintree he was proved right. Despite 12-7 Prince Regent started hot favourite at 3/1 and landed over the last fence with a commanding lead. But he was exhausted and had no answer to the late challenge of lightly-weighted Lovely Cottage and Jack Findlay. The public were shattered and his defeat marked the decline in the fortunes and popularity of the National not halted until the 1960s when the sloping of the fences, the tightening of entry qualifications, the reduction of top weight to twelve stone and a massive injection of prize-money, first arrested and then reversed it.

Prince Regent won five more races including the Champion Chase, Liverpool (1946) and was fourth in the 1947 Grand National. At the end of season 1947-48 an attempt was made to retire him but he viewed this programme with disapproval and eventually returned to Druid's Lodge because it was felt more conditions races would be available for him in England. He retired just before Christmas in 1949.

PRUDHOMME

Chestnut horse, 1877, Cymbale—Preude (Cobnut). Bred by M. Massé, in France.

A very classy hurdler owned by the fifth Lord Rosebery, Prudhomme won the Great Sandown Hurdle (1882), the Grand Annual Handicap Hurdle, Sandown (1882) and the Kempton Park Grand Hurdle (1883). He was almost always ridden by that most polished amateur, Mr Arthur Coventry.

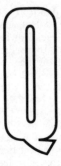

QUARE TIMES

Bay gelding, 1946, Artists Son—Lavenco (Flamenco). Bred by Mr P. P. Sweeney.

Quare Times, whose female line traces to the great jumping influence of Jackdaw, was bought as a yearling by Mrs W. E. Welman and sent as a three-year-old to Vincent O'Brien. Here he was very slow to show any signs of ability. He did not race until he was six and went through two seasons unplaced before winning a chase at Gowran Park shortly after his eighth birthday. In all he won seven races including the National Hunt Chase (1954) and the 1955 Grand National, 11-0 (P. Taaffe), 100/9, by 12l, 4l, from Tudor Line, 11-3 (G. Slack) and Carey's Cottage, 10-11 (T. Taaffe). Con-ditions have seldom been worse for the big race and despite the water jump being dolled off and fence 13 halved, the rain-sodden ground was barely raceable.

After his victory he was sold to Mrs John Rogerson but unsoundness curtailed his career and he won only two more races.

Although Quare Times was admirably suited to testing conditions and extreme distances, he must not be dismissed as a mere plodding stayer for he ran several fine races, notably his two-length second to the subsequent Gold Cup winner, Limber Hill, in the 1955 National Hunt Handicap Chase.

QUEEN'S TASTE

Bay gelding, 1946, Queen's Eyot—Lass of Tullaherin (Torlonio). Bred by Mr G. W. Williams.

An Irish-bred gelding, Queen's Taste was bought at Goff's for 280 guineas as a four-year-old. He proved a tough, versatile chaser winning 13 races from 2m to 3m, 7f, including the Scottish Grand National three times (1953, 1954 and 1956). He was owned by Mr W. Bailey and trained by H. Clarkson at Bishop's Sutton, Yorkshire.

RACECOURSE ASSOCIATION

The Racecourse Association was formed in 1907, comprising 63 of the 76 existing courses. Absentees included Newmarket, Liverpool and several small National Hunt Courses. In 1963, by which time only Newmarket and Liverpool continued to abstain, the authorities announced that they would henceforth issue licences only to courses belonging to the Association.

For administrative purposes it is divided into three zones, Northern, Midland and Southern. Each area appoints four members to the Council which has regular meetings at the Association's London office in Portman Square and is in close contact with the Jockey Club, the Levy Board, the Tote and the various associations of racing's estates.

The Association's offices are at 42 Portman Square, London W.1.
Chairman: Air-Commodore W. T. Brooks, A.F.C., D.S.O.
Chief-Executive: Col. J. Cameron-Hayes.

RACECOURSES, Current National Hunt

Racecourses, with respective Clerks of the Course:

Ascot Capt. the Hon. E. N. C. Beaumont
Ayr Col. W. W. McHarg and Maj. C. D. Patterson
Bangor on Dee Maj. J. Moon
Carlisle Maj. C. D. Patterson
Cartmel Capt. T. J. C. Mordaunt
Catterick Maj. C. D. Patterson
Cheltenham Maj. P. W. F. Arkwright
Chepstow J. P. V. Hughes
Devon & Exeter Cmdr E. W. Sykes, D.S.C.
Doncaster Maj. George Boon

Fakenham P. B. Firth
Folkestone D. Cameron
Fontwell Park Derek Hubbard
Haydock Park P. B. Firth
Hereford J. Williams
Hexham Maj. C. D. Patterson
Huntingdon H. Bevan
Kelso Col. W. W. McHarg
Kempton Park Maj. George Boon
Leicester Capt. N. Lees
Lingfield Park R. N. Fabricius
Liverpool J. V. Hughes
Ludlow Maj. J. Moon
Market Rasen J. P. U. Lucas
Newbury Capt. C. B. Toller
Newcastle A. C. Newton
Newton Abbot C. C. Whitley
Nottingham David Heyman
Perth Col. W. W. McHarg
Plumpton B. E. Robinson
Sandown Park Maj. P. Beckwith-Smith
Sedgefield Col. C. Egerton
Southwell K. S. Ford
Stratford-on-Avon Lt.-Cdr. J. W. Ford
Taunton Cdr. E. W. Sykes
Teesside Park Capt. T. C. J. Mordaunt
Towcester D. W. Bushby
Uttoxeter Lt.-Cdr., J. W. Ford
Warwick David Heyman
Wetherby Maj. J. Moon
Wincanton Maj. H. W. Hibbert
Windsor D. W. Bushby
Wolverhampton Lt.-Cdr. J. Ford
Worcester H. Bevan

Steeplechase Courses

In all Steeplechase courses:

(i) All fences, except those at water-jumps, must be not less than four feet six inches in height.

(ii) In the first two miles there shall be at least twelve fences, and in each succeeding mile at least six fences.

(iii) For each mile there shall be at least one ditch six feet wide and two feet deep on the take-off side of a fence, guarded by a bank and rail not exceeding two feet in height.

(iv) There shall be a water-jump at least twelve feet wide and two feet deep,* guarded by a fence not exceeding three feet in height and this water-jump may be regarded as one of the fences prescribed by section (ii).

*NOTE The shelve from the floor of the water on the landing side to begin six feet from the landing edge. A horizontal turfed shelf two inches below the surface of the water to extend inwards from the landing edge of the water for eighteen inches to meet the top of the shelve.

Hurdle Race Courses

Rule 83 of the Rules of Racing –
In all Hurdle race courses:

(i) All hurdles must be not less than three feet six inches in height from the bottom bar to the top bar.

(ii) In the first two miles there shall be at least eight flights of hurdles with an additional flight of hurdles for every complete quarter of a mile beyond that distance.

RACECOURSE TECHNICAL SERVICES

The Racecourse Technical Services Company is a subsidiary of the Horserace Betting Levy Board and is responsible for the photo-finish, the camera patrol, the race-timing service, the public-address system, closed-circuit television and the starting stalls in the United Kingdom. The company was formed in 1967 as a strengthening and modification of the Race Finish Recording Company Ltd. In addition the R.T.S. have carried out numerous installations abroad. The board is composed as follows:
Chairman: Sir Raymond Brown O.B.E.
Directors: Sir Denys Hicks O.B.E., Maj. W. D. Gibson, Miss M. E. Meades; Managing Director: J. C. S. James.

RACEGOERS CLUB

The Racegoers Club is run by the Racing Information Bureau and its object is simply to get more people to go racing more often. Many courses offer concessions to club members. Expeditions have been organized to places of racing interest including France, for the Prix de l'Arc de Triomphe, and to America, for the Washington International, as well as a tour of the major studs. The club also owns horses and sponsors races. It has an office at 42 Portman Square, London W.1. The Chairman is Mr Anthony Fairbairn.

RACEHORSE OWNERS ASSOCIATION

The Racecourse Owners Asociation's board for 1974 was as follows:
Chairman: D. D. Sieff, Esq.
Secretary-General: J. S. Biggs, Esq.

The council is composed of elected members, co-opted members and in addition, past-presidents can be nominated to the council.

RACING CALENDAR, The

The Racing Calendar is the official publication of the Jockey Club. It is published by Messrs Weatherbys and issued every Thursday. It contains particulars of every race, that is to say the conditions, entries, handicaps, forfeit stages, and final acceptances. It lists all race-meetings; gives the registration of colours and names of horses, names of persons and horses on the Forfeit List, and reports all objections and disqualifications. Apprentice jockeys and their masters are listed and so are all licensed jockeys and trainers. The first public intimation of any 'warning off' is the official notice in *The Racing Calendar* on the Thursday after the ban has come into force.

RAG TRADE

Chestnut gelding, 1966, Menelek—The Rage (Cagire II). Bred by Mr I. Williams, in Ireland.

A typical product of his sire, the strongly constructed Rag Trade needed plenty of time to mature and won only one race before his eighth birthday. He amply repaid the patience shown him and won eight chases including the Joe Coral Welsh Grand National, Chepstow (1976) and the 1976 *News of the World* Grand National, 10-12 (J. Burke) 14/1, by 2l, 8l, from Red Rum, 11-10 (T. Stack) and Eyecatcher, 10-7 (B. Fletcher).

When he first came to England he was trained by George Fairbairn for his owner-breeder Ian Williams, a son of Evan Williams *(q.v)* and himself a distinguished amateur rider. For them he won the Haydock National Trial and following his spectacular last-fence fall when an assured winner of the Kim Muir Chase at the 1975 National Hunt Meeting, he was sold at Doncaster's pre-Aintree sale, with his National engagement, for an incredible 18,000 guineas. The purchaser was Jack Doyle, on behalf of a syndicate headed by Mr P. B. Raymond, the flamboyant Mayfair hairdresser and tycoon, who had owned Ayala. He completed his training with Arthur Pitt and ran in the National, finishing tenth and last behind L'Escargot.

He was transferred to Fred Rimell

during the summer but took time to find his form the following season and was beginning to look distinctly expensive when, profiting from the last fence fall of Gylippus, he won the Joe Coral Welsh Grand National. This race evidently put him cherry ripe for the Grand National and, skilfully ridden by John Burke, he produced a good turn of speed from the last to hold the persistent challenge of Red Rum by two hard-fought lengths.

He was then beset by leg problems and a dispute arose between owners and trainer over presents for the National victory. He was therefore put up for sale again to dissolve the partnership and Mr Raymond bought him outright for 5,000 guineas and returned him to George Fairbairn. After a long slow preparation on the Northumberland hills, he re-appeared in fine fettle to win the Vaux Breweries Chase at Teesside on the strength of which he was made favourite for the 1978 Grand National. Unhappily he broke down so badly on the second circuit that he had to be put down.

RANK, James Voase (1881-1952)

Mr J. V. Rank was the eldest son of Joseph Rank who developed modern methods of milling flour at Hull. He inherited and extended the business and during the 1930s set about channelling some of his vast resources into fulfilling his triple ambition to win the Derby, the Grand National and the Waterloo Cup. Between 1935-38, he was second in all three. Scottish Union was second in the 1938 Derby, Cooleen was second in 1937 Grand National and Joker's Resort was second in 1935 Waterloo Cup at Altcar.

He owned a number of really good horses, notably Southern Hero (*q.v.*) (18 chases, including three Scottish Grand Nationals) and one really great one in Prince Regent (*q.v.*) (1946 Cheltenham Gold Cup, the Irish Grand National and third and fourth in the Nationals of 1946 and 1947). He nearly bought Reynolds-town (*q.v.*) but was dissuaded by a friend who disliked black horses and, even more ironically, he owned Early Mist (*q.v.*), but died just a year before that horse won the National in the colours of Mr J. Griffin.

A blunt but immensely kind man, he was one of the nicest of chasing's big owners. His trainers included Bobby Renton, Bill Payne, Gwyn Evans, Noel Cannon and latterly, Tom Dreaper.

Colours: royal blue and primrose quarters, primrose sleeves, royal blue cap.

RATHCOOLE

Chestnut gelding, 1917, not in the General Stud Book, Rathurde—Barbara.

A popular, consistent horse owned by Mrs Chester Beatty, Rathcoole won a total of 29 races, culminating in the 2-mile Coventry Cup at the 1929 National Hunt Meeting.

RAYSON, Thomas (1882-1952)

Tommy Rayson trained near Winchester in Hampshire. He produced Davy Jones as a young horse and won three Flat races, a hurdle and two chases with him before selling him to Lord Mildmay. His biggest success was to win the 1946 Grand National with Lovely Cottage, which made him Leading Trainer for the season 1945-46 with two winners of five races worth £9,933.

REARDON, John Michael (1891-1974)

Jack Reardon won the 1916 'war' National on Vermouth. After the First World War he set up a small stable at Epsom where he trained for 40 years. He produced a number of successful Flat jockeys including Brian Swift.

RED ALLIGATOR

Chestnut gelding, 1959, registered in Miss Prior's Half-Bred Stud Book, Magic Red—Miss Alligator (Hyacinthus). Bred by Mr William Kennedy, in Northern Ireland.

One of the only pair of half-brothers to have won the Grand National, Red Alligator's pedigree is discussed under his dam's entry. He was sold as a yearling for 360 guineas and during his first three seasons, in which he won a solitary hurdle race from 27 outings, gave little indication of having been a bargain. However he became a fine, reliable jumper and a resolute stayer who showed vast improvement when switched to fences.

In all he won 11 chases including the 1968 Grand National, 10-0 (B. Fletcher), 100/7, by 20l, a neck, from Moidore's Token 10-8 (B. Brogan) and Different Class, 11-5 (D. Mould). Red Alligator who was owned by Mr John Manners and trained at Bishop Auckland by Denys Smith, also ran third to Foinavon in the dramatic 1967 National.

RED APRIL
Bay gelding, 1937, April the Fifth—Red Maru (Kosciusko). Bred by Lord Stalbridge.

A half-brother to the 1945 Cheltenham Gold Cup winner, Red Rower, Red April raced in the colours of Lady Stalbridge and won a total of 23 races. The most important of these were the Queen Elizabeth Chase, Hurst Park (1951), then the second most valuable race in the Calendar and, appropriately the Lord Stalbridge Memorial Cup, Wincanton. Red April, who was by the 1932 Derby winner, also ran third to Brains' Trust in the 1945 Champion Hurdle. He was trained by Vernon Cross.

RED PRINCE II
Chestnut horse, 1889, Kendal—Empress (Blood Royal). Bred by Mr H. E. Linde.

A son of the 1880 National winner, Red Prince II proved a high-class two-year-old, winning the National Produce Stakes at the Curragh. He went on to prove a brilliantly precocious four-year-old over fences, winning four races including the £2,000 Lancashire Chase (the most valuable race in the Calendar) by eight lengths.

Unfortunately he was thick-shouldered and top-heavy and became difficult to train, characteristics that he passed on at stud. Nevertheless he was an extremely successful sire of jumpers and reliable sources state that he was the leading sire of chasers from 1904-9, although no printed statistics can be found to corroborate this.

RED ROWER
Bay gelding, 1934, Rameses the Second—Red Maru (Kosciusko). Bred by Lord Stalbridge.

A half-brother to the smart Red April (q.v.), Red Rower was leased to Lady Sybil Phipps for the early part of his career. Trained by Ivor Anthony, he won two hurdle races and six chases including the Cheltenham Grand Annual. He was also third to Poet Prince in the 1941 Cheltenham Gold Cup and an unlucky second to Medoc II in 1942, after nearly being brought down.

After the war he returned to his owner-breeder, Lord Stalbridge, who trained him to win two more chases including the 1945 Cheltenham Gold Cup (D. Jones), 11/4, by 3l, 1½l, from Schubert (C. Beechener) and Paladin (P. Conlon).

RED RUM
Bay gelding, 1965. Bred by Mr Martin McEnery.

		Gold Bridge
	Vilmorin	
		Queen of the
Quorum		Meadows
		Bois Roussel
	Akimbo	
Red Rum		Bulolo
		Link Boy
	Magic Red	
		Infra Red
Mared		
		Anwar
	Quinta	
		Batika

A deep-bodied, robust, attractive horse of medium size, Red Rum was formerly owned by Mrs Lurline Brotherton and trained by Bobby Renton. Although quite useful – he had won three Flat races, three hurdle races and five chases – he had not lived up to his early promise, was by no stretch of the imagination top class, had shown unmistakable signs of disinclination to struggle, and, worst of all, had suffered an attack of pedalostitis. All in all he looked very well sold at 6,000 guineas when in August 1972, Southport garage proprietor and trainer, Donald McCain, acquired him for Mr le Mare in an effort to fulfil his octogenarian patron's lifelong ambition to win the National.

Apparently revitalized by the Lancashire sea breezes and an unorthodoxly stringent preparation on Southport Sands, Red Rum proceeded to win 16 more chases including a record three Grand Nationals, besides being second in two more. He also won a Scottish Grand National, Ayr (1974) and was only beaten inches by Red Candle, to whom he was conceding 14lb, in the 1973 Hennessy Gold Cup at Newbury.

Grand National 1973: 10-5 (B. Fletcher) 9/1 jt-f, ¾l, 25l, from Crisp, 12-0 (R. Pitman) and L'Escargot, 12-0 (T. Carberry). Red Rum who was leading the rest of the field and thus had nothing to race with, made up the best part of a fence from the Canal Turn to catch and beat the gallant Crisp in the last 50 yards. The pair of them beat Reynoldstown's 38-year record by over 18 sec. Red Rum recording 9 min. 1.90 sec. Grand National 1974: 12-0 (B. Fletcher), 11/1, won by 7l, a short head, from L'Escargot, 11-13 (T. Carberry) and Charles Dickens, 10-0 (A. Turnell).

This was the first dual victory since

Reynoldstown and only the eighth in the history of the race. Furthermore, Red Rum was the first horse since Reynoldstown in 1936 to carry 12 stone successfully. Red Rum pulled out so fresh after his second victory that his trainer had no compunction in saddling him for the Scottish National and his confidence was rewarded by an easy win. Red Rum, who was ridden as usual by Brian Fletcher, thus became the first horse to win both English and Scottish Nationals in the same year and a statue of him was commissioned to stand on Ayr Racecourse commemorating this feat.

Despite pressure from many sections of the Press and public that he should be retired, Red Rum continued to race and although his star was somewhat dimmed on park courses, Aintree still brought the swagger back to his walk and the spring to his heels. In 1975 he ran a gallant second to the dual Gold Cup winner L'Escargot to whom he was conceeding 11lbs. In 1976, now ridden by Tommy Stack, after a mid-season dispute had severed his long and successful partnership with Brian Fletcher, he came to the last locked level with Rag Trade. A magnificent jump gained him ½ a length but Rag Trade would not be denied and despite heroic efforts, he was 2 lengths adrift at the winning post.

In 1977 no one presumed to steal his glory. Even the weather relented and the cold, wet spring produced a dry, sunny day specially for him with good ground under his feet. The fates (or some other machination) felled the fancied horses and left him clear at Becher's on the second circuit. From then on the race became a procession and in the end Red Rum, 11-10 (T. Stack), 9/1, won by 25l, 6l, from Churchtown Boy, 10-0 (M. Blackshaw) and Eyecatcher, 10-1 (C. Read.

Still he was not done with. Although at 13 he was too slow to win away from Aintree, he was enjoying himself, in marvellous physical shape and running well enough to suggest to his connections that, in what looked to be a substandard year, he could win a fourth National. However, a week before the big race he bruised a heel on the beach and after a dramatic week of touch and go to which the media gave unprecedented attention, he was withdrawn on the eve of the race and his retirement was announced forthwith.

As he has been made into a limited company the first racehorse to achieve such distinction it seems likely that plenty more will be seen of him.

RED SPLASH
Chestnut gelding, 1919, Copper Ore—La Manche (Wavelet's Pride). Bred by Capt. E. H. Wyndham.

An exceptionally good-looking horse of a quality rare among chasers of his age, Red Splash was a precocious youngster and by the end of his fifth year had won five chases including the Coventry Novices Chase, Cheltenham (1923) and the inaugural Cheltenham Gold Cup (1924) (F. B. Rees), 5/1, by a head and a neck from Conjuror II (Mr H. Brown) and Gerald L (I. Morgan). Red Splash who had made nearly all the running and won in the gamest fashion seemed all set for a great career but unfortunately he became unsound and did not win again.

Red Splash was one of only three five-year-olds to win the Gold Cup, the others being Patron Saint and Golden Miller.

He was raced by his breeder, Capt. (later Col.) the Hon. E. H. Wyndham of the Life Guards, and trained by Fred Withington who had also trained both his sire and dam.

REES, Frederick Bilbo (1894-1951)
Dick Rees was a son of a Pembrokeshire veterinary surgeon. He and his older brother, Lewis, grew up in a hunting and point-to-pointing atmosphere and before the World War I they rode a little for D. Harrison's Tenby stable.

In 1914 he enlisted in the Sussex Yeomanry. He was then commissioned into the Manchester Regiment and finally seconded to the Royal Flying Corps. On his demobilization he rode as an amateur until 1920 when he turned professional. He rode chiefly for George Poole and established himself with astonishing rapidity. A natural horseman, he was also a supreme tactician and was held to be the finest all-round jockey of the inter-war period.

He was Champion Jockey five times, in 1920 (64 winners), 1921 (65), 1923 (64), 1924 (108, a record from only 348 mounts) and 1926-27 (59).

His principal victories included:

The Grand National (1921) Shaun Spadah

The **Cheltenham Gold Cup** (1928) Patron Saint; (1929) Easter Hero
The **Grand Steeplechase de Paris** (1925) Silvo
The **Champion Hurdle** (1929) Royal Falcon

He is one of seven jockeys to have won all of chasing's classics. Always a *bon viveur*, he was beset by weight problems and retired comparatively early.

REES, Lewis Bilby
Bilby Rees, elder brother of Dick (*q.v.*), inevitably suffered by comparison but he was a fine rider in his own right. His principal successes were the 1922 Grand National on Music Hall and 1928 Champion Hurdle on Brown Jack.
He is the father of well-known National Hunt jockey, Bill Rees (*q.v.*).

REES, Lewis William (b.1934)
Bill Rees was born into chasing. The son of Bilby Rees, (*q.v.*), he was apprenticed to Walter Nightingall and then to Bob Turnell for whom he won the 1960 Cheltenham Gold Cup on the brilliant but slightly unpredictable Pas Seul.
Next season he was retained to ride first jockey to Peter Cazalet and for several years they had a very successful association. He rode 51 winners for H.M. the Queen Mother and won the 1965 Mackeson Gold Cup on Dunkirk. The twilight of his career was clouded by two dreadful leg injuries and he retired in 1972. The following year he began a career as a racing official.

REGAL
Black gelding, 1871, Saunterer—Regalia (Stockwell). Bred by Mr W. Graham.
The son of the 1865 Oaks winner, Regal proved only moderate on the Flat, winning two small races but he went on to be a good-class staying chaser and won seven chases including the Warwick Grand Annual (1876), the Great Sandown Chase (1876), the Grand International Chase, Sandown (1880 and 1881) and the 1876 Grand National, 11-3 (J. Cannon), 25/1, by a neck, 3l from Congress, 11-3 (Mr E. P. Wilson) and Shifnal, 10-3 (R. I'Anson).
Regal, who thus became one of five five-year-olds to win the race, was owned by Capt. Machell (*q.v.*).

RENTON, Robert (1888-1975)
Bobby Renton was the son of a parson.

His family owned Oxclose Farm, Ripon, Yorkshire, and he was brought up to run it. As a young man he hunted, point-to-pointed, made young horses and rode as an amateur on the Flat and over fences. He began training in a small way in 1919.
The advent of Mrs Brotherton (*q.v.*) brought him to the fore and throughout the 1950s his stable was one of the most important in the country. He favoured big, old-fashioned steeplechasers and they were all beautiful jumpers.
He won:

The **Grand National** (1950) Freebooter
The **Scottish Grand National** (1952) Flagrant Mac; (1955) Bar Point
The **Lancashire Chase** (1951) Q.E.D.; (1955) Tudor Line
The **Grand Sefton** (1949) Freebooter; (1951) Freebooter; (1960) Ernest
The **Champion Chase** (1949) Freebooter
The **Champion Novices Chase** (1956) Glorious Twelfth
The **National Hunt H'cap Chase** (1954) Holly Bank
The **Topham Trophy** (1954) Little Yid; (1962) Dagmar Gittal

He continued to have the occasional ride while training and rode his last race at Hexham when 75 years old.
He retired in 1971, handing over his yard briefly to his last retained jockey, Tommy Stack. Stack soon found out that he could not ride and train to his own satisfaction and it was then taken over by Tony Gillam. Renton's last winner was, ironically, the triple National winner Red Rum.

REUGNY
Chestnut horse, 1868, Minos—Reine Blanche (The Baron). Bred in France.
Reugny won a hurdle race and three chases for Lord Aylesford as a four-year-old and was then bought by Captain Machell in a package deal with Defence and Disturbance for a total of £1,200. He was so footsore that he was turned out at the Limber Magna establishment of Machell's associate and jockey, John Maunsell Richardson.
Reugny did not race prior to the 1874 Grand National but was well galloped at home and started 5-1 favourite, 10-12 (Mr J. M. Richardson) and won by 6l, 4l, from Chimney Sweep, 10-2 (J. Jones) and Merlin, 10-7 (J. Adams). His victory caused a rift between owner and jockey

as result of which Richardson never raced again.

Reugny, Defence and Disturbance were sold on at an enormous profit but Reugny who evidently was difficult to train, did not run for two seasons and never won again.

REYNOLDSTOWN

Brown or black gelding, 1927, registered in Miss Prior's Half-Bred Stud Book, My Prince—Fromage (Frontina). Bred by Mr R. Ball.

As a young horse Reynoldstown was nearly sold to Mr James Rank who was at the time avidly scouring the countryside for sons of My Prince. But Mr Rank would not buy a black horse and Reynoldstown became the property of Maj. Noel Furlong whose horses were trained by himself and ridden by his son Frank, a subaltern in the 9th Lancers.

Reynoldstown, unkindly described as a "long-backed, narrow-gutted brute", was quick to show ability and won four hurdle races before going on to win eight chases including the Grand National two years in succession:

1935 11-4 (Mr F. Furlong), 22/1, by 3l, 8l, from Blue Prince, 10-7 (W. Parvin) and Thomond II, 11-13 (W. Speck).
1936 12-2 (Mr F. Walwyn), 10/1, by 12l, 6l, from Ego, 10-8 (incl. 11lb overweight) (Mr H. Llewellyn) and Bachelor Prince, 10-9 (J. Fawcus).

In 1935 Golden Miller, the previous year's winner was favourite at 2/1 but unseated his rider at Valentine's on the first circuit. Reynoldstown was less fancied than the stable's other runner, Really True who started at 18/1. Reynoldstown beat Golden Miller's record for the race by one-fifth sec. and his time of 9 min. 20.20 secs. stood until 1973.

In 1936 Frank Furlong was unable to do the weight so a brother-officer, Mr Fulke Walwyn, took the ride. Not until 1974 did another horse win the National in successive years or carry 12 stone successfully.

RICHARDS, Gordon W. (b.1930)

Gordon Richards was born in the West Country and apprenticed to J. C. Waugh and subsequently to Ivor Anthony. For a period he was attached to Mrs Louie Dingwell and rode on the Flat. He then moved north and switched to fences in which sphere he was beginning to make a name for himself, riding for Arthur Stephenson when back injuries, sustained in a fall at Perth, ended his career in the saddle.

Having established himself in the north, he bought a farm at Bamburgh, Northumberland, and set up a small stable of hunters and liveries. One of his enterprises was to provide the horses for the film *Becket*. However the pull of steeplechasing was too strong to be denied and in 1964 he took out a licence to train. A year later he moved to the stables at Greystoke Castle, a beautiful fourteenth-century building on the edge of the Lake District, where Tommy Robson had previously trained. Here, assisted from 1966-75 by Ron Barry, and 1975-77 by Jonjo O'Neill, his team blossomed into one of the most powerful in the North.

His first good horse, his favourite and he still maintains the best, was Playlord (12 races including the 1969 Scottish Grand National and Great Yorkshire).

His major successes include:

The Grand National (1978) Lucius
The King George VI Chase (1969) Titus Oates
The Whitbread Gold Cup (1971) Titus Oates
The Massey-Ferguson Gold Cup (1969) Titus Oates
The Scottish Grand National (1969) Playlord
The Great Yorkshire Chase (1969) Playlord
The Cheltenham Trial Hurdle (1975) Sea Pigeon
The Victor Ludorum Hurdle (1978) Mixed Melody

In 1975-76 he became the second trainer to saddle over 100 winners in a season. He finished third in the Trainer's List with 45 winners of 105 races worth £75,454, while in 1977-8, boosted by the fine National win of Lucius, he finished third with 29 winners of 54 races worth £88,091.

RICHARDSON, John Maunsell (1846-1912)

John Maunsell Richardson was born at Limber Magna in Lincolnshire. He was educated at Harrow where he proved a natural athlete and played in the cricket team that beat Eton by an innings and 67 runs. He went on to Cambridge where he started hunt racing. Although he progressed to become an amateur of the very highest class, hunting remained his first love. He was Master of the Cambridge Drag and later shared a 'box' in Leicestershire with his brother and Rolly Meglund (later Earl of Minto and Viceroy of India).

He was a polished natural horseman and disapproved violently of short leathers and the forward seat. He won the National Hunt Chase (1870) on Schiedam, the Scottish Grand National (1871) on Keystone and the 1873 Grand National on Disturbance and 1874 on Reugny, after which he had a blazing row with that horse's owner, James Machell (*q.v.*) and rode racing no more. He was Champion Amateur in 1872 riding 56 winners.

He later married the widowed Countess of Yarborough and became Unionist M.P. for Brigg. He was reckoned a great authority on the conformation of both horse and hound and regularly judged at both Dublin and Peterborough. He also wrote for the *Daily Telegraph* and Finch Mason's *Heroes and Heroines of the Grand National* is dedicated to him.

RIMELL, Thomas Frederick (b.1913)

The son of the successful Kinnersley trainer Tom Rimell (*q.v.*) and brother-in-law of Gerry Wilson, Fred Rimell grew up in the world of hunting and steeplechasing. He was apprenticed to his father and rode 34 winners on the Flat before turning to jumping in 1932. The combination of his hunting background and Flat polish made a formidable N.H. jockey and he was Champion Jockey on four occasions, 1938-39 with 61 winners, 1939-40 with 24, 1944-45 with 15 (equal with 'Frenchie' Nicholson) and 1945-46 with 54. In 1947 he broke his neck twice in eight months which terminated his riding career. The second occasion was on the afternoon of the Cheltenham dinner given annually in honour of the previous season's Champion Jockey. He should have been the guest of honour but spent the night in hospital instead.

He had already taken out a licence to train and now began to develop at Kinnersley what became one of jumping's 'big three' stables.

His major victories include:

The Cheltenham Gold Cup (1967) Woodland Venture; 1976) Royal Frolic

The Grand National (1956) E.S.B.; (1961) Nicolaus Silver; (1970) Gay Trip; (1976) Rag Trade

The Champion Hurdle (1973) Comedy of Errors; (1975) Comedy of Errors

The Irish Sweeps Hurdle (1969) Normandy; (1973) Comedy of Errors; (1974) Comedy of Errors

The Daily Express Triumph Hurdle (1969) Coral Diver; (1972) Zarib; (1978) Connaught Ranger

The Scottish Grand National (1967) The Fossa

The Scottish Champion Hurdle (1972) Coral Diver; (1975 Comedy of Erors

The Welsh Grand National (1957) Creola; (1968) Glenn; (1970) French Excuse; (1976) Rag Trade

The Welsh Champion Hurdle (1972) Comedy of Errors;

The Mackeson Gold Cup (1968) Jupiter Boy; (1969) Gay Trip; (1970) Chatham; (1971) Gay Trip

The Lancashire Chase (1949) Coloured School Boy; (1950) Coloured School Boy

The Liverpool Hurdle (1949) Ballandine; (1958) Tokoroa

The Grand Sefton (1961) Nicolaus Silver; (1964) Red Thorn; (1965) The Fossa

The Victor Ludorum Hurdle (1972) North Pole; (1975) Zip Fastener

The Fighting Fifth Hurdle (1971) Inishmaan; (1972) Comedy of Errors; (1973) Comedy of Errors; (1974) Comedy of Errors

The Great Yorkshire Chase (1975) Rough House

The Whitbread Gold Cup (1977) Andy Pandy

The Greenall-Whitley Chase (1976) Royal Frolic

The Royal Doulton H'cap Hurdle (1978) Royal Gaye

In 1976 he brought off the Grand National/Cheltenham Gold Cup double, which had not been achieved since Basil Briscoe, with Golden Miller in 1934, ridden, by an odd coincidence, by his brother-in-law Gerry Wilson (*q.v.*).

The Rimell horses are always impeccably schooled and turned out and many are of a clearly recognizable pattern. Deep-bodied, short-legged, active horses of medium size are what the 'Master of Kinnersley' appears to like best, the obvious example being Gay Trip.

He has been Leading Trainer on four occasions. In 1975-76 he became the second trainer to win £100,000 for his patrons in the season.

1960-61	28 winners of 58 races worth	£34,811
1968-69	32 „ „ 62 „ „	£38,344
1969-70	35 „ „ 77 „ „	£61,864
1975-76	30 „ „ 49 „ „	£111,740

RIMELL, Thomas Reginald (d.1967)

Tom Rimell was head-lad to Joe Butters and took out a licence to train at Kinnersley in 1924. His biggest success was to win the 1932 Grand National with Forbra. His son, Fred (q.v.) rode many winners for the stable and took it over after World War II. His daughter, Vera, married Gerry Wilson.

RIDDEN FOR HIRE

Any person who has held a professional jockey's licence from any recognized Turf Authority or who has ever been paid directly or indirectly for riding in a race or who, within the period of the previous three years has been paid either as a stable employee in a licensed stable or as a groom in a Hunt, private, livery or horse-dealer's yard or as a Hunt Servant, is considered to have ridden for hire and is not eligible to hold an Amateur Riders Permit.

ROBERTS, John Frederick (1917-74)

The son of the Cheltenham trainer, Ben Roberts, John Roberts succeeded his father and retired in 1970, having held a licence for 25 years. By far his biggest success was winning the 1954 Cheltenham Gold Cup with Four Ten.

ROBINSON, George William (b.1934)

An Irishman and a very polished, all-round horseman, Willie Robinson began riding as a amateur but soon turned professional. He rode his first winner at Navan in 1955 and shortly afterwards joined Dan Moore. With a riding weight of under 9st for most of his career, he was able to ride on the Flat and was second in the 1958 Derby on Paddy's Point.

In the early 'sixties he came to England and was retained by Fulke Walwyn.

His principal victories were:

The Cheltenham Gold Cup (1963) Mill House

The Grand National (1964) Team Spirit

The Champion Hurdle (1962) Anzio; (1965) Kirriemuir

The King George VI Chase (1963) Mill House

The Hennessy Gold Cup (1961) Mandarin; (1963) Mill House; (1968) Man o' the West

The Grand Sefton (1963) Team Spirit

The Mildmay Memorial (1960) Team Spirit

He relinquished his licence in 1970 and now lives in Ireland where he does a good deal of hunting and show-jumping.

ROBSON, Thomas William, M.R.C.V.S. (b.1924)

Tommy Robson was born on a farm on the Duke of Northumberland's estate and qualified at the Royal Veterinary College, Edinburgh, in 1950. He learnt a great deal from Stewart Wight and rode as an amateur from 1942-60 and as a professional from 1961-63. He took out a permit to train in 1952 and a full licence at the beginning of 1953-54 with stables at Penrith in Cumberland.

He won the Scottish Grand National twice, on Queen's Taste in 1953 and Sham Fight, who he also trained, in 1962. He also trained Brasher to win the race in 1965, the last year it was held at Bogside. He rode and trained his wife's Merry Windsor to win the Wetherby H'cap Chase (1955) while his two biggest successes were the Scottish Champion Hurdle (1968) with Al Alawi and the 1964 Champion Hurdle with Magic Court.

He also won some good races on the Flat, chiefly with well-bred 'cast-offs' from fashionable Newmarket stables. Since 1973 he has assisted Barry Hills at Lambourn.

RODDY OWEN

Bay gelding, 1949, Owenstown—Desla's Star (Cygnus or Bachelor's Heir). Bred by Mr A. Nolan.

Roddy Owen, a massively handsome horse, was bought by Lord Fingall as an unbroken five-year-old. He won a total of three hurdle races and 13 chases including the Leopardstown Chase (1958) beating the subsequent National winner, Mr What, by eight lengths giving him 26lb, and the 1959 Cheltenham Gold

Cup, (H. Beasley), 5/1, by 3l, 10l, from
Linwell (F. T. Winter) and Lochroe (A.
Freeman). He was undoubtedly a fortunate winner for Pas Seul had a clear
lead when he fell at the last, badly in-
terfering with Linwell and Lochroe.

Roddy Owen had a tremendous duel
with Lochroe in the 1958 King George
VI Chase which Lochroe won by a head.
He was trained by Danny Morgan.

RODDICK, Brig. Mark G., D.S.O. (d.1959)

Mark Roddick served with the Royal
Artillery during World War I and transferred to the 10th Hussars in 1932. During the 1930s he rode very successfully as
an amateur rider, winning the Grand
Military Gold Cup three years in succession, in 1937 with Buck Willow, 1938
with Kilstar and 1939 with Fillip, all of
whom he trained himself. He served with
great distinction during World War II
and rose to command the 4th Light Armoured Brigade in the Western Desert.
He was wounded after Alamein. After
the war he retired in Ireland.

ROGERS, Charles (1899-1971)

Charlie Rogers is best remembered
for his association with that most
unorthodox owner, Miss Dorothy Paget,
which began at the N.H. meeting of 1939
when she asked him to find replacements
for Golden Miller and Insurance. He
found her Roman Hackle and Solford,
respective winners of the 1940 Gold Cup
and Champion Hurdle.

She nicknamed him Romeo and he
remained her racing manager until her
death. He also trained her horses in
Ireland and won her the 1943 Irish National with Golden Jack (see DAN
MOORE) and the 1946 Champion Hurdle
with Distel. He had previously won the
Irish National twice with Impudent Bar-
ney (1931) and Copper Court (1932).

He also managed her studs at
Ballymacoll and Killeen. Other great
horses who passed through his hands
were Brown Jack (q.v.) who he bought as
a yearling and Royal Mail (q.v.), whom
he bred.

His horses were always beautifully
schooled and turned out and he insisted
on a very high standard of stable
management. A gay, kind, witty man, he
was a delightful companion and a fine
judge of both horse and man.

ROIMOND

Chestnut gelding, 1941, Roidore—
Ellamond (Loch Lomond). Bred by
Mrs W. J. Fennell.

A grand stamp of horse built on the
lines beloved by the 1st Lord Bicester,
Roimond raced for seven seasons, won
15 chases and was second to Russian
Hero in the 1949 Grand National.

Among his best victories were the
Mildmay Memorial, Sandown (1951), the
Gold Cup Trial Chase, Birmingham
(1949), and the New Year Chase, Chel-
tenham (1949), He was also second to
Cottage Rake in the 1948 King George
VI. Roimond was trained by George
Beeby and usually ridden by Dick
Francis.

ROMAN HACKLE

(Late Samurai.) Bay gelding, 1933,
Yutoi—Wanoya (Wavelets Pride). Bred
by Capt. and Mrs G. Hastings.

A large, rather plain, raw-boned individual, Roman Hackle was bought by
Charlie Rogers for Miss Dorothy Paget
(q.v.) for whom he won nine races
including the Leopardstown Chase, the
Broadway Novices Chase (1939) and the
1940 Cheltenham Gold Cup (E.
Williams), evens, by 10l, 2l, from Black
Hawk (T. Rimell) and Royal Mail (D.
Morgan). At the time Roman Hackle was
thought to be an exceptional horse but he
proved disappointing. He was favourite
for the 1941 Gold Cup but finished down
the field behind Poet Prince.

ROMAN OAK

Bay gelding, 1884, not in the General
Stud Book by Ascetic, dam by
Whistlebinkie.

Roman Oak won six races including
the 1891 Champion Chase, Liverpool,
with 12-9, the Irish International Handicap Chase, Leopardstown (1891) and
the Lancashire Chase, Manchester
(1892).

ROQUEFORT

Brown gelding, 1879, Winslow—Cream
Cheese (Parmesan). Bred by Mr J.
Gretton.

A small, well-made horse, an excellent
jumper with plenty of speed, Roquefort's
considerable ability was tempered by
great cunning which combined with his
hard-pulling propensities made him an
extremely difficult horse to ride.

As a four- and five-year-old he won

three Hunter Flat races, a hurdle and two steeplechases and was third in the Grand National. The following year, 1885, 11-0 (Mr E. P. Wilson), 100/30f, he won by 2l, 4l from Frigate, 11-10 (Mr H. Beasley) and Black Prince, 10-5 (T. Skelton).

He maintained his form through 1886 winning the Champion Chase and the Grand Sefton with big weights but the next year he bolted and ran off the course in all his starts. In 1889 he relented briefly and won the Champion Chase with 12-10 but the following season he reverted to his bad old ways and ran out in two of his three races.

Roquefort had many changes of owner and trainer but spent the greater and certainly the most successful part of his career in the Bishops Sutton yard of Arthur Yates for whom John Swatton held the licence.

ROSE PARK
Chestnut gelding, 1946, Pactolus—Primulas (Glanmerin). Bred by Mr F. Purcell.

Mr Guy Lawrence's Rose Park, a fast, bold-jumping front runner won two hurdle races and 18 chases. Basically a two-miler, he was forced through the lack of opportunities at that distance, to attempt the classic distances of three miles and upwards and by a combination of blinding speed, courage and enterprising tactics he achieved considerable success. Among his victories were the Gainsborough Chase, Sandown (1957) and the King George VI Chase, Kempton (1956). Moreover he was in the lead and looking all over the winner when he fell at the second last in the 1953 Cheltenham Gold Cup.

Rose Park went to America for the International Chase in 1954 but after a prolonged and exhausting journey he failed to show anything approaching his proper form. He was trained by Peter Cazalet.

ROSYTH
Chestnut horse, 1958, Admiral's Walk—Rossenhall (Chamossaire). Bred by Maj. T. Dixon.

After a modest career on the Flat during which he won four races in three seasons for Ryan Jarvis, Rosyth was sold for 430 guineas at Doncaster to Mr J. K. Sankey and went to Ryan Price.

Rated "none too consistent" (Timeform) on the Flat, he displayed similar characteristics over hurdles but fortunately for his connections he was able to produce his best form at the right time. In four seasons he won only three races but these included the first two runnings of the Schweppes Gold Trophy (1963 and 1964) by far the most valuable handicap hurdle race in the Calendar.

His second victory was a remarkable performance for the field of 24 included three Champion Hurdlers, Salmon Spray second, Magic Court fourth and Another Flash sixth. In both these races he was ridden by Josh Gifford.

Rosyth stood as a stallion at his owner's Calehill Stud, Charing, Kent.

ROUCH, William Albert (1863-1947)
William Rouch was head of the world-famous horse photography business. His father founded the firm, which were originally manufacturing chemists and dealers in photographic apparatus and invented portable dark-room tents, Collodian dry-plates and the 'Eureka' camera. William Rouch brought the firm to world-wide prestige and gained a Royal Warrant through his portraits of the royal Derby winners, Persimmon and Minoru. He was succeeded by his nephew, Basil Wood.

ROWLAND ROY
Bay gelding, 1939, Monktown—Laurel Lady (Sundari). Bred by Mr M. Halloran.

Mr A. G. Boley's Rowland Roy arrived unheralded in Fulke Walwyn's yard in a job lot of four horses. Three of them were palpably not racehorses and were returned forthwith but Rowland Roy remained and won eight chases including the Scottish Grand National (1947), the King George VI Chase, Kempton (1947) and the Ewell Chase, Sandown (1949).

ROWLANDS, Dr Fothergill (d.1878)
The son of a Monmouthshire doctor, 'Fogo' Rowlands qualified himself and practised until 1844 when he gave up the medical profession and became one of the leading amateurs of his generation. He rode frequently for Lord Strathmore and is seen on that peer's The Switcher in Herring's *Steeplechase Cracks*. He won the old Baden-Baden Hunt Chase in 1862 on Medora and once won at a race at Loo for the King of the Netherlands. He was one of the men responsible for the revival of chasing in the 'sixties and

instigated the National Hunt Chase, first run at Market Harborough in 1859.

Later he became a trainer with headquarters at Prestbury Park, Cheltenham. He rented Prestbury House from Christopher Capel and his owners included the Duke of Hamilton, Mr Reginald Herbert and Sir John Astley (The Mate). He won the Cheltenham Grand Annual 1866 with Columbia and the Croydon Hurdle with The Scamp. Later he moved to Pitt Place, Epsom, and added the Prince of Wales and Lord Marcus Beresford to his patrons.

ROYAL APPROACH

Brown or black gelding, 1948, King's Approach—Flotation (Felicitation). Bred by Mr John Flannery.

When Lord Bicester's Royal Approach, who won a hurdle race at five years, won the Irish Grand National in 1954 after an unbeaten season of six races including the Carrickmines Chase, Leopardstown, and the Cathcart Chase, National Hunt Meeting, he was thought to be a world beater who might achieve his owner's lifelong ambition to win the National. Tragically he broke a bone in his hind leg when out to grass that summer and although he recovered sufficiently to run and indeed to be placed in 1956-57 the brilliance was gone and he never won again. Royal Approach was trained by Tom Dreaper and ridden by Pat Taaffe.

ROYAL FALCON

Chestnut horse, 1923, White Eagle—Queen Mother (Diamond Jubilee). Bred by the National Stud.

A most resolute and supremely consistent horse, Royal Falcon won nine races on the Flat and six hurdle races including the Imperial Cup, Sandown (1928) and the 1929 Champion Hurdle (F. B. Rees), 11/2, by 4l, 5l, from Rolie (W. Stott) and Clean Cash (G. Pellerin). Royal Falcon was trained by F. Leach when owned by Mrs G. Drummond. After his Imperial Cup victory he was sold to Miss Williams-Bulkeley and went to Robert Gore. After his Champion Hurdle victory he went to America.

ROYAL FROLIC

Bay gelding, 1969, Royal Buck—Forward Miss (Flyon). Bred by John Seymour, in Ireland.

An imposing individual, standing over a lot of ground, who won the Yearling Championship at the Royal Dublin Show. Royal Frolic was having only the 12th race of his career when he won the 1976 Piper Heidsick Cheltenham Gold Cup (J. Burke), 14-1, by 5l, the same, from Brown Lad (T. Carberry) and Colebridge (F. Berry).

He was bought for 5,200 guineas by Fred Rimell for Sir Edward Hanmer at the Doncaster August Sales in 1972 and after just one run at the end of the year, he had an attack of liver fluke which resulted in him missing a year. He came back in 1974-75 and has to date won a hurdle race and nine chases, of which the most important after the Gold Cup was the Greenall-Whitley Handicap Chase, Haydock (1976).

Until his facile win in that race he had not been generally regarded as an immediate Gold Cup prospect. However the absence of both Captain Christy and Easby Abbey prompted trainer, Fred Rimell, to run him.

Royal Frolic provided the first leg of a Gold Cup/Grand National double completed by Rag Trade for Fred Rimell and stable jockey, John Burke. He missed season 1976-77 but came back the following year to win two chases and run a fine race for the Cheltenham Gold Cup in which he would almost certainly have been second had he not fallen at the last.

ROYAL MAIL

Black gelding, 1929, registered in Miss Prior's Half-Bred Stud Book, My Prince—Flying May (Flying Hackle). Bred by Mr C. A. Rogers.

Royal Mail was bought as an unbroken three-year-old by Hubert Hartigan who sold him on to Mr Hugh Lloyd-Thomas, a former assistant secretary to the Prince of Wales and a member of the British Embassy Staff. Mr Lloyd-Thomas sent his purchase to Ivor Anthony who saddled him to win the two hurdle races and 14 chases including the Becher Chase and the 1937 Grand National, 11-13 (E. Williams), from Cooleen, 11-4 (Mr J. Fawcus) and Pucka Belle, 10-7 (Mr E. W. Bailey). He was also second to Golden Miller in the 1936 Cheltenham Gold Cup and third to Roman Hackle in 1940.

Royal Mail was ridden on more than one occasion by his owner who proposed to ride him in the 1938 National. Tragically he was killed from a fall in a chase at Derby a month before and

Royal Mail was put up for sale. He was bought for £6,500 by Mrs Evans and ran in the National ridden as before by Evan Williams. Carrying 12-7, he finished unplaced.

ROYAL MARSHAL II
Brown gelding, 1967. Registered in Miss Prior's Half-Bred Stud Book, Marshal Pil—Princess Puzzlement (Gregalach's Nephew). Bred by Mrs Lloyd-Thomas.

A half-brother to the 1972 Grand National winner, Well To Do (q.v.), and three other winners, Royal Marshal II is owned by Mr John Sumner and trained by Tim Forster. An inveterate breaker of blood vessels, he has to be very carefully handled and can only be satisfactorily prepared for an autumn campaign. From limited opportunities he has won three hurdle races and five chases including the Hennessy Cognac Gold Cup, Newbury (1974) and the King George IV Chase, Kempton (1976). Royal Marshal II is always ridden by stable jockey Graham Thorner.

ROYAL RELIEF
Bay gelding, 1964, Flush Royal—French Colleen (Lobau). Bred by Mr E. R. Courage.

A member of Mr Edward Courage's famous Drumrora family (q.v.), Royal Relief, a chunky, attractive gelding of medium size, raced for 10 consecutive seasons winning two hurdle races and 14 chases, including the National Hunt Two Mile Champion Chase twice (1972 and 1974) and the Stone's Ginger Wine Chase (1972). A somewhat lazy horse who needed some give in the ground, he seemed to produce his best at Cheltenham. Besides his two victories in the Champion Chase he was placed four times in the race, 2nd in 1970 to Straight Fort, beaten ¼l when only a novice, in 1971 third to Crisp, in 1973 when beaten ¾l by Inkslinger and in 1975 when second to Lough Inagh. Like all his family he was trained by his owner-breeder.

ROYAL TAN
Chestnut gelding, 1944, registered in Miss Prior's Half-Bred Stud Book, Tartan—Princess of the Birds (Prince Hermes). Bred by Mr J. Toppin in Co. Tipperary, Ireland.

At one stage of his career the blaze-faced Royal Tan seemed destined to be one of the Grand National bridesmaids who litter the Calendar. In 1951 he came to the last with his race won only to be unbalanced by his excited amateur rider and blunder away his chance leaving the plodding Nickel Coin to win easily. The following year he fell at the very same fence when challenging strongly for the lead, after which he did not run for a year. However his turn came in 1954 when, 11-7 (B. Marshall), 8/1, he prevailed by a neck and 10l, over Tudor Line, 10-7 (G. Slack) and Irish Lizard, 10-5 (M. Scudamore).

His former rider, 'Phonsie' O'Brien, brother of trainer Vincent, had come to the conclusion that Royal Tan would not tolerate dictation from the saddle and that had the horse been left to his own devices the two fateful errors would not have occurred.

Royal Tan who won the National in the colours of Joe Griffin ('Mincemeat Joe') won a total of eight chases including the National Hunt Handicap Chase (1952). He was also third to E.S.B. in the 1956 National.

ROYAL TOSS
Brown gelding, 1962, registered in Miss Prior's Half-Bred Stud Book, Royal Challenger—Spinning Coin II (Artist's Son). Bred by Mr H. Handel.

Royal Toss, who was owned and trained under permit by his breeder, was out of the very able, but somewhat erratic West Country mare, Spinning Coin II, winner of 10 point-to-points and two hunter-chases. A big, handsome horse, always impeccably turned out, he won a hurdle race and 11 chases including the Welsh Grand National, Chepstow (1971), the Whitbread Gold Cup, Sandown (1970), the Mildmay Memorial, Sandown (1972) and finished second, beaten ¾l, to Glencaraig Lady in the 1972 Cheltenham Gold Cup.

He broke down in preparation for the 1973 Gold Cup and although he raced and won again he was past his best. Royal Toss was ridden in most of his races by Nigel Wakley.

RUBIO
Chestnut gelding, 1898, Star Ruby—La Toquera (Sir Mordred). Bred by the Rancho del Paso Stud, California, U.S.A.

Of all the strange, romantic stories behind Grand National winners, few can match the tale of the 1908 winner, Rubio. Bred in America, he came to this country as a yearling and despite his dam being a half-sister to the mighty Sceptre, fetched a mere 15 guineas at the Newmarket Sales. He was later resold for 95 guineas to Maj. F. Douglas-Pennant as a hunter and proved such a success that he was sent to Bernard Bletsoe to be trained. In 1903 he won three chases but then broke down. When he regained soundness he was sent to the Prospect Arms, Towcester, to pull the hotel bus. This drastic treatment was entirely successful and by the end of 1906 he was back in training, this time with Fred Withington. In 1907-08 he won four races including the 1908 Grand National, 10-5 (H. Bletsoe), 66/1, by 10l, 6l, from his stable companion Mattie McGregor, 10-6 (W. Bissill) and The Lawyer III, 10-13 (Mr P. Whitaker). Rubio broke down approaching the water in the 1909 National and was retired.

RULES OF RACING

The first-published set of Rules for Steeple Chases appear in the preface of Mr Henry Wright's *Steeplechase Calendar* of 1826-44.

Mr Wright comments: "the aim, object and practice of Steeple Chasing correspond in the main features so exactly with Racing, that the same Rules and Regulations have generally been found applicable to either sport; in some minor particulars, however, the Laws of the steeple chase differ and go farther than such as have hitherto been deemed amply sufficient for flat racing ... ".

Among his suggestions are that any rider going "upwards of 100 yards on any high-road, lane or public thoroughfare" will be disqualified. Similarly anyone pusillanimous enough to go through a gate.

If the term 'Gentleman Riders' must be used – and Mr Wright strongly deprecates it, it should allude only to persons received in society as gentleman: "Members of the leading London Clubs, Foxhunting or Racing Clubs, Officers in the Army or Navy, Barristers, Solicitors, Medical Men or others so considered by position and profession and who do not and never have been in the habit of receiving remuneration for riding, either directly or in a form of travelling expenses or any other indirect manner."

He further stipulated that in the event of a rider falling and not being able to continue, some other rider could complete the course provided he could draw the weight. The state of the weather and ground was at all times to be at the discretion of the Stewards who could postpone or cancel as they thought fit. Bets would only stand if the race were decided on the day fixed, except by mutual agreement.

The Committee, set up by Viscount Andover (later Earl of Suffolk and Berkshire), Mr B. J. Angell, Mr E. C. Burton and Mr W. G. Craven in 1863, grew into the Grand National Hunt Committee that by 1867 had a published set of rules and official returns entitled *Steeplechases Past.*

From then on the National Hunt Committee gradually extended their authority until they had achieved a comprehensive control of the sport.

In 1879 it was announced that every jockey must have an annual licence which could be obtained by application to Weatherbys and for which they had to pay one sovereign to the Bentinck Benevolent Fund. Jockeys' fees were to be five sovereigns a ride, ten sovereigns a winner, one sovereign expenses. Shortly afterwards a directive went out that all races must be advertised in *The Racing Calendar* as being subject to the Rules of the Grand National Hunt Committee. Every meeting had to be attended by at least two Stewards and a Judge, Clerk of the Scales, Handicapper and Starter.

By 1889 registration of colours was compulsory. In 1890 an inspector of courses was appointed by the Stewards of the N.H. Committee and regulations were laid down for courses.

No race was to be less than two miles. In all steeplechases "there shall be 12 fences in the first two miles and six in every mile thereafter. In every mile there shall be at least one open ditch six feet wide and three feet deep, in front of a fence of four feet six inches, guarded by a single rail or left open. There shall be a water jump at least 12 feet wide and 2 feet deep, open or guarded by a perpendicular fence not exceeding two feet in height".

For hurdle races there were not to be no less than eight flights in the first two miles and an additional flight for every quarter-mile. The hurdles were to be not less than three feet six inches.

In 1904 rules against doping were introduced.

By 1910 Trainers, Clerks of Courses,

Handicappers, Stakeholders, Clerks of
the Scales, Starters and Judges all
required licences from the N.H. Committee, who had also turned their attention to race programmes. They laid down
that half the guaranteed prize money
must be given in steeplechases and that
every programme must contain at least
two steeplechases, one of more than three
miles. Within ten years Racecourse Staff
Managers, Ring Inspectors, Gate
Keepers and Checktakers had come into
the net and required licences if employed
at more than one meeting per year.

In 1947 the photo-finish camera was
introduced.

In 1966 Mrs Nagle won her case
against the Jockey Club and henceforth
ladies were allowed to hold licences to
train under both Jockey Club and
National Hunt Rules.

In 1967 Passports were introduced as a
compulsory documentary identification
for all thoroughbreds.

In 1968 the Jockey Club and the
National Hunt Committee amalgamated
and the following year a combined set of
rules were drawn up.

In 1976 as a result of the Sex
Discrimination Act, ladies were permitted to ride in steeplechases.

The Rules of Racing for 1978 are
reproduced here and elsewhere in this
book by kind permission of the Jockey
Club. Portions referring solely to Flat
racing have been omitted.

RUSSIAN HERO
Bay gelding, 1940, Peter the Great

—Logique (Lex). Bred by Mr F. W.
Williamson.

Despite having hunted and won
point-to-points in his youth, Russian
Hero was an erratic jumper who stayed a
maximum of $2\frac{1}{2}$ miles on park courses so
it was not surprising that, despite his
eight previous victories, he was allowed
to start at 66/1 for the 1949 Grand National.

His stable companion, Lord Bicester's
Roimond was much preferred in the
betting but Russian Hero, 10-8 (L.
McMorrow), 66/1, won by 8l, 1l, from
Roimond, 11-12 (R. Francis) and Royal
Mount, 10-12 (P. Doyle). Russian Hero,
who was tipped only by the *Daily
Worker*, was raced by his breeder Mr
Williamson and trained by George
Owen, He did not win subsequently.

RUTTLE, J. J. (1877-1948)
Jack Ruttle, an Irishman, was a fine
cross-country rider in his youth. He then
became a trainer, at first in a private
capacity for the Dixon family and later
setting up a public stable at Ringwood.
His biggest success was to win the 1939
Grand National with Workman, whom
he bought after seeing him run at a local
point-to-point. He persuaded Tim Hyde
(*q.v.*), who was more of a showing and
show-jumping rider than a jockey, to ride
the horse because "only Hyde was right
for Workman". He also won the Irish
Grand National twice, with Halston in
1920 and 1922.

SAFFRON TARTAN

Bay or brown gelding, 1951, Tartan —Kellsboro' Witch (Jackdaw of Rheims). Bred by Mr C. C. Thompson.

A very handsome gelding whose dam was a half-sister to Kellsboro' Jack and also to the grandam of Flame Gun (*q.v.*), Saffron Tartan won a bumper, three hurdle races and seven chases, including the Gloucester Hurdle, the King George VI Chase (1960) and the 1961 Cheltenham Gold Cup (F. Winter), 2/1f, by 1½l, 3l, from Pas Seul (D. Dick) and Mandarin (P. G. Madden).

Owned by Colonel Westmacott, he was trained to start with by Vincent O'Brien, who thought him the best chaser to pass through his hands and later, when the maestro had given up his National Hunt interests, by Don Butchers.

Fred Winter also rated him among the two best he had ridden and he was perhaps unlucky in that respiratory and leg troubles prevented him from achieving a more impressive record. He was hobdayed in 1959 and broke down in preparation for the 1961 King George VI Chase.

He was also a smart hurdler and won a division of the Gloucester Hurdle and was third in the 1960 Champion Hurdle.

SALAMANDER

Bay or brown gelding, 1859, Fire-eater —Rosalba (Colwick). Bred by Mr J. Bouchier.

Salamander, who was reputed to have a crooked foreleg, was bought cheaply, as part of a job lot, by Mr Edward Studd as a hunter. If his portrait is to be believed he was a lovely stamp of horse with both quality and substance and soon showed his new owner that he had ability to match his looks.

Mr Studd engaged crack amateur Alec Goodman to ride Salamander in the 1866 Grand National and backed him to win

£40,000 at 40/1. His confidence was richly repaid for Salamander, 10-7 (Mr A. Goodman), 40/1, won pulling up by 10l, 4l, from Cortolvin, 11-6 (J. Page) and Creole, 10-10 (G. Waddington). The following week he won the important Warwick Grand Annual but in April he fell in a minor race at Crewkerne and broke his back.

SALES

The principal sales at which National Hunt Bloodstock is offered are J. P. Botterill's, The Windsor Forest Stud who sell at Ascot, Doncaster Bloodstock Sales Ltd. who sell at the Sales paddocks, Doncaster and Tattersalls who sell at the Park Paddocks, Newmarket. Many British buyers deal at Robert J. Goff and Company, Kill and Ballsbridge International Bloodstock Sales Ltd, Dublin.

SALMON SPRAY

Chestnut gelding, 1958, Vulgan—Fly Book (Flyon). Bred by Mr W. H. Corry.

A full-brother to the dual Whitbread winner Larbawn, Salmon Spray was a chunkily built, attractive individual, a beautiful mover and at his best a brilliant hurdler. Owned by Mrs John Rogerson and trained for her by Bob Turnell, he won a total of two chases and 12 hurdle races including the Liverpool Hurdle and the 1966 Champion Hurdle (J. Haine), 4/1, by 3l, ¾l, from Sempervivum (J. King) and Flyingbolt (P. Taaffe). He was favourite for the 1965 Champion Hurdle but caused a sensation by falling at the second flight. Salmon Spray twisted his gut and had to be put down in May 1970.

SANDOWN (Group 1)

In 1867 a committee, including the Duke of Hamilton and the Earl of Rosebery, was formed with the object of constructing a racecourse in the wooded grounds of Sandown Park on the outskirts of the village of Esher. Two grandstands were built, one for the general public and one for club members, to a design borrowed from France. A £2,000 fence was then erected round the perimeter and the inaugural meeting, a three-day affair comprising both Flat races and steeplechases was held in April 1875. The National Hunt Chase was held at Sandown that year although the Grand National Hunt Committee were doubtful of the propriety of it being held on an enclosed, artificial course.

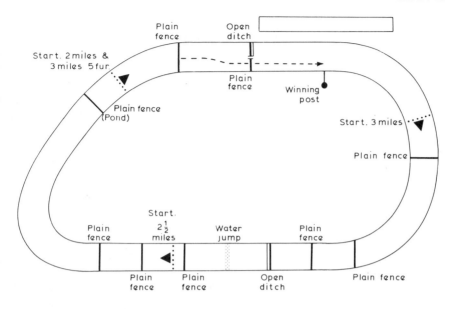

The Grand International Steeplechase was the first big race to be instituted. It was run over four miles (later altered to 3½ miles and finally 3m, 5f, 25y) and £1,200 was added, making the total value over £2,000. This was swiftly followed by the Great Sandown Hurdle Race, the Great Sandown Chase and the Prince of Wales Chase in honour of the Prince who was a loyal patron of Sandown from the beginning. He won the Sandown Military Gold Cup in 1887, with Hohenlinden ridden by Roddy Owen but, greatly to the embarrassment of the stewards, was objected to by the second on the grounds that horses must be the property of officers on full pay. As His Highness was demonstrably not, they were obliged to uphold the objection. The Grand Military Gold Cup came to Sandown in 1877 and apart from visits to Rugby in 1880, Aylesbury in 1866 and Aldershot in 1887, has remained there ever since.

In 1885 the course became a limited company and a year later Hwafa Williams became Clerk of the Course. Under his direction several innovations were introduced, including the charging of a half-crown admission fee and a club membership scheme. Each member was given two lady's badges in the hopes of enticing the fair sex to come steeplechasing. Hwafa Williams was also responsible for the establishment of the Eclipse Stakes in 1886. At £10,000 it was

the richest race in the world, the prize being nearly double that of the Derby.

Sandown maintained its lead into the twentieth century. The Imperial Cup (1907) became the most valuable and competitive handicap of the year for hurdlers, a position it maintained until the introduction of the Schweppes Gold Trophy in 1963. The Mildmay Memorial, contributed by friends of Lord Mildmay, was instituted in 1951. In 1974 it became known as the Anthony Mildmay, Peter Cazalet Memorial.

The first sponsored race, The Whitbread Gold Cup (1957) also went to Sandown. It was staged at the otherwise Flat April meeting and despite the considerable misgivings as to the lateness of the season for top-class chasers, the disinterest of Flat racegoers in watching slow, staying chasers and the unwillingness of the jumping fraternity to come racing for just one steeplechase, the race has been a resounding success. It has never failed to attract a good-sized, high-quality field and a bumper crowd, there is nearly always a good finish and it has never been won by a bad horse.

The course is right-handed, oval in shape and about 1m, 5f round. The fence away from the stands is downhill. The three fences in the back straight, known as the Railway fences, are very close together and put a considerable premium on accurate jumping.

Best Times

Distance	Time	Horse-age-weight	Date
2m H	3m 43	Irish Imp 5-10-12	24-3-62
2m 5f 75y H	5m 6	Hindu Flame 7-11-5	23-3-62
2m 18y C	3m 47.90	Tingle Creek 12-11-11	4-11-78
2½m 68y C	5m 4.20	Chacon 6-10-11	21-10-70
3m 118y C	5m 59	Arkle 8-12-7	6-11-65
3m 125y C	6m 9.80	Gold Wire 10-10-9	24-3-62
3m 5f 25y C	7m 11.5	The Dikler 11-11-13	27-4-74

Grand Military Gold Cup (3m 118y)

	COURSE	HORSE	OWNER	RIDER
1867	Liverpool	Tally Ho	Mr George	Mr Gerard
1868	Rugby	King Arthur	Capt. Brabazon	Col. Knox
1869	Rugby	Juryman	Capt. Coleman	Mr Pritchard
1870	Rugby	Knockany	Lord C. Innes-Ker	Col. Knox
1871	Windsor	Donato	Mr H. R. Ray	Mr Pritchard
1872	Rugby	Charleville	Maj. Byrne	Mr H. Browne
1873	Rugby	Revirescat	Mr Heron Maxwell	Mr W. Hope-Johnstone
1874	Rugby	Marc Antoine	Capt. Ray	Col. Harford
1875	Rugby	Lady Sneerwell	Col. Byrne	Mr W. Hope-Johnstone
1876	Rugby	Earl Marshall	Lord Downe	Mr W. Hope-Johnstone
1877	Sandown	Chilblain	Mr Fitzroy	Mr W. B. Morris
1878	Sandown	Chilblain	Capt. A. Paget	Mr W. B. Morris
1879	Sandown	Boyne Water	Mr H. Fenning	Mr M. J. Hartigan
1880	Rugby	Cymrw	Mr H. S. Dalbiac	Owner
1881	Sandown	Lobelia	Mr F. Waldron	Mr Lee-Barber
1882	Sandown	Lord Chancellor	Lord Manners	Owner
1883	Sandown	Beaufort	Col. Murray	Mr Lee Barber
1884	Sandown	Larva	Maj. Tidswell	Mr J. B. Murdoch
1885	Sandown	Scorn	Capt. C. B. Childe	Mr Barton
1886	Aylesbury	Standard	Capt. Childe	Mr T. Hone
1887	Aldershot	Dalesman	Capt. Fisher	Owner

Thereafter at Sandown

	HORSE	OWNER	RIDER	TRAINER
1888	Bertha	Mr H. T. Fenwick	Mr Onslow	——
1889	St Cross	Mr B. W. J. Alexander	Capt. E. R. Owen	——
1890	Lady Sarah	Lord Annaly	Capt. Little	——
1891	Hollington	Capt. A. E. Whitaker	Capt. C. Lambton	——
1892	Ormerod	Capt. A. E. Whitaker	Capt. Bewicke	——
1893	The Midshipmite	Mr H. L. Powell	Maj. Burn-Murdoch	——
1894	Aesop	Capt. M. Hughes	Sir C. Slade	——
1895	Field Marshal	Mr Eustace Loder	Mr Crawley	——
1896	Nelly Gray	Capt. J. A. Orr-Ewing	Mr D. Campbell	——
1897	Parapluie	Col. G. H. Gough	Mr D. Campbell	——
1898	County Council	Maj. Fenwick	Maj. Onslow	——
1899	Lambay	Capt. Murray-Threipland	Owner	——
1900-02	No Race			
1903	Marpessa	Maj. E. Loder	Maj. Onslow	——
1904	Dunboyne	Mr H. E. Brassey	Maj. Richardo	——
1905	Ruy Lopez	Rear-Admiral Lambton	Capt. Stacpoole	——
1906	Royal Blaze	Mr R. F. Eyre	Capt. L. S. Denny	——
1907	Old Fairyhouse	Mr C. Bewicke	Owner	——
1908	Mount Prospect's Fortune	Capt. G. Paynter	Owner	——
1909	Sprinkle Me	Capt. E. Christie-Miller	Capt. C. W. Banbury	——
1910	Sprinkle Me	Capt. E. Christie-Miller	Capt. C. W. Banbury	——
1911	Vinegar Hill	Mr D. McCalmont	Owner	——

HORSE	OWNER	RIDER	TRAINER
1912 Another Delight	Mr E. H. Wyndham	Owner	——
1913 Another Delight	Mr E. H. Wyndham	Owner	——
1914 Jack Symons	Capt. G. Paynter	Owner	——
1915-19 *No Race*			
1920 White Surrey	Admiral of the Fleet Sir Hedworth Meux	Maj. Walwyn	——
1921 Pay Only	Mr W. Filmer-Sankey	Owner	——
1922 Pay Only	Mr W. Filmer-Sankey	Owner	——
1923 Annie Darling	Mr R. L. McCreery	Owner	——
1924 Lee Bridge	Mr R. G. Shaw	Owner	——
1925 Ruddyglow	Mr W. Filmer-Sankey	Owner	Owner
1926 Foxtrot	Capt. H. Lumsden	Owner	Owner
1927 Scotch Eagle	Capt. A. F. W. Gossage	Owner	Owner
1928 Dash o' White	Mr P. S. Ackroyd	Capt. R. L. McCreery	Owner
1929 Drin	Capt. A. F. W. Gossage	Owner	Owner
1930 Drintyre	Mr C. N. Brownhill	Owner	Owner
1931 Slieve Grien	Capt. R. B. Moseley	Owner	Owner
1932 Castledown	Sir P. Lawson	Owner	——
1933 Backsight	Mr R. B. T. Daniell	Owner	Owner
1934 Crafty Alice	Mr T. Wallis, jun	Owner	Owner
1935 Young Cuthbert	Mr R. Courage	Owner	Owner
1936 Misdemeanour	Sir P. Lawson	Owner	Owner
1937 Buck Willow	Mr M. G. Roddick	Owner	Owner
1938 Kilstar	Capt. M. G. Roddick	Owner	Owner
1939 Fillip	Maj. M. D. Roddick	Owner	Owner
1940-48 *No Race*			
1949 Demon Vino	Maj. J. W. Phillips	Owner	R. Brignell.
1950 Klaxton	Mr W. D. Gibson	Owner	I. Anthony
1951 Klaxton	Capt. W. D. Gibson	Owner	I. Anthony
1952 Klaxton	Capt. W. D. Gibson	Owner	I. Anthony
1953 Atom Bomb	Maj. P. Fielden	Owner	C. Mitchell
1954 Pointsman	Maj. C. Blacker	Owner	A. Kilpatrick
1955 Skatealong	Maj. P. Fielden	Owner	C. Mitchell
1956 Cottage Lace	Maj. W. D. Gibson	Owner	R. Turnell
1957 Easter Breeze	Maj. R. Dill	Owner	H. Thomson Jones
1958 Stalbridge Park	Capt. Sir N. Nuttall	Owner	A. Kilpatrick
1959 Golden Drop	Capt. S. Bradish-Ellames	Capt. P. Upton	C. Mitchell
1960 Joan's Rival	Capt. P. Bengough	Owner	A. Kilpatrick
1961 Stalbridge Park	Capt. Sir N. Nuttall	Owner	A. Kilpatrick
1962 Cash Desire	Lt.-Col. T. Wallis	Mr P. Greenwood	H. E. Smyth
1963 Baxier	Lord Fermoy	Owner	A. O'Brien
1964 Threepwood	Capt. N. Ansell	Owner	Owner
1965 Rueil	Mr B. Leigh	Mr B. Leigh	T. Forster
1966 Willow King	Capt. G. C. Perry	Owner	J. N. Barrett
1967 Indian Spice	Lt.-Com. J. G. Beyfus	Owner	F. Winter
1968 Ballyverine	Capt. G. Vere-Nicoll	Owner	K. Cundell
1969 *No Race*			
1970 Charles Dickens	Col. P. Bengough	Owner	A. Kilpatrick
1971 Charles Dickens	Col. P. Bengough	Owner	A. Kilpatrick
1972 Charles Dickens	Col. P. Bengough	Owner	A. Kilpatrick
1973 Ziguenor	Maj. D. Chesney	Owner	Owner
1974 Pakie	Maj. A. Parker-Bowles	Owner	F. Walwyn
1975 *No Race*			
1976 Lucky Edgar	Lord Ullswater	Maj. A. Cramsie	Lord Ullswater
1977 Double Bridal·	Maj.-Gen. Sir J. d'Avigdor-Goldsmid	Mr C. Price	F. Walwyn
1978 Mr Snowman	Lord Leverhulme	Mr C. Sample	T. Forster

The William Hill Imperial Cup (2m)

	HORSE	OWNER	RIDER	TRAINER
1907	Carnegie	Lord Carnarvon	J. O'Brien	——
1908	Perseus II	Mr H. Reynolds	Mr S. J. Bell	——
1909	*No Race*			
1910	Black Plum	Mr J. B. Joel	F. Mason	——
1911	Bendy-Tree	Mr Sol Joel	J. Hare	——
1912	Meridian	Mr G. A. Prentice	W. Escott	——
1913	Rathlea	Mr T. Nolan	E. Piggott	——
1914	Vermouth	Mr P. F. Heybourn	G. Duller	J. Bell
1915-19	*No Race*			
1920	Trespasser	Mr P. F. Heybourn	G. Duller	J. Bell
1921	Trespasser	Mr P. F. Heybourn	G. Duller	J. Bell
1922	Trespasser	Mr P. F. Heybourn	G. Duller	J. Bell
1923	North Waltham	Mr J. White	G. Parfremont	——
1924	Noce d'Argent	Mr Siegmond Cohen	F. Wooten	——
1925	Scotch Pearl	Mr A. Howeson	F. Rees	——
1926	Peeping Tom	Sir M. McAlpine	G. Duller	J. Bell
1927	Zeno	Mr A. C. Howeson	W. Speck	W. Nightingall
1928	Royal Falcon	Mrs G. Drummond	T. Leader	F. Leach
1929	Hercules	Sir M. McAlpine	G. Duller	J. Bell
1930	Rubicon II	Mr V. Emanuel	G. Duller	P. Donaghue
1931	Residue	Mr B. Warner	G. Pellerin	O. Anthony
1932	Last of the Dandies	Mr J. Westgate	W. Hollick	W. Payne
1933	Flaming	Mr G. H. Bostwick	Owner	I. Anthony
1934	Lion Courage	Mr W. R. Read	G. Wilson	Owner
1935	Negro	Mr J. R. King	W. Speck	George Wilson
1936	Negro	Mr J. R. King	S. Ingham	George Wilson
1937	Le Maestro	Mrs J. V. Rank	J. Fawcus	G. Evans
1938	Bimco	Mr J. Ismay	E. Vinall	H. Turner
1939	Mange Tout	Prince Aly Khan	G. Wilson	G. Duller
1940-46	*No Race*			
1947	Tant Pis	Miss J. Maguire	H. Nicholson	J. Goldsmith
1948	Anglesey	Mr P. Watson	J. Gilbert	S. Ingham
1949	Secret Service	Mr R. Sweeney	J. Gilbert	F. Walwyn
1950	Secret Service	Mr R. Sweeney	T. Cusack	F. Walwyn
1951	Master Bidar	Mr W. H. Watts	R. Emery	R. Smyth
1952	High Point	Mr F. J. Richmond	H. Sprague	J. Dennistoun
1953	High Point	Mr F. J. Richmond	H. Sprague	J. Dennistoun
1954	The Pills	Mr H. C. Nias	J. Dowdeswell	P. Rice-Stringer
1955	Bon Mot II	Mr S. Wootten	M. Haynes	Owner
1956	Peggy Jones	Group-Capt. H. Hanmer	A. Oughton	S. Palmer
1957	Camugliano	Mr H. T. Smith	R. Emery	Owner
1958	Flaming East	Mrs R. D. Vallance	Mr J. Lawrence	G. Vallance
1959	Langton Heath	Mr C. R. Fenton	R. Martin	W. Stephenson
1960	Farmer's Boy	Mr A. H. Birtwhistle	D. Nicholson	W. Stephenson
1961	Fidus Achetus	Mrs T. M. Stack	C. Chapman	M. James
1962	Irish Imp	Mrs O. Negus-Fancey	G. Ramshaw	R. Smyth
1963	Antiar	Contessa di St Elia	D. Mould	P. Cazalet
1964	Invader	Maj. D. Wigan	T. Jones	L. Dale
1965	Kildavin	Mr A. W. Wood	J. King	L. Major
1966	Royal Sanction	Mr A. Walking	R. Pitman	F. Winter
1967	Sir Thopaz	Mr H. Joel	J. Haine	R. Turnell
1968	Persian Empire	Mr H. Alper	B. Scott	C. Davis
1969	*No Race*			
1970	Solomon II	Mr E. Weidermeyer	B. R. Davies	D. Barons
1971	Church Wood	Mrs H. Hawkins	D. Barrott	M. Goswell

(Renamed William Hill Imperial Cup)

HORSE	OWNER	RIDER	TRAINER
1972 Spy Net	Mr E. Cohen	G. Lawson	L. Dale
1973* Lanzarote	Lord Howard de Walden	R. Pitman	F. Winter
1974 Flash Imp	Mrs O. Negus-Fancey	J. King	R. Smyth
1975 *No Race*			
1976 Nougat	Mr M. Vickers	G. Enright	J. Gifford
1977 Acquaint	Sir H. Ingram	Mr N. Henderson	F. Winter
1978 Winter Melody	Mr J. Hanson	W. Smith	Owner

*Run at Kempton

1907-71 run as The Imperial Cup

The Mildmay Memorial (H'cap) Chase (3m 5f 118y)

HORSE	OWNER	RIDER	TRAINER
1951 Roimond	Lord Bicester	T. Molony	G. Beeby
1952 Cromwell	Hon. Mrs Mildmay-White	B. Marshall	P. Cazalet
1953 Whispering Steel	Mrs M. H. Kilpatrick	R. Emery	A. Kilpatrick
1954 Domate	Mr E. Stanning	A. Corbett	F. Cundell
1955 *No Race*			
1956 Linwell	Mr D. Brown	R. Hamey	C. Mallon
1957 Much Obliged	Mr H. Draper	H. East	N. Crump
1958 Polar Flight	Mrs P. Pleydell-Bouverie	G. Slack	G. Spann
1959 *No Race*			
1960 Team Spirit	Mrs D. R. Brand	G. W. Robinson	D. Moore
1961 Mac Joy	Mr W. C. Simpson	M. Scudamore	K. Bailey
1962 Duke of York	Mr J. Tilling	Mr D. Scott	J. Tilling
1963 *No Race*			
1964 Dormant	Mrs Wells-Kendrew	P. Buckley	N. Crump
1965 Freddie	Mr R. R. Tweedie	P. McCarron	Owner
1966 What A Myth	Lady Weir	P. Kelleway	H. R. Price
1967 *No Race*			
1968 Stalbridge Colonist	Mr Blindell	S. Mellor	K. Cundell
1969 *No Race*			
1970 Larbawn	Mr M. Marsh	J. Gifford	Owner
1971 *No Race*			
1972 Royal Toss	Mr H. Handel	N. Wakley	Owner
1973 Midnight Fury	Mr C. Payne-Crofts	V. Soane	F. Winter
1974 High Ken	Mr R. Hickman	B. R. Davies	J. E. Edwards
1975 Money Market	Lord Chelsea	J. King	C. Bewicke
1976 Money Market	Lord Chelsea	R. Barry	C. Bewicke
1977 Zeta's Son	Mr M. Buckley	R. Barry	P. Bailey
1978 Shifting Gold	Mr R. Russell	J. Francome	K. Bailey

Whitbread Gold Cup (3m 5f 118y)

HORSE	OWNER	RIDER	TRAINER
1957 Much Obliged	Mr H. Draper	H. East	N. Crump
1958 Taxidermist	Mrs Peter Hastings	Hon. J. Lawrence	F. Walwyn
1959 Done Up	Mr J. U. Baillie	H. Sprague	H. R. Price
1960 Plummers Plain	Mr F. Clay	R. Harrison	L. Dale
1961 Pas Seul	Mr J. Rogerson	D. Dick	R. Turnell
1962 Frenchman's Cove	Mr S. Joel	S. Mellor	H. Thomson Jones
1963 Hoodwinked	Lady Joicey	P. Buckley	N. Crump
1964 Dormant	Mrs Wells-Kendrew	P. Buckley	N. Crump

	HORSE	OWNER	RIDER	TRAINER
1965	Arkle	Anne, Duchess of Westminster	P. Taafe	T. Dreaper
1966	What a Myth	Lady Weir	P. Kelleway	H. R. Price
1967	Mill House	Mr Gollings	D. Nicholson	F. Walwyn
1968	Larbawn	Mr M. Marsh	M. Gifford	Owner
1969	Larbawn	Mr M. Marsh	J. Gifford	Owner
1970	Royal Toss	Mr H. Handel	R. Pitman	Owner
1971	Titus Oates	Mr P. Cussins	R. Barry	G. W. Richards
1972	Grey Sombero	Mr F. Cauldwell	W. Shoemark	D. Gandolfo
1973	Charlie Potheen	Mrs B. Heath	R. Barry	F. Walwyn
1974	The Dikler	Mrs D. August	R. Barry	F. Walwyn
1975	April Seventh	Mrs B. Meeham	S. Knight	R. Turnell
1976	Otter Way	Mr O. Carter	J. King	Owner
1977	Andy Pandy	Mrs S. Mulligan	J. Burke	F. Rimell
1978	Strombolus	Mr M. Buckley	T. Stack	P. Bailey

SASSOON, Capt. Reginald Ellis (d. 1933)

Capt. Sassoon did not learn to ride until he joined the Irish Guards. He began chasing about 1925 and was at first a very indifferent horseman but his slight frame and modest demeanour hid a lion's heart. He transferred his horses to Percy Woodland who effected a most remarkable improvement and made his protégé one of the leading amateurs of his generation. He bought West Indies in the hopes of winning the Grand National and on her achieved at least part of his ambition by winning the Valentine Chase over part of the course. He was mercifully too ill to ride when she killed herself at Newbury in 1932 but only a year later he met a similar fate and died from the injuries sustained when Clear Nite fell at Lingfield. He was elected to the National Hunt Committee in 1932.

SAUCY KIT

Bay horse, 1961, Hard Sauce—Reckitts (Mieuxcé). Bred by the Sassoon Studs.

A grand stamp of horse standing 16.2 h.h., Saucy Kit won two Flat races and 10 hurdle races including the N.H. Centenary Hurdle, Kempton (1967) and the 1967 Champion Hurdle, (R. Edwards), 100/6, by 5l, 1½l, from Makaldar (D. Mould) and Talgo Abbess (F. Carroll).

A great jumper with a fine turn of foot Saucy Kit was usually held up for a late run and at his best was very effective indeed. He retired in 1969 and now stands at the Blakeley Stud, near Shrewsbury, where he is managed by Roy Edwards who rode him to victory in the Champion Hurdle.

SCOTT, Gerald (b.1938)

A very popular Northern jockey, Gerry Scott came from a point-to-pointing family who ran a pub in Durham and usually trained a N.H. horse under permit. He was apprenticed to Capt. Crump in 1954 and remained with the stable until he retired in 1972. He rode his first winner in 1956 and although his career was bedevilled by breaking his leg on no less than six occasions he was extremely successful.

His principal victories were:

The Grand National (1960) Merryman II
The Scottish Grand National (1959) Merryman II
The Hennessy Gold Cup (1962) Springbok
The Wetherby H'cap Chase (1959) San Lorenzo

During his prolonged spells of injury he did sterling work for the Injured Jockeys Association. In 1973 he was appointed a racing official and now acts as a starter.

SCOTTISH MEMORIES

Chestnut gelding, 1954, Scottish Union—Souvenir d'un Ami (Tai-Yung). Bred by Mrs F. Blacker.

A versatile, consistent and popular gelding, Mr G. B. Saunderson's Scottish Memories won 12 hurdle races and 16 steeplechases including the Cheltenham Trial Hurdle (1963), the Cathcart Challenge Cup, National Hunt Meeting (1965), and the Mackeson Gold Cup (1961).

He was one of the horses that Paddy Sleator and Arthur Thomas managed so skilfully between them. He kept his form marvellously over a number of years and was equally at home in 2-mile hurdles as 3-mile steeplechases. He was particularly effective at 2-2½ miles and loved Cheltenham. He was usually ridden by Bobby Beasley.

SCUDAMORE, Michael John (b.1932)

A farmer's son, Michael Scudamore came to chasing from the point-to-point field and rode as an amateur before turning professional. A very fine horseman, he was particularly skilful at getting horses to jump confidently and accurately and his services were soon in great demand.

His successes included:

The Cheltenham Gold Cup (1957) Linwell
The Grand National (1959) Oxo
The King George VI (1956) Rose Park
The Triumph Hurdle (1956) Square Dance
The Welsh Grand National (1957) Creola II
The Mildmay Memorial (1961) Mac Joy
The Topham Trophy (1963) Barberyn

His best season was 1956-57 when he rode 58 winners and finished second in the Jockeys' Championship. He was also fifth in 1958-59 with 45.

He retired in 1966 after a particularly nasty fall had damaged his eyesight and now trains a small string of jumpers from his Herefordshire home. As might be expected, he is notably successful with his well-schooled chasers of whom the best to date have been Fortina's Palace (10 races including the Grand Annual, 1970) and Bruslee (seven chases including the 1974 Mackeson Gold Cup).

SEAMAN

Bay gelding, 1876, Xenophon—Lena Rivers (Brockley). Bred by Capt. Gubbins.

Seaman, a small but beautifully proportioned, quality individual was chronically unsound and had to be fired as a two-year-old when trained on the Curragh by Henry Eyre Linde.

During 1880-81 when his stable was carrying all before it in France and England, as well as at home he won four races, including the Conyngham Cup, Punchestown, and the Grande Course des Haies, Auteuil. He was, however, considered unlikely to stand a preparation for the National and was therefore sold for £2,000 to English Guards officer, Lord Manners.

Seaman's new trainer, Capt. Machell shared Linde's view and sent his charge to Aintree for the 1882 National only three-parts fit. Seaman however overcame his lack of fitness, his rider's inexperience and his own breakdown after the last and with 11-6 (Lord Manners), 10/1, prevailed in a desperate finish by a short head, a bad third over Cyrus, 10-9 (Mr T. Beasley) and Zoedone, 10-0 (Capt. Smith).

Cyrus was trained by Linde and thus the stable reject prevented him completing the hat-trick initiated by Empress (1880) and Woodbrook (1881). Seaman never ran again but recovered sufficiently to serve as a much-loved hack to his owner and family.

SEA PIGEON

Brown gelding, 1970, Sea Bird II—Around the Roses (Round Table). Bred by the Greentree Stud Inc. (U.S.A.).

The classically bred Sea Pigeon, by one of the great post-war Derby winners out of a winning half-sister to the 1000 Guineas second, Rosalba, won the Duke of Edinburgh Stakes, Ascot, on his only outing as a two-year-old. However the handsome, American-bred colt then trained by Jeremy Tree, proved a bitter disappointment as a three-year-old and despite the ability that took him into seventh place in Morston's Derby, failed to reach the frame on any of his five outings.

He was then sold privately to Mr Muldoon, a patron of Gordon Richards' shrewd Penrith stable and ran in two amateur Flat races as a four-year-old, in the second of which his enthusiasm looked extremely suspect. However hurdling transformed his outlook and in the capable hands of Ron Barry, he won four of five races in his first winter and only went under by 1½ lengths to Bird's Nest in the fifth.

Since then he has won a further eleven hurdle races including the Scottish Champion Hurdle, Ayr (1977 and 1978), the Bellway Fighting Fifth Hurdle, Newcastle (1978), the Cheltenham Trial Hurdle (1975) and the Allied Manufacturing Handicap Hurdle, Liverpool (1977). He was unable to run in the 1976 Champion Hurdle and for the first time in his hurdling career, looked irresolute when finishing fourth to Night Nurse in 1977. A more charitable interpretation would be that he was unsuited by the dead ground, a view substantiated when he ran a game second to Monksfield in 1978.

At the start of 1976-77 he was transferred, with all Mr Muldoon's horses, to the Malton Yard of M. H. (Peter) Easterby, since when he has almost always been ridden by Jonjo O'Neill.

His hurdling success has given him a new outlook on Flat racing and he has won 8 races including the Chester Cup (1977 and 78).

SEDGEFIELD (Group 5)

A Durham course dating from 1867, Sedgefield is a left-handed, rectangular track, about one mile, two furlongs in length with some undulations. It is a sharp track which sets a premium on jumping ability. There is a great deal of racing, mostly of a very modest nature, which provides opportunities for less than high-class northern horses.

The most important races are The Bradbury H'cap Chase, (December, 3m 250 yds, £1,305) and The Durham National H'cap Chase (March, 3½m, £1,604).

Irish Lizard, winner of 12 chases including the Grand Sefton and twice placed in the Grand National. He was elected to the N.H.C. in 1936 and was also a member of the Jockey Club. Colours: white, primrose sleeves, black cap.

SELLING RACE

A selling race is one in which the conditions demand that every horse running, if a loser, may be claimed and if a winner, must be offered for sale by auction. The lowest price at which the winner can be sold is laid down in the Rules of Racing and varies according to the value of the race. If, at the auction, the winner is sold for more than the stipulated selling price, the surplus goes to the Race-course except that the winning owner shall be paid 10% of any surplus between the selling price and £1000 and 25% of any further surplus. A loser in a selling race can be claimed for the stipulated selling price plus the value of the plate. No person can claim more

Best Times

Distance	Time	Horse-age-weight	Date
2m H	3m 59	Molly Fay 4-11-12	11-9-71
2½m H	5m 1.9	Gilmarsh 5-10-0	30-5-74
2m C	4m 3.5	Basket 9-10-0	15-9-73
2½m C	5m 12.70	Fine Fellow 9-11-8	26-5-78
3m 250y C	6m 15.50	Tilston 6-12-1	26-5-78
3½m C	7m 14	Tembo 7-9-7	10-3-73

SEFTON, Hugh William Osbert Molyneux, 7th Earl (1898-1972)

Lord Sefton was educated at Harrow and Sandhurst and served with the Royal Horse Guards. His family had owned Aintree racecourse since its founding but in 1947 he sold it to Mrs Topham, whose family had managed the course for almost as long a period, subject to the condition that it should always be kept for agricultural and racing purposes. When Mrs Topham attempted to sell it for redevelopment in 1964 he applied for an injunction to restrain her and was given judgement. The House of Lords upheld the decision but reversed it on appeal.

Lord Sefton was a great supporter of National Hunt racing and did not really achieve the success he deserved. His biggest success was to win the 1942 Cheltenham Gold Cup with Medoc II and he also owned that popular stayer,

than one horse and each claim must be accompanied by a fee of £10. The claim has to be made in writing to the Clerk of the Course within fifteen minutes of the winner passing the scale or the judge announcing the decision on all placings, whichever be later. If two or more persons claim the same horse, the auctioneer holds an auction between the claimants in the office of the Clerk of the Course. Any surplus above the claiming price is divided between the Race-course and the Jockey Club except that the owner of the horse shall first receive 10% of that surplus.

SENECA

Chestnut gelding, 1937, Caligula— Facette (Cid Campeador). Bred by Sir Malcolm McAlpine.

Seneca was raced by his breeder and trained by Victor Smyth at Epsom. After winning on the Flat at three-years, he won two hurdle races in 1941 including the Champion Hurdle (R. Smyth), 7/1, by a head, 2l, from Anarchist (M. Jones) and Ephorous (H. Nicholson). It was a remarkable performance for a four-year-old in only his second run over hurdles and Ron Smyth rated him the best he ever rode.

Seneca broke down shortly after the Champion and although he recovered and raced after the war, he did not win again. He won the Champion Hurdle as an entire but was later cut.

SENSIER, W. (d.1894)

A native of Alresford, Hampshire, Billy Sensier started life as a stable lad and rose to be first jockey to Arthur Yates, who spoke of him as "a very finished, brainy jockey". Although accurate figures are hard to come by, Sensier was certainly Champion Jockey on more than one occasion, including 1884.

He was associated with the consistent The Midshipmite (q.v.) on whom he won the 1893 Champion Chase. He was killed following a fall at Plumpton.

SERGEANT MURPHY

Chestnut gelding, 1910, General Symons—Rose Graft (Ascetic). Bred by Mr G. L. Walker.

An Irish-bred son of the good chasing mare, Rose Graft, Sergeant Murphy won 10 chases including the Scottish Grand National, Bogside (1922) and the 1923 Grand National, 11-3 (Capt. G. H. Bennet) 100/6, by 3l, 6l, from Shaun Spadah, 12-7 (F. B. Rees) and Conjuror II, 11-11 (Mr C. Dewhurst). He was 13 years old at the time and remains the oldest horse to have won the race. Previously he had been seventh to Poethlyn in 1919, fourth to Troytown in 1920 and fourth in 1922 after refusing the Canal Ditch and losing his bridle at the second attempt.

Sergeant Murphy won the National in the colours of Mr Stephen ('Laddie') Sanford, an American and a Cambridge polo-blue. Mr Sanford bought him in 1920 for £1,200 to hunt but found him rather too much of a handful and put him back into training. Sergeant Murphy was trained by George Blackwell who had won the 1903 Derby with Rock Sand and thus joined the select group of five trainers who have won both the Derby and the National. The others are James Jewitt, Richard Dawson, Willie Stephenson and Vincent O'Brien.

SHANNON LASS

Bay or brown mare 1895, not in the General Stud Book, Butterscotch—Mazurka (Uncas).

Shannon Lass ran on the Flat at three years but did not win and was subsequently sold to Mr Ambrose Gorham for whom she won eight chases including the 1902 Grand National, 10-1 (D. Reed) 20/1, by 3l, the same, from Matthew, 9-12 (W. Morgan) and Manifesto, 12-8 (E. Piggott). Shannon Lass was trained by Jem Hackett. She did not win subsequently.

SHAUN GOILIN

Chestnut gelding, 1920, not in the General Stud Book, reputedly Shaun Aboo—Golden Day (Golden Measure).

The result of an unplanned mating, ensuing from his dam's escape from her conventional paddock and subsequent service by an unknown colt, thought to have been Shaun Aboo, Shaun Goilin was slow to come to hand and did not win till he was seven years old. He went on to win six chases including the Grand Sefton, Liverpool (1929) and the 1930 Grand National, 11-7 (T. Cullinan), 100/8, by a neck, 1½l, from Melleray's Belle, 10-0 (J. Mason) and Sir Lindsay, 10-6 (D. Williams).

The finish was one of the closest on record and the result marked a notable treble for jockey Tim Cullinan, who had won the Gold Cup on Easter Hero and the Champion Hurdle on Brown Tony.

Shaun Goilin, a handsome, rangy, pale chestnut was sixth in the 1931 National and third in 1932. He was owned by Mr W. H. Midwood, Master of the Cheshire hounds, and trained at Weyhill by Frank Hartigan.

SHAUN SPADAH

Brown or bay gelding, 1911 Easter Prize—Rusialka (Bushey Park). Bred in Ireland by Mr P. McKenna.

Shaun Spadah, a long-backed, roman-nosed bay with a prominent white blaze, won 19 races including the Coventry Chase, Kempton (1921), the Becher Chase, Liverpool (1923), the Prince of Wales Chase, Sandown (1919) and the 1921 Grand National. 11-7 (F. Rees) 100/9. He was the only horse to finish without a fall although The Bore, 11-8 (Mr H. Brown) and All White, 10-13 (R. Chadwick) were remounted to finish second and third. The fall of the The

Bore at the second last when going particularly well was undoubtedly fortunate for Shaun Spadah. Shaun Spadah was formerly owned by Frank Barbour but in 1918 was bought by Mr (later Sir) Malcolm McAlpine. He was trained at Lewes by George Poole.

SHEILA'S COTTAGE
Bay mare, 1939, registered in Miss Prior's Half-Bred Stud Book, Cottage—Sheila II (Pageant). Bred in Co. Limerick, Ireland, by Mrs J. H. Daly.

Sheila's Cottage had won a point-to-point and four chases when she was purchased early in 1948 for £3,500 by Neville Crump on behalf of Mr John Proctor with a view to running in the Grand National. This she won, 10-7 (A. Thompson) 50/1, by 11, 61, from First of the Dandies, 10-4 (J. Brogan) and Cromwell, 10-11 (Lord Mildmay). Whether she would have done so, had not Eddie Reavey on Zahia taken the wrong course and missed out the last fence or if Lord Mildmay (q.v.) had not been afflicted by paralysing cramp throughout the last half mile, remains a matter for conjecture.

Sheila's Cottage, who was once described by her ungallant trainer as an "ornery old cow", celebrated her victory by removing the top of Arthur Thompson's finger when he went to congratulate her that evening.

Her stud record is as follows:

1951 bay gelding (Arco) **Lucky Cottage**
1953 bay gelding (Iceberg II) **Polar Palace**
1955 bay filly (Monsieur L'Amiral) **Young Sheila**
1956 bay filly (Napoleon Bonaparte) **The Wren**
1958 bay filly (Blue Chariot) **Blue Cottage**
1960 bay gelding (Umid) **Cottager** (one hurdle, four chases and a point-to-point).

SHEPHERD, Richard (b.1947)
Richard Shepherd, an amateur rider from the V.W.H. country in Gloucestershire has a unique record in the Cheltenham Foxhunter Challenge Cup which he has won three times, in 1966 on his father's Straight Lady when only 19, and in 1977 and 1978 on that mare's sons, Long Lane, and Mount Olive both of whom he owns and trains.

His other successes include:

The United Hunts Challenge Cup (1977) Long Lane

The Mercedes-Benz United Hunts Challenge Cup (1978) Mount Olive
The B.M.W. Gentlemen's Championships (1977) Mount Olive

SHIFNAL
Brown horse, 1869, Saccharometer—Countess Amy (St Albans). Bred Mr J. Eyke.

Shifnal was brought out of a 'seller' at Alexandra Park by John Nightingall who trained him to win nine chases, including the United Kingdom Handicap Chase, Croydon (1876), the Surrey Grand Open Chase, Sandown (1876), the Grand International Chase, Sandown (1878) with 12-7 and the 1878 Grand National, 10-12 (J. Jones), 100/15, by 21, 10l, from Martha, 10-9 (Mr T. Beasley) and Pride of Kildare, 11-7 (J. Moore). He was also third to Regal in the 1876 Grand National.

SILVER FAME
Chestnut gelding, 1939, Werwolf—Silver Fairy (He Goes). Bred Mr J. W. Osborne and Capt. E. L. Mansfield.

A deep-bodied, short-legged, pale chestnut with a prominent white blaze, Silver Fame epitomized the 'Bicester' stamp of chaser and was probably the best horse that great sportsman ever owned. He was an easy horse to underestimate for he would never exert himself unnecessarily and would beat good and moderate by the same margin. Game, consistent and very popular, he won a 'bumper' and 27 chases including the Emblem Chase, Manchester (1947), the Golden Miller Chase, Cheltenham (1950), the National Hunt Handicap Chase, National Hunt Meeting (1950) and the 1951 Cheltenham Gold Cup (M. Molony), 6/4f, by a short head, 2l, from Greenogue (G. Kelly) and Mighty Fine (J. Bullock). Silver Fame was trained by George Beeby.

SILVO
Bay gelding, 1916, Minter—Ever True (Perigord). Bred by Mr M. Dawson.

A handsome, quality dark bay, Silvo was reckoned by many to be the best chaser in England during the mid 'twenties. He won 18 chases including the Grand Sefton, Liverpool (1923), the Champion Chase, Liverpool (1923) the Grand International, Sandown (1925) and the Grand Steeple, Auteuil (1925).

At one time owned in partnership by Sir E. Edgar and Mr W. H. Midwood, he was bought outright by Mr Midwood for £10,500 at the beginning of the season 1925-26. Silvo who was trained by Percy Whitaker, was also third in the 1924 Grand National and third in the 1927 Gold Cup.

SIRES, LEADING

1911-12	Hackler	winners of	34	races	worth	£5,376
1912-13	Hackler	,, ,,	29	,,	,,	£6,043
1913-14	Wavelet's Pride	,, ,,	37½	,,	,,	£3,852
1914-15	Travelling Lad	,, ,,	4	,,	,,	£3,942
1915-16	Barcadale	,, ,,	3	,,	,,	£1,401
1916-17	Santoi	,, ,,	18	,,	,,	£2,051½
1917-18	Rydal Head	,, ,,	4	,,	,,	£2,247
1918-19	Rydal Head	,, ,,	4	,,	,,	£5,655
1919-20	Zria	,, ,,	15½	,,	,,	£7,019
1920-21	Easter Prize	,, ,,	3	,,	,,	£7,564
1921-22	Clifton Hall	,, ,,	6	,,	,,	£8,026
1922-23	General Symons	,, ,,	1	,,	,,	£7,850
1923-24	Moorside II	,, ,,	4	,,	,,	£8,666
1924-25	Roi Herode or Day Comet	,, ,,	6	,,	,,	£8,727
1925-26	Cyllius	,, ,,	8½	,,	,,	£8,421
1926-27	Marco	,, ,,	2	,,	,,	£8,477
1927-28	Cipango	,, ,,	5	,,	,,	£12,106¾
1928-29	My Prince	,, ,,	12	,,	,,	£14,934
1929-30	Achtoi	,, ,,	25	,,	,,	£5,034
1930-31	Jackdaw	,, ,,	20	,,	,,	£11,513½
1931-32	Foresight	,, ,,	9	,,	,,	£9,445
1932-33	Jackdaw	,, ,,	29	,,	,,	£10,223½
1933-34	Goldcourt	,, ,,	3	,,	,,	£8,174
1934-35	My Prince	,, ,,	26	,,	,,	£9,349¾
1935-36	My Prince	,, ,,	12	,,	,,	£8,507
1936-37	My Prince	,, ,,	16	,,	,,	£7,226
1937-38	Man o'War	,, ,,	5	,,	,,	£8,454
1938-39	Cottage	,, ,,	30	,,	,,	£10,502½
1939-40	Werwolf	,, ,,	7	,,	,,,	£5,297
1940-41	Tommy Atkins	,, ,,	7	,,	,,	£1,826
1941-42	My Prince	,, ,,	11	,,	,,	£1,696¼
1942-43	*Loch Lomond	,, ,,	9	,,	,,	£1,402½
1943-44	*Wavetop	,, ,,	4	,,	,,	£1,628
1944-45	Knight of the Garter	,, ,,	12½	,,	,,	£1,516
1945-46	Cottage	,, ,,	29	,,	,,	£12,823
1946-47	Within-the-Law	,, ,,	6	,,	,,	£10,847
1947-48	Cottage	,, ,,	51	,,	,,	£23,465¾
1948-49	Cottage	,, ,,	30	,,	,,	£12,395
1949-50	Steelpoint	,, ,,	44	,,	,,	£20,444
1950-51	Pay Up	,, ,,	11	,,	,,	£12,110
1951-52	Bimco	,, ,,	8	,,	,,	£11,177
1952-53	Domaha	,, ,,	23	,,	,,	£10,185½
1953-54	Tartan	,, ,,	24½	,,	,,	£12,596½
1954-55	Artist's Son	,, ,,	6	,,	,,	£9,602½
1955-56	Bidar	,, ,,	12	,,	,,	£11,826¼
1956-57	Straight Deal	,, ,,	22	,,	,,	£10,246½
1957-58	Grand Inquisitor	,, ,,	6	,,	,,	£15,441½
1958-59	Bobsleigh	,, ,,	9	,,	,,	£16,040¼
1959-60	Vulgan	,, ,,	38	,,	,,	£14,061½
1960-61	Nicolaus	,, ,,	18½	,,	,,	£24,252½

1961-62	Zalophus	„	„	1	„	„	£20,238½
1962-63	Supertello	„	„	8	„	„	£23,500
1963-64	Vulgan	„	„	59	„	„	£42,172
1964-65	Archive	„	„	28	„	„	£38,384
1965-66	Vulgan	„	„	90	„	„	£45,737
1966-67	Vulgan	„	„	94	„	„	£62,265
1967-68	Vulgan	„	„	82	„	„	£37,781
1968-69	Vulgan	„	„	76	„	„	£44,911
1969-70	Vulgan	„	„	76	„	„	£60,914
1970-71	Vulgan	„	„	66	„	„	£42,760
1971-72	Vulgan	„	„	64	„	„	£51,945
1972-73	Escart III	„	„	73	„	„	£42,611
1973-74	Vulgan	„	„	51	„	„	£50,858
1974-75	Escart III	„	„	23	„	„	£53,889
1975-76	Menelek	„	„	57	„	„	£93,198
1976-77	Master Owen	„	„	34	„	„	£85,202
1977-78	Master Owen	„	„	40	„	„	£56,168

*Ireland only

SIR KEN

Bay gelding, 1947, Laëken—Carte Grise II. Bred in France by M. M. Chenorio.

Certainly the most successful, if not the greatest hurdler to run under National Hunt rules, Mr Maurice Kingsley's Sir Ken won 20 hurdle races, including three Champion Hurdles in successive years and four chases.

A great big, raking horse, Sir Ken, who was trained by Willie Stephenson, went through his first three seasons completely dominating his contemporaries and won 16 races without meeting defeat. His Champion Hurdle victories were as follows:

1952 (T. Molony), 3/1f, by 2l, 4l, from Noholme (B. Marshall) and Approval (D. Dillon).
1953 (T. Molony) 2/5f, by 2l, 1½l, from Galation (B. Marshall) and Teapot II (P. Taaffe).
1954 (T. Molony), 4/9f, by 1l, 3l, from Impney (M. Pumprey) and Galation (P. Taaffe).

In 1955-56 Sir Ken was switched to fences with at first very successful results. His four victories included the Cotswold Chase (N.H. Meeting) and the Mildmay Chase, Liverpool. However the following season he registered disapproval of the bigger obstacles and failed to complete on three of his four outings.

SIR WILLIAM

Alan McDonough's Sir William, "a lightly made horse, almost unmanageable" won several races including the 1838 Liverpool Steeplechase, in some circles thought to have been the second Grand National. In this race he was ridden by Henry Potts, his owner having had a bad fall and been dragged on their previous outing. If his portrait is to be believed, Sir William was a far from imposing individual with a most deplorable hind-leg.

SKEAPING, John (b.1902)

John Skeaping was born into an artistic family. His father was a painter and his mother a pianist. He attended the Goldsmith's College of Art and the Royal School of Art from where he won a gold medal and a travelling scholarship in 1920. In 1924 he won the *Prix de Rome*.

He served with the S.A.S. during World War II and afterwards became Professor of Sculpture at the Royal College of Arts, a post which he held until 1959. He became a Royal Academician in 1959. He now lives and works in the Camargue district of France, while his paintings and sculptures command a world-wide market. Most of his painting is in pastel or colour wash, in which mediums his work has a delicacy and rhythm reminiscent of Eastern art.

SKELTON, T.

Tommy Skelton was a good-looking, delicate man, lacking in strength but with the "hands of an angel and the determination of the devil". Contemporaries thought him better over hurdles than fences but results do not bear this theory out.

His successes included:

The Grand National (1886) Old Joe
The Grand Sefton (1887) Savoyard
The Lancashire Chase (1887) Savoyard
The Prince of Wales' Chase (1889) Scottish Minstrel
The Sandown Grand Prize (1888) Astrakan

SKYMAS

Brown gelding, 1965, Skyros—Red Mimas (Red Shaft). Bred and owned by Mr M. Magee.

A rangy, rather plain but extremely tough gelding, Skymas has, to date, won six hurdle races and 18 steeplechases over distances ranging from 2-3 miles.

Skymas's pedigree is undistinguished to say the least. His sire was unraced and has produced no other remotely top-class horse while his dam was a point-to-pointer whose only other winning produce is the moderate point-to-pointer, Miss Mimas. Nevertheless Skymas has had a long and meritorious career hallmarked by his versatility and resolution.

His principal victories have been the National Hunt 2-mile Champion Chase (1976 and 1977), the Mackeson Gold Cup, Cheltenham (1973) and the Sun Ratings Chase, Liverpool (1977). He was also second to Tartan Ace in the 1973 Irish Distillers Grand National.

He has been trained throughout his career by Brian Lusk in Co. Antrim and is usually ridden by the former Irish Champion Amateur, 'Mouse' Morris.

SLACK, George

An accomplished Northern jockey who rode principally for W. A. Hall and R. Renton, George Slack was particularly effective round Liverpool. He had the misfortune to find one too good in no less than three Nationals, being second on Tudor Line in 1954 (beaten a neck by Royal Tan) and 1955, and on Tiberetta in 1958. He was also second, beaten $\frac{1}{2}$ length on Polar Flight in the 1958 Gold Cup.

His successes included:

The Lancashire Chase (1955) Tudor Line
The Mildmay Memorial (1958) Polar Flight
The Emblem Chase (1952) Stormhead: (1959) Knightsbrook

The Great Yorkshire Chase (1960) Knightsbrook
The Haydock Grand National Trial (1953) Witty
The Topham Trophy (1954) Little Yid

SLEATOR, Patrick Joseph

A shrewd, likeable and extremely clever man, Paddy Sleator runs a large mixed stable at Grange Conn in Co. Wicklow. In the early 1960s he used to send a string of fit, well-schooled horses to Arthur Thomas's Warwickshire establishment, from where, ridden by Bobby Beasley, they were launched on the good autumn and early-winter races. Strings of races were won by such as Black Ice, Harwell and Scottish Memories. English trainers, outraged by this piracy, made representations to the authorities and the profitable enterprise was stopped.

Among the good races he has won are the 1960 Champion Hurdle with Another Flash, several divisions of the Gloucester Hurdle and the 1961 Mackeson Gold Cup with Scottish Memories.

SLOAN, George (b.1939)

A health hydro proprietor from Nashville, Tennessee, whose father is Master of the Hillsboro Foxhounds. George Sloan sounds an unlikely Champion Amateur for British steeplechasing to throw up. Finding insufficient outlets for his talents and ambitions in the restricted chasing opportunities in the States, the tall, gentle, soft-spoken Southerner determined to try for the British title.

To this end he purchased a string of horses which he placed chiefly with Josh Gifford (but a few with George Fairbairn), acquired a house two miles from the Giffords and proceeded to commute across the Atlantic to ride the winners. And in this unheroic age his gamble came off gloriously. By the end of season 1977-8 he had ridden 23 winners thus earning himself the title, a consignment of Bollinger champagne and a tiny niche in the record books.

SMITH, Crompton (b.1939)

An American amateur who had twice won America's timber classic, The Maryland Hunt Cup (once in record time) as well as the Grand National point-to-point and My Lady's Manor Cup on Jay Trump, Tommy Smith became in 1965 the first of his countrymen to ride the winner of the Grand National.

He had come to England with Jay Trump the previous autumn, and entrusted their joint preparation to the hands of the dual National winner Fred Winter, who had only just set up his training establishment at Lambourn. Obeying the maestro's instructions to the letter, he rode a cool, patient race and wore down the indomitable Freddie and Pat McCarron in the last 100 yards to win by half a length.

The pair went on to Paris to challenge for the Grand Steeplechase and adapting themselves remarkably well to yet another totally different type of course and fence, ran a sterling race to be third, after which they returned to America.

SMITH, Denys (b.1924)

Denys Smith has a large, mixed stable run on extremely business-like lines at Bishop Auckland. He started with a permit in 1957-58, trained his first winner in 1960 and went public the following season. In 1968 he won the Grand National with Red Alligator, the Great Yorkshire with Sixty-Nine and finished Leading Trainer with 55 winners worth £37,944. Other good winners include the top-class but fated hurdler, Dondieu (seven races including the Scottish Champion Hurdle (1971) and the Fighting Fifth (1971)). He is increasingly successful on the Flat and has won both the Lincolnshire Handicap and the William Hill Gold Cup.

SMITH, Richard

In 1972-73 Richard Smith became Champion Amateur, having ridden 56 winners, a total which took him into fifth place in the Jockeys' Table. No amateur since World War II had ridden over 50 winners and none since Lord Mildmay in 1949-50 had gained a place in the professional list. His principal success was the 1971 Foxhunters on Hope Again. At the beginning of season 1973-74 he turned professional, riding principally for Les Kennard's strong Taunton stable, for whom he won the Lloyds Bank Hurdle in 1974 on Highland Abbe.

Sadly this very talented young man broke his neck right at the end of his first professional season, in which he had ridden 35 winners, and was not able to ride racing again.

SMITH, William J.

A Cheltenham-based jockey, William Smith won the 1914 Grand National on Sunloch when comparatively inexperienced. He went straight to the front and stayed there, survived a nasty last fence blunder and won by 8 lengths. He also won the Stanley Chase (1915) on Limerock and was desperately unlucky not to win the 1917 War National on that horse who was well in the lead when he crossed his forelegs and fell on the run-in. He rode very long even by the standards of his day and was Champion Jockey in 1917, riding 15 winners.

SMITH, William Morris (b.1948)

One of the most successful of the present generation of N.H. jockeys, Bill Smith has had a curious rise to the top. He started conventionally enough by going to Fred Rimell as a 15-year-old school-leaver but left after only a month. He then left racing and worked in a branch of Moss Bros. After riding a couple of point-to-point winners he took out a licence to ride as an amateur and rode his first winner under Rules on 1968 on Silver Meteor. He turned professional at the beginning of 1969-70 and rode for W. C. Marshall. He has since ridden for Edward Courage, Fred Rimell and currently Fulke Walwyn.

His principal victories include:

The Champion Hurdle (1973) Comedy of Errors

The National Hunt Two-Mile Champion Chase (1972) Royal Relief; (1974) Royal Relief

The Welsh Champion Hurdle (1973) Comedy of Errors

The Irish Sweeps Hurdle (1971) Kelanne; (1973) Comedy of Errors

The Triumph Hurdle (1973) Zarib

The S.G.B. Chase (1971) Spanish Steps

The Fighting Fifth Hurdle (1972) Comedy of Errors; (1973) Comedy of Errors

The Stone's Ginger Wine Chase (1972) Royal Relief

The Schweppes Gold Trophy (1975) Tammuz

The Imperial Cup (1978) Winter Melody

SMYTH, Roland Victor (b.1915)

A member of the famous Epsom racing family, Ron Smyth was apprenticed to his father, H. E. Smyth, and rode on the Flat until becoming too heavy. He then switched to N.H. Rules with conspicuous success, becoming a particularly fine hurdles rider. He won the Champion Hurdle three times, 1941 on Seneca, 1942 on Forestation and 1948 on National Spirit. He also won several races on Lord Bicester's Silver Fame (*q.v.*) and Kempton's valuable Lonsdale Hurdle (1947) on Sammy's Rock. He was Champion Jockey in 1941-42 riding 12 winners, an achievement which caused his father to comment that he was evidently "the best of a bad lot".

He took out a licence to train in 1947 and successfully runs a medium-sized mixed stable at Clear Height Downs Road, Epsom. He specializes in big hurdle handicaps and has won the Imperial Cup three times, in 1951 with Master Bidar, 1962 with Irish Imp and 1974 with Flash Imp. He has also won the Triumph Hurdle twice: 1965 with Blarney Beacon and 1971 with Boxer.

SMYTH, Victor

An uncle of Ronald Victor (*q.v.*), Victor Smyth was apprenticed to Richard Wootten (a younger brother of Stanley) and was a very successful Flat jockey. He won the Oaks (1923), on Brownhylda, the Ascot Gold Cup (1923) on Happy Man and the Cambridgeshire H'cap (1916) on Eos before giving up around 1924 because of increasing weight.

He subsequently became a successful trainer and saddled over 1000 winners under both Rules. He won the Champion Hurdle three times, in 1941 with Seneca, 1942 with Forestation and 1948 with National Spirit, all of whom were ridden by his nephew, Ron. National Spirit won a total of 33 races including the Cheltenham Hurdle and the Princess Elizabeth Hurdle and in 1965 he and Mr Leonard Abelson (the horse's owner) presented the National Spirit Trophy to Fontwell Racecourse. He also saddled Bronze Arrow to win the Lancashire Chase in 1948.

In 1965 he retired and handed the stable over to his son, Paul Victor.

SOCIETE DES STEEPLECHASES DE FRANCE

The Société des Steeplechases de France is the controlling body of French chasing. It is an independent, non-profit-making administrative body, recognized by the Government, to which all racecourse societies must belong. An Act of 1891 provided a Tote Monopoly making all betting, other than through the Paris-Mutuel, illegal. A deduction of 15½% on all wagers is statutory and of this over half goes back into the sport, which is why French racing is currently in a much healthier economic situation than British.

Although chasing had taken place in France since the 1830s – Jem Mason, Tom Olliver and the McDonough brothers all rode successfully in France – it was not until 1863 that any controlling body was formed. This was the Société Général des Steeplechases under the presidency of S.A. Prince Joachim Murat. Its racecourse was at Vincennes and it ran 10 meetings a year. In 1866 it became responsible for all chasing in France. The Franco-Prussian war of 1870 brought the first Société to an end and in 1873 it was reconstructed as the Société Anonyme des Courses. In 1878 it became the Société des Steeplechases de France.

SOLFORD

Bay gelding, 1931, Soldennis—Margaret Beaufort (Swynford). Bred in Ireland by Mr P. J. Hartigan.

Solford, a late-maturing horse, won twice on the Flat at four years and a maiden hurdle at Naas in 1937-38 before being purchased for the Hon. Dorothy Paget (*q.v.*).

Sent to Owen Anthony, he won six hurdle races including the International Hurdle, Gatwick (1939), Jubilee Hurdle, Manchester (1940) and the 1940 Champion Hurdle (S. Magee), 5/2f, by 1½l, 4l, from African Sister (*q.v.*) (K. Piggott) and Carton (F. Rickaby). Solford broke his back in a novice chase at Worcester in January 1942 and had to be destroyed.

SOUTHERN HERO

Bay gelding, 1925, Bachelor's Jap—Torfrida (Speed). Bred in Ireland by Mr John Ennis.

A thoroughly game performer, who, while lacking the speed to make his presence effective in absolutely top-class company, retained winning form right through the 1930s, Southern Hero won 19 chases including the Conyngham Cup, Punchestown 1932, the National Trial Chase (Gatwick) 1934, the Prince of Wales's Chase (Sandown) 1935 and the Scottish Grand National three times (1934, 1936 and 1939). He was also second in that race in 1937 and 1938.

During his novice career in Ireland he

was owned by Lady Helen McCalmont but in 1932 he was bought by Mr James Rank (*q.v.*) and came to England where he was trained by Gwyn Evans until the latter's death when he was moved to Harry Brown. Southern Hero was usually ridden by Jack Fawcus.

SOUTHWELL (Group 5)
A flat, left-handed course, just over 1¼ miles, Southwell in Nottinghamshire dates from 1867. It is a sharp course favouring speedy, handy horses. It provides a generally modest standard of racing, the principal events being, the Annesley H'cap Hurdle (March, 2m 4f, £1,092), the Colonel R. Thompson Memorial Trophy H'cap Chase (October, 3m 110y, £1,690) and the Danethorpe H'cap Chase (March, 2m 4f, £1,378).

turn of foot. Although age later blunted his speed, his staying powers remained unimpaired and he finished fourth and third under big weights in the Grand Nationals of 1974 and 1975.

Spanish Steps was trained under permit by his owner-breeder. In most of his big triumphs he was partnered by John Cook.

SPECIFY
Brown gelding, 1962, Specific—Ora Lamae (Skoiter). Bred by Mr A. P. Parker.

A neatly made, brown horse of no more than medium size, Specify won three hurdle races and six chases including the Mildmay of Flete Challenge Cup, National Hunt Meeting (1969) and the

Best Times

Distance	Time	Horse-age-weight	Date
2m H	3m 48.60	Heluan 5-11-6	27-5-78
2m 80y H	3m 45	Beautiful Boy 6-11-6	6-6-66
2½m H	4m 45.60	Beautiful Boy 7-11-6	29-8-67
3m H	5m 41.80	Seething Lane 5-11-3	31-8-71
2m C	3m 53	Touch Line 8-10-5	6-6-66
2m 74y C	4m 0.50	Roslevin 6-11-5	23-5-70
3m C	5m 59.40	Nether Place 6-10-5	6-6-66
3m 110y C	6m 4	Golden Crisp 8-10-2	23-5-70

SPANISH STEPS
Bay gelding, 1963, registered in Miss Prior's Half-Bred Stud Book, Flush Royal—Tiberetta (Tiberius). Bred by Mr Edward Courage.

A member of the remarkable Drumrora family (*q.v.*), Mr Edward Courage's Spanish Steps, like his first cousin and stable-mate, Royal Relief, raced for ten consecutive seasons winning four hurdle races and 12 chases including the Totalisator Champion Novices, National Hunt Meeting (1969), the Gainsborough Chase, Sandown (1970), the Benson and Hedges Gold Cup, Sandown (1969), and the Hennessy Gold Cup, Newbury (1969). He was also third to L'Escargot in the 1970 Cheltenham Gold Cup and fourth to Glencaraig Lady in 1972. In 1971 he was inadvertently withdrawn from the race at the four-day acceptance stage, which was generally held to be a grave misfortune as he had looked to hold a first-rate chance.

A fine jumper and a most resolute battler, Spanish Steps did possess a nice

1971 Grand National, 10-13 (J. Cook), 28/1, by a neck, 2l, from Black Secret, 11-5 (Mr J. Dreaper) and Astbury, 10-0 (J. Bourke).

Previously Specify had appeared more effective at distances of less than three miles, but in one of the most closely contested finishes for years – six horses jumped the last with a chance – Specify lasted home best.

Specify, who won in the colours of Mr F. W. Pontin, was trained by J. E. Sutcliffe. He did not win subsequently but ran a good race to finish sixth to Well To Do in the 1972 National.

SPECK, William (d.1935)
Lewes-born Billy Speck learnt his trade with Harry Escott and Stanley Wootten and rode on the Flat before turning to fences. He rode conspicuously short and was said to be unequalled among his contemporaries at winding a horse up for the last.

His principal successes included:

The Champion Chase (1935) Double
Crossed
The Imperial Cup (1935) Negro
The Lancashire Chase (1934) Avenger
The Stanley Chase (1934) Double Crossed

He was also associated with Mr Jock
Hay Whitney's great-hearted Thomond
II, on whom he won the Becher Chase
three years in succession, was twice
placed in the Grand National and who
was involved in the epic duel with Golden Miller for the 1935 Cheltenham
Gold Cup. After the excitement of the
race had died down he said to his
conqueror, Gerry Wilson: "Well done
mate. Well here's one thing, when we are
old and grey, sitting back and enjoying a
drink, we can tell them how we did ride
at least one great horse race, one day in
our lives."

Tragically he was never to enjoy that
drink. He broke his back in a fall from a
bad horse in a seller at the following
Cheltenham meeting and died six days
later. Cheltenham had become his
adopted town and it turned out to
honour him. His funeral procession was
two miles long and they buried his saddle, whip and colours with him. His son,
Victor, rode under N.H. Rules and
trained near Melton Mowbray and his
grandson is showing promise as a N.H.
jockey.

SPENCER, George
George Spencer owned and trained the
1963 Champion Hurdler, Winning Fair.
He had been given the horse who was
one-eyed and was at the time one of only
four horses in his Co. Tipperary yard.

SPRAGUE, Harry
Harry Sprague rode principally over
hurdles although he was a particularly
strong horseman and very effective over
fences as well.

He won the Imperial Cup twice, in
1952 and 1953 on High Point, and the
1958 Triumph Hurdle on Pundit. Over
fences his principal successes were the
Grand International, Sandown (1952) on
Legal Joy and the 1959 Whitbread Gold
Cup on Done Up in which he beat
Mandarin a short head after a
magnificent piece of riding on an incorrigibly lazy horse. It was his last ride

and he is reported to have been sick from
his exertions afterwards.

SPRIG
Chestnut gelding, 1917, Marco—Spry
(Galloping Simon). Bred by Capt.
R. C. B. Partridge.

Capt. Partridge was killed at the very
end of World War I and, believing it to
be her son's wish, Mrs Partridge under-
took the racing career of Sprig with
the long-term objective of the Grand
National.

Sprig won a total of five hurdle races
including the Victory Hurdle,
Manchester (1922) and 11 chases including the Stanley Chase, Liverpool (1924),
the National Hunt Handicap Chase
(1926) and the 1927 Grand National,
12-4 (T. Leader), 8/1f, by 1l, the same,
from Bovril III, 10-12 (Mr G. W. Pennington) and Bright's Boy, 12-7 (J.
Anthony). He was also fourth to Double
Chance in 1925 and fourth to Jack
Horner in 1926.

A big, strong, imposing horse, Sprig
was far from easy to train. His trainer
Tom Leader described him as having
"very nasty, gummy forelegs" and he was
also subject to bouts of mysterious illness
accompanied by high temperature.

SPRINKLE ME
Bay gelding, 1900, registered in Miss
Prior's Half-Bred Stud Book, Rapallo—
mare by Hackler. Bred by Mr T. S. Kirk.

An Irish-bred horse bred in Co.
Meath, Capt. Christie-Miller's Sprinkle
Me was tough and consistent and
reckoned about the best of his age at up
to $3\frac{1}{2}$ miles. His 19 victories included the
Grand International, Sandown (1909),
and the Grand Military, Sandown (1909
and 1910).

STACK, Thomas Brendan (b.1945)
Like the majority of champion jockeys,
an Irishman, but unlike them not reared
in a hunting, point-to-point background,
Tommy Stack was born in Co. Kerry,
educated at a Jesuit College and became
an insurance clerk in Dublin. His introduction to the mercurial sport of N.H.
racing was fostered by his school friends
Bobby Barry and Barry Brogan (q.v.) and
he found himself spending weekends at
the training establishment of Brogan's
father, Jimmy.

On the sudden and unexpected death

of Jimmy Brogan, Tommy Stack became more and more involved with the Brogan stable, now controlled by his friend, until he determined, despite staunch family disapproval, to seek his own fortune in the racing game. A letter sent to ten top English N.H. trainers, offering his services free on the chance of a ride, proved unproductive as only one of the trainers, Capt. Neville Crump, bothered to reply and he could not help. A chance introduction to veteran Yorkshire trainer Bobbie Renton was more fruitful and to his Oxclose, Ripon, establishment young Stack, aged 19, with the clothes he stood up in and £50, arrived in the summer of 1965.

He rode his first winner, as an amateur, barely two months later and continued to ride as an amateur for two years before turning professional. He was still at Oxclose in the summer of 1971 having made something of a name for himself and ridden 50 winners the previous season, when Renton informed him that he proposed to retire and suggested that Stack should take over the stable. For a few weeks he performed the dual functions of trainer and jockey, winning in both capacities. Among his charges was his future National partner, Red Rum (q.v.), whom he had several times ridden to victory. However he did not like the arrangement, found that he could not do both jobs to his satisfaction and by November had handed the stables over to Anthony Gillam. His riding career resumed its momentum and his hunger for rides became proverbial. In 1974 he became first jockey to the huge and powerful stable of W. A. Stephenson and that season he became Champion Jockey riding 82 winners, a feat he repeated in 1976-77 with 97 winners. His quest for the Championship became an obsession. He travelled hundreds of miles for rides and twice in the brief midsummer close season he went to the U.S.A. to ride over fences there.

His principal successes include:

The Grand National (1977) Red Rum
The Schweppes Gold Trophy (1977) True Lad
The Whitbread Gold Cup (1978) Strombolus
The Mildmay Chase (1972) Explicit
The Greenall-Whitley Chase (1972) Young Ash Leaf
The Cheltenham Grand Annual H'cap Chase (1977) Tom Morgan

In the autumn of 1977 he suffered a horrific fall at Hexham when his mount reared over backwards in the paddock, shattering his pelvis. After three months on traction, he staged an astonishing recovery and at the beginning of March announced himself fit enough to ride Red Rum in the forthcoming Grand National. In the event, Red Rum bruised a foot and had to be withdrawn and his substitute mount, Hidden Value, illrepaid his heroic efforts by falling at the third fence. He continued to ride his customary flow of winners during April, including a characteristically determined effort on Strombolus in the Whitbread Gold Cup, but in May announced his retirement.

He has joined the company which runs the Coolmore Castle Hyde and Associated Studs in Ireland and will be based at the Longfield Stud, Co. Tipperary.

STALBRIDGE, Rt. Hon. Hugh Grosvenor, M.C., 2nd Baron (d.1949)

The eldest son of a younger brother of the Duke of Westminster, Lord Stalbridge was educated at Eton and served with the 14th Hussars and afterwards the Northamptonshire Yeomanry in the Boer War and World War I. A keen supporter of steeplechasing he bred, owned and trained horses right up to his death.

He won the Cheltenham Gold Cup twice, in 1927 with Thrown In, whom he trained himself and was ridden by his son, Hugh, and in 1945 with Red Rower whom he also bred. Lady Stalbridge had considerable success with Red Rower's half-brother, Red April (q.v.). He also won the 1940 Grand National with Bogskar. Bogskar's National Cup was presented by his widow to Wincanton Racecourse and forms the trophy for the Lord Stalbridge Memorial Chase.

He was elected to the National Hunt Committee in 1926 and served two terms as a Steward.

Colours: dark blue, orange sash and cap. *See also* VERNON CROSS.

STALBRIDGE COLONIST

Grey gelding, 1959, Colonist II—Eesofud (April the Fifth). Bred by Mr Harry Dufosee.

An attractive grey, bred at Lord Stalbridge's family home in Dorset, Stalbridge Colonist won four hurdle races and 13 chases including the Mild-may Memorial, Sandown (1968), and the Hennessy Gold Cup, Newbury (1966) in which he beat Arkle, a feat emulated by only five other horses after the latter's first season.

Stalbridge Colonist also ran second, beaten ½ length, to Woodland Venture in the 1967 Cheltenham Gold Cup. He did not win during his last two seasons and when, at the age of 12, he was offered at Ascot Sales as a potential point-to-pointer in June 1971, he was bought back by his 82-year-old breeder for 680 guineas, in order that he might spend a peaceful retirement. Stalbridge Colonist was trained by Ken Cundell.

STARTER AND STARTING

29.(i) The Starter shall obtain a list of runners for each race from the Clerk of the Scales in the Weighing Room.

(ii) Every horse shall be at the Post ready to start at the appointed time. In races confined to apprentices, horses shall not be led to the Start.

(iii) All riders who arrive at the Starting Post must immediately place themselves under the control of the Starter.

(iv) The horses must be started by the Official Starter or his authorized substitute.

    (a) All Flat races shall be started from Starting Stalls, or, if they are not available, with a flag.

    (b) All Steeple Chases and Hurdle races shall be started by a Starting Gate approved by the Stewards of the Jockey Club unless they have given permission for a flag to be used.

Except that, in the case of emergency, by permission of the Stewards or the Starter, *any* race may be started with a flag.

(v) The Starter shall call over the names of the runners and for Flat races assign the horses to the places drawn by lot, all horses to take their places at the Start in the order drawn for them. The rider who has drawn No. 1 must always be placed on the left and other riders must take their places in consecutive numbers from the left.

(vi) The Starter, shall give all orders necessary for securing a fair start. The horses must be started, as far as possible, in a line, but they may be started at such reasonable distance behind the Starting Post as the Starter thinks necessary.

(vii) In a start from a Starting Gate or with a Flag, the Starter has full power to remove an unruly horse and should he do so, he must place it at such distance to one side of or behind the other runners that it cannot gain, any advantage itself or cause danger to, or prejudice the chances of the other horses and riders engaged in the race. Permission may be given by the Starter for a horse to be held or the Starter may himself order an unruly horse to be held, but in all cases the horse must be held 'at a stand' behind the other runners at a position to be designated by the Starter. Should any unruly horse cause undue delay it may be 'left'.

(viii) In a start from Starting Stalls the Starter has full power to remove an unruly horse but no horse shall be permitted to start from outside the Stalls, nor is it permitted for a horse to be held in the Stalls. A horse which refuses to enter the stalls, or a horse which enters and through its unruly behaviour damages its stall shall be withdrawn by the Starter.

(ix) The Starter shall order the white flag denoting that the horses are under Starter's orders to be hoisted:

    (a) for races started from Starting Stalls when all the horses are in the Stalls.

    (b) for races started from a Starting Gate when he has mounted his rostrum.

    (c) for races started by Flag when he has taken up his position to start the race.

(x) Should the Starter consider that through any cause a horse is unable to start he shall at once notify the Clerk of the Scales that the number must be withdrawn and shall inform him whether the horse came under Starter's orders or not. No horse which has come under Starter's orders shall be withdrawn except under the provisions of Sub-Rules (x) or (xiii) of this Rule.

(xi) Misconduct by a rider at the start is an offence under the Rules of Racing and the Starter has the power to inflict a fine not exceeding £17.50 for such an offence. Should a rider be so fined the Starter shall report the fact at once to the Stewards. He shall also report to the Stewards any rider whom he considers to have been guilty of misconduct at the start.

(xii) Should the Starter consider that

through any faulty action of the Starting Gate or Starting Stall a fair Start has not been effected he shall declare it a false Start and order any riders, by means of a recall flag, to return to the Post. The Starter's decision on these points shall be final.

(xiii) A start in front of the Starting Post, or on a wrong course, or before the appointed time, is void.

(a) For Flat races the horses must be started again as soon as practicable but, in the event of any horse, running the course from a false start, or from a void start, the owner may, with the consent of the Stewards, withdraw his horse from the race; the horse shall, nevertheless be considered as having come under Starter's Orders.

(b) In Steeple Chases or Hurdle races, unless at least one rider returns to the Starter after the recall flag has been raised for a false start, the race shall be void. Should only one rider return to the Starter, and satisfy him as to his having obeyed the recall flag, his horse shall be considered as having walked over for the race. Should more than one return the race shall be started again as soon as the course is clear. Horses which complete a circuit of the course or fall shall not be considered as having obeyed the recall flag. All horses which were recalled by the Starter shall, nevertheless, be considered as having come under Starter's Orders. The Starter's decision on all matters covered by this sub-Rule shall be final.

(xiv) The Starter shall report to the Stewards, for transmission to the Racing Calendar Office, all cases in which he has dispensed with the Starting Stall or Starting Gate or made any notification under sub-Rule (x), and his reasons for doing so, the time at which the race was started and by whom or by what cause any delay was occasioned.

STEPHENSON, William (b.1911)

Willie Stephenson came from a family long associated with hunting, breeding and point-to-pointing. He was brought up at Crawleas, Bishop Auckland with his cousin, Arthur Stephenson (*q.v.*), and was apprenticed to Major Beatty. It was a hard but good school. He learnt his craft thoroughly and was taught to know every muscle and bone in a horse's body. He was immediately successful and became a much sought after lightweight, "cool, beautifully balanced and neatly crouched . . . with magic hands". At the age of 16 he dead-heated for the Cambridgeshire on Niantic. In the winter of 1929 he broke his pelvis in a hunting accident and the enforced inactivity was the start of his weight problems. By 1932 he was riding over hurdles.

During World War II he served with the Gunners and in 1946 he took out a licence to train, starting with two horses. His Royston stable quickly expanded and was equally successful under both Rules. His principal N.H. successes are:

The Grand National (1959) Oxo
The Champion Hurdle (1952) Sir Ken; (1953) Sir Ken; (1954) Sir Ken
The Imperial Cup (1959) Langton Heath; (1960) Farmer's Boy
The Grand Sefton (1956) Key Royal
The Topham Trophy (1963) Barberyn
The Lancashire Hurdle (1947) Sussex Martlet; (1951) Sir Ken; (1954) Baby Don
The National Hunt Chase (1963) Time
The Fred Withington Chase (1960) Vivant

He also trained Arctic Prince to win the 1951 Derby and thus belongs to the select group of five to have achieved the National-Derby double. (*See also* JEWITT, MARSH, BLACKWELL and O'BRIEN.)

Together with Ken Oliver he was responsible for the revival of Doncaster Sales in 1962 and is a partner in Doncaster Bloodstock Sales. He also owns the Tudor Stud, which is managed for him by ex-jump jockey, Rex Hamey. He is married to Frenchie Nicholson's sister Barbara and has five daughters. Colours: maroon, pale-blue stripes, maroon cap.

STEPHENSON, William Arthur (b.1920)

A cousin of Willie Stephenson (*q.v.*), Arthur Stephenson farmed the family land at Bishop Auckland and rode as an amateur and did not take out a licence to train until 1959. Success came very quickly and he currently handles a large, mixed stable, run on very professional lines. Although it is predominantly N.H., it has won such races as the July Cup, the Gimcrack (Rapid River, 1972) and The Middle Park (Tudenham, 1972).

In 1969-70 he became the first N.H.

trainer to turn out 100 winners and he has repeated the feat every season, apart from 1974-75, since. In 1973-74 he won 105 races worth £50,729.

His principal victories include:

The Scottish Grand National (1961) Kinmont Wullie
The Welsh Grand National (1964) Rainbow Battle
The Mackeson Gold Cup (1966) Pawnbroker
The Topham Trophy (1971) Rigton Prince
The Haydock Grand National Trial (1966) The Ringer
The Wetherby H'cap Chase (1962) Cocky Consort; (1964) Mr Jones
The Cheltenham Trial Hurdle (1969) Celtic Gold
The Wills Hurdle (1969) Celtic Gold
The Liverpool Foxhunters (1972) Credit Call; (1975) Credit Call
The Cheltenham Foxhunters (1972) Credit Call
The Grand Pardubitz Chase (1973) Stephen's Society

He also trained that splendid old warrior Supermaster to win 34 races. Colours: yellow, black hooped sleeves, black and white quartered cap.

STEVENS, George (1833-71)
George Stevens holds the record of riding five Grand National winners. He won in 1856 on Freetrader, 1863 on Emblem, 1864 on Emblematic and 1869 and 1870 on The Colonel.

He was born near Cheltenham and, like nearly every boy of promise in the area, was coached by Tom Olliver. From a letter written by Olliver to a friend of Steven's just before the 1869 National, we learn something of the old maestro's approach to the big race. "If Stevens lays away from his horses and be not interfered with, it will be like a lot of terriers leading a staghound a gallop – tell him it is a long way from home the last half mile. I have no doubt he will say I am a d——d old fool but recollect old Tom Olliver's words. Be cautious and go not too soon, the post is the place to win at."

Stevens obeyed these instructions to the letter and won by three lengths. In fact he customarily rode a waiting race. He also won the Cheltenham Steeplechase three times, in 1863 and 1865 on Emblem and 1870 on Daisy. A frail-looking man, of delicate health he weighed less than nine stone and rode

only occasionally. He won only 76 chases in 22 seasons but his winner percentage was extraordinarily high.

He was killed in June 1871 when his hat was blown off riding down Cleeve Hill, causing his staid cob to shy violently and whip round, flinging the best cross-country jockey in England head-first against a stone.

STORMHEAD
Bay or brown gelding, 1944, Pactolus— Stormchild (Knight of the Garter). Bred by Mr B. Macabe.

A good staying chaser owned first by Mr Rank (*q.v.*) and then by Mr Clifford Nicholson, Stormhead won a hurdle race and twelve chases including the Leopardstown Chase (1951) the Molyneux Chase twice, the Topham Trophy, Liverpool (1955) and the Emblem Chase, Manchester (1952 and 1953). He was trained by W. A. Hall and usually ridden by Paddy Farrell.

STOTT, W. (d.1933)
A small, strong and irrepressibly cheerful man, Billy Stott was Champion Jockey from 1927-32 inclusive (1927-28, 88 winners; 1928-29, 76; 1929-30, 77; 1930-31, 81; 1931-32, 77). Trained like his friend Billy Speck, in the Wootten academy, he came to prominence in the late 1920s.

He won:

The Cheltenham Gold Cup (1933) Golden Miller
The Champion Hurdle (1933) Insurance
The Lancashire Chase (1928) Tusker
The Hurst Park National Trial (1932) Bicester
The Coventry Chase (1933) Forbra

After winning the 1933 Gold Cup on Golden Miller he was taken off in favour of Ted Leader for the Grand National. Accepting a chance ride on Pelorus Jack, he led Kellsboro' Jack into the last but fell.

Shortly afterwards he was forced to stop riding because of heart-trouble and he died later that year following a car crash.

STRAKER, Clive
A member of an old, sporting Northumbrian family, Clive Straker and his brother, John, rode in point-to-points and as amateurs for years. Clive was

Champion Amateur in 1951-52 riding nineteen winners. His successes included the 1952 National Hunt Chase on Frosty Knight. After he retired from the saddle he continued to ride and train a few point-to-pointers from his home near Hexham.

STRATFORD-ON-AVON (Group 3)

Stratford-on-Avon in Warwickshire dates from 1880. It is an enterprisingly run little course that owes a great deal to the late Gay Sheppard (Clerk of the Course, 1949-73). The track of 1¼ miles is left-handed, conical shaped and flat. The clay soil can get very heavy but a watering system is available to alleviate dry spells. Although the racing is for the most part of a fairly modest quality, the races are invariably well filled and the attendances excellent. The course is paired with Overöll, in Norway, who have been presented the Oslo Trophy to a H'cap Hurdle (September, 2m 6f, £897). Other big races include the Courage Brewery H'cap Chase (October, 2m 6f, £3,016), the Ladbrokes H'cap Hurdle (February, 2m, £1,858), the S.K.F. Hurdle Future Champions (May, 2m, £1,872) and the Horse and Hound Cup Final Champion Hunters Chase (June, 3¼m, £3,660).

Best Times

Distance	Time	Horse-age-weight	Date
2m H	3m 40.40	Chusan 6-11-12	7-5-56
2½m H	4m 45.80	Sea Cash 8-10-12	17-4-58
2¾m H	5m 14.3	Roi-Dal 5-11-6	2-9-72
3¼m H	6m 26.2	Vitbe 8-10-13	1-6-74
2m and few y C	4m 1.40	Fact and Fiction 7-11-11	12-10-63
2f 110y C	4m 18.40	Crescendo III 8-10-10	5-5-56
2¾m C	5m 30.40	Chandigar 7-11-10	31-5-75
3m C	6m 8.20	Sailors Warning 9-11-11	12-10-63
3m 2f C	6m 34.20	Bonhomie 7-10-5	29-3-56
3m 4f 110y C	7m 34.50	Happy Morn II 11-11-9	8-5-58

SUNDEW

Chestnut gelding, 1946, Sun King—Parsonstown Gem (J'Accours). Bred by Mr N. McArdle.

Sundew, a slashing big chestnut standing 17.2 h.h., was bred in Co. Meath and sent up to Ballsbridge as a yearling where he was bought for 370 guineas by Pat Grey. Fortunately for himself he was given plenty of time to mature and did not run until he was seven when he made a winning debut over fences in Ireland. He then came to England and won seven chases including the Haydock Park National Trial (1956), the Grand International, Sandown (1957) and the 1957 Grand National, 11-7 (F. Winter) 20/1, by 8l, 6l, from Wyndburgh, 10-7 (M. Batchelor) and Tiberetta, 10-0 (A. Oughton).

Sundew was bought by Mrs Kohn for £3,000 on the eve of the 1955 National in which he fell. After he had fallen again the following year, she sent him to the December Sales but failed to get a bid. An offer to sell him privately at £2,500 found no takers and so Mrs Kohn perforce still owned him when he finally triumphed in 1957.

Sundew was trained by Fred Hudson and was at the time the only chaser in the small yard. He broke a shoulder after dropping his hindlegs in the water at Haydock Park in November 1957 and had to be destroyed.

SUNLOCH

Bay gelding, 1906, Sundorne—Gralloch (Trayles). Bred by Mr H. S. Black.

Sunloch, who descended on his dam's side from Pocahontas (q.v.), won six chases including the 1914 Grand National, 9-7 (W. J. Smith), 100/6, by 8l, the same, from Trianon III, 11-9 (C. Hawkins) and Lutteur III, 12-6 (A. Carter). He went off in front and made all the running and was at one stage 40 lengths clear.

Sir Charles Assheton-Smith who had owned Cloister, Jerry M. and Covertcoat, tried hard to buy Sunloch before the 1914 National. Had he been successful he would have completed a hat-trick. Sir Charles did in fact buy Sunloch after the National, but he died within the year and the horse never won for him. Sunloch won the National in the colours of Tom Tyler, who also trained him.

SUTCLIFFE, John Earnshaw (1906-1975)

John Sutcliffe senior, so called to distinguish him from his son, John Robert (*q.v.*), also a fine trainer, trained a small but very successful mixed stable near Ashtead in Surrey. He was also a company director and a member of Lloyds. He did not take out a licence until 1965, three years after his son. His principal successes were the 1971 Grand National with Specify and the Schweppes Gold Trophy 1971 with Cala Mesquida and 1973 with Indianapolis. Specify and Cala Mesquida were owned by Mr F. W. Pontin. He was largely responsible for the saving of Lingfield Park in 1974 and made the approach to Ladbrokes who finally bought it.

SUTCLIFFE, John Robert Earnshaw (b.1940)

The son of John Sutcliffe senior (*q.v.*), John Sutcliffe junior rode successfully as an amateur and as a professional under National Hunt Rules and was Champion Amateur in 1958-59 riding eighteen winners. His victories included the Coronation Hurdle, Liverpool, on Ocarina.

He took out a licence to train at Woodruffe House, Epsom, in 1962 and is chiefly known for his Flat horses. He handled the dual classic winner Right Tack, and the tough miler Jimmy Reppin. His biggest success under National Hunt rules was the Schweppes Gold Trophy (1965) with Elan. Colours: dark green, light blue hoops and armlets, cerise cap.

SWATTON, John (1840-1909)

John Swatton was head-lad and licence-holder to Arthur Yates (*q.v.*), and is therefore officially credited with the National victories of Roquefort (1885) and Cloister (1893). He had been with Yates since both were small boys and when Yates began riding over fences as an amateur, unbeknown to his parents, used to help smuggle his things out of the house.

A first-class stableman, he was totally uninterested in racing, never had a bet and rarely went to the races. He did accompany stable-jockey William Dollery to Aintree when the latter was having his first National ride and in the absence of Yates, walked the course with him. He pointed out all the weak spots and marked them with string, happily oblivious of the fact that the course he had charted was probably over five miles long. Dollery took his own course and finished prominently, though not among the placed horses.

SWEET JOE

Chestnut gelding, 1972, Joe Price—Honey's Flight (Misty Flight). Bred in the U.S.A. by Mr Milton Ritzenberg.

Although bred in the U.S.A. Mr Milton Ritzenberg's Sweet Joe has done all his racing in Great Britain. After winning twice on the Flat at three years, Sweet Joe had a most successful hurdling campaign with four victories culminating in the Victor Ludorum Hurdle, Haydock (1976). At this point his career hesitated. He lacked the speed to make his presence felt among the fiercely competitive crop of top hurdlers and he clearly found the transition to fences difficult. Once he fell with a good race at his mercy and on another occasion blundered himself out of contention. However by 1978 he had got himself sorted out and won two good chases in impressive fashion, namely the Nottingham Champion Novices Chase and the Sun Alliance Chase, N.H. Meeting. Sweet Joe is trained at Newmarket by Tom Jones and ridden by his increasingly stylish young jockey, Stephen Smith-Eccles.

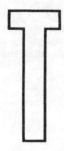

TAAFFE, Patrick (b.1930)

Pat Taaffe, a lanky, soft-spoken Irish jockey was the most effective horseman seen on British tracks since World War II. His ability to get horses jumping confidently and well has rarely been surpassed and while his somewhat unorthodox, apparently untidy finishes have been criticized, he won more big races than anybody else.

The son of trainer Tom Taaffe, he grew up in the world of hunting and showing and progressed, via the point-to-point field, to steeplechasing proper. After a successful spell as an amateur, he was offered, in 1950, the job of first jockey to Tom Dreaper and accepted with alacrity.

The partnership lasted 20 years and ended with his retirement. During that time they won every important race in England and Ireland and produced the horse of the century, Arkle.

Taaffe's principal successes include:

The Cheltenham Gold Cup (1964) Arkle; (1965) Arkle; (1966) Arkle; (1968) Fort Leney
The Grand National (1955) Quare Times; (1970) Gay Trip
The King George VI (1965) Arkle
The National Hunt Two-Mile Champion Chase (1960) Fortria; (1961) Fortria; (1964) Ben Stack; (1966) Flyingbolt; (1970) Straight Fort
The Tote Champion Novices Chase (1970) Proud Tarquin
The Irish Grand National (1954) Royal Approach; (1955) Umm; (1959) Zonda; (1961) Fortria; (1964) Arkle; (1966) Flyingbolt
The Whitbread Gold Cup (1965) Arkle
The Hennessy Gold Cup (1964) Arkle; (1965) Arkle
The Mackeson Gold Cup (1962) Fortria
The Massey-Ferguson Gold Cup (1965) Flyingbolt

The Black and White Gold Cup (1965) Flyingbolt; (1966) Dicky May
The Grand Sefton (1953) Coneyburrow

He retired in 1970 and took out a licence to train. Success has come instantly and he has produced the brilliant if unpredictable Captain Christy to win the Irish Sweeps Hurdle (1972), Scottish Champion Hurdle (1973), the King George VI Chase (1974 and 1975), and the Cheltenham Gold Cup (1974).

TAAFFE, Thomas J.

Tom Taaffe trained at Rathcoole, Co. Dublin. He won the 1958 Grand National with Mr What and produced the famous jockey brothers (subsequently trainers), Pat (q.v.) and Tos. The 1955 Grand National was a great triumph for him for the winner, Quare Times, was ridden by Pat and the third, Carey's Cottage, was trained by himself and ridden by his younger son, Tos.

TASKER, J.

Information about J. Tasker is remarkably hard to come by but he evidently had a field day in 1854, winning the Grand National on the 4/1 favourite, Bourton and the Cheltenham Steeplechase on Trout. Both horses were owned by Mr Martin Moseley. In 1855 he was killed in a fall at Warwick.

TATE, Richard

The son of shrewd Worcestershire trainer Martin Tate, Richard Tate rode very successfully as an amateur and was Champion Amateur 1967-68 (30 winners) and 1968-69 (17 winners). A bad fall waterskiing damaged his neck so badly that he was obliged to give up race-riding. He now farms and assists his father, Martin Tate.

TATTERSALLS

Tattersalls' enclosure on a racecourse is situated next to the club or members' stand and it is there that the main volume of on-course betting takes place. The public who pay to go into Tattersalls have access to the paddock.

TAUNTON (Group 5)

A most attractive, small, West-country course, Taunton is right-handed, oval and more-or-less flat except for a dip three furlongs out, followed by a steady rise to the winning post. The circuit is only 1¼ miles round but the turns are easy and it is a galloping track.

There are no important races, among the most valuable being the Staplehay H'cap Hurdle (April, 3m 1f, £1,082), the West Monkton H'cap Hurdle (March, 2m 3f, £1,017) and the Wedmore H'cap Chase (May, 3m 1f, £1,005).

points and a hunter-chase as a nine-year-old. He was then sold to Mr Henry Lane and sent to Neville Crump for whom he won four chases including the Honeybourne Chase, Cheltenham, and the 1952 Grand National, 10-12 (A. P. Thompson), 100/7, by 5l, a bad third, from Legal Joy, 10-4 (M. Scudamore)

Best Times

Distance	Time	Horse-age-weight	Date
2m H	3m 39.80	Cantlie 10-11-4	7-5-76
2m 3f H	4m 24.20	Shahr Aly 7-10-0	7-10-71
3m 1f H	5m 20.30	Brimful 6-11-3	27-12-69
2m C	3m 47.60	Dun Oir 8-10-2	11-11-71
2m 3f C	4m 29.40	Kasim Baba 7-12-0	11-5-73
3m 1f C	6m 3.50	Landway 10-10-4	11-5-73

TAXIDERMIST

Bay gelding, 1952, Ujiji—Rage Bleu (Plassy). Bred by the Knockaney Stud.

After winning a modest race on the Flat at three years, Taxidermist was bought by Peter Hastings-Bass for £250 and sent to Fulke Walwyn, whose wife Kathleen took a half share. His first season under N.H. Rules yielded only a humble seller after which he was somewhat dubiously retained for £170 against the advice of shrewd ex-trainer Ivor Anthony (*q.v.*). However better things were in store for Taxidermist who went on to win 12 chases including the Whitbread Gold Cup, Sandown (1958) and the Hennessy Gold Cup, Newbury (1958) in which he beat the Gold Cup winner, Kerstin, a short head.

Taxidermist had a habit, disconcerting to his supporters, of dropping himself out in the early stages of a race and coming with a great rattle at the end. He was usually ridden by the Hon. John Lawrence (*q.v.*).

TAYLOR, W.

W. Taylor won the 1846 Grand National on the unquoted Pioneer and the Cheltenham Steeplechase 1848 on Standard Park.

TEAL

Bay gelding, 1942, Bimco—Miltown Queen (Soliman's Orb). Bred by Mr G. Carroll.

After changing hands on several occasions for two-figure sums, Teal came into the possession of Mr Ridley Lamb, of the sporting Northumbrian family, who produced him to win two point-to-

and Wot No Sun, 11-7 (D. Dick). The following year he ran a great race to be second in the Great Yorkshire and was much fancied for the Cheltenham Gold Cup. Sadly he dropped his hind legs in the water and ruptured himself and despite an operation, died ten days later.

TEAM SPIRIT

Bay gelding, 1952, Vulgan—Lady Waleskwa (Knight of the Garter). Bred by Mr P. J. Coonan in Ireland.

A small, chunkily built horse, typical of his sire, Team Spirit won four hurdle races and seven steeplechases. He spent the early part of his career in Ireland where, as a good-class eight-year-old, trained by Dan Moore, whose victories included the Mildmay Memorial, Sandown (1960) and the Hurst Park National Trial (1960), he looked a very live National contender. However after he had fallen while attempting to refuse Becher's (second circuit), finished a remote ninth in 1961 and fallen again in 1962, these hopes seemed unlikely to be fulfilled.

At the beginning of season 1962-63 he was bought by an American partnership comprising Mr J. K. Goodman, Mr Gamble North and Mr R. B. Woodard and came to England to be trained by Fulke Walwyn in whose hands he prospered anew. He won the National Hunt Handicap Chase (1963), was fourth in that year's National, and went on to win the Grand Sefton, Liverpool (1963) and the 1964 Grand National, 10-3 (G. W. Robinson), 18/1, by ½l, 6l, from Purple Silk, 10-4 (J. Kenneally) and Peacetown, 10-1 (R. Edwards).

TEESSIDE PARK (Group 4)

Teesside in Durham, formerly known as Stockton, used to stage National Hunt racing in the nineteenth century, but it was not until 1967 that a new jumping circuit, which several leading northern trainers helped to design was laid out. The circuit is left-handed, oval, flat and about one mile six furlongs in length. The most important races are the Ladbroke Racing H'cap Chase, (December, 3m 31y, £1,010) and the Joe Coral H'cap Hurdle (February, 2m 176y, £2,106).

TEN UP

Bay gelding, 1967, Raise You Ten—Irish Harp (Owenstown). Bred by Mr J. W. Osborne.

Ten Up, a rangy son of the Goodwood Cup winner Raise You Ten, was bought by Tom Dreaper on behalf of Anne, Duchess of Westminster for 5,000 guineas as a three-year-old at Ballsbridge.

A dour stayer and a real mud-lover, he won a Flat race, three hurdle races and nine steeplechases including the Sun Alliance Chase, Cheltenham (1974), The

Best Times

Distance	Time	Horse-age-weight	Date
2m H	4m 0.30	Mickey Acklam 7-10-8	10-5-77
2m 176y H	3m 47.50	Sword Thrust 8-9-7	7-10-72
2m 5f 104y H	4m 56.80	Pearl's Lad 6-10-12	12-3-76
3m 1f 134y H	6m 54.2	October 5-11-6	6-1-68
2m C	3m 55	Roselevin 7-10-5	9-10-71
2m 4f 66y C	5m 1.2	J.F.K. 8-12-1	1-11-69
3m 31y C	6m 7	Chester Moor 7-10-0	9-10-71
3m 4f 71y C	7m 36	Sovereign Gale 6-10-0	24-4-70
4m 137y C	8m 31.6	Great Noise 6-10-7	24-4-70

TELEVISION

Direct televised coverage of races started in 1946 and has been gradually increasing over the years. There is no doubt that television does, in some degree, reduce attendances at race-meetings, particularly in inclement weather, but this disadvantage is offset by the interest in racing which television stimulates among the public and by the volume of off-course betting that it creates.

In May 1964 a television committee set up by the Racecourse Association recommended that in relation to television, the object of the Association was to negotiate block contracts with the B.B.C. and with independent television authorities. This object has not yet been achieved. Its purpose was not merely to benefit those courses whose meetings were being televised, but to form a fund in which those courses whose meetings were not televised would share. In the meantime, racecourses continue to negotiate their own contracts, many of which are of a long-term character. The report by Sir Henry Benson's Committee of Inquiry into the Racing Industry suggested that racing is not receiving as much income from television contracts as it could. Finally, it is worth bearing in mind that without television coverage, there would be very few sponsored races.

Whitbread Trial Chase, Ascot (1975) and the 1975 Cheltenham Piper Champagne Gold Cup, (T. Carberry) 2-1, by 6l, ¼l, from Soothsayer (R. Pitman) and Bula (J. Francome).

Ten Up thus provided a first Gold Cup for Jim Dreaper, although the sixth for the stable which had already sent out Prince Regent (1946), Arkle (1964, 1965 and 1966) and Fort Leney (1968). Ten Up's later career was bedevilled by breaking blood vessels, a tendency which created drama at the 1976 Cheltenham Festival. He had previously raced successfully with the assistance of a pre-race injection of the coagulant, Estro, which was permissible in Ireland provided the Stewards were notified in advance. Dreaper requested permission for this injection to be administered by a Jockey Club vet prior to the Gold Cup. After deliberation the Stewards informed him that this would be in contravention of Rule 53, for under no interpretation could such an injection fall into any category other than "a substance (other than a normal nutrient) which could alter its racing performance". On receiving this advice, Dreaper withdrew Ten Up, who as he freely admitted, could not go a mile without the injection. As the Irish Stewards subsequently brought their policy into line with those of England, Ten Up's racing career was badly affected. The Duchess then gave him to her god-son, Capt. J. Hodges and after a rest and a spell of hunting he had some great rides in hunter-chases, winning the Royal Artillery Gold Cup (1978).

THE BENIGN BISHOP
Bay gelding, 1967, Arctic Slave—Honeytown (Fortina). Bred by Mr J. K. M. Oliver.

A fine, big, strong horse and a most genuine performer, The Benign Bishop won a total of three hurdle races and 13 chases including the Greenall-Whitley Chase, Haydock (1975), the Great Lancashire Chase, Haydock (1975) and the Welsh Champion Chase, Chepstow (1973). Sadly he then slipped the tendon off his hock and although he was got fit to race again, he was not successful. He was trained in Scotland by his breeder, after whose nickname he is named.

THE CALLANT
Grey gelding, 1948, St Michael—Windywalls (Shining Tor). Bred by Mr C. W. Scott.

A successful and very popular Scottish hunter-chaser, Mr Scott's almost white The Callant won six point-to-points and 16 hunter-chases including the Heart of All England, Hexham (1955) and the Cheltenham Foxhunters (1956 and 1957). The Callant was qualified with the Jedforest and invariably ridden by Jonathon Scott-Aiton. His excursions into top handicap company were not successful and after falling in the 1957 Whitbread Gold Cup and again in the 1958 Eider Chase he was off the course for two years.

THE CAPTAIN
Bay gelding, 1878, Lothario—Catherina (Uncas). Bred in Ireland by Mr C. L. Ellison.

The Duke of Hamilton's The Captain was one of the best horses in England at distances from 2½-3 miles. His victories included the Prince of Wales Chase, Sandown (1885), the Champion Chase, Liverpool (1885) and the Baden-Baden Hunt Steeplechase (1885).

His trainer, Richard Marsh, reckoned him one of the best horses he ever trained and declared that he never fell. The Captain was usually ridden by Dennis Thirlwell but George Lambton

also won on him and described him as "a champion up to three miles, a beautiful, short-legged horse up to any weight and a glorious jumper".

THE COLONEL
Brown horse, not in the General Stud Book, Knight of Kars—Boadicea. Bred by Mr John Weyman.

An elegant, almost black entire, The Colonel won eight races in the colours of his Shropshire breeder, including the Grand Nationals of 1869 and 1870.

1869 10-7 (G. Stevens), 13-1, by 3l, 1l, from Hall Court, 10-12 (Capt. Tempest) and Gardener, 10-7 (Ryan).

1870 11-12 (G. Stevens), 4/1 f, by a neck, 3l, from The Doctor, 11-7 (G. Holman) and Primrose, 10-12 (Mr Brockton).

The Colonel, who was trained at Bishop's Castle by a farmer named Roberts was then sold for £2,600 to Baron Oppenheim and went to Berlin. He was not a success however and returned to run fourth carrying 12-4 to The Lamb in the 1871 National. He afterwards returned to Germany and may or may not have served as a charger to Wilhelm I. It is certain that he stood as a stallion at Beberbeck where he had considerable influence. His grandsons Optimus and Obelisk were notable stallions whose line exists to this day.

THE DIKLER
Bay gelding, 1963, Vulgan—Coronation Day (Grand Weather). Bred by Mr J. F. Moorhead.

A massively proportioned bright bay, who for years was regarded as the *enfant terrible* of British steeplechasing, The Dikler finally adopted a more mature attitude to life and won a total of two point-to-points and 14 chases, including the King George VI Chase, Kempton (1971), the Whitbread Gold Cup, Sandown (1974) and the 1973 Cheltenham Gold Cup (R. Barry), 9/1, by a short head, 6l, from Pendil (R. Pitman) and Charlie Potheen (T. Biddlecombe). He was also third to Glencaraig Lady in the 1972 Gold Cup and second to Captain Christy in 1974.

As a four-year-old, The Dikler was so impossible that he was returned to his owner, Mrs D. August, with the recommendation that he should be shown and hunted. This programme achieved some measure of success and two years later he made his debut in point-to-points. He ran in four, winning two and running off the course in one other when holding an unassailable lead. In 1969 he was put back into training with Fulke Walwyn, who, it was felt, was the one man capable of channelling his wayward abilities. Still remarkably difficult to hold and steer, prone to the odd diabolical blunder and occasionally to downright sulks, he was one of the most exasperating characters in training and one of the best loved. Pendil's admirers have never understood how he came to be beaten by The Dikler in the 1973 Gold Cup. Certainly at distances up to and including three miles, the latter lacked the speed to get within hailing distance of the Winter champion but there were no visible excuses for Pendil that day and it must be accepted that the extra quarter-mile and the Cheltenham hill tipped the scales in favour of The Dikler.

In 1975 and 1976 The Dikler made gallant attempts at the Grand National, but although he jumped superbly, giving Ron Barry a memorable ride and on each occasion was there with a chance at the second last, he failed to stay the final half-mile and could not finish nearer than sixth. He was retired in the spring of 1976.

THE HERON
Chestnut gelding, 1941, Flamenco—Lady Loch (Loch Lomond). Bred by Mr Dan O'Gorman.

In an all-too-brief career, Mr Clifford Nicholson's smart hurdler, The Heron won six races including the Princess Elizabeth Handicap Hurdle, Doncaster (1948), the Princess Royal Handicap Hurdle, Doncaster (1949) and the Victory Hurdle, Manchester (1949 and 1950). He was trained first by Mr Nicholson himself and then by W. A. Hall.

THE HUNTSMAN
Bay horse, 1853, not in the General Stud Book, by Tupsley. Bred in Ireland.

The Huntsman was one of those Liverpool hardy annuals that litter the history of the race, and was faster than most. After changing hands several times early in his career, he became the property of old Ben Land and in 1859 ran third in the National, ridden by young Ben. The following year he was bought by a young Army officer, Tom

Townley, 10th Hussars and ridden by a brother officer, Capt. Hunt, ran a great race to be second, beaten just half a length by Anatis, to whom he was giving 26lb. On the strength of this bright showing, he was bought by ex-patriate Harry Lamplugh (*q.v.*) on behalf of his French patron, the Vicomte de Namur, whose ambition to win the National had been narrowly thwarted on several occasions.

In 1862 The Huntsman fulfilled these ambitions and gave France her first victory in the race (H. Lamplugh), 3/1f, by 4l, a bad third, from Bridegroom, 10-13 (Ben Land) and Romeo, 8-12 (C. Bennett).

THE LAIRD
Brown gelding, 1961, Border Chief—Pré Fleurie (Mieuxcé). Bred by Mr W. J. Bebbington.

The Laird, Mr H. J. Joel's attractive and popular gelding, was a superlative jumper who kept his form remarkably well over nine seasons. His twenty victories included the Cathcart Challenge Cup, National Hunt Meeting (1971), the Stone's Ginger Wine Chase, Sandown (1967), the Gainsborough Chase, Sandown (1968), the Coventry Chase, Kempton (1971) and the Massey-Ferguson Gold Cup, Cheltenham (1966). He also ran second beaten a neck to Fort Leney in the 1968 Cheltenham Gold Cup. The Laird was trained by Bob Turnell and usually ridden by Jeff King.

THE LAMB
Grey horse, 1862, not in the General Stud Book, Zouave—dam by Arthur. Bred by Mr Henchy, in Co. Limerick, Ireland.

A very small, delicately fashioned grey with the chiselled head of the Arab race, The Lamb won four races and in 1871 became the third horse to win a second Grand National.

As a youngster he was so small and weedy that a racing career was not envisaged for him. He was offered to the prominent English owner, Mr Edward Studd (who owned Salamander, (*q.v.*)) as a hunter for his son and was contemptuously rejected as being "not fit to carry a man's boots".

However The Lamb thickened and strengthened with age and at five years, now the property of Dublin veterinary surgeon Joseph Doyle, he won the valuable Kildare Hunt Plate at Punchestown. He was then leased to Lord Poulett and came to England.

His National victories were as follows:

1868 10-7 (Mr Edwards), 9/1, by 2l, the same, from Pearl Diver, 10-12 (Tomlinson) and Alcibiade, 11-10 (Colonel Knox).
1871 11-4 (Mr Thomas), 11/2, by 2l, 3l, from Despatch, 10-0 (G. Waddington) and Scarrington, 11-4 (Cranshaw).

Mr Edwards was the professional name of George Ede (*q.v.*), the Hampshire-born, old Etonian pupil of The Lamb's trainer, Ben Land.

The Lamb was off the course for two years between his National victories, suffering from a wasting disease of his quarters and when he returned to training both his confederates had departed from the scene. Ben Land had renounced chasing in favour of the Flat and George Ede had been killed in a horrible fall at Liverpool.

Their replacements were Chris Green, who had won the National in 1850 on Abd-el-Kader and in 1859 on Half-Caste, and Tommy Pickernell (Mr Thomas), who was engaged as result of a dream of Lord Poulett's in which he saw The Lamb ridden by Pickernell winning. "He won four lengths and you rode him and I stood close to the winning post at the turn. I saw the cerise and blue sleeves and you as plain as I write this."

The Lamb ran fourth in the 1872 National carrying the welter burden of 12-7 and at about this juncture – whether just before or after the National is not clear – was sold for £1,200 to Baron Oppenheim. Like The Colonel, he went to Germany and was easily winning the Grosser Preis von Baden-Baden when he ran into a boggy patch of ground barely a 100 yards from the post. His rider, Count Nicholas Esterhazy, frantically urged him on and as The Lamb gamely tried to accelerate, one of his forelegs stuck in the mud and snapped. He was destroyed on the spot.

THE LIBERATOR
Bay gelding, 1865, not in the General Stud Book, Dan O'Connell—Mary O'Toole. Bred by Mr Stokes in Annendale, Ireland.

An enormous horse, standing 17 h.h., with a long back, great shoulders, very little body and curious, donkey-like feet, The Liberator won three races, including the 1879 Grand National, 11-4 (Mr G. Moore), 5/1, by 10l, 2l, from Jackal, 11-0 (J. Jones) and Martha, 10-13 (Mr Beasley).

He ran in seven Nationals, the last when he was 17, and finished third to Austerlitz in 1877 and second to Empress, to whom he was conceding 2 st., in 1880.

The Liberator, whose sire was bought at auction for 30s. and covered his mares for 7s. 6d., was part owned by Garrett Moore (*q.v.*), of the famous Irish chasing family. At one stage this partnership with Mr Plunkett Taaffe came into dispute and an application was in fact made to restrain The Liberator from running in the 1879 National.

THE MIDSHIPMITE
Bay gelding, 1886, not in the General Stud Book, Torpedo—Lady Piggot (New Oswestry).

A top-class chaser at distances up to three miles, The Midshipmite won 40 chases and was almost unbeatable on park tracks. Sandown, Kempton and Gatwick were his favourite haunts and although he could jump Liverpool – he won the Champion Chase in 1893 – he could not last out the distance of the National. Among his other notable victories was the Grand Military, Sandown (1893) with 13-7.

The Midshipmite was owned by Mr H. L. Powell and trained by Arthur Yates, with whom he was a great favourite. Yates claimed that The Midshipmite won 50 races but the author can only find 40 in *Steeplechases Past!*

THE O'DELL
Grey gelding, 1922, Book—Scapegoat II (Morganatic). Bred by Mr J. O'Dell.

One of the best-loved hunters of all time, Maj. H. P. Rushton's The O'Dell won over 40 point-to-points and hunterchases, including the Liverpool Foxhunters (1937 and 1938) over the full National course, twice. At the time of his second victory in 1938 he was 16 years old and he was second the following year. The O'Dell was trained by his owner and ridden by Maj. Otto Prior-Palmer.

THE SCOT
Chestnut gelding, 1876, Blair Athol—Columba (Charleston). Bred by Mr R. H. Combe.

First produced by Capt. Machell (*q.v.*), The Scot won twice at five years and was then sold to Mr Leigh, for whom he won three good chases during 1881-82, the Great Metropolitan, Croydon, the Great Sandown Chase and the Grand International, Sandown. He was sent to Germany in 1883 but was subsequently bought for the Prince of Wales in whose colours he started favourite for the 1884 National but fell at Becher's.

THE SOARER
Bay gelding, 1889, not in the General Stud Book, Skylark—Idalia (Lurgan). Bred by Mr Doyle.

The Soarer was bought in Ireland as a four-year-old by 9th Lancer subaltern David (later Sir David) Campbell, and sent to the Weyhill establishment of Willie Moore, whose licence was held by head-lad John Collins. The Soarer proved an immediate success and won seven races as a five-year-old but thereafter became difficult to train. He got very poor and lost his form as a six-year-old but came back in 1896 to win the Great Sandown Chase and the Grand National, 9-13 (Mr D. Campbell), 40/1, by 1½l, the same, from Father O'Flynn, 10-12 (Mr C. Grenfel) and Biscuit, 10-0 (Matthews). Just before the race Mr Campbell had sold his horse to Colonel Hall-Walker, later Lord Wavertree. The Soarer did not win again and fell in both his subsequent Nationals.

THIRLWELL, Dennis (b.1860)
A high-class amateur of the late nineteenth century, Dennis Thirlwell was Richard Marsh's brother-in-law and rode principally for him and the Duke of Hamilton. He was an amusing and talented man, a musician, of delicate health and an intuitive horseman. He was at his best on highly strung, nervous horses and less effective on the rough ones.

His victories included:

The Paris Hurdle (*c.*1885) Marc Antony; (1886) Jannock
The Prince of Wales Chase (1884) Eau de Vie; (1885) The Captain
The Old Baden Hunt Chase (1885) The Captain
The Liverpool Hurdle (1884) Zeus
The Champion Chase (1884) Eau de Vie
The Grand National Hurdle (1885) Fenelon
Grand International Hurdle (1886) Bolero

THOMAS, E.
E. Thomas trained Kirkland to win the 1905 Grand National. Kirkland who had previously been fourth and second, won twelve other races including the Grand Sefton (1902).

THOMOND II
Chestnut gelding, 1926, registered in Miss Prior's Half-Bred Stud Book, Drinmore—mare by St Luke. Bred by the Duc de Stacpoole in Co. Meath, Ireland.

A small, blood-like horse, Thomond II is said to have been out of a thoroughbred mare but she lived in troubled times and in fact lost an eye in a shooting incident caused by the Black and Tans and not until the indefatigable Miss Prior did some research, was the family registered.

After winning five chases at country meetings, Thomond II was bought by Charlie Rogers for American millionaire, Mr 'Jock' Hay Witney and came to England to be trained by Jack Anthony.

He won 17 chases including the Seven Springs Chase, N.H. Meeting (1932), and the Becher Chase, Liverpool, three years in succession (1932, 1933 and 1934), but it was for his defeats in the 1935 Cheltenham Gold Cup and Grand National, that this great-hearted, delicate little horse is best remembered.

The decision to run Thomond II in the 1935 Gold Cup was a last-minute one. It was assumed that he would by-pass Golden Miller and go for the two-mile Coventry Cup which was at his mercy. But with the arrival of his owner from America, Thomond II who had beaten Golden Miller once and whom the prevailing hard ground suited much better than his heavier rival, was re-routed or the Gold Cup and his challenge produced the most thrilling finish ever recorded for that historic race. The battle was joined three fences out and not until 100 yards from the winning post did Golden Miller's superior strength assert itself and he inched ahead to win by ¾ length.

Both horses were due to run in the Grand National 15 days later and while the chances of neither had been improved by this titanic struggle, it was generally assumed that the frail constitution of Thomond II would suffer worst. This assumption proved incorrect and while Golden Miller, hot favourite at 2/1, withdrew himself from the contest after less than half a circuit, Thomond II, whom one unkind racing correspondent described as "no more than a ham sandwich", ran a heroic race and in fact landed over the last fence just in front of the eventual winner, Reynoldstown. For a few yards he maintained his momentum but he was very tired and weakened on the run-in to finish third. He had occupied the same position the previous year behind Golden Miller.

Thomond II was invariably ridden by Billy Speck.

THOMPSON, A. P.

Arthur Thompson was apprenticed to John Kirwan in Co. Kilkenny and came to England in 1936. He based himself at Middleham and rode winners for Matt and Harry Peacock and for Col. Lyde. At the outbreak of war, he joined up. He was captured in France but escaped on a bicycle.

After the war he rode for Capt. Neville Crump for whom he won the Grand National twice, in 1948 on Sheila's Cottage and 1952 on Teal. He was also second to Freebooter on Wot No Sun on whom he won the Scottish Grand National (1949). Other good wins include the Haydock Park National Trial (1955) on Goosander and the Welsh Grand National (1951) on Skyreholme. Sheila's Cottage is buried at the bottom of his garden. His daughter, Shirley, is married to Bobby Beasley (*q.v.*).

THORNER, G. E. (b.1949)

Graham Thorner comes from a Somerset farming family. He joined Capt. Forster as a 15-year-old school-leaver and has been attached to the stable ever since. He had his first rides in 1966-67 as an amateur and rode three winners. He turned professional the following season and within four years was Champion Jockey (1970-71) with 74 winners. The following year, 1972, he won the Grand National on his guv'nor's Well To Do and achieved his best-ever total of 75.

A thoughtful, intelligent jockey, he is also strong and forceful and is particularly effective on staying chasers.

Other major successes include:

The King George VI Chase (197) Royal Marshall II
The Arkle Trophy (1973) Denys Adventure; (1978) Alverton

The Hennessy Gold Cup (1974) Royal Marshall II
The Mildmay of Flete Challenge Cup (1972) Mocharabuice

THOROUGHBRED BREEDERS ASSOCIATION

President: The Duke of Devonshire
Chairman: Mr R. J. McCreery
Secretary: Mr S. G. Sheppard

The Thoroughbred Breeders Association officially exists to promote the science of producing and improving the thoroughbred horse and to represent the interests of breeders. They have an office with an extensive research library, available to members, at 168 High Street, Newmarket.

In practice, their activities extend a good deal further than this. They arrange courses and seminars for Stud Owners, managers and grooms, contribute to the publishing of the *Statistical Record*, arrange all Breeders Prizes and both maintain and finance a team of veterinary scientists who research into infertility, the findings of which they publish. They also maintain close links with Weatherbys, the leading auctioneering firms, the Levy Board and the Equine Research Station and represent Breeders' interests on a variety of committees including the Bloodstock (V.A.T.) Committee and the British Racing Industry Council.

THRALE, Peter Ralph Alwen (1886-1959)

A qualified veterinary surgeon, Peter Thrale had an Epsom practice for many years. He served with the R.A.V.C. from 1914-18 and took out a licence to train in 1926. At first he trained at Shirley near Croydon but later moved to West Horsley in Surrey.

He trained the good staying chaser, Drintyre (20 chases including the 1930 Scottish Grand National and Grand Military Gold Cup) and won the Military Gold Cup again in 1938 with Buck Willow. He produced Monave'en (*q.v.*), and after World War II won the Triumph Hurdle twice, in 1957 with Meritorious and 1959 with Amazon's Choice.

Colours: black, cerise cross-belts, black cap.

THROWN IN

Chestnut gelding, 1916, Beau Bill—Va Largo (Long Tom). Bred by Mr G. C. Sharpe.

After a mediocre Flat career, Thrown In won seven races for Mrs Sanday, when still an entire. In 1925 he was sold to Lord Stalbridge for his son, Hugh Grosvenor, to ride. He was cut and during the next two seasons proceeded to win eight chases, including the Valentine Chase, Liverpool (1926), and the 1927 Cheltenham Gold Cup (Hon. Hugh Grosvenor), 10/1, by 2l, 1½l, from Grakle (J. Molony) and Silvo (F. Rees).

Shortly after this momentous victory, Hugh Grosvenor took up an appointment in Australia and in 1928 he was killed in a plane crash there. His stricken father sold Thrown In who did not win again and was exported to Denmark.

TIBERETTA

Bay mare, 1948, registered in Miss Prior's Half-Bred Stud Book, Tiberius—Drumrora (Friar Gray). Bred by Mr E. R. Courage.

A tough, honest, staying mare not over-endowed with speed, but a marvellous jumper, Tiberetta won 11 chases including the Becher Chase, Liverpool (1957) and the Grand Sefton, Liverpool (1958) and finished third, second and fourth in successive Grand Nationals. In 1957 she was third to Sundew, in 1958 she was second to Mr What and in 1959 she was fourth to Oxo after landing on top of the Chair.

At stud she has been equally successful. Her breeding record is as follows:

1960 bay filly (Chamossaire) **Chamoretta** (three chases, three point-to-points).
1961 bay filly (Chamossaire) **Tamoretta** (one hurdle race, five chases).
1963 bay gelding (Flush Royal) **Spanish Steps** (four hurdle races, 12 chases).
1964 bay gelding (Flush Royal) **Trajan** (eight chases).
1966 brown gelding (Quorum) **Quintus** (four chases).
1967 Bay horse (Right Boy) **Lictor** (one hurdle race and two chases, including Topham Trophy H'cap, Liverpool).
1968 bay filly (Quorum) **Roman Meeting**
1971 bay gelding (Tycoon II) **Mafia King** (three chases).
1973 bay filly (Tycoon II). **Lavilla**

Tiberetta was put down in 1976.

TINGLE CREEK

Chestnut gelding, 1966 (U.S.A.), Goose Creek—Martingale (Flushing II). Bred by Mrs Wallace Whitaker.

Tingle Creek, a handsome, racy-looking, bright chestnut was bred in the U.S.A. and won five races before Mrs Whitaker sent him to England in the autumn of 1972 to the Newmarket stable of Tom Jones (*q.v.*). In this country he has won twenty-two chases including the Benson & Hedges H'cap Chase (1973), the Drogheda H'cap Chase, Punchestown (1974), the Express Chase, Sandown, and the Nottingham Champion Chase (1973 and 1974) and the Sandown Pattern Chase (1973 and 78). This last splendid victory in which he broke his own course record was his swansong and he was retired forthwith.

The most spectacular jumper of fences to be seen in the British Isles for years, Tingle Creek needed good to firm conditions underfoot to show his best, although he won on soft ground. Moreover he seemed more effective, particularly in later seasons, at conceding lumps of weight in lower-class handicaps than in condition races. He never performed up to his best in the National Hunt Two-Mile Champion Chase at the National Hunt Meeting.

Tingle Creek holds the 2-mile course record at Doncaster and Sandown.

TINKLER, Colin Harwin (b.1954)

A member of a sporting Yorkshire family, Colin Tinkler was more or less brought up in the saddle. His father is a permit-holder and his mother a very successful point-to-point and amateur rider who won the Newmarket Town Plate and was Ladies' Amateur Champion in 1978. He began riding as an amateur and rode his first winner at Hexham in 1970. He turned professional in 1973 and became attached to Ken Oliver's Hawick stable, first as second jockey and from 1976 as first jockey. In 1977-78 he joined Fred Rimell's stable, sharing the rides with John Burke. His best season to date has been 1974-75 when he rode 67 winners to finish fourth in the Jockeys' Table. In 1975-76 he was fifth with 56.

A fine horseman for whom horses jump very sweetly, he has gained most of his big successes in chases. They include:

The Arkle Trophy (1975) Broncho II

The Mildmay Chase (1975) Tom Morgan
The Greenall-Whitley Chase (1973)
Tregarron
The Berni Inns Chase Final (1975) Shirlath
The Bass H'cap Chase (1974) Meridian II
The Royal Doulton H'cap Hurdle (1978)
Royal Gaye
The Topham Trophy H'cap Chase (1978)
Canit
The William Hill Yorkshire Chase (1978)
Autumn Rain

TIPPERARY TIM

Brown gelding, 1918, Cipango—Last Lot
(Noble Chieftain). Bred by Mr J. J.
Ryan.

After proving useless as a two-year-
old, Tipperary Tim was cut and 'stored'
for jumping. He was bought by Mr C. F.
Kenyon and sent to Shropshire trainer, J.
Dodd. Later Mr Kenyon sold all his
horses and Tipperary Tim was acquired
by his brother, Mr H. S. Kenyon, for 420
guineas.

A dour stayer and a notably sure-
footed performer, Tipperary Tim won
nine chases including the notorious 1928
National in totally unforeseen circumstances. He was in fact the only horse to
finish without a fall, and with 10-0 (Mr
W. P. Dutton), at 100/1, won by a distance from the remounted Billy Barton,
10-11 (T. Cullinan) who was upsides and
going the better when he fell at the last.

TITUS OATES

Bay gelding, 1962, Arctic Slave—
Cacarina (Cacador). Bred by Mr J. Kent.

After Mr Christopher Collins's Titus
Oates had won a hurdle race and seven
chases, he was sent up to the July Ascot
Sales and fetched a then record 14,750
guineas. The handsome, quality six-
year-old had to date been qualified with
the Zetland and trained by Arthur
Stephenson. He was bought by Mr Philip
Cussins, a patron of Gordon Richard's
Penrith stable, for whom he won a
further 17 chases, including the Coventry
Pattern Chase, Kempton (1970), the King
George VI Chase, Kempton (1969), the
Massey-Ferguson Gold Cup, Cheltenham (1969) and the Whitbread Gold
Cup, Sandown (1971). Titus Oates, who
continued to race zestfully until 1973-74,
was extremely popular, and was usually
ridden by Ron Barry.

TOTE, The

Under the Racecourse Betting Act of
1928, the Racecourse Betting Control
Board was set up to operate the Tote. No
capital was advanced for the project nor
was the company permitted to accept
credit bets. It was directed that all profits
were to go into a fund to be used for the
general benefit of racing and breeding.

On 2nd July 1929 the Tote operated
for the first time at Carlisle and Newmarket. The staff were housed in tents
and although no one let the guide ropes
down, as had been feared, their
telephone wires from Newmarket were
cut.

In the first few years turnover was very
meagre while operating costs were
correspondingly high. Not until the formation of the Tote Investors Ltd, as a
private company to offer Tote credit
facilities in 1930, did the project begin to
thrive. By 1934 every racecourse in Britain was equipped with Tote facilities
and in 1939 the turnover reached £7
million.

Between 1929-61 the Racecourse Betting Control Board made contributions
totalling £9,725,470 to the racing industry. The money was spent on
improved accommodation and amenities,
increased prize-money and subsidies
towards the cost of transporting horses to
meetings. In 1961 the Horserace Betting
Levy Board (q.v.) was established and at
once took over the distributive functions
of the Tote. For the first annual levy, the
Tote, who at the time were estimated to
handle five per cent of the nation's betting, contributed £927,993, while the
Bookmakers achieved £892,617.

Another change brought about by the
'sixties was that the Betting and Gaming
Act (1960) legalized off-course betting
shops. Therefore in 1962 the Horserace
Totalisator Board acquired the capital of
Tote Investors Ltd and, at the same time,
Tote Offices Ltd was formed as a subsidiary of Tote Investors Ltd with the aim
of developing a chain of such shops.

These shops were soon in difficulties.
The Betting Tax of 2½ per cent on turnover imposed in 1966, which the Tote as
a statutory body had perforce to impose,
sent many big Tote backers to the larger
bookmaking organizations who were able
to stand the tax. This was followed by the
foot-and-mouth epidemic of 1967-68
which lost 81 meetings and the adverse
weather conditions of the following year
which put paid to a further 96. These
were crippling blows to an organization

which could only offer betting on horseracing in Great Britain. The final catastrophe was the imposition, in 1969, of Rateable Value Tax, a special levy of three times the takeable value on all off-course betting premises.

Faced with bankruptcy, the Tote hived off 50 of their 61 shops into a separate organization run by City Tote (Mecca), who added 50 of their own shops and offered a full bookmaking service from which the Tote received an authorization fee based on turnover.

Reprieve came in the form of the Horserace Totalisator and Betting Levy Board Act which put the Tote on an equal footing with the bookmakers, enabling them to offer starting price and ante-post odds on football, boxing, cricket, golf and greyhounds as well as horseracing.

The Tote now operates 154 betting shops. Its turnover for the year ending 31st March 1978 was £65,743,025, an increase of nearly £17 million on the previous year.

small, country meetings where they act as a great draw, providing more competitive fields than would normally be attracted. From 1964-73 they sponsored the Totalisator Champion Novices Chase (3m, 100y) at the National Hunt Meeting which was the biggest and most prestigious novice prize of the year.

TOWCESTER (Group 4)

Towcester in Northamptonshire is charmingly situated in the grounds of Easton Neston Park. It dates from 1880. The right-handed, 1¾-mile track is undulating with steady climbs over the last six furlongs which make it a severe test of stamina. The soil is clay, so extremes of going are likely. The level of prize money is comparatively high and there are several sponsored races. The most valuable is the Robert Horne Paper Co. Novice Chase (March, 3m 190yds, £1,800).

Best Times

Distance	Time	Horse-age-weight	Date
2m H	3m 43.70	Divinity 3-10-12	1-10-77
2m 5f 26y H	5m 8.20	Slievereagh 5-10-10	17-4-76
2m 50y C	3m 59	Silver Night 6-10-1	25-5-74
2m 5f 110y C	5m 33	Tartan Slave 11-11-11	26-5-78
3m 190y C	6m 15	Crofter 6-11-9	26-5-78

The Tote staff are operated from 45 local teams. They normally travel to meetings by coach, being picked up at pre-arranged points. In addition a large number of part-time staff are employed for occasions such as bank holidays when a very extended service is provided. On Easter Monday the Tote is operated at 16 race-meetings and 10 point-to-points requiring a staff of 2,700, while a further 2,000 are required for the London office and the credit and cash offices.

New ideas are being formulated to cope with the Tote's rapid expansion, particularly on the field of transmitting bets. The scheme is to link ticket machines to a mobile computer which would in turn transmit them to the central computer in London. All bets could thus be collected and collated by the 'Off' and dividends could be calculated seconds after the result is known and relayed back to the course.

For some years now the Tote have sponsored a number of races, many at

TRAINERS

Trainers have been required to be licensed since 1905.

50. Every trainer in Great Britain of a horse running under these Rules must obtain from the Stewards of the Jockey Club subject to such restrictions as they consider necessary, either:

(i) a licence to be applied for annually on the prescribed form, which may be granted for any period up to a year, or,

(ii) in the case of persons training only those horses which are the sole property (free of all lease or other joint arrangement, except between those persons for whom he is entitled to train) of themselves, or of their spouses, parents, sons or daughters (or the Executors or Administrators of such persons), for Steeple Chases and Hurdle races a permit to train to be applied for each season on the prescribed from, which may be granted for any period up to a year; except that, for the purposes of Hunters' Steeple Chases and the Grand Military

Gold Cup, a horse may also be trained privately without licence or permit (subject to the provisions of Rule 186) by the proprietor of the stable from whence the horse was regularly and fairly hunted during the current season, but in that event the owner shall be treated as trainer for all purposes under these Rules.

The fees (including V.A.T.) to be paid in respect of each licence or permit shall be such as the Stewards of the Jockey Club shall from time to time decide. The sum of £4 from each fee for a licence and £1 for each fee from a permit shall be allocated to the Jockey Club Charities as directed by the Stewards of the Jockey Club.

51. Every trainer shall conduct his business of training racehorses with reasonable care and skill and with due regard to the interest of his owners and to the safety of his employees and agents and of the horses in his charge.

52. (i) Every owner and part owner of a horse in training with a licensed trainer must, before the horse is entered or run in races, enter into a Training Agreement on the prescribed form with his trainer and this agreement must be registered at the Racing Calendar Office.

(ii) Subsequent alterations to the fees to be charged must be notified to the owner and to the Racing Calendar Office by the trainer on the prescribed forms which will be registered unless the owner notifies the Racing Calendar Office within 21 days of receipt of such form that he does not accept the alteration. In the event of an owner not acepting the alteration the original Agreement shall be deemed to be at an end and the horse or horses concerned may not be entered or run in races until a new agreement is registered.

(iii) A registration fee of £1 (plus V.A.T.) is payable by the trainer in respect of each new registration and of each notification of alteration of fee.

(iv) Failure to register a Training agreement will be regarded as a breach of the Rules of Racing by both the owner and the trainer.

(v) Any trainer who has not received settlement of an account for training fees due from an owner for whom he trains or has trained under a Training agreement horses under a written agreement within three months of the date of despatch of the account may report the matter to the Stewards of the Jockey Club. Such report shall be in writing, signed by the trainer concerned, giving details of the name and address of the owner, the nature and the amount of the debt and the date upon which the account was rendered.

(vi) Provided that not more than twelve months have elapsed since the date upon which the account was rendered, the Secretary of the Jockey Club shall, upon receipt of a complaint, notify the registered owner concerned that payment should be made or a written explanation sent to the Stewards of the Jockey Club within eight days of the despatch of the notification.

(vii) Should the owner fail to make the payment or should the Stewards of the Jockey Club consider that this explanation is not satisfactory the amount due will, after thirty days have elapsed from the date of the despatch of the notification, be considered to be arrears due under these Rules and his name will be added to the Unpaid Forfeit List.

(viii) It shall be a breach of the Rules of Racing for a trainer to submit an unjustified or frivolous report.

53. Where any horse has been declared to run under Rule 141 (i) and an examination under Rule 14 (vi) shows the presence in its tissues, body fluids or excreta of any quantity of any substance which is either a prohibited substance or a substance the origin of which cannot be traced to normal and ordinary feeding and which could by its nature affect the racing performance of a horse the trainer of the horse in question shall be fined not less that £250 or, at the discretion of the Stewards of the Jockey Club, his licence or permit shall be withdrawn. However the Stewards may waive the fine if they are satisfied that the substance was administered unknowingly and that the trainer had taken all reasonable precautions to avoid a breach of the Rule.

54. (i) No trainer shall employ any person to work in his stable who has previously been in a training stable without referring to the last trainer to employ him and receiving a reply. Any person prevented by this Rule from obtaining or retaining employment shall have the right of appeal to the Stewards of the Jockey Club.

(ii) No trainer shall engage or retain any person in respect of whom a current Identity Card has not been issued by or on behalf of the Stewards of the Jockey Club.

(iii) (a) Identity cards are issued only upon the joint application of the trainer concerned and the proposed employee. Every such application shall be in writing in a form prescribed by the Stewards of the Jockey Club and shall contain a signed undertaking by the proposed employee to be bound by the Rules of Racing. Identity Cards are the property of the Stewards of the Jockey Club; they are returnable on demand and may be granted subject to conditions, refused or cancelled at any time at their absolute discretion.

Note: Application forms for Identity Cards must be obtained from the Registry Office.

(b) The following fees are payable: for the initial issue and each annual renewal of an Identity Card, 50p (plus V.A.T.); for the replacement of a lost Identity Card, £2 (plus V.A.T.).

(c) When issued, Identity Cards must be signed by the employee and the employer.

(iv) Save when they are reasonably required for production to any persons entitled to inspect them, Identity Cards shall be kept in the possession and custody of the trainer but on termination of employment such cards must be returned to the Registry Office immediately, endorsed with the date of termination.

(v) Any trainer infringing this Rule shall be reported to the Stewards of the Jockey Club.

N.B. For the purposes of this Rule, 'trainer' shall be understood to mean a person holding a licence or permit to train under Rule 50.

55. Every licensed trainer is required to take part in the Benefit Scheme established by the Horserace Betting Levy Board for persons engaged in the Racing Industry and payments due for the scheme constitute sums due under these Rules. Payments due from permitted trainers who have voluntarily entered the Scheme are also due under these Rules.

56. If a trainer becomes a disqualified person his licence or permit is thereby revoked, except that if the disqualification is incurred under Rule 137 or Rule 203 his licence or permit shall remain valid for a period of 14 days from the date of publication in the Forfeit List or from the date of disqualification under Rule 203, after which it shall be revoked unless the disqualification has been rescinded before that period has elapsed.

57. Every horse sent by a trainer to an equine swimming pool shall be deemed to be in care of the trainer whilst visiting the pool, whether it is an Approved pool or otherwise and the trainer will be held responsible for any breaching of the Rules committed in relation to the horse whilst so visiting.

TRAINERS, LEADING

	Name	Horses	Races	Total £
1940-41	R. C. Hobbs	8	19	2,005
1941-42	R. C. Hobbs	6	10	2,035
1942-45	*No Racing*			
1945-46	T. Rayson	2	5	9,933
1946-47	F. T. Walwyn	36	60	11,115
1947-48	F. T. Walwyn	40	75	16,790
1948-49	F. T. Walwyn	36	64	15,563
1949-50	P. Cazalet	29	75	18,427
1950-51	T. F. Rimell	24	60	18,381
1951-52	N. Crump	22	41	19,356
1952-53	M. V. O'Brien	4	5	15,514
1953-54	M. V. O'Brien	7	8	14,274
1954-55	H. R. Price	24	47	13,888
1955-56	W. Hall	18	41	15,807
1956-57	N. Crump	19	39	18,495
1957-58	F. T. Walwyn	14	35	23,013
1958-59	H. R. Price	29	52	26,550
1959-60	P. Cazalet	25	58	22,270
1960-61	T. F. Rimell	28	58	34,811
1961-62	H. R. Price	34	64	40,950

	Name	Horses	Races	Total £
1962-63	K. Piggott	4	6	23,091
1963-64	F. Walwyn	30	59	67,129
1964-65	P. Cazalet	34	82	36,153
1965-66	H. R. Price	29	65	42,276
1966-67	H. R. Price	34	73	41,222
1967-68	Denys Smith	26	55	37,944
1968-69	T. F. Rimell	32	62	38,444
1969-70	T. F. Rimell	35	77	61,864
1970-71	F. T. Winter	29	73	60,840
1971-72	F. T. Winter	37	71	62,863
1972-73	F. T. Winter	37	85	79,066
1973-74	F. T. Winter	41	89	101,781
1974-75	F. T. Winter	39	81	74,205
1975-76	T. F. Rimell	30	49	111,740
1976-77	F. T. Winter	33	76	83,405
1977-78	F. T. Winter	44	90	145,915

TRESPASSER

Bay horse, 1916, Kildare II—Intrusive (Isinglass). Bred by Lord Ellesmere.

Mr P. F. Heybourn's Trespasser was indisputably the best hurdler to race in England between the wars and was in fact unbeaten. He was also very fair performer on the Flat, winning a total of seven races at two, three, four, five and six years, including the Queen's Prize and the Bibury Cup. His six hurdles victories included the £1,000 Coventry Hurdle, National Hunt Meeting (1920) and the Imperial Cup, Sandown (1920, 1921 and 1922), the last twice carrying 12-7. In 1921 he won by 10 lengths giving the second 35lb. Trespasser was trained by James Bell and always ridden by ace hurdles rider George Duller. At stud he bred a few National Hunt winners and his daughter, Tickets, bred the Champion Hurdler, Victor Norman.

TREVETHIN and OAKSEY, John Geoffrey Tristram, 4th Baron (b.1929)

John Lawrence won his first race at the Pegasus club point-to-point in 1951. As he so characteristically phrased it, "the distinguished judges and barristers who organized the bar point-to-point had quite unwittingly deprived their profession of my services". It was a grievous loss to the bar. It was N.H. racing's incalculable gain for since the death of Lord Mildmay, no one has done more for the sport.

To begin with he was an amateur rider of the highest class and, like good claret, he improved with age. He was Leading Amateur twice, in 1957-58 (18 winners) and 1970-71 (17).

His major successes include:

The Whitbread Gold Cup (1958) Taxidermist
The Hennessy Gold Cup (1958) Taxidermist
The Imperial Cup (1958) Flaming East
The National Hunt Chase (1959) Sabaria
The Liverpool Foxhunters (1966) Subaltern;
(1973) Bullock's Horn
The Cheltenham Foxhunters (1973)
Bullock's Horn

He was also a close second on Carrickbeg in the 1963 Grand National. Until his enforced retirement as the result of an accident in 1975 he rode principally for Mr J. J. Astor, Colonel Whitbread and Roddy Armytage.

He is also an I.T.V. commentator, a newspaper correspondent, writing with vision, clarity and something of a crusading spirit in the *Sunday Telegraph*, as "Marborough" in the *Daily Telegraph* and as "Audax" in *Horse and Hound*. He is a trustee of the Injured Jockeys Fund and works unceasingly on their behalf, as he does for all those employed in the sport that he loves. He lives the lives of three hard-working men and is, in addition, a brilliant after-dinner speaker. His wife, Victoria, is a daughter of former N.H. trainer 'Ginger' Dennistoun. Colours: white, black diamond, red sleeves and cap.

TRODMORE HUNT

The case of the Trodmore Hunt Meeting is one of the most audacious hoaxes ever perpetrated on the bookmakers.

The *Sporting Times* were asked to print a card of the Trodmore Hunt meeting for 1st August, 1898. As they had insufficient representatives to cover all the minor meetings that day they were glad to accept an offer from a responsible racegoer to cable in the results. The following day there was a discrepancy in the returns published by the two principal sporting papers. The *Sporting Life* returned one winner at 5/2 while the *Sporting Times* quoted 5/1. An enquiry followed as result of which it was discovered that the Trodmore Hunt fixture was totally fictitious.

TROYTOWN

Brown gelding, 1913, Zria—Diane (Ascetic). Bred by Maj. T. G. Collins in Ireland.

A really grand stamp of horse who could only be faulted in that his mighty front made him look a trifle light about the loins, Troytown was half-brother to two useful National Hunt performers, Wilkinstown and Kenia. In a tragically brief career, Troytown won four chases for Maj. Gerrard, including the most important races in England and France before having to be put down at the age of seven.

After winning a maiden chase in Ireland, Troytown came to Liverpool for the Spring Meeting of 1919. His jockey took the wrong course in the novice Stanley Chase but the pair came out two days later to win the Champion Chase by 6 lengths. That summer Troytown went to France for the Grand Steeplechase de Paris and starting at 37/10 (A. Escott) he made every yard of the running and won easily. In 1920 he won the Grand National in sensational style, 11-9 (Mr J. Anthony) 6/1, he won by 12l, 6l, from The Turk, 9-7 (R. Burford) and The Bore, 10-1 (Mr H. Brown. He went straight to the front, pulling like a steam engine, made two appalling blunders that would have felled any lesser horse and was still pulling as he passed the winning post. He in fact carried the shattered Anthony round to the start again before he could be pulled up.

He went to France again that summer and after running third in the Grand Steeple, took the field for the Prix des Drags six days later. Crashing through a post-and-rails on the far side of the course, he broke a bone above his knee and had to be destroyed.

Troytown was trained in Ireland by Algy Anthony. Despite the briefness of his career, he was undoubtedly a very great horse indeed.

TRUDGILL, Robert

A West-country jockey of iron nerves, Bob Trudgill won the 1924 Grand National on Master Robert who had been rejected by stable-jockey Peter Robert. Trudgill would ride anything and in consequence had some really dreadful falls including one, the day before the National, which necessitated extensive stitching in his leg. He rode like a demon to get Master Robert home, burst the stitches and collapsed on dismounting.

The joint-owners gave him a present of £2,000 and trainer Aubrey Hastings commented that "no other jockey but Trudgill would have won on Master Robert".

TUDOR LINE

Chestnut gelding, 1945, King Hal—Miss Lucy Glitters (Diligence). Bred by Mr David Murphy.

A handsome, well-balanced chestnut, Mrs E. Truelove's Tudor Line was slow to mature but went on to win six chases including the Victory Chase, Manchester (1953), the Mildmay of Flete, National Hunt Meeting (1954) and the Lancashire Chase, Manchester (1955). He also ran second in two successive Nationals. In 1954 he was beaten a neck after a driving finish with Royal Tan and in the quagmire conditions of 1955 he was beaten 12 lengths by Quare Times. Tudor Line was trained by Bobby Renton and usually ridden by George Slack.

TURNELL, Andrew (b.1948)

Andy Turnell, son of trainer Bob (q.v.), is one of the most successful of the younger generation of N.H. jockeys. He was apprenticed to his father, understudied Jeff King and Johnny Haine for years and now rides as first jockey for the stable.

He is easily recognizable for he rides so short that it looks impossible for him to stay on, let alone balance and steer his mount. Yet he does these things very effectively; horses jump well for him and he is able to establish a beautifully fluid rhythm through the air.

His principal victories to date are:

The Lloyds Bank Champion Novice Hurdle
(1976) Beacon Light
The Massey-Ferguson Gold Cup (1972)
Arctic Bow
The Wills Premier Chase (1973) Balinese
The Whitbread Trial Chase (1973) Balinese

The Fred Withington Chase (1972) The Ghost
The National Hunt H'cap Chase (1974) Cuckolder
The Great Yorkshire Chase (1974) Cuckolder
The Hennessy Cognac Gold Cup (1975) April Seventh
The Black and White Gold Cup Novices Chase (1976) Tree Tangle
The Mackeson Gold Cup (1974) Bruslee
The Fighting Fifth H'cap Hurdle (1977) Bird's Nest

His best season to date was 1972-73 when he rode 45 winners, coming ninth in the list.

TURNELL, Andrew Robert (b.1914)
A former N.H. jockey, Bob Turnell runs a large and extremely successful stable at Ogbourne Maisey near Marlborough in Wiltshire. His success has not been lightly earned. After an apprenticeship with Geoffrey Bennett (father of 'Tuppy' Bennett) (*q.v.*) he rode as a professional from 1926-57 and it was not until after World War II that fortune so much glanced in his direction. His victory in the 1946 Grand Sefton on the Rogerson's War Risk paved the way for some better rides and he went on to win the Great Yorkshire Chase (1949) on Old Mortality and the Sandown Open Chase on Prince Blackthorn.

When he took out a licence to train in 1954, Mr and Mrs John Rogerson became his principal patrons and each owned a really good horse. Mr Rogerson had Pas Seul (*q.v.*) and Mrs Rogerson, who as Miss Joel had won the Newmarket Town Plate in her youth, had Salmon Spray (*q.v.*) He has also been very successful for Mr H. J. Joel.

The stable's principal successes are:

The Cheltenham Gold Cup (1960) Pas Seul
The Champion Hurdle (1966) Salmon Spray
The National Hunt Two-Mile Champion Chase (1967) Drinny's Double; (1968) Drinny's Double
The Champion Novices Chase (1958) Pas Seul
The Tote Champion Novices Chase (1964) Buona Notte
The Whitbread Gold Cup (1961) Pas Seul; (1975) April Seventh
The Hennessy Gold Cup (1967) Rondetto; (1974) Cuckolder; (1975) April Seventh
The Massey-Ferguson Gold Cup (1966) The Laird

The Black and White Gold Cup (1971) Jabeg; (1976) Tree Tangle
The W. D. & H. O. Wills Premier Chase (1973) Balinese
The Topham Trophy (1970) Charter Flight
The Stone's Ginger Wine Chase (1965) Rondetto; (1967) The Laird; (1968) Bowgeeno
The Fighting Fifth Hurdle (1976) Bird's Nest; (1977) Bird's Nest

He still finds time to hunt with the Beaufort and does not hesitate to take valuable racehorses out if he feels they would benefit. He is a noted teacher of jockeys as besides his son, Andrew, he has produced Jeff King (*q.v.*), and Johnny Haine (*q.v.*).

He has regularly finished high up in the Trainers List, being second in 1963-64 with 59 races worth £32,937 and fifth in 1972-73 with 43 races worth £42,186. An outspoken member of his profession, he has a poor regard for much of racing's management and does not hesitate to air his views.

TWEEDIE, Robert Reginald (b.1911)
Reg Tweedie rode as an amateur from 1932-49 with considerable success, winning over 100 races including the Cheltenham Foxhunters (1934) on his father's Ballybrack (*q.v.*). He then took out a permit to train and had enormous success with Freddie (*q.v.*), who started in point-to-points, won the Cheltenham Foxhunters (1964) and went on to become a staying chaser of the highest class, winning the Mildmay Memorial, the Great Yorkshire and the Gallagher Gold Cup and being twice second in the Grand National.

His wife runs a small stud at their home at Middlethird, Berwickshire, and from the game mare, Rosie Wings, has bred the good winners Mount Athos, Scottish Sinbad and John Splendid. He was elected to the N.H.C. in 1969.
Colours: blue, red sleeves, blue cap.

TYLER, Thomas
Tom Tyler, a sporting farmer from Loughborough, Leicestershire, owned and trained the 1914 Grand National winner Sunloch, after refusing tempting offers from slate magnate Sir Charles Assheton-Smith. After Sunloch's victory, he was induced to sell but Sir Charles died that autumn and his new purchase did not win in his colours.

The **Schweppes Gold Trophy** (1968) Persian War

The **Irish Sweeps Hurdle** (1970) Persian War

The **Triumph Hurdle** (1967) Persian War:
(1968) England's Glory: (1971) Boxer

He retired at the end of 1973-74.

UTTOXETER (Group 3)

Uttoxeter, a popular little Staffordshire track has survived some difficult moments. Steeplechasing has been staged there for upwards of 130 years but it was only in 1907 that the present course began to operate. Before the war the Racecourse Company owned all but 140 yards of the course which was privately owned. Afterwards the owner refused to re-lease on acceptable terms so in 1952 the Urban District Council stepped in and bought it under a compulsory purchase order. The course is left-handed, undulating, oval in shape and just over $1\frac{1}{4}$ miles. The bends are easy and despite its size it is quite a galloping course.

The level of prize money is comparatively high and the principal races are the Midlands Grand National H'cap Chase (April, 4m, 4f, £3,496), and the Bass Worthington H'cap Hurdle (April, 2m, 1f, £2,127).

UTTLEY, James (1939)

Jimmy Uttley was born in Lancashire and was apprenticed to Staff Ingham. He rode successfully on the Flat, winning about 50 races before becoming too heavy. He did his National Service with the Royal Horse Artillery and then turned his attention to N.H. racing. Basing himself at Ashtead, Surrey, where he helped Staff Ingham with his yearlings and two-year-olds. He rode only over hurdles and in that sphere became the most polished and effective rider of his generation.

His successes included:

The **Champion Hurdle** (1968) Persian War:
(1969) Persian War: (1970) Persian War

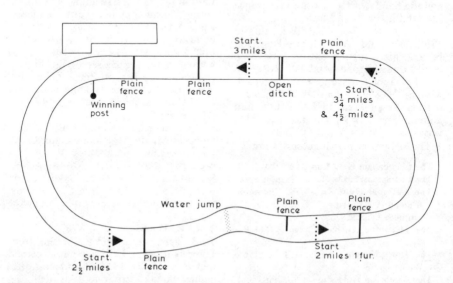

Best Times

Distance	Time	Horse-age-weight	Date
2m 180y H	3m 56.20	Jackie Little 7-10-12	9-10-71
2m 1f H	3m 56.40	The Flak Bomber 5-10-3	29-4-76

2½m H	4m 42.9	{ Irish Special 6-10-12	13-5-71
		{ Tamalin 7-10-1	27-4-74
3m H	5m 48.30	Honey Blue 8-10-12	19-4-76
2m 40y C	3m 57	Effendi 7-10-4	26-9-53
2m 1f C	4m 16.80	Master H 7-11-12	19-4-76
2½m C	4m 54.2	McKenzie 8-11-8	27-4-74
3m C	5m 58.60	Rodway Belle 8-9-8	13-4-71
3m 2f C	6m 25.40	Hidden Value 10-11-4	18-5-78
3m 3f C	7m 0.7	Fighting Chance 6-10-0	6-4-74
4½m C	9m 47.80	Burrator 7-10-1	10-4-76

VANGUARD

Bay gelding, not in the General Stud Book, by Old Advance or Belzoni.

Vanguard won six chases including the 1843 Grand National, 11-10 (T. Olliver), 12/1, by 3l, ½l, from Nimrod, 11-0 (Scott) and Dragsman, 11-3 (Crickmere). His ownership is vague and he appears in *Steeplechases Past* as the property of Mr King, Lord Chesterfield and lastly of Tom Olliver himself. Vanguard was a great favourite of Olliver's who had a sofa made from his hide.

VAULX

Brown gelding, 1914, Benvenuto—Bairgen Breac (The Baker). Bred by Sir P. Walker.

Vaulx, who was bought by Charles Piggott as a yearling for £10, was named after the village of Vaulx-Vraucourt on the Somme. A good staying chaser, he won 13 races including the National Hunt Handicap Chase, Cheltenham (1922 and 1924) and the Welsh Grand National (1925). Vaulx was owned and trained by Charles Piggott (*q.v.*), and ridden by the latter's nephew, Keith.

VERMOUTH

Bay gelding, 1910, Barcaldaile—dam of Bushey Park ex Meanus. Bred by Mr P. J. Hartigan.

A talented and versatile young horse whose career was severely hampered by World War I. Vermouth has rarely been given credit for his achievements.

Trained by shrewd James Bell, he won six races including the County Hurdle, National Hunt Meeting (1914), the Imperial Cup, Sandown (1914), the Lancashire Chase, Manchester (1915) and the 1916 War National, 11-10 (J. Reardon), 100-8, by 2l, 6l, from Irish Mail, 12-5 (C. Hawkins) and Schoolmoney, 10-2 (A. Saxby), before his seventh birthday. After that he trained off abruptly and failed to win in 19 outings over the next three seasons.

VICTOR NORMAN

Grey gelding, 1931, King Sol—Tickets (Trespasser). Bred by Mr W. J. Peek.

A grandson of crack hurdler, Trespasser. Victor Norman won twice on the Flat, seven hurdle races including the International Hurdle, Gatwick (1935) and the 1936 Champion Hurdle, (H. Nicholson), 4/1, by 3l, 1½l, from Free Fare (G. Pellerin) and Cactus II (G. Wilson).

He was owned by Mrs M. Stephens and trained by Morgan de Witt Blair when he won the Champion Hurdle. He later won three steeplechases for Henry Turner.

VIVIAN

Bay gelding, not in the General Stud Book, by Fencer.

Capt. Lamb's Vivian and Captain Becher were among the most prominent partnerships in the early days of steeplechasing and feature in many prints of the day. Among their victories were the Northamptonshire Steeplechase (1834), the Vale of Aylesbury (1834), a £2,000 match at Market Harborough against the Marquis of Waterford on Cock Robin, and the Cheltenham Steeplechase (1837).

VOLUPTUARY

Bay gelding, 1878, Cremorne—Miss Evelyn (Orlando). Bred by Her Majesty Queen Victoria

Voluptuary's background was rather more glamorous than many of his contemporary National winners. Bred at the Royal Stud, he was sold to Lord Rosebery as a yearling and won him three good-class Flat races at three years. He was thought good enough to run in the Derby but did not gain a place. He was then sold to Mr H. F. Boyd and sent to the Warwickshire establishment of William and Ted Wilson, to be trained for jumping.

He won a hurdle race in December 1883 and although he was reputed to have jumped "every fence in Warwickshire", he did not have a preliminary outing over fences before winning the 1884 Grand National, 10-5 (Mr E. P. Wilson), 10/1, by 4l, 6l, from two subsequent winners Frigate, 11-3 (Mr H. Beasley) and Roquefort, 10-5 (J. Childs).

Voluptuary did not run again and ended his career in Drury Lane where nightly he jumped the water jump in the Grand National scene from *The Prodigal Daughter,* if possible shedding his partner, Len Boyne, in the process, which earned the poor man an extra five shillings.

VULGAN
Bay horse, 1943. Bred in France by M. J. Lambert

			Gainsborough
		Sir Nigel	
	Sirlan		Lady Elinor
			Antivari
		Laniste	
Vulgan			Loetitia
			Radames
		Motrico	
	Vulgate		Mastiques
			Sans Souci
		Vodka	
			Viranka

A neat, compact horse standing just under 16 h.h., Vulgan was bred in France and raced there until he was four years, winning five races over distances up to 3,000 metres. He came to England in 1948 to be trained by John de Moraville and won his only hurdle race, the Gloucester Hurdle, National Hunt Meeting, and the Queen Alexandra Stakes at Royal Ascot. He continued to race until he was six, winning one further race and being placed several times in good-class staying races.

Sent up to the Newmarket Sales, he was bought for 510 guineas by the British Bloodstock Agency acting on behalf of Mr Frank Latham who wanted a small, quality, agile horse of proven soundness who would refine the big, rangy Irish jumping mares. Vulgan stood at Mr Latham's Blackrath Stud at Athy, Co. Kildare, starting at a fee of 40 guineas which rose ultimately to 250 guineas, then a record for a National Hunt sire.

His success was instant and phenomenal. By 1959-60 he was heading the Sires List, a feat he repeated on nine subsequent occasions. It is not an exaggeration to say that he has had more influence on National Hunt breeding than any other stallion in its history. He stamped many of his stock with his compactness, quality and activity.

His principal winners include the Cheltenham Gold Cup winner, The Dikler (*q.v.*), the Grand National winners Team Spirit (*q.v.*) (1964), Foinavon (*q.v.*) (1967) and Gay Trip (*q.v.*) (1970) perhaps the prototype Vulgan, and the 1966 Champion Hurdler Salmon Spray (*q.v.*).

Others include Colebridge ('.'/ills Premier Chase Final, 1970, Irish Distillers Grand National, 1974), Into View (Heinz Chase and Black and White Gold Cup, Ascot, 1970), Kinloch Brae (Cathcart Chase, National Hunt Meeting, 1969), Larbawn (*q.v.*) (Whitbread Gold Cup, 1968 and 1969) and Gay Vulgan (National Hunt Chase, 1977).

In June 1968 Vulgan fractured a hock and had to be destroyed.

By the end of 1978 he had sired the winners of 1,055 races worth £634,322. Details of his Leading Sire figures are:

1959-60	winners of	38	races worth		£14,061½
1963-64	,,	,,	59	,,	,,	£42,172
1965-66	,,	,,	90	,,	,,	£45,737
1966-67	,,	,,	94	,,	,,	£62,265
1967-68	,,	,,	82	,,	,,	£37,781
1968-69	,,	,,	76	,,	,,	£44,911
1969-70	,,	,,	76	,,	,,	£60,914
1970-71	,,	,,	66	,,	,,	£42,760
1971-72	,,	,,	64	,,	,,	£51,945
1973-74	,,	,,	51	,,	,,	£50,858

WALWYN, Fulke (b.1910)

Fulke Walwyn was born in Monmouthshire. His father was a soldier and Master of the Monmouthshire Hounds and his twin-sister became Mrs Helen Johnson-Houghton. He was commissioned into the 9th Lancers, a regiment with a fine chasing tradition, and began riding as an amateur. He was Leading Amateur on three occasions and won the 1936 Grand National on Reynoldstown. The next season he turned professional and rode for George Beeby but a badly broken arm put him out for the greater part of the season. In 1938 he had a dreadful fall at Ludlow, fracturing his skull for the second time and being unconscious for a month, after which he was forbidden to ride racing any more.

He immediately took out a licence to train at Delamere, Lambourn, and had trained 18 winners before war broke out. He returned to the Army forthwith although the medical authorities refused to pass him fit for operational service.

In 1944 he bought Ted Gwilt's Saxon House, secured the services of Joe Lammin as head-lad and hoped that the horses would come. They did. In season 1945-46, he was Leading Trainer. In 1946 Miss Paget sent him six horses and he repeated the feat. In all he has been Leading Trainer five times, 1945-46, 1946-47, 1947-48, 1957-58 and 1963-64 and, even more remarkable, has failed to make the leading six on only eight occasions in thirty-three seasons' training.

His major successes have been:

The Cheltenham Gold Cup (1952) Mont Tremblant; (1962) Mandarin; (1963) Mill House; (1973) The Dikler

The Grand National (1964) Team Spirit

The Champion Hurdle (1962) Anzio; (1965) Kirriemuir

The King George VI (1947) Rowland Roy; (1957) Mandarin; (1959) Mandarin; (1963) Mill House; (1971) The Dikler

The Imperial Cup (1949) Secret Service; (1950) Secret Service

The Scottish Grand National (1947) Rowland Roy; (1964) Popham Down

The Scottish Champion Hurdle (1969) Mugatpura

The Triumph Hurdle (1956) Square Dance

The Whitbread Gold Cup (1958) Taxidermist; (1967) Mill House; (1973) Charlie Potheen; (1974) The Dikler

The Hennessy Gold Cup (1957) Mandarin; (1958) Taxidermist; (1961) Mandarin; (1963) Mill House; (1968) Man of the West; (1972) Charlie Potheen

The Grand Steeplechase de Paris (1962) Mandarin

The Schweppes Gold Trophy (1975) Tammuz

This last-named horse belonged to H.M. Queen Elizabeth the Queen Mother who transferred her horses to him in 1973 after the death of Peter Cazalet.

A charming, unpretentious and shrewd man, he is infinitely patient, treats all his horses as individuals and is a wizard with doubtful legs. It is unlikely that any other trainer could have achieved what he did with Mont Tremblant, Mandarin and Mill House. He commands immense loyalty from his staff and heads one of the best teams in the country.

WANDERER

Bay horse, about 1845, not in the General Stud Book, Verulam—Mrs Stapley (Ambo). Bred in Ireland.

Mr Dennis's Wanderer was a distinctly dark horse when he came over from Ireland with the stable fancy, Boundaway, to contest the 1855 Grand National. Unquoted in the betting, carrying 9-8 (J. Hanlon) he was always prominent, was given a breather coming on to the racecourse and pounced at the final hurdle to win by 2l, 4l, from Freetrader, 9-4 (Meaney) and Maurice Daley, 9-6 (R. James).

Bells Life described Wanderer as a "rough, undersized common-looking hunter" and queried whether "a worse field had ever started".

WARWICK (Group 3)

The county town of Warwick was one of the earliest centres of steeplechasing and the Warwick Grand Annual over four miles, one of the important chases of the nineteenth century. The National Hunt

Chase was held at Warwick in 1902 and 1903 and from 1906-10. The course is left-handed, roughly triangular and chiefly flat, except for a short, sharp rise and following descent just beyond the winning post. The circuit is about 1 mile 6 furlongs.

The principal races are The Brooke Bond Oxo National H'cap Chase (January, 4m 1f, £3,397), The Crudwell Cup (March, 3m 4f, 300 y, £1,844) and the Sherbourne H'cap Chase (January, 2m 4f, £2,078).

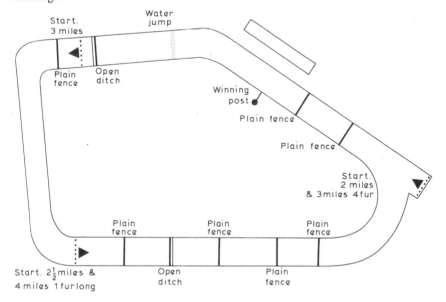

Best Times

Distance	Time	Horse-age-weight	Date
2m H	3m 33.60	Exstream 5-12-1	16-9-72
2m 5f H	4m 43	Carrymore 7-10-0	19-9-70
2m C	3m 49.60	Eagles Nest 6-12-0	19-9-70
2½m C	4m 58.40	Kalyan 6-11-0	19-9-70
2m 5f C	5m 48.10	Old Smokey 9-10-10	7-3-78
3m C	5m 59.10	April Seventh 12-12-0	20-5-78
3m 4f 300y C	7m 23	Popham Down 7-10-11	26-11-64

WATER-JUMP

The Rules of racing state that "there shall be a water-jump 12 feet wide and 2 feet deep, guarded by a fence not exceeding 3 feet in height". The previous ruling was that "The shelve from the floor of the water on the landing side to begin 6 feet from the landing edge. A horizontal turfed shelf, two inches below the surface of the water to extend inwards from the landing edge of the water for 18 inches to meet the top of the shelve." This did not prevent a series of fatal mishaps at the water jump, Sundew, Mr Jones and Master Garter being among the victims and the Jockey Club sought for some way of modifying it.

During 1972-73, Sport Surfaces made three test installations at Windsor, Towcester and Newcastle which featured a well-sloped pit shallowing out from 1 foot to 7 inches, cushioned with 7 inches of sand and surfaced with a proprietary band of shock-absorbent rubber called 'jump turf'.

WATKINSON, Ian (b.1948)

Ian Watkinson rode his first winner in 1966 but his career was slow to prosper. By sheer perseverance, good horsemanship and willingness to ride work, schooling and thoroughly bad horses he gradually made his way up. The turning point of his career came when he began to ride work for Newmarket trainer, Tom Jones. He made the most of the opportunity, rode several winners on the stable's second rides and, on the retirement of David Mould (*q.v.*), stepped into the first jockey slot. In his first season he finished 12th in the jockey's list with 45 winners, more than his total for the previous five seasons. At the beginning of 1977-8 he accepted a retainer to ride first jockey to Peter Bailey

His principal successes include:

The Hennessy Cognac Gold Cup (1976) Zeta's Son

The Victor Ludorum Hurdle (1976) Sweet Joe

The Greenall-Whitley Chase (1977) General Moselle

The Embassy H'cap Hurdle (1977) Sea Pigeon

The Bass H'cap Chase (1976) Jolly's Clump

The Bellway Fighting Fifth Hurdle (1978) Sea Pigeon

WATKINSON, William (d.1926)

William Watkinson was born in Tasmania of Irish parents. He was apprenticed to W. P. Cullen at the Curragh and later rode for Lindsay Fitzpatrick. In 1912 he moved to Scotland and was thereafter attached to the Ayrshire stable of John McGuigan.

He won the Champion Chase 1920 on Always and was second in the 1922 National on Drifter. In 1926 he bought Jack Horner home to win the big race for American Charlie Schwartz. Schwartz was dissuaded from giving him a £4,000 present in favour of £1,000 annually for four years. Poor Watkinson never enjoyed the fruits of this generosity for he was killed in a fall at Bogside just three weeks later.

WEBBER, Anthony

Anthony Webber, one of the few old Etonian professional jockeys riding, is a member of a sporting Oxfordshire family. His grandfather, Capt. Jack Webber was a very well-known showjumper who ran the B.S.J.A. for years. He began riding in point-to-points while still at school and, as soon as he left, began riding the horses trained by his father, John.

In 1973-74 he became Champion Amateur, riding 21 winners, after which he took out a professional licence. His most prolific winner has been Ballyrichard Again, a one-time cripple who with patience and care was got right to win eight races.

WELL TO DO

Chestnut gelding, 1963, registered in Miss Prior's Half-Bred Stud Book, Phebus—Princess Puzzlement (Gregalach's Nephew). Bred by Mrs H. Lloyd-Thomas.

Well To Do, who was bred by the widow of Royal Mail's owner, traces back on the dam's side to the grand jumping line of My Prince. He was bought as an unbroken three-year-old by Capt. Tim Forster on behalf of Mrs Heather Sumner.

A neat gelding of no more than medium size, Well To Do was slow to mature but proved genuine, consistent, a safe jumper and a sound stayer and had won his owner a hurdle race and five chases before her tragic death from cancer in June 1971.

Under the terms of her will, Well To Do then passed to her trainer, Capt. Forster for whom he won four races including the 1972 Grand National, 10-1 (G. Thorner), 14/1, by 2l, 3l, from Gay Trip, 11-9 (T. Biddlecombe) and Black Secret, 11-2 (S. Barker).

His record of sure-footedness and consistency must be almost unparalleled for he never fell, only once unseated his rider, and finished unplaced only seven times in seven seasons' racing.

His half-brother, Royal Marshal II (*q.v.*), owned by Mr John Sumner and also trained by Capt. Forster, is also a distinguished staying chaser whose victories include the King George VI Chase, Kempton (1976) and the Hennessy Gold Cup, Newbury (1974).

WERWOLF

Chestnut horse, 1919. Bred by Sir R. W. B. Jardine.

		Marco
	Marcovil	
		Lady Villikins
Hurry On		
		Sainfoin
	Toute Suite	
Werwolf		Star
		Isonomy
	Isinglass	
		Wenlock
Forest Lassie		
		Ladas
	Baroness La Flêche	
		La Flêche

Werwolf, whose pedigree combined the proven jumping strains of Marcovil and Pocahontas (through Isinglass) with the classic quality of La Flêche, was disappointing on the racecourse. He won two modest races on the Flat at four years and two hurdle races at six years.

He retired to stud in Ireland, being stood first by Mr Christopher Roche and from 1926 by Mr Joseph McDonald at a fee of 19 guineas. He was a prolific sire of jumping winners, getting Silver Fame (*q.v.*) (Gold Cup 1951), Bogskar (*q.v.*) (Grand National 1940), Free Fare (*q.v.*) (Champion Hurdle 1937), Timber Wolf (Welsh National and Lancashire Chase) and Aigeard Sios (*q.v.*).

He was Leading Sire in 1939-40, siring four winners of seven races worth £5,297 and was put down in December 1941.

WEST INDIES
Bay mare, 1924, Jackdaw—Isle of the Blessed (St Brendan). Bred by Maj. D. Dixon.

A brilliantly fast and very popular mare, West Indies suffered from lack of opportunities at her distance which was two miles. Nevertheless she won three hurdle races and four steeplechases including the International Hurdle, Gatwick (1930), and the Sandown Open Hurdle (1930) with 12-7. One of her most scintillating efforts was her six-length

victory in the 2-mile Sefton Chase at Newbury, carrying 12-12.

In 1931 she was bought by leading amateur, Capt. Sassoon (*q.v.*), and realized a long-cherished ambition for him by winning the Valentine Chase, Liverpool, by 10 lengths.

In January 1932, West Indies fell and broke her neck in the Winchester Handicap Chase at Newbury, to the great grief of the racing public.

WETHERBY (Group 2)
An old-established, well-run Yorkshire track dating from 1867, Wetherby is a left-handed, oblong track, 1½ miles round and flat apart from a sharp rise just past the winning post and a slope down to the back straight. It is a course that sets a premium on stamina and good jumping and horses possessing these qualities are well catered for.

The Wetherby H'cap Chase (3m 100y) used to be very important in the 1950s and was won by such good horses as Bramble Tudor and Much Obliged. It is now run at the April meeting and is worth £3,495. Other important races are the Rowland Meyrick H'cap Chase (January, 3m 100y, £3,765), and the Wetherby Pattern Novices Chase (November, 3m 100y, £2,970).

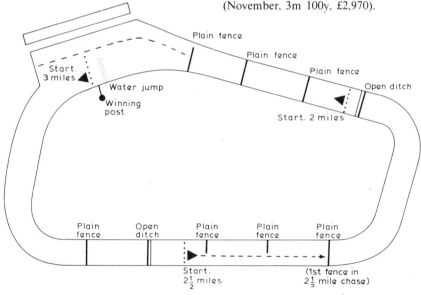

Best Times

Distance	Time	Horse-age-weight	Date
2m H	3m 43	Somerville 8-11-1	15-10-69
2½m H	4m 47.80	Supermaster 5-11-4	3-6-68

3m H	6m 3.40	Glorious Day 6-10-13	17-1-53
2m 50y C	3m 50.20	Basket 6-10-6	14-10-70
2m 70y C	4m 8.80	Ace of Trumps 11-11-7	31-10-59
2½m C	5m 23	Irish Imp 6-11-7	9-11-63
2½m 100y C	5m 12.50	Anthony Watt 6-11-2	18-11-72
3m 100y C	6m 18.60	Collingwood 9-10-6	26-5-75
3½m C	7m 36.60	Tant Pis 10-10-13	13-2-65

WHAT A DAISY
Chestnut mare, 1955. Bred by Mrs B. O'Neill.

```
                              Duncan Grey
                His Reverence
                              Reverentia
   Grand Inquisitor
                              Prince Galahad
                High Prestige
                              Prestige
What a Daisy
                              Rustom Pasha
                J'Accours
                              More Haste
   Lady Sunderlin
                              Duke of
                              Buckingham
                Duchess of Pedulas
                              Pedulas
```

Mrs O'Neill's unraced mare, whose dam was half-sister to the Grand National winner Mr What, died in 1974 after a most remarkable career at stud. She is principally remembered for the exploits of her son L'Escargot, but all her seven foals to race have been good winners, viz.

1959 bay gelding (Richard Louis) **Havago** (one flat race, four hurdles including the Gloucester Hurdle and one chase).

1961 filly (dead).

1962 bay filly (Vulgan) **What A Honey** (unraced; dam of Wolverhampton – one hurdle and seven chases) and Streetfold – three hurdle races).

1963 chestnut gelding (Escart) **L'Escargot** (two Flat races, three hurdles including Gloucester Hurdle and nine chases, including the Cheltenham Gold Cup (1973 and 1974) and the Grand National (1975).

1964 chestnut gelding (Beau Rossa) **Red Rossa** (one race).

1967 bay gelding (Royal Buck) **What A Buck** (two hurdle races, nine chases including the S.G.B. Chase and the Tote Northern Handicap Chase).

1968 bay gelding (Royal Buck) **The Pilgarlic** (three hurdle races and five chases).

1969 chestnut filly (Royal Buck) **Rathganny** (one Flat race and one hurdle).

1971 chestnut gelding (Master Buck) **Flitgrove** (three hurdle races and two chases).

1972 bay colt (Master Buck).

1973 bay colt (No Argument).

WHAT A MYTH
Chestnut gelding, 1957, Coup de Myth—What a Din (Taj ud Din). Bred by Mr D. J. Muir.

A dour stayer who relished soft ground, Sir Archibald James and Lady Weir's What a Myth won four hurdle races and 17 chases in a long and honourable career that spanned nine seasons.

Among his important victories were the Whitbread Gold Cup, Sandown (1966), the Mildmay Memorial, Sandown (1966), the Rhymney Breweries, Chepstow, and the Mandarin Chase, Newbury. By 1968 both his ability and his enthusiasm seemed on the wane and his astute trainer, Capt. H. R. Price sent him to Leicestershire for a spell of hunting. After winning two small hunter-chases without being extended, What a Myth returned to Cheltenham invigorated and on the soft ground he loved, won the 1969 Gold Cup (P. Kelleway), 8/1 by 1¼l, 20l, from Domacorn (T. Biddlecombe) and Playlord (R. Barry). He remains the only 12-year-old to win the race.

WHITAKER, Capt. Percival Aynton Ouley (1870-1944)
Percy Whitaker was educated at Wellington and served with the Sussex Hussars and the Essex Militia. A very keen man to hounds, he was Master of the Essex and Suffolk from 1895-97 and of the Oakley from 1897-1904.

He was a distinguished amateur heading the list in 1908 with 26 winners and winning that year's National Hunt Chase, on Rory O'Moore, whom he later trained to win the Champion Chase (1911). He trained first at Royston and later at St Giles, near Salisbury, and among his good winners was Silvo (q.v.), 1923 Champion Chase (ridden by Whitaker), Grand Sefton (1923) and Grand Steeplechase de Paris (1925). His stepson

Peter Roberts was also a leading amateur.

WHITE, Kenneth Brian (b.1943)

Ken White was apprenticed to J. P. Yeomans and rode his first winner in 1959. For years he was attached to the Rimell stable, becoming the first jockey on Bill Smith's transfer to Fulke Walwyn. He thus took over the ride on Comedy of Errors, with whom he established a particularly harmonious relationship and gained his biggest successes. These included:

The **Champion Hurdle** (1975) Comedy of Errors

The **Irish Sweeps Hurdle** (1974) Comedy of Errors

The **Fighting Fifth Hurdle** (1974) Comedy of Errors

The **Scottish Champion Hurdle** (1972) Coral Diver; (1975) Comedy of Errors

The **Welsh Grand National** (1967) Happy Spring

The **Haydock Grand National Trial** (1969) Game Purston; (1970) French Excuse

The **Victor Ludorum Hurdle** (1972) North Pole

The **Mackeson Gold Cup** (1970) Chatham

Nicknamed 'Stoker', he was a tremendously strong rider with a great sense of timing and was particularly effective on large or lazy horses. He was obliged to retire in 1976 as a result of a recurring shoulder injury.

WHY NOT

Bay gelding, 1881, Castlereagh—Twitter (Durham). Bred by Miss Nugent in Ireland.

A grand stamp of chaser with well-laid shoulders and a fine hind leg, Why Not won 23 chases including the Lancashire Chase, Manchester (1891), the Grand Sefton, Liverpool (1893), the Metropolitan Chase, Gatwick (1893) and the 1894 Grand National, 11-13 (A. Nightingall), 5/1, by 1½l, a head, from Lady Ellen II, 9-10 (T. Kavanagh) and Wild Man from Borneo, 10-9 (Mr J. Widger).

In his earlier days, Why Not was ridden by crack amateur, Charlie Cunningham for whom he won 10 races and was second in the 1889 Grand National. In 1893 he was bought by Capt. C. H. Fenwick and sent to Willie Moore at Weyhill. Thereafter he was usually partnered by Arthur Nightingall who thought

the world of him: "He was such a game old chap. He stood all my punching like a hero ... he struggled to the bitter end with unflinching resolution."

In all Why Not ran in seven Nationals and apart from his victory in 1894, he was second in 1889, third in 1893 and fifth on three occasions, 1890, 1895 and 1896.

WIDGER, Joseph (1864-1923)

Joe Widger was a member of a very famous and popular dealing family from Co. Waterford. The family supplied most of the countries in Europe with remounts and their turnover was in the region of 3,000 animals a year.

Thus Joe grew up in the saddle and won his first race under rules when only 14, at Bangor, whither he had run away from his Queen's County School.

From an early age he cherished an ambition to win the National and to this end bought, in 1893, Wild Man From Borneo on whom he finished third in the following year's National. He and his brother, Mike then settled themselves at Alfriston to lay themselves out to win in 1895. This they accomplished for Wild Man From Borneo, ridden by Joe, won by 1½ lengths.

After this sterling victory he did little more race-riding but confined himself to hunting and the family business.

WIGHT, John Stewart (1897-1963)

Stewart Wight served in the 1914-18 War with the Lothian and Border Horse. He rode as an amateur from 1919-26 and then for one year as a professional. He took out a licence to train in 1924. He handled Lord Joicey's brave mare Bramble Tudor (*q.v.*) (19 races including The Great Yorkshire Chase, 1955), Inversible (Grand Sefton, 1937), Ballybrack (*q.v.*) (Cheltenham and Liverpool Foxhunters), Happymint (Cheltenham Foxhunters 1954 and Liverpool Foxhunters, 1955) and The Callant (*q.v.*) (Cheltenham Foxhunters, 1956 and 1957).

He also won the Scottish Grand National twice, in 1950 with Sanvina and 16 with Fincham. In season 1954-55 he trained the winners of 59 races, heading the list of number of races won.

He possessed a fine eye for a potential jumper and admired the big, old-fashioned sort. He used rigorous training methods and his horses all jumped well.

On racecourses he was a familiar figure with his bowler hat and neat side-whiskers giving him the air of an old-fashioned sportsman, which indeed he was. He coached several jockeys, professional and amateur, including Dick Curran, Mick Batchelor, Ken Oliver, Reg Tweedie, Danny Moralee and Tommy Robson. He retired in 1960 because of ill-health.

WIGHTMAN, William Gilbert Rowell (b.1914)

Bill Wightman was educated at Dulwich and assisted Laing Ward training ponies. He was encouraged into racing proper by Geoffrey Gilbey and took out a licence in 1937. From 1939-46 he served with the Royal Artillery; he was imprisoned by the Japanese and came out weighing less than eight stone.

After the war he resumed training at Upham, Southampton, and had his first big successes with Hallowe'en with whom he won the Cheltenham Foxhunters (1951), the Hurst Park Grand National Trial (1952) and the King George VI Chase (1952 and 1954). He also won the Welsh Grand National (1958) with Oscar Wilde.

His stable has always been a mixed one and is nowadays almost exclusively Flat. He had a great deal of success with the fine sprinter, Runnymede. Colours: black and white hoops, red sleeves, black cap.

WILD MAN FROM BORNEO

Chestnut gelding, 1888, registered in Miss Priors Half-Bred Stud Book, Decider—Wild Duck (Sheldrake). Bred by Mr G. Keays in Ireland.

Wild Man From Borneo who came from a grand Irish jumping family unravelled by Miss Prior, was sold as a foal to that great judge Mr J. J. Maher and thence to the Widgers, a prominent sporting family who were later to produce Jerry M. Ridden by young Joe Widger, he won eight chases including the Great Midland Chase, the Great Bangor Chase and the 1895 Grand National, 10-11 (Mr J. Widger), 10/1, by 1½l, a bad third, from Cathal, 10-9 (H. Escott) and Van de Berg, 9-13 (Dollery).

WILLIAMS, Dudley

A Welshman, Dudley Williams came from Carmarthenshire as did the Anthony brothers for whom he rode a good deal. The highlight of his career was to win the 1933 Grand National on Kellsboro' Jack. He also won the Stanley Chase (1932) on that horse, the Grand Sefton (1933) on Kilcash Hill, and the Welsh Grand National (1930) on Boomlet.

He was very unlucky in the 1930 National on Mr Jock Hay Whitney's Sir Lindsay who hit the last fence hard and blundered, causing Williams to lose both stirrups, and still finished third, beaten only a neck and 1½ lengths, to Shaun Goilin and Melleray's Belle.

WILLIAMS, Evan

Evan Williams, a Welshman, is the son of starter Fred Williams. He first rode as an amateur, turned professional in 1933 and was attached to Owen Anthony's Letcombe Bassett stables when fame was thrust upon him in totally unexpected circumstances. Less than three weeks before the 1936 Cheltenham Gold Cup, Golden Miller ran out with Gerry Wilson in a race at Newbury. Wilson was promptly axed and Williams, who was then comparatively unknown, co-opted to ride the horse at Cheltenham. He won all right but he must have had some anxious moments finding himself in front and alone, fully three fences from home. He got the ride at Aintree but after being knocked over at the first fence, the Miller declined to proceed beyond Valentine's.

Williams won the Gold Cup again in 1940 on Roman Hackle and the 1937 Grand National on Royal Mail. After the war he trained on the Flat at Kingsclere and won the Festival of Britain Stakes (later the King George VI and Queen Elizabeth) with Supreme Court.

He retired young and went to live in Co. Limerick where he became a Master of Hounds. His wife, a sister of Kim Muir, owns the Knockaney Stud. Their son, Ian, is a fine amateur rider and won the Cheltenham Foxhunters (1974), on Corrie Burn.

WILLIAMSON, George

George Williamson won the 1899 Grand National on Manifesto, after surviving a near-fatal slip on some hay put down on the landing side of the Canal Turn as a precaution against the frost. He also won Sandown's important Grand International Chase (1897) on the same horse. Other good victories included the Liverpool Hurdle in 1892 on Prince Frederick and in 1895 on Miss Patty. He rode abroad a great deal and won the Bohemian Grand Steeplechase four times running on Handy Andy. He settled in Vienna and died only just before World War I.

WILLOUGHBY de BROKE, John Henry Peyto Verney, M.C., 20th Baron (b.1896)

Lord Willoughby de Broke has served racing in a number of capacities for many years. After a service career in the 17/21st Lancers he rode as an amateur and owned the good hurdler Carryduff whose victories included the International Hurdle at Gatwick.

He was elected to the N.H.C. in 1940 and has served three terms as a Steward, 1942-45, 1950-53 and 1964-67. He is Chairman of Cheltenham and Wolverhampton racecourses and previously at Birmingham. He serves as a Steward at a number of courses including Cheltenham and was Chairman of Racecourse Technical Services from 1959-70. Colours: yellow, chocolate hooped sleeves, chocolate cap.

WILSON, Edward, P. (1846-1918)

Ted Wilson was the leading amateur of the 1880s. He was short-legged and tremendously strong in the back and rode very short which was considered ugly at the time.

He won the Grand National twice in successive years. In 1884 with Voluptuary trained by his brother William (*q.v.*) at their Ilmington, Warwickshire, home, and 1885 with the very difficult Roquefort. He was unlucky on Congress in 1876, being beaten a neck by Regal, after being interfered with.

Other good victories included:

The National Hunt Chase (1877) Bear;
(1881) Pride of Prussia; (1882) Llantarnam; (1883) Satellite; (1884) Equity)
The Birmingham Grand Annual (1867) Tiger; (1869) Equity
The Sandown Grand International (1875) Goldfinder
The Grand Sefton (1873) Congress; (1886) Roquefort
The Leamington Grand Annual (1875) Congress; (1876) Congress

He was Champion Amateur twice, in 1877 with 37 winners and in 1883 with 27. In later life he ran a pub at Loughborough and continued hunting until 1905.

He was considered something of a rough diamond and was very short of cash until Voluptuary set him up. Nevertheless he was very kind and possessed great charm and a particularly infectious smile.

WILSON, Gerald (d.1969)

Gerry Wilson was Champion Jockey seven times which is a record.

1932-33	with	61	winners
1933-34	,,	56	,,
1934-35	,,	73	,,
1935-36	,,	57	,,
1936-37	,,	45	,,
1937-38	,,	59	,,
1940-41	,,	22	,,

The son of a famous Whaddon Chase dealer he was apprenticed to Frank Hartigan at Weyhill and in his early days rode a good deal for 'Sonny' Hall. The combination of his marvellous hands, with courage, toughness and unquenchable will to win proved unbeatable and he was soon at the top.

His victories include:

The Cheltenham Gold Cup (1934) Golden Miller; (1935) Golden Miller
The Grand National (1934) Golden Miller
The Champion Hurdle (1934) Lion Courage
The Imperial Cup (1935) Lion Courage; (1939) Mange Tout
The Welsh Grand National (1932) Miss Gaynus
The Champion Chase (1931) Coup de Château (dead-heated with Easter Hero)

The tragedy of his career was his senseless axing from Golden Miller as a result of that horse's débâcle in the 1935 Grand National and subsequent run-out at Newbury. After his previous year's record-breaking victory and his sterling defeat of Thomond II in the Gold Cup, Golden Miller went to Liverpool the hottest favourite ever. Wilson was offered a substantial bribe to stop him and with his characteristic honesty, immediately informed both owner and trainer and the Stewards. As for the race itself, Wilson's contention that the horse tried to stop, pitched and bucketed over the fence, giving him no conceivable chance of remaining in the saddle, has been incontrovertibly borne out by on-the-spot witnesses, the evidence of the film camera and Golden Miller's subsequent performances at Liverpol.

After his retirement from the saddle, he became a trainer and turned out the 1945 Champion Hurdler Brains Trust. He retired in 1956 and ran the Marquis of Granby, near Newbury, until his death.

WILSON, Maj. John Philip (1889-1959)
Wilson won the 1925 Grand National on Double Chance. A Yorkshireman, he played for the Yorkshire Gentlemen until 1928, and after he retired from the saddle ran a small stable in the East Riding. At one stage of his career he represented Ladbrokes on the rails.

WILSON, William
The younger brother of Ted Wilson (*q.v.*), William Wilson trained Voluptuary to win the Grand National of 1884. It was a considerable feat for Voluptuary had never jumped a fence in public, although he was reputed to have been schooled over every fence in Warwickshire. He also owned Congress and

trained him to win many races including the Grand Sefton (1876). Congress had been sold to Lord Lonsdale when he won the Grand Steeplechase de Paris.

WINCANTON (Group 3)
Wincanton, the most accessible of the West-country courses has been well served by the M4 and an enterprising executive. Meticulous care of the track and imaginatively framed races have attracted top-class horses to this modest but sporting little track. The course is right-handed, virtually flat and 1 mile, 3 furlongs round on well-drained soil. The present course was laid out in 1927.

The principal races are the Badger Beer H'cap Chase (November, 2m, 5f, £2,057), the Lord Stalbridge Memorial Cup H'cap Chase (November, 3m, 1f, £1,234), the Mendip Hills Novices Chase, (November, 2m, £2,113), and the Ladbroke Kingwell Pattern Hurdle (February, 2m, £2,267). This last has been used by Bula and Lanzarote as a stepping-stone to Cheltenham, Royal Frolic, Canasta Lad and Moonlight Bay are other top-notchers to have run there in recent years.

Best Times

Distance	Time	Horse-age-weight	Date
2m H	3m 37.60	Exstream 5-12-0	29-9-72
2½m H	4m 54.80	Avemaure 6-10-11	15-3-56
2¾m H	5m 13.2	Cool Affair 7-10-3	1-11-74
2m C	3m 53	Fitzcard 12-10-7	7-9-71
2m 5f C	5m 7.20	Maniwaki 10-10-6	13-9-77
3m 1f C	6m 21	Quantock Hill 7-10-7	2-10-70

WINDSOR (Group 3)
A very pretty Thameside course within easy reach of London, Windsor, which

dates from 1867, has always been very popular. The track is in the form of a long, narrow figure-of-eight and although

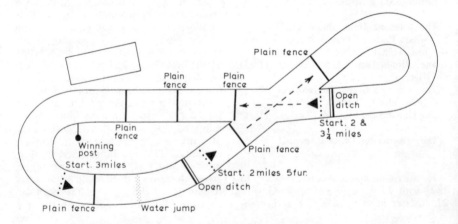

some of the early bends are quite sharp, the long six-furlong run to the finish redresses the balance in favour of long-striding horses.

There are no races of outstanding importance but the racing is usually competitive and the level of prize money quite moderate. The principal prizes are the Royal Windsor H'cap Chase (January, 3m, £1,693) and the New Year's Day Hurdle (January, 2m, 30y, £4,383).

Best Times

Distance	Time	Horse-age-weight	Date
2m 30y H	3m 43.90	Gay Manicou 8-10-6	11-11-72
2m 40y C	3m 56.40	Stone Thrower 10-10-7	5-11-77
2m 5f C	5m 18.50	New Formula 7-11-13	5-11-77
3m and few y C	5m 58.90	Alu-Alu 9-10-13	10-11-71

WINNING FAIR
Brown or black gelding, 1955, Fun Fair—Winning Hazard (Atout Maitre). Bred by Mr P. Finn.

A one-eyed gelding, owned and trained in Ireland by Mr G. Spencer, Winning Fair won six hurdle races and three chases, his most notable victory being the 1963 Champion Hurdle (Mr A. Lillingstone), 100/9, by 3l, a neck, from Farrney Fox (P. Powell) and Quelle Chance (B. Wilkinson).

WINTER, Frederick Thomas (b.1926)
Fred Winter is one of only two men training (the other is Fred Rimell) to have been Champion Jockey and Leading Trainer and the first trainer to win over £100,000 for his patrons in one season, which he did in 1973-74.

The son of a famous Flat-jockey turned trainer, Fred Winter was apprenticed first to his father and then to H. Jelin at Newmarket. He rode winners on the Flat but soon became too heavy. He began riding over fences in 1947. He gained his first win from his first ride on his father's Carton but a month later he broke his back in a novice hurdle at Wye. It was nearly the end of his career for not only was he off the course for over a year but his nerve was badly shaken. However he came back the following season with 18 winners and began to ride for Ryan Price. It was the start of one of the most famous jockey-trainer combinations of them all and the start of the Winter cult. He is a man who exercises natural dominance over people. His contemporaries swore he was unique and even those whose memories stretched back to Rees, Wootten, Duller and Piggott, reckoned they had never seen his equal. His strength and will was almost superhuman and he seemed physically to lift horses past the post. He could also adapt himself remarkably to different horses and situations. He was the only man, apart from the horse's original owner, who could ride Hallowe'en, for the small, bouncy ex-hunter would not tolerate dictation from the saddle and invariably rewarded the skilled efforts of top-class riders by putting them on the floor. Winter left him entirely to his own devices and won 17 races including two King George VI Chases. And who will ever forget his epic ride on Mandarin to win the Grand Steeplechase de Paris when he completed nearly four miles of Auteuil's tortuous, twisting track with the bit dangling uselessly from Mandarin's anyway wooden mouth?

His principal victories were:

The Cheltenham Gold Cup (1961) Saffron Tartan; (1962) Mandarin

The Grand National (1957) Sundew; (1962) Kilmore

The Champion Hurdle (1955) Clair Soleil; (1959) Fare Time; (1961) Eborneezer

The Grand Steeple de Paris (1962) Mandarin

The King George VI Chase (1952) Hallowe'en; (1954) Hallowe'en; (1960) Saffron Tartan

The Hurst Park National Trial (1952) Hallowe'en; (1959) Done Up

The Champion Novices Chase (1959) Flame Gun

The Triumph Hurdle (1953) Clair Soleil; (1961) Cantab

He was Champion Jockey on four occasions:

1952-53	with	121	winners (a record)
1955-56	„	74	„
1956-57	„	80	„
1957-58	„	82	„

He retired in 1964 and was awarded the C.B.E. for his services to racing, the first N.H. jockey to be so honoured. He applied to become an assistant starter but was turned down, the authorities in their wisdom, feeling that he would not command the necessary respect.

Later that year he took out a licence to train and made his headquarters at Uplands, Lambourn. He started his career in quite unprecedented fashion, saddling two Grand National winners in his first two seasons training Jay Trump (1965) and Anglo (1966) and has never looked back. He became Leading Trainer in 1970-71 a position he held for six of the next seven years. In 1973-74 he became the first N.H. trainer to top £100,000.

1970-71	29 winners of	73 races worth		£60,739
1971-72	31 ,, ,,	72 ,, ,,		£62,863
1972-73	37 ,, ,,	85 ,, ,,		£79,066
1973-74	41 ,, ,,	89 ,, ,,		£101,781
1974-75	39 ,, ,,	81 ,, ,,		£74,205
1976-77	33 ,, ,,	76 ,, ,,		£83,405
1977-78	44 ,, ,,	90 ,, ,,		£145,915

His principal victories are as follows:

The Cheltenham Gold Cup (1978) Midnight Court
Grand National (1965) Jay Trump; (1966) Anglo
The King George VI Chase (1972) Pendil; (1973) Pendil
The Champion Hurdle (1971) Bula; (1972) Bula; (1974) Lanzarote
The National Hunt Two-Mile Champion Chase (1971) Crisp
The Tote Champion Novices Chase (1973) Killiney
The Sun Alliance Chase (1975) Pengrail
The Arkle Trophy (1970) Soloning; (1972) Pendil
The W. D. and H. O. Wills Premier Chase (1974) Credibility
The Embassy Premier Chase (1976) Floating Pound; (1978) The Dealer
The Black and White Gold Cup (1970) Into View; (1972) Pendil; (1973) Bula
The Heinz Chase (1969) Beauchamp; (1970) Into View
The S.G.B. Chase (1972) Soloning
The Imperial Cup (1966) Royal Sanction; (1973) Lanzarote; (1977) Acquaint
The Massey-Ferguson Gold Cup (1973) Pendil
The Victor Ludorum Hurdle (1977) Rathconrath

The Liverpool Foxhunters (1977) Happy Warrior
The Welsh Champion Hurdle (1975) Lanzarote

Like Fulke Walwyn, his success is based on marvellous team-work. From John Francome down to the youngest lad, an *esprit de corps* runs through the yard. It is regarded as an honour to work there and nobody leaves voluntarily.

There have been disasters to check the unbroken tidal sweep of success. The fatal fall of Killiney at Ascot in the Spring of 1973, the last-gasp defeats of Pendil and Crisp in the Gold Cup and Grand National of the same year, the fall of High Ken that brought down Pendil when lined up to win the 1974 Gold Cup, and the fatal falls of Lanzarote and Bula at the 1977 National Hunt Meeting. Perhaps the gods ordained them lest they be thought to bestow their favours unfairly.

WITHINGTON, Frederick (1869-1951)
The son of a parson, Fred Withington was born at Fringford, Oxfordshire, and was educated at Eton. He rode successfully as an amateur, winning the Champion Chase (1896) on Greig Olway. He began training at the turn of the century, at first at Fritwell for Lord Fitzwilliam and Lord Hugh Grosvenor. He later moved to Danebury and sent out Rubio and Mattie McGregor to be first and second in the 1980 Grand National. Mattie McGregor was the more fancied of the two and was ridden by the stable jockey, W. Bissell.

After World War I he moved back to the Bicester area and reduced his string, training only for Mr Vivian Smith (later Lord Bicester) and Major Wyndham for whom he saddled Red Splash to win the first Cheltenham Gold Cup (1924).

He retired in 1930 and was elected to the N.H.C. the following year and later to the Jockey Club although he never had a runner on the Flat. He served a term as a Steward, the first N.H. trainer

to do so and acted as a Steward at Sandown, Cheltenham, Fontwell, Nottingham, Windsor, Kempton and
Towcester. He was also a J.P. and an
Oxfordshire County Councillor.

He was a very upright man who had
the knack of making people want to do
things for him – hence his success as an
organizer.

WOLVERHAMPTON (Group 3)

A left-handed, triangular course, more-
or-less flat and just over 1½ miles round,
Wolverhampton is excellently managed.
The course is always in good order and
they rarely have to abandon however wet
it is; the amenities which include a paddock in front of the stand and a
children's playground, are excellent.

The races are framed to give several
medium-sized prizes rather than one
large one and the principal races are the
Wolverhampton Champion Hurdle Trial
(February, 2m, £2,075), the Stourbridge
Hurdle (January, 2m, £2,399), the Astbury Novices Chase, (December, 2m, 5f,
£2,467) and the Reynoldstown Pattern
Hurdle (November, 2m, 4f, £1,638).

WOODBROOK

Chestnut gelding, 1874, The Lawyer
(half-bred)—The Doe (Roebuck). Bred
by Capt. Kirkwood.

Woodbrook, who was raced by his
breeder, was yet another brilliant young
horse produced by H. E. Linde at
Eyrefield Lodge, the Curragh, who failed
to withstand the prevailing stringent
training methods. He won the 1881
Grand National, 11-3 (Mr T. Beasley),
6/1 by 4l, 4l, from Regal, 11-12 (J.
Jewitt) and Thornfield, 10-9 (R. Marsh),
having taken up the running from
Valentine's (first circuit) and never being
headed thereafter. Subsequently he was
sold to Mr Oeschlager for £1,300 but he
died the following year without running
again.

Prior to his National victory Woodbrook won six races. He also won the
Grand Sefton, Liverpool (1879) but after
this race he was objected to on the
grounds of insufficient description. The
matter was referred to the Stewards of
the National Hunt Committee who
upheld the objection.

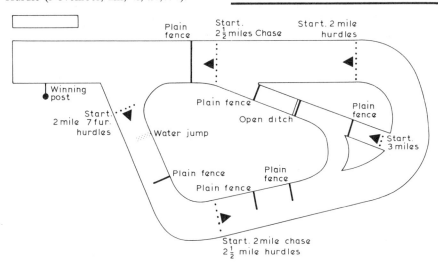

Best Times

Distance	Time	Horse-age-weight	Date
2m H	3m 46	Penisola 9-10-0	13-3-68
2½m H	4m 67.60	Aethon 8-10-3	11-3-68
3m 160y H	6m 2	{ Rodway Belle 8-9-10	20-5-71
		{ Arctic Count 7-11-12	21-5-70
2m C	3m 57.60	Heroic Lad 5-11-11	9-11-70
2½m C	4m 59.50	Game Purston 6-9-11	17-11-64
2m 5f C	5m 31.90	Casamayor (Arg) 7-11-1	28-11-77
3m C	6m 6.20	Mighty Fine 8-10-7	13-3-50
3m 140y C	6m 13.50	Astbury 7-10-9	22-10-70

WOODLAND, Percy (1882-1958)

A great and much-loved character of dry wit, suave manner and debonair appearance, Percy Woodland is the only man to have ridden two National winners (Drumcree, 1903, and Covertcoat, 1913), two Grand Steeple winners (Dandolo, 1904, and Canard, 1905) and two French Derby winners (Maintenon, 1906, and Or du Rhin, 1910).

The son of a Hendon dealer and trainer, he was small, neat and very effective on the Flat and rode his first winner at 13. He was Champion N.H. Jockey in 1903, riding 54 winners. He rode markedly short and could balance a horse and extract the last ounce from it without apparent effort. He lived in France for a while where he rode and trained a great many winners.

After World War I he settled at Cholderton, Wiltshire, and trained. He was hard on his horses who always appeared light, trace-clipped and untrimmed but well-schooled and hard as nails. He was a friend to scores of young officers who he trained as well as their horses. One of his protégés was Capt. Sassoon who did him the greatest credit, while he saddled at least five winners of the Grand Military Gold Cup. He trained two brilliant young horses both of whom had the misfortune to come up against champions in their prime. El Hadjar had a glittering novice career and after winning the Coventry Chase was well fancied to beat Golden Miller in the 1934 Gold Cup in which he fell. He fell again and was killed in the Champion Chase. Gib was another such who after giving Gregalach 6lb and a decisive beating at Lingfield, was seriousy fancied to beat Easter Hero in the 1930 Gold Cup. He ran a heroic race and was still upsides at the second last, when he fell and like many a good horse sapped by a great one, was never the same again.

He alo trained the flying West Indies but reckoned Leinster (twelve chases including the Grand Sefton and the Champion Chase twice) the best he ever had. After World War II he acted as a N.H. starter.

WOODLAND VENTURE

Bay gelding, 1960, Eastern Venture—Woodlander (Lancewood). Bred by Mr H. H. Collins.

A product of the point-to-point field, the home-bred Woodland Venture was sent to Fred Rimell at Severn Stoke as an unruly five-year-old and won seven chases including the closely-fought 1967 Cheltenham Gold Cup (T. Biddlecombe), 100/8, by ¾l, 2l, from Stalbridge Colonist (S. Mellor) and What A Myth (P. Kelleway).

He was off the course for the whole of season 1967-68 and, after winning one race the following year, died of liver-fluke during his summer holiday.

WOOTTEN, Frank (1894-1940)

The son of a distinguished Australian trainer and brother of Stanley (*q.v.*). Frank Wootten came to England just after the turn of the century. He was Champion Jockey on the Flat in 1909, 1910, 1911 and 1912. His victories included the Oaks (Perola, 1909), the St Leger (Swynford, 1910) and the Grand Prix de Paris and he rode seven winners at Royal Ascot in 1912.

During World War I he served in Mesopotamia and after it he was too heavy to continue on the Flat therefore switched to N.H. racing. He rode chiefly over hurdles and was very successful. His best season was 1921 whenhe rode 60 winners. Some thought him even better than George Duller and the *cognoscenti* long treasured the finish of the 1924 Imperial Cup when, on Noce d'Argent, he beat Duller on Spinney Hill, a neck. He also won that year's Liverpool Hurdle on Stuff Gown.

He trained at Epsom for a while but in 1933 he returned to Australia and remained there till his death.

WOOTTEN, Stanley M. C.

Stanley Wootten and his bother Frank (*q.v.*), were sons of a distinguished Australian trainer and came to England at the beginning of the century. He rode successfully for a few years before becoming too heavy and then trained under both Rules at Tredwell House, Epsom, until 1963. His N.H. interests were chiefly confined to hurdling. He owned and trained the versatile Noholme, who won 15 Flat races, 10 hurdle races and two steeplechases, including the Nuneaton Hurdle twice, and the New Century Chase at Hurst Park, and who numbered Sir Ken, National Spirit and Knock Hard among his victims. He also won the Imperial Cup (1955) with Bon Mot II and the County Hurdle (1932) with Fouquet.

Cool, precise and a stern disciplinarian, he placed moderate horses very shrewdly and landed some substantial gambles. He was a very fine teacher of jockeys and 'the Wootten touch' lives on for his protégés included 'Frenchie' Nicholson (*q.v.*), currently the most prolific producer of successful apprentices, Staff Ingham (*q.v.*), who subsequently trained for him and who in his turn has produced Jimmy Uttley, and Johnny Gilbert, (*q.v.*), who since 1973 has held the post of Racing Instructor to the Joint Board Training Scheme. Colours: cerise, gold sleeves, light blue cap.

WORCESTER (Group 3)

The attractive river-side course of the county town of Worcester dates officially from 1867 although there is recorded steeplechasing at a much earlier date than that. The Royal Worcester Chase was an important feature of the 1830s and 'forties and nearly all the early steeplechasing cracks rode there including Tom Olliver, Jem Mason, the McDonoughs, and Josie Little. The track is left-handed, oval and flat, about one mile, five furlongs round.

The general level of prize money is high for a Group 3 course and the principal races are the Sir Ken Pattern Hurdle (October, 2¼m, £2,680) and the Royal Worcester Spode H'cap Chase (March, 3m, £2,453).

A massive rebuilding operation took place at Worcester in 1974.

Alexander Maguire and ran third in the Irish Grand National.

Between 1937 and 1939 he won four races including the 1939 Grand National, 10-6 (T. Hyde), 100/8, by 3l, 15l, from Macmoffat, 10-3 (I. Alder) and Kilstar, 10-3 (G. Archibald).

Thereafter Workman's form tailed off badly and he failed to win again in four seasons racing.

Workman was the first of three horses by Cottage to win the National.

WOT NO SUN

Bay gelding, 1942, Sun-Yat-Sen—Hopeful Lass (My Prince). Bred by Mr T. C. Plunkett.

Capt. T. D. Wilson's Wot No Sun came from the same female as Kellsboro' Jack. He was a consistent staying chaser who won 12 races including the Emblem Chase, Manchester (1949), the Grand Sefton, Liverpool (1952), and the Scottish Grand National, Bogside (1949). He was also twice placed in the Grand National, being second to Freebooter in 1950 and third to Teal in 1952. Wot No Sun was trained by Capt. Neville Crump.

WRIGHT, Joseph Stanley (b.1906)

Stan Wright who trains near Bromyard in Herefordshire took out a permit in 1952 and a full licence in 1959. His biggest success was to win the 1958 Champion Hurdle with his wife's Bandalore, who was at the time one of only six horses in the yard.

Best Times

Distance	Time	Horse-age-weight	Date
2m H	3m 40.20	Volante 8-12-9	9-10-63
2¼m H	4m 7.10	Molly Fay 5-12-2	19-8-72
2½m H	4m 48.90	Swift Shadow 8-11-10	15-9-77
3m H	5m 42.20	Candid Camera 5-10-0	10-4-68
2m C	3m 48.20	Colonius 7-11-7	10-5-76
2½m C	5m 6.50	⎰ Casamayor (Arg) 7-11-12 ⎱ Eastern Harvest 10-11-2	29-10-77 12-4-67
3m C	5m 49.40	Great Opportunity 7-10-12	7-9-75

WORKMAN

Brown gelding, 1930, Cottage—Cariella (Caricato). Bred by Mr P. J. O'Leary in Ireland.

A grand, big plain horse with a lot of power behind the saddle, Workman first drew attention to himself by winning the big hunter chase at Punchestown in 1936. The following year he was bought by Sir

Other good victories include:

The Welsh Grand National (1967) Happy Spring
The Golden Miller Chase (1963) Happy Spring
The Rhymney Breweries Chase (1962) Happy Spring
The Tote Investors H'cap Chase (1957) Château Pavie

WYNDBURGH
Brown gelding, 1950, Maquis—Swinnie (Haining). Bred by Miss Rhona Wilkinson.

A stout-hearted stayer, bred and owned by Miss Wilkinson (later Mrs Ken Oliver) and in fact trained by her although the permit was held by her father, Wyndburgh graduated to chasing from the hunting field.

As a six-year-old he was placed in a point-to-point, ridden by his owner, and won a hunter chase. Thereafter he ran in handicap company and won 13 chases including the Grand Sefton and the 4-mile Tote Investors Handicap Chase (now the Eider Chase), Newcastle, twice.

He also ran in six Grand Nationals finishing sixth, fourth and second three times. In 1957 he was second to Sundew; in 1959 he was beaten 1½ lengths by Oxo, after his rider, Tim Brookshaw, had broken a leather at Becher's (second circuit) and ridden the rest of the way without stirrups; lastly in 1962 he was beaten by Kilmore, after which he was retired back to the hunting field.

WYNE, Denny
An Irish jump jockey, Denny Wynne won the 1847 Grand National on Matthew. He was also third on Crabbs in 1854. His son James was also a jockey but died following a fall from O'Connell in the 1862 National.

YATES, Arthur (1841-1922)

Arthur Yates was a great-nephew of John Elmore (*q.v.*). Despite this racing background, his parents greatly disapproved of him riding as an amateur, which he did with considerable success winning approximately 460 races. He won the very valuable Bristol Hurdle twice on Cramoisie in 1873 and Palm in 1874, and the Great Metropolitan Chase at Croydon on Harvester (1871). He thought himself unlucky not to win the 1872 National with Harvester whom he had had shod with studs because of the very heavy going. Harvester held a winning chance at the last but as he landed, caught one of his front heels with the stud and tore it practically off. He once won a race a Croydon after falling at the water by catching his horse's tail and leaping back into the saddle over its quarters.

In racing reports it is oft-times said
A jockey has cleverly won by a head
But Yates has performed, when all other arts fail
A more wonderful feat, for he won by a tail.

He later trained at the family home of Bishop's Sutton, Alresford, Hampshire, and with headman John Swatton holding the licence, the stable was phenomenally successful. He was undoubtedly Leading Trainer although there are no records to prove it. He trained 106 winners in 1891, 124 in 1892 and claimed to have saddled a total of 2,955. Among his best horses were Gamecock (*q.v.*), The Midshipmite (*q.v.*), Roquefort (Grand National, 1885) and the mighty Cloister (*q.v.*) (Grand National 1893). His jockeys were all home-produced and two of them, Dollery (*q.v.*) and Sensier (*q.v.*) became outstanding.

He had a particular talent of keeping horses sound and fresh over a long period and had a box built over a stream at the bottom of a water meadow, in which any horse with leg problems could be stood.

He continued training until 1913, becoming very much the grand old man of chasing, and his beautifully run establishment, where he kept a menagerie of zebras, deer and rare birds, besides his substantial training establishment, became a place of pilgrimage.

ZEUS

Bay gelding, 1879, Kingcraft—Wildfire (Artillery). Bred by Mr M. Dawson.

A top-class handicap hurdler in an age when they were very competitive owing to the good prize money available, Zeus was owned by the doomed Marquess of Hastings.

After a very moderate Flat career, he won 6 races, including the Great Sandown Prize (£725) and the 1884 Liverpool Hurdle. He also dead-heated for the 1883 running but was beaten a length on the re-run.

ZOEDONE

Chestnut mare, 1877, not in the General Stud Book, by New Oswesty—Miss Honiton.

A really game, safe jumping mare standing about 15.3 h.h. and very hard to fault, Zoedone had a successful five-year-old career, winning two chases and running third to Seaman in the 1882 Grand National despite being short of work due to coughing. She was then sold for £1,000 to Prince Charles Kinsky and sent to Upton trainer, W. Jenkins.

Starting at 100/8, 11-0 (Prince Kinsky) she won the 1883 National by 10l, 6l, from Black Prince, 10-4 (Canavan) and Downpatrick, 10-7 (Mr T. Widger). The following year carrying top-weight of 12-2, Zoedone ran an excellent race on ground faster than she cared for and finished fourth to Voluptuary.

In 1885 she was greatly fancied for the race and had been extensively coupled with the Lincoln winner Bendigo. Advance warnings of doping had been received and every possible security measure had been observed. The mare was saddled in the racecourse boxes and mounted on the course. Prince Kinsky did notice a speck of blood on her muzzle and a minute puncture but nevertheless continued. Zoedone fell heavily at the practice hurdle and arrived at the start with her legs tucked up with pain. She was allowed to take her chance and survived for a circuit and a half, jumping apparently from memory until Bechers on the second circuit where she shot vertically upwards and crashed to the floor. She was found to have been poisoned and was never able to run again.

Index

Abbott, T., 9
Abd-el-Kader, 9, 107, 149, 197, 257
Acthon, Major 98
Adam, Emil, 9
Adams, James, 9, 218; principal successes, 9
Adare, 175
African Sister, 9-10, 205, 243; successes, 9
Airgead Sios, 10, 275; victories, 10
Al Alawi, 166, 221
Albergo, 10, 12
Alcazar, 10, 25; successes, 10
Alcibiade, 10, 12, 69, 86, 180, 257
Alder I, 33, 285
All White, 46, 237
Allowances, 10
Ally Sloper, 10-11, 13, 25, 112, 149
Amateur: definition of, 11; licences, 11; licence fees, 11; riders' fees, 11; champions, 11-12
Amazon's Choice, 259
Ambush II, 12, 13, 29, 207; successes, 12
Anarchist, 94, 237
Anatis, 12, 117, 119, 256
Angell, Benjamin John ('Cherry'), 10, 12, 35, 179-80
Angers, 28
Anglesey, 121
Anglo, 12, 97, 172, 192, 282; successes, 12
Annandale, 106
Anne, Duchess of Westminster, 15, 80, 92
Another Flash, 10, 12, 13, 158, 223, 241
Anthony, Algernon, 12-13, 165, 266
Anthony, Ivor, 13, 25, 40, 57, 60, 112, 128, 134, 177, 208, 216, 219, 224, 253; principal success, 13
Anthony, John Randolph (Jack), 11, 13, 38, 60, 79, 85, 103, 126, 149, 164, 245, 258, 266; as Champion Jockey, 13
Anthony, Owen, 13, 69, 105, 178, 200, 243, 278
Anzio, 13; successes, 13
Apple Peel, 9
Approval, 240
April Seventh, 14, 168; victories, 14
Arbury, 86
Archer, Frederick, 14, 79
Archer, William, 14, 34, 79, 148, 196
Archibald, G., 208, 285
Archive, 14, 15; as leading sire, 14
Arctic Slave, 14-15, 168; successes, 14-15
Ardoon, 15; as leading sire, 15
Argo, 15; success, 15
Arkle, 14, 15-16, 40, 43, 47, 79, 80, 92, 103, 111, 140, 171-2, 200, 201, 211, 247, 253; principal victories, 15-16
Armour Bright, 41

Armytage, Roderick, 16-17, 26, 92, 145, 265; successes, 16-17
Arthur, 127
Ascetic, 17
Ascetic's Silver, 17; 112, successes, 17
Ascot, 17-18; valuable races run at, 18
Assaroe, 19, 118, 189; successes, 19
Assheton-Smith, Sir Charles, 128, 267
Astbury, 244
Asterabad, 167
Aunt May, 17, 202
Austerlitz, 19, 65, 117, 121, 287; successes, 19
Auteuil, 10, 19-20: The Grand Steeplechase de Paris winners, 19-20; see also SOCIÉTÉ DES STEEPLECHASES DE FRANCE
Autocar, 202
Ayala, 20, 38, 205, 214; successes, 20
Aylin, A., 11
Ayr, 20-3; winners of principal races at, 21-3

Baby Don, 78
Bacchus, 24; successes, 24
Bachelor Prince, 219
Bachelor's Hall, 24, 95; victories, 24
Badanloch, 169
Bailey, Mr E. W., 224
Bailey, Peter, 24, 42, 274; successes, 24
Balchin, F., 12, 148
Balding, Gerald, 24, 67, 112, 115, 175: principal successes, 24; as Chairman of National Hunt Trainers' Association, 24, 186
Ballinode, 10, 24-5, 176; successes, 24-5
Ballot Box, 25, 206; successes, 25
Ballybogan, 208
Ballybrack, 25, 267, 277
Ballyhackle, 109
Ballymacad, 25, 81, 112, 158, 208; victories, 25
Bampton Castle, 95
Bandalore, 25, 108, 132, 285
Bangor-on-Dee, 25; important race at, 25
Barbour, Frank, 26, 31, 88
Barker, S., 101, 274
Barona, 26
Barrott, Douglas, 26; victories, 26
Barry, Mr M., 134
Barry, Ronald, 26, 43, 65, 83, 197, 219, 235, 255-6, 261, 276; principal successes, 26
Barsac, 12
Batchelor, Mick, 278
Bates, R., 113
Battleship, 26-7, 64, 116, 117, 126, 149, 175; victories, 27
Baulking Green, 27, 94; successes, 27, 94
Beacon Light, 27; victories, 27
Bear's Slipper, 40, 96

Beasley, Harry H., 13, 27, 28, 43, 62, 64, 65, 142, 143, 158, 191, 195, 198, 222, 223, 270
Beasley, H. H., 27, 64
Beasley, Henry Robert, 12, 27-8, 43, 235, 241, 259; successes, 27-8
Beasley, Mr J., 28
Beasley, Patrick (Rufus), 27
Beasley, T., 27, 28, 99, 146, 149, 162, 235, 238, 257, 283
Beaver II, 19, 28, 161; successes, 28
Becher, Capt. Martin, 28; successes, 28
Beeby, George, 28-9; major successes, 29
Beeby, Harry, 29
Beechener, C., 216
Bell, James, 29, 265, 270
Bell Tower, 175
Benazet, 85
Bengough, Lt.-Col. Piers, 29; successes, 29
Benign Bishop, The, 255; successes, 255
Bennet, Capt. Geoffrey, 29, 32, 69, 237, 267
Bennett, Mr C., 119, 256
Beresford, Lord Marcus Talbot de la Poer, 12, 29, 59, 132, 173, 191, 224
Berry, F., 30, 103, 174; important successes, 30
Bertha, 119
Betting shops, 30
Bevill, Mr, 46
Bewicke, Maj. Calverly, 30, 114, 136; best wins, 30
Bewicke, Capt. Percy, 30; successes, 30
Bicester, Hugh Vivian Smith, 1st Baron, 30-1, 96
Bickley, J., 26, 31
Biddlecombe, Anthony, 31
Biddlecombe, Terence, 31, 39, 43, 96, 139, 255, 274, 276, 284; principal victories, 31
Billy Barton, 31, 71, 149, 261; successes, 31
Billykin, 190
Birch, A., 31, 173
Bird's Nest, 27, 31-2, 192, 235; victories, 32
Biscuit, 258
Bissill, L. W., 33, 282
Black Duncan, 57
Black Hawk, 222
Black Ice, 241
Black Justice, 202
Blacklock, 32
Black Prince, 223
Black, Richard, 32, 95
Black Secret, 79, 244, 274
Blackshaw, M., 217
Blackwell, George, 32, 237
Blagueur II, 200
Blair, Morgan de Witt, 32
Blaris, 32-3, 37, 202; victories, 32
Blennerhasset, 82
Blessington Esquire, 190
Bletsoe, Bernard, 33, 226
Bletsoe, Morgan, 33; successes, 33
Bloodstone, 67
Bloomer, 33
Blue Prince, 219
Bobby Corbett, 166
Boddam, 32
Bogskar, 33, 70, 101, 133, 162, 246, 275
Bon Mot II, 284

Bona fide meetings, 33
Bonnie Lassie, 33; victories, 33
Boomlet, 278
Border Flight, 90
Border Incident, 34; victories, 34
Bore, The, 37, 237-8, 266
Bountiful Charles, 71
Bourke, J., 244
Bourton, 34, 252
Bovril III, 245
Boxall, 76
Boxer, 39
Boyce, Charles, 34, 86, 172
Brabazon, Aubrey, 34, 47, 67, 113; successes, 34
Brains Trust, 34, 216, 280; successes, 34
Bramble Tudor, 34, 72, 131, 277; victories, 34
Brasher, 95, 221
Brave Cry, 110
Breeder, definition of, 34
Brendan's Cottage, 34-5, 66, 177, 198; victories, 34-5
Bretherton, R., 35, 127
Brewis, Robert, 35, 44
Brick, 117
Bridegroom, 10, 12, 31, 119, 179, 256
Bright's Boy, 126, 245
Briscoe, Basil, 13, 35, 47, 103-5, 122, 200, 220
Bristol, steeplechasing at, 35
British Racing Industry Council, 259
British Yeoman, 46
Broadcasting of races, 35
Brockton, Mr, 255
Broderick, Patrick, 20, 35-6, 192; principal successes, 36
Brogan, J., 27, 245-6
Brogan, J. B., 36, 103, 145, 203, 215, 238, 245; major successes, 36
Bronze Arrow, 243
Brookshaw, S. J. ('Tim'), 36, 73, 91, 122, 198, 199
Brotherton, Mrs Lurline, 37, 218
Brown, Frank Atherton, 37; best wins, 37
Brown, Harry, 15, 37, 82, 208, 237, 244, 266; successes, 37
Brown Jack, 37-8, 40, 112, 218, 222; successes, 37-8
Brown Lad, 38, 80, 169, 224; successes, 38
Brown Tony, 13, 38, 71, 237
Bruno II, 71
Bruslee, 235
Buckaway, 139
Buckingham, John, 38, 92
Buckley, Pat, 20, 38; victories, 39
Buck Willow, 222, 259
Buffalo Bill, 108
Bula, 39, 42, 43, 47, 65, 254, 282; successes, 39
Bullock, J., 40; victories, 40
Bullock's Horn, 40, 96; victories, 40
Bulteel, Sir John Crocker, 40, 119, 162, 171; Clerk of the Course, 40
Bumper, definition of, 40
Buona Notte, 40, 96; successes, 40
Burford, R., 40, 208, 266
Burke, John, 40-1; successes, 41
Burns, T. P., 12, 60, 90
Butchers, Donald, 34, 41, 228

Cackler, 42, 69, 81, 109; victories, 42
Cactus, 11, 257
Cala Mesquida, 251
Callant, The, 115, 255, 277; victories, 255
Campbell, Lt.-Gen. Sir David, 42, 99, 258; successes, 42
Canard, 283
Canasta Lad, 24, 42; successes, 42
Candy II, 35
Cannon Ball, 210
Cannon, Joe, 19, 42, 150, 158, 218
Captain Christy, 28, 38, 39, 42-3, 64, 65, 224, 252, 255; victories, 42-3
Captain Dreyfus, 208
Captain Fox, 113
Captain, The, 255; victories, 255
Carberry, Tommy, 30, 38, 41, 43, 47, 74, 79, 122, 145, 146, 169, 216, 224, 254; successes, 43
Carey, T., 167
Carey's Cottage, 212, 252
Carlisle, 43
Carmen IV, 35, 44; successes, 44
Carnival Boy, 76
Carrickbeg, 20, 41, 265
Carroll, F., 234
Carsey, 69, 202
Carter, A., 250
Cartmel, 44; valuable race at, 44
Carton, 243
Cartwright, D., 39
Casse Tête, 44, 200; successes, 44
Cathal, 81, 278
Catterick, 44
Caubeen, 64, 156
Caughoo, 45, 74, 167; successes, 45
Cazalet, Peter, 45, 70; success achieved by, 45
Celtic Gold, 45-6; victories, 46
Chadwick, Robert, 46, 103, 127, 156, 237; victories, 46
Chandler, 46, 196; successes, 46
Chang, 25
Charity, 46, 204
Charles I, 46
Charlie Potheen, 14, 36, 46-7, 209, 255; victories, 47
Cheltenham, 47ff; principal races and results at, 47-57
Chenango, 57; victories, 57
Chepstow, 57; important races and results at, 57-9
Chester, 86
Chimney Sweep (half-bred), 29, 59, 218; victories, 59
Chimney Sweep, 59; victories, 59
Chisman, Peter, 59-60
Chorus, 203
Christie, Hector, 60, 95
Chuchoteur, 198
Churchtown Boy, 217
Cigar, 46
Clair Soleil, 60, 90; victories, 60
Clancy, G., 103
Clanricarde, Marquis of, 174
Clare County, 120
Clark, F. Ambrose, 60, 117, 134

Claymore, 73
Clean Cash, 38, 224
Clear Cut, 110
Clear Profit, 169
Clerk of the Course, duties of, 60-1
Clerk of the Scales, duties of, 61
Clinker, 61-2
Cloister, 17, 27, 62, 64, 73, 88, 91, 121, 128, 146, 198, 207, 250, 251, 287; successes, 62
Clonave, 62; successes, 62
Cloringo, 82
Cocky Consort, 161
Colebridge, 38, 195, 224, 271
Coleman, Thomas, 28, 63
Colledge Master, 63; victories, 63
Colliery Band, 202
Collingwood, 87
Collins, Christopher, 63, 69, 126, 200, 261; successes, 63
Collins, R. John, 63, 175, 258
Collis, Lt.-Col. Robert, 63-4, 103
Colonial Cup, The, 64; winners of, 64
Colonel, The, 10, 117, 149, 207, 249, 255, 257; victories, 255
Coloured School Boy, 40, 64, 67; victories, 64
Columbia, 224
Columbine, 76
Come Away, 27, 62, 64, 121, 198; victories, 64
Comedy of Errors, 42, 47, 64-5, 83, 142, 192; victories, 65
Congress, 19, 65, 218, 279, 280; victories, 65, 280
Conjuror II, 37, 180
Conlon, P., 216
Connors, M., 186
Cook, John, 65, 145, 203, 244; successes, 65
Cool Alibi, 73
Cool Customer, 65, 67, 91; victories, 65, 91
Coolleen, 224
Corbett, Hon. Thomas, 66; successes, 66
Corrie Burn, 278
Cortolvin, 66, 90, 200, 228
Costello, W., 66
Cottage, 35, 66, 162, 285; successes of stock, 66
Cottage Rake, 34, 35, 47, 65, 66-7, 113, 195, 222; victories, 67
Cotton, Gilbert, 67, 205
Coulthwaite, Tom, 46, 67, 87, 107, 118, 127, 149, 189; major successes, 67-8
County Council, 119
Courage, Edward, 38, 68, 81, 122, 203, 242; major successes, 68
Couvrefeu II, 68; successes, 68
Coventry, Arthur, 68, 211
Coventry, George, 9th Earl of, 68-9, 86, 180
Coventry, Capt. Henry, 10, 68-9
Covertcoat, 69, 109, 158, 250, 283
Covert Hack, 119
Cowley, P., 69, 206; successes, 69
Cox, Mr J., 78, 169
Crabbs, 34, 286
Cramoisie, 287
Crank, R., 169
Crash helmets, compulsory use of introduced, 29, 69
Credit Call, 63, 69; winner of 37 races, 69
Creole, 228

Crickmere, Mr, 69
Crisp, 69-70, 145; successes, 70
Crisp, Kitty, 72, 154
Cromwell, 45, 70, 171, 238; successes, 70
Cross, Vernon, 70
Croydon, 70
Cruachan, 60
Crudwell, 66, 70-1, 72, 82, 96; victories, 70-1
Crump, Capt. Neville, 16, 38-9, 60, 71, 131, 149, 169, 177, 234, 238, 246, 253, 259; major successes, 71
Culverthorpe, 205
Cullinan, Thomas, 38, 41, 57, 71, 122, 143, 237, 261
Cunard, Sir Guy, 7th Bart., 71; successful point-to-point rider, 71
Cundell, Frank, 16, 24, 65, 71-2, 205; important successes, 72
Cundell, Ken, 28, 247
Cundell, Peter, 24
Cunningham, C. J., 72, 99, 277
Cunningham, T., 72
Curate, The, 46, 148
Cure-All, 72, 126, 154, 204
Curran, Richard, 72; successes, 72
Cusack, Thomas, 72, 96, 101; victories, 72
Cushenden, 60
Cyrus, 28, 146, 162, 235

Dagmar Gittel, 37
Dainty, 201
Daisy, 249
Daly, James, 73
Dandolo, 283
Dandy Tim, 91
Dane, The, 126
Daniels, William, 73, 100
D'Arcy, Capt., 204
Dark Sultan, 60
Dash o'White, 167
Davenport, Stephen, 73; victories, 73
Davies, Bertram, 73, 155-6; victories, 73
Davies, Colin, 73
Davy Jones, 45, 73-4, 170-1, 215
Davy Lad, 74, 118; successes, 74
Dawson, Matt, 32
Dawson, Richard, 32, 74, 106, 237
Defence, 76, 158
Delaneige, 173
Dempsey, Edward, 45, 74
Denys Adventure, 94
Derrinstown, 191
Despatch, 44, 257
Detail, 81
Devon and Exeter, 74; important races at, 74
Devon Loch, 45, 75, 87, 97; victories, 75
Dewhurst, C., 237
Diane, 17
Dick, David, 13, 25, 75, 83, 87, 171, 174, 228, 253; successes, 75
Dickinson, Anthony, 75-6; principal successes, 75
Dickinson, Michael, 75-6; principal victories, 76
Different Class, 215
Dikler, The, 30, 36, 43, 96, 103, 122, 145, 202, 209, 255-6, 271; victories, 255

Dillon, D., 240
Discount, 69, 76; successes, 76
Distel, 76, 197, 200, 222
Disturbance, 76-7; victories, 76
Dixon, Mr, 86
Dockeray, George, 155
Doctor, The, 255
Dodd, John 77
Dollery, William, 62, 77, 251, 278, 287
Domacorn, 276
Dominion, 96
Don Bradman, 163
Doncaster, 77-8; principal races and results, 77-8
Dondieu, 92, 202, 242
Done Up, 78, 245; victories, 78
Donoghue, Steve, 38
Donzelon, 157
Doorknocker, 78, 109, 190
Dormant, 16, 79, 171; victories, 79
Dormer, Mr J. C., 91
Double Chance, 14, 79, 126, 196, 245, 280; victories, 79
Douglas, 72
Dowdall, 17
Dowdeswell, John, 79
Downpatrick, 87, 288
Doyle, Maj. Edward, 79, 126
Doyle, P., 227
Dragsman, 69, 270
Drake, Mr H., 69
Dreaper, Jim, 38, 79-80, 244; successes, 80
Dreaper, Tom, 15, 30, 36, 47, 79, 80-1, 92, 95, 96, 145, 211, 215, 224, 251, 254; major winners, 80
Drifter, 178, 274
Drintyre, 259
Driscoll, Edmund, 25, 81; successes, 81
Drogheda, 74, 81; successes, 81
Drumcree, 17, 81, 194, 283
Drumikill, 202
Drumroan, 156
Drumrora V, 68, 81, 225, 244; founder of successful family, 81; daughters of, 81
Dubaythorn, 40
Dudley, 37, 81-2, 176; successes, 82
D.U.K.W., 186
Duller, George, 32, 37, 82, 265, 281, 284; victories, 82
Dunkirk, 40, 82, 218
Dutton, William, 82, 261
Dyas, Harry, 162, 176

Earl Marshal, 117
Early Mist, 31, 83, 108, 123, 164, 174, 195, 215; successes, 83
Easby Abbey, 65, 83, 192, 224; successes, 83
East, Henry, 83; best victories, 83
Easter Hero, 13, 26, 47, 71, 82, 84-5, 106, 107, 135, 143, 178, 237, 284; successes, 84-5
Easter Pirate, 114
Easterby, Miles Henry, 47, 83-4, 236; principal victories, 84
Eborneezer, 85; successes, 85; stock, 85
Ede, George, 85, 117, 148, 180, 257; as noted Gentleman Rider, 85

Edwards, Lionel, 86
Edwards, Roy, 85, 234, 253
Ego, 111, 219
Egremont, 94
El Hadjar, 284
Elizabeth, H.M. Queen, 170, 174
Elizabeth, H.M. the Queen Mother, 45, 75, 97, 98, 107, 161, 174, 177, 195, 272
Elliman, 161
Elmore, John, 35, 101, 127, 155, 164, 174
Embarrassed, 35
Emblem, 12, 37, 69, 86, 172, 180, 249; successes, 86
Emblematic, 10, 12, 69, 86, 172, 180, 249
Emery, René, 86, 149, 169
Emigrant, 34, 86
Emperor, 105
Empire Night, 163
Empress, 28, 86-7, 146, 175, 176, 207; victories, 87
Encoroli, 186
England's Glory, 121
Ephorous, 237
Equine Research Station, Newmarket, 116, 259
Eremon, 73, 87, 118, 189; victories, 87
Ernest, 37
E.S.B., 75, 87, 97, 225; achievements, 87
Esban, 87
Escart III, 87; as prolific sire, 87
Escott, Anthony, 88, 208, 266; principal victories, 88
Escott, Harry, 88, 208, 244, 278
Eternal, 36, 88; victories, 88
Evans, Gwyn, 80, 88, 211, 215, 244
Even Dawn, 88
Even Keel, 36, 88
Even Melody, 88
Even Money, 88; successes, 88
Everett, Lt. Robert, 89, 107
Exquisite, The, 72
Eyecatcher, 214, 217

Fairbairn, George, 214-15, 241
Fairy Hill, 79
Fakenham, 90
Fan, 90
Far Flight, 37
Fare Time, 12, 90; success, 90
Farmer's Boy, 85
Farrney Fox, 281
Farrell, Paddy, 36, 90-1, 122, 191, 249; major victories, 90
Fashion House, 137
Father Confessor, 11
Father O'Flynn, 62, 91, 121, 198, 258; successes, 91
Fawcus, Capt. John, 91, 103, 106, 219, 224, 244; principal successes, 91
Fawley, 175
Fees, jockeys, 91
Fidele, 117
Fighting Fifth Hurdle, 242
Fighting Line, 96
Filibert, 161
Fillip, 222
Filmer-Sankey, Mr W., 140

Filon d'Or, 176
Finnure, 30, 67
Firing operation, 91
First of the Dandies, 238
Fitzgerald, P., 57
Flag, 41
Flame Gun, 91-2, 115, 228; successes, 91
Flash Bulb, 12
Flashaway, 12
Flash Imp, 65, 192, 243
Fletcher, Brian, 92, 146, 149, 214, 215, 216-17; victories, 92
Flood, Francis, 30, 92, 103
Fly Mask, 79, 165
Flyingbolt, 80, 92, 228; successes, 92
Flying Wild, 40, 43
Foinavon, 92, 135, 215, 271
Folkestone, 93; principal race at, 93
Fontwell Park, 93; principal race at, 93
Forbra, 94, 110, 156, 221; successes, 94
Ford, James, 94
Ford of Fyne, 163
Forest King, 94; victories, 94
Forest Prince, 12
Forestation, 94, 243; successes, 94
Forster, Capt. Timothy, 27, 94, 225, 259, 274
Fort Devon, 95; successes, 95
Fortina, 32, 34, 60, 94-5, 96, 168; successes as sire, 95
Fortina's Palace, 235·
Fortleney, 95-6, 254, 256
Fortria, 16, 95, 96, 161, 171; successes, 96
Forty Secrets, 95
Foster, Eric, 96
Foulkes, Charles, 96
Fouquet, 284
Four Ten, 72, 96, 101, 209, 221; successes, 96
Frail, John, 35
Francis, Richard, 71, 73, 75, 198, 222, 227
Francome, John, 97, 169, 254, 282; successes, 97
Freddie, 12, 63, 97, 126, 166, 267
Freddy Fox, 186
Freebooter, 37, 97-8, 175, 210, 259, 285; victories, 98
Free Fare, 98, 108, 16, 198, 202, 270, 275; successes, 98, 108
Freeman, Arthur, 98, 177, 222
Freetrader, 32, 98, 117, 174, 249, 272
French Colonist, 26
Frenchman's Cove, 98-9; successes, 98
French Tan, 143
Frigate, 28, 99, 146, 206, 223, 270
Frisby, J., 9, 72
Furlong, Lt.-Cdr. Francis, 99, 134, 204, 209, 219

Galation, 240
Galloway Braes, 100, 137, 140, 174; successes, 100
Gamecock, 73, 100, 195, 287; victories, 100
Game Field, 91
Game Spirit, 43
Garde Toi, 67
Gardener, 255
Gatland, James, 100
Gatwick, 100-1

Gauntlet, 81
Gay Donald, 94, 101, 107, 137, 201; victories, 101
Gay Lad, 32, 101, 196, 204
Gay Light, 148
Gay Record, 195
Gay Spartan, 101; successes, 101
Gay Trip, 31, 101-2, 220, 271, 274; victories, 101
General Peace, 30
Gentle Ida, 134
Gentle Moya, 87, 170
Gerald, 217
Gib, 284
Gibson, Maj. W. D., 102, 139
Gifford, Joshua, 26, 92, 102, 203, 210, 223, 241; victories, 102
Gifford, Macer, 102, 142
Gilbert, A., 32
Gilbert, John, 102, 285; successes, 102
Gill, A., 113
Giolla Mear, 30
Glencaraig Lady, 30, 95, 102-3, 110, 225, 244, 255
Glenkiln, 166
Glenside, 13, 64, 103
Globule, 117
Golby, Tom, 86
Gold Arrow, 33
Gold Legend, 143
Gold Wire, 167
Golden Cygnet, 103
Golden Fleece, 11
Golden Miller, 13, 35, 47, 68, 103-5, 106, 146, 156, 173, 174, 176, 191, 200, 217, 219, 220, 222, 245, 249, 258-9, 278, 279-80, 284; successes, 103-5
Gone Dry, 202
Good Date, 79
Goodgame, J., 76
Good Review, 195
Goodman, Alexander, 86, 105, 204, 228; victories, 105
Goosander, 259
Gordon, Robert, 106, 204
Gore, Robert, 69, 101, 106, 224; victories, 106
Goswell, G., 165
Gourlay, John, 81, 106
Gracious Gift, 189
Grakle, 68, 104, 106-7, 156, 173, 260; successes, 106-7
Grand Canyon, 64, 142
Grand National, 1-0; first race to be broadcast, 149; winners of, 151-3
Grantham, Anthony, 101, 107; victories, 107
Grayling, 196
Green, Christopher, 9, 86, 109, 257
Greenall, Peter, 107, 132; principal winners, 107
Green Drill, 170, 177
Greenogue, 238
Greenogue Princess, 178
Gregalach, 68, 106, 107, 143, 149, 156, 173, 178, 284; successes, 107
Greig Olway, 282
Grenfel, Mr C., 258
Grifel, 107, 149, 200

Griffin, Mr J. H., 83, 108, 215, 225
Grosvenor, Hon. Hugh, 108, 260, 282
Grudon, 31, 81, 108, 117, 191; victories, 108
Gubbins, Roderic, 108
Gunner, The, 173
Gwilt, Edward, 79, 98, 108, 272
Gyi Lovam, 200

Hackett, J. F., 109
Hackler, 73, 109, 158
Hackwatch, 109; successes, 109
Haine, John, 109, 228, 266, 267; major victories, 109
Half-Caste, 32, 107, 109, 257
Hall, Mr R. H., 127
Hall, W. A., 78, 90, 109-10, 190, 241, 249, 256; victories, 109-10
Hall Court, 10, 255
Hallowe'en, 96, 101, 110, 140, 146, 209, 278; victories, 110
Halsey (jockey), 12
Hamey, James, 94, 110, 140
Hamey, Rex, 110, 248
Handel, Herbert, 110; successes, 110
Handicap, definition of, 111
Handicappers, duties of, 111
Hanlon, J., 111, 272
Happy Home, 67, 95
Happymint, 111, 115, 176, 277; successes, 111
Happy Spring, 111; victories, 111
Harding, Maj.-Gen. Sir Reginald, 98, 108, 111
Harlech, 113
Harpist, 32
Harrison, Herbert, 111
Hart Royal, 112
Hartigan, Frank, 83, 101, 111-12, 176, 237, 279
Harty, Edward, 112, 116; victories, 112
Harvester, 287
Harwell, 241
Hastings, Hon. Aubrey, 13, 17, 25, 31, 38, 101, 112, 149, 166, 266
Hastings-Bass, Peter, 13, 65, 112, 253
Hathaway, Mr, 201
Hatton's Grace, 34, 47, 112-13, 186, 195, 203; victories, 112-13
Hawa's Song, 20
Hawkins, C., 250, 270
Haydock Park, 113; principal races, and winners of, 113-14
Hayhurst, S. G., 114, 137
Head, A., 186
Head, Richard, 34
Head, W., 208
Herbert, Edward Ivor, 75, 92, 114-15, 147
Herbert, Capt. P., 35
Hercules, 29
Hereford, 115; important races at, 115
Herod Bridge, 163
Heron, The, 190, 256; successes, 256
Hexham, 115; principal races at, 115
Hickey, O., 115
Hidden Mystery, 194
High Ken, 43, 64, 168, 282
High Point, 245
Highland Abbe, 242
Highland Wedding, 112, 115-16; victories achieved, 115-16

Hill House, 46, 102, 116; successes, 116
Hill Song, 148
Hill, William, 116
Hinterland, 96
Hislop, J., 45
Hobbs, Bruce, 27, 116-17
Hobbs, Reginald, 27, 60, 116, 117, 167
Hobson, Fred, 19, 117
Hogan, J., 140
Holland, J., 33, 117
Holman, George, 117, 165, 255
Holman, William, 12, 47, 117, 148, 172, 196, 204
Honey End, 92
Hope Again, 242
Hope-Johnstone, Capt. Wentworth, 117-18, 195; successes, 117-18
Horserace Betting Levy Board, 118, 261
Horserace Totalisator Board, 118; composition of, 118
Howard, Stanley, 118, 189
Hudson, Frank, 118
Hughes, Desmond, 74, 118-19, 197; principal victories, 118
Hughes-Onslow, Maj. Arthur, 119; victories, 119
Hunters' Steeplechase, 119
Huntingdon, 119; prizes, 119
Hunts: Atherstone, 208; Bicester, 208; Heythrop, 208; Pytchley, 208; Worcestershire, 208
Huntsman, 12, 109, 119, 142, 256
Hurst Park, 119; principal races, 119-20
Hyde, Timothy, 120, 137, 155, 211, 227, 285

I'Anson, Robert, 24, 44, 46, 121, 200, 218; major victories, 121
Ilex, 64, 121, 191, 192; victories, 121
Impney, 240
Indian Salmon, 122
Indian Spice, 205
Indianapolis, 251
Ingham, Staff, 9, 38, 98, 121, 122, 148, 268, 285
Injured Jockeys Fund, 36, 68, 91, 122, 168, 234, 265; Trustees, 122
Inkslinger, 122, 225; successes, 122-3
Insurance, 47, 122, 222; victories, 122
Interview II, 87
Into View, 271
Invader, 132
Inversible, 277
Irish Coffee, 138
Irish Lizard, 83, 122-3, 191, 225, 236; successes, 122
Irish Mail, 13, 69, 270
Irish racing, 123: principal courses, 123; principal races and results, 123-5
Isaacs, T., 94
Ivy Green, 90

Jack Dummer, 122
Jack Finlay, 155
Jackal, 29, 257
Jackdaw of Rheims, 207
Jack Horner, 32, 126, 143, 196, 245, 274
Jacobus, 11, 67
James, R., 98, 272

Jarvis, Jack, 30
Java Fox, 132
Jay Trump, 63, 97, 126, 149, 241-2, 282; victories, 126
Jealousy, 32, 126-7
Jean du Quesne, 109, 142
Jenkins, W. H. P., 127, 138, 288
Jenkinstown, 46, 73, 81, 109, 118, 127, 258
Jerry, 35, 127, 166, 167
Jerry M, 19, 69, 81, 127-8, 146, 200, 205, 207, 250; victories, 128
Jewitt, James, 32, 150, 158, 237, 283
Jockey Club, The, 130; officials of, 130-1
Jockeys: licensing of, 128; fees, 128-9; champion, 129
Jockeys Association, 129-30: National Hunt, 130; constitution of, 130
Johnny Longtail, 100, 131; victories, 131
Joicey, Lt.-Col. Hugh Edward, 3rd Baron Joicey, 131; owner of high-class chasers, 131
Jones, Arthur, 132; victories, 132
Jones, D. L., 32, 132; successes, 132
Jones, George, 107, 132
Jones, Harry Thomson, see THOMSON-JONES, HARRY
Jones, J. G., 132, 218, 257; victories, 132
Jones, Mervyn Anthony, 33, 132-3, 237
Jones, T. M. ('Buck'), 132; victory, 132
Judas, 156
Judge, the, duties of, 135
Jupiter Jones, 27

Kami, 45
Kari Sou, 146, 176
Kavanagh, T., 134, 161, 277; victories, 134
Keep Cool, 88
Kelleway, Paul, 26, 39, 134, 284; successes, 134
Kellsboro' Jack, 13, 60, 91, 134, 149, 228, 249, 278, 285; successes, 134
Kelly, C., 17
Kelly, G., 238
Kelso, 134-5; principal races, 134
Kempton, John, 92, 135
Kempton Park, 135; important races, 135-6
Kenneally, J., 253
Kerstin, 114; 136-7, 147, 170; successes, 136-7
Keystone, 220
Kidney, W., 155
Kilcash Hill, 278
Kilcoleman, 138
Killiney, 71, 112, 137, 282; victories, 137
Kilmore, 137, 177, 286
Kilpatrick, Alex, 29, 100, 137; victories, 137
Kilstar, 222, 285
Kinane, Thomas, 137-8, 174, 192
Kindersley, Gay, 41, 138
King, Jeffrey, 74, 96, 116, 138, 228, 256, 266, 267; victories, 138
Kinloch Brae, 271
Kinsky, Count (later Prince), 9, 127, 138-9, 288
Kirkland, 139, 173, 258
Kirriemuir, 139, 158, 192; successes, 139
Klaxton, 102, 139; victories, 139
Knight of Gwynne, 9, 72, 204
Knight of Rhodes, 88
Knight of the Garter, 139-40; successes as sire, 140

Knock Hard, 140, 195, 284; victories, 140
Koko, 26, 31, 84, 110, 140, 196, 202; important victories, 140

Lad, stable, 141
Lady Helen, 30
Lady Helen II, 277
Lady of the Lake, 175
Lady riders, 141
Lady Sneerwell, 117
Lady Villikins, 100
Laird, The, 96, 256; victories, 256
Lamb, Ridley, 141, 156
Lamb, The, 107, 149, 180, 205, 256-7; victories, 256-7
Lambton, Hon. George, 19, 29, 42, 98, 126, 141-2, 158, 255; principal victories, 141
Lamplugh, Harry, 66, 109, 119, 142, 256
Land, Ben, 85, 86, 107, 109, 119, 256, 257
Lanzarote, 64, 65, 142, 282; victories, 142
Lara, 64
Larbawn, 102, 142, 163, 228, 271; victories, 142
Larraun, A., 113
Larry Finn, 60
Last Link, 95
La Veine, 200, 201
Lawrence, John, see TREVETHIN AND OAKSEY, JOHN GEOFFREY TRISTRAM, 4TH BARON
Lawyer III, The, 226
Lay, P., 33
Leader, Harvey, 142-3
Leader, Thomas Edward, 25, 37, 68, 104, 122, 142-3, 178, 197, 245, 249
Leader, Thomas Richard, 143; principal winners, 143
Leap Frog, 143, 195
Legal Joy, 253
Lehane, Johnny, 137, 143; principal victories, 143
Leicester, 143-4; principal races at, 144
Leinster, 17, 144, 284
Lemon, Mr B., 25
Leney Princess, 95, 144-5, 167; foaling record, 145
Le Paillon, 145, 186; victories, 145
L'Escargot, 47, 64, 87, 137, 145-6, 175, 190, 214, 216-17, 244, 276; victories, 145-6
Le Vermontois, 102
Liberator, The, 19, 87, 175, 257; victories, 257
Lillingstone, Alan, 108, 146, 176, 281
Limb of the Law, 79
Limber Hill, 82, 96, 100, 146, 209, 210, 212; victories, 146
Limerock, 242
Limestone Edward, 190
Linde, Henry, 12, 19, 28, 87, 99, 134, 146, 149, 162, 235, 283
Lindley, J., 25
Lindsay-Gordon, Adam, 14, 32, 47, 106, 197, 198, 205
Lingfield Park, 146-7; valuable races, 146
Linwell, 95, 96, 110, 115, 136-7, 147, 209, 222; victories, 147
Lion Courage, 147-8; successes, 148
Liquidator, The, 90
Little, Capt. James, 46, 148, 180, 196; successes, 148

Little Charley, 12, 14, 32, 117, 148
Liverpool, 148-54; first running of Grand National at, 148; important races, 148, 150; winners of important races, 151-4
Llewellyn, Mr H., 219
Lobau, 198
Lochroe, 45, 98, 154, 201, 222; victories, 154
Loft, W. J., 154
Lomax, Mrs Rosemary, 112
Lord Chancellor, 27, 162
Lord Marcus, 28, 200
Lottery, 47, 101, 111, 127, 154-5, 167, 193; victories, 155
Lough Conn, 45
Lough Inagh, 225
Lovely Cottage, 66, 155, 204, 211, 215
Lucius, 73, 155-6, 219; success in 1978 Grand National, 156
Luck-All, 111
Lucky Purchase, 156; victories, 156
Ludlow, 156
Lutteur II, 88, 149, 156, 200, 250
Lyall, F., 128
Lyall, Robert, 104, 106-7, 156-7
Lyford Cay, 39
Lynn, J., 87
Lynn, William, 148, 157

Macauley, 176
Machell, Capt. James, 42, 76, 150, 158, 218, 220, 235, 258
MacMoffat, 33, 115, 285
Madden, Peter, 158, 228
Magee, Sean, 158, 243
Maghull, 196
Magic Court, 158, 166, 221, 223; victories, 158
Magnier, Clem, 10
Maguelonne, 19
Maguire, J., 186
Maher, James, 158-9; victories, 158-9
Maiden, definition of, 159
Major Rose, 39, 202
Makaldar, 234
Mallon, Charles, 95, 115
Man of the East, 132
Manchester, 159-60; results of principal races at, 159-60
Mandarin, 19, 78, 147, 158, 161, 177, 228, 245, 272, 281; victories, 101
Manicou, 161; victories, 161
Manifesto, 63, 81, 128, 134, 139, 146, 149, 161-2, 166, 176, 207, 237, 278; successes, 161-2
Mann, R., 192
Manners of Foston, Lord John, 3rd Baron, 9, 158, 162, 235
Marco, 162, 165
Maria Day, 9
Mariner's Log, 96
Market Rasen, 162-3; principal races at, 163
Marpessa, 119, 202
Marsh, Alec, 163; victories, 163
Marsh, Michael, 163
Marsh, Richard, 62, 81, 163-4, 283
Marshall, Bryan, 83, 108, 164, 225, 240; successes, 164
Marshall, W. C., 242

Martha, 28, 238, 257
Mask Off, 201
Mason, F., 13, 103, 139, 156, 164; principal victories, 164
Mason, James, 13, 111, 155, 164-5, 167, 172, 173, 237, 243; principal victories, 165
Master H., 165, 169
Master Monday, 165, 192
Master Mowbray, 117, 165, 169, 192
Master of Foxhounds Association, 209
Master Owen, 165; as good sire, 165
Master Robert, 112, 165-6, 266; successes, 166
Mathet, F., 60
Matthew, 166, 237, 286
Mattie McGregor, 33, 66, 73, 226, 282
Maurice Daley, 172, 272
Mawson, George, 166, 206; victories, 166
McAuliffe, Willie, 162, 166
McCann, Donald, 45, 166, 216
McCarron, Patrick, 12, 97, 126, 158, 166, 242; victories, 166
McCreery, Robert, 166-7, 176; victories, 167
McDonagh, Desmond, 167; successes, 167
McDonough, Alan, 46, 127, 167, 175, 210; victories, 167
McDowell, Hector, 167
McMorrow, Liam, 167, 227
McNally, Owen, 112
Medoc II, 117, 145, 167, 190, 216, 236; victories, 167
Medora, 223
Melleray's Belle, 198, 218, 237
Mellor, Stanley, 39, 73, 130, 167-8, 169, 193, 198; awarded MBE, 168; important victories, 168
Menelek, 168
Menton, 98
Menzies, 60
Mercer, Syd, 26, 87
Meritorious, 259
Merlin, 218
Merry, 138
Merry Deal, 108, 132, 168-9, 200; victories, 168-9
Merryglass, 72
Merryman II, 169, 191, 209; victories, 169
Metropolitan Racecourse Bill, 169
Midnight Court, 38, 169; victories, 169
Midnight Steeplechase, 169-70
Midshipmite, The, 237, 257, 287; victories, 257
Mighty Apollo, 35
Milburn, George, 87, 147, 170, 177; victories, 170
Mildmay of Flete, Lord Anthony Bingham, 2nd Baron, 45, 70, 74, 161, 170-1, 174, 215, 229
Mill House, 14, 16, 36, 39, 79, 96, 111, 171-2, 190, 201, 272; victories, 171-2
Minerva, 98
Minos, 98
Miss Alligator, 12, 172; breeding record, 172
Miss Batty, 172; breeding record, 172
Miss Hungerford, 19
Miss Hunter, 101
Miss Mowbray, 105, 142, 172, 204
Miss Patty, 279
Moidore's Token, 215

Moiffa, 29, 31, 115, 139, 149, 172-3; successes, 173
Moloney, Jack, 106, 107, 173; victories, 173
Molony, Martin, 67, 96, 113, 173, 238
Molony, Tim, 47, 78, 112, 140, 173, 240; principal successes, 173-4
Monave'en, 107, 119, 174, 259; successes, 174
Monksfield, 167, 174, 192, 236; successes, 174
Mont Tremblant, 75, 83, 101, 140, 174, 200, 272; victories, 174
Moonlight Escapade, 87
Moonraker, 174; victories, 174
Moore, Daniel, 27, 43, 64, 95, 98, 101, 122, 146, 167, 175, 221, 222, 253; principal races won by, 175
Moore, Garrett, 35, 87, 106, 175, 257; principal successes, 175
Moore, J., 238
Moore, W. H., 24, 63, 111, 121, 131, 162, 175-6, 277; principal successes, 175
Moralee, Andrew (Danny), 111, 167, 176, 278; victories, 176
Morgan, Danny, 35, 57, 167, 176, 186, 208, 222; principal victories, 176
Morgan, Frank, 25, 176
Morgan, I., 217
Morgan, T., 106
Morgan, W., 237
Morrow, Robert, 100, 140, 174, 176
Morse Code, 35, 105, 176-7; successes, 176
Moss Bank, 85
Mould, David, 177, 201, 203, 215, 234, 274; principal victories, 177
Mount Prospect's Fortune, 81
Mount Royal, 42, 69, 109, 177
Moylan, J., 165
M.P., 99, 121
Mr Fitz, 191
Mr Jones, 63
Mr What, 98, 137, 177, 199, 221, 252, 260, 276
Mr Wonderful, 94
Much Obliged, 177; successes, 177
Muir, 70
Mullins, K. 113
Munnings, Sir Alfred, 177
Murphy, H., 87
Murphy, P. J., 67
Music Hall, 13, 178, 218; victories, 178
My Prince, 100, 162, 178, 207, 211, 219; victories, 162, 178
Mythical, 40

Napper Tandy, 139
National Association of Bookmakers Ltd., 179; members of, 179
National Head Lads Association, 179; officials of, 179
National Hunt Chase, 10, 179-80; hunts subscribing to, 179
National Hunt Committee, 68, 130, 180, 208-9; composition of, 180; names of past and present members, 180-6
National Hunt Trainers' Association, 24, 186; chairman, 186
National Trainers' Federation, 186

National Spirit, 47, 145, 186, 243, 284; victories, 186
Nellie Gray, 42
Newbury, 186-8; important races at, 187-8
Newcastle, 188; important races at, 188
Newey, Alfred, 11, 87, 118, 139, 189; successes, 189
Newman, Gerry, 43, 156
Newton Abbot, 189; principal races at, 189-90
Nicholls, G., 147
Nicholson, Clifford, 78, 122, 190, 256
Nicholson, David, 16, 76, 85, 117, 139, 190; successes, 190
Nicholson, Herbert, 167, 176, 190-1, 200; successes, 190-1
Nickel Coin, 40, 191, 195, 225; victories, 191
Nicolaus Silver, 137, 169, 191; successes, 191
Night Nurse, 32, 36, 47, 84, 142, 174, 192, 235; victories, 192
Nightingall, Arthur, 25, 64, 72, 81, 91, 99, 108, 121, 149, 166, 191, 277; victories, 191
Nightingall, John, 191, 192
Nightingall, Walter, 25, 192, 206, 218
Nightingall, William, 25
Nimrod, 270
Noce d'Argent, 284
Noholme, 240
Norman, Timothy, 12, 192
North Waltham, 201
Notting Hill, 193
Nottingham, 192-3; important races at, 193
Novice, definition of, 193
Nugent, Sir Charles, 5th Bart., 81, 194
Nugent, Mr H., 108

Oaksey, see TREVETHIN AND OAKSEY, JOHN GEOFFREY TRISTRAM, 4TH BARON
O'Brien, Mr A., 191
O'Brien, Val, 195; major successes, 195
O'Brien, Vincent, 32, 34, 41, 47, 76, 83, 88, 108, 113, 140, 145, 164, 195, 212, 228, 237; successes, 195
O'Dell, The, 257; victories, 257
O'Donaghue, Jack, 191, 195
Odor, 127
O'Grady, Eddie, 103
O'Halloran, Martin, 24
Old Ben Roe, 126
Old Buck, 33
Old Joe, 195-6; victories, 195
Old Mortality, 267
Old Tay Bridge, 79, 112, 126, 140, 196
Oliver, James Kenneth, 36, 92, 196, 248, 260, 278; victories, 196
Olliver, Tom, 14, 46, 76, 101, 106, 143, 148, 149, 155, 166, 196-7, 198, 204, 243, 270
Olympia, 95
O'Malley Point, 90, 191
O'Neill, John Joe, 127, 197, 219, 236; principal successes, 197
O'Ryan, Robert, 76, 98, 197
O'Toole, Michael, 74, 118, 197; main successes, 197
Ormerod, 30
Osborne, Joseph, 9, 197
Oscar, 204
Oscar Wilde, 278

Our Hope, 98, 108, 111, 132, 146, 197-8
Owen, Maj. E. R., 27, 62, 64, 91, 100, 198, 229; principal victories, 198
Owen, George, 35, 36, 73, 96, 168, 198, 227; victories, 198
Owners, leading, 1940-78, 199
Oxo, 36, 177, 199, 260, 286; successes, 199

Page, D., 12
Page, John, 44, 66, 200, 201, 228
Page, The, 117
Paget, Hon. Dorothy, 13, 15, 34, 35, 47, 75, 76, 104-5, 122, 158, 174, 175, 200, 222, 243, 272
Paget, Mr E., 94
Paladin, 216
Pampero, 191
Pappageno's Cottage, 36
Parapluie, 42
Parasang, 19
Pardubitz Steeplechase, Czechoslovakia, 63, 200
Parfremont, Georges, 156, 200-1
Parvin, W., 122, 219
Pas de Quatre, 201
Pas Seul, 16, 45, 101, 147, 154, 191, 201, 218, 222, 228, 267; victories, 201
Passport, 201
Pathfinder, 201, 205
Patlander, 87
Patron Saint, 111, 201-2, 217; victories, 201-2
Patsey V, 25
Pau, 121
Paulina, 155
Payne, W. H., 32, 202, 215
Peace River, 37
Peacetown, 253
Pearl Diver, 257
Peeping Tom, 29
Peertoi, 38
Peggy Jones, 74
Pellerin, George, 38, 98, 122, 148, 202, 224, 270; successes, 202
Pelorus Jack, 249
Penarth, 117
Pendil, 43, 122, 202, 206, 255, 281; victories, 202
Pennington, Mr G. W., 245
Percy, 72
Permit scheme, 202-3
Permit-holders Association, 203
Perseus II, 29
Persian Empire, 73
Persian War, 39, 47, 73, 112, 203; victories, 203
Persse, Henry, 17, 70, 164, 203; principal achievements, 203
Perth, 203-4; important races at, 203
Peter Simple, 46, 72, 101, 148, 172, 196, 204
Peter Simple (Old Peter), 204; victories, 204
Petre, Capt. Robert, 204, 209; successes, 204
Pickernell, Tommy, 12, 86, 196, 201, 204-5, 257; victories, 205
Piggott, Charles, 10, 205, 270
Piggott, Ernest, 42, 128, 149, 161-2, 205, 208, 237, 281; successes, 205
Piggott, Keith, 9, 20, 205, 243, 270; principal successes, 205

Pigott-Brown, William Brian, 3rd Bart., 205; victories, 205
Pills, The, 79
Pioneer, 205-6, 253
Pippin II, 06; successes, 206
Pitman, Richard, 65, 79, 97, 116, 142, 202, 206, 216, 254, 255; successes, 206
Plaine, M., 198
Plastic fences, introduction of, 206
Playfair, 42, 99, 166, 206
Playlord, 276
Plummer, Sir Desmond, 118
Plumpton, 206-7; valuable races at, 207
Pocahontas, 12, 19, 62, 87, 139, 162, 207, 250, 274
Poet Prince, 40, 208, 216, 222; victories, 208
Poethlyn, 128, 149, 205, 207-8, 237; victories, 208
Point-to-Point Steeplechases, 209; principal races, 209; officers of Secretaries Association, 209
Point-to-pointing, 208-9; rules formulated, 209
Pointsman, 71, 137, 176
Polar Flt, 137, 241
Pollen, 208
Polly Steven, 121
Pompelmoose, 57
Pontin-Go, 143
Poole, George, 10, 86, 88, 209-10, 217, 238
Portago, Marquis de, 67
Potts, Henry, 210, 240
Powell, A., 46, 210
Powell, P., 281
Power, A., 191
Power, James, 98, 146, 210; victories, 210
Power, Mr 127
Price, Ryan, 28, 47, 60, 78, 90, 102, 116, 134, 137, 171, 210, 223, 276, 281; principal successes, 210
Pride of Kildare, 238
Primrose, 255
Prince Blackthorn, 95, 257
Prince Frederick, 278
Prince George, 204
Prince Hindou, 113
Prince of Wales, H.R.H. (later King Edward VII), 12, 13, 29, 35, 37, 164, 173, 191, 198, 224, 229, 258
Prince Regent, 74, 80, 120, 155, 178, 211, 215, 254; principal victories, 120, 211
Prior-Palmer, Maj. Otto, 257
Privy Seal, 202
Professor, The, 198
Provocative, 110
Prudent King, 90
Prudhomme, 211; successes, 211
Pucka Belle, 224
Pumphrey, M., 240
Pundit, 121, 245
Purple Silk, 253
Pyrrhus III, 113

Quare Times, 180, 195, 212, 252, 266; successes, 212
Q.E.D., 37
Queen's Taste, 212; victories, 212
Quelle Chance, 13, 281

Quick Reply, 141
Quita Que, 78, 169

Racecourse Association, 213; formation of, 213
Racecourse Betting Control Board, 261
Racecourse Technical Services Co., 214; board of, 214
Racecourse: current National Hunt and Clerks of Courses, 213; steeplechase courses, rules for, 213; hurdle courses, rules for, 214
Racegoers Club, 214
Racehorse Owners Association, 214; board of, 214
Racehorse Owners Compensation Fund, 91
Racing Calendar, The, 214
Rackley (jockey), 206
Radical, 62
Rafferty, J., 85
Rag Trade, 41, 112, 168, 214-15, 217, 224; successes, 214-15
Rank, Mr J. V., 31, 37, 80, 83, 88, 108, 215, 219, 244, 249
Rathcoole, 215; successes, 215
Rathlea, 205
Rathnally, 46, 103
Rayson, Thomas, 155, 215
Read, C., 217
Really True, 99, 134
Reardon, John, 215, 270
Reavey, E., 238
Red Alligator, 12, 92, 172, 215, 242
Red April, 34, 70, 72, 216, 246; victories, 216
Red Lad, 17
Red Prince II, 87, 146, 176, 216; successes, 216
Red Rower, 70, 132, 167, 208, 216; successes, 216
Red Rum, 37, 70, 92, 103, 137, 145, 146, 149, 150, 166, 214-5, 216-7, 218, 246; successes, 216-17
Red Splash, 217, 282; victories, 217
Reed, D., 237
Rees, F. B., 10, 25, 29, 32, 47, 85, 143, 173, 202, 217-18, 224, 237, 260, 281; principal victories, 217-18
Rees, Lewis Billy, 37, 178, 202, 218
Rees, Lewis William, 218
Regal, 65, 150, 158, 218, 238, 279, 283; successes, 218
Rejected IV, The, 205
Reljef, 149
Renton, Robert, 37, 98, 210, 215, 216, 218, 241, 246, 266; successes, 218
Residue, 202
Retour de Flamme, 25
Returned, The, 111
Reugny, 29, 76, 158, 218-19, 220
Revirescat, 117
Reynoldstown, 99, 149, 170, 178, 211, 215, 216-17, 219, 259, 272; successes, 219
Richards, Gordon, 26, 197, 219, 235, 261; major successes, 219
Richardson, John Maunsell, 76, 158, 218-20
Rickaby, F., 94, 243
Ridden for Hire, 221

Rimell, Fred, 31, 34, 40, 59, 64, 76, 87, 94, 101, 112, 149, 191, 214, 220, 224, 242, 260, 277, 281, 284; major victories, 220
Rimell, Thomas, 94, 220-1, 222
Roberts, John, 96, 221
Robin O'Chantry, 76
Robin-a-Tiptoe, 99
Robinson, George W., 13, 16, 139, 143, 158, 171, 201, 221, 253; principal victories, 221
Robson, Thomas, 158, 219, 221, 278; successes, 221
Rock Sand, 32
Roddick, Brig. Mark, 222
Roddy Owen, 147, 154, 176, 221-2; victories, 221-2
Roderic Random, 167
Rogers, Charles, 37, 76, 175, 200, 222; successes, 222
Roimond, 30, 96, 222, 227; victories, 222
Rolie, 224
Roman Hackle, 13, 200, 222, 278; victories, 222
Roman Oak, 30, 100, 222; victories, 222
Romeo, 119, 256
Rondetto, 116
Roquefort, 99, 222-3, 251, 270, 279, 287; successes, 222-3
Rory O'More, 202
Rose Graft, 17
Rose Park, 147, 223; victories, 223
Rosyth, 102, 223
Rouch, William, 223
Rowland Roy, 32, 223; successes, 223
Rowlands, Dr Fothergill, 132, 179, 208, 223-4
Royal Approach, 30, 80, 224; victories, 224
Royal Chancellor, 96
Royal Danieli, 27, 175
Royal Epic, 70
Royal Falcon, 224; victories, 224
Royal Frolic, 39, 41, 224; successes, 224
Royal Gaye, 174
Royal Mail, 178, 222, 224-5, 274, 278; victories, 224
Royal Marshall II, 94, 225, 274; successes, 225, 274
Royal Meath, 17, 19, 146
Royal Phoebe, 102
Royal Relief, 70, 225, 244; victories, 225
Royal Sanction, 205
Royal Tan, 87, 108, 123, 164, 191, 195, 225, 249, 266; successes, 225
Royal Toss, 30, 103, 110, 225; victories, 225
Roycroft, Mr W., 16
Rubio, 33, 66, 108, 126, 225-6, 282
Ruddyglow, 140
Rueil, 94
Rules of Racing, 226-7
Russian Hero, 167, 227; victories, 227
Ruttle, J., 120, 227
Ryan, J., 9
Ryshworth, 76

Saffron Tartan, 12, 41, 228; victories, 228
Sage Merlin, 107
Salamander, 66, 105, 228, 256
Sales, principal, 228
Salmon Spray, 223, 228, 267, 271

Sammy's Rock, 243
Sandown, 228; important races and results at, 229-34
San Michele, 71
Sanvina, 196
Sassoon, Capt. Reginald, 234, 275, 284
Saucy Kit, 85
Savon, 208
Savoyard, 100
Saxby, A., 270
Scamp, The, 224
Scarlet Letch, 35
Scarrington, 44, 257
Schiedam, 220
Schoolmoney, 270
Schubert, 216
Schwartz, Charlie, 126, 143, 274
Scot, The, 257-8; victories, 258
Scots Grey, 35, 175
Scott, Gerald, 12, 38, 169, 234; principal victories, 234
Scott-Aiton, Jonathon, 255
Scottish Memories, 234-5, 241; successes, 234
Scottish Sea, 37
Scudamore, Michael, 16, 70-1, 147, 199, 225, 235, 253; successes, 235
Seaman, 150, 158, 162, 235, 288; successes, 235
Sea Pigeon, 142, 174, 192, 235-6; successes, 235-6
Sebastian V, 156
Secret Service, 72
Sedgefield, 236; important races at, 236
Sefton, Hugh William, 7th Earl, 236
Selling race, definition of, 236
Sempervivum, 228
Seneca, 236-7, 243; success, 236-7
Sensier, W., 237, 287
Sergeant Murphy, 17, 29, 32, 237; victories, 237
Seventy-Four, 101, 127, 155
Shady Girl, 103
Shaef, 174
Shakespeare, 105
Shangarry, 66, 105
Shannon Lass, 109, 237
Shaun Goilin, 71, 94, 112, 237, 278
Shaun Spadah, 37, 210, 237-8; successes, 237
Sheila's Cottage, 35, 66, 70, 171, 238, 259; stud record, 238
Shepherd, Richard, 238; successes, 238
Shifnal, 192, 218, 238; victories, 238
Shortt, F., 101
Silver Fame, 30, 161, 162, 173, 238, 243, 275; successes, 238
Silvo, 19, 88, 238, 260, 276; victories, 238
Sir Henry, 196
Sir John, 9
Sir Ken, 47, 112, 174, 203, 240, 284; victories, 240
Sir Lindsay, 237, 278
Sir Peter Laurie, 117, 172
Sir William, 210, 240
Sires, leading, from 1911-78, 239-40
Skeaping, John, 240
Skedaddle, 146
Skelton, Tommy, 100, 223, 240-1; successes, 241

Skish, 143
Skymas, 241; principal victories, 241
Skyreholme, 259
Slack, George, 25, 60, 96, 98, 137, 177, 212, 225, 241, 266; successes, 241
Slater, 134
Sleator, Patrick, 12, 28, 78, 92, 176, 190, 234, 241
Sloan, George, 241
Sly, Jnr., 98
Smith, Capt. 235
Smith-Crompton (Tommy), 126, 241-2
Smith, Denys, 92, 215, 242; successes, 242
Smith, Richard, 242
Smith, William J., 25, 242, 250
Smith, William Morris, 65, 142, 146, 192, 242, 277; principal victories, 242
Smyth, Roland Victor, 47, 94, 186, 236, 242-3; successes, 243
Smyth, Victor, 47, 94, 186, 236, 243; successes, 243
Snaigow, 16
Soarer, The, 42, 63, 176, 258; successes, 258
Société des Steeplechases de France, 243
Socks, 105
Solanum, 88
Solford, 9, 13, 158, 200, 222, 243; victories, 243
Soliman, 30
Solomon II, 73
Song of Essex, 122
Soothsayer, 64, 254
Southern Hero, 37, 101, 104, 135, 149, 215, 243-4; successes, 243
Southport, 94
Southwell, 244; principal races at, 244
Spahi, 146
Spanish Steps, 81, 145, 146, 244; successes, 244
Speciality, 113
Specify, 156, 244, 251
Speck, William Morris, 32, 104, 219, 244-5, 249, 259; principal successes, 245
Spencer, George, 245, 281
Splash, 95
Sprague, Harry, 78, 245; successes, 245
Sprig, 35, 143, 149, 162, 245; successes, 245
Spring, 34
Springbok, 131
Sprinkle Me, 245; victories, 245
Stack, Thomas, 65, 97, 214, 217, 218, 245-6; principal successes, 246
Stalbridge Colonist, 96, 246-7, 284; successes, 246-7
Stalbridge, Rt. Hon. Hugh Grosvenor, 2nd Baron, 246
Standard Park, 253
Stanmore, 47, 117
Starter and starting, duties of, 247-8
Statecraft, 107
State Secret, 90
St Caradec, 200
Steel Bridge, 116
Stenquill, 40
Stephens, W. E., 195
Stephenson, William, 26, 32, 47, 110, 199, 237, 240, 248; principal successes, 248
Stephenson, William Arthur, 46, 63, 90, 107, 219, 246, 248-9, 261; principal victories, 249

Stevens, George, 10, 86, 98, 117, 126, 149, 196, 249, 255; record of riding five Grand National Winners, 249; successes, 249
St George, 27
St George II, 204
St Leger, 166
Stobbs, C., 161
Stoney Crossing, 16
Stormhead, 90, 249; victories, 249
Stott, W., 107, 122, 224, 249; successes, 249
Straight Fort, 225
Straker, Clive, 249-50; successes, 250
Stratford-on-Avon, 250; principal races at, 250
Stroller, 60
Stuff Gown, 284
Summerville, 74
Sundew, 118, 250, 260, 273, 286; successes, 250
Sunloch, 242, 250, 267; successes, 242
Super Flash, 196
Sutcliffe, John Earnshaw, 244, 251; principal successes, 251
Sutcliffe, John Robert, 251; victories, 251
Swatton, John, 251, 287
Sweet Joe, 251; successes, 251
Sweet Lavender, 202
Switcher, 205

Taaffe, Pat, 16, 28, 47, 79, 80, 90, 95, 96, 101, 145, 161, 171, 199, 212, 224, 228, 240, 252, 257; principal successes, 252
Taaffe, Thomas, 87, 177, 212, 252
Tabor, C., 10
Taffytus, 178
Talgo Abbess, 234
Tant Pis, 191
Tartan Ace, 122, 241
Tasker, J., 252
Tate, Richard, 252; success of, 252
Tattersalls, 252
Taunton, 252-3; valuable races at, 253
Taxidermist, 14, 137, 253; victories, 253
Taylor, Alec, 14
Taylor, George, 14
Taylor, H., 108
Taylor, W., 81, 253
Teal, 115, 209, 253, 259, 285; successes, 253
Team Spirit, 175, 253, 271; victories, 253
Teapot II, 240
Teesside Park, 254; important races at, 254
Television coverage of races, 254
Templescoby, 37, 79
Tempest, Capt., 10, 255
Ten Up, 39, 64, 80, 254-5; controversy over running of, 80
Thirlwell, Dennis, 255, 258; victories, 258
Thomas, Arthur, 234
Thomas, E., 258
Thomas, Mr, 19, 66
Thomond II, 13, 104-5, 110, 219, 243, 258-9, 279; successes, 258
Thomondgate, 69
Thompson, Arthur, 28, 98, 238, 253, 259; successes, 259
Thompson, Marcus, 37
Thomson-Jones, Harry, 98, 177, 251, 273; major victories, 132

Thorne, Miss Diana, first lady rider to ride winner, 141
Thorner, Graham, 94, 225, 259, 274; major successes, 259
Thornfield, 164, 283
Thoroughbred Breeders Association, 259
Thrale, Peter, 259
Thrown In, 106, 108, 246, 260; victories, 260
Tiberetta, 81, 177, 241, 250, 260; success, 260; breeding record, 260
Tied Cottage, 74
Timber Wolf, 37, 116
Timmie's Battle, 107
Timothy Titus, 13
Tingle Creek, 193, 260; successes, 260
Tinkler, Colin, 174, 260-1; successes, 260-1
Tipperary Tim, 31, 71, 77, 82, 84, 261; victories, 261
Titus Oates, 15, 63, 261; successes, 261
Tokoroa, 25
Tom West, 87
Too Good, 19, 146, 195
Topham, Mrs Mirabel, 150, 236
Tote, The, 261-2
Tout ou Rien, 169
Towcester, 262; valuable races at, 262
Townley, Capt., 12
Trainers; leading, from 1940-78, 264-5; rules governing, 262-4
Treachery, 86
Tree Tangle, 65
Trespasser, 29, 146, 265, 270,; victories, 265
Trevethin and Oaksey, John Geoffrey Tristram, 4th Baron, 20, 40, 96, 130, 253, 264-5; major successes, 265
Trianon III, 250
Trodmore Hunt, 265-6
Trout, 252
Troytown, 13, 17, 19, 146, 165-6, 237, 266; successes, 266
Trudgill, Robert, 165-6, 266
Trump Card, 205
Tudor Line, 212, 225, 241, 266; victories, 266
Turco, 28
Turf Board, 180
Turk, The, 266
Turnell, Andrew, 32, 65, 192, 203, 216, 266-7; principal victories, 266-7
Turnell, Andrew Robert, 14, 27, 32, 40, 83, 95, 109, 138, 139, 201, 218, 228, 256, 266, 267; principal successes, 267
Tweedie. Robert Reginald, 25, 97, 267; successes, 267
Tyler, Thomas, 250, 267

Ultimatum, 200
Uncle Jack, 88
Upton Lad, 82
Uttley, James, 39, 47, 121, 203, 268, 285; successes, 268
Uttoxeter, 92, 268; principal races at, 268-9

Valentine, 127, 148
Van de Berg, 278
Vanguard, 32, 76, 196, 270
Vatelys, 113
Vaulx, 205, 270; victories, 270

Vermouth, 29, 215, 270; victories, 270
Victor II, 28
Victor Norman, 32, 98, 190, 265, 270; successes, 270
Vidi, 34, 117
Vigor, 86, 146
Vinall, E., 9, 67
Vincent, Miss Lorna, first lady rider to win as professional, 141
Vitement, 9
Vive, 202
Vivian, 28, 167, 270; victories, 270
Voluptuary, 99, 270-1, 279, 280, 288; successes, 270-1
Vulgan, 168, 271; victories, 271; as leading sire, 271
Vulture, 101

Waddington, G., 44, 126, 228, 256
Walwyn, Fulke, 13, 36, 46-7, 75, 95, 99, 105, 108, 139, 158, 161, 171, 174, 200, 204, 208, 209, 219, 221, 223, 242, 253, 256, 272, 277, 282; major successes, 272
Walwyn, Peter, 24, 175
Wanderer, 111, 272
Ward, Mr R., 81
War Risk, 116, 267
Warwick, 272-3; principal races at, 273
Water-jump, rules regarding, 273
Watkinson, Ian, 273-4; principal successes, 274
Watkinson, William, 126, 178, 274
Weathercock, 86, 148
Weathervane, 121
Webber, Anthony, 274
Well To Do, 31, 94, 101, 225, 244, 259, 274; successes, 274
Werwolf, 274-5; successes, 274-5
West Indies, 275, 284; victories, 275
Wetherby, 275-6; principal races at, 275
What a Buck, 190
What a Daisy, 276; winners by foals of, 276
What a Myth, 276, 284; victories, 276
Whinstone Hill, 35
Whisper Low, 19, 28, 146
Whitaker, Capt. Percival, 101, 226, 239, 276-7
White, Kenneth, 41, 65, 277; principal successes, 277
White, W., 86, 126
Whitney, 'Jock' Hay, 13, 85, 104, 258, 278
Why Not, 63, 72, 73, 99, 176, 180, 191, 277; successes, 277
Widger, Joseph, 277, 278
Widger, Mr J. W., 173
Widger, Mr T., 288
Wight, John Stuart, 34, 72, 111, 131, 221, 277-8; successes, 277
Wightman, William, 110, 278; successes, 278
Wild Man From Borneo, 100, 158, 277, 278; successes, 278
Wild Monarch, 200
Wilkinson, B., 169, 281
Williams, Dudley, 94, 134, 237, 278
Williams, Evan, 47, 65, 214, 222, 224-5, 278; successes, 278
Williams, Hwafa, 229; Clerk of the Course at Sandown, 229

Williamson, George, 12, 81, 161, 278-9; victories, 278-9
Willoughby de Broke, John Henry Peyto Verney, 20th Baron, 279
Wilson, Edward, 65, 218, 223, 270, 279, 280; victories, 279
Wilson, Gerald, 34, 41, 47, 104-5, 143, 148, 220, 221, 245, 270, 278, 279-80; victories, 279
Wilson, Maj. John Philip, 79, 280
Wilson, William, 280
Wincanton, 280; principal races at, 280
Windermere Laddie, 122
Windsor, 280-1; principal races at, 281
Winning Fair, 132, 146, 245, 281; successes, 281
Winter, Fred, 12, 28, 39, 41, 47, 60, 64, 70, 72, 75, 78, 85, 90, 97, 100, 101, 102, 110, 112, 134, 137, 140, 142, 143, 146, 161, 168, 169, 171, 174, 192, 197, 202, 206, 210, 222, 228, 242, 250, 281-2: principal victories (as jockey), 281; principal victories (as trainer), 282
Withington, Frederick, 30, 66, 101, 160, 161, 217, 226, 282
Witty, 190
Wolverhampton, 283; principal races at, 283
Woodbrook, 28, 146, 283; victories, 283
Woodland, Percy, 69, 81, 139, 144, 194, 210, 234, 283-4: record held by, 283-4; victories, 284
Woodland Venture, 96, 209, 247, 284; victories, 284

Wootton, Frank, 284; victories, 284
Wootton, Richard, 243
Wootton, Stanley, 190, 243, 244, 281, 284-5; victories, 284
Worcester, 285; principal races at, 285
Worcran, 139
Workman, 27, 35, 66, 120, 173, 227, 285; victories, 285
Wot No Sun, 98, 253, 259, 285; victories, 285
Wrack, 112
Wright, Joseph Stanley, 25, 111, 285; successes, 285
Wyndburgh, 137, 196, 199, 250, 285-6; victories, 286
Wynne, Denny, 9, 34, 166, 205, 286

Xanthus, 12, 148
Xeno, 117

Yaller Girl, 86
Yates, Arthur, 19, 62, 77, 100, 117, 223, 237, 251, 257, 287; successes, 287
Yenisei, 142
Young Ash Leaf, 64

Zahia, 238
Zeta's Son, 24
Zeus, 288; victories, 288
Zitella, 27
Zoedone, 127, 138, 235, 288; successes, 288
Zonda, 201